SUMMARY OF COMMON UNIX COMMANDS (Continued)

COMMAND	ACTION
egrep	"Extended" version of grep
expr	Evaluate Boolean and arithmetic expressions
false	Return nonzero (*false*) exit status
fgrep	"Fast" version of grep
file	Report type of file
find	Find matching files and perform specified actions
finger	Report user information
format	Format disks and cartridge tapes
ftp	Transfer files to and from remote systems
grep	Search files for regular expression matches
haltsys	Gracefully shut down system (root)
head	Display first few lines of a file
join	Display the join (lines with common field) of two files
kill	Send a signal to process (by default, terminate the process)
ksh	Invoke the Korn shell
lc	List directory contents in columns
line	Read a line (shell script usage)
ln	Create link to a file
logname	Get login name
lp, lpr	Send request to printer
lprint	Print on local printer
lpstat	Report printer status
ls	List contents of a directory
mail	Send and receive mail
man	Print reference pages from online manual
mesg	Grant or deny permission to receive write messages from other users
mkdir	Create a new directory
mknod	Build a special file
more	Display a file one page at a time
mount	Mount a special file, or report its status
mv	Move (rename) a file

(continues on last page of the book)

UNIX COMPLETE

Peter Dyson

Stan Kelly-Bootle

John Heilborn

SAN FRANCISCO ► PARIS ► DÜSSELDORF ► SOEST ► LONDON

Associate Publisher: Gary Masters

Contracts and Licensing Manager: Kristine O'Callaghan

Compilation Acquisitions & Developmental Editor: Tracy Brown

Compilation Project Editor: Gemma O'Sullivan

Compilation Editor: Kristen Vanberg-Wolff

Acquisitions & Developmental Editors: John Read, Gary Masters, Dianne King

Project Editors: Kathleen Lattinville, Valerie Potter, Brenda Frink

Editors: Odile Sullivan-Tarazi, Armin Brott, Nancy Crumpton

Compilation Technical Editor: Brian Horakh

Technical Editors: Dan Tauber, Aaron Kushner, Raymond John Felton

Book Designer: Happenstance Type-O-Rama

Graphic Illustrator: Tony Jonick

Electronic Publishing Specialist: Franz Baumhackl

Production Coordinators: Lisa Haden, Nathan Johanson, Chris Meredith, Teresa Trego

Indexer: Nancy Guenther

Cover Designer: Design Site

Cover Photographer: Mark Johann

Library of Congress Card Number: 99-61310
ISBN: 0-7821-2528-X

Manufactured in Canada

10 9 8 7 6 5 4

ACKNOWLEDGMENTS

This book incorporates the work of many people, inside and outside Sybex.

Gary Masters and Tracy Brown defined the book's overall structure and contents. John Heilborne compiled and adapted all the material for publication in this book and wrote Chapter 19 especially for it. Kris Vanberg-Wolff edited the final text.

A large team of editors, developmental editors, project editors, and technical editors helped to put together the various books from which *Unix Complete* was compiled: Dianne King and John Read handled developmental tasks; Odile Sullivan-Tarazi, Armin Brott, Nancy Crumpton, Kathleen Lattinville, Valerie Potter, and Brenda Frink all contributed to editing or project editing; and the technical editors were Dan Tauber, Aaron Kushner, and Raymond John Felton.

The *Unix Complete* production team of electronic publishing specialist Franz Baumhackl and production coordinators Teresa Trego and Chris Meredith worked with speed and accuracy to turn the manuscript files and illustrations into the handsome book you're now reading. Finally, our most important thanks go to the contributors who agreed to have their work excerpted into *Unix Complete*: Stan Kelly-Bootle, Peter Dyson, and John Heilborn. Without their efforts, this book would not exist.

CONTENTS AT A GLANCE

Introduction   xix

Part I   Unix Tutorial   **1**

Chapter 1   Are You Online Yet?   3
Chapter 2   Simple Commands   15
Chapter 3   Meet the Unix File System   23
Chapter 4   Creating Your Own Files   37
Chapter 5   Electronic Mail   57
Chapter 6   Your Own Personalized Unix   81
Chapter 7   Your Own File System   101
Chapter 8   Processes and Multitasking   117
Chapter 9   Printing and Spooling   143
Chapter 10   The vi Family of Editors   159
Chapter 11   Advanced vi Techniques   177
Chapter 12   Exploiting the Shell   199
Chapter 13   Dipping into the Toolbox   239
Chapter 14   grepping, sedding, and a Little awking   273
Chapter 15   Advanced Shell Scripts   321
Chapter 16   Reaching Out to Remote Computers   365
Chapter 17   Basic System Administration   399
Chapter 18   X Windows Exposed   421
Chapter 19   Out of the Vacuum:
             The Door to Mainstream Applications   441

Part I   Unix Desktop Reference   **461**

Chapter 20   The Complete Unix Desk Reference   463

             Index   964

TABLE OF CONTENTS

Introduction   xix

Part I ▶ Unix Tutorial   1

Chapter 1 □ Are You Online Yet?   3

Gaining Access—What You Need to Get Started   4
    Terminals   4
    Keyboards   5
    Screens   6
Who Does What?   7
Logging In   7
Typing Errors   8
The Enter Key   9
Login Errors   9
Logged In at Last!   10
    Defaults   10
    Login Greetings   10
Commands   11
Logging Out Already?   12
Choice of Passwords   13
What's Next   13

Chapter 2 □ Simple Commands   15

Files—A Quick Introduction   16
Command Arguments   17
    Who Do People Say That I Am?   17
    Instant Calendars   19
    Pipelines   20
    More Calendars   20
What's Next   21

Chapter 3 □ Meet the Unix File System   23

Directories   24
    The Name of the File   26
    Trees and Hierarchies   27

The root of the Matter   31
   Absolute Path Names   32
   Home Is Best   32
   You Are Here   33
What's Next   35

Chapter 4 □ Creating Your Own Files   **37**

Standard Input and Output   38
Redirecting Output   39
The ls Command   40
   Wildcards   41
   Exploring ls with the man Command   43
The cat Command   45
Using Output Redirection with Other Commands   46
Using cat to Create Files   47
The lc Command   48
Counting Words with wc   49
Redirecting Input   50
Comparing Redirection and Pipelines   51
   Erasing Files with rm   52
   Indirection with Input, Output, and Pipelines 54
   Appending Output to Your Files   54
   Standard Errors   55
What's Next   55

Chapter 5 □ Electronic Mail   **57**

Superusers Unite!   58
You Haven't Written to Me Lately   59
   Off the Wall   63
   Final Warning   63
The Mailperson Cometh   64
   Read Your Mail!   64
   Leaving the mail Program   66
   Printing Your Mail Messages   67
   Message Headers   67
   Message Selection   68
   Saving and Deleting Messages   70
   Reading Mail from Another Source   72

Sending Mail 72
Using Other Email Programs 77
What's Next 78

Chapter 6 ◻ Your Own Personalized Unix **81**

Changing Your Password 82
   The passwd Command 83
   Good and Bad Passwords 83
   The /etc/passwd File 84
Choosing Your Shell 88
   The Path to Success 89
   The Names of the Shells 90
Login Profiles 91
   Bourne Shell Login Profiles 92
   C Shell Login Profiles 92
Your Own Login Profile 93
   Shell Variables—An Introduction 93
   Setting Terminal Options with stty 97
   Viewing Your .profile File 98
What's Next 99

Chapter 7 ◻ Your Own File System **101**

Home Rule 102
Permissions 103
   The Owner 104
   File Permissions 104
   Directory Permissions 105
   Permissions for Owner, Group, and Others 107
   Default Permissions 110
Changing Owners and Groups 111
Changing Permissions 112
What's Next 114

Chapter 8 ◻ Processes and Multitasking **117**

Multijargon 118
Multiprogramming Operating Systems 118
Multitasking 120

Unix Images and Processes   121
    Process Biography   122
    Forks and Spawns   123
The Shell As a Process   124
Background Processes Using &   125
    The wait Command   126
Killing Processes   127
    Hello, I Must Be Going!   128
Checking Your Processes with ps   130
Have a Nice Process   133
Multicommand Lines   134
The sleep Command   137
Scheduling Processes   138
What's Next   141

Chapter 9 □ Printing and Spooling   **143**

Central and Local Printers   144
Save a Tree   145
Overcoming the Printer Jungle   145
The lp Command   147
    Printer Options   148
    A Simple Shell Script   150
    The C Shell alias Command   151
    The -c Copy Option   153
The lpstat Command   154
Changing Print Requests with lp -i   155
    The cancel Command   156
The lprint Command   156
Simple Formatting with pr   156
What's Next   157

Chapter 10 □ The vi Family of Editors   **159**

Preliminaries   160
Meet the Family   164
    The Three+Four Modes   166
    Mode Navigation   168
Creating a Text with vi   169
    Text Entry   170
    Cursor Movement   173
What's Next   175

Chapter 11 □ Advanced vi Techniques   177

Screen Controls   179
More on Text-Entry Modes   180
Text Deletion   181
Changing Text   183
Yanking and Putting Text   184
Searching Text   186
The ex Command Mode   187
Using the Shell within vi   188
Assorted ex Commands   188
Abbreviations   189
Entering and Leaving vi   195
What's Next   196

Chapter 12 □ Exploiting the Shell   199

Shell Scripts   201
Your First Shell Script   202
Exploiting dw   204
Executing dw Directly   205
Shell Script Summary   207
Script Debugging   207
Special Commands   208
New Commands from Old   208
The Dot Command   210
Shell and Subshell Variables   210
Setting and Unsetting Variables   214
Exporting Variables   216
How Shell Scripts Work   218
The Positional Parameters   220
echo and the Shell Metacharacters   222
Familiar Quotations   223
Backquotes   224
More on Metacharacters   226
Escaping with \   226
The Comment Character #   227
Double Quotes   228
Metacharacter Sequences   229
The Shell Game   234
What's Next   237

Chapter 13 □ Dipping into the Toolbox   **239**

The sort Command   240
    Over There!   242
    The sort f Option   243
    The sort d Option   244
    The sort i Option   244
    The sort n Option   245
    Multiple File Sorts   246
    The sort u Option   246
    The uniq Command   247
The head Command   250
The tail Command   251
The split Command   252
The cut Command   253
The paste Command   255
The find Command   257
The tr Command   264
The dd Command   266
Putting It All Together   267
What's Next   270

Chapter 14 □ grepping, sedding, and a Little awking   **273**

The grep Family   274
    Quoting the Search Pattern   275
    Word Searches and the -w Option   275
    Case-Sensitive Searches   276
Regular Expressions   278
    Substitute Command Revisited   282
    Global Commands   283
    Inverse Global Commands   284
    Tagged Regular Expressions   287
The fgrep Command   288
The egrep Command   289
    Who Takes Precedence?   290
The grep Family Summary   292
The sed Stream Editor   295
sed Syntax   295
    The edit_command   297

Come All Ye Tramps and 'awkers   301
   awk Fields   303
   awk Records   304
   The -F Option   306
   awk Relational Operators   308
   Multiple Tests   309
   Begin and End   311
   awk and Math   313
   awk Flow Control   316
   awk Round Up   319
What's Next   319

Chapter 15 ▫ Advanced Shell Scripts   **321**
The Menu, Please   322
   Helpful Comments   323
   The while Loop   324
   The test Command   329
   The read Command   342
   if Only   344
   Error Handling   346
   The Best case Scenario   349
   Branching with && and || 351
   More Menu   352
   Positional Parameters   354
   Doing Sums   362
   Script Review   363
What's Next   363

Chapter 16 ▫ Reaching Out to Remote Computers **365**
UUCP   366
   Making Contact   367
   UUCP Applications   368
UUCP Security   374
   The uucp Command   379
Unix and Networking; Reaching the Promised LAN   384
   Introducing TCP/IP and Ethernet   385
   Distributing Files over the Network   386
   Client-Server Computing   387

Accessing the Internet   388
   What Is the Internet, Anyway?   388
   UUCP Addressing versus Domain Addressing   389
   Transferring Files with ftp   390
   Connecting to a Remote Computer with telnet   394
   World-Wide Web   395
   Talk, Talk, Talk   395
   Introducing USENET   396
   Using News Readers   396
What's Next   397

Chapter 17 ▫ Basic System Administration   **399**

Unix System Administration   400
What's Involved   401
Superuser Rules OK?   402
   Assuming Power   404
Putting the Boot In   405
   Cleanup Time   405
   Single-User Mode   406
   Multiuser Mode   406
The Halting Problem   406
File Systems and Filesystems   409
Backing Up   410
   When?   411
   What?   411
   Who?   412
   How?   413
New Accounts   417
What's Next   418

Chapter 18 ▫ X Windows Exposed   **421**

An Introduction to X   422
   Clients and Servers Revisited   423
   How the X Protocol Works   425
   X Compared with Other Windowing Systems   425
   What the Users See in X   425
   X-Terminals and PC X Servers   426
   X Benefits   427

X Window Managers: Open Look and Motif 427
Using X 429
    Logging In 430
    X Resources 430
    Using the xterm Terminal Emulator 431
    Using Other X Clients 434
    Killing an X Client 436
X Marks the Spot: The Future of X 436
What's Next 438

Chapter 19 ▫ Out of the Vacuum:
The Door to Mainstream Applications 441
Samba 442
    smbd 442
    smb.conf & swat 443
    nmbd 444
    smbclient 445
    Running Samba 448
mtools 452
    Configuring mtools 452
Setting Drive Parameters 453
    Running mtools 455
And One More Thing: SCO, VisionFS, and Merge 459
What's Next 459

Part II ▸ Unix Desktop Reference 461

Chapter 20 ▫ The Complete Unix Desk Reference 463

Index *964*

INTRODUCTION

Unix Complete is a one-of-a-kind computer book—valuable both for the breadth of its content and for its low price. This thousand-page compilation of information from two Sybex books provides comprehensive coverage of the popular Unix operating system used in universities and research centers, as well as at many Fortune 500 companies. This book, unique in the computer book world, was created with several goals in mind.

Enormously powerful, Unix is also complex and requires everyone who uses it to first read a tutorial and then keep a reference handy for specialized commands. *Unix Complete* provides both for only $19.99. It will help you become familiar with the capabilities and uses of Unix so you'll know which additional Unix books will best suit your needs. It will also acquaint you with some of our best authors—their writing styles and teaching skills, and the level of expertise they bring to their books—so you can easily find a match for your interests as you delve deeper into Unix programming.

With *Unix Complete*, you'll learn all about getting the most out of Unix System V—from building file systems to connecting to remote computers, the Internet, and using mainstream programs. As you become more proficient with Unix, you'll find the reference section in Part II to be an invaluable daily tool. This comprehensive reference quickly puts every command, option, and control at your fingertips.

If you've read other computer "how-to" books, you've seen that there are many possible approaches to the task of showing how to use software and hardware effectively. The books from which *Unix Complete* was compiled represent two different approaches to teaching that Sybex and its authors have developed—the comprehensive tutorial style of the *Understanding* series and the quick, concise style of the *Desk Reference* series. You'll see that these books have in common a commitment to clarity, accuracy, and practicality.

You'll find in these pages ample evidence of the high quality of Sybex's authors. Unlike publishers who produce "books by committee," Sybex authors are encouraged to write in individual voices that reflect their own experience with programming, with real-world applications, and with the evolution of today's personal computers. Each author has written and fine-tuned the programs included in his chapters, and has supplied tips and warnings born of his own direct experience.

In adapting the source materials for inclusion in *Unix Complete*, the compiler preserved these individual voices and perspectives. Chapters were edited only to add helpful explanations of topics otherwise not covered here in depth, and to update references as needed so you're sure to get the most current information available.

Who Can Benefit from This Book?

Unix Complete is designed to meet the needs of a wide range of computer users. Therefore, while you *could* read this book from beginning to end, all of you may not *need* to read every chapter. The Table of Contents and the Index will guide you to the subjects you're looking for.

Students   Even if you have only a little familiarity with Unix, this book will enable you to log on and use essential Unix commands, customize your start-up options and file system, send and receive e-mail, and access the Internet from your Unix system.

Intermediate users   If you already know the basics of Unix, this book will give you more sophisticated skills and a deeper understanding of the capabilities of Unix. You'll learn how to navigate and use remote systems using ftp and telnet, understand the X Windows system and X utilities, and perform basic system administration and security tasks.

Advanced users   You, too, will find much useful information in this book. You'll explore all of the Unix shells, master system commands and tools, create commands, and build advanced shell scripts.

How This Book Is Organized

Unix Complete is made up of two parts:

Part I: Unix Tutorial   Part I consists of 19 chapters in a tutorial format. With the exception of Chapter 19, Part I is taken exclusively from *Understanding Unix*. It contains essential information for all Unix users, from basic operating principles to system optimization.

Part II: Unix Desktop Reference   Excerpted from *The Unix Desk Reference,* Part II is a handy alphabetical reference covering Unix terms, utilities, and commands.

A Few Typographical Conventions

When an operation requires a series of choices from menus or dialog boxes, the ➢ symbol is used to guide you through the instructions, like this: "Select Programs ➢ Accessories ➢ System Tools ➢ System Information." The items the ➢ symbol separates may be menu names, toolbar icons, check boxes, or other elements of the Windows interface—anyplace you can make a selection.

This typeface is used to identify programming code and Internet URLs, and **boldface type** is used whenever you need to type something into a text box.

You'll find these types of special notes throughout the book:

TIP

You'll get a lot of these Tips—for quicker and smarter ways to accomplish tasks—based on the authors' long experience using Unix.

NOTE

You'll see these Notes, too. They usually represent alternate ways to accomplish a task or some additional information that needs to be highlighted.

WARNING

In a very few places you'll see a Warning like this one. When you see a warning, pay attention to it!

For More Information...

See the Sybex Web site, www.sybex.com, to learn more about the books that went into *Unix Complete.* On the site's Catalog page, you'll find links to any book you're interested in.

We hope you enjoy this book and find it useful. Happy computing!

PART I

UNIX TUTORIAL

```
echo "2.      Show Date"
echo "3.      Display a file"
echo "4.      Change working director
echo "5.      Return to original dir
echo "Q.      Quit
echo
echo -n "Enter choice: .\b"
read choice
case $choice in
1) who | more
   pause;;
2) date
   pause;;
3) echo "Enter file name: \c"
   read fil
   if [ -r "$fil" -a -f "$fil ]
   then
      clear
      more -d $fil
   else
      echo "Cannot di
   fi
   pause;;
4) echo "En
   read di
   if test      "  dir    pwd`
   then
      cd $dir
   else
      echo "$dir: no such di
   fi
   pause;;
5) if test "$dir" != "$p
   then
      cd $prevdir
   fi
   pause;;
```

Chapter 1

Are You Online Yet?

T he first stage of your journey is a mental one. You must accept that Unix is a large, complex system to tackle. Unless you take one careful, diligent step at a time, it is easy to become somewhat overawed. If you flip aimlessly through the mountains of official documentation, you can be forgiven for feeling daunted by the number of commands and options, and by the sheer weight of quirky detail. The good news is that you need learn only a few Unix basics in order to become productive. As you build on this solid foundation, layer by layer, the climb becomes more gentle. This book stresses constant practice with useful examples so that you see cause and effect rather than ponder textbook abstractions. It also emphasizes motivation: knowing *why* the Unix designers provided certain features often clarifies *how* they are implemented. It proves much easier to assimilate facts when they are interrelated in some way, rather than picked up in isolation.

We can certainly discount any rumors that Unix is impossibly arcane unless you have an advanced degree in computer science. The proof can be found in thousands of ordinary office installations worldwide. Although Unix dominates the academic and research arenas, its presence in the business world has been growing rapidly on every platform from mainframe to PC.

GAINING ACCESS—WHAT YOU NEED TO GET STARTED

As with any computer system, there are several prerequisites before you can gain access and start using Unix. You obviously need a suitable terminal correctly connected to a computer that is running Unix. (The latter caution is not as dumb as it seems—many computers nowadays are capable of running several operating systems, so you need to be sure that you are talking to the right one.) Each Unix vendor supplies precise documentation for installing a particular combination of hardware and version of Unix.

When you are connected and ready to go, you are said to be *online* to the computer. When you lose connection for any reason, you go *offline,* and life becomes simple again. Your terminal may be local, directly cabled (or *hardwired*) to the computer, or it may be remotely connected via modems and telephone lines. The difference affects only the way you establish a connection; once you are online, the type of connection, local or remote, does not normally affect the way you work.

Remote connection is made by dialing the number of the Unix system just as you would make a normal telephone call. In most cases, the dialing is automated with suitable telecommunications software. The actual procedures are very much site-dependent, so you will need to consult your local guru or Unix vendor. Operating remotely, of course, exposes you to the random gremlins of the telecommunications underworld—glitches on the lines, electrical interference, broken connections, and so on—as well as the psychological stresses of isolation if things go wrong.

Terminals

Unix supports almost every type of terminal ever invented, and indeed is designed so that terminals not yet invented can be handled by simple software changes. As far as the beginner is concerned, a terminal can be looked on as a device with a *keyboard* for typing in instructions and data to the computer (*input*), and a CRT or monitor screen to *echo* your input and display messages or responses from the computer (*output*). The computer itself usually has a hard-wired terminal referred to as the *console* or *systems console*.

Terminals can be *dumb* or *intelligent,* although it is not always easy to tell the difference. A dumb terminal has a keyboard and CRT but no local processing power—it relies on the central computer for all its processing needs. An intelligent (or *smart*) terminal, in addition to a keyboard and CRT, has some built-in processing power and local memory. With the low costs of microprocessors and integrated circuits, the completely dumb terminal is now quite rare. The same cost factor has also led to the widespread use of PCs (personal computers) as very intelligent devices capable of working both online as Unix terminals and offline as stand-alone PCs. Indeed, with the advent of superfast microprocessors such as the Intel Pentium and Motorola G3, which can handle high-capacity disks and lots of RAM, your Unix may well be running on a PC or workstation while supporting other terminals and PCs.

Keyboards

Whether you have a dumb or intelligent terminal, an online PC, or a PC running Unix, you will have a keyboard for input and a screen for output. With all the varieties of keyboard layout and key labeling currently on the market, you will appreciate that the instructions in this book may need some adjustment for your particular keyboard. To further complicate matters, most smart terminals allow you to personalize the keyboard in various ways. In other words, you may be able to *remap* the keyboard, thereby changing the action of certain keys or sequences of keys.

An extreme form of remapping is the use of *emulation* software that makes a brand X terminal behave like a brand Y model. Whatever tricks you perform, Unix needs to know the type and mode of the terminal being used so it can correctly interpret the stream of characters you are sending. The normal alphanumeric printable characters are fairly standard (usually the so-called ASCII set), but the invisible control characters, like Ctrl, Alt, Shift and Insert, are subject to the more diverse interpretations of the hardware jungle of keyboards, screens, and (especially) printers. The parts of Unix that cope with these vagaries are, perforce, correspondingly messy. Until you know more, therefore, it is best to have your vendor or system administrator set up Unix for your particular terminal.

To avoid too many diversions, I will assume the standard PC keyboard conventions. When we encounter the need for special keystrokes other than the universal alphanumeric keys, I will point out some of the most common variants. For example, the key called Enter on the PC plays an essential role in Unix input. Your Enter key may be marked as Return, CR, Car Ret, or ↵.

Screens

Although Unix was originally developed for systems using monochrome, text-based displays, today most versions of Unix use some kind of GUI (Graphical User Interface). GUIs are, like Microsoft Windows, designed to make using the computer more intuitive to you, the user.

This book was written for monochrome text displays using standard 25-line-×-80-column displays. Unless specifically stated otherwise, this is the configuration you should be using to work through the examples in this book. The reason we use a text-based approach instead of a GUI-based approach is twofold. First, virtually every one of the functions and commands for operating Unix are text-based or have a text-based equivalent. And second, although Unix has many graphical operations that correspond to the text commands, there are many that have no graphical equivilant and would therefore be impossible to show in a graphics-only environment. Additionally, although almost all Unix systems today use some variation of X-Windows for their GUI, there are several variations that could make these initial descriptions quite difficult to follow. As such, we'll leave the discussion of how X-Windows operates for later on in this book. For the moment, you need to get to a text window to proceed.

To access a text window, you should do one of the following:

- ▶ Open a Terminal window on your GUI. In most X-Window systems, when you initially log in, the system will automatically open a terminal window for you in the GUI. If your systems does not automatically open a terminal window for you, you can open one by clicking the appropriate icon on the Control Panel.

- ▶ Switch to a text-only screen. In SCO Unix you can accomplish this by holding down the Ctrl and Alt keys and then pressing one of the function keys: F1–F12.

When you get to the new text screen, you will need to log in again. Don't let this throw you, just enter your login name and password again.

WHO DOES WHAT?

In larger installations, there are staff specially assigned to manage the system, so you would not normally be concerned with such mundane tasks as installing terminals and ensuring that Unix is set to handle them. In particular, you'll find a system administrator (SA for short) who will be the chief liaison between you as user and the Unix system. Whether system administration is a single full-time job or spread among staff members according to shifts or particular responsibilities will depend on the size and complexity of your Unix site. At smaller installations, the system administrator may simply be a designated user selected (or sentenced) to play this role in addition to other duties. The system administrator may even be you! Fear not, this book explains the chief responsibilities of the SA. For the moment, I will assume that you have someone who can get you online.

The first sign that your terminal awaits you is that your screen displays the *prompt*

    login:

with the cursor blinking impatiently after the colon. A prompt is any message or symbol that indicates that input is expected—in other words, you are being *prompted* to type something! The cursor is a distinctive symbol on the screen indicating where your next typed character will appear.

Although you are online to Unix and Unix is talking to you, you are not yet an active user. You must first log in (some say log on) and satisfy Unix that you are a legitimate user. Let's see how.

LOGGING IN

In a single-user environment, such as DOS, anyone booting up the system can usually start operating it without permission. DOS itself just doesn't care. If you want to control access, you must install some additional security system (either mechanical locks or software barriers). With a multiuser system such as Unix, the need for security has to be taken more seriously since access may be possible from terminals beyond your immediate control. Unix offers a host of built-in security features that allow the system administrator to control who can get online as well as what the users can and cannot do when they get online. The system administrator is free to decide how much security is appropriate for a given installation, but there is a minimum level found at most sites.

The basic idea is that the system administrator assigns each user a unique *user name*, also called a *logon*, and an initial *password*. The SA sets up your logon and password on the system and tells you what they are. Once you have logged on (you'll see how soon), you are free to change your password but not your logon name. The latter is usually your first name in lowercase letters, such as `stan` or `mary`. In larger installations, it may be necessary to use fuller names and/or initials to ensure uniqueness. Whatever scheme is adopted, your logon *must* be in lowercase, and it serves to identify you to Unix at all times.

The choice of passwords needs careful consideration and we'll be discussing this in detail later on. For now, make sure you know your password and keep it to yourself. And try not to forget your password—it means more work for the system administrator, who may be annoyed enough to issue you a temporary, deflating password such as `dummy`.

At the `login:` prompt, type your logon. As you type, you'll see your keystrokes echoed on the screen. The stream of characters you type is actually going to a temporary storage area inside Unix known as a *buffer*. Each character in turn is sent back to the screen as you type—hence the terms *echo* and *echoing*. Most of your keyboard entries will be echoed in this way, but there are important exceptions, as you'll see shortly.

TYPING ERRORS

Your keyboard entry builds up in the buffer until you press Enter, at which point Unix starts examining what you have typed. You therefore have a chance to correct your input *before* you press the Enter key.

If you make a conscious typing error, there are two ways to recover: erase and retype characters or scrub the entire entry and start over again.

To erase characters to the left of your cursor, you can press the Backspace key. If your keyboard lacks a Backspace key, use Ctrl-H. Ctrl-H means holding down the Ctrl key and pressing the H key. You may see this written ^H in Unix documentation.

To delete a whole line, type Ctrl-U, then retype from the beginning. (Your system may allow the use of # to delete the previous character, or @ to delete the whole line. Check with your system administrator or experiment!)

THE ENTER KEY

When you think you have correctly typed your user name, press the Enter key. Until you press Enter, Unix will simply wait for more keystrokes. This is a general rule: pressing Enter signals the end of your typing and asks Unix to process what you have typed. Unix responds with the prompt

`Password:`

The password is case-sensitive. Carefully type your password exactly as the system administrator set it up (using the proper upper- and lowercase letters); then press Enter. (This is the last time I'll remind you that Enter is needed after every completed line of input.) I stress the word *carefully* for two reasons:

▶ What you type in the password field is *not* echoed on the screen, lest Peeping Toms are lurking behind you.

▶ Passwords are (or should be) strange, un-English, hard-to-type combinations.

Unix now checks both your logon name and your password. If the logon is valid and matches the password previously assigned, you will be logged into Unix.

LOGIN ERRORS

If you make a login error, you get the message

`Login incorrect`

followed by another login prompt:

`login:`

Note that Unix plays its cards pretty close here. If you type `stam` in place of `stan`, followed by Stan's password, Unix will not say `logon name invalid`. If you type `stan` followed by Mary's password, Unix will not say `password invalid`. All you know is that either the logon name, the password, or both do not match. This withholding of clues is all part of the cloak and dagger game—no help for the potential intruder. If you keep getting `Login incorrect` messages, check the Caps Lock key; you may be using the wrong case. If this doesn't help, you'll have to double-check with your system administrator.

Part i

LOGGED IN AT LAST!

Once you've passed the login hurdle, Unix can respond in many ways depending on the way your system is set up. Both you and the system administrator can tailor your environment to suit your lifestyle. This is the two-edged sword of Unix: infinite flexibility! In the simplest case, your successful login is greeted by a single character, known as the *shell prompt*. A $ symbol indicates that you have the Bourne shell; a % means you have the C shell. (There are other shells and other prompts, but these two are the most common.)

The differences between the Bourne shell and C shell will not affect you until we reach more advanced Unix operations. The examples here display the Bourne shell, so when you see the $ prompt in the following examples, make the mental adjustment to % if you are using the C shell.

I'll have more to say about shells later. For now, look on them as special Unix programs that will interpret your typed commands and pass them on for further action. A Unix shell is something like the command-line interpreter, COMMAND.COM, in DOS. Most Unix systems now offer you a choice of shells so that you or your system administrator can select the default shell to suit your tastes. The word *default* crops up frequently in data processing, so let's take a brief time-out to discuss what it means.

Defaults

If you have a simple situation where the computer expects a yes or no response, it may be that 90 percent of the time yes is the more appropriate response, as in Are you sure you want to Exit? y/n?. If the program has been arranged so that the Enter key works as though y had been entered, we say that y is the *default*. More generally, if one option among many is the one programmed to be selected in the absence of user input to the contrary, that option can be the default. In many Unix situations, you can change a default permanently or for a particular session. In the latter case, you would revert to the default default, as it were, in subsequent sessions.

Login Greetings

In addition to the shell prompt, Unix may reward you with a message or two. If Unix is uncertain as to your type of terminal, it may prompt you for information before proceeding:

```
TERM = unknown)
```

or

```
TERM = vt100)
```

In the latter case, the vt100 (or some similar set of characters in parentheses) represents the default terminal type for your system. To pass this hurdle, you need to confirm this default name by pressing Enter or supply the actual terminal type. Your system administrator can help you here. Each terminal type supported by Unix has a mnemonic name such as vt100 (the DEC VT-100), wyse60 (for the Wyse 60), and so on. In most cases, the system administrator can set up the system so that the TERM message does not appear or simply requires you to press Enter.

The system administrator can also set up a message of the day (known as *motd* in Unix jargon) that will be displayed to all users when they log in. The message may be an important newscast (The system will be down next Friday) or a cheery Welcome aboard! My SCO UNIX also tells me useful facts about disk usage. You may see the message

```
You have mail.
```

This alerts you to the fact that the Unix electronic mail service has received one or more messages since the last time you cleared your incoming mailbox. Mail can originate from users on your system (you can even send yourself a letter) or from users on any other remote system that has your Unix mailing address and the right connections.

COMMANDS

What is the shell prompt prompting you for? The answer is Unix *commands.* These commands come in all shapes and sizes, from simple and common to rare and hellish. The command itself is a rather brief set of letters (usually, but not always, with a hint of mnemonicity), possibly followed by *options* and/or *arguments.* I'll explain these terms in the next chapter, but for now, let's try a few simple commands. I'll use boldface to show what you type and lighter type to indicate the response. First, enter the command date. The dialogue will look something like this:

```
$ date
Tue Feb 16 09:35:12 PST 1999
$ _
```

Note that after the date, time, and time zone are displayed, the shell prompt reappears ready for your next command. Next enter who to see who is on the system. The response is a list of all active users, the terminals they are logged on, and the date and time they last logged on.

```
$ who
iwonka ttyla Feb16 10:05
stan   tty2a Feb16 15:23
$ _
```

Unix lets you enter two or more commands on the same line. Simply enter a semicolon between each command; then press Enter after the final command:

```
$ date; who
Tue Feb 16 09:35:12 PST 1999
iwonka ttyla Feb16 10:05
stan   tty2a Feb16 15:23
$ _
```

The next example shows what happens if you enter a nonexistent command.

```
$ amelia
amelia: not found
$ jimmy_hoffa
jimmy_hoffa: not found
$ _
```

No, Unix is not an expert in aviation and trade union history. If you enter a command that is unknown to Unix, you get the not found message, followed by the shell prompt.

It is important at this early stage to realize that it is almost impossible to damage a computer system by mistyping a command. There are, to be sure, a few dangerous commands, such as rm and rmdir, that if used rashly, can erase files you may not want to erase. I'll show you how to avoid such calamities, so there is no need to develop computophobia.

LOGGING OUT ALREADY?

WARNING

Be sure to log out after each Unix session.

After logging in and typing a few commands, it may seem premature to show you how to log out (some say log off). In fact, it is an essential operation to master as soon as possible. The whole point of security and passwords is lost if you leave your terminal in an active logged-in state, whether remotely or locally. Anyone can take advantage of your hard-gained access, and who knows what evil lurks in the hearts of men and women? In addition, some sites charge you real money or set quotas for connect time. The logging out procedure varies according to the shell you are using. The Bourne shell logout works as follows:

```
$ exit
```

The C shell requires this command to log out:

```
% logout
```

At most sites, you can also log out with Ctrl-D. (Remember to hold down the Ctrl key and press D.) A successful logout is signaled by the appearance of the login prompt, so if you or anyone else wishes to become an active user, the full logging in sequence is required. If you are connected by modem, you must follow the vendor's instructions for hanging up. Many online Unix systems will hang up for you when you log out, but check this before you run up unnecessary phone bills.

Choice of Passwords

Passwords must strike a balance between memorability and lack of obviousness. These aims conflict somewhat. Passwords should be reasonably memorable; otherwise you'll have to write them down in too many accessible places. They should also be fairly long, say, six characters minimum. You have probably heard all the stories of hacker break-ins. Often the passwords were broken because the user used obvious words such as names of husbands, wives, dogs, or children. The SCO UNIX and other Unix systems offer the automatic generation of "pronounceable" but otherwise highly obscure passwords such as klibrugak, which you would remember in syllables as "kli-bru-gak." Another useful trick is to mix alphanumeric characters with punctuation or even invisible control characters.

What's Next

Chapter 2 introduces the Unix kernel, some of the more commonly used shells, and the basic organization of data within Unix: files directories and subdirectories. You'll also get to try out a few simple Unix commands.

```
echo "2.    Show Date"
echo "3.    Display a file"
echo "4.    Change working director
echo "5.    Return to original dir
echo "Q.    Quit
echo
echo -n "Enter choice: .\b"
read choice
case $choice in
1) who | more
   pause;;
2) date
   pause;;
3) echo "Enter file name: \c"
   read fil
   if [ -r "$fil" -a -f "$fil ]
   then
     clear
     more -d $fil
   else
     echo "Cannot d
   fi
   pause;;
4) echo "En
   read di
   if test       $dir       pwd`
   then
     cd $dir
   else
     echo "$dir: no such di
   fi
   pause;;
   5) if test "$dir" != "$p
      then
        cd $prevdir
      fi
      pause;;
```

Chapter 2

Simple Commands

In Chapter 1, you logged in to Unix and entered the two commands `date` and `who`. In this chapter, I'll introduce a few more simple commands and give you a better idea of what is going on when Unix receives and obeys your instructions. This discussion will introduce or expand on several important topics, including shells, kernels, programs, files, and permissions, although fuller treatments await you in later chapters. As in all pursuits of knowledge, a general framework is needed upon which you can slot in the nitty details.

FILES — A QUICK INTRODUCTION

Computer *files* are so called because they bear a nodding relation to the old-fashioned manila files people once used to store bits of paper. Such files had tab markers with headings such as "Gas Receipts, 1908–1909," allowing a primitive form of *random access*. For the moment, you can think of a computer file simply as a place for storing data and programs on your disk. Disk files also have tab markers known as *filenames*. Groups of files are stored in *directories*, which also have names. Both you and Unix use these directory and filenames when locating a file and accessing its contents. You'll see how in Chapter 3.

A major service offered by Unix (and most other operating systems) is handling files by name. You usually do not need to be concerned with the physical location or structure of a file–Unix keeps track of these boring details. Your accounts payable data may reside on cylinder 87 starting at sector 102, and it may even move about during processing. All you need to know is the directory name, `/usr/payables` or whatever, and the filename, say, `ac.payable`.

You (or your application program) may want to access a data file to examine or update its contents. Data or *text* files normally contain visible, printable characters encoded in ASCII format. You'll meet commands that will display or print the contents of a text file by reading a sequence of characters from the disk. There are yet more commands that allow you to write to the disk in order to create and modify text files. You can also copy and rename files, or append one file to another. You can, dare I mention it, all too easily erase (or *kill*) files.

Multiuser systems need to offer safeguards to prevent users from reading and/or erasing other users' files without due authority. Unix has an elaborate scheme of file ownerships and permissions whereby users and groups of users can protect their files. Each file in the system carries read, write, and execute permissions that dictate who can do what with a file.

Binary files, unlike text files, which are easily readable by most humans, contain program code in a form understood only by your CPU. Although some groups of characters in binary code may coincide with ASCII characters, printing or displaying a binary file will give you gibberish and may even lock up your printer or terminal.

If you want to run a program, Unix needs to locate it by name. When you enter the command `date`, for example, Unix looks for a program file called `date`. It looks in various places, as you'll see in Chapter 5. If it fails to find the target file, you get a *filename: not found* message, as you saw with `amelia` in Chapter 1.

COMMAND ARGUMENTS

Unix is not just the kernel and shell. Even the most basic versions of Unix come with a set of utility programs for editing and manipulating files: searching, sorting, and so on. Each of these can be invoked by entering the appropriate command, usually followed by additional, optional information known as *command arguments* and *options* (or *switches*). To reduce verbosity, the term *argument* is often applied to any extra information you type after a command, whether it is a filename or the symbol for a switch. Even when you enter a command such as `date` with no arguments, Unix usually supplies a default argument behind your back. You'll find that some arguments are needed simply to override or modify such defaults.

The precise nature and format for these arguments and options varies from command to command, and getting to know their quirks is a major part of mastering Unix. Each command has a *syntax,* or set of rules, governing its legal arguments. In addition, of course, you need to learn the semantics behind each syntactical variation: what does the command do, and how is the action modified by the presence of arguments? And, as I mentioned earlier, most commands have default arguments that you need to know about.

The bulk of the Unix documentation, in fact, is devoted to listing the syntax and semantics of the commands and their permissible arguments. Some commands you will use daily so they become familiar friends. Others are quite esoteric, requiring even the experts to take a sly peek at the manual to refresh their memory. Most systems have some or all of the Unix command reference manual online for instant access via the `man-` command.

Who Do People Say That I Am?

Try adding the arguments `am i` to the command `who`:

```
$ who am i
stan     tty01    Mar 23 13:07
$ _
```

NOTE

Unix distinguishes arguments from commands and, in most cases, other arguments by the spaces that separate them.

Your response, I imagine, will be different. Note the space between the command and its first argument. This is a general rule, otherwise Unix would be unable to distinguish the command name from what follows. We also have a space between the two arguments am and i, but other commands may accept arguments with or without spaces or other separating symbols.

In the interests of gooder English, Unix also accepts who am I with a capital *I*. The extra arguments alter the normal action of who. Rather than list all active users, it tells you about yourself: your login name, the name of the terminal or *line* you are wired to, and the date and time you logged in. The question is not as dumb as it may seem, by the way. You may be working away from home on a strange terminal and need to know its name; you may be registered under several user names; you may want to check when you logged in; or you may encounter a terminal that has been rashly left by someone in a logged-in state. (In the latter case, the who am i really asks "Who *was* that fool?")

Here is a useful shorthand to show the syntax of the who command so far presented:

```
who [am i]
who [am I]
```

We use the square brackets to enclose any argument or arguments that can be legally omitted. Note carefully that it would be wrong to write who [am] [i], since this would imply that who am and who i are legal (which is not true).

Now enter the command

```
$ who
```

immediately followed by the command

```
$ who -s
```

NOTE

A hyphen usually indicates that the following symbol is an option.

Can you spot any difference in the responses displayed by Unix? Unless someone logged in or out between your two entries, the two commands will give you the same result. They are equivalent because the switch -s (s here means short) is the default option for who. This option tells Unix to display just the name, line, and time fields of all active users. Unless you use another option that overrides the -s, who will assume you want the short option. The - sign (minus or hyphen) is commonly used in Unix to indicate that the following symbol is an option. When more than one option is allowed, you often find that a single - can be followed by a string of option symbols.

Instant Calendars

Next we'll try the calendar display command cal to illustrate another use of arguments and defaults. Enter cal as follows:

```
$ cal
     February 1999
 Su Mo Tu We Th Fr Sa
     1  2  3  4  5  6
  7  8  9 10 11 12 13
 14 15 16 17 18 19 20
 21 22 23 24 25 26 27
 28
```

The full syntax for cal is:

```
cal [[month] year]
```

Notice the positions of the square brackets used to indicate optional groups of arguments. They indicate that you can enter cal, cal *year*, or cal *month year*, but you are not allowed to enter cal *month*. Try some of the following combinations:

```
$ cal 1999
```

Whoops, the calendar for a whole year quickly scrolls off the screen. Time for a ReadSpeed enrollment? Not really. Unix offers a trick whereby you can display one screenful of text at a time:

```
$ cal 1999 | more
```

After the first part of the calendar fills the screen, you'll see the legend -- More --, and scrolling halts until you press the spacebar. Scrolling then resumes until another screen is full, and so on until the output is over and the prompt reappears. You can scroll one line at a time by pressing the Enter key.

Pipelines

The | (vertical bar) symbol represents a *pipeline* that takes the output of one program and sends it as input to another program. The second program is known as a *filter*. The output from a filter can either be displayed, or it can be passed on to another filter by using the pipeline symbol again. In $ x | y | z, the output from program x feeds into filter y, the output of y feeds into filter z. The output of z, if any, would normally be displayed on the screen.

In the above example, | redirects the output of `cal` from the screen to the filter called `more`. We won't delve deeply into this important mechanism just now—suffice it to say that `more` soaks up the data coming from `cal` and passes it on one screen or line at a time with a convenient pause and prompt. Other filters, provided by Unix or user-created, allow a wide range of data manipulation to and from files and screens.

More Calendars

The optional month argument can be entered numerically:

    $ cal 9 1999

or alphabetically:

    $ cal sep 1999

Both will display the calendar for September 1999. This is less than a screenful, so the `more` trick is not required. Unix is quite tolerant over the format for the month. Try

    $ cal s 1999

Since s (or S) uniquely determines September (no other month can claim this initial letter), September is what you get. With June, you need at least jun to avoid clashing with July. May needs three letters because of March, and so on. The rule for the month entry is this: either a number between 1 and 12, or enough letters (lower- or uppercase) to uniquely identify the name of a month.

A common error is to type the year as 99 when you mean 1999. The Unix calendar goes back to 1 C.E. (Common Era, also known as A.D.), so 99 is taken as, well, 99! The legal range for year is 1 to 9999, so you can play around with calendars past and future. I confirmed, for example, what my mother told me: I was born on a Sunday. Run your birth month and year past cal and check your day of birth. And if you're interested in getting a little surprise, try running the calendar for September, 1752 (talk about your leap years!)

To explore more useful Unix commands, you need to know more about the Unix file system. This forms the subject of our next chapter.

WHAT'S NEXT

In the next chapter, we'll take a closer look at directory structures (hierarchies), adding and deleting files and directories, and ways to navigate within the Unix file structures. We'll also take a look at a few housekeeping functions, such as making new directories and moving files in and out of them.

```
echo "2.      Show Date"
echo "3.      Display a file"
echo "4.      Change working director
echo "5.      Return to original dire
echo "Q.      Quit
echo
echo -n "Enter choice: .\b"
read choice
case $choice in
1) who | more
   pause;;
2) date
   pause;;
3) echo "Enter file name: \c"
   read fil
   if [ -r "$fil" -a -f "$fil" ]
   then
      clear
      more -d $fil
   else
      echo "Cannot di
   fi
   pause;;
4) echo "En
   read di
   if test    d "$dir       pwd`]
   then
      cd $dir
   else
      echo "$dir: no such dir
   fi
   pause;;
   5) if test "$dir" != "$pr
      then
         cd $prevdir
      fi
      pause;;
```

Chapter 3

MEET THE UNIX FILE SYSTEM

Files play an important and pervasive role in Unix. In Chapter 2, you learned that the file is a place where data and programs are stored. In this and the following chapter, you'll see how Unix extends this simple idea so that files can also represent devices, such as printers, terminals, and disk drives, and even less tangible objects such as *processes*.

To recap the four most important facts about files that were introduced in Chapter 2:

- ▸ Files are grouped into directories.

- ▸ Files and directories have names.

- ▸ Within a directory, each file has a unique name.

- ▸ The command names you type correspond to the names of program files that are interpreted by the shell.

Let's delve more deeply into files and directories by exploring a familiar analogy: your home filing system.

DIRECTORIES

A typical home filing system might start life with separate manila folders filed alphabetically:

Cajun Recipes

Dad's Recipes

Gas Receipts 1997

Gas Receipts 1998

Gas Receipts 1999

IRS 1997

IRS 1998

IRS 1999

John's Recipes

John's School

Mary's College

Mom's Recipes

For a small collection of files, this organization might be adequate, but as the number of files increases, your access time and frustration would grow—with most of the time spent in trying to recall the exact name of the folder holding your target data. Suppose now that you buy some larger folders and label them

> Education
>
> Gas Receipts
>
> IRS
>
> Recipes

Within each large folder you store the appropriate files. Your new file might be restructured and relabeled to look like this:

> Education
>
> > John
> >
> > Mary
>
> Gas Receipts
>
> > 1997
> >
> > 1998
> >
> > 1999
>
> IRS
>
> > 1997
> >
> > 1998
> >
> > 1999
>
> Recipes
>
> > Cajun
> >
> > Dad
> >
> > John
> >
> > Mom

In Unix terms, the larger folders represent directories, while the individual folders represent the files. Notice that the "search time" is reduced, mainly because you are better organized! You can go quickly to, say, *Education* by thumbing through the major categories, then quickly locate *John* or *Mary*.

You will immediately note that there are now two files named *John*. However, the two *John* files are distinct: one is under *Education* and the other is under *Recipes*. Similarly, the filenames *1997*, *1998*, and *1999* each appear twice but represent different sets of data. In Unix, you can indicate these distinctions as follows:

Education/John	The John file in the Education directory
Education/Mary	The Mary file in the Education directory
Recipes/John	The John file in the Recipes directory
Gas.Receipts/1998	The 1998 file in the Gas.Receipts directory
IRS/1998	The 1998 file in the IRS directory

and so on. Each directory/file combination, you'll notice, is unique, although the filenames may be duplicated.

The Name of the File

The period in Gas.Receipts, by the way, is not a typo. Unix file and directory names cannot have intervening spaces, so you tend to use a symbol such as . or _ or - to increase legibility: GasReceipts, Gas.Receipts, Gas-Receipts, and Gas_Receipts are all permitted, but Gas Receipts would look like two separate names to Unix. Most of the naming rules we'll be looking at apply equally to file and directory names, so to reduce verbiage, I'll often just refer to filenames. In fact, you'll see that Unix, being file-centered, treats directories rather like files in many situations.

In DOS, the period is reserved to show a file *extension*. In the filenames CONFIG.SYS or WS.COM, for example, SYS and COM are extensions, limited to three characters at most, used to tell you something about the nature of the file. Unix is more flexible: periods are optional, but if used, they can be placed anywhere in a file or directory name and you can use as many of them as you wish with one exception: A period at the *beginning* of a filename does have a special significance, so we'll avoid using names such as .thingy until I've explained this usage.

Unix names can have up to 255 character filenames, depending on the limitations created by the system administrator. There are, however, a few symbols that are illegal or inadvisable. For instance, using the / character within a name would confuse Unix and everyone else, as it is used to distinguish directory names from filenames; something like `Gas/Receipts` would be interpreted as a file called `Receipts` in a directory called `Gas`.

WARNING

Avoid * / ? ¨ ´ ` [ ] and any control characters in your Unix filenames. Though spaces are acceptable in Unix, you do, however, need to put single quotes around the filenames that use them so Unix doesn't think its dealing with multiple files when it encounters them.

Similarly, the invisible control characters should not be used, again for obvious reasons. The other forbidden characters are * ? ¨ ´ ` [and], for reasons that will emerge later.

You should strike a balance between a short, ambiguous filename, such as `things` or `stuff`, that barely indicates its contents, and a long-winded essay that may prove difficult to recall and type consistently. Of course, if your directories are succinctly named, the filenames can be short and simple, as in the examples above.

NOTE

The prepackaged command names of Unix are often notoriously short and cryptic. There are sound historical reasons for this. In the late 1960s, when Ken Thompson and Dennis Ritchie were developing the first Unix, the available terminals were slow, 10-character-per-second teletypewriters, so it made sense to keep both command lines and error messages as short as possible. They also had very little memory to work with...an even more compelling reason.

Remember too that Unix, unlike DOS, distinguishes upper- and lower-case letters in file and directory names. The files `irs`, `Irs`, and `IRS` are different, so watch your Shift and Caps Lock keys. Traditionally, though, programmers have never been slick touch typists, so command names have tended to be short and in lowercase.

Trees and Hierarchies

As you've seen, Unix uses the symbol / (forward slash) between the directory name and the filename. (DOS users will recognize this trick—see the next section.) It provides a file structure known as *hierarchical*, which simply means that the files are organized like the folders in a filing cabinet. So far, you've only seen a two-level hierarchy, directory_name/ filename, but both DOS and Unix build on this in a natural way: a directory (like a file folder) can itself hold other directories (like one folder can hold other folders). But instead of calling the folders *folders*, Unix calls them *directories* and *subdirectories*. Directories can hold subdirectories and subdirectories can hold *subsubdirectories* (usually just called subdirectories), and so on. And finally, subdirectories and directories can hold files.

NOTE

Subdirectories are often simply called *directories*.

NOTE

DOS borrowed the Unix hierarchical file structure when DOS matured from Version 1.0 to Version 2.0. For some obscure reason, though, DOS uses a \ (backslash) rather than the / (forward slash) used in Unix. DOS would use IRS\1998.DAT, for example, for a file in the IRS directory. This difference can be a nuisance if you are constantly switching between DOS and Unix. Either system will quickly tell you if you use the wrong slash, and usually no real damage results: you'll just get an annoying file not found or similar message.

Paths

The Unix notation for these hierarchies is quite simple. If you see a file named usr/stan/memo, you know at once that usr is a directory with a subdirectory called stan that holds a file called memo. The *path* to memo is the sequence of directories you need to traverse to reach memo, namely usr/stan/. You can also say that the path to stan is usr/. The path concept turns out to be of great practical importance when working with Unix files. If this concept is a little fuzzy to you, have patience. There will be plenty of examples before long.

Figure 3.1 shows a *tree* diagram, a common and convenient way of looking at paths and file hierarchies. Unlike Mother Nature's trees, file trees traditionally grow upside down, with the branches spreading downwards away from the light.

Quick test: what is the path to mail? Yes, you climb down the tree via the directories usr and mary to mail, so the path is usr/mary/. What is the path to temp? Ah, gotcha! Both stan and mary have a file called temp, so the question needs reframing.

You Call That a File?

The labels in Figure 3.1 identify which names are directory names and which are filenames. Without these labels, you could certainly deduce that usr, stan, and mary are directories. How? Well, they are each shown holding (or providing a path to) a named object on the lower level: usr holds stan and mary, stan holds memo and temp, and so on. Only directories can hold other directories and files. Files can hold data (not shown in the tree), but they cannot hold directories or other files.

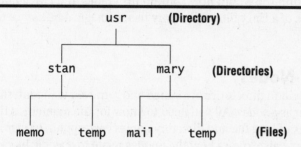

FIGURE 3.1: The file tree

If I removed the label showing memo as a file, however, you could not tell from the tree whether memo was a file or an *empty* directory. As you can guess, an empty directory is a perfectly valid directory that by some quirk of fate happens not to hold any subdirectories or files. If you erased the files stan/memo and stan/temp, for instance, stan would still exist, but it would now be an empty directory.

You'll be pleased to learn that Unix offers commands that tell you whether a given name is a file or a directory. There are also commands to create and remove both directories and files, as well as commands that let you "move" around the tree in all directions and explore the contents of directories and files (limited only by any security restrictions imposed by other users and the system administrator). Before rushing into these commands, you need a little more background on Unix file organization.

Filename Duplicates

Although you can have more than one Unix file called John, each must reside in a different directory. In the manila folder world we looked at earlier, there's nothing to stop you from misfiling *John's Education* stuff in the *Recipe* section. The two files marked *John* would just sit there. This would be a nuisance and would hinder prompt retrieval, but it would not violate the known Laws of Physics.

In this area, Unix files are less tolerant, and here the manila folder analogy starts breaking down. Two John files cannot coexist in the Recipes directory. Putting a second file named John into the Recipe directory would overwrite the existing John file with the second John file, regardless of the relative sizes of the two files. By overwriting, I mean *completely* replacing the contents of one file with another. The original data is lost: the Recipe/John file would now contain his grades and curriculum vitae! The name of a Unix file or directory has no magical influence over its contents.

Files and i-Nodes

In fact, Unix files and directories are stored and retrieved using internal numbers known as *i-nodes*. All you need to know for the moment is that Unix keeps track of how file and directory names correspond, or *map*, to their i-nodes. Unix also knows how the i-nodes relate to specific blocks and tracks on your disk. The sequence of steps taken by Unix when you key in a filename is (briefly) as follows:

1. Use the path to get to the relevant table.

2. Find the name in that table.

3. Note the corresponding i-node.

4. Use the i-node to locate the file on the disk.

5. Manipulate the data in the file (read, write, and so on) according to your command.

Flat Files

Unix files are what we call *flat files*. You can think of them as simple streams of characters or bytes without any intrinsic format or structure. They can grow and shrink freely as they are manipulated and massaged in various ways. Unix maintains in its tables a number giving the current length in bytes of each file, and this is updated whenever the file size changes. When a program tries to read beyond the end of a file, Unix generates an EOF (end-of-file) message—end of reading!

Other operating systems have elaborate sets of formats defining specific headers and fields for different files, strict rules that must be adhered to by all user programs. With Unix, it is up to individual application programmers to impose some structure on the string of bytes sitting in a Unix flat file. When we come to editing text files, you'll see that the usual layout codes, such as tab and carriage return, are written into files by the editor program just like normal characters. It is the editor, not Unix itself, that interprets them to give you nicely formatted documents.

Two Names for the Same File?

The chunk of flat data sitting in a file "knows" only its unique i-node. You could not determine its Unix name by reading this data; you would have to trace back to the tables where Unix keeps its lists of i-nodes and names. Each name has a unique i-node, but several different names can reference the same i-node value. So, if, for example, two different file-names, stan and joe, are linked, they could both access the same file. Changes to stan would immediately show up if you worked with joe, and vice versa. How did stan and joe achieve this strange status? Well, Unix provides a command called ln (link) that lets you link an existing file to another name. Assuming you set up stan first, you could enter

```
$ ln stan joe
```

Thereafter, the names joe and stan will both access the same file, essentially giving you two names for the same physical file. Why would you want to do this? Because you can save keystrokes by linking files with long names to a shorter "alias."

THE ROOT OF THE MATTER

The tree in Figure 3.1 is just a part of the total Unix file tree. At the base of the whole tree is a special directory appropriately called the root. Remember that file trees are inverted with respect to natural timber, so the root will be shown at the top!

Changing the symbolism to family trees, you can see that other directories have one (unique) parent and may possibly have children, but the root has only children. The root is the only directory with no parent. The whole tree grows (down!) from the root, the Adam of the family.

The symbol for the root is /, which beginners find rather strange at first. Yes, the selfsame slash that is used to separate directory and file-names when listing paths and path names. You may think it confusing and ambiguous to use the one symbol in two apparently conflicting ways, but once you start using the root symbol, it soon emerges as a natural and indeed elegant approach.

First, let's add the root to our earlier tree. The result is shown below in Figure 3.2.

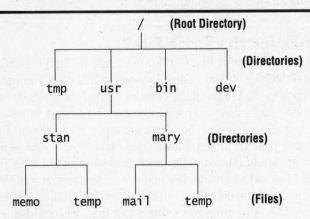

FIGURE 3.2:   File tree with root

Notice that usr is now a subdirectory of root, and that I have added a few more subdirectories to root, namely tmp, bin, and dev. These three standard directories have many branches, but I've omitted them to avoid clutter.

Absolute Path Names

We can now give the full path names for our four files as follows:

```
/usr/stan/memo
/usr/stan/temp
/usr/mary/mail
/usr/mary/temp
```

The first / is the root. This is a fixed point of reference. The subsequent / symbols are our familiar directory/file separators.

Path names starting with /, the root, are called *absolute* path names: they specify the file completely.

Home Is Best

The beauty of the Unix file hierarchy is that you do not always have to specify these lengthy, absolute path names. If you are already partway down the path to your target file, all you need to specify is the *rest* of the path. Unix knows where you are, and will construct the full, absolute path name for you. If you are already "sitting at" mary, say, you can access the file /usr/mary/mail by simply asking for mail. Unix supplies the /usr/mary/ part for you.

To see how this works, you need to understand two new concepts: the *home* directory and the *working* directory.

Every user is assigned a home directory by the system administrator. When you first log in, you are placed in this home directory. Home is your starting point in the file tree. From there you can roam around the tree, up, down, and sideways, landing in different directories, and returning home for love and dinner. The directory you happen to be in at any point in your odyssey is called your *current* or *working* directory, and has the special nickname (or alias). (pronounced *dot*). Most times, this will be your own, home, dedicated, private directory. Here you are king or queen, free to establish your own subdirectories and files, set visiting rights (permissions) for other users, and so on. Only the system administrator can override your protective shield. Otherwise, your home directory is safe and cozy. It is almost always named /home or /usr. My home directory, for example, is called stan just like my login name, so I start at /usr/stan.

How do you know where you are in the file tree as you move around? Read on.

You Are Here

The pwd command means "print working directory." In Unix, the word "print" often means "display," another hangover from the early teleprinter terminal days.

The response to pwd gives you the absolute path name of your current place in the file tree, namely your working directory. For example:

```
$ pwd
/usr/stan
$ _
```

Next, try creating your own subdirectory and moving to it, as in

```
$ mkdir test
$ cd test
$ pwd
/usr/stan/test
$ _
```

Since I was already in /usr/stan, the mkdir test (make new directory called test) command created a new, empty subdirectory with the absolute path name of /usr/stan/test. Its name *relative* to /usr/stan, my home directory, is simply test. So while I'm in my home directory, I can refer to the new directory "just below me" simply as test—there is no need to use the longer absolute path name. Knowing where you are in the tree is therefore vital: your current, working directory quietly "adds" its path to any relative directory or filename arguments you type.

The cd test (change working directory to test) command therefore moves me from /usr/stan to /usr/stan/test. I could have used

```
$ cd /usr/stan/test
```

with exactly the same results but with more keyboard effort.

You can use cd without an argument to get to your home directory at any time. For example:

```
$ pwd
/usr/stan/test
$ cd
$ pwd
/usr/stan
```

After cd returned me to my home (also called root) directory, I used pwd to confirm my present whereabouts. While you are getting used to navigating the directories, it's an excellent idea to use pwd frequently. Remember that if, for example, you have several files called John, the one you are accessing is the one in your current directory, unless you explicitly supply an overriding path name. If you are working in /usr/joe/Education, the name John refers to /usr/joe/Education/John. If you want to access the other John without changing directories, you could type its full, absolute path name: /usr/joe/Recipes/John. Or, you could change your working directory with this command:

```
$ cd /usr/joe/Recipes
```

Now, of course, you can access /usr/joe/Recipes/John by using good old plain John. Confused? Well, it does take some practice. Like riding a bike, some things are easier to do than to write about. The key point to watch is that absolute path names start with the root symbol /. They take you all the way back to the root, then lead you down to your target. Relative path names do not have an initial /, so they lead you from where you are to your target.

Back Home

Suppose I'm in /usr/stan/test/temp. To get back to the parent directory, /usr/stan/test, I could use this command:

    $ cd /usr/stan/test

but Unix offers a simpler method. The special argument.. (two periods, pronounced *dot-dot*) always means "the parent of the current directory." So

    $ cd ..

gets me to /usr/stan/test a little sooner!

Wherever you are, cd .. moves you one level back towards the root. If you are already at root, then cd .. has no effect.

Removing a Directory

Let's get rid of the test directory. It's empty and has served its purpose. The command to use is rmdir (remove directory):

    $ rmdir test

If test had contained any files or directories, Unix would warn you and would refuse to delete the directory. Now that test has been deleted, try cd test for a giggle. Yes, you get a directory: does not exist error message. You may get this error message on occasions when you are convinced that the target directory *does* exist. The usual reason is that you are not in the correct working directory. If you are in /usr and type cd memo, Unix looks in vain for /usr/memo. Now memo does exist, but it's a subdirectory of /usr/stan. So, either supply the full path name, or make /usr/stan your working directory.

With the commands pwd, mkdir, cd, and rmdir, you can gain some useful insights into the Unix file tree. To progress further, you'll need to know how to create files. This is the subject of our next chapter.

What's Next

In Chapter 4, we'll show you how to create your own files from the keyboard and from other files. Additionally, we'll take a look at some basic file maintenance, such as displaying the contents of a subdirectory and deleting files that you no longer need.

```
echo "2.      Show Date"
echo "3.      Display a file"
echo "4.      Change working director
echo "5.      Return to original dire
echo "Q.      Quit
echo
echo -n "Enter choice: .\b"
read choice
case $choice in
1) who | more
   pause;;
2) date
   pause;;
3) echo "Enter file name: \c"
   read fil
   if [ -r "$fil" -a -f "$fil" ]
   then
      clear
      more -d $fil
   else
      echo "Cannot di
   fi
   pause;;
4) echo "En
   read di
   if test      "$dir"    pwd`
   then
      cd $dir
   else
      echo "$dir: no such di
   fi
      pause;;
   5) if test "$dir" != "$p
      then
         cd $prevdir
      fi
      pause;;
```

Chapter 4

CREATING YOUR OWN FILES

Now that you know how to navigate the Unix file hierarchy, it's time to create some files of your own. In this chapter, you'll learn how to store the output of commands in disk files and how to key text into files. You'll also meet the `ls` and `lc` commands that list the names and attributes of your files in various formats, as well as the `cat` (catalog) command, which lets you read the contents of files. As the number of commands you learn continues to grow, you'll see how they can be combined to create useful tools.

STANDARD INPUT AND OUTPUT

Recall my earlier comment that files are omnipresent in Unix. In fact, you have already been using two special files without being aware that they *were* files. Since a Unix file can represent any stream of characters, it is not surprising to find that the characters you enter on the keyboard and the characters displayed on your screen can be associated with two files called *standard input* and *standard output*. For brevity, I'll call them stdin and stdout, the internal names used by C programs and their programmers. (Note that you do not use these names as filename arguments in commands—more on this later.)

▸ For most users, the stdin file, the command's standard input, refers to your *keyboard*.

▸ For most users, the stdout file, the command's standard output, refers to your *monitor screen*.

You do not have to create or name these two standard files as you do with normal user disk files. Unix automatically *opens* them for you whenever a command that needs them starts to operate. Opening a file simply means priming it for action, an internal Unix operation the mechanics of which are of no immediate concern to us.

The stdin and stdout files are clearly different in many ways from the disk files you met in Chapter 3. Unless you save your keystroked input somewhere, your default stdin file is simply a source of characters that the system discards as soon as they have served their purpose. Likewise, the characters sent to the default stdout file appear fleetingly on the screen, then move on to oblivion.

It can be useful, however, to treat the data streams coming from stdin and going to stdout in exactly the same way as data traveling to and from conventional files. Here's a simple example.

In the dialogue below, the first line uses the pwd command introduced in Chapter 3. The pwd command prints the name and path of the directory that you are logged in to—in this example, /usr/stan. Your own home directory will usually be /usr/xxx, where xxx is your login name. If you are not in your home directory, you should use cd on its own to get there. Recall that cd without an argument defaults to your home directory: /usr/xxx, or whatever your home directory happens to be. In this chapter, you'll be creating and using test files that you won't want to keep later, so it's safer to be in your own personal directory where you cannot bother other users.

```
$ pwd
/usr/stan
$ date
Mon Apr 3 17:33:28 PDT 1995
$ date >today.test
$ _
```

WARNING

Using $ `command` > *filename* without care may overwrite valuable data in *filename*!

The first date command displays the current date on the screen in the time-honored fashion, similar to the example shown above. But where is your date display from the fifth line?

The answer lies in the way the greater-than symbol (>) works in Unix. The > symbol tells Unix to take the output from the first parameter and put it into the location specified by the second.

So in the fifth line above, we have asked Unix to *redirect* the output from date into a file called today.test. In response, Unix quietly and temporarily reassigned stdout from your screen to this file. If this file already exists, all exisiting data in the original file will be overwritten. If it doesn't exist, Unix will create a new file called today.test. So be very careful when you use this directive, as you could easily lose valuable data if you are not careful about naming your target file.

REDIRECTING OUTPUT

NOTE

DOS users will probably recognize the use of > and < for redirection—another case of DOS-Unix flattery by imitation.

The greater-than sign (>) is a redirection operator (on PC keyboards, you'll find that > is shift-period). Note that spaces before and/or after > or < are optional. Once again, as its name and shape suggest, > effectively takes the stream of characters produced by date and redirects them *from* the screen file *to* the disk file, today.test.

We'll concentrate on output redirection for a while, but it should come as no surprise to hear that Unix can also redirect `stdin` using the symbol < (note the direction), so that many commands can take their input data either from the keyboard or from a disk file.

Before I go any further, let's verify that your redirection has worked as planned. Enter the following commands:

```
$ ls
...
lp0
mbox
today.test
...
$ cat today.test
Mon Apr  3 17:33:50 PDT 1995
$ _
```

There are two new important commands here: `ls` and `cat`.

THE ls COMMAND

`ls` stands for "list" because it lists the names of the files and subdirectories in your current directory. `ls` has many options that I'll discuss later. For now, I am using the plain `ls` without options to prove that a new file called `today.test` has indeed been created. When you type the `ls` command, you may well get a different list from mine. The ellipses in the last example indicate that there may be other filenames showing, since I've no way of knowing what files exist in your current directory. What I do know is that if you entered `date >today.test` correctly, then `ls` will reveal the new file, `test.today`. Furthermore, you'll find it listed in the correct alphabetical sequence, since `ls` kindly sorts the names alphabetically for you by default. Later you'll see how to vary this ordering by supplying options.

Note also that `ls` without options lists both your files and subdirectories by name only, without telling you which is a file and which is a directory.

Another way of using `ls` to check the existence of files (or directories) is as follows:

```
$ ls today.test
today.test
$ ls teddy.bear
teddy.bear not found
$ _
```

Here you've supplied a filename argument, and `ls` will list just that file if it exists; otherwise you get a `name not found` message, where *name* is the filename you specified. In our simplified notation, the syntax for `ls`, so far, is

    ls *name*

Omitting the optional `name`, the names of all files and subdirectories in your current directory are listed. It's easy to extend this syntax by adding an optional path:

    ls *path/name*

For example, `ls/usr` or `ls/usr/` will list all the files and subdirectories of `/usr` even if your current directory is `/usr/stan`.

Similarly, `ls/usr/memo` will tell you if `memo` exists in `/usr`, whatever your current directory may be. A good way to picture this is that when you omit the optional path name, Unix assumes your current directory by default. You simply override this default by adding a specific path name.

Wildcards

NOTE

DOS users will observe that `ls`, as used so far, bears a close resemblance to the DOS *dir* command. The use of * and ? for wildcards is also very similar.

`ls`, like many Unix commands, also supports *wildcard searches*. Try the following:

```
$ ls *
...
lp0
mbox
today.test
...
$ ls *test
today.test
$ ls ??day.test
today.test

$ls *
lp0
mbox
today.test

$ _
```

In the example above, there are three files in the current directory: 1p0, mbox and today.test. By specifying *test, the first line returns today.test since it's the only file that contains the string test. The second command, ??day.test, returns today.test because it's the only file that contains a dot and the specified characters. (The ??'s will match any two characters that precede day. So, if they were present, this line would also match files named inday, upday, or myday.)

In the third line, all three files are returned because the * will match any filename.

FOR ADVANCED USERS ONLY

Unix also provides a more sophisticated pattern-matching argument format for 1s and similar commands. 1s [abc]*, for example, will list all files starting with "a", "b", or "c", and 1s *[vqz] will match all files ending with "v", "q", or "z". 1s [a]??[s] will match all four-letter names starting with "a" and ending with "s". I'll have more to say on matching in Chapter 9.

Within the [and] you can place any sequence of characters for *individual* matching. More interestingly, you can ask for a *range* of characters as follows: 1s [a-m]* will match any file starting with a letter in the range a to m inclusive. You could use 1s [s-u]???[1-9] to list any five-letter files starting with "s", "t", or "u" and ending with a digit between "1" and "9".

The shell turns arguments featuring wildcards into sets of matching names for 1s to process. 1s *itself*, contrary to appearances, does not receive wildcard arguments. You'll see the implications of this when I discuss echo and other commands.

An interesting quirk of Unix wildcards concerns the matching of names beginning with a period. You may recall that I warned you in Chapter 3 against using an initial period when naming files and directories. The reason is twofold.

First, any file such as .profile that starts with a period is *not* normally reported by 1s and similar commands. So I lied when I said that * matched all character strings! Such files are *hidden* for various reasons. To "see" them, you must use

    1s .*

CONTINUED ➡

Second, as you saw in Chapter 3, Unix uses the period in its short-hand for two important directories: one period for your current directory, and two periods for the parent of your current directory. So, `ls .` and `ls ..` list the contents of your current and parent directories respectively. If `ls *` also matched initial periods, it would generate a host of unwanted names. Try

```
ls .*
```

It will find list files such as `.profile`, then all the files and subdirectories of your current directory (also known as `.`), then finally it will list all the files and subdirectories of `..`, the parent of your current directory. Better use `ls .* | more` to give you a pause after each screenful.

I mentioned the many options available with `ls`. Although this is not the place to enumerate them, I will now take a brief detour to show you how to learn more about `ls` without having to comb the documentation.

Exploring ls with the man Command

Although Unix has the reputation of being user-indifferent, it has one eminently friendly facility that has been widely imitated, without acknowledgment, by other suposedly user-friendly systems. From the earliest days, the man command has provided easy access to an online manual. Its size and quality, however, may vary from site to site, depending on factors such as available disk space and the system administrator's devotion to updates. Try entering the command

```
$ man ls
```

The online manual pages for `ls` will scroll by one screenful at a time, with a pause for digestion. At the end of each screen, a colon appears. Press the Enter key to see the next page. Eventually, you'll get back to the $ prompt.

Any command name will serve as the man argument. Commands are uniformly explained under the following sequence:

Name (Section)	LS(C)
Command	Ls
Syntax	`ls [-ACFRabcdfgilmnopqrstux]` `[names]`

Description	Describes the effect of each option and lists the default options
Files	Lists any associated files, e.g., files where defaults may be stored
See Also	Lists related commands
Notes	Gives additional information or samples of usage
Standards Conformance	Lists the Unix standards with which the command conforms, e.g. AT&T SVID, X/Open

The online manual uses a standard Unix section coding scheme to facilitate reference to the Unix cornucopia. The header LS(C) means that the ls command is in the C (command) section; CRASH(ADM) references the crash command in ADM, the system administration section; TERMINFO(M) is all about terminfo in the Miscellaneous section, and so on. A LOCAL section documents all commands that are specific to your installation. You'll gradually become familiar with which section holds which command. You can ask man to search all or selected sections. From now on, when I introduce a new command, I will provide the section code to guide you.

Digesting the Syntax

The syntax line usually looks daunting. The twenty-two letters shown inside [and] after ls mean that you can use either some, all, or none of them with ls. Note that case is important: a and A are different options. A single option would be written as ls -l [*names*], for example, with a hyphen before the chosen letter and a space after the command and before the file or directory names (if any). The - has no negative connotations: some options are subtractive while others are additive.

Multiple options can either be written out in full

    ls -l-a *name*

or combined with a single hyphen:

    ls -la *name*

The option letters are sometimes mnemonics: -l means list in the *long*, comprehensive format. Sometimes they are less so: -a means list the hidden files and directories (those beginning with a period), so you can think of a as standing for *all*. Sometimes no obvious mnemonic appears: -u means sort the list by time of last access.

In the syntax line, [*names*] means that one, several, or no names are all admissible. So both `ls` and `ls -la name1 name2 name3` are legal.

Table 4.1 lists some of the more popular `ls` variants.

TABLE 4.1   Common options for `ls`, `l`, and `lc`

Option	Description
Default	Lists in alphabetic sequence, excluding `.`names (that is, names starting with a period)
`-a`	Lists all matching entries, including `.`names
`-l`	Provides a long listing showing type of entry (file or directory), permissions, owner, size, and date last modified
`-r`	Reverse listing order
`-s`	Gives size of each file
`-t`	Lists in order of time-date last modified (latest first)
`-u`	Lists in order of time-date last accessed (latest first)

The `man` command itself has many options for customizing and printing the manual in different formats. Naturally, you can read all about these by typing

```
$ man man
```

Be warned that `man` can become quite addictive. For now, just note that the manual text files are stored in `/usr/man`; your system administrator can add to these for any local commands or instructions.

THE cat COMMAND

Returning to the `date >today.test` experiment outlined in the section "Redirecting Output," you'll recall that we used `cat today.test` to prove that redirection worked as promised.

The `cat` command (in `man` section C), used with a single filename argument, simply displays the *contents* of the given file. So `cat today.test` displays the sequence of characters stored in `today.test`. As you saw earlier, `cat` gave a display on your screen similar to

```
Mon Apr 3 17:33:50 PDT 1995
```

which was exactly like the original `date` command with no redirection. Ah, not exactly! The time of the second `date` entry was a few seconds later! However, you must agree that the output from date was success-fully redirected into today.test. It's quite neat to realize that you have created a file and filled it with meaningful data without resorting to word processors or text editors!

The name cat is short for *catenate*, which in turn is short for *concatenate*, a fancy, $500 term for joining things together. You have seen cat display only a single file, so you may wonder what this has to do with concatenation. The reason is that cat can be used with several filename arguments: cat x y will display the contents of file x, followed by the contents of file y. Using our newfound friend >, cat x y > z will concatenate the two files x and y into one new, big file called z.

USING OUTPUT REDIRECTION WITH OTHER COMMANDS

Redirection works with any command that generates output to stdout. We often talk about a command *writing* to its standard output. Try the following:

```
$ who >who.dat
$ cat who.dat
iwonka tty1a Apr5 10:04
stan   tty2a Apr5 10:32
$ ls >list.dat
$ cat list.dat
list.dat
lp0
mbox
today.test
who.dat
$ cat who.dat list.dat >combo
$ cat combo
iwonka tty1a Apr5 10:04
stan   tty2a Apr5 10:32
list.dat
lp0
mbox
today.test
who.dat
$ _
```

Your displays will differ somewhat, but they should convince you that with redirection, commands such as who and ls can create useful files.

Note how cat with two filename arguments concatenates the files to the third argument, combo. The second argument, list.dat, although nearer to combo in the command line, appears at the end of combo. The reason for this is that cat reads and transfers its arguments from left to right.

You should experiment on your own by creating a calendar file using cal > cal.dat or cal 1990 > cal.year. Note that the optional arguments for cal are entered before the redirection arguments. Use ls and cat to check your new files.

The syntax for output redirection is simple:

commandname [*options*] [*>filename*]

Omitting the optional > *filename* arguments gives the default: command output goes to the screen. (Note that you should never actually use >stdout as an argument. Unix would take date >stdout literally, creating a disk file called stdout!)

Before I move on from output to input redirection, let's see a simple way of creating a file from keyboard input. You'll be using cat in a new way. So far, we have been creating files with data determined by other commands, such as date, cal, and who; it would be nice to have some files with our own written texts in them. You'll meet some new commands: lc and wc (both in man section C).

USING cat TO CREATE FILES

Enter the following sequence:

```
$ cat >poem.1
Mary had a little lamb,
Its feet were white as snow;
^d
$ _
```

Press Enter after typing poem.1, lamb, and snow; to get line spaces as shown. During text entry Unix stores the Enter key action as the ASCII *newline* code (value 10). When text files are read back to screens or printers, the newline code gives you the familiar carriage-return/linefeed action.

After the final Enter, you should hold down the Ctrl key and type a d or D. Ctrl-D, traditionally written as ^d or ^D, is the Unix EOF (end-of-file) character, telling the command that input is finished. Let's see the result of our efforts:

```
$ cat poem.1
Mary had a little lamb,
```

```
Its feet were white as snow;
$ _
```

The miracle is readily explained: cat was reading data from your default standard input, the keyboard, and passing it to its redirected standard output, the file poem.1. Let's try another:

```
$ cat >poem.2
And everywhere that Mary went,
The lamb was sure to go.
^d
$ cat poem.2
And everywhere that Mary went,
The lamb was sure to go.
$ _
```

Now it's concatenation time:

```
$ cat poem.1 poem.2 >poem
$ cat poem
Mary had a little lamb,
Its feet were white as snow;
And everywhere that Mary went,
The lamb was sure to go.
$ _
```

cat will not replace WordPerfect, but at least we have a file with a poem in it.

To test your ls and wildcard skills, try the following:

```
$ ls poem.?
poem.1
poem.2
$ ls poem*
poem
poem.1
poem.2
$ _
```

THE lc COMMAND

Now for a new command from the ls family:

```
$ lc poem*
poem      poem.1    poem.2
$ _
```

NOTE
lc is standard for SCO UNIX, but may not be available on your system.

Yes, lc (in man section C) means "list in columns," but otherwise works very much like ls. Without any name arguments, lc lists the files and sub-directories of your current directory.

Normally, lists are sorted lexicographically (in dictionary order). You can vary this with the -t option, giving time-of-last-data-modification order, with the latest modified file listed first:

```
$ lc -t poem*
poem      poem.2    poem.1
$ _
```

The -u option sorts by time of last access, with the most recently accessed file first. Here is a case where two options conflict, so avoid the combination -ut. The -r option reverses the order given by the other options, so -rt (sort by time modified, with earliest first) and -ru (search by time accessed, with earliest first) are legal and useful.

```
$ lc -rt poem*
poem.1    poem.2    poem
$ _
```

COUNTING WORDS WITH WC

You can also determine some statistics about your file contents using the wc (word count) command (in man section C):

```
$ wc poem
              4  22 108 poem
$ wc poem.1
              2  11  53 poem.1
$ wc poem.2
              2  11  55 poem.2
$ _
```

wc gives you the number of lines, words, and characters in the target file. Note that the number of characters is more than you might expect because the newline codes count as characters.

It's interesting, and in the true spirit of Unix, to combine commands. Try ls | wc. The output of ls (a list of your files) will be counted by wc and the result displayed. The first number from wc is the number of files in your current directory.

REDIRECTING INPUT

If you feel comfortable about output redirection using >, the next topic, input redirection, should present no real obstacles. Since the directions are reversed, the input redirection symbol is naturally reversed also: you use

    command < filename

to indicate that the command will take its input from the file filename rather than from the default standard input, namely your keyboard.

To illustrate this concept, I'll introduce a useful command called pr (in man section C) that performs relatively simple text formatting for screen display or hardcopy printers. As I mentioned earlier, many Unix names reflect the days of yore when most terminals were printing devices, so the pr (print) command should not be taken literally. You still find Unix folk talking about "printing on the screen" when they really mean "displaying." Anyway, pr accepts text from stdin and writes the formatted output to stdout, which as you now know can be the screen, a disk file, or a special file representing a hardcopy printer. You can see that pr meets all the criteria for being a filter (see Chapter 2), and such it is.

NOTE

A filter is a program that reads from the standard input and writes to the standard output. Either input or output or both can be redirected to files.

pr has options for "printing" titled, paginated, multicolumn reports with optional line numbers, tab expansion, and a host of other tricks. (Try man pr to see the full story.) The default options for pr give the following format:

- ▶ 66-line pages with page number, date, time, and filename at the top of each page
- ▶ 5-line header and trailer
- ▶ Single-column layout
- ▶ Single-line spacing

(Unix has more sophisticated text formatters, but pr is adequate for simple listings.)

I will use the following option arguments to vary these defaults:

-d   Uses double-line spacing

-t   Suppresses the header and trailer and stops after last line of file without spacing to next page

The object is to take a text file, say i text, format it, and display the result on the screen. Our command line will have the following pattern:

```
pr options <itext
```

Note carefully the layout: the options must immediately follow the command. pr will read its input from itext because of the < symbol. The output has not been redirected, so pr writes to the screen. To capture the output of pr in a file, you simply redirect the output by adding a > symbol and a filename. It may appear strange at first, but the general format combining both input and output redirection is as follows:

```
pr options <itext >otext
```

Note the sequence carefully. You can picture the output "emerging" from the command pr options <itext and going into otext. You can practice with the following example:

```
$ pr -t-d <poem >d.poem
$ cat d.poem

Mary had a little lamb,

Its feet were white as snow;
And everywhere that Mary went,

The lamb was sure to go.
$ _
```

COMPARING REDIRECTION AND PIPELINES

You met the pipe symbol | in Chapter 2, where we used cal | more to gain a pause between each screen-load of calendric data. The output of cal becomes the input of the filter more, and the output from more is directed to the default standard output, your screen. Compare this example with

```
$ date >today.test
$ _
```

in which the output of date is sent to a file.

The two actions are closely related, but you must not confuse the pipe-line action of | with the redirection achieved using > and <. All three symbols affect the way the shell deals with input and output. Both > and | effectively take the output of a command and "divert" it from the default stdout, namely your screen. The big difference is that | must be followed by the name of a special program, known as a *filter*, whereas > is followed by a filename.

Filters are special in that they take their input from stdin and send their output to stdout. You can often simulate the action of a filter by using > and < with a temporary file acting as a bridge. For example,

```
$ ls >temp
$ pr -t<temp
1p0
poem
poem.1
poem.2
$ rm temp
$ _
```

can be more elegantly performed with

```
$ ls | pr -t
1p0
poem
poem.1
poem.2
$ _
```

In the first example, we created an intermediate file called temp. To illustrate that this file was of no further use to us, we use rm temp to erase it. What the user maketh, the user can taketh away! This command needs a section!

Erasing Files with rm

The rm (remove) command (in man section C) is a vital but potentially dangerous command that deletes, zaps, and removes.

```
$ lc file*
file1     file2     file3
$ rm file1 file2 file3
$ cat file1
cat: cannot open file1
$ lc file*
file* not found
$ _
```

They've all gone!

```
$ ls tmp*
tmp1
tmp6
tmp89
$ rm tmp?
$ ls tmp*
tmp89
$ _
```

Still one left!

rm is therefore a rapid, irrevocable way of getting rid of many files and their contents. rm just quietly removes the files with no fuss or feedback.

There are some safeguards, however, which depend on what *write permissions* you have for the directory and the files involved. These permissions are intended to prevent you from erasing the files of others without their prior consent (a practice that people tend to frown on). Usually, you do have these write permissions on your own files, but care is still needed.

A useful trick is to use the -i (inquire) option. With rm -i file*, say, you are asked to confirm the deletion of each matching file. You can answer n or N to preserve the file, or y or Y to remove it.

A dangerous option is -r (recursive), which takes a directory as argument. rm -r stan, where stan is a directory, would erase the directory stan, every file in stan, every subdirectory of stan *and* their files, and so down the hierarchy. The part of the file tree branching from stan downwards is utterly zapped. (This is called *recursive* because rm keeps calling itself with subdirectory arguments.) Clearly this is powerful stuff, but occasionally useful when severe pruning is called for. Happily, you can control the felling of your tree by combining the i and r options: rm -ir stan will seek confirmation before each deletion.

▶ Use rm with care!

▶ rm -i is safer.

▶ rm with * and ? needs extreme care! Use ls first, and ask: do I need any of these files?

▶ rm -i * and rm -i ?? is safer.

▶ rm -r *directory* is highly dangerous!

▶ rm -ir *directory* is less dangerous!

You met `rmdir` in Chapter 3. This is a milder way of removing directories: if the directory `stan` has any files in it, `rmdir stan` will not delete `stan`.

In addition to the dangers of losing files completely (name and contents) with the careless use of `rm`, indirection can lose you the contents of a file, which is really just as frustrating, possibly more so. The file seems to be there, at least by name, but the data within may not be as planned. So let's return to redirection and filters for a few more insights.

Indirection with Input, Output, and Pipelines

In `cal | more`, the output from `cal` provides the input to `more`, which processes (filters) it, then passes it on. The output from `more` is therefore available for further processing. In our example, the output from more is simply passed on to `stdout`, but you are free to add further pipe symbols and filters. The output of the final filter of such a chain can go to `stdout`, or it can be redirected to a file.

With `date >today.test`, the output from `date`, on the other hand, is written into the file `today.test`. Examine the following dialogue:

```
$ date | today.test
today.test: execute permission denied
$ _
```

Unix has been asked to treat `today.test` as an executable filter, and is unable to oblige. You'll see later how Unix determines which files are data files and which are executable programs.

Try to guess what would happen with

```
$ date > more
```

Well, you have now created a file called `more` in your current directory! Sorry about that. A previously existing file called `more` would now be overwritten with the date. The next section explains how possibly dangerous overwrites can be avoided.

Appending Output to Your Files

The danger of > overwriting an existing file, with the possible loss of valuable data, may be worrying you. Unix offers a simple remedy. You can *append* data using the special redirection operator >> (two adjacent > symbols with no intervening spaces). By append, I mean adding the redirected data to the end of an existing file without disturbing the existing data. Appending to a nonexistent file works just like >, that is, Unix creates a new, empty file first. Try the following:

```
$ who >who.dat
$ cat who.dat
iwonka tty1a Apr3 10:04
stan   tty2a Apr3 10:32
$ date >>who.dat
$ cat who.dat
iwonka tty1a Apr3 10:04
stan   tty2a Apr3 10:32
Mon Apr 3 17:33:28 PDT 1995
```

The first line creates or overwrites who.dat. The second line confirms the contents of who.dat. The fifth line appends the output from date to the previous contents of who.dat. The following cat confirms our prediction.

Reversing the append symbols (to give <<) provides a special feature called *in-line input.* You'll see this in action when I cover advanced shell programming.

Standard Errors

In addition to stdin and stdout there is a third standard file created by Unix called standard error, or stderr for short. This is for displaying error or diagnostic messages. Like stdout, stderr is opened and linked to your screen whenever a command starts executing. In the following example

```
$ cat pandora.box >junk
cat: cannot open pandora.box
$ cat junk
$ _
```

the error message is actually sent to the default stderr, namely your screen, and not to the file junk. In fact, junk is empty, as shown by the second cat command. The key point is that if you redirect stdout to a file, stderr remains linked to the screen: you do not want the file picking up a strange mix of good data and error diagnostics.

WHAT'S NEXT?

In Chapter 5, you'll learn how to create network mail; how to manage your messages; and how to read, save, and delete messages.

```
echo "2.      Show Date"
echo "3.      Display a file"
echo "4.      Change working director
echo "5.      Return to original di
echo "Q.      Quit
echo
echo -n "Enter choice: .\b"
read choice
case $choice in
1) who | more
   pause;;
2) date
   pause;;
3) echo "Enter file name: \c"
   read fil
   if [ -r "$fil" -a -f "$fil ]
   then
      clear
      more -d $fil
   else
      echo "Cannot d
   fi
   pause;;
4) echo "E
   read di
   if test   d "$dir  pwd`
   then
      cd $dir
   else
      echo "$dir: no such di
   fi
   pause;;
5) if test "$dir" != "$p
   then
      cd $prevdir
   fi
   pause;;
```

Chapter 5
ELECTRONIC MAIL

Unix lets you exchange messages with other users on your machine and, with the proper connections, users on other Unix systems. Indeed, many of the world's largest intercomputer networks are those running under various Unix protocols using SMTP (Simple Mail Transfer Protocol) and similar commands (to be discussed in Chapter 16). I'll use the general term *email* (short for electronic mail) to cover the many different user-to-user telecommunications methods available, including not only the traditional mailing of letters and memos but also the transfer of text and binary files.

Before you tackle the details of email under Unix, you need to know a little more about access rights and privileges.

SUPERUSERS UNITE!

Normally, Unix shields you and your terminal from other active users, and vice versa. However, the system administrator, or anyone else blessed with the password to the special login name root, has the awesome ability to bypass this protective barrier of read, write, and execute permissions. For this reason, any user privileged to log in as root is also called a *superuser*. A superuser can peek into and erase any of your files and directories, interrupt your work at any time with warning messages, kill any or all of your running jobs, ban you from the system by changing or removing your logins and passwords without prior consultation, and generally play God or Devil as the mood takes her or him.

Superusers even boast a special prompt symbol. Rather than seeing the everyday $ or % prompts for the Bourne or C shell, when you log in successfully as root, you see a #. This distinctive root or superuser prompt, #, reminds you that you have gained special access to the system. Of course, all the normal user commands and options can be used. What distinguishes the superuser is the additional arsenal of commands and options that Unix withholds from non-superusers. For obvious reasons, therefore, the root password must be guarded closely and changed regularly. Being admitted to the inner circle brings both power and responsibility. In fact, abuse by a superuser is rare, and when it does happen, it is more likely to be the result of human error than a deliberate assault. As you'll see in Chapter 17, many quite mundane but necessary chores can only be achieved by root, including backing up, changing peripherals, adding users, software updates, and gracefully closing down the system.

Although you cannot protect yourself against intrusions from superusers, you can decide whether you want to exchange messages with other normal users. If you are a natural recluse, you can simply refuse to read your email. You can also put up an electronic equivalent to the Do Not Disturb sign.

Unix offers two commands that permit users to send and receive messages. The mail command (in man section C) gives you a sophisticated store-and-forward mailbox. The simpler write command (in man section C) lets you send messages directly to any user who is willing to be interrupted. I'll discuss the write method first.

You Haven't Written to Me Lately

The write *login* command sends a message from your keyboard to the screen of the user whose login you specify, provided that the target user is logged onto the system and is "open" to receiving messages. Every user starts life in this receptive state, but at any time you can use the mesg command to close the door—or perhaps taking your phone off the hook is a better metaphor:

```
$ mesg n
$ _
```

The argument n means no messages accepted—Go Away!—¡No molestar! If you change your mind later on, you can reverse your choice as follows:

```
$ mesg y
$ _
```

The y, for yes, tells the other users on the system that you are now *writable,* that is, willing to accept incoming messages from anybody's write commands. As I mentioned, you are normally in the writable state when you first log in, so mesg y is only needed to undo an earlier mesg n. You (or the system administrator) can arrange matters so that you default to mesg n when you log in—I'll show you how in Chapter 6. If you are ever in doubt as to your writable status, just enter mesg without an argument and Unix will tell you:

```
$ mesg
mesg is y
```

NOTE

Yes, as you may have guessed, a superuser can disturb anyone with a write or wall command regardless of writability. In an emergency, the system administrator may need to grab everybody's attention: I'm halting system in 30 secs! Save your work!

Commands such as mesg that can both alter and report the status of something are quite common in Unix. Used with an argument, they set or change some parameter; used without an argument, they tell you the current value. But recall the important exception: cd without an argument changes the current directory to your home directory.

Suppose you are logged in as mary and want to send user stan a message. The first sensible thing to do is to check if stan is online and active. To do this, enter

```
$ who -u
jane    tty03 Mar 14 12:34
```

```
joe      tty12 Mar 15 10:09 1:12 169 store
mary     tty02 Mar 15 09:03 .    110 r&d
stan     tty01 Mar 15 11:09 .    170 engineering
stan     tty34 Mar 15 11:15 0:30 172 engineering
$ _
```

The familiar who command with the –u option tells you a little more than the plain who you've used so far. Each section, or column, is usually called a *field*. The fields shown are as follows:

Login name	Name of active user.
Terminal	Name of terminal or line.
Date/time	When user logged in.
Activity	Hours:minutes since line was last used. A period indicates some activity within the last minute, that is, the user is probably at work right now.
Pid	Process id number: unique number assigned by Unix to each running process or task. Ignore this for now.
Comment	Optional information often used to identify a terminal's location.

The two occurrences of stan may seem strange, but there's no cause for alarm. Stan is perfectly free to log in as stan on as many terminals as he wishes. Stan may even have several different login names (for accounting and auditing purposes, for example). who shows you all currently logged-in users, so you now know that stan is logged in on both tty01 and tty34. Furthermore, the symbol in the activity field is a period, so you know that stan has been doing something on tty01 within the last minute but tty34 has been idle for a while. Joe, it seems, has left his terminal unattended for over an hour—let's hope he has a good excuse.

If stan were active and writable on only one terminal, you could just enter

```
$ write stan
```

and Unix would figure out the destination. Since stan is active on two terminals, we must tell Unix which one to write to by adding the terminal name as a second argument. If you try

```
$ write stan tty34
permission denied
$ _
```

Unix quickly tells you that stan on tty34 is incommunicado (not writable). So let's try

```
$ write stan tty01
_
```

The absence of the permission denied message is your clue that Stan is writable. The prompt is also absent, but the cursor indicates that Unix is ready for your message. You could immediately start typing your message on this and subsequent lines, but you'll see in a moment that this can be confusing and even wasteful—Stan may respond before you have finished. Both parties need to follow an agreed protocol to avoid those maddening mix ups you get on delayed long distance phone calls. So wait after the write command until you receive an acknowledgment from Stan. Supposing that he was in the middle of something, his screen display would be rudely interrupted mid-job with a warning message and bleep:

```
$ cat poem
Mary had a little la
        Message from mary (tty02) [Tue Apr 13 01:32:15]
mb
...
...
$ _
```

Some formatting commands such as pr and nroff have a built-in protection against such interruptions, since they can cause havoc with your layout.

If Stan wishes to engage in conversation with Mary, he enters

```
$ write mary
Mary! Stan here, what's up? o
```

He knows for sure that Mary is active and on tty02, but it is possible that Mary has inadvertently left herself *unwritable*. Note that you can issue write commands without being writable! It's not a sensible thing to do, but many dumb things are legal in Unix as in other walks of life. It may also be the case that Mary is logged in on terminals other than tty02, in which case Stan could play safe by adding the argument tty02: write mary tty02. This is the terminal where Mary is awaiting your reply. The message following this command appears on Mary's screen as follows:

```
$
        Message from stan (tt01) [Tue Apr 13 01:13:42]
Mary! Stan here, what's up? o
_
```

The two terminals are now "connected" and will remain so until both users enter Ctrl-D (the usual way of terminating a program). More precisely, if Stan presses Ctrl-D, he terminates his write connection to Mary but will continue to receive Mary's messages until she uses Ctrl-D. When you terminate with Ctrl-D, your screen will say (end of message); you press Enter to get back to prompt level.

Returning to the exchange of messages, notice the final letter o in Stan's first response. This means "over" and tells Mary that Stan is ready for her message. She, in turn, will end her reply with an o, then wait for Stan's rejoinder. Typing back before you see this o can lead to strange clutter on the recipient's screen. To signal that you have no more to say, you end your last line with oo meaning "over, out."

When Mary sees the o in Stan's acknowledgment, she types

```
It's your turn to make the coffee! o
```

Stan now types

```
OK, over in ten minutes. oo
```

Mary now knows from the oo that Stan has no more to say. Mary has the last word:

```
Fine, Stan, see you here soon, Mary. oo
```

Both parties can now safely press Ctrl-D and Enter to return to their normal prompts.

I should stress that o and oo are merely common conventions between Unix users: the symbols have no programming significance.

If you do not have a colleague willing to let you play with the write command, you can always write to yourself:

```
$ mesg
mesg is y
$ mesg n
$ mesg
mesg is n
$ write your_login
permission denied
$ mesg y; write your_login
Hello to myself o
Hello to myself o
Must fly oo
Must fly oo
```

Press Ctrl-D and Enter to return to the prompt.

Note the two-command line using a semicolon separator. Note also that each line you write to yourself is repeated immediately. One of the miracles of modern computer science, but admittedly the novelty soon wears off.

Off the Wall

I mentioned that the system administrator can override the mesg n setting of any user. If you are logged in as root, you can send an urgent message to every active user with one invocation of the wall command (in man section ADM). wall stands for "write all." As with write, wall reads your standard input, so you can either type your global warnings, as in

```
# wall
Closing down the system at 5:00pm sharp
```

and then press Ctrl-D and Enter, or redirect your warnings with wall < warn1.msg, where warn1.msg is a pre-prepared text file. When sending a file message, you do not have to terminate with Ctrl-D, since the file generates an EOF (end-of-file) automatically. Recipients of a wall message are interrupted with the warning

```
Broadcast Message from root [Tue Apr 13 01:35:02]
Closing down the system at 5:00pm sharp
```

The wall command, unlike write, is not intended to set up a dialogue, so the o and oo conventions are not observed. Some implementations of wall ensure that even inactive users will get the message when they log in.

Final Warning

I leave this topic with a brief but firm warning not to abuse the write command. You would normally need an excellent reason for writing to a complete stranger's screen—Your printer is on fire might suffice, but not Hi, welcome aboard! My name is Joe, and I work down the hall from you....

NOTE

Don't play the fool with write and wall! Use mail unless your message requires immediate attention.

For more organized and civilized intercommunication, you need the mail command. Even with this, certain conventions and good habits must be observed for success. Unlike `write`, `mail` lets you send messages to both active and inactive users, whether they like it or not. Whether they read your mail is another matter! And whether they respond is yet another kettle of fish.

THE MAILPERSON COMETH

Contrary to its public image, Unix has always been popular in certain office automation applications. The first Unix application was, in fact, multiuser document preparation at AT&T Bell Labs. The need for interuser communication soon sparked the development of an email system. The growing team of Unix programmers also found it essential to share messages, so the `mail` program has grown like Topsy, acquiring many features (some more useful than others).

As a result, the options offered by the `mail` command, and the names used for a given function, now vary considerably among different Unix implementations. The phrase *blatant featurism* is sometimes used to describe the situation. An emerging solution is to offer all the existing synonyms for a given function, so you may find that `ignore` and `discard`, different names for the same function, are both accepted.

`mail` is a complex command that controls both the receiving, sending, and saving of mailed messages. In addition to text messages, `mail` can send and receive files of any kind. I'll concentrate on the core features that should be available on most systems, possibly with minor variations in syntax.

Read Your Mail!

Whenever you log in, Unix checks a central repository, a sort of electronic post office called the `system mailbox`, to see if there is any mail there addressed to you. The system mailbox maintains files for each user in a special directory called `/usr/spool/mail`, so that Mary's mail is held in the file `/usr/spool/mail/mary` and so on. Do not confuse this directory with Mary's home directory, `/usr/mary`. Mail can be received and held for Mary even if her home directory is erased for any reason. Some systems may store this file in a different directory like /var/spool/mail. If mail is found for you, you will see the message `You have mail` before your prompt appears. Some systems will also give you a `You have mail` message if mail arrives during a session.

To read your mail, you simply enter the command `mail`. If there is no mail, a `no messages` response is invoked. For the user with login `iwonka`, a typical mail-reading session might proceed as follows:

```
$ mail
SCO UNIX System V Release 3.2 Type ? for help.
"/usr/spool/mail/iwonka": 2 messages 1 new 2 unread  >N 2
stan@kelly.UUCP Tue Apr 13 02:01 13/2446 Hello
U 1 stan@kelly.UUCP Tue Apr 13 01:30 27/1306
? _
```

This response tells you the name of your system mailbox, in this case `/usr/spool/mail/iwonka`, and the number and types of messages waiting for you. Next you are shown the *header* information, summarizing each piece of your mail in reverse chronological order, that is, the most recent mail comes first. You may also see a list of users who have been sent copies of a particular message. The `mail` command now awaits your further instructions. The `?` beside the cursor is a special prompt indicating that you are in *command* (or mail-reading) mode. (Later on, you'll encounter another mode called *input* mode, used when you are sending mail.)

What you type in command mode will determine how your mail is displayed, printed, stored, and/or erased. Each message has a header followed by a *body* that carries the meaty text of the message. `mail` has commands that display either header, body, or both. The command options are extensive and differ between different versions of Unix. Most of the commands have long and short versions—with some exceptions, you need only enough letters of the command to ensure uniqueness. For example, `h` gives you `header`, `hel` is equivalent to `help`, and so on.

Many of the default values taken by `mail` can be preset by placing an appropriate value in an *environment variable.* In fact, this approach is common for most Unix commands. This makes life extremely flexible for the user, but it complicates matters for Unix book authors! What a command actually does is often up to you and/or your system administrator. Certain global, or system-wide, defaults are set by the system administrator, while each user may have the power to override these locally. Chapter 6 deals with the various ways you can personalize your system, including the setting of environment variables. In this chapter, I will occasionally mention the effect of a certain environment variable. This will alert you to the fact that your `mail` command may not work exactly as stated.

The header display says `Type ? for help`. So why not start by entering

```
? ?
```

You can also type the equivalent commands help or hel. You'll get quite a list of available commands and optional arguments. The command list or li also gives you a list of available commands but with no explanation. This is a useful aid when you're on an unfamiliar system.

I'll concentrate on the simple, everyday commands that let you read and save your mail. Be aware that some of the commands used inside mail look very much like normal Unix commands, but the options and defaults often differ.

Many system administrators kindly send you a welcome message to greet you when you first log in. If so, you have an early opportunity to gain familiarity with the mail command. If not, you should ask a colleague to send you some test messages. Failing that, you can write to yourself (see "Sending Mail" later in this chapter).

The absolute simplest entry you can make at the ? prompt is to press Enter! This is equivalent to typing p (for print, meaning display) or t (for type, also meaning display). Enter, p, and t all produce the same effect: They display the *current* message, after which the ? prompt reappears. The next message in the header list now becomes the current message. By just pressing Enter, you can quickly scan your mail until a no next message appears followed by the ? prompt. Rather than pressing Enter after each message, you can try

    ? *

which displays all messages, with a pause after each screenful. Messages displayed on your monitor are piped by default through the more filter, so you'll get the familiar pause if a long message fills your screen. You can specify your own filter for fancier displays, but more is usually more than adequate. If not, ask your system administrator to check the PAGER setting. This defaults to more, but can be set to give more elaborate mail display formatting.

Leaving the mail Program

You can leave the mail program by typing ex, exit, or x. This style of departure leaves your mail undisturbed—you can return to mail and find all your messages still in your system mailbox. In fact, the You have mail reminder will still appear whenever you log in until you have cleared the system mailbox (you'll see how soon).

You can also leave the mail program with a quit or q, but this deletes from the system mailbox any message you have read during this session.

However, such deleted messages are saved automatically in a special default file in your home directory called mbox. Saving in mbox is done by *prepending* (that is, adding to the start of the file) rather than by appending or overwriting. Prepending ensures that mbox retains your read mail in the same most-recent-first order as the system mailbox. mail allows you to read and delete messages in your mbox, so you don't have to keep mail there forever.

There are ways of varying this default behavior, as you'll soon discover. You can save mail in files other than mbox, and you can delete (and undelete) selected messages during a session. But for now, the key lesson is that exit leaves the system mailbox as is, while quit prunes all read mail, leaving a local copy in /usr/*your_login*/mbox. After reading all your mail and departing with a quit, you will not be bothered with a You have mail greeting until some new mail pours in.

Note again that the file /usr/spool/mail/stan is part of Unix's central system mailbox, from which mail pulls your mail by default. Your local, user mailbox for storing selected mail that you may want to keep is called /usr/ *your_login* /mbox.

Having seen the simple, default approach to reading your mail, we'll look at some useful variants in the following sections.

Printing Your Mail Messages

lpr or l (line printer) entered in command mode (after the ? prompt, remember) will print the current message on your default printer. lpr * or l * will print all your messages, one after the other. Here, print really means print—real, black-on-white, ink-and-paper printing! The name lpr suggests another Unix anachronism, stemming from the days when all hardcopy printers were tabulators or line printers. mail will usually be set up to print your messages prettily with page numbers. If this is not the case, your system administrator will be able to help. I'll have a lot more to say about printing in Chapter 9.

Message Headers

The fields in the header need to be understood to exploit the more advanced mail facilities. Take another look at the headers you first encountered in the "Read Your Mail" section:

```
>N 2 stan@kelly.UUCP Tue Apr 13 02:01 13/2446 Hello
 U 1 stan@kelly.UUCP Tue Apr 13 01:30 27/1306
```

The > symbol in column 1 indicates the current message. This is the message that will be displayed by default if you do not specify a message identifier argument in certain commands. Each message header is tagged with a letter in column 2: N means a new message since you last read your mail; U means unread mail; O means old, and so on. mail keeps track of what you are doing, so these status letters are updated during each session. Each message is numbered in column 3, with higher numbers signifying more recent mail.

The remaining fields are fairly obvious. They tell you the sender, date and time sent, size (lines/characters), and optional subject matter. The latter appears only if the sender entered a line giving the subject title when composing the message. Such titles, as in traditional interoffice memos, can be useful on a heavily used email system. An added benefit is that mail lets you select messages by searching the subject field for a given string. For example, you could display all mail with Urgent anywhere in the subject field. You can also select just the mail from a given user.

If you are not connected to other Unix systems, the sender field may just show the sender's login name. The above example shows the sender as stan@kelly.UUCP meaning user stan on the Unix system (or node) called kelly. Your own site may have such a name. It allows users at other sites to exchange mail with you and your colleagues. I'll discuss this in much more detail in Chapter 16.

Message Selection

You can also display or print each message by selecting the message number. If the headers reveal a letter from the boss at the bottom of the pile, you may feel inclined to read this first before wading through all the valentines. To display message number 9, for instance, you can type p 9, t 9, or just 9. Again, note that display is the default.

```
? p 9
From: boss Tue Apr 13 09:03:23 1995
To:   iwonka
Subject: Layoffs
It has come to my attention that...
  ...
? _
```

To print message 6, you would use lpr 6 or l 6. You can also display or print a range of messages as follows:

```
? p 3-7
```

displays messages 3, 4, 5, 6, and 7. Equivalently, you can use `? t 3-7` or simply `? 3-7`.

> `? lpr 2-4`

prints messages 2, 3, and 4. To display or print all the mail from `mary`, you can enter `p mary` or `lpr mary`. As before, the `p` is optional.

Other useful display options are listed below:

`? p ^`	Displays first undeleted message
`? p $`	Displays last message
`? p *`	Displays all messages
`? p /string`	Displays all messages with the specified character string `string` in the subject line (also matches `String`, `STRING`, and so on)
`? p :n`	Displays all new messages
`? p :r`	Displays all read messages
`? p :o`	Displays all old messages
`? p :u`	Displays all unread messages
`? p :d`	Displays all deleted messages

You can replace the `p` with a `t`, or omit it altogether. The print versions use `lpr` or `l` in place of `p`.

Sometimes you may want to read the first few lines of messages before deciding where your priorities lie. The `top` command, or `to` for short, used with the usual message arguments, displays the first five lines of selected messages:

> `? top *`

displays the first five lines of all messages.

> `? to 1-3`

displays the first five lines of messages 1 through 3.

> `? top mary`

displays the first five lines of all messages from Mary.

If you have a heavy mailbag, the following header commands are handy for rechecking message numbers, senders, and subjects:

`? =`	Displays current message number
`? h`	Displays screenful of current headers

? h *n*   Displays header for message number *n* (You can also use a range of message numbers here.)

? h+   Displays next screenful of headers

? h-   Displays previous screenful of headers

The number of headers per screenful is yet another value that can be preset in an environment variable; in this case you set a value in the screen variable. You'll see how in the next chapter.

Alternatively, once you know your target messages, you may wish to avoid screen clutter by skipping past the headers. The command for this is ignore or ig for short.

Saving and Deleting Messages

You saw earlier that using quit deletes read messages from the system mailbox and saves them in your mbox. Here are some commands that allow you to save and mark particular messages for deletion during a mail session whether read or not:

? **save**

saves the current header and message in mbox and flags the message for deletion from your mailbox.

? **s**

does the same as save.

? **save tempbox**

saves the current header and message in a file named tempbox and flags the message for deletion from your mailbox.

? **save 1-3   tempbox**

saves headers and messages 1–3 in a file named tempbox and flags messages 1–3 for deletion from your mailbox.

If you use write or w in place of save or s, the action is the same except that the headers are not saved, just the message bodies. A variant of save called Save (a capital "S" makes the difference) lets you save selected messages in a file named for the sender found in the header. Assuming you are stan, the Save command, or S for short, works as follows:

? **Save mary**

saves all messages from Mary in /usr/stan/mary and flags all messages for deletion from your mailbox.

? **S 1-3**

saves messages 1–3 in /usr/stan/*author-of-message-1* and flags messages 1–3 for deletion from your mailbox.

If you want saved messages to go to a directory other than your default, home directory, there is an environment variable called folder you can preset.

All the messages you save using the save, write, or Save commands are flagged so that when you enter quit, they will be deleted from the system mailbox. A command called copy, or c for short, lets you save messages in mbox or a designated file without losing them from the system mailbox when you enter quit. In other words, copy saves without flagging the message(s) for deletion. A variant of copy naturally exists called Copy (or C), which works like Save but does not incur deletion when you quit. You can also delete a message directly from the system mailbox, whether saved or not, by using the delete or d command. The message list arguments follow the established pattern:

? **delete**

deletes the current message from the mailbox without saving it in mbox. The next undeleted message becomes the current message.

? **d 3-4**

deletes messages 3 and 4 from the mailbox without saving them in mbox. The next undeleted message after message 4 becomes the current message.

? **d boss**

Danger! This deletes from the mailbox all messages from boss without saving them in mbox. The next undeleted message becomes the current message.

? **d** *

Danger! This deletes all messages from the mailbox without saving them in mbox.

A useful composite command, dp or dt, lets you delete the current message then display the following undeleted message.

WARNING

Once you leave the mail program, you cannot undelete a deleted message.

If you rashly delete messages and want to undo your mistake, you can restore them using the undelete command (u for short) provided you do not leave the mail session:

? **undelete**

undeletes the current message. The next undeleted message becomes the current message.

> ? **u 3-4**

undeletes messages 3 and 4. The next undeleted message after message 4 becomes the current message.

> ? **u ***

undeletes all messages.

Reading Mail from Another Source

All my examples have assumed that mail will read from the standard system mailbox. If you want to read mail from some other file, you use the -f option as follows:

    mail -f mail_filename

A common application would be reading mail saved in your mbox, since this file has the same format as the system mailbox. *mail_file-name* can have a path; otherwise your current directory is assumed. You can also use -f in those instances when you have saved mail by sender name with Save and you want to study it and respond to it later. Which leads us to the next topic: how to send mail.

SENDING MAIL

You've been busy reading, printing, saving, and deleting incoming mail in command mode. It's time to return the favor by sending mail to other users. Once again, the options are numerous, so I'll concentrate on the basics. The simplest approach is to use mail with a user name as argument:

    $ mail mary
    Subject: Backups
    Thanks for your memo on backups. Let's meet after work.
    Regards, Stan

Pressing Ctrl-D brings up the $ prompt.

As you can see, mail determines from the user-name argument that you are in *compose* (or input or send) mode, and responds by asking you to enter a single-line subject. This is optional, so you can just press Enter if you have no subject in mind. It's good form to supply a pithy, relevant subject—it can provide a useful searching tool as your mailbag grows.

After the subject line, you simply type away until your message is complete. You then bring the cursor to the start of an empty line and press Ctrl-D (or type a period on some systems). Your missive now wends its speedy way to Mary's system mailbox. Mary will receive a `You have mail` notice and can do all the good things with your message that I discussed earlier.

If the message cannot be delivered for any reason, `mail` attempts to return it to your system mailbox with a suitable explanation. In the event of some interruption during transmission, partial messages are saved in the file `dead.letter` in your home directory.

If you want to send the same message to several users, all you need is to list their names after `mail` separated by a space like this:

```
$ mail mary joe fred iwonka
Subject: Party Time!
My place at 6:00pm tonight.
Regards, Stan
```

Pressing Ctrl-D sends the message and brings up the $ prompt. All four users will receive the same message in their respective system mailboxes.

It is important to distinguish *command* mode (reading mail) from *compose* mode (sending mail). The commands and options are quite different. To complicate matters, while you are in command mode, you can switch to compose mode in order to respond to mail that you have just read. For example:

```
$ mail
```

puts you in command mode in the `mail` program.

```
? p
```

allows you to read the first letter. Let's say that Joe sent you this letter. To respond to his mail message right away, you would enter

```
? mail joe
```

This puts you in compose mode. Type your subject line and message; then press Ctrl-D to send your missive and return to command mode.

As you can see, `mail` is a valid command from within `mail`! A neat variant is `Mail` (capital "M"). If you had used `Mail joe` in the above example, Unix would save *your* message in a file named `joe` (rather like the `Save` command explained earlier).

There is an even quicker way of responding to the current message. After the ? prompt, you can enter `reply`, `respond`, or `r` for short. For example, let's say you have just read the first letter in your mailbox. Entering `r` after the ? prompt puts you in compose mode, adds the subject of the first letter to your subject line, and treats the sender of the first letter as the recipient of your letter. The r trick saves you entering the recipient's name and the subject line.

Returning to the original task of writing to Mary, you might prefer to compose your letter using a text editor, especially if it is a long message needing careful thought. While you are keyboarding mail directly, you can only correct errors on the current line—not too helpful for precise composition. There are two approaches. First, you can use redirection as follows:

```
$ mail mary < mary.lett1
$ mail joe fred < memo.3
$ _
```

where mary.lett1 and memo.3 are prepared text files. mail will read from these files as explained in Chapter 4. The message is terminated by the EOF (end-of-file), so you don't need a manual Ctrl-D. If you want to add a subject line, use the -s option:

```
$ mail -sHello mary < mary.lett1
$ mail -sPayday joe fred < memo.3
$ _
```

As an alternative to the redirection of a pre-edited file, you can invoke and use a text editor while composing a message. But if you are in compose mode, how can mail distinguish your commands from real message characters in your letter? The solution requires the use of a special *escape* character to warn mail that what follows is not message text, but a command entry. The default escape character for mail is the ˜ (tilde). To invoke the vi editor, for example, you would type ˜v; and to get the ed editor, you would enter ˜e. (Environment variables can be set to give you other editors, but these are the defaults.) You can call the editor at any time to edit a partial message.

Here are two more examples of tilde escape commands:

```
$ mail joe
˜c mary bill
˜b boss
```

After entering these tilde escape commands, you type and send your letter as usual. The ˜c command adds the names mary and bill to the *carbon copy* or *Cc* list in your message header. Your message will go to them, as well as to joe, and all recipients will know that Mary and Joe were "copied" on this message. The header will appear as follows:

```
To: joe
Cc: mary bill
```

The ˜b command is a little sneaky. It sends a *blind copy* to boss! Only you and boss know of this furtive maneuver: the header does not reveal the recipients of blind copies.

While in compose mode you can use the ˜! combination to execute a shell command:

```
$ mail joe
˜!ls
poem mbox memo.3
```

After the list appears, you are returned to compose mode. See Table 5.1 for a summary of the main mail commands.

TABLE 5.1: Summary of mail Commands

MAIL COMMAND AT ? PROMPT	ACTION
Enter	Displays the current message
p	Displays the current message
t	Displays the current message
*	Displays all messages
p *	Displays all messages
t *	Displays all messages
n	Displays message number *n*
p *n*	Displays message number *n*
t *n*	Displays message number *n*
m-n	Displays messages number *m* to *n*
p *m-n*	Displays messages number *m* to *n*
t *m-n*	Displays messages number *m* to *n*
lpr *n*	Prints message number *n*
l *n*	Prints message number *n*
lpr *m-n*	Prints messages number *m* to *n*
l *m-n*	Prints messages number *m* to *n*
user_name	Displays all messages from *user_name*
p *user_name*	Displays all messages from *user_name*
t *user_name*	Displays all messages from *user_name*

TABLE 5.1 continued: Summary of mail Commands

MAIL COMMAND AT ? PROMPT	ACTION
lpr *user_name*	Prints all messages from *user_name*
l *user_name*	Prints all messages from *user_name*
p */pattern*	Displays all messages matching *pattern* in subject line
p :n	Displays all new messages
p :r	Displays only messages already read
p :o	Displays all old messages
p :u	Displays all unread messages
p :d	Displays all deleted messages
to[p] *	Displays top (first 5 lines) of all messages
=	Displays current message number
h	Displays screenful of current headers
h *n*	Displays header for message number *n*
h+	Displays next screenful of headers
h-	Displays previous screenful of headers
ig[nore]	Bypasses headers
s[ave]	Saves current header and message in mbox and flags for deletion
c[opy]	Saves the current header and message in mbox but does not flag for deletion
S[ave]	Same as save, but saves in special mbox file using sender's login name
C[opy]	Same as copy, but copies to special mbox file using the sender's login name
s[ave] *filename*	Saves current header and message in *filename* and flags for deletion
w[rite]	Same as save, except headers are not saved
q[uit]	Exits mail and deletes all messages flagged for deletion
d[elete] [*arg*]	Deletes current message by default (*arg* can specify * (delete all); *name* (delete all messages from *name*); or a range of message numbers)
dp	Deletes the current message then displays the next
dt	Deletes the current message then displays the next

TABLE 5.1 continued: Summary of mail Commands

Mail Command at ? Prompt	Action
u[ndelete] [*arg*]	Undeletes current message by default (*arg* as in delete command)
mail *name*	Sets you into compose mode for sending a message to *name*
mail -s *subname*	Same as mail *name*, but adds a subject line
r[eply]	Puts you into compose mode to reply to the current message sender
r[espond]	Puts you into compose mode to reply to the current message sender

Using Other Email Programs

There are many other Unix email programs available, and I'll briefly describe some of them in this final section.

mailx is based on an earlier program called Mail (note the initial capital "M"), and offers many commands for mail preparation and for replying to mail. mailx is similar to mail, but uses tilde (~) escape sequences to separate special commands from the regular text of a message. When you use a tilde escape, it must be the first character on the line. The ~? command displays a summary of all the tilde escape commands. And to add a confusing note, on some Unix systems, mailx has been renamed as mail.

NOTE

The mail programs that you work with directly are known as *mail user agents*, and most of them use more primitive mailers called *mail transport agents* such as sendmail to handle the actual mail transmission.

The MH message handling system, developed by Bruce Borden, Stockton Gaines, and Norman Shapiro, with later versions by Marshall Rose and John Romine, uses a very different approach from mail and mailx, in that it provides a set of separate programs for specific mail functions that you can call from an ordinary shell prompt.

The elm mailer, written and placed in the public domain by Dave Taylor, is screen-oriented rather than line-oriented like the other mailers covered in this chapter. It allows you to reply to a message; forward, delete, or move a message; group messages together; and create aliases for the mail addresses you use most often.

Finally, the emacs editor also includes its own mailer, known as rmail. The format of emacs mail files is incompatible with the standard Unix mail-file format, but emacs provides commands for converting between the two.

There are also several excellent email packages available from independent software vendors, in addition to the email components of popular graphical user interfaces such as SCO's Open Desktop or the DeskSet from Solaris.

Chapter 16 offers more information on mailing to remote computers.

WHAT'S NEXT

In Chapter 6, you'll learn how to customize your version of Unix. You'll learn how to change your password and login profile, switch shells, and modify the way that you operate within Unix.

```
echo "2.      Show Date"
echo "3.      Display a file"
echo "4.      Change working directo
echo "5.      Return to original dir
echo "Q.      Quit
echo
echo -n "Enter choice: .\b"
read choice
case $choice in
1) who | more
   pause;;
2) date
   pause;;
3) echo "Enter file name: \c"
   read fil
   if [ -r "$fil" -a -f "$fil" ]
   then
      clear
      more -d $fil
   else
      echo "Cannot di
   fi
   pause;;
4) echo "En
   read di
   if test  d "$(dir= pwd`)"
   then
      cd $dir
   else
      echo "$dir: no such di
   fi
      pause;;
   5) if test "$dir" != "$pr
      then
         cd $prevdir
      fi
      pause;;
```

Chapter 6

YOUR OWN PERSONALIZED UNIX

Unix is unique in the way it lets you create your own tools and working conditions. In this chapter, I'll show you some of the ways you can tailor Unix to suit your particular hardware and work profile. Your system administrator will establish certain overall conditions, but as you become more experienced, you will want to modify the way Unix behaves when you log in. In the current jargon, you will be creating your own personal *environment*. Along the way, you'll learn quite a few new relevant facts about passwords, shells and shell variables, paths, and login profiles.

CHANGING YOUR PASSWORD

One of the first personal touches you may wish to apply is to change your password. In Chapter 1, I assumed that the system administrator had given you your login name and initial password. At most sites, this initial password is a temporary one that you are expected to change as soon as possible. At other sites, they may start you off with no password at all, leaving you to assign a password if you so desire. The procedures for changing old passwords and assigning new passwords both use the `passwd` command, as I'll explain in the following section. Until you do have a password, most systems will not bother you with the `password:` prompt. Some systems will prompt you for a password whether you have a password or not. If you have no password, pressing Enter at the password prompt is the only acceptable response!

For single-user Unix systems, of course, the whole question of passwords and security may be irrelevant—only you can decide whether they are worthwhile. Even if your present situation does not call for password protection, you should still become familiar with the simple `passwd` command.

For obvious security reasons, passwords should be changed from time to time whether you suspect intruders or not. Clearly, if you have reason to suppose that someone has been using your account illegally, you should immediately contact your system administrator rather than simply changing your password. The system administrator may prefer to give you a fresh login name and password and then set some traps for the intruder on your old login name and password.

Password administration varies widely between different sites. Exactly when passwords need to be changed and by whom can be mandated in different ways depending on the security level of the installation. Some sites specify a maximum lifetime for each password. If so, you will be prompted to change your password periodically, and you may be locked out if you fail to respond. There may also be a minimum change time for a password, in which case you will be warned if you try to change your password too often.

Furthermore, at some sites, password changes are made only by the system administrator. If your installation is one where individual users are not allowed to change their passwords, the following section will not be relevant.

The passwd Command

The passwd command (in man section C) is used to change a password. It can also be used to establish a password if you do not have one. The following dialog illustrates the procedure:

```
$ pwd
/usr/stan
$ passwd
Changing password for stan
Old password:
```

At this prompt, you type in your old password, or press Enter if you don't have a password. Unix then asks you to type in your new password. Type your new password carefully; then retype it when prompted.

As with passwords entered during login, Unix does not echo passwords keyed in during the passwd procedure. The next thing to note is that you need to know your old password (if any) before you can change it! This is abundantly sensible, of course. Slightly less obvious is the need to type the new password twice. The idea is that with a single, non-echoed entry, you might mistype the intended password and then have great trouble recalling what you typed. If your two new password entries differ, Unix responds with

```
Mismatch - password unchanged
$ _
```

or some similar warning. You must then enter passwd again and repeat the exercise more carefully. You will also get a warning if your old password is entered incorrectly. Note that some systems will not prompt you for the old password if you do not have a password. The absence of warnings tells you that you have successfully changed your password. In the event of a warning, passwd leaves your password unchanged.

Good and Bad Passwords

While on the subject of changing passwords, it is worth recapping the rules for good password construction. A poorly devised password is almost as bad as having none at all, leading to complacency and a false feeling of security. If your system offers automatically generated passwords, you should take advantage of this feature. There has been much research on what constitutes a good password based on measuring the "obviousness" and "ease of guessing" of character strings. Since serious intruders can quickly generate millions of password combinations, you clearly need to avoid short and simple passwords.

A minimum password length can be specified by the system administrator, typically six characters. Passwords should contain at least two alphabetic characters and at least one numeric or special character. You should avoid telephone numbers, birthdays, and car registration numbers. Passwords that correspond to login names (or their anagrams) or to names in a dictionary can be automatically rejected. The system administrator can also set the maximum number of retries when you attempt to enter or change a rejected password (the default is usually three or four).

The latest versions of the passwd command provide optional tests for obviousness. In addition, SCO UNIX offers a command called goodpw (in man section ADM) that subjects a proposed password to a variety of sophisticated tests.

The /etc/passwd File

Passwords are stored in an ASCII file called /etc/passwd, not to be confused with the executable file /bin/passwd. The directory /etc, by the way, is pronounced "et-see" rather than "et cetera." It contains various administrative data files and programs. Try ls /etc for a quick look at their names. In addition to the file passwd you'll also see the file motd (message of the day) that I mentioned in Chapter 1.

The file Command

The existence of two files of different types, both called passwd, may prompt you to ask if there's a quick way to determine the type of a file. The directory name often gives you a clue: /bin/passwd is likely to be a program (binary) file. Certain file-naming conventions also help: the file qsort.c is likely to be the source code of a C language program, and so on. However, these clues are not wholly reliable, since any directory can store any kind of file, and users need not abide by file-naming conventions. A useful command called file (in man section C) comes to the rescue. file takes one or more file (or directory) name arguments and tells you what kind of file each one is likely to be.

```
# file /etc /bin/passwd /etc/passwd /usr/src/qsort.c
/etc:      directory
/bin/passwd:   pure executable
/etc/passwd:   ascii
/usr/src/qsort.c:   c program text
# _
```

Note that `file` cannot always determine the file type exactly. It reads the first few lines looking for clues, but recall that Unix files have no pre-ordained structure other than that determined by users and their programs.

/etc/passwd lists all active users including `root` and `bin`. Each user entry occupies a separate line with seven fields separated by colons. Many routines, including those used by the login program, need to read the /etc/passwd file. Only `root` can write to the /etc/passwd file directly, but changes are usually made indirectly via special commands, some of which are available to ordinary users. For example, the `passwd` command outlined previously works by changing a field in /etc/passwd.

An emerging trend is the provision of menu-driven system administration, reducing the need to know the quirks of individual commands. SCO UNIX, for example, provides `sysadmsh` (system administration shell), an easy-to-use, menu-based interface that `root` can run to set up and change almost every system parameter, including user passwords. These types of tools are the ideal solution for small Unix sites without a full-time system administrator.

WARNING

It is dangerous to even *think* about editing the /etc/passwd file directly! You can peek but don't poke!

Any user can examine the contents of /etc/passwd by using `cat`:

```
$ cat /etc/passwd
root:gf54JQxxZ32Fd:0:1::/:/bin/sh
...
stan:oIg65rfRdffn8:24:12:Stan Kelly-
Bootle:/usr/stan/:/bin/sh
fred:qEsgs3324Fcc2:25:12:Frederick
Lemaitre:/usr/fred/:/bin/csh
joe::27:14:Joseph Lussac:/usr/joe:
...
$ _
```

Your listing will be different, but the seven fields (separated by six colons) should be recognizable. Two adjacent colons indicate an empty (or null) field. The field after the final colon may also be empty, as in the case of Joe's entry above.

All seven fields in /etc/passwd are listed in Table 6.1 for reference. Their full significance will emerge later in this chapter.

TABLE 6.1: /etc/passwd Fields

Field Number	Field Name	Description
1	login name	Name assigned to each user.
2	encrypted password	User's password as encrypted by Unix (shown as an * in many Unix versions).
3	uid	Unique user identification number assigned to a user (root is 0).
4	group id	Number indicating the user's group.
5	Gecos	A miscellaneous field usually used for additional user information, for example, full name, telephone number, etc. The finger command is used to display this field.
6	login dir	The home directory that the user is logged into automatically after login.
7	default shell	The name of the shell that will run for this user after login.

Every user, you will recall, is allocated a home directory, usually a sub-directory of /usr. It is field 6 of /etc/passwd that determines your home directory when you first log in.

Field 3, the user id (uid), also deserves a mention here. Your login name is used by the login routines to determine your numerical uid. Thereafter, Unix uses only your uid for the internal checking of your identity. It is possible for two login names to share the same uid (and therefore be effectively the one user), but two different uids cannot have the same login name.

Field 2, if nonempty, is deliberately peculiar! When I said that /etc/passwd was an ASCII file visible to all users and that it contained each user's password (including root's), you may have guessed there would be a catch somewhere! The jumble of characters in the second field of stan's entry is an *encrypted* version of Stan's password.

The encryption mechanism works as follows: if your password is, for example, mazkywu, then the Unix encryption algorithm might produce a6Fc76HGGdsS1. In this direction, encryption is fast, simple, and gives a unique mapping. In other words, distinct passwords cannot produce the same encrypted result. So when you log in and type a password, the system does not check your entry against your current password; rather, Unix encrypts your entry and compares the result with the encrypted version found in /etc/passwd.

Since the encrypted password is "public," you may wonder if the original password can be determined. In theory the answer is yes; in practice, to recover `mazkywu` from `a6Fc76HGGdsS1` requires computing resources far beyond those in most nongovernment agencies. Note that even the superuser cannot decrypt your password. If you forget your password, the superuser (and no one else) can erase your password and provide you with a new one.

When selecting a password, make sure it is not a word found in any dictionary or on any type of printed media. People called crackers will often run dictionary files against the password files, which are readable by any user. Running dictionary files against a password file often takes only a few hours on today's high-speed personal computers and weak passwords are easily broken. If you pick a password that is not in a dictionary, you make the challenge exponentially harder, and the cracker must resort to a brute force attack. A brute force attack requires the cracker to try every possible password, starting at "A" and going to "ZZZZZZZZ."

If brute force decryption takes your run-of-the-mill supercomputer more than, say, a year, it is fair to say that your password is safe! Of course, no encryption scheme is 100 percent satisfactory for all circumstances, and as computing price/performance ratios improve, encryption algorithms need to respond. For this reason, some Unix systems no longer store the encrypted passwords in the accessible `/etc/passwd` file. In place of the encrypted password, you may find a * symbol. Documentation about high-security systems is naturally hard to come by!

NOTE

The file that is not readable by anybody but the kernel and superuser is called the shadow password file. The location of the password file varies from system to system. Consult your system documentation for specifics on location of the shadow password file.

In the above example, note that Joe's password field is empty, possibly indicating that he or she has no password at present. This means that other users (and spies) are aware of Joe's vulnerability. The moral is clear! Get yourself a password as soon as possible.

The crypt Command

While on the subject of security, I should mention that Unix provides a `crypt` command (in man section C) that lets you encrypt entire files. The same command is used to decrypt encrypted files. You select a string of characters known as your *encryption key*. This key controls the conversion of your readable text (known in the spy trade as the *plain* or *clear* text) into the encrypted or enciphered version. The latter, of course, is pure gibberish, and only those knowing the key can use the `crypt` command to decrypt (or decipher) this gibberish back to the original plain text. If you keep your key to yourself, nobody (not even the superuser) will be able to read your encrypted secrets. Again, one must add the proviso that a suitably determined spy equipped with CIA/NSA computer power may be able to crack your code. (Incidentally, the U.S. government regulates the distribution of the Unix encryption utilities, so they are not normally available to unauthorized sites overseas.)

A typical encryption/decryption session might look as follows:

```
$ crypt <plain >encrypted
Enter key:
```

At this prompt, you type your key. (The screen will not echo the string you enter.) Enter the following command:

```
$ rm plain
$ _
```

The text in the file `plain` is now enciphered in the file `encrypted`, and to be safe you have erased the original! Note the redirections, needed because `crypt` reads from your standard input and writes to your standard output. Decryption requires the entry of the same key (so better not forget it) and a natural reversal of redirection:

```
$ crypt <encrypted >plain
Enter key:
$ _
```

At this prompt, you enter your key to decrypt the text in `encrypted` and redirect the decrypted text to `plain`.

It is worth mentioning here that the Unix tradition has never been overly paranoid regarding security. The original intent was to protect individual users without hindering the cooperation needed for joint program development. You'll see presently how groups of users can be defined, able to share access to certain directories and files, while keeping out other users.

CHOOSING YOUR SHELL

As I explained in Chapters 1 and 2, most of your work with Unix is performed in cooperation with a shell. You will recall that a shell is a special

Part I

program that interprets your commands and provides a programming interface to the kernel. Until fairly recently, the choice of shells was limited; however, the current trend is toward implementations giving you a choice of shells. (Chapter 19 discusses the evolution of Unix in more detail.) Some sites offer the Korn shell in addition to the Bourne and C shells. An early decision you (or your system administrator) can make is which shell should be your default shell, that is, the shell that is activated when you log in. Of course, this choice does not prevent you from switching shells during a session.

Your default shell is determined by the last field of the file you have just been studying, /etc/passwd. Look again at the example I gave earlier:

```
stan:65rfRdffn8:24:12:Stan Kelly-
Bootle:/usr/stan/:/bin/sh
fred:qEs324Fcc2:25:12:Frederick
Lemaitre:/usr/fred/:/bin/cshjoe:RDff43SXz3:27:14:Joseph
Lussac:/usr/joe:
```

The field after the final colon, if not empty, is the full filename of the default shell program for each user. Such programs are usually in the bin subdirectory of root. The directory name bin stands for *binary*. You may recall from Chapter 2 that binary (executable) files, as opposed to text files, contain executable programs or commands in a special format—you may not be able to display their contents with cat, but the kernel knows how to interpret them as instructions. If you run ls /bin, you can list the names of a large number of Unix commands stored in /bin. Some of these will be familiar. Most of the general Unix commands reside in the /bin directory. To appreciate the significance of the /bin directory, a small digression is needed to discuss paths.

The Path to Success

Each user has an individual sequence of directories called a path that tells Unix where to look for an entered command. When you enter date, for example, the shell will first search for the program date in the first directory listed in your path statement. If it's not there, a search is made in each of the subsequent path directories and the first date file encountered will be executed. (I assume here that the permissions set for date and its directory allow you to access and run it—I'll have more to say about such permissions in Chapter 7.)

If date is not found, of course, you'll get a command-unknown message. Such a message does not necessarily mean that there is no date rogram on your system; it may simply mean that there is no date program in your current directory, nor in any of the directories specified by your path. I'll show you soon how to check and change your path. For now, it should be clear that /bin, where all the common commands reside, must be one of the directories in your path. If not, you are in for a frustrating time! Another directory that holds commonly used commands is called /usr/bin, so this is also normally found in path.

NOTE

DOS users will recognize the Unix path mechanism, since it was borrowed by DOS with a few syntactical changes.

Your *current* directory, by the way, is usually in your path by default or by design (you'll see how later). The path mechanism conveniently lets you run programs that reside in directories other than your current directory (the one given by pwd). Of course, if you know that prog resides in the directory /xxx/tyy/zzz, you can (provided the permissions are right) run it by entering the full path name, /xxx/tyy/zzz/prog, regardless of your path and your current position in the file tree.

The name bin crops up frequently in Unix in different contexts, causing possible confusion to the unwary. There is the login name bin, representing a user who has some but not all of the privileges of root. You also have several bin directories such as /bin and /usr/bin available to all users.

When you come to create your own programs and commands, they will usually be for your own private use, so they would not normally reside in /bin or /usr/bin. They could go into your home directory, but rather than clutter that up, it is sometimes helpful to have your own binary directory of executable programs. If you are mary, for instance, you would create a directory called /usr/mary/bin. By adding this directory to your path, you ensure that you can run your personal programs from any directory.

With this path digression behind us, let's return to the default shells.

The Names of the Shells

The Bourne shell is an executable file called sh. Since it resides in the /bin directory, its full name is /bin/sh. Assuming that /bin is in your path, and you have no other program called sh in an earlier directory of your path sequence, then the Bourne shell can be invoked with sh or, as you'll see later, with optional arguments: sh args.

Similarly, the C shell is stored in the file /bin/csh and the Korn shell in /bin/ksh. There is also a /bin/rsh and /bin/bash available on many Unix versions. This is a *restricted* version of the Bourne shell that the system administrator may mandate in order to limit a user's access to certain commands. The bash is the "Bourne Again shell" and has an extended shell scripting language that includes advanced loop constructs and other neat functionality you won't find in the standard bourne shell. bash often completely replaces the standard bourne shell on newer systems. You should try ls /bin/*sh to check which shells you have on your system.

The last entry in your line of /etc/passwd will be /bin/sh if your default shell is the Bourne shell, or /bin/csh if your default is the C shell. Similarly, the Korn shell is indicated by the entry /bin/ksh. No entry after the final colon usually means that your default shell is the Bourne shell. In the /etc/passwd example, users stan and joe will default to the Bourne shell, while fred defaults to the C shell.

Later on, when you start looking at shell scripts, I will point out some of the differences between these shells. Until then, simply accept the default shell that your system has provided. The differences will not affect your work significantly until you reach more advanced operations.

Since shells can be run like normal programs, you can enter the commands sh, csh, or ksh to run the Bourne, C, or Korn shells, respectively. However, note that there can be differences between the way the C shell is invoked automatically during login compared with invoking it manually with a command. These differences will be clarified in the next section, where I discuss the login profile.

LOGIN PROFILES

There are usually several site conventions determined by your system administrator. These provide what might be called global actions, or defaults affecting all users. They are placed in a special file known as the *global login profile*. The shell executes the commands in this file whenever you log in.

NOTE

Unix login profiles are similar to the AUTOEXEC.BAT files of DOS. Various parameters can be set and commands can be executed automatically when you "start" the system. AUTOEXEC.BAT is executed when you boot DOS, but Unix login profiles are executed each time you log in.

You can elect to modify some or all of these defaults either temporarily during a given session, or permanently for all sessions. The general idea is that you can run commands of your own choosing to modify your environment during a given session: such changes will last until you log out. Or you can place these commands in a special file in your home directory known as your *personal login profile*. When you log in, the shell will first execute the global login profile (if one is found), and then execute your personal login profile (if one is found). The net result of executing these two sets of commands gives you your "permanent" start-up environment each time you log in.

Since you can change your personal login profile at any time, it is not quite correct to use the word *permanent*. As you gain familiarity with Unix, however, your login profile will settle down to reflect your usual needs. Note the tremendous flexibility of having a global profile for everyone followed by personalized profiles for each user.

The profile names and mechanisms vary between the Bourne and C shells as outlined in the following sections.

Bourne Shell Login Profiles

When you log into the Bourne shell, it looks for a file called /etc/profile. This is the global (or system-wide) login profile. If found, all the commands in /etc/profile are executed. Next, the shell looks for a file called .profile in your home directory. This is your personal login profile. If found, the shell executes all the commands in .profile. Then the prompt appears to signal the start of your session. The normal Bourne shell prompt is $, but this can be modified by login profile commands, as you'll see presently.

C Shell Login Profiles

Whenever you run the C shell, it first looks for a file called /etc/cshrc. This is the C shell equivalent to the Bourne global login profile. If found, all the commands in /etc/cshrc are executed. Next, the shell looks for the file called .cshrc in your home directory. This is your personal C shell run command file. If found, the shell executes all the commands in .cshrc. If the C shell is being run at login time, an additional login profile called .login is sought in your home directory. If found, the commands in .login are executed. Finally, the prompt appears to signal the start of your session. Usually the C shell prompt is %, but this can be changed by commands in any of the three profiles listed above.

Typically, the global login profile calculates and displays disk usage information, displays the motd (message of the day), checks your mailbox and tells you if you have any mail, and displays any news bulletins. It also usually sets a umask that determines the default permissions for any files and directories you may create. More on this in Chapter 7.

For the moment, I'll concentrate on setting personal profiles for the Bourne shell. Apart from the profile name differences, there are several differences in the commands available in the C shell and how certain parameters are set.

YOUR OWN LOGIN PROFILE

What sort of commands can you usefully run from a login profile? Well, you can display the date and time (with date), call for a daily aphorism from the fortune cookie jar (with usr/games/fortune), check who else is logged in (with who), invoke a personal memo service (with calendar), modify your prompt symbol, and a host of other useful tasks. Your profile can contain any sequence of commands with appropriate arguments and pipes, and the effect is the same as if you were to key these commands each time you logged in. In addition to running any of the standard utility commands available, or commands that you have created yourself, many of the tricks performed by your profile depend on setting values in *shell variables*.

Shell Variables—An Introduction

Shell variables are rather like the variables used in conventional programming languages such as BASIC. Remember that Unix shells are not only command interpreters but also offer many features of a programming language. The shell variable is your first gentle exposure to shell programming. The key notion of a variable is that you can provide a name, or *variable identifier*, for some entity, such as PATH or doc. Variable names with capital letters are usually reserved for standard variables with predetermined Unix meanings, as listed in Table 6.2. You have already met the path mechanism. Now you know how the path sequence of directories is stored: in a shell variable, conveniently named PATH!

TABLE 6.2: Built-In Bourne Shell Variables

VARIABLE	DESCRIPTION
CDPATH	Search path for the cd command
PATH	Search path for user commands
MAIL	Name of the mail file that the shell will check to see if you have mail
MAILCHECK	Frequency with which the shell checks for new mail
MAILPATH	List of mail files to be checked by shell, together with optional messages to be displayed (default is "You have mail")
PS1	Primary prompt symbol (default is " $ ")
PS2	Secondary prompt symbol (default is "> ")
IFS	Internal field separators (default is space, tab, newline)
SHACCT	Name of file used for accounting purposes
TERM	Your terminal name
HOME	Your home directory

NOTE

The shell variables discussed here are for the Bourne shell only. The C shell has its own predefined variables that are similar but different.

Your own personal variables should have names with small letters. This rule is simply a useful convention, by the way. As long as you avoid using the built-in variable names for your own variables, you can use any names you like. However, keeping to the Unix traditions will make your shell scripts more legible.

The value of a shell variable can be set by means of an assignment statement. For example,

```
PATH=:/bin:/usr/bin:/usr/stan/bin
doc=/usr/stan/document
PS1='Enter your command:'
```

sets the variable PATH to the expression:/bin:/usr/bin/:usr/stan/bin; similarly, doc and PS1 are given the values /usr/stan/document and 'Enter your command: ' respectively. Note carefully that the direction of assignment is from right to left. The initial : in path indicates your current directory and is equivalent to writing dot colon (. :).

There are no $ prompts shown in the above snippet. Each line is part of a *shell script*, rather than a sequence of manually entered commands. When a script is executed, each of the above lines would be interpreted exactly as if you had typed them in yourself. However, there is no prompt or pause, unless the script specifically requests input. You can picture a script as an invisible typist, rapidly entering a sequence of commands. There's a good deal more to shell scripts, of course, but the first essential concept is that of simulating a sequence of manual commands.

NOTE

Spaces aren't allowed before or after the = assignment operator.

Setting PS1 to any character string will change your primary prompt. You can even set your prompt to #, the usual superuser prompt. Please resist the temptation—it will not increase your powers and will certainly cause much angst and confusion.

In the last example, your prompt would be changed from '$ ' to 'Enter your command: '. Note the use of single forward quotes when setting PS1; these ensure that the spaces within the new prompt string are transferred to PS1. Great care is needed to distinguish forward quotes from backquotes. Unix is quite picky about these two symbols: entering the wrong quotes can have disconcerting effects! (More on this in Chapters 13 and 16.) Note also the space at the end of the prompt string for added legibility:

```
$ PS1='Enter your command: '
Enter your command: _
```

Later on, you'll see other reasons for placing quotes around certain characters. The general idea is that the shell treats some characters, known as *metacharacters,* in a special way (recall the use of * and ? as filename wildcards, for example), but when such characters are *quoted* (that is, surrounded by single or possibly double quotation marks), the shell treats them literally.

Once set, any variable name, prefixed by a $, can be used in expressions. The leading $ symbol (not to be confused with the default prompt symbol) tells the shell to convert the name to its current value before performing an operation. For example,

```
Enter your command: cd $doc
Enter your command: pwd
```

```
/usr/stan/document
Enter your command: echo PATH
PATH
Enter your command: echo $PATH
:/bin:/usr/bin:/usr/stan/bin
Enter your command: echo '$'PATH
$PATH
Enter your command: echo PS1
PS1
Enter your command: echo $PS1
Enter your command:
Enter your command: PS1='$'$ _
```

The effect of cd $doc is exactly the same as cd /usr/stan/document since $doc evaluates to the expression assigned to doc earlier. One immediate advantage of such personal variables is to save typing! Once doc is assigned, you can use $doc as a convenient abbreviation.

The echo PATH example illustrates the importance of the $ prefix. The echo command (in man section C) simply echoes its arguments by sending them to your standard output. echo PATH therefore displays PATH quite literally, but with echo $PATH, the shell evaluates the variable PATH and echoes the value stored therein, namely:/bin:/usr/bin:/usr/stan/bin. Putting forward quotes around the $, you'll notice, removes the special interpretation of the $ as a variable evaluator, so that '$'PATH echoes as $PATH. Similarly, note how the metacharacter $ changes the result of echoing PS1 and $PS1.

The echo command is more useful than at first meets the eye! As the path example shows, echo lets you examine the contents of a variable, a useful operation when debugging a program. Even with nonvariables, echo is useful when you want a shell script to display a message:

```
echo 'Please enter Y or N '
```

Another useful application for echo is to send a fixed string to a file using redirection:

```
$ echo'** Hello Mary! ** ' >junk
$ cat junk
** Hello Mary! **
$ _
```

We'll make use of this trick occasionally to create small files without bothering with a text editor. The result is similar to the cat >>poem.1 trick you used in Chapter 4.

You can include newlines in a quoted string as follows:

```
$ echo 'Workers of the
> World, Unite!'
Workers of the
World, Unite!
$ _
```

After pressing Enter (newline) at the end of the first line, the shell displays its *secondary prompt*, in this case a > symbol, and waits for more input. After the final quote and newline, the shell knows that the command is complete, so it echoes the complete string, including the embedded newline, then displays its primary prompt, $. The secondary prompt is stored in the predefined shell variable PS2. By default, PS2 contains '>', but you can set it to any string using the assignment operation:

```
$ PS2='More input: '
$ _
```

As you saw in the case of PS1 earlier, a variable can be assigned another value at any time, hence the origin of the term "variable."

Variable names are usually chosen to indicate the type of value stored. As in the case of filenames, you should avoid certain characters that may confuse the shell, such as spaces, > < * ? $ " ' ' and \. Remember, too, to avoid using any of the predefined shell variables listed in Table 6.2.

A common command found in login profiles is stty (in man section C), a command that lets you customize your terminal in various ways. This is especially useful if you are using a dumb terminal with limited features.

Setting Terminal Options with stty

The command stty stands for "setting options for your teletypewriter," a reminder of the ancient origins of Unix! As the number and complexity of terminals has continued to blossom since the early 1970s, the stty command has grown in size to match. I will simply list some of the common stty options. The simplified syntax is

```
stty [-a] [options]
```

Using stty with no arguments will simply display a list of certain current settings. With the -a argument, stty displays all the current option settings. To set options, you use stty with various mnemonics as arguments. For example,

```
$ stty -tabs
$ _
```

will cause any tab codes to be converted to spaces when outputted to your terminal. This is useful if your terminal does not handle tab codes automatically. Similarly, you can vary the keystrokes used for erasing characters and killing lines:

```
$ stty erase[backspace] kill @
$ _
```

Here, the notation [backspace] means you press the Backspace key, since it is difficult to show you this action on the printed page! Alternatively, you could enter $ stty erase '^h' since Unix interprets '^h' as Ctrl-H, the ASCII code for backspace. The net result of this command is to assign the backspace key to the character erase function, and the @ key to the line delete function. A Berkeley version of stty called tset may be available on your system. The syntax is different, but the same options are generally available.

Viewing Your .profile File

Until you have developed some editing skills (see Chapters 10 and 11), you will not be able to play around with your login profile. However, you can list your current profiles and see what they are doing for you by entering

```
$ cat .profile
```

You'll probably find entries similar to the following in your .profile file:

```
PATH=:/bin:/usr/bin:$HOME/bin:
MAIL=/usr/spool/mail/ 'logname '
export PATH MAIL
umask 077
```

Note that $HOME will be converted to your home directory, say /usr/ stan, resulting in a path set to:/bin:/usr/bin:/usr/stan/bin:.

The second line illustrates an important use of the backquote mark ' (also known as the *grave* accent), not to be confused with the single forward quote '. Expressions within backquotes are taken as commands to be run by the shell, and the resulting value of the executed command replaces the backquoted expression. Easy for me to say! To see what this means, consider what happens when the shell encounters the backquoted expression 'logname'. The shell pauses to run the command logname, a simple command that returns your login name, say stan. Magically, the line

```
MAIL=/usr/spool/mail/'logname'
```

is transformed to

```
MAIL=/usr/spool/mail/stan
```

This line then establishes the name of the file that will be examined periodically to see if mail has arrived (see Table 6.2). The ability to invoke commands within commands, as it were, takes some getting used to, but it gives Unix shell scripts considerable power and elegance (not found in DOS BAT files, for example!). More on this in Chapters 12 and 15.

The `export` command tells the shell that the following list of variables, `PATH` and `MAIL`, will be needed in other programs. To understand this technicality requires an understanding of how shells can spawn subshells, so I'll spare you the details until Chapter 12. The `umask` (short for "user mask") line sets a default for permissions on files and directories that you may create. (More on this in Chapter 7.) With this background, you should be able to get some idea of what your own `.profile` is up to. Similarly, you can examine `/etc/profile` to see what global settings have been arranged for all users.

In the next chapter, I move on to another vital aspect of personalizing your Unix: setting up your own directories and files.

What's Next

Chapter 7 shows you how to organize your personal files. You'll learn how to create subdirectories, copy files, and switch from one directory to another. Additionally, you'll see how to change the permissions on your files so you can determine who can look at them, use them, and/or modify them.

```
echo "2.      Show Date"
echo "3.      Display a file"
echo "4.      Change working director
echo "5.      Return to original dir
echo "Q.      Quit
echo
echo -n "Enter choice: .\b"
read choice
case $choice in
1) who | more
   pause;;
2) date
   pause;;
3) echo "Enter file name: \c"
   read fil
   if [ -r "$fil" -a -f "$fil ]
   then
      clear
      more -d $fil
   else
      echo "Cannot d
   fi
   pause;;
4) echo "E
   read di
   if test -d "`dir      pwd`
   then
      cd $dir
   else
      echo "$dir: no such dir
   fi
   pause;;
5) if test "$dir" != "$p
   then
      cd $prevdir
   fi
   pause;;
```

Chapter 7

YOUR OWN
FILE SYSTEM

I've mentioned several times that Unix presents you with certain global resources under the general care and nourishment of the system administrator, while at the same time giving you your own home directory where you are, more or less, sovereign. Your home directory is your normal starting point in the Unix file hierarchy. From this node you are free to grow your own branches by sprouting subdirectories and files of your own choosing. Furthermore, you can determine with great precision who can access your home territory: you can prevent outside access to particular files or to whole directories. This chapter, therefore, covers both the creation of your own file system and the setting of permissions.

These are major steps in getting Unix on your side. Unix revolves around files, so you need to create a tree of directories with names that help you to organize your files. Many beginners simply let their files build up in their home directory. This is as chaotic as shoving all your papers into one big folder; storage effort is reduced at the expense of retrieval effort. As a simple suggestion, you could organize your files as follows:

`/usr/stan`	Home directory
`/usr/stan/bin`	Subdirectory for private programs
`/usr/stan/memo`	Memo subdirectory
`/usr/stan/memo/fred`	Directory for all memos to/from Fred
`/usr/stan/memo/mary`	Directory for all memos to/from Mary

The files representing your correspondence with Fred, say, can now have helpful names with a subject and date, such as `inv091290`. Since they are in the `fred` directory, the filenames do not have to be saddled with references to Fred. Your freedom to create files and directories is absolute in your own home!

HOME RULE

If you are user `stan` logged into `/usr/stan`, for instance, you can create a new file called `/usr/stan/copy.poem` or a new empty subdirectory called `/usr/stan/memo` ready to hold more files and subsubdirectories:

```
$ cd
$ pwd
/usr/stan
$ cp poem copy.poem
$ mkdir memo
$ cd memo
$ pwd
/usr/stan/memo
$ cp ../poem copy2.poem
$ mkdir fred
$ cd fred
$ pwd
/usr/stan/memo/fred
$ _
```

Remember that cd with no arguments puts you into your home directory.

NOTE

Remember, every directory holds two special directory "names": . (dot) means the directory itself, and .. (dot-dot) means the parent directory.

cp (in man section C) is the copy command. Used here in its simplest format, it copies the first named file (known as the *source*) to the second named file (known as the *destination*), overwriting the latter if it already exists. The source file for cp must exist; the destination file may or may not exist. Unless you specify otherwise, cp assumes that the files are in your current directory. Notice that in the second use of cp in the last example, I want to copy /usr/stan/poem. Since the current directory was /usr/stan/memo, I had to "step back" a level to the parent, using the .. notation. Of course, I could have typed the full path name:

```
$ cp /usr/stan/poem copy2.poem
```

but the ../ trick is simpler once you get used to it.

You have already met mkdir, which tries to create a subdirectory given by its argument. The parent of the newly created directory is your current directory. Note that mkdir does not automatically change to the directory you just created. After mkdir memo, you are still in /usr/stan. Remember that if you want to work within any new directory that you create, you need to cd to it first.

mkdir can fail for several reasons, for example, Unix will present you with an error message if the subdirectory already exists. Additionally, if you tried to cd to someone else's home directory to perform the above sequence of commands, the chances are that Unix would object with a permission denied message or similar brick wall. Unless you are logged into root as a superuser, the right to mess around outside your home directory and its children is under the control of others. In the same way, you have the power to admit or keep out any nonroot users. I have mentioned permissions several times in a general context. It is time to explore this crucial topic in greater detail.

PERMISSIONS

There are, in fact, eighteen different permission classes, so you are facing an area of Unix which most beginners find confusing at first assault. The different types of permissions fall into three categories, and the permission classes arise from the possible combinations of permissions from these categories:

- ► File and directory permissions
- ► Read, write, and execute permissions
- ► Owner, group, and public (or others) permissions

Before I list them exhaustively, let's review the basic concepts.

The Owner

Every file and directory has a designated *owner*, usually the original creator. Let's consider first a file that you own. You can grant or withhold its three permissions (read, write, and execute) in any way you wish. These three, also known as *access modes*, are quite independent. You can set these three permission levels differently for three sets of users: yourself, members of your group, and others.

Naturally, you grant yourself, as owner, read and write permissions (in fact, you usually get these two permissions by default). Where appropriate, you can give yourself execute permission with a single chmod command, as you'll see later.

File Permissions

Read permission means you can list the contents of files with cat or pr or any other command that accesses the data inside the file. Write permission means that you can change the contents of a file. If the file is executable (either a binary program or a shell script), execute permission means that you can run it as a program. Note that as a safety precaution, you may want to withhold write permission from your important files. This is rather like breaking off the plastic write-protect tab on an audio or video tape. If the need arises, you can always restore the write permission by covering the opening with a piece of tape (or in the case of Unix, by changing the permissions with chmod, a handy command that we'll be looking at soon. In the meantime, just be aware that any file can have any combination of permissions, allowing you to read them, change them, or execute them. And just because you have one permission does not necessarily mean you have the others.

You can now decide who else should have these access rights. If you belong to a group (assigned by the system administrator), group members may enjoy any, all, or none of the three permissions. This can be decided on a file-by-file basis. Finally, all other users outside your group can be granted any, all, or none of the three permissions on a global or user-by-user basis. Permissions granted outside the group and owner are sometimes called *public* permissions.

Directory Permissions

The three permissions can also be applied to directories, although the meanings of read, write, and execute have to be interpreted slightly differently. I'll explain these subtle differences in several ways to ensure that you understand their significance.

Read and write directory permissions are fairly obvious. You need read permission to determine the *contents* of a directory with ls or a similar command. ls has to read the various fields in a directory in order to give you the *names* of its files and subdirectories. This is quite different from the act of reading the contents of a file or the contents of a subdirectory. Directory read permission is quite independent of, and must not be confused with, any of the permissions set on the files and subdirectories themselves. If you grant others read permission on your directory, but withhold read/write permissions on your files, then other users will be able to see all your filenames but will be unable to read or change the contents of your files. Conversely, you could (in theory) withhold directory read permission but grant file read and/or write permissions. If so, other users would not be able to determine your filenames with ls, yet if they somehow managed to learn the name of one of your files, they might be able to read and/or change it.

Directory write permission lets you alter the contents of a directory. Without such permission, therefore, you cannot add or remove files or subdirectories.

Directory execute permission is not the same as file execute permission. While file execute permission lets you run a file, directory execute permission is often called directory *search* permission. This permission allows a user to access any file or subdirectory, since such access calls for a search of the directory in order to locate that file or subdirectory.

In order to cd into a directory, you also need directory execute permission in that directory; and even with this permission, you would further require write permission in that directory in order to alter its contents, that is, create and erase files, or create and erase its subdirectories.

Stan was able to create the subdirectory memo and create and access files therein because he has read, write, and execute permissions in his own home directory, /usr/stan, and its children. Yes, each user acquires these and similar permissions on their own directories and files as a sort of birthright, and only root can take them away. (You, as the owner, could also remove some or all of these permissions from yourself, or even relinquish your ownership, but that might border on the suicidal!)

Whether you have permission to cd into /usr/mary, for example, is entirely up to mary and root, since only they can change the permissions on Mary's files and directories.

Mary may well grant group members and/or others execute permission on her home directory but withhold other permissions. If so, such users could cd to /usr/mary, but without directory write permission, would not be free to create files and subdirectories there. Stan could not even list the files in /usr/mary unless Mary grants him directory read permission there. Note that if you happened to know the name of a program file in usr/mary and she gave you execute permissions on both the directory and the program, you could run it without needing directory read permission. If you find this confusing, be patient. All will be clear soon.

If Mary had a file called poem, other users could not read or copy it unless Mary granted them file read permission for that file. Nor could they write over or change a file in /usr/mary without specific file write permission on that file. When write permission is withheld on a file, we say that the file is *write protected*, and similarly for reading permission, we use the phrase *read protected*.

Once again, under normal circumstances, you can have full read, write, and execute permissions (as appropriate) on the files and subdirectories that you create in your home directory (and its branches), but outside this, other users can withhold or modify these permissions. To change the contents of a directory you must have *write* permission on that directory. This includes making, erasing, and renaming files, and creating subdirectories with mkdir. To copy a file with cp, you need to have *read* permission on the source file and *write* permission on the destination file, assuming the file exists. If the destination file does not exist, you must have *write* permission for that directory so you can create the target file there.

It's time to classify all these permissions and then see how you can set and change them.

Permissions for Owner, Group, and Others

Like Caesar's Gallia, Unix offers three divisions of access permissions:

Owner   Permissions granted to the current owner of a file or directory. The owner is usually the original creator of the file or directory, but ownership may be alterable using the chown (change owner) command (discussed later in this chapter).

Group   Permissions granted to a set of consenting users forming a group. Groups are given a group name by the system administrator, who also arranges for individual users to join or leave each group.

Public   Permissions granted to all users. Public file and directory permissions apply to any legal user.

In each of these divisions, there are three types of permission available: *read, write,* and *execute.* The terms, coded as r, w, and x, are reasonably intuitive, but you must be aware that they each mean slightly different things when applied to files and directories. There are therefore six types of permission to digest: file read, directory read; file write, directory write; file execute, directory execute.

As I mentioned earlier, the last combination looks peculiar, since one does not normally think of directories as being executable. Shell scripts and program files are executable, but surely a directory such as /usr/ stan cannot be "run" like a program? The answer is that the "execute" in the directory execute category has a special interpretation, sometimes known as directory search permission.

A Unix directory, as you may have noticed, is very much like a file: both have names and both store data. The difference, of course, is that the data inside a directory is a list of file and subdirectory names together with certain control information to help Unix locate them on your disk. To discover the file and subdirectory names in a directory, using ls for instance, requires *read* permission on that directory. To add or remove files or subdirectories requires *write* permission on the directory. Even to rename a file, you must have *write* permission on the directory. And to access a file requires *execute* permission; when a filename is a command argument, for example, the directory must be searched before the file can be located on your disk.

NOTE
By withholding directory execute (or search) permission, you can prevent access to any file in that directory, since accessing a file requires a search of its directory.

Here's something that confuses many beginners: provided you have write permission on a directory, you can remove one of its files even when the file is *write protected*. Write protection of a file protects only its contents; the file itself is vulnerable unless its directory is write protected.

The following listing should clarify the situation:

Permission	Symbol	Meaning
no permission	–	Permission withheld.
Read	r	Read permission on a file allows access to its contents.
		Read permission on a directory allows the determination of the names of its files and subdirectories, for example, with ls.
write	w	Write permission on a file allows change to its contents.
		Write permission on a directory allows change to the contents of that directory by adding or deleting files and subdirectories.
execute	x	Execute permission on a file allows use of that file as a command.
		Execute permission on a directory allows a search of that directory for a file.

The four symbols r, w, x, and - (no permission) are used to specify the permission rights for each file and directory. To examine file permission rights, you use the ls-l command. The -l argument means "long" or "full" listing. For directories, you use ls-ld, where the combined -ld argument means long directory listings. Here are some examples:

```
$ ls -l openhouse
-rwxrwxrwx 1 stan prog 245 May 20 10:15 openhouse
```

The leftmost field of ten symbols is the permissions field. The first symbol indicates the type of file as follows:

Symbol	Type of file
-	Ordinary file
d	Directory
b	Block I/O device
c	Character I/O device

For the moment, you can ignore the I/O device files. My examples will be limited to ordinary files and directories.

The remaining nine symbols show the three sets of three permissions for owner, group, and others. In the example above, the display shows the following permission field:

► The first symbol, -, means openhouse is a *file* (a d here would indicate a directory).

► The first rwx means that the owner, stan, has read, write, and execute permissions.

► The second rwx means that all members of stan's group have read, write, and execute permissions.

► The third rwx means that all others have read, write, and execute permissions. (This group is also called the public permissions group.)

As you can see, openhouse is accessible to everybody. All can read, change, and run this file as a program or command provided that its directory has execute permission for all.

Without too much diversion from our study of permissions, let's look briefly at the other fields displayed by ls-l.

Field	Description
1	The file has only one link. This means that the file is known only as openhouse. A 2 here would mean that the file can be accessed via two different names (or links).
Stan	The file is owned by stan.
Prog	The file belongs to the group called prog.

Field	Description
245	The file has 245 bytes.
May 20 10:15	The file was last modified at this date/time.
openhouse	The filename is openhouse.

Here's another example:

```
$ ls -l myprog
-rwxr-x--- 1 stan prog 645 May 21 12:15 myprog
```

The owner of myprog, namely stan, enjoys rwx permissions, so he can read, write, and execute this file. Members of the prog group, however, can only read and execute myprog, as indicated by the group permissions r-x. The lack of write permission means that group members cannot modify myprog. Their ability to erase myprog will depend on permissions in the directory. All others are given permissions of ---, namely no permissions at all! Outsiders cannot read, change, or execute myprog. Attempts to do any of these operations will invoke the message

```
myprog: permission denied.
```

To allow members of the prog group to check filenames and access files in /usr/stan, the directory permissions must be set appropriately:

```
$ ls -ld /usr/stan
drwxr-x--- 5 stan prog 780 May 19 09:25 /usr/stan
```

Note the initial d indicating a directory. The owner has rwx permissions, allowing stan to read, write, and search /usr/stan. Group members are denied directory write permission, so they cannot create or erase files and subdirectories in /usr/stan. However, they have read permission, so they can use ls to discover all the filenames. They also have execute permission, so they can access the files they want to read and run.

Default Permissions

When you acquire your home directory, it normally comes with the following default permissions set by the system administrator:

```
drwx------
```

These permissions will also be acquired by any subdirectories you create. They imply that, initially, you have sole control over your directories. Only you can read, write, and search them. Nobody else can cd to your directories, alter their contents by adding or removing your files or subdirectories, or search them to access your files.

Any files you create will usually default to

```
-rw-------
```

Once again, nobody can interfere in any way (except `root`, of course). Note, however, that your script files do not acquire execute permission by default. If you create shell scripts and wish to run them, you must set execute permission yourself. (Binary program files become executable automatically when you compile and link them.) You'll see how to do this in the next section.

NOTE

It's a good idea to create a file and a directory and check their permissions with `ls`. This will reveal the current defaults.

These initial permission defaults can be varied by you and/or the system administrator by changing a parameter known as the `umask` (or user mask). This requires a knowledge of the octal numbering system used to encode the `rwx` pattern of each permission set, so I'll spare you the details until later.

CHANGING OWNERS AND GROUPS

The key point to note is that only you, the owner, and the omnipotent `root` can vary your permissions. Likewise, you cannot go around changing anyone else's permissions! You can, however, relinquish ownership of a file (subject to the system administrator's approval). You use the `chown` (change owner id) command (in `man` section C) as follows:

```
$ chown mary poem memo
$ _
```

Provided that `poem` and `memo` are found and you are their owner, the above line will change the ownerships to Mary. You can list as many filenames as you wish, separated by spaces. The second argument can be any valid login name, or you can use the corresponding numerical uid (user id). The file is still in your directory, so Mary may not be able to do much with her new possession. One thing she can now do as the new owner is to change the permissions of these files, if she so desires.

A similar command, `chgrp` (change group id—also in `man` section C), lets you change the group id of a file.

```
$ chgrp systems poem memo
$ _
```

will change the group of the two files to systems. Providing that the directory permissions allow, members of the systems group acquire new access rights on these two files.

Changing Permissions

The chmod command (in man section C) is used by the owner of a file or directory (or by root) to change its access permissions.

There are two distinct ways of using chmod, best described by a few examples. The first method is called the *absolute* method because it changes all of the permission settings:

```
$ ls -l myprog
-rwxr-x--- 1 stan prog 645 May 21 12:15 myprog
$ chmod 0777 myprog
$ ls -l myprog
-rwxrwxrwx 1 stan prog 645 May 21 12:15 myprog
```

The first argument of chmod is called the *mode*. Here, a mode of 0777 has somehow managed to set the permissions to -rwxrwxrwx (that is, read, write, execute for owner, group, and public). The trick works as follows:

Permission	Numeric Value
-	0
r	4
w	2
x	1

For each of the three sets, you add up the numbers corresponding to the permission required:

rwx = 4 + 2 + 1 = 7

rwx = 4 + 2 + 1 = 7

rwx = 4 + 2 + 1 = 7

This gives you the mode argument of 777 (the leading 0 is optional).

If you are familiar with the octal and binary notations, the mode argument in chmod is easy to figure. Each rwx group is expressed as an octal number. Write each octal number in binary, for example:

```
777 <F113>=<F255> (111)(111)(111) <F113>=<F255>
(rwx)(rwx)(rwx)
```

```
666 <F113>=<F255> (110)(110)(110) <F113>=<F255> (rw-)(rw-)(rw-)
542 <F113>=<F255> (101)(100)(010) <F113>=<F255> (r-x)(r--)(-w-)
```

1 means permission granted; 0 means permission denied.

A few more examples may help:

Mode	Permission
0600	-rw-------
0666	-rw-rw-rw-
0222	--w--w--w-
0555	-r-xr-xr-x
0744	-rwxr--r--

The other chmod method is called the *relative* or *symbolic* method. Here, you select just the permissions to be changed; the other permissions are unaltered. The syntax is

```
chmod [who] [+|-|=] [permissions] filename
```

The optional first argument, *who*, can be any of the following symbols (or combinations of them):

Who	Meaning
A	All users (the default)
G	Group
O	Others (public)
U	User (owner)

The second argument can be either + (to add a permission), - (to remove a permission), or = (to assign a given permission and remove any others that might be there). Note the syntax: | is read as OR (exclusive).

The third argument, permissions, can be any combination of the familiar r, w, and x symbols.

The final argument is the name of the target file or directory. As you can guess, the total number of variants is astronomical, but here are a few simple examples:

```
$ ls -l myprog
-rwxr-x--- 1 stan prog 645 May 21 12:15 myprog
$ chmod o+x myprog
$ ls -l myprog
-rwxr-x--x 1 stan prog 645 May 21 12:15 myprog
```

```
$ chmod ug-r myprog
$ ls -l myprog
--wx--x--x 1 stan prog 645 May 21 12:15 myprog
$ chmod a+r myprog
$ ls -l myprog
-rwxr-xr-x 1 stan prog 645 May 21 12:15 myprog
$ chmod u=r myprog
$ ls -l myprog
-r-------- 1 stan prog 645 May 21 12:15 myprog
```

As you can see, o+x adds execute permission to others (leaving the rest unchanged); ug-r removes read permission from user (owner) and group; and a+r adds read permission to owner, group, and others. Note that +r would give the same effect as a+r since a is the default. To combine a series of permissions, separate each with a comma, for example,

```
$ chmod o+x, ug-r myprog
```

The u=r example sets read permission to user (owner), but clears all other permissions. Use this format with care! Play around with chmod to get the feel for it. In spite of the apparent complexities, it soon becomes natural. There are just a handful of common combinations. Two you'll be using a lot when we discuss shell programming later are

```
chmod u+x filename
```

and

```
chmod +x filename
```

The first format makes filename executable by you (the user); the second version makes filename executable by everyone!

WHAT'S NEXT

In Chapter 8, we'll take a look at multitasking, multiprogramming and multiprocessing. You'll discover how Unix manages the processing needs of all the users on a network simultaneously. You'll also learn how to set up tasks that can run in the background while you work on other projects and how to schedule things to happen when you want them to happen.

```
echo "2.      Show Date"
echo "3.      Display a file"
echo "4.      Change working director
echo "5.      Return to original dire
echo "Q.      Quit
echo
echo -n "Enter choice: .\b"
read choice
case $choice in
1) who | more
   pause;;
2) date
   pause;;
3) echo "Enter file name: \c"
   read fil
   if [ -r "$fil" -a -f "$fil ]
   then
      clear
      more -d $fil
   else
      echo "Cannot di
   fi
   pause;;
4) echo "En
   read di
   if test   d "$dir    pwd`
   then
      cd $dir
   else
      echo "$dir: no such di
   fi
   pause;;
5) if test "$dir" != "$p
   then
      cd $prevdir
   fi
   pause;;
```

Chapter 8

PROCESSES AND MULTITASKING

I n this chapter, I'll explore the significance of Unix's multitasking capabilities, clarify the somewhat murky terminology, and show you how you can exploit multitasking in your daily activities.

MULTIJARGON

Before I explain multitasking, you should be aware of two older, related terms. The first is *multiuser,* which simply means that the system can simultaneously service more than one online terminal. The other, *multiprogramming,* means that the system can run several programs at the same time. A multiprogramming system is not necessarily multiuser (take a single-user PC under OS/2, for example), but a multiuser system certainly needs multiprogramming. Unix, of course, is both a multiprogramming and a multiuser operating system. Naturally, to cope with several concurrent users, Unix must be installed on a system with the necessary multichannel I/O (input/output) boards.

Note that multiprogramming includes the situation where 300 users are each running `date`, as well as the situation where one user is running `date`, `who`, and `lp` at the same time.

Some computers, known as *symmetrical multiprocessing* systems (SMP for short), achieve multiprogramming by using several processors (either running independently or tightly coupled), but we will be concerned with multiprogramming on a single-processor system with the aid of a suitable operating system. A multiprocessor system can literally run several programs simultaneously; with a single processor, multiprogramming is, in fact, a clever illusion. Deep down inside a single-processor system, only one machine instruction can be executed at any instant. A sufficiently powerful central processing unit (CPU), however, can devote a *time slice* to one program, then switch to service another, and so on, giving the appearance of simultaneity.

MULTIPROGRAMMING OPERATING SYSTEMS

The multiprogramming operating system must be designed to perform a delicate juggling trick. It must allocate *resources,* such as CPU cycles and memory, and assign priorities so that each program receives adequate attention. Urgent jobs must be granted larger and/or more frequent CPU time slices without unduly neglecting lesser jobs. Also, jobs differ in their requirements. Number-crunching programs tend to be CPU intensive, while many business applications are I/O bound, with relatively little computation. The operating system needs to handle mixes of such jobs as efficiently as possible.

A program that is waiting for user input, for example, can be safely suspended regardless of priority. Remember that between each of your tentative keystrokes, your 100 MHz CPU is capable of many millions of useful cycles.

A program that is actually executing must have a copy of some or all of its object code loaded in main memory so that the CPU can access the program instructions. For most PCs, the system's main memory is made of integrated circuits called RAM (Random Access Memory). Depending upon the version that you're using, when running Unix, it is recommended that you have a minimum of 32MB (million bytes) of RAM. In fact, your system will run best if you have at least 64MB on systems like SCO Unix. Whereas, for systems like Linux, you can have as little as 16MB for good operation.

For this reason, main memory is an important resource that needs to be carefully managed by the operating system. At any particular moment, your computer's main memory will hold not only the object code (the actual, binary commands) of your currently running program, but also the object code for a number of suspended programs, together with various data areas that contain the intermediate results of these programs. Most if not all of the operating system kernel must also be resident in main memory. As far as the CPU is concerned, the kernel is also simply a set of programs that needs to be executed on demand. Of course, since the kernel is in charge, the kernel is not just another program: it maintains its own priorities to avoid being upstaged by user programs.

How many programs can coexist in primary memory depends on the amount of memory in your computer and the size of the programs you are running.

Some suspended programs and their data (or selected portions of these) may have to be *swapped* out from main memory to the hard disk to make room for the next scheduled program. Later, when the operating system selects them for execution, the swapped items must be restored from disk to memory. Much research has been devoted to the art of scheduling and swapping active programs and data since the immediate effect of excessive swapping is performance degradation. Disk I/O is relatively much slower than memory reads and writes. And remember that the CPU itself gets involved in the swapping activity. An extreme case known as *thrashing* can bring the system to a snail's pace: in this instance, the system is so preoccupied with swapping information between main memory and the hard disk that little or no productive processing takes place.

The inner details of these gymnastics are happily hidden from the average user, but having a general feel engenders some sympathy for the folks who design operating systems. Also, in practical terms, it explains the old adage that you can never have too much RAM (main memory).

The situation is further complicated by the need to remember which programs are suspended, when, and for what reason. The operating system needs to store the *context* of each suspended program so that execution can resume at the right point with the same values prevailing at the time of suspension. Contexts are really snapshots of the CPU's program counter and registers, and contexts are being saved and restored regularly by the operating system as programs are switched.

MULTITASKING

The more modern term *multitasking* includes the idea of multiprogramming but extends the concept to include the ability to run different parts of the same program (also known as *threads*) simultaneously. The basic idea is that most programs can be treated as a sequence of smaller elements called *tasks.* Sometimes these tasks must be executed and completed in order, one at a time. For example, task 2, say, may need the results from task 1 before it can proceed. On other occasions, some or all of the tasks in a program can be usefully tackled independently, without regard to the other tasks that are running. And, of course, you will encounter mixed situations where task 1, task 2, and task 3 can be run independently, but task 4 must await their completion.

Another element in the jigsaw is that many peripherals, such as tape and disk drives, can also operate independently. An I/O task (such as reading from a disk) can be triggered by a system call in program A and left to run independently while the operating system prepares to run another task or program. The operating system scans its table of suspended jobs and determines which of those that are "runnable" has the highest priority, say program B. The context of program A is then stored together with a flag indicating its wait status (waiting for a disk read). The previously saved context of program B is then restored and program B starts executing. But how will the suspended program A ever get restarted? Well, the I/O device needs to signal that its operation is complete, and this is done by a *device interrupt.* Device interrupts are messages that system peripherals send to the CPU, telling it that they need its attention. For example, when you press a key on your keyboard, the keyboard stores the value of the keystroke and sends an interrupt to the CPU, telling it that it has data waiting for it. As the name implies, an interrupt can occur at any time, and the kernel must take note of it even if no immediate restart of program A is possible. The kernel's reaction to the interrupt in this case would be to change the status of program A from "waiting for disk read" to "runnable." This restores program A as a candidate for execution, and eventually, depending on its relative priority, program A will regain its place in the sun.

Peeling off these deeply nested onion layers is a complex business—the key is to have an overall picture and lots of faith. Luckily, Unix offers you some simple commands that let you run as many programs as you wish and keep track of their progress. But first, more jargon!

Unix Images and Processes

The terms *program* and *task* are rather vague: a piece of code can be divided in many ways, both conceptually and practically. A programmer can construct a program by compiling and linking many smaller programs or modules. During execution, such programs can invoke other programs and subroutines, some of which may be *system calls*. These are basic service routines provided by the operating system. So at one level of discussion, a program is a source code text prepared by a programmer. At another level, a program is a compiled, binary file on a disk. And at yet another level, a program is a piece of binary code sitting in your RAM waiting to be *dispatched* (that is, executed) or possibly temporarily swapped out to disk through lack of available memory.

To reduce this ambiguity, Unix uses two precise terms, *image* and *process*. To set the scene before precision strikes, repeat the following mantra: The process is the execution of the image.

NOTE

The terms *process* and *processor* are still a tad confusing. A multiprocessor system has several CPUs, but a single-processor Unix system can process several Unix processes! Also, the term *process control* can refer to real-time systems at chemical and other plants, as well as to the part of the kernel that controls Unix processes.

More technically, the image represents the executable program in binary form (misleadingly called the *text segment*), together with various data structures holding the context of the program, and two work areas (called the *data segment* and the *stack*). Figure 8.1 shows a simplified version of a Unix image. All you need to know for now is that the text segment in memory is strictly read-only: the kernel ensures that it cannot be written over or changed during execution. The other areas can be freely accessed *and* changed during execution. The image must be resident in memory while its process is executing.

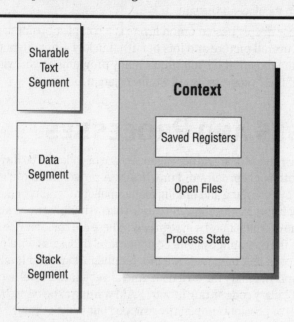

FIGURE 8.1:   Image Layout

Process Biography

When you invoke the wc (word count) command, for example, the shell (via calls to the kernel) loads an image and starts a new process with a unique numerical *pid* (process identifier). All subsequent references to this process (both by users and other processes) are made via its pid rather than by the name of the original command. You met a similar situation with user and group identifiers, and the theme appears in many other Unix situations. The pid's 0 and 1, by the way, are reserved for special processes created when Unix first boots.

If another user invokes the wc command, a fresh process is created with a different pid. (A completely new image, by the way, is not always needed with a new process, since processes are able to share the text segment of an image when running the same program.)

You could even invoke wc again while your first wc is still running (you'll see how soon), and the second wc would create a separate process with its own pid. The point to stress is that programs and processes are distinct entities. There can be many processes independently executing the same program.

Each runnable process will be selected for execution according to its priority (later you'll see how priorities are set and altered). The state of a process can change many times during its lifetime. It may be put in a *sleeping* state, meaning that it is suspended temporarily for various reasons, such as waiting for I/O or for other processes to finish. Usually, a process will run to completion and then disappear from the scene. A process may also terminate through some error condition or as a result of a signal (such as kill) from the user or from another process. However it is terminated, a completed process is removed from the table of processes, and the RAM it occupied is freed for new processes.

Forks and Spawns

While a process A is running, it may *spawn* another process, B. B is said to be the *child* of A, and A is called the *parent* of B. Spawning is achieved by a system call known as fork, so we often talk about processes being forked. A child process can itself spawn children, and so on ad infinitum. A detailed understanding of spawning mechanism is not essential for your day-to-day Unix operation, but the following brief summary will give you a helpful background.

Initially, the child and parent processes are virtually identical. They each start with independent, identical copies of the original RAM image but, being separate processes, they do have distinct pid's. The child also has access to any files that the parent has opened. Processes can also share special I/O channels called *pipes* that behave rather like files, as you saw in Chapter 4 (more on this soon).

The child then calls exec using the command name and its arguments (if any) inherited from the parent. exec is a system call that revamps the child's image so that the child process starts executing the inherited command. Child and parent processes are now free to go their own way and do their own things by executing their now different images. Because they can both access the same open files and pipes, though, there are opportunities for *interprocess* communication and cooperation.

The pipes and filters you saw in Chapter 4, in fact, were simple examples of two cooperating processes. In ls | wc, for example, the ls process writes to the pipe while the wc process reads from the pipe. The kernel buffers and synchronizes this activity, and will delay the reading process if the buffer is empty. Similarly, the writing process is held up if the buffer is full.

The parent process also has an important option: it can choose to *wait* for its child to terminate. The parent makes this choice by invoking the system call `wait`, which is so arranged that the parent is informed when the child process has terminated and the reason for termination. Since a parent may spawn several children before going into a wait state, `wait` also tells the parent which of the child processes has terminated. The full relevance of this parental "wait for the kids" privilege will emerge in future sections when you see how the shell process spawns children.

The fork is a fundamental operation in Unix: when you first boot Unix, there are just two basic processes created called `swapper` (or `sched`) and `init`, with pid's 0 and 1 respectively. All other user processes are spawned by calls to `fork`! For example, `init` forks several background processes called *daemons* (more on these later) and a set of `getty` processes that monitor each terminal looking for user logins.

In some ways, the hierarchy of processes, from parents to children, to grandchildren, is comparable with the file hierarchy outlined in previous chapters. Before I enlarge on this theme, there is an important parent process to consider—one you have been quietly using since Chapter 1!

The Shell As a Process

Although I did not make a splash about it, you have already been exposed to Unix processes and their forks. Whenever you type a command, the shell spawns a process that executes that command. Running the shell itself, as you may have guessed, is a process.

The shell process can run some commands under its own steam, but more often than not it spawns a child process to execute the programs and commands you enter. Being a patient parent, the shell usually waits for this child process to complete, after which the shell displays its prompt, inviting a new command.

But what if you could tell the shell *not* to wait for the child process to finish? What if you could get the prompt back immediately, while the child process continued on its own? Clearly, you could then run another command while the child process was running in the *background*. Unix offers a simple way of achieving this desirable feat. In fact, you can easily set up as many commands as you wish, all running "simultaneously."

Some processes do not lend themselves to background execution, of course. Text editors such as ed require constant keyboard and screen interaction, and must be run in the *foreground*. Similarly, commands producing screen displays can cause chaos if run in parallel. Some jobs that seem to be ideal for background processing are in fact handled correctly by Unix without special user intervention. For example, you'll see that Unix can automatically *spool* printing jobs. Spooling means that all print requests are queued up centrally so that you don't have to wait for the printer to print your job before you execute another command.

Of course, there may be a limit to the number of background commands you can have at one time, depending on RAM size, the complexity of the commands, and what other users are up to. Many Unix systems now use demand-paged virtual memory. This extends the effective main memory size by using available disk space as if it were a part of your computer's main memory. The only practical limit on how many processes you have running using virtual memory is that computer response time may become unacceptable because of excessive swapping of data between the hard disk and main memory.

With these provisos in mind, let's return to the keyboard and do some single-processor multitasking!

BACKGROUND PROCESSES USING &

The simplest way to create simultaneous processes is with the & command terminator. When you terminate a command with & (followed by Enter), the shell spawns a child process as usual, but does not wait for the child to terminate. Rather, the shell displays the pid (process identifier) of the new process, then immediately displays the prompt for another command:

```
$ wc chapter* >chap.count &
2676
$ ed stan.data
?stan.data
a
_
```

The number 2676 is the unique pid of the process spawned to execute the image loaded by the shell in response to the wc command. This process, counting the lines, words, and characters in all the files matching `chapter*`, will run in the background while you are busy editing `stan.data` in the foreground. The output of the `wc` process was redirected to the file `chap.count`. Without redirection (accomplished with the > command), the results of the count would go to your standard output (the screen), and strange numbers would appear mixed up with your `ed` displays!

The above example can be extended:

```
$ wc chapter* >chap.count &
2676
$ ls -l accounts/inv* >invfiles &
3125
$ ed stan.data
345
a
_
```

You now have two background processes running while you do some more text editing. Note that the 345 is *not* a pid, but the number of characters in `stan.data`!

There are many candidates for background processing. For example, some of the tasks that a typical user might want to make background processes include long sorts, database imports, and large spreadsheet recalculations. For programmers, lengthy compilations and links can putter along out of sight while new code is being edited in the foreground.

The wait Command

What if you initiate one or more background processes with & and then decide that you need to wait until they have all terminated? For example, you may realize that you need the results of the word count process in order to start the next job. One answer is to use the `wait` command (in man section C). The `wait` command takes no arguments. If the prompt appears immediately after entering `wait`, you can be sure that all your background processes are complete. Otherwise, there must be background processes still running, and you and your screen must simply wait for the prompt! Alert readers may wonder if `wait` is executed in the normal way by a child process spawned by the shell. The answer is no! `wait` must be executed by the shell itself by using the system call (also called `wait`) and exercising the parental "wait for the children" privilege I discussed earlier.

Alternatively, you can use the `fg` (foreground) command to bring a background job into the foreground. A really powerful trick in Unix (which is supported by most shells), is the `ctrl-z` (suspend) functionality, which allows you to take a process that's in the foreground and suspend it. A suspended process will not run until you type `fg` to run it in the foreground. The opposite of `fg` is `bg` , which puts a suspended process in the background. To get an idea of how these work, lets say you start a process and after waiting a while, you realize its going to take a little longer than you expected. You can press `ctrl-z` while the program is running and you will be returned to a shell. Be aware, though, that the process has been suspended and will get no CPU time until you type `fg` to resume it (at which point you will lose your shell). If you want to keep your shell and let your process run in the background, type `bg` instead of `fg` and you're done.

What if you initiate a long background process and change your mind? Or supposing a process gets into that bane of all programmers, an endless loop or some other kind of wild state? (It is remarkably easy to write a shell script that will run forever without achieving anything useful.) The next section reveals the essential but lethal `kill` command.

KILLING PROCESSES

You can kill any or all of *your own* processes with the `kill` command, so caution is urged. The superuser, as you might guess, can kill any user's processes, and sometimes has to exercise this power in emergencies (viral or trojan horse invasions, for instance).

A killed process just disappears: its image is cleared and it ceases to qualify for scheduling by the kernel. Killing your own processes, though, is not quite as fatal as zapping the wrong file. If you inadvertently kill a background process running a long `wc`, for example, you can simply reissue the command and only time has been lost. Nevertheless, killing the wrong process can be a nuisance.

The `kill` command, for historical reasons, is rather misleadingly named. The `kill` command actually sends a *signal* to your processes. Some of these signals do, in fact, request or enforce process termination, but other signals sent by `kill` have no connection with killing at all! Some defense for the name is that, by default, if no signal is specified, `kill` does send a signal requesting process termination; for most users, this is the only situation where `kill` is ever used. Let's look at the `kill` syntax to clarify matters:

```
kill [-signal] pid1 [pid2 ...pidn]
```

The kill command sends the signal given by the optional signal argument to each process indicated in the list of process identifiers. You must indicate at least one pid. The special value 0 can be used for pid1, in which case the signal is sent to all processes created from your current login, excluding your shell process.

The default signal happens to be 15—this is the request-process-termination signal. So,

```
$ kill 2676
```

is the same as kill -15 2676, which sends a termination request to the process with pid 2676. In our earlier example this pid was running wc, so you may wonder why Unix does not allow a simple kill wc format. The reason is that you may have several processes running wc jobs, whereas the pid is unique.

To check the success of your kill request, you need to run the ps (process status) command, the subject of a later section. Under most circumstances, kill pid will actually kill the process, but there are exceptions. First, a process can be run under the nohup (no hangup) regimen. This deserves a small digression.

Hello, I Must Be Going!

Suppose you want to start a mammoth job, log out, switch off your terminal, head home, and crack an ice-cold Fosters. You can do all this and leave your job running. You simply type nohup and a space, followed by your command and its arguments (if any), ending with & to create a background process:

```
$ nohup bigjob args &
3421
$ logout
```

The process running bigjob carries on in the background at low priority. And by including the nohup option in your command, if someone other than the superuser logs in on your terminal, the process is immune from an accidental or intentional kill 3421. Likewise, you yourself cannot use kill 3421 to stop the process.

But what if you *need* to stop a process? There may be some pathological cases in which the process staggers on unheeding, never ending and ignoring simple kill attempts. Is there no way of terminating such processes?

Yes!

Unix provides a big blaster signal that guarantees sudden death to both running-wild and nohup processes:

```
$ kill -9 3421
```

So, signal value 9 is the real killer.

Similarly,

```
$ kill -9 0
```

is a rather heavy-handed way of stopping all your active processes, excluding the parent shell.

The system administrator, as mentioned earlier, can kill any or all processes, regardless of "ownership." There is a special signal used only by the superuser to curtail all user activity, reducing the system to a single-user state prior to making major system changes or closing down for the night.

```
# kill -1 1
```

The signal value 1 means *hangup,* and is only used after issuing a prior warning (for example, wall) to all active users. (Some systems have a killall command, for use by root only, which also kills all active processes, with the exception of those processes involved in the shutdown procedure. More on this in Chapter 17.)

The other values for signal are for advanced users, but you may want to take a peek at the man pages for kill.

Before moving on to the ps command, one more piece of process jargon is needed. Your shell process is considered to be the group *leader* of all the spawned processes you may be running. In more complex situations, there may be other group leaders, possibly other shells running under your shell with their own children. The ! (bang) command "escapes" you temporarily to the shell. In fact, ! spawns a fresh copy of sh. When you exit this shell, you return to its parent, the original sh. The group concept lets you consider just those processes running from a certain parent (usually your shell) without the confusion of any earlier generation of processes.

CHECKING YOUR PROCESSES
WITH PS

To keep track of what processes are active, you use the ps (process status) command. The ps command is one of those that has attracted many dialectal variants, so your version may differ from mine. The prevalent syntax is as follows:

    ps [options]

The most common options are

None	Lists processes of your terminal only in short format
-d	Lists all processes except process group leaders
-e	Lists all processes
-a	Lists all terminal processes except group leaders and nonterminal processes
-t tlist	Restricts list to the terminals in tlist
-p plist	Restricts list to the pid's in plist
-g glist	Restricts list to the pid's in the groups given by glist
-u ulist	Restricts list to pid's belonging to uid's in ulist
-f	Provides full listing
-l	Provides long listing

Some options determine *which* processes will be displayed; other options determine *how much* information you'll get. You can combine some of these options, or rely on the various defaults. Consider the following example:

```
% ps
PID    TTY    TIME    CMD
1801   tty3   0:04    csh
2452   tty3   0:04    ps
% _
```

For a change of scenery, I've switched from my SCO UNIX to a dialup BSD (Berkeley Software Distribution) system called basis. Note the C shell prompt.

There are two processes active on my terminal: pid 1801 is running csh, the C shell, and pid 2452 is running ps. The latter, of course, is the selfsame ps command that is reporting the state of my processes! The other fields shown are quite obvious: TTY tells you the name of the controlling terminal; TIME gives the accumulated execution time in minutes:seconds.

ps with no options confines its attention to processes running from your own terminal and gives a short listing. This is by far the most common format you will need. Usually, you will invoke ps simply to find a pid for the kill command or to verify that a kill has been successful. The TIME field is also useful for checking on possible endlessly looped processes.

For a fuller account of your own processes, use the -f option:

```
% ps -f
UID       PID  PPID  C   STIME     TTY  TIME CMD
bin      8371  5386  127 16:14:35  tty3 0:03 ps -f
polemic  5386     1    5 03:06:56  tty3 0:04 -csh
% _
```

The CMD field is now a bit more informative: it shows not only the command name but the arguments and options used when it was called. The additional fields are as follows:

UID   The login name of the process owner

PPID   The pid of the parent process

C   The processor utilization for scheduling

STIME   The starting time for the process

In the above example, the PPID (the pid of the parent) of ps is given as 5386, which can be confirmed by checking the reported pid of csh, also 5386.

To see what the system itself and the other users are up to, you can use the -a option:

```
% ps -a
PID   TTY   TIME   CMD
100   co    0:03   timehack
79    co    6:34   dqueuer
81    co    6:34   cron
83    co    16:53  update
5386  tty3  0:04   ps
% _
```

Note first that co, the systems console, is running several mysterious processes that are none of your business! Unless you are a superuser, of course, you are not allowed to `kill` any process you do not own, so do not try.

The process called `cron` is an example of a *daemon* (pronouced daymon) process. The spelling indicates that such processes are amiable spirits rather than evil *demons*. Daemons run ceaselessly in the background performing various essential tasks. `cron` is the clock daemon responsible for scheduling other processes (more on this when you meet the `at` and `batch` commands later in this chapter). The `update` process is another daemon, responsible for updating the disk system at specified intervals. (The daemon names vary according to Unix version.)

The above `ps -a` display seems to have forgotten the `csh` shell process. The reason is that the a option excludes group leader processes such as your shell. You should experiment with other option combinations: `-ag` will extend the a listing above by showing you the shell processes and other group leaders; `-alg` will tell you more than you might care to know about all processes.

The `l` option adds status and state fields to the `ps` listing, interpreted as follows:

Process Status Bit	Meaning
01	Process image is in RAM.
02	System (internal) process.
04	Process image is locked in RAM.
10	Process is being swapped.
20	Process is being traced (waited upon) by another process.

The value displayed is the sum of these bits, so that 06 means the process is a system process (02) and is locked in RAM (04). Certain processes, such as those for physical I/O, may need to be locked in RAM to prevent the kernel from swapping them out to disk at an injudicious moment.

Process State Field	Meaning
0	Nonexistent
S	Sleeping
R	Running

I	Intermediate
Z	Terminated
T	Stopped
B	Waiting

The long l listing also tells you the priority assigned to each process. The higher the number, the lower the priority. The default priorities for all processes are set and adjusted by the system administrator. You can *lower* the priorities on your own processes individually when you run commands, but only the superuser can *increase* them. The nice command is used to adjust scheduling priorities. Read on.

HAVE A NICE PROCESS

When the system tries to run too many high-priority jobs at the same time, computer response time deteriorates and everybody suffers. The prevailing Unix philosophy is to be kind and gentle and reduce the need for system administrator intervention by lowering the priorities on long-winded, not-so-urgent jobs. Be nice to other users, and they'll be nice to you—thus the name for the nice command. The nice syntax is

```
nice [-inc] command [args]
```

This will run the given *command* with its optional *args* at a priority level determined by the optional number *inc*. A terminating & is quite common to put the process in the background but is not part of the nice syntax. To understand the impact of the *inc* argument, you need to know that each process has a *nice number* in the range 0–39, from which the kernel calculates the actual scheduling priority. The value 0 represents the highest priority, 39 the lowest. The default nice number is 20, right down the middle. To lower your priority, you have to increase the nice number, hence the name *inc* I've given to the option. The number you supply for *inc* increases the current nice number by *inc* up to a maximum of 39. The default value for *inc* is 10, so that

```
$ nice -10 wc inv* >count.inv &
2654
$ _
```

and

```
$ nice wc inv* >count.inv &
2654
$ _
```

both increase the nice number by 10 (usually from 20 to 30), thereby lowering the priority assigned to the wc process. The ps -l (long format) command, by the way, tells you the current nice number. The nohup command, introduced earlier, automatically adds 10 to its process's nice number, so nohup jobs always run at a lower priority (the price you pay to avoid termination).

A not-so-nice property of nice, however, is that the superuser can also use *negative* values of *inc* in order to lower the nice number and increase the priority of any process:

```
# nice -15 bigjob &
5431
# _
```

This entry makes bigjob run with a nice number of (20-15) = 5. Note that ordinary users are not allowed negative values of *inc*, whereas superusers can use positive or negative values.

If you or the system administrator use *inc* values that try to push the nice number outside the range 0–39, the shell quietly adjusts a negative result to 0, and a result greater than 39 is reduced to 39.

In the final sections of this chapter, I'll cover some useful command-line variants and introduce the tee, sleep, at, crontab, and batch commands.

NOTE

On some systems, the values for nice range from 19 to –19 instead of 0 to 39. As mentioned above, ordinary users can use only positive values for nice.

MULTICOMMAND LINES

It is important to distinguish the multicommand line from the background command line. The following entry:

```
$ wc chapter* ; who
      123   677   3488 chapter1
      223  1090   4560 chapter2
      ...
      stan tty1 Oct 13 00:34
      mary tty2 Oct 13 10:24
      ...
$ _
```

has two commands separated by a semicolon. The shell executes each command in the foreground and in sequence as though you had entered them on separate lines. Consider next the following situation:

```
$ wc chapter* ; who | wc
     123   677  3488 chapter1
     223  1090  4560 chapter2
     ...
     2 10 46
$ _
```

The pipe symbol | acts only on the who command, producing the 1ine, word, and character counts of Chapters 1 and 2 as before, as well as the counts for the listing of who is currently online. If you want to analyze the output from *both* commands, you can add parentheses as follows:

```
$ (wc chapter* ; who) | wc
     983 7140 36545
$ _
```

The two commands still execute in the foreground, one after the other, but their output is combined by the wc filter, resulting in the line, word, and character counts for all files combined..

This seems a natural place to show you the tee command. The name comes from the t-pipe familiar to all plumbers and gardeners. In Unix, a t-pipe has one input and two identical outputs (unlike the plumbing version where each output carries a fraction of the input flow). Placing a tee in a pipe allows two copies of the input data to be tapped. One output must go to a file; the identical output carries on down through the filter. Figure 8.2 illustrates the following example:

```
$ who | tee save.it | wc
     2 10 46
$ cat save.it
     stan tty1 Oct 13 00:34
     mary tty2 Oct 13 10:24
     ...
$ wc <save.it
     2 10 46
$ _
```

As you can see, tee sends the output from who to the file save.it and also to the pipe to wc, displaying the line, word, and character counts of who.

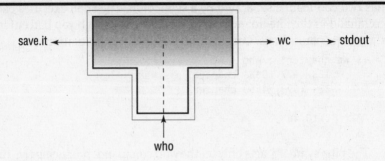

save.it ◄─────────────────────────► wc ─────► stdout

who

FIGURE 8.2:   tee Command T-pipe

Returning to background processes, you can set up several background processes on the one line by repeating the &:

```
$ wc chapter* >chap & ls -l acc/inv* >invfiles &
2676
3125
$ ed stan.data
345

_
```

You can also mix background and foreground jobs as follows:

```
$ who >whodat & date
5421
Fri July 21 13:01 PST 1995
$ cat whodat
stan tty1 July 21 00:34
mary tty2 July 21 10:24

...

$ _
```

Here, who runs in the background while date is a foreground process. With tiny jobs like these, of course, the difference is somewhat metaphysical.

You can see now that there are three command terminators:

Newline (Enter)	Process foreground, prompt on next command line
;	Process foreground, but stay on command line (no prompt)
&	Process background, prompt on next command line

THE SLEEP COMMAND

Sometimes you may want to put a sequence of commands in the background. An instructive example uses the sleep command (in man section C). sleep n simply cycles idly for *n* seconds (not exceeding 65,535 seconds) and can be most useful in shell scripts where you want to slow down a sequence of displays:

```
echo Hope you have time to read this line
sleep 5
echo before I show you this line
```

Now play with the following example, using different numbers for the sleep argument:

```
$ (sleep 10; date) & date
6734
Fri July 21 13:01 PST 1995
$ Fri July 21 13:11 PST 1995
```

The process, with pid 6734, will first execute sleep and then execute date, both in the background. The second date command is in the foreground, so it displays right away followed by the prompt. Approximately ten seconds later, the second date displays. The timing can be slightly wrong depending on how busy the system is—remember that processes receive time slices according to their priorities.

Notice that the output from the second date simply appears wherever the cursor happens to be at the time. In this example, no harm is done, but recall my earlier warning about background processes that may ruin your screen layout.

The sleep command can be used to create a primitive alarm system:

```
$ (sleep 3600; echo Jeopardy on TV!) &
$ _
```

After approximately one hour, the screen will display the chosen message. If you embed one or more Ctrl-G characters in the message string, you will ring the bell on your terminal. Remember that the message may appear anywhere on the screen, mixed up with any foreground displays you may be generating at the time.

SCHEDULING PROCESSES

A related command called at (in man section C) lets you schedule jobs to run at some future date:

```
$ at 4:30am tomorrow
wc chapter* >chap.count
```

You next enter Ctrl-D to terminate your input. Once you enter Ctrl-D, at assigns a job id, such as 6A, and displays it together with the date scheduled to run the list of commands you have submitted:

```
6A 04:30 Jan 23 1995
$ _
```

If you decide to cancel the request, you enter

```
at -r job-id
```

You can cancel only your own scheduled jobs unless you are the superuser.

The at command syntax for scheduling future jobs is

```
at time [date] [increment]
```

The list of commands will be executed at the time and date arguments supplied (as modified by the optional increment). These arguments can take many forms, best illustrated by the following examples. Unix makes sensible assumptions as to when the jobs should run. If you enter 8 or 8:00am with no day specified, you'll be scheduled for today if possible (that is, if it's not yet 8:00 a.m.); otherwise the jobs will run at 8:00 a.m. the following day. Similarly with months and years!

Without a colon between hours and minutes, time must be 1, 2, or 4 digits. A 24-hour military format is assumed unless you add the optional am or pm. 1- and 2-digit entries are taken as hours; 4-digit times are taken as hours and minutes. (A 3-digit entry is clearly ambiguous.) at also accepts words such as tomorrow and next as well as day and month names.

If you entered any one of the following as the time argument:

```
8
08
0800
8:0
08:0
8am
8:0am
08:00am
```

your scheduled jobs will be executed at 8:00 a.m. today if you entered the at command before 8:00 a.m., or at 8:00 a.m. tomorrow if the at command was entered at 8:00 a.m. or later. Similarly, the following time arguments will cause your scheduled jobs to run the next time the clock strikes 11:00 p.m.:

```
22
2200
1100pm
11:00pm
```

You can also use these special time arguments with at: now, noon, and midnight.

The optional *date* argument takes any one of the following formats to specify the day you want the scheduled jobs to run:

```
Feb 23
today
tomorrow
Sunday
```

You can even specify the year you want the scheduled jobs executed:

```
Jun 23, 1999
```

will run your jobs on June 23, 1999.

To use an optional increment, enter a + followed by a number and one of the following unit arguments:

```
minute(s)
hour(s)
day(s)
week(s)
month(s)
year(s)
```

Combining these gives you an enormous battery of scheduling schemes. Here are a few suggestions:

```
at 0800 Feb 12
at now +2 days
at tomorrow +3 hours
at 11:00am Monday next week
at 5:00pm Sep 15 next year
```

The cron daemon that you met earlier has the task of keeping tabs on all the at jobs in the works, and dispatching them when their due date/time arrives.

The system administrator has the power to select which users are permitted to use the at facility.

Redirection in both directions is useful with the at command. at takes its input from stdin, so if you set up a file with a list of your jobs (one command per line), you can simply enter

```
$ at now +1 month <command.file
23S 08:34am Jan 23 1999
$ _
```

The scheduled times of waiting jobs can be displayed using at with the -l option:

```
at -l [job-id1 job-id2 ...]
```

If you omit the job-id arguments, you get a list of all the jobs currently scheduled; otherwise you get just the jobs requested.

Jobs scheduled with at are not background processes in the strictest sense: they are simply earmarked for future processing, and when the scheduled date/time arrives, they are entered for execution (background or foreground) as though you had just typed their commands yourself.

You can even write a shell script that will schedule itself to run at regular intervals. The following line embedded in a shell-script file called myshell will generate a request to run itself at 8:00 a.m. every Monday:

```
echo "myshell" | at 0800 Mon next week
```

You'll learn more of these tricks in Chapter 12.

More elaborate methods of scheduling recurring jobs are possible with crontab. The details are beyond our immediate scope, but briefly, crontab lets you set up a list of commands in a file called /usr/spool/cron/crontab/username. Each line in this file specifies a command, and the time and interval for execution. The cron daemon then scans this file regularly and schedules the jobs as required. The superuser can control which users are allowed to use this facility.

The batch command (providing the superuser gives you permission) is a much simpler scheduling mechanism that lets you set up big jobs to be run whenever the system loading permits:

```
$ batch
bigjob >bigjob.stats
```

Pressing Ctrl-D enters the command line and returns you to the system prompt. Unlike at, batch does not specify a scheduling date/time. All you know is that bigjob will run as soon as conditions allow.

WHAT'S NEXT

Printing is the subject of the next chapter. Among the things you'll learn are how to print a file on local and remote printers and how to choose between the printers available on your network. We'll also look at some basic print formatting commands.

```
echo "2.      Show Date"
echo "3.      Display a file"
echo "4.      Change working director
echo "5.      Return to original dir
echo "Q.      Quit
echo
echo -n "Enter choice: .\b"
read choice
case $choice in
1) who | more
   pause;;
2) date
   pause;;
3) echo "Enter file name: \c"
   read fil
   if [ -r "$fil" -a -f "$fil" ]
   then
      clear
      more -d $fil
   else
      echo "Cannot d
   fi
   pause;;
4) echo "En
   read di
   if test      d "$dir:      pwd`
   then
      cd $dir
   else
      echo "$dir: no such dir
   fi
      pause;;
   5) if test "$dir" != "$p
      then
         cd $prevdir
      fi
      pause;;
```

Chapter 9

PRINTING AND SPOOLING

The subject of printing has cropped up several times in previous chapters—usually in the context of *displaying* information on the screen. In this chapter, I'll be using the word "print" in its normal sense: the act of putting characters on paper.

As I warned you, Unix clings to the confusing anachronism of the term "print" to mean "output to terminal." This is a vestige of times past when terminals were teleprinters that produced user input and system responses in the form of printed paper, known as *hard copy*, to distinguish it from more volatile representations like video displays. And to make matters worse, teleprinters clattered along at only 7 characters or less per second on cheap rolls of unperforated paper!

The word teletypewriter was usually abbreviated to TTY (pronounced "tit'ee"), and this has survived into the 20th century: the general terminal interface is known as `dev/tty`, hence the current Unix joke: What do you call a $20,000 high-resolution, 30-inch, 3-D color monitor? Answer: `tty01`! (If you don't see the humor in this, just wait— you will!)

When CRTs were introduced they were promptly dubbed "glass tit'ees." The commands and mnemonics for sending output to the new terminals, CRTs, retained their old "printing" associations. In normal conversation, too, the word "print" often means "display," depending on the context. In passing, note another annoying ambiguity: "blank" means "space" rather than "null" or "empty."

The early "real" printers for lengthy listings were usually *line printers* based on punched card tabulators that printed a line at a time, at speeds ranging from 100 to 600 lines per minute, and with very limited, uppercase fonts. For this reason, you find that many Unix hardcopy print-control commands include the mnemonic `lp` (line print) even if you are using character-serial (one character at a time) printers or page-based laser printers. So you'll meet commands such as `lpstat`, `lprint`, `lpadmin`, `lpfilter`, `lpsched`, and so on, as well as `lp` itself used as a command and a subdirectory.

CENTRAL AND LOCAL PRINTERS

The cost of high-speed line and page printers often dictates that a central pool of such devices be shared by many users. At the same time, many terminals have *printer ports* that permit the attachment of slower, cheaper printers as a dedicated local service. You'll see that Unix supports both configurations. The central printer approach, of course, requires special arrangements so that printing jobs can be prioritized and scheduled if several users request a printout at the same time. This is achieved by *spooling,* whereby copies of the print image are stored (queued) temporarily until the printer is ready. "Spooling" is yet another anachronism stemming from the predisk days when all but the tiniest files were stored on reels (or spools) of magnetic tape. SPOOL as a fancy acronym of Simultaneous Peripheral Operation On-Line is a piece of reverse engineering! Tape drives are still with us, of course, but are now mainly used as high-volume data backup devices, agents for transferring data between alien systems, and distribution media for software.

Spooling means that you do not have to wait for your print request to be completed. Your print command and options are placed in a queue, leaving your terminal free for other jobs. The queue is scanned periodically by a system daemon, known as the *LP (line printer) request scheduler,* running in the background.

Each site has a default printer to which print requests are sent in the absence of contrary instructions. Larger sites may have clusters of similar printers, called *classes,* that can share the load—a request will be handled by whichever printer in the class becomes available first. Printers can also be addressed by name, and Unix offers flexible control when you have printers that are loaded with preprinted forms, such as invoices or checks.

SAVE A TREE

I've delayed dealing with the topic of real printing in a vain effort to preserve our dwindling forests. Ironically, unless you tell Unix otherwise, the typical printing defaults can be quite wasteful for small runs; you are likely to get extra *banner* pages at the front of your listings telling you all about your print request. I should not have to urge caution in the overproduction of hard copy. The early dream of the paperless office has become the nightmare of huge piles of unread (unreadable) reports. When a listing *is* essential, avoid the temptation of producing that "spare" copy.

OVERCOMING THE PRINTER JUNGLE

You are probably aware of the bewildering diversity of printing devices. As with the CRT market, attempts at standardization are bedeviled by rapid technological progress. The result is that Unix has a great deal of irksome but essential baggage devoted to handling the hundreds of different printer models currently available. It is the job of the system administrator, aided possibly by the printer vendor if the model is peculiar, to set up a central printer service.

Briefly, this involves allocating an appropriate port (serial or parallel) and ensuring that this port is disabled from normal terminal logins. After physically attaching the printer to this port, the device can be accessed as `/dev/ttyn`, where *n* is the number of the serial port. Parallel ports (usually attached to Centronics-compatible printers) are accessed via `/dev/lp0`.

The directory `/dev` contains special files which represent your peripherals: terminals, printers, disk drives, and so on. Unix, as I mentioned earlier in this book, treats many different objects as though they were files. The ordinary disk files you've been using have this essential property; sequences of characters (bytes) can be read from them and written to them. Since you can also send and receive streams of bytes to and from peripheral devices, Unix gives each I/O device a special file-like interface. This elegant idea was another Unix innovation subsequently adopted by DOS and other operating systems. The advantage is that the input and output of many commands can be redirected not only to standard output (screen) and from standard input (keyboard) but also to and from other devices on your system.

Of course, devices differ considerably in how they physically handle input and output. Each type of peripheral must have its own software interface, called a *device driver,* linked into the kernel, to translate its individual quirks. The driver absolves both the kernel and the user from having to know too much about the device's internal nuts and bolts. The result is that normal file operations such as opening, closing, reading, and writing can be equally applied to devices. (Of course, not all such operations make equal sense with all devices: reading data from a printer, for example, is restricted to receiving handshaking signals such as "ready," "paper low," "paper jammed," and so on.)

Output can be redirected to a cooperative special file using the normal > operator. If you are `root`, a simple test of the newly installed printer's physical connections can therefore be made as follows:

```
# who >/dev/tty3a
# _
```

for serial ports, or

```
# who >/dev/lp0
# _
```

for parallel ports. The exact /dev argument, of course, will depend on the port number and type selected.

This simple redirection bypasses the Unix print services such as spooling, so it is not recommended for normal production printing jobs. The characters from who (or any other command that produces output) will print "as is" with no formatting, page jumps, or page numbers. Worse still, there is no protection against the printer receiving data from other users. The collision could be messy!

To establish proper service, the system administrator has several additional chores to perform. The printer must be given a name, optionally assigned to a class, and provided with an interface program. Details of the printer's characteristics must be placed in the terminfo file if not already there. There may also be a need to define or change one or more *filter* programs. I'll discuss filters in more detail later. For now, look on them as programs that can adjust the output files of applications to match and exploit the features of particular printer models. Filters can also help in detecting and reporting printer errors. Unix comes with several standard filters, but new applications and printer models may require special versions. These are often provided by the printer or application vendor.

If you lack an experienced system administrator, nearby guru, or helpful vendor, you may be lucky enough to have a Unix implementation with a friendly system administration shell. The SCO Unix System V/386, for example, has sysadmsh, which offers simple menus for adding and configuring printers (and many other tasks, of course). The menus avoid the need to master the intricacies of the /usr/lib/lpadmin command (in man section ADM).

Assuming you do have an established printer service, let's look at the commands available to exploit it.

THE lp COMMAND

The lp command (in man section C) submits a request to the print service. The syntax is

```
lp [options] [file1 file2 … fileN]
```

Without the options, this command will spool and then print the given files on the default printer. In the absence of any filenames, lp takes its input from your keyboard—giving you a rather expensive typewriter! The following entry will print the contents of stan.data on the default printer:

```
$ lp stan.data
request id laser-24 (1 file)
$ _
```

The command responds by assigning and displaying a *print request id*, showing the printer name, a unique number that increments with each request, and the number of files in the spool. The print request id can be used in subsequent commands to identify and control the printing in various ways. Because the request is spooled, the prompt immediately returns, and you can enter more commands.

If you have more than one printer and do not want to print on the default printer, you can use the -d option:

```
$ lp -ddaisy stan.data
```

```
request id daisy -26 (1 file)
$ _
```

Here, I've elected to print on a printer called daisy. The printer name follows the -d with no intervening white space. Note that with some installations the name after the -d may refer to a class—that is, a cluster of identical printers. In this case, the request will be serviced by whichever printer in the class first becomes free.

Wildcard filename arguments are useful with lp:

```
$ lp chapter.*
request id laser-34 (12 files)
$ _
```

will request the printing of any files in your current directory that match chapter.*. You can also print several files by listing their names with spaces as separators:

```
$ lp chapter.1 chapter.5
request id laser-36 (2 files)
$ _
```

If you use continuous sprocket-fed stationery, you will, by default, get a form feed after chapter.1 has printed.

Printer Options

Before studying the lp options, you should print a few small files to see what global defaults may have been established for your system. An /etc/default/lpd file set up by the system administrator controls certain options that interact with the options you enter with an lp command. For example, the usual global default for printing banner pages will give you an extra page in front of your printout. Banner pages summarize the print request, showing the date, user id, the request id, and the filenames being printed. In large installations with a central printing facility, the banner pages serve the essential function of identifying who gets what. In smaller sites, you may want to inhibit the banner pages:

```
$ lp -onobanner chapter.1 chapter.5
request id laser-36 (2 files)
$ _
```

The lp options vary from site to site, so check your local manual. The options shown here are available on SCO Version V and similar versions.

The -o option is followed by the nobanner suboption. Other -o suboptions are listed below:

Suboption	Description
-onofilebreak	Omits the form feed between file listings
-olength=*n*	Sets page length to *n* lines
-olength=*n*i	Sets page length to *n* inches
-olength=*n*c	Sets page length to *n* centimeters
-owidth=*n*i	Sets page width to *n* inches
-owidth=*n*c	Sets page width to *n* centimeters
-olpi=*n*	Set line pitch to *n* lines per inch
-ocpi=*n*	Sets printer to *n* character(s) per inch
-ocpi=pica	Sets printer to 10 characters per inch
-ocpi=elite	Sets printer to 12 characters per inch
-ocpi=compressed	Sets printer to maximum possible characters per inch

Some printers, of course, cannot respond to all of these options. A single font printer with fixed character size, for example, could not honor certain pitch-changing options.

You can enter as many separate -o suboptions as you wish provided you repeat the -o:

```
$ lp -onobanner -ocpi= elite chapter.1
request id laser -38 (1 file)
$ _
```

Other useful lp options are as follows:

Option	Description
lp -n[*number*]	Prints *number* copies of each file requested. The default is one copy.
lp —m	Sends a mail message to you when the printing is complete.
lp —w	Displays a message on your terminal when the printing is complete. If you happen to be logged out when this message arrives, it will be diverted to your mailbox.

Option	Description
lp -q[*priority*]	Sets a priority level for your print request. The default is set by the system administrator. Zero is the highest priority, 39 is the lowest.
lp -s	Suppresses the normal "request id" message.
lp -R	Erases the file(s) when they have been printed. Use this with care, of course!
lp -L	Uses the local printer attached to your terminal. See also the lprint command described later.

A Simple Shell Script

As you can see, combining various lp options can lead to hideously complex commands. If you are loath to type such long-winded commands on a regular basis, Unix offers the shell script, which merits a brief detour. You'll see shell scripts and procedures in more detail in Chapters 12 and 15, but this is a good opportunity to show you a simple but practical example. You can readily devise your own myprint procedure, say, so that myprint chapter.1 performs a complex command with less typing effort.

Using ed or cat >myprint, create a file called myprint containing the single line

```
lp -onobanner -ocpi=elite $1
```

The expression $1 (familiar to DOS batch file programmers) is called a *positional parameter*. If you invoke myprint with the argument chapter .1, the shell replaces $1 with chapter.1, giving you the same effect as the longer lp command and its options. There are two ways of invoking your new command. With the first method, the following command

```
$ sh myprint chapter.1
```

spawns a Bourne shell that reads the file myprint, replaces $1 with the argument chapter.1, then executes the resulting command:

```
lp -onobanner -ocpi=elite chapter.1
```

The second method involves first making myprint directly executable by changing its mode with chmod:

```
$ chmod u+x myprint
```

Thereafter, myprint can be invoked without the need for sh:

```
$ myprint chapter.1
```

Your current shell now does the work, but the end result is the same as in method 1.

The u+x option in chmod gives you alone, as the owner, execution permission for myprint, as explained in Chapter 7. If you want to grant all users permission to use myprint, you would vary the chmod option as follows:

```
$ chmod a+x myprint
```

or equivalently,

```
$ chmod +x myprint
```

since a (all users) is the default. Alternatively, you may wish to limit usage to members of your group with

```
$ chmod g+x myprint
```

After using chmod, you should run ls -l myprint to check that it has the correct x fields for your purposes.

Shell scripts are available for both the Bourne and C shells, although the syntax and available features are different (see Appendix A). Peculiar to the C shell, though, is another keystroke-saving ploy called the alias command. Let's make another detour before we return to the printing commands.

The C Shell alias Command

The C shell alias command is rather like a *macro* in other languages. You save keystrokes by replacing a long command string with a shorter one:

```
% alias myprint lp -onobanner -ocpi=elite
% _
```

Thereafter, until you leave the shell, myprint acts as a synonym or alias (hence the name) for the command and options entered above. The C shell replaces myprint with

```
lp -onobanner -ocpi=elite
```

so that myprint can take additional options as well as the usual file arguments:

```
% myprint -olength= 55 chapter.2
request id laser-39 (1 file)
% _
```

has the same impact as entering

```
% lp -onobanner -ocpi=elite -olength=55 chapter.2
request id laser-39 (1 file)
% _
```

Your aliases are not "remembered" from one session to the next, so if you want to use them regularly, the appropriate alias commands must be placed in your .cshrc file. You'll recall from Chapter 6 that .cshrc, the C shell read command file, is read each time a new subshell is created. You could place your list of aliases in your .login file, but this is read only once, when you first log in. Any subshells spawned during a session would not know about these aliases unless they were also present in .cshrc.

If you forget which aliases have been set up, alias with no arguments will tell you:

```
% alias
bye      clear;logout
c        clear
dir      ls -al
g        grep
gb       set gb=`/bin/pwd`; cd $gt;set gt=$gb
gt       set gt=`/bin/pwd`; cd !^
h        history
la       ls -F
ll       ls -l
m        more
motd     more /etc/motd
p        ps -ef
reserv   taper
rm       rm -i
rot13    tr "[A-M][N-Z][a-m][n-z]" "[N-Z][A-M][n-z][a-m]"
myprint  lp -onobanner -ocpi =elite
mytemp   cd /usr/stan/tmp
% _
```

(See Appendix A for details.) Some of the above aliases, by the way, are supplied globally by the system administrator. They are so common in the C shell world that they assume the character of "standard" commands. It can be a tad confusing for beginners who look up dir, say, in the man pages and find it missing. Well-run sites, though, will have local man pages that document all aliases and other local quirks.

Note especially the rm alias. By aliasing an *existing* command you are effectively overriding its standard definition. Naturally, great caution is needed! You would not want cd to remove all your files, would you? In the case of rm, the alias is a common safety ploy: the -i argument warns you before erasing files.

Note also that you can alias a group of commands as in bye, which will invoke clear followed by logout.

You can examine a particular alias as follows:

```
% alias mytemp
```

```
mytemp   cd /usr/stan/tmp
% _
```

You can kill off an alias by using `unalias` followed by the name of the alias:

```
% unalias mytemp
% mytemp
mytemp: Command not found
% _
```

Of course, if `mytemp` is aliased in your `.cshrc`, it will be revived the next time you spawn a new shell.

The `unalias` command also accepts wildcards, so `unalias *` will remove all existing aliases, and `unalias ??print` will kill off `myprint` as well as `skprint`, and so on.

The full power of `alias` emerges when you combine several commands, possibly including previously defined aliases, under the one alias:

```
% alias pjob mytemp; myprint
% _
```

It's time to return to the `lp` command.

The -c Copy Option

Since print requests are queued (spooled), you may wonder what happens if you reedit or erase a file before the print service has had a chance to extract the file from the queue and print it. The answer is that under normal circumstances the printout reflects the latest state of your file. If you erase it too soon, you'll lose the listing! If you edit it before the print is complete, the results can be unpredictable; you may be editing a part of the file that has already been printed, or not, as the case may be. There are two solutions: leave the file alone until it's fully printed; or use the `-c` (copy) option.

You can check the status of your print requests using the `lpstat` command. You'll see how in the next section.

The `-c` option tells the shell to make immediate copies of all the files in the `lp` command. It is these copies that will eventually print regardless of what you do with the original files. The `-c` option, like the other `lp` options, can be placed in any order in the options sequence. The following commands will work the same—both send a copy of `chapter.2` to the print service:

```
$ lp -onobanner -c -ocpi=elite -olength=55 chapter.2
$ lp -onobanner -ocpi=elite -olength=55 -c chapter.2
```

You can now edit (or erase!) `chapter.2` without affecting the listing.

THE lpstat COMMAND

Whenever processes are pushed into the background, you need some way of following their progress. Just as ps and pstat tell you the status of processes in general, lpstat (in man section C) keeps you informed regarding the fate of your print requests. As with pstat there are options that affect the amount of information to be displayed. You can check individual or groups of print requests by user name or id, request id, and/or printer name or class. The default is to report on all your requests that are still in the queue.

```
$ lpstat
laser-36   stan 4567 Aug 23 15:56 on laser
laser-40   stan  678 Aug 23 16:08
laser-45   stan 1243 Aug 23 16:23
$ _
```

The display tells you when each request was submitted, by whom, and the size in bytes of each file. The legend "on laser" indicates that request laser-36 is currently printing a file of 4,567 bytes on the printer called laser.

The most common options are listed below. The options can be combined in any sequence. You can actually type all as a list argument, but since this is the normal default list, there is no pressing reason to do so.

lpstat option	Meaning	Description
-a[list]	Acceptance	Displays status of printer or class names in optional list. Default is all printers and classes. The list can be entered as laser,daisy or laser daisy.
-c[list]	Class	Lists class names and their members. Default is all classes.
-d	Default	Displays the name of the default printer.
-o[list][l]	Output	Displays status of requests in list (default option is all). The list can be any mix of printer/ class names and request ids. The l (long) option gives a more complete display.

lpstat option	Meaning	Description
-r	Request	Displays the status of the LP request scheduler, for example, Scheduler is running. If the scheduler is not running for any reason, the spooling service is not available, and you will need to print directly using cat> dev/xxx.
-s	Summary	Displays a complete summary of the printer service: default printer, class lists, character sets, and so on.
-t	Total	Gives a complete LP status display: all users and all printers.
-u[list]	User	Displays status for the users in list (default is all users).
-v[list]	Device	Displays printer names and dev/xxx paths for printers named in list (default is all printers).

CHANGING PRINT REQUESTS WITH lp -i

The lp -i command lets you change the options on a print request after it has been submitted—provided, of course, that you act before the printing is complete. You'll need to know the print request id, so if you haven't made a note of this, you'll need to run lpstat first. If the printing has started but has not finished, the printing will halt and a new request with the revised options will be submitted, that is, you start again from the beginning of the file. You use the -i option as follows:

    lp -i print_id new_options

The new_options arguments can be any valid lp print options, and they replace the original options to form a revised request. The designated files are not changed.

The cancel Command

You use the `cancel` command to cancel any printer requests. The syntax is

```
cancel [id1 id2 id3…idn] [prname1 prname2…prnamex]
```

Specifying the optional id arguments will cancel requests with those id numbers. Specifying the optional printer names will cancel requests made on particular printers. If a file is currently printing, `cancel` stops it in its tracks. If you specified several files in the same request, any not yet printed will not be printed.

THE lprint COMMAND

Many terminals nowadays have a built-in port allowing you to connect a printer. These are called *local* printers to distinguish them from the central *spool* printer(s). As an alternative to the `lp -L` option mentioned earlier, you can print a file on your local printer with the `lprint` command (in man section C). There are two formats:

```
lprint -
```

will print the following keyboard entries (until you enter Ctrl-D).

```
lprint filename
```

will print the argument file. Your `etc/termcap` file must be set correctly with your terminal and printer parameters.

SIMPLE FORMATTING WITH pr

The `pr` command (in man section C) can be used to format your listings in various ways. `pr` sends formatted text to the standard output by default, so you need to pipe this to `lp` to get formatted hardcopy printouts:

```
$ pr chapter.1 | lp
request id laser-69 (1 file)
$ _
```

In the absence of `pr` options, the above prints `chapter.1` with simple page breaks, with each page numbered, dated, and headed by the filename. The following options are available:

Option	Description
+k	Starts printing at page k (default is page 1).
-k	Prints in k columns (default is single column).

Option	Description
-d	Prints in double-line spacing.
-e[*k*]	Expands tab codes in file to give tabs at character positions *k*+1, 2×(*k*+1),.... The default gives tabs at every 8th position.
-n[*k*]	Adds *k*-digit line numbers. Default is 5, that is, line numbers up to 99999.
-w[*k*]	Sets line width to *k*. Default is 72.
-o[*k*]	Offsets (indents) each line by *k* character spaces. Default is 0.
-l[*k*]	Sets page length to *k* lines. Default is 66.
-h[*header*]	Replaces filename *header* by the string header at top of each page.
-p	Screen only: pauses after each page.

As you can see, some of the pr options match similar options available in the lp command, so you need to avoid unnecessary duplications. Setting the options in pr (and possibly creating a shell script or alias) has the merit that you can have a screen preview before piping out to lp. The -p (page pause) option is useful here. A typical pr example might be:

```
$ pr +10 -e9 -d -h"Chapter 1" chapter.1 | lp
```

This would print the header Chapter 1 on each page, starting at page 10 of the chapter.1 file. Tabs would be ten character positions apart, and the printout would be double-line spacing.

WHAT'S NEXT

In Chapter 10, we'll discuss text editing using a program that is a standard part of virtually every version of Unix today: vi. The vi editor is a full-page editor designed to provide Unix users with a simple, yet fairly powerful means of creating and editing text files, programs, and most importantly, script files.

```
echo "2.      Show Date"
echo "3.      Display a file"
echo "4.      Change working director
echo "5.      Return to original dire
echo "Q.      Quit
echo
echo -n "Enter choice: .\b"
read choice
case $choice in
1) who | more
   pause;;
2) date
   pause;;
3) echo "Enter file name: \c"
   read fil
   if [ -r "$fil" -a -f "$fil" ]
   then
     clear
     more -d $fil
   else
     echo "Cannot d
   fi
   pause;;
4) echo "En
   read di
   if test -d "$dir      pwd`]
   then
     cd $dir
   else
     echo "$dir: no such di
   fi
     pause;;
   5) if test "$dir" != "$p
      then
         cd $prevdir
      fi
      pause;;
```

Chapter 10

THE vi FAMILY
OF EDITORS

This chapter covers several evolutionary stages in Unix text editing, beginning with a program called vi (pronounced "vee-eye"). The name vi stands for "visual," and this points to its most visible feature; you get to see a whole screenful of the text you are editing. vi was originally developed by Bill Joy (who also designed the C shell) for the BSD (Berkeley Software Distribution) versions of Unix. If your system claims "Berkeley extensions," this usually means that you have vi and csh (the C shell) available. The standard Unix (System V) also includes vi, so it's almost certain that you will find it on your system.

The vi family of editors inherits most of the concepts found in ed. In particular, both ed and vi are modal editors with *text-entry* and *command* modes. They also offer the same elaborate text searching methods based on *regular expressions.* The historical reason for this overlap is that vi makes use of a line editor called ex, which in turn is an enhancement (superset) of ed. In fact, vi is really ex with a fancy, screen-oriented user interface. You'll see later that from within vi you can use the colon (:) escape command to switch to ex command-line mode. In this mode, the familiar ed commands found in ex are all available!

Some users still prefer to use ex (or a simplified version of ex called edit) as a sort of supercharged ed, but the visible screen interface has made vi the editor of choice at most Unix sites. Programmers in particular like the *autoindent* feature that helps create structured, legible source code. They also relish the ability to create wild macros and the opportunity of escaping temporarily to the shell in order to test the program being edited. vi bristles with options and legerdemain but is easily customized so that it fires up with your personal preferences preset as defaults. Those who persevere and master vi achieve remarkable editing feats at high speed and will brook no criticism of vi, however mild.

I have tried to make this chapter as self-contained as possible. The pace, however, will be brisker since by now you should be familiar with Unix command syntax. vi is a large program to which entire books have been dedicated (as well as posters, coffee mugs, and reference cards), so I make no claim to a comprehensive treatment. The vi man pages (all thirty-eight of them) should be consulted for the less common options.

PRELIMINARIES

vi uses some special key combinations for cursor and display control, so you need to make sure that Unix knows about your terminal and all its quirks. Each terminal has its own peculiar software interface with the outside world. The output codes generated by, say, the Delete key or by combinations such as Ctrl-U are far from standard. Similarly, the input code sequences needed to clear the screen or delete to the end of a line vary among manufacturers (and often between monitors from the same manufacturer). Your terminal, therefore, must be correctly identified to the Unix system before the vi-specific keystrokes will work as planned. vi makes use of the following special keys (the actions are described briefly and may depend on the current mode as indicated; I'll elaborate later).

NOTE

Keyboards do vary greatly, so you should check the given mappings of keystroke-to-action on your own system and make the necessary adjustments to this chapter's instructions.

Name	Action
Esc	Returns you to command mode or cancels commands. Also terminates an ex command.
Return	Terminates an ex command or starts a newline in text-entry mode. (Return is sometimes labeled Enter or ↵.)
Interrupt	Aborts a command (often labeled Del, Delete, or Rubout).
Bksp	*Text-entry mode:* Backspaces the cursor by one character on the current line. Removes the previously typed character from the edit buffer, but does not remove it from the display (sometimes labeled as Left Arrow). The current line is defined as the line containing the cursor.
	Command mode: Backspaces cursor without deletion (can take a preceding count parameter).
Ctrl-D	*Command mode:* Scrolls down a half-screen.
Ctrl-F	*Command mode:* Scrolls page forward.
Ctrl-B	*Command mode:* Scrolls page backward.
Ctrl-N	*Command mode:* Moves cursor down one line (alternative to cursor arrow key).
Ctrl-P	*Command mode:* Moves cursor up one line (alternative to cursor arrow key).
Bell or Ctrl-G	*Command mode:* Displays vi status.
Ctrl-R or Ctrl-L	*Command mode:* Redraws the screen (choice depends on terminal type).
Ctrl-U	*Text-entry mode:* Restores cursor to the first character inserted on the current line (further insertions can then be made from that point).
	Command mode: Scrolls up a half-screen.

Name	Action
Ctrl-V	*Text-entry mode:* Used to insert control characters into the text by suspending the normal action of that control character (some exceptions).
Ctrl-W	*Text-entry mode:* Moves the cursor to the first character of the last inserted word.
Ctrl-T	*Text-entry mode:* If autoindent is on, gives an indent of shiftwidth spaces from left-hand margin. (shiftwidth can be preset or varied by vi commands.)
Ctrl-@	*Text-entry mode:* When entered as first character of an insertion, vi replaces Ctrl-@ with the last piece of text inserted (unless this exceeds 128 characters). Similar to . (dot) in command mode.

Because keys can be labeled in so many different ways, I'll use the vi generic names that appear in the left-hand column.

The secret to getting these vi special keys to work as shown lies in having an entry in the file /etc/termcap that provides Unix with details of your terminal's capabilities (hence the name termcap). The /etc/ termcap file is a database describing all the terminals in your system (and possibly some ancient ones that have long since vanished). To speed access to this large database, a condensed (compiled) version of termcap is created in the usr/lib/terminfo directory.

termcap is a text file that you can view, print, and (God forbid) edit. My alarm here stems from the potential Catch-22; how to edit a file that may need editing before you can edit a file! Happily, editors such as ed are fairly undemanding, so there are usually "generic" termcap entries that give you sufficient features to create a termcap entry that will support vi.

Each termcap entry can take from one line for simple terminals to as many as thirty lines for more complex models. With the advent of color and graphics, the situation is growing even more complicated. Each entry starts with a two-character abbreviation followed by a set of alternative names (separated by |). Next comes a sequence of highly cryptic, comma-delimited entries representing that terminal's characteristics.

NOTE

If vi does not know your terminal type, you may get garbled screens or a message saying "Using open mode." In either case, exit with :q! and check your termcap file and TERM variable setting, as explained below.

To add a new terminal to termcap, you try to find an existing entry for a similar terminal, then copy and edit that entry. The man pages for termcap are in section F (for files). Listed there are several hundred coded capabilities that you can add to a termcap entry. To give you the merest flavor, consider the entry

    cl<F102P8>| adm3| 3| lsi adm3:bs:am:li#24:co#80:cl=^Z

This is for the Lear Siegler ADM-3 terminal, known to Unix as either cl, adm3, 3, or lsi adm3—hence the first four entries separated by | (| is read as "or"). For historical reasons, the first terminal name is always two characters, while the second name is the most common abbreviation for that terminal. vi always uses the second name, in this case, adm3. As you'll see, this is also the name that is usually set in your shell variable, TERM. The final name is a fuller description intended solely as a visual aid to humans, so spaces are allowed.

Following the name fields, there are as many capability fields as required. You use the backslash at the end of a line if you need to continue your entry on the next line. The above example has five capability fields: bs for backspace/erase; am for automargin (also known as wraparound); li#24 and co#80 to indicate a 24-line, 80-column screen. vi needs to know your screen size, of course, so it can scroll and position the cursor correctly. Finally, the cl=^Z field means that Ctrl-Z will clear the ADM-3 screen. Note that not every program requires that every available capability of your terminal be set in termcap. For example, you could run ed without having the clear screen capability defined. Usually, though, Unix will come with a generous termcap selection, and your terminal will be fully described somewhere in the list. The point is that if vi appears to work fine on your terminal, then the termcap fairy has blessed you already. If vi works erratically, the chances are that termcap needs attention. Other applications, such as Lyrix and Multiplan, also refer to /etc/termcap, so sooner or later you should get your terminal in the database.

NOTE

Before vi can be used, your terminal must be correctly registered in /etc/ termcap and /usr/lib/terminfo, and your shell variable TERM must be set with your terminal name.

From now on, I will assume that your system administrator, supplier, or local guru has established a suitable `termcap` entry for your terminal.

It is also necessary to set the shell variable TERM to the terminal name used in `termcap` (usually the popular name found in the second name field). This is normally achieved by an entry in your `.profile` (Bourne shell) or `.login` (C shell) file, as explained in Chapter 6. If you are using the Lear Siegler ADM-3 terminal, a typical `.profile` entry might be

```
TERM=adm3
export TERM
```

for the Bourne shell, or

```
setenv TERM adm3
```

for the C shell (more on these differences in Appendix A).

MEET THE FAMILY

There are three editors in the `vi` family: `view`, `vedit`, and `vi` itself. They all offer full, navigable screen displays of your text. Gone are the traps of "hidden" line addresses that vary as you edit your files (although you can use line addresses if you wish by escaping to `ex` mode). With `vi` and her siblings, you are closer to the modern WYSIWYG (What You See Is What You Get, pronounced "wiziwig") school of editing. With this added power, of course, comes a heavy baggage of commands and features. You can, however, get by with just a handful of basic commands. And, since the effects of your actions are more immediately visible than with `ed`, the learning curve is that much easier.

Before you start worrying about whether you have three distinct sets of commands to learn for each member of the `vi` family (which cynics might say is par for the Unix course), let me reassure you that `view` and `vedit` are simple subsets or variants of `vi`—they all share the same command structure. The differences are as follows:

`view`   The "read-only" version of `vi`. Allows a file to be displayed, scrolled, and searched but not altered in any way.

`vedit` The "novice" version of `vi`. It offers the *showmode* feature by default, provides more help, and reduces the complexity of certain operations.

All three editors are invoked using the same syntax:

```
vi [-option...] [command...] [filename...]
```

```
view [-option...] [command...] [filename...]
vedit [-option...] [command...] [filename...]
```

Later in this chapter I'll explain the various options and command sequences available. Many of them will not make much sense until you've seen how vi works. Unless stated specifically, you can assume that all three editors treat these options and commands in the same way.

In many ways, you can look on view and vedit as invocations of vi with certain default options and settings built in. For example,

```
view filename
```

is entirely equivalent to

```
vi -R filename
```

since the -R option specifies read-only mode, that is, you can look at the contents of a file, but you can't make any edits.

The vedit variant runs vi in novice mode with certain options set on or off by default as shown in the list below. How and where you can vary these options with the set command will be covered later; for now, note that there are *switch* options and *string* options. The ex and vi convention is that each switch option has an "on" version and an "off" version distinguished by the prefix no. For example, to set magic on, you use set magic; to turn it off, you use set nomagic. By contrast, string options are set to specific values, for example, set report=6. Each string option has a default value that it assumes in the absence of an explicit set assignment. The vedit defaults are listed below:

no magic	Reduces the number of special characters allowed in regular expressions.
report=1	Sets the report threshold to 1. This means that any command that changes more than one line will invoke a visual report after the command. The normal vi default is report=5. The idea is that beginners are warned immediately after modifying two or more lines so they can use undo promptly to cure any inadvertent editing errors. Experienced users can set the threshold higher.
showmode	The legends INSERT, APPEND, CHANGE, or OPEN MODE will be displayed whenever you activate one of the text-entry modes.
redraw	If you have a dumb terminal, the editor will vary its display output to simulate an intelligent terminal. This option is becoming less useful as dumb terminals become extinct.

You can turn novice mode off and on from within `vedit` with `set nonovice` and `set novice`, but you cannot directly control `novice` mode from within `vi` (or `ex`). What you can do from within `vi` (or `ex`) is to set or unset any or all of the above options. Beginners are advised to use `vedit` with `novice` set on (the default), or use `vi` with `showmode` set on. The latter (assumed in this chapter) requires the following steps:

1. When `vi` first fires up, you are in command mode.

2. Type: (colon)—do not press Return.

3. A colon appears on the status line, with the cursor immediately following. You are now in `ex` mode.

4. Type `setshowmode` followed by Return.

5. You are now back in `vi` command mode.

6. `vi` will now display the appropriate text-entry legend (INSERT, APPEND, and so on) whenever you switch to insert, append, change, or open modes.

`vi` remains in `showmode` for this session only. You can make `showmode` or any other selectable option permanent by putting suitable commands in a file called `.exrc` (ex resource). We'll see how in a moment.

Another example of setting defaults is the `mesg` option. While using `vi`, it is most unpleasant to receive messages from other users. You can control email write permission during `vi` sessions only, with the commands `setmesg` and `setnomesg` (the default is `nomesg`). These choices override your current writeability only while `vi` is being used.

The six steps listed above may not be immediately understandable, so let's look closer at the various modes mentioned so far.

The Three+Four Modes

`vi` is a modal editor with three main operational modes: *text-entry, command,* and `ex` *escape.* In addition, the text-entry mode can be further divided into *insert, append, change,* and *open* submodes. Modalism means that the program interprets your keystrokes depending upon which mode the program is in at the time.

WARNING

Watch out for some ambiguity in the literature: text-entry mode is often referred to as text-insert mode (or just insert mode). It is less confusing to think of text-entry mode having four submodes: insert, append, change, and open (as indicated with showmode on).

The following list summarizes the differences between the three main modes and provides some audio-visual clues that may help you to distinguish them:

Text-entry mode
: Typed characters go to a temporary file known as the editing buffer (and eventually to a permanent file if the buffer is saved). Visual clues: printable characters that you type will appear on the screen. If showmode is on, the appropriate legend INSERT, APPEND, CHANGE, or OPEN MODE will be displayed at the bottom right of the screen. Audible clue: pressing Esc will exit text-entry mode without bleeping.

Command mode
: Keystrokes are interpreted as vi editing commands. Each command is usually a single or double keystroke (with possible modifiers), performing such operations as cursor movement, screen scrolling, text deletion, change and movement, string searching, and switching to the other modes. Visual clues: the typed commands do not immediately show on the screen. If showmode is on, the absence of the mode legends is significant! Audible clues: typing a character that does not correspond to a command will sound a bleep. Pressing Esc will always bleep (and you remain in command mode).

ex Escape mode
: Your input is interpreted as an ex command. Visual clues: the ex command prompt : (colon) will be displayed at the beginning of the status line. The cursor appears after the colon. ex commands are displayed as you type them but have no effect until you press Return or Esc.

I'll call this third mode the ex mode. The ex mode is always visually apparent; a colon prompt is displayed on a line known as the status line. This is where you will enter any ex commands followed by the Return or Esc keys. After completing an ex command, you usually return to command mode. The showmode feature controls a helpful display on the right-hand side of the status line that tells you when you are in text-entry mode. In fact, you are told the submode: INSERT, APPEND, CHANGE, or OPEN. Initially, you'll find it useful to have a visual "mode reminder," but before long, you'll probably prefer to have a bit more editing space.

Mode Navigation

You normally fire up in command mode. You need to learn the following set of simplified mode-switching maneuvers (I'll elaborate later):

NOTE
Alphabetic commands are case-sensitive.

From Mode	To Mode	Command, Key, or Action Needed
Command	Text-entry	i, I (insert)
		a, A (append)
		o, O (open new line)
		s, S (substitute)
		c, C (change)
		r, R (replace)
Text-entry	Command	Esc
Command	ex	: (colon)
ex	Command	Return or Esc after ex command
Text-entry	ex	Must go via command mode with Esc, then : (colon)
ex	Text-entry	Must go via command mode with Return or Esc after ex command, followed by a text-entry switch

After this general background, it's time to use vi on some simple texts. The first example illustrates simple text entry, cursor movement, and file saving. The only way to learn vi is by constant practice. It is not easy to describe all the vi features using words alone. What may take several long sentences to explain precisely is often immediately apparent when you experiment with vi.

CREATING A TEXT WITH vi

First, we'll create a special trash directory to keep our vi experiments out of harm's way. You should set up vi to give you showmode on, as described earlier.

```
$ cd
$ pwd
/usr/stan
$ mkdir trash
$ cd trash
$ vi test.data
```

The screen will now show twenty-three tildes, one in the extreme left-hand column (column 1) of each line, from line 2 to line 24. The cursor will appear in column 1 of line 1. Line 25, the status line, will say "test .data" [New file]. Line 25 is reserved for status messages and for entering ex commands.

I am assuming an 80-column × 25-line screen, of course. vi looks at the terminfo file to determine each terminal's screen size, and displays are adjusted accordingly.

The tildes are simply place markers indicating empty lines. They are not text characters to be saved in a file, and they will disappear one by one as you enter text on successive lines.

If test.data is an existing file, vi test.data will initially display some or all of its contents depending on the file size and your screen size. If the text requires less than a screenful, tildes will indicate the unused lines. If the text exceeds the capacity of the screen, you initially see the top "screen's worth" (no tildes) and you will have to scroll down to reveal the rest of the file. vi provides many scrolling and searching commands (up and down, by line, half-page, full-page, multiple pages, and so on) for rapid scanning of large files.

The status line is used not only to report various conditions, but for entering ex commands. You can clear this line at any time, provided you are in command mode, by pressing Ctrl-L. (On some terminals, you must use Ctrl-R.) This useful command is known as *screen refresh* or *screen redraw.* You can also use it to remove any spurious rubbish from the screen, such as those random characters that arise from glitches in a communications line, or unwanted, unstoppable messages from root! Remember that you can block other users from writing to you, either permanently or just when you are using vi.

Pressing Ctrl-G (or Bell, if you have such a key) when in command mode will display a status message giving you the name of the file you are editing, whether or not it has been modified since the last save, and a number representing the percentage of the amount of the file (measured in lines) that lies in front of the current character (that is, the character at the current cursor position). Ctrl-G is therefore called the *status* command.

NOTE

The innocent word *blank* is not always used consistently in Unix literature. It can mean empty when describing the "line" between successive end-of-line characters. It can also mean spaces or tabs.

The cursor is initially placed under the first nonblank character found in the first line, so status would show 100%. If the first line is completely blank, the cursor appears in column 1. The cursor position plays a vital role in vi editing. It controls where your entered text will be positioned in the target file.

Text Entry

The editor fires up in command mode. Before you can enter, change, or rearrange text, you must switch from command mode to one of the text-entry modes. Adding fresh text is done in either append mode (the a command) or insert mode (the i command). These modes differ only in where the text is added: you append *after* the current character but insert *before* the current character. In some situations, such as initially when the buffer is empty, this distinction is irrelevant. On other occasions, the difference is vital. For example, to add text at the end of a line, you must use append mode (you'll see shortly that some cursor movement commands do not allow the cursor to be moved beyond the last character of a line).

1. Type a (lowercase) without a Return. The "a" will not appear–show no surprise!

Part i

2. You are now in text-entry mode. In particular, you are in append mode, and the APPEND MODE legend should appear on the right side of the status line, line 25. (If not, perhaps you are using vi with the showmode off? To fix this, type Esc, colon, then type set showmode followed by Return. Now repeat from step 1.)

3. Type the following text with Returns at the end of each line:

```
At last, I am using vi, the visual editor.
I am in append mode, so my keystrokes are
being stored (appended) into the editing
buffer. Later on, after further editing, I
will save this text by writing from the
buffer to the file test.data.
```

I have entered a final newline (Enter) and two spaces after each period to match the definition of a sentence in vi. Certain vi commands rely on this convention when moving the cursor one sentence at a time.

Notice how the tildes have disappeared from lines 2 to 6, but on the unused lines, 7 to 24, there are still tildes in column 1. If you make any typing errors, ignore them for the moment. I'll explain how to make corrections after you've learned some cursor movement commands.

The above text is stored in the editing buffer. Until you write it out to disk, the file test.data remains empty. During long editing sessions, it is sound practice to save the buffer at regular intervals. To do this, follow these steps:

1. Press Esc to leave append mode and return to command mode.

2. Type a colon. You are now in ex mode. The status line will echo this colon. It serves as the ex mode prompt.

3. Type w (the ex write command) followed by Return. This writes the editing buffer to disk. Since you did not specify a filename, the buffer is written to the current file, namely test.data. You are now back in command mode.

You can save the buffer in any directory/filename combination for which you have write permission. For example, if the file test.temp does not exist, :w test.temp will create such a file and then write the buffer to it. If test.temp exists, the :w command will *not* overwrite it, but you can force an overwrite with :w! test.temp. The current filename is not changed by the :w command, so subsequent writes would still default to test.data in the absence of a filename argument. A useful variant is `:w>>filename`, which appends the `vi` buffer to `filename`. There are three convenient ways to write and exit `vi`:

`:wq` (Return)	Same as `:w` (Return) followed by `:q` (Return).
`:x` (Return)	Same effect as above.
`ZZ`	Same effect as above, but note that you do not need to type the colon or press Return. When you are in command mode, as opposed to `ex` mode, no Return is needed after a command; your input takes effect immediately once the command is completed. The status line will confirm your write operation:

```
"test.data" [New file] 5 lines, 237 characters
```

From now on, the above sequence will be described as "type :w" or simply `:w`, as though it were a single command. Such commands are sometimes called colon commands—they consist of the colon escape to `ex` mode, then an `ex` command followed by a Return (or Esc), which executes the `ex` command and usually returns you to command mode. I say "usually" because there are colon commands that exit `vi` or escape temporarily to the shell. With such commands, you will receive clear visible clues (the shell prompt, for instance) that you are *not* back in `vi` command mode.

NOTE

If you want to abort a partially entered `ex` command, press the Interrupt key (either Del, Delete, or Rubout on most terminals).

Now that you are back in command mode, you'll notice that the APPEND MODE display has disappeared. There is no explicit COMMAND MODE legend, but there's a simple trick available to confirm your command-mode status (especially useful if `showmode` is off). Just press Esc again, and you will hear a beep. If you are already in command mode, Esc is an invalid selection. And if you weren't in command mode, you are now! Some find this Esc probing a viable substitute for the `showmode` feature. We can summarize the preceding session as

```
a[text]Esc[:w<Return>]
```

It started in command mode, switched to text-entry (append) mode, escaped to command mode, detoured to `ex` mode, then returned to command mode. The clue to mastering `vi` is gaining fluency with such sequences to the point where you move between the modes without thinking about them. You even reach the stage where `vi` seems eminently intuitive!

Finally, let's exit vi. Since you have just saved your work, a simple : q (quit) will bring you back to the shell from which vi was invoked. If you try : q before all current changes have been saved, you will be warned and vi will not exit until you either write your changes or tell vi to discard them. You overrule the warning with : q ! (quit and discard recent changes without complaint). As noted earlier, you can write and quit in one fell swoop using : wq, : x, or ZZ.

If you now invoke vi with test.data, the text will appear and the status line will announce

```
"test.data" 5 lines, 237 characters
```

Note that the legend [New file] is now missing.

Cursor Movement

It's time to explore the major cursor movement commands, which are listed below. Note carefully that many vi commands are case-sensitive (for example, l and L perform different functions):

Command	Action
l or spacebar or →	Moves cursor to the right, but not beyond the end of a line (note the warning beep). The spacebar does not blank out any characters being traversed.
h or Bksp or ←	Moves cursor to the left, but not beyond the start of the current line (a beep sounds). (The current line is the line containing the cursor.)
+ or Return	Moves cursor to the start of the next line. Beeps if no next line.
j or Ctrl-N or Ctrl-J or LF or ↓	Moves cursor down one line in same column. (Note: LF is the Line Feed key found on older terminals). Beeps if no next line. If column in the lower line is beyond the end of the line, the cursor will move to the last character of that line. The cursor will never move down to an empty position beyond the end of a line.

Command	Action
k or Ctrl-P or ↑	Moves cursor up one line in the same column. Beeps if you are on the first line. If column in the upper line is beyond the end of the line, the cursor will move to the last character of that line. The cursor will never move up to an empty position beyond the end of a line.
–	Moves cursor up to the start of the previous line. Beeps if no previous line.
^	Moves cursor to the first nonblank character of the current line.
0 (zero)	Moves cursor to column 1 of the current line (whether blank or not).
$	Moves cursor to the last character of the current line.
w	Moves cursor forward to the start of the next word. Words are taken to be strings separated by whitespace (newlines, spaces or tabs) or punctuation symbols, so "heavy,metal,rock" and "heavy metal rock" both count as three words. Repeated application will scan words on next line (if any).
W	As for w, but words are taken as strings separated by whitespace (punctuation alone does not count). If you were scanning forward with W, "heavy,metal,rock" would be skipped as one word. "Heavy, metal, rock" would need three Ws to skip. Repeated application will scan words on next line (if any).
b	Works like w, but moves cursor backwards to the start of the previous word.
B	Works like W, but moves cursor backwards to the start of the previous word.
e	Works like w, but cursor stops under the last character of the next word. If the cursor is already inside a word, it will stop at the end of that word.

Command	Action
E	Works like W, but cursor stops under the last character of the next word. If cursor is already inside a word, it will stop at the end of that word.
(	Moves cursor to the start of the current sentence, or to the start of the previous sentence if the cursor is already at the beginning of a sentence.
)	Moves cursor to the start of the next sentence. vi looks upon a sentence as any string terminating with a period, question mark, or exclamation mark that is followed by either two spaces or a newline. The two-space requirement is a nuisance for those who prefer single spacing between sentences.
H	Moves cursor to home, sweet home, namely column 1 of the top line of the screen.
L	Moves cursor to the bottom line of the screen.

Using `test.data`, practice these cursor movements until you feel comfortable with them. In the next chapter we'll start some serious vi editing.

What's Next

Now that you've gotten a feel for how vi works, you're ready to proceed with Chapter 11, in which you'll learn some advanced vi operations, including screen controls, and more on the ex command modes.

```
echo "2.      Show Date"
echo "3.      Display a file"
echo "4.      Change working directory
echo "5.      Return to original dire
echo "Q.      Quit
echo
echo -n "Enter choice: .\b"
read choice
case $choice in
1) who | more
   pause;;
2) date
   pause;;
3) echo "Enter file name: \c"
   read fil
   if [ -r "$fil" -a -f "$fil ]
   then
      clear
      more -d $fil
   else
      echo "Cannot di
   fi
   pause;;
4) echo "En
   read di
   if test     "${dir:  pwd`
   then
      cd $dir
   else
      echo "$dir: no such d
   fi
      pause;;
   5) if test "$dir" != "$p
      then
         cd $prevdir
      fi
      pause;;
```

Chapter 11

ADVANCED
vi TECHNIQUES

Three aspects of vi affect the learning curve. First, the commands you type do not appear on the screen, so you lack the familiar, direct visual confirmation of your keystroke. (Did I type "b" or "B"?) Of course, you do see the result of the command, and with time, the blind keystroke and the resulting cursor movement meld in a natural way. Second, the habit of keying a command followed by a Return must be broken: in command mode, the valid command keys are "instant" and a spurious Return can be a nuisance. Finally, the different actions arising from a case shift are not consistent or memorable. Invalid commands always beep, so expect some noise during your apprenticeship. However, note that most keys have some command assignment, so the danger of errors is quite high.

NOTE

Unclear on the concept! People often complain about *steep* learning curves. In fact, steep means fast! See Fig 11.1.

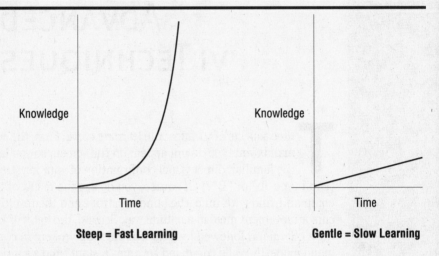

Steep = Fast Learning   Gentle = Slow Learning

FIGURE 11.1:   Comparison of learning curves

Some of these commands are usefully mnemonic, but others are not: the lowercase l for cursor right is particularly inappropriate. (Yet such is the quirk of human memory that this soon becomes unforgettable!) Once you have played with these, you are ready to jazz up the action by adding a *count* number in front of the cursor movement command. Whenever it makes sense you can multiply the movement as follows:

3l   Moves 3 characters right (if possible—the end of the current line is the limit).

6h   Moves 6 characters left (but never beyond the start of the current line).

2+   Moves down 2 lines, ending at the start of the line. Beeps if move is impossible.

4$ Moves to end of the line that is 3 lines beyond the current line. (The 4 is needed because moving to the end of the current line counts as one move.)

The full syntax of the cursor-movement commands is therefore

```
[count] command
```

with a default *count* of 1. The *count* option is the general rule, so I will only mention it when it does not apply or when the meaning is unusual.

Screen Controls

With the small text entered so far, the screen-control commands, such as scrolling and paging, are singularly unimpressive. So let's use a nice vi trick to increase the file size. Position the cursor under the final period of the last line of the test.data example in Chapter 10. Press Esc to ensure that you are in command mode; then type a (append) followed by Return to put you on line 6. Now type

```
This line is being added to test.data.
```

and then press Return to bring the cursor to line 7.

Now press Esc to return to command mode and simply type a period (the repeat command). The text of line 6 will be repeated on line 7:

```
At last, I am using vi, the visual editor. I am in append
mode, so my keystrokes are being stored (appended) into the
editing buffer.  Later on, after further editing, I will save
this text by writing from the buffer to the file test.data.
This line is being added to test.data.
This line is being added to test.data.
```

The rule is that a period typed in command mode repeats your last insert (or delete) command.

Next try the u (undo) command. Line 7 clears. Press u again. Line 7 reappears! So, u tells vi to undo the effects of the *previous* command. If the previous command was a u, u undoes the effect of that undo, thereby restoring the previous file state. Three successive u's are the same as one u; four u's effectively do nothing, and so on. (Contrast this with the nested undo command found in some editors that can progressively restore each previous state.) The vi undo command allows you to toggle between two states. This can be useful after a text change. You can quickly compare the old and new versions, and retain the one that appeals.

Use the period again and again to repeat the last inserted line, and notice how the screen scrolls up when you reach line 24. You can now usefully explore the following screen-control commands:

Command	Action
[*n*] Ctrl-U	Scrolls the screen up *n* lines. The default gives a half-screen scroll up.
[*n*] Ctrl-D	Scrolls the screen down *n* lines. The default gives a half-screen scroll down.
[*count*] Ctrl-F	Pages the screen forward, leaving two lines between pages for continuity, if possible. Note that *count* gives the number of *pages,* with a default of 1.
[*count*] Ctrl-B	Pages the screen backward, leaving two lines between pages for continuity, if possible. Note that *count* gives the number of *pages* with a default of 1.
Ctrl-G or Bell	Displays the status line.
z<Return>	"Zeroes" the screen by redrawing the display with the current line placed at the top of the screen. This is an apparent exception to the "no Return" rule. In fact, the z command can be followed by a Return, ., or - with different effects (see below).
z.	As z<Return>, but places the current line in the middle of the screen.
z-	As z<Return>, but places the current line at the bottom of the screen.
Ctrl-R or Ctrl-L	Refreshes the screen, clearing any spurious displays; also clears the status line message. Test to see which variant works on your terminal.

More on Text-Entry Modes

Once you can move the cursor about, you are ready to practice the four basic text-entry modes: append, insert, open, and change. You have already used the a (append) command, so the following variants should be straightforward. Remember that the following commands switch you to text-entry mode, so after typing the required text, you need to press Esc to return to command mode.

Command	Action
a[*text*]	Appends *text* after cursor
A[*text*]	Appends *text* at end of current line no matter where the cursor is
i[*text*]	Inserts *text* before cursor
I[*text*]	Inserts *text* in front of current line no matter where the cursor is
o[*text*]	Opens a new line below the current line and inserts *text*
O[*text*]	Opens a new line above the current line and inserts *text*

Note especially the lowercase and uppercase variants. In addition to these commands, you can use the J (join) command, which joins (combines) the current line with the line following, but does not switch you to text-entry mode.

Text Deletion

You can delete characters from the screen and/or the buffer in text-entry and command modes, but the methods used in command mode are far more flexible. In text-entry mode, you can use the Backspace key to erase immediately noticed errors. Each time you press Backspace, the cursor moves to the left, erasing one character from the buffer but not from the screen. This can be disconcerting at first (and even at second or third). The screen is refreshed when you press Esc and return to command mode. Using Ctrl-R or Ctrl-L (refresh) also tidies up the screen. The following command-mode deletion methods have the merit of keeping the display and buffer in synch. Note that delete commands do *not* switch you to text-entry mode. After a command-mode delete, you are still in command mode.

Command	Action
x	Deletes the character at the cursor
[*count*]x	Deletes *count* characters forward starting at the cursor
X	Deletes the character ahead of the cursor
[*count*]X	Deletes *count* characters backward starting at the one ahead of the cursor
dd	Deletes the current line
D	Deletes from the cursor to the end of the current line
d<*cursor_movement*>	Deletes from cursor or from current line to a point determined by the *cursor_movement* argument

The d<*cursor_movement*> method is best explained by some examples. Before you try these, keep the u key in mind in case things get out of hand: you can undo (restore the damage of) any deletion immediately with u. If you mess up a line beyond repair, the U variant can be used: U restores all the changes you may have made on a line since you first moved the cursor there. Also, vi has special delete buffers that save deleted text, so you can recover your most recent nine deletions, as I'll explain shortly. The cursor-movement command following the d determines the extent of the deletion, as listed below:

Command	Deletion
dw	From the cursor to the end of the word
db	From the cursor to the beginning of the word
d<Return>	Current line and the *following line*
d0	From the cursor to the beginning of line
d^	From the cursor to the first printable character of line
d$	From the cursor to the end of line
d)	From the cursor to the end of sentence
d(	From the cursor to the start of sentence
dL	From the cursor to the end of screen
dH	From the cursor to the start of screen

On top of these powerful monsters, you can add a count argument:

Command	Deletion
d4w	Four words forward
d3b	Three words backward

You may be puzzled by the placement of the *count* argument, but vi is logical here. The cursor-movement format is 4w to skip four words, so d4w will delete four words.

Changing Text

Change-text commands work rather like delete commands with two major differences: they mark the area of text to be changed, and they switch you to insert mode so you can enter the replacement text. The way vi marks your text is by displaying a $ sign in place of the last character of the block to be changed. For example, if you place the cursor on the first character of "visual" in test.data, and enter cw (change word), the screen will show visua$. The c command, as you may guess, can take any of the cursor-movement arguments (and the usual count arguments as well). You are now in text-insert mode. If you type "exciting", these characters will replace visua$ on the screen (and in the buffer). So the general syntax is

c[*count*]<*cursor_movement*>[*text*]<Esc>

which brings you back to command mode. (The < > symbols are used to improve legibility; they are not to be typed when they surround a typical entry.) Here are some common variants.

NOTE
With r and R the buffer is not updated until you leave insert mode.

Command	Action
[*count*]r<*char*>	Overstrikes the character at cursor with *count* copies of another character you specify, *char*, while remaining in command mode (default is 1).
[*count*]R<*text*><Esc>	Overstrikes the current line with *count* copies of *text* (default is 1).

cc<*text*><Esc> or C<*text*><Esc>	Changes current line and replaces it with *text*.
s<*text*><Esc>	Substitutes current character with *text*.
[*count*]s<*text*><Esc>	Substitutes *count* characters with *text*.
S<*text*><Esc>	Substitutes current line with *text*.
[*count*]S<*text*><Esc>	Substitutes *count* lines with *text*.
><*cursor_movement*>	Shifts all lines determined by *cursor_movement* to the right by shiftwidth spaces (8 by default).
<<*cursor_movement*>	Shifts all lines determined by cursor_movement to the left by shiftwidth spaces (8 by default). You can change the default with a set command (see Table 11.1 later in this chapter).
>>	As for >, but shifts current line only.
<<	As for <, but shifts current line only.

NOTE

A general rule is that doubled operators affect the current line, for example, dd (delete line), cc (change line), << (shift line to left), and so on.

Yanking and Putting Text

vi offers several auxiliary buffers that help you to "cut and paste," that is, move text fragments from one part of the file to another (or even between different files). There are 26 named buffers known as *a*, *b*,...*z* and nine delete buffers labeled 1–9. In addition there is an *unnamed* buffer that serves two roles: it acts as the default buffer in many operations, and it serves as the receptacle for the most recently deleted piece of text. For this reason it is often referred to as delete buffer 0.

You can *yank* text from the editing buffer into one of the 26 named buffers, or into the unnamed buffer, as follows:

`["<letter>]y<cursor_movement>`

If you specify a letter, text will be yanked into that named buffer. Using a lowercase letter gives you a destructive yank (known as a *General Sherman*), whereby previous buffer contents are overwritten; using the uppercase letter leads to an appending yank (or *Lincoln*), where the yanked text is added to the buffer.

By default, the unnamed buffer is used. The amount of text saved is determined by the `cursor_movement` argument. For example, `"ayw` will yank the current word into buffer a, replacing a's previous contents. `"Ay(` will yank and append a sentence to buffer a. The following variants will not surprise you:

`["<letter>]yy`

or, equivalently,

`["<letter>]Y`

will yank the current line.

Each time you delete text, it is moved automatically to the unnamed buffer and also loaded onto the stack of delete buffers 1–9. The nine most recent deletions are therefore accessible by number just as the yanked texts are accessible by letter.

To transplant the yanked or deleted text, you use the p (put) command. This moves the contents of a buffer to the editing buffer at the current cursor position. The syntax is

`["<letter<F2M>|<F255M>number>]p`

or

`["<letter<F2M>|<F255M>number>]P`

where, as before, the default buffer is the unnamed buffer. For example, `"3p` will put the contents of delete buffer 3 into the edit buffer, while `"sp` will put in the contents of buffer s. Exactly where the recovered text will appear in your final document depends on whether the yanked or deleted text contains a partial line or not. Also, the choice of p or P has an effect. The p form will place the buffer text below the current line or after the cursor, while P places it above the current line or before the cursor. A little experimentation will clarify these differences.

Because of the defaults, a common cut-and-paste strategy is to delete, move the cursor, then retrieve the buffer contents with a p.

An important point to note is that these buffers retain their contents until you exit vi. Since you can switch files during a vi session, it is possible to cut from one file and paste to another.

Searching Text

Searching in vi is similar to the approach you saw in the ed editor. The syntax has four basic formats:

```
/[pattern]/[ offset]<Return>
/[pattern]<Return>
```

or

```
?[ pattern]?[ offset]<Return>
?[ pattern]<Return>
```

The / symbol gives forward searches, while ? gives backward searches. The pattern argument can be any regular expression. If no pattern is given, vi uses the previously entered pattern (if none exists, you get an error beep). offset is a positive or negative number that modifies your search as follows:

```
/sun/+2
```

will stop two lines after the line having the first occurrence of "sun" after the current cursor.

```
?sun?-4
```

will stop four lines prior to the line having the first match with "sun" during a backward search from the current cursor.

You can use the set ignorecase (or set ic is also acceptable) ex command if you want a case-insensitive search. In this case, /sun/ will match "Sun", "SUN", and so on. The default setting is noic, which results in case-sensitive searches.

Having located a match, a simple n repeats the last search command in the same direction. Use N to repeat a search in the opposite direction.

To search for a given character in the current line, you can use

```
f<character>
```

for a forward search, and

```
F<character>
```

for a backward search. Useful shorthands let you use a semicolon to repeat the last character search, while a comma repeats the search in the opposite direction.

A slight variation on f and F will move the cursor to the character just before a match:

t<*character*>

for a forward search, and

T<*character*>

for a backward search. As with f, you can use a semicolon to repeat the last character search, while a comma repeats the previous search in the opposite direction.

Another trick associated with searching is the ability to *mark* text. With large files, you may want to place "bookmarks" or "place markers" to speed up future references. The m (mark) command has the following syntax:

m<*lowercase_letter*>

The current cursor is associated with the given letter. The letter marks give you 26 placeholders (not to be confused with the named buffers). Later on, after editing elsewhere, you can revisit a marked place in the edit buffer by using the ' (forward quote) or ' (backquote) commands:

'<*lowercase_letter*>

will move the cursor to the start of the line containing the position previously marked with the argument letter. The backquote variant takes you to the exact spot previously marked. An error beep will greet attempts to find a nonexistent mark. vi treats '<*letter*> and '<*letter*> as valid cursor-movement commands, so, with due care, you could combine them with d (delete) commands.

THE EX COMMAND MODE

When you enter a colon in command mode, you pass to ex command mode. Subsequent commands appear after the colon prompt on the status line. In practice, ex command mode is usually reserved for those jobs that cannot be done easily in vi command mode. Text insertions, changes, and searches are best done with the vi visual interface. ex is better employed with file manipulations (reading and writing), setting global options, and temporary escapes to the shell.

Using the Shell within vi

You can run any Unix command without leaving vi. The syntax is

    :!<unix_command> <Return>

In the unix_command argument you can use % as a shorthand for the name of the current file, # for the name of the last edited file, and ! for the previous command. For example, if you entered

    :!cp # stan.temp<Return>

this would copy your last edited file to stan.temp. Then later on, you could repeat this command with

    :!!

Note, though, that since you can switch files during a vi session, the meaning of # (the last edited file) can change!

You can also spawn a shell and run any number of Unix jobs, then return to vi where you left it with the following command:

    :sh

When you have finished your shell excursions, Ctrl-D returns you to the previous vi session.

When you escape to the shell, vi will warn you if you have changed your edit buffer since the last write:

    [No write since last change]

You can avoid this constant nagging with

    :set nowarn

and turn it back on with

    :set warn

The idea behind the warning is that many unforeseen events can occur during a temporary escape to the shell. Also, if you want to make use of the file being edited, it is clearly sensible to make sure that the file is updated. When you are "out in the shell," you cannot usually access the vi buffer, but you can access the edited file on the disk.

ASSORTED EX COMMANDS

The following sections discuss some useful miscellaneous vi features available in ex mode. If you are in command mode, you'll recall, you need to prefix these commands with a colon.

Abbreviations

The abbr (or ab for short) command lets you set up time-saving abbreviations. If you find yourself typing "SCO UNIX" frequently, you can enter the command:

```
:abbr scx SCO UNIX
```

or

```
:ab scx SCO UNIX
```

Now you need only type "scx" to bring up the full phrase. Some care is naturally needed: using an abbreviation such as "SCO" might misfire if you use "SCO" in other contexts. You usually enter all your standard abbreviations in the .exrc file (ex resource or start-up file) that I mentioned in Chapter 10. I'll discuss .exrc in detail at the end of this chapter. You can remove an abbreviation with the unab (or equivalently, una) command:

```
:una scx
```

Macros with the map and map! Commands

The two map commands are rather similar to abbr. They let you set up *macros* to speed your input. A macro, as far as the map command is concerned, is a *single* printable or control character (excluding digits, Esc, and Enter) that triggers a whole sequence of commands or characters. The map command sets up macros that work in command mode, while the map! variant is used for text-entry macros. As with abbr, your macro assignments can be temporary (all or part of the current session) or "permanent" (set up in .exrc and effective during each session unless temporarily turned off).

Suppose you find yourself frequently using the :!who shell escape sequence to see who else is logged in. You can map (or assign) any nondigit keyboard or control character (excluding Esc and Enter) to achieve this job with one keystroke rather than five. If you assign a key that already has a vi meaning, expect some confusion! Your newly mapped macro will override the normal vi function assigned to that character. Since the vi commands have commandeered most of the printing keys, the choice is rather limited. Of course, it's your call: you may find a better use for a letter than the standard function assigned by vi. The most promising unassigned printing keys are g, q, v, K, V, and Z together with the punctuation symbols [,], @, #, and *. Of the control combinations, you should avoid (or use with care) the following in vi macros, since they have special meanings in one or more modes:

Ctrl-B   Ctrl-R   Ctrl-L   Ctrl-W

Ctrl-D	Ctrl-S	Ctrl-M	Ctrl-]
Ctrl-F	Ctrl-U	Ctrl-N	Ctrl-@
Ctrl-G	Ctrl-V	Ctrl-Q	

A simple but instructive map example is

```
:map V xp
```

The colon is not needed if you are already in ex command mode. Typing V in command mode will trigger the command sequence xp. The x will delete the character at the cursor, and the p (put) command will display the deleted character (from the unnamed buffer where deletions are stored) after the new cursor position. The net result is to reverse two characters: the original cursor character and the one to its right. You have only saved one keystroke, but the V is mnemonically superior to px. Some users even map a lowercase letter to a single uppercase letter command in order to save a shift!

As a more complex example, we'll assign Ctrl-Z to the !who sequence as follows:

```
:map <Ctrl-Z> :!who<Ctrl-M>
```

Before I show you how to do this, let's examine the results. Thereafter, pressing Ctrl-Z in command mode will have the same effect as entering : !who. Note that the Ctrl-M provides the Return keystroke needed to complete the command—without the Ctrl-M, the system would sit there waiting silently for an Enter. The Ctrl-M was not required in the xp example since the x and p commands do not need the Return key. With all mapping applications you must carefully match the actual keystrokes needed for each macro in the appropriate modes. If your macro is invoked in command mode and contains an i, for example, the following macro keystrokes will be interpreted in text-insert mode until an Esc is reached.

To insert the two control codes in the above sequence, you need a special trick: just pressing Ctrl and Z or Ctrl and M will *not* work! You must first enter Ctrl-V followed by the appropriate control combination. Ctrl-V is vi's control code escape character. It warns vi that the next entered character is to be taken literally with no special interpretation. (There are a few exceptions: Ctrl-Q and Ctrl-S are always trapped by Unix before vi sees them. They are used to "pause" and "restart" certain processes, so it is wise to avoid using Ctrl-Q and Ctrl-S in macros.) The actual keystrokes needed to achieve the mapping are therefore

```
:map <Ctrl-V><Ctrl-Z> :!who<Ctrl-V><Ctrl-M>
```

followed by Return. Your screen will show:

```
:map ^Z :!who^M
```

since vi translates the Ctrl-V to ^ (caret), the traditional visible symbol for the Ctrl key.

As an alternative to entering <Ctrl-V><Ctrl-M>, you can try <Ctrl-V><Return>—if this works on your system, vi will also echo the string ^M.

If your macro needs the Esc key, you'll need the same Ctrl-V trick to enter it as a map argument. vi will echo ^[on the screen to confirm your entry.

The macro you set up need not be a complete command. You can map part of a command and enter the balance manually. For example,

```
:map Y "ay
```

maps part of the yank-into-buffer-*a* command. After entering Y, you need to complete the command with a cursor-action command specifying how much text is to be yanked. Typing Y) will expand to "ay), which yanks from the cursor to the start of the next sentence. But, I hear you cry, Y is already a valid vi command: it usually yanks the current line. However, overriding a standard command is quite reasonable here since there is a synonym for Y, namely yy—both usually yank the current line. So with the new macro in place, typing Yy will give you "ayy with no loss of features or keystrokes.

You make your macros permanent by entering them into your .exrc file along with your favorite abbreviations.

If you want to remove a macro during a session, you use the unmap command. The following commands will remove the V and Ctrl-Z macros we set up earlier:

```
:unmap V
:unmap <Ctrl-V><Ctrl-Z>
```

If they are in your .exrc file, of course, they will be reestablished when you next fire up vi. There is another way of storing any permanent vi settings. The environment variable EXINIT can be assigned abbreviations, maps, and set commands:

```
EXINIT='set nowarn|abbr SKB Stanley|map V xp'
```

Note the single quote marks and the separator | between successive commands. You may recall meeting environment variables such as HOME, MAIL, and PATH, and how they are assigned, in Chapter 6. Such assignments are usually placed in your .profile file, followed by

```
export HOME MAIL PATH EXINIT
```

so they become effective when you log in, and available to your Bourne shell and any child shells. Recall that the C shell uses the `setenv` command in the `.cshrc` file. I'll have more to say on this subject in the next chapter.

The version of `map` used so far gives you macros that work only in command mode. For example, you could not expect the V macro to work in text-entry mode! For macros that work in text-entry mode, you need the `map!` variant, but otherwise the syntax and philosophy is the same. The `map!` variant is really an alternative to `abbr`. As with `map` and `abbr`, be very careful that the macros you assign do not impede normal typing—the characters you map lose their normal significance. There is an `unmap!` variant for unmapping `map!` type macros.

To see what macros and abbreviations are in force, you simply enter `:map`, `:map!`, or `:ab` with no arguments.

The set Command

You've met several attributes that you can turn on and off, or assign values to, with the `set` command. There are many more of varying degrees of importance depending on the type of editing you are engaged in. Recall that `set` works only in `ex` command mode, so you need to type `:set` if you are in command mode, or < Esc>`:set` if you are in text-entry mode. Table 11.1 gives a list of the more common arguments you can use with `set` together with their defaults. Some attributes, known as *switch* options, default to either off or on. Others, known as *string* options, default to certain values.

TABLE 11.1: Common set Arguments

set ARGUMENT	DEFAULT	ACTION OR PROPERTY
autoindent, ai	noai	Each line you create is indented to match the indent of the previous line. To back up to the preceding tabstop, enter Ctrl-D. Tabbing is controlled by the value of `shiftwidth` (see set `shiftwidth` below).
autoprint, ap	ap	Displays the current line number after certain ex commands. Equivalent to adding a p after such commands.
autowrite, aw	noaw	Writes the buffer to disk after certain commands if the buffer has changed.
beautify, bf	nobf	Discards all control characters except tab

TABLE 11.1 continued: Common set Arguments

set ARGUMENT	DEFAULT	ACTION OR PROPERTY
directory, dir	dir=/tmp	set dir=*path* specifies the directory for the edit buffer.
errorbells, eb	noeb	Rings the bell before an error message.
ignorecase, ic	noic	Case is ignored when matching regular expressions.
list	nolist	Displays tabs as ^I and end-of-lines as $.
magic	magic	set nomagic reduces the number of metacharacters available in regular expressions so that only ^, \, and $ have special significance.
mesg	nomesg	set nomesg turns off e-mail write permission during vi sessions.
number, n	nonumber	All output lines will display with their line numbers.
report	report=5	set report=*n* will provide a warning if your command modifies more than *n* lines.
scroll	scroll=1/2 window	Sets the number of lines scrolled when Ctrl-D is received in command mode. Also sets the number of lines displayed by the z command to twice the value of scroll. The default is W/2 where *W* is the value used in set window=*W*.
shell, sh	sh=/bin/sh	set sh=*pathname* sets the path name of the shell to be spawned by the ! and shell commands. If the SHELL variable is present, this gives the default, otherwise /bin/sh is assumed.
shiftwidth, sw	sw=8	set sw=*n* sets tabwidth to *n* spaces (see set autoindent).
showmatch, sm	nosm	When) or } is typed, the cursor will move to the previous matching (or { for one second. Useful when editing source code where matching pairs of nested ( )and { } are important.
showmode	noshowmode	Displays the text-insert mode, for instance, INSERT, APPEND, CHANGE, OPEN.
term	term=TERM	set term=*XXX* changes the terminal type of the output device to *XXX*.

TABLE 11.1 continued: Common set Arguments

set ARGUMENT	DEFAULT	ACTION OR PROPERTY
terse	noterse	Reduces the amount of error diagnostics for the experienced user.
warn	warn	set nowarn removes the [No write since last change] warning when you escape to the shell.
window	Default varies	set window=n sets the number of displayed text lines to n. The default depends on the speed and screen size of your terminal: typically 8 for slow terminals, 16 for medium speed terminals, and (max-1) for fast terminals. Most modern terminals will default to 24 lines of text with line 25 reserved for ex commands and messages. The default value for set scroll is half the set window value (see setscroll).
wrapscan, ws	ws	Regular expression searches will wrap around past the end of the file and back to the start of the file. set nows will prevent search wrap around.
wrapmargin, wm	wm=0	set wm=n will set the margin to n spaces during automatic newline insertion while in text-entry mode.
writeany, wa	nowa	Suspends the normal checks made before a write command, so that provided you have permission, you can write to any file.

For example, unless you set autoindent, vi assumes that autoindent is off, and unless you set noautoprint, vi assumes that autoprint is on. For switch options, you use set *argument* to turn on the property, and set no <*argument* to turn it off. String options use the syntax

    set *argument*=*value*

I list the default values that vi assumes in the absence of contrary instructions. Some arguments can be abbreviated as indicated. You'll find that any reasonable abbreviation will work provided there is no ambiguity.

You can use set with no arguments to get a list of all current settings. Recall, also, that vedit invokes vi with various novice options already preset.

The .exrc File

In most cases, the defaults will be adequate while you are learning vi.
When you want to personalize your editing, you can start adjusting these
options in the .exrc file—a wonderful way to try out your vi skills in fact!
This file is always scanned (if present) when vi (or ex) is fired up. You can
look on .exrc as a sort of .profile or .cshrc file for vi sessions.

A typical .exrc file might contain lines such as

```
set nowarn
set eb
set report=3
abbr SYB Sybex Books
map V xp
map Y "ay
map T "ap
```

Entering and Leaving vi

There are several useful options you can add when you invoke vi with an
existing file. If you type vi *filename* and *filename* exists, you fire up
ready to start editing at the first line of the file. Often it saves time to enter
vi with the cursor at some more convenient point, for instance, the end of
the file, or at the last sentence you were working on.

The syntax for invoking vi allows the following variants:

```
vi + filename
```

This loads *filename* as usual but displays the last screenful with the
cursor at the end of the file.

```
vi +n filename
```

places the cursor at the start of the *n*th line.

```
vi +/pattern filename
```

takes you to the start of the line holding the first occurrence of *pattern*
in the file. If *pattern* contains spaces, you must surround it with double
quotes:

```
vi +/"Yours faithfully" myletter.skb
```

Once vi has located a match, you can use the n command for repeat
forward searches and then use N for repeat backward searches.

You can switch files without leaving vi by using the :e for edit command (just like the e command in ex and ed). Suppose you have edited
and saved myletter.skb with :w, and want to edit poem. You simply type

```
:e poem
```

and you start with the cursor at the beginning of poem, which now becomes your new default filename. You can also use the variants

```
:e + poem
:e +/winter poem
```

or

```
:e +20 poem
```

to place the cursor in your preferred starting point.

For more advanced cursor location when editing multiple files, vi offers a tag system. This is beyond the scope of this book, but you may wish to consult the man vi section for details. I also recommend *A Guide to vi* by Dan Sonnenschein (Prentice-Hall, 1987) and *Learning the vi Editor,* Fifth Edition, by Linda Lamb (O'Reilly & Associates, 1990).

WHAT'S NEXT

Chapter 12 is an introduction to shell scripts. Shell scripts are custom text files that add to Unix commands. By creating your own shell scripts, you can automate the way Unix works for you.

```
echo "2.      Show Date"
echo "3.      Display a file"
echo "4.      Change working director
echo "5.      Return to original dire
echo "Q.      Quit
echo
echo -n "Enter choice: .\b"
read choice
case $choice in
1) who | more
   pause;;
2) date
   pause;;
3) echo "Enter file name: \c"
   read fil
   if [ -r "$fil" -a -f "$fil" ]
   then
      clear
      more -d $fil
   else
      echo "Cannot di
   fi
   pause;;
4) echo "En
   read di
   if test -d "$[dir= pwd`]
   then
      cd $dir
   else
      echo "$dir: no such di
   fi
   pause;;
   5) if test "$dir" != "$p
      then
         cd $prevdir
      fi
      pause;;
```

Chapter 12

EXPLOITING THE SHELL

The Unix operating system was designed by programmers for programmers. More precisely, the very first version of Unix was devised by Ken Thompson (joined later by Dennis Ritchie), who was "dissatisfied with the available computer facilities, discovered a little-used PDP–7 [an early DEC minicomputer], and set out to create a more hospitable [programming] environment." This background helps to explain the unique flavor of Unix. The limited hardware resources demanded a compact, efficient kernel and a flexible file-handling system. Starting, as it were, with a clean, nonproprietary slate, Thompson was free to combine "a carefully selected set of fertile ideas" with no immediate commercial or marketing considerations. The sole predefined objective was a system that was programmer-friendly.

Programmers are by nature independent and creative souls. They are seldom content to use a fixed set of tools to achieve a given result. Programmers are usually more fascinated by the tools themselves rather than by the applications they create with those tools. They want to forge and reforge their tools, so they welcome an operating system that offers freedom to those smart enough to "hack" it. The word "hacking," by the way, originally referred to this benign propensity to tinker with programs, prizing clever and even arcane tricks above the needs of the "despised user." The hacker as network intruder and criminal is a recent and unfortunate semantic deterioration of the term. Anyway, as a result of this, Unix therefore evolved into a tool-making tool for programmers, with few concessions to the end user at the bottom of the DP food chain.

Where does all this leave the non-programmer with payrolls to run, debts to collect, and disks to back up at the end of the day? To put it differently, since you're reading this book, we can only assume you'd like a little help. Fortunately, these days, Unix has become a lot more friendly. This is primarily due to the efforts of the folks who brought you the various shells that accompany most versions of Unix today. In fact, not only can you choose between different shells, you can even choose different user interfaces, ranging from a simple text-only version to something that resembles Windows. Shells are the outer layers of software that lie between the user (you) and Unix. They parse your command line, perform wonderful transformations on command arguments, and locate and interpret your commands. But the shell is also a powerful programming language providing the tool-making facility I referred to. With the shell, you can create your own commands and even build a completely new environment.

To many users, the Bourne or C shell *is* Unix: the familiar prompt for character-based commands with cryptic, inconsistent syntaxes. Yet as you've seen in previous chapters, a shell is "just" another Unix program rather than an integral part of the operating system. The "real" Unix is the kernel, and via system commands (usually accessed via C or assembly language), programmers can tap the power of Unix without using the standard shells, if they so choose.

A popular in-joke among programmers is "If you don't like the Unix interface, write your own shell." In fact, you can control your interface without delving directly into the kernel. The available shells, sh, csh, and ksh, are sufficiently powerful and flexible to allow you to build more friendly interfaces using shell scripts. These interfaces will still be character-oriented, but they can present menus, simple windows, and even point-and-select features using a mouse. For the more elaborate GUIs (graphical user interfaces) with icons, resizable windows, dialog boxes, and the other trimmings associated with Microsoft Windows, new, complex shells are needed. And, in fact, this is exactly what has been happening since Unix migrated from the labs to the world of business, where the needs and desires of ordinary users attract more respect; see Chapter 18 for more information.

There are now thousands of sites where the non-programmer is seldom, if ever, prompted by a $ or % symbol. The new interfaces range from simple shell script menus to elaborate GUIs such as SCO's Open Desktop (based on OSF/Motif), Apple's A/UX, AT&T's Open Look, KDE, and many others. Some of these are more like separate operating-system layers on top of Unix than traditional shells. Others simply exploit the facilities offered by one of the standard shells. The thrust of this chapter is to show you how shell scripts can, paradoxically, protect you from the rigors of the shell and provide your own personalized user interface.

SHELL SCRIPTS

As the name indicates, a shell script is a text file that guides and coaxes the shell into performing a sequence of actions. A script can hold any series of commands (both internal shell commands and external Unix commands, with or without arguments), programs, or even other previously written scripts. Scripts can use redirections and pipes, allowing you to write your own *filters.* You might compare this concept to a movie script, where each action, speech, and camera angle is carefully listed. As you study a shell script, you try to imagine how the shell will react to each piece of text, as though you were entering the script on the keyboard. If you've been exposed to DOS, the analogy with .BAT (batch) files will be helpful, except that Unix shell scripts have a much richer armory of features.

There are, alas, small but nagging differences between the Bourne and C shells and these affect the shell script syntaxes and available features. This chapter will deal with Bourne shell scripts for several sound reasons. First, the Bourne shell, /bin/sh, was the first of all the Unix shells and is available on most, if not all, Unix installations. Further, Bourne shell scripts will "run" under the C shell, /bin/csh. What happens, in fact, is that the C shell can recognize a Bourne shell script and invoke the Bourne shell to execute it. Bourne shell scripts will also run under the Korn shell (/bin/ksh). The latter combines most of the features of the Bourne and C shells, and is now bundled with the popular SCO UNIX and other implementations. There are also utilities available that can translate shell scripts from one shell format to another.

/bin/sh is a complex program and many large books have been devoted to its features. I will tackle the most important aspects in the next two chapters. This chapter will give you an overall grasp of shell scripting, offering a host of simple but effective strategies for improving your life without incurring the pain of the arcane shell-programming features. In Chapter 15, I'll delve a little deeper with more advanced shell scripts.

You have already encountered examples of shell scripts. The .profile and .login files I discussed in Chapter 6 are all shell scripts, used to preset various parameters and perform other setup tasks.

Shell scripts can prompt for input and take different actions depending on the keyed response. Similarly, commands can be triggered with user-supplied arguments and, depending on the results of such commands, select the appropriate steps from your script. This concept of selective or conditional execution, common to all programming languages, is known as *flow control*. Some of your simple shell scripts will just carry out a fixed sequence of operations, serving rather as a keystroke-saving macro, while others can guide you through a maze of choices. Recall that a shell script can invoke other programs and shell scripts, so there is, in fact, no limit to what you can achieve.

Shell scripts, once written and debugged, actually reduce your shell-shock by replacing complicated command lines with simpler entries of your own choosing. If you are new to programming, shell scripts offer a reasonably gentle introduction to the art. There is no compilation phase: the shell immediately interprets your scripts, and you can develop them progressively, testing and debugging section by section.

Your First Shell Script

As a first, somewhat naive illustration, suppose you regularly wanted to show the date, list the current logged-in users, and check their status. You could, of course, enter the commands date and who (with suitable arguments) each time, but why not make the shell do the work with a script file? Simply create a file called dw (using vi or ed) containing the five following lines (the first three of which are optional, and cosmetic, but are highly recommended):

```
:
# @(#)dw -- show date and users -- SKB 11/13/95
#
date
who -u
```

Anatomy of dw

The initial solitary colon is not essential, but rather a long-established convention indicating that the text that follows is a Bourne shell script. The colon is treated as a NOP (no operation) by the Bourne shell—in nonjargon terms, the colon is successfully ignored by the Bourne shell. The C shell *does* make use of the first character found in a script. An initial # (also known as the *comment* character) tells the C shell that the following text is intended as a C shell script. Any initial symbol other than # will cause the C shell to invoke the Bourne shell to execute (or try to execute) your script as a Bourne shell script.

WARNING

The two worst things you can do are to start a Bourne shell script with a # and to omit the # at the start of a C shell script! For maximum portability, always start your Bourne scripts with a colon. C shells must start with a #.

Of all the non-# symbols available to start your Bourne script, the most sensible (and therefore the hallowed tradition) is the harmless NOP (colon). This gives both humans and C shells a clear warning of the nature of your script. Avoid blank lines at the start of your scripts: an initial newline is certainly a valid non-# character but it does not provide a strong visible clue.

The next two lines are optional comments signaled by a leading #. (The # is quite safe now that we are past the initial character in the file.) The Bourne shell ignores any word starting with # and also ignores all subsequent characters up to the next newline. You use comments to annotate your scripts (author, date, version number, and so on). I'll have more to say later about the need to develop good commenting habits. The @(#) string is a useful trick used by the what command to extract the title and purpose of a script. what scans an argument file and displays information from any commented section containing the sequence @(#):

```
$ what dw
    dw:
    dw -- show date and users -- SKB 11/13/95
$ _
```

For this reason, @(#) is often known as the *what string*. After a what string, you should enter a succinct description of the script, preferably with version date and author. You can use as many what strings as you wish at any part of your script. The what command will display all such marked legends.

The third line, a single #, is just for improved legibility. A blank line here would be equally acceptable. The fourth and fifth lines do the real work by invoking `date` and `who`. The `who -u` option provides additional user data as explained in Chapter 5.

The Naming Problem

The name you give the file needs some thought because that name will be used to invoke the script file. You should avoid existing command names, of course, and you should, in the Unix tradition, keep your script names as succinct as possible! Calling the script `date_and_who`, for example, makes its intentions clear, but errs in the direction of volubility—after all, the idea is to save typing effort. I therefore elected to call the file `dw`, which provides some clue to its purpose. We'll first check the contents of `dw`:

```
$ cat dw
:
# @(#)dw -- show date and users -- SKB 11/13/95
#
date
who -u
```

Exploiting dw

There are several ways of exploiting the `dw` file. Since `sh`, the Bourne shell, is a program that accepts input from its standard input (usually your keyboard), you can simply redirect input as follows:

```
$ sh <dw
Mon Nov 13 15:33:50 PDT 1995
root    tty02    Nov 13 11.08        . 168
stan    tty01    Nov 13 14:45        . 169
iwonka  tty06    Nov 13 12:32   0:02 170
$ _
```

The result is quite intuitive: `sh` accepts the commands from the `dw` file (ignoring `:` and skipping the comments), just as though you had keyed `date; who -u`. A tad less intuitive is the following variation:

```
$ sh dw
Mon Nov 13 15:33:51 PDT 1995
root    tty02    Nov 13 11.08        . 168
stan    tty01    Nov 13 14:45        . 169
iwonka  tty06    Nov 13 12:32   0:03 170
$ _
```

Even without the redirection, sh has accepted dw as an argument, extracted from it the two commands, and executed them with identical results. The program sh (like many other Unix programs) can take its input from a file named as an argument whether you use < for redirection or not. Although these two examples give the same result, there is a technical difference. In the sh dw example, the shell retains your keyboard as standard input; with sh <dw, the standard input has been redirected to the file dw.

The Bourne shell, as I've mentioned several times, is a program called sh, so you can invoke it at any time by entering sh with or without arguments. The fact that your login shell, usually sh too, is now asked to "run" sh seems a little spooky at first encounter. If you recall the discussion in Chapter 8 on parent and child processes, the situation should not worry you unduly. The sh that processes dw is a child process forked by your login (or home) shell that also happens to be an sh process. When one shell forks another shell, the child is called a *subshell*. The full implications of this situation will emerge as I proceed. For the moment, accept on faith that the subshell you have invoked with sh dw takes the characters from dw rather than from the keyboard. The result is what you might expect from actually typing the commands you stored in dw.

Executing dw Directly

After showing you two ways of exploiting dw, I must now spring a surprise on you. dw is not yet a proper shell script. A shell script, by definition, is an *executable* text file that can be run like a normal command. Having to invoke dw with an explicit sh is rather a nuisance. Yet, if you try dw from the shell prompt, you'll get an execute permission denied message. Before you (or anyone else) can run your new dw script as a regular command you *must* make the file executable. You'll recall that the usual default permissions for the files you create are simply read/write for you, the owner. Let's check this fact:

```
$ ls -l dw
-rw------- 1 stan other 13 Nov 13 13:32 dw
$ _
```

(Depending on the ruling default permissions, you may find differences in the first field. Some systems may be set to give, say, read/write permissions to you and read permission to your group, for example, -rw-r-----. Other sites may default to -rw-r--r--, offering read permission to every user. You can even set your umask to override these defaults either temporarily or permanently.)

The easiest way to add execution permission for you as user-owner is

```
$ chmod u+x dw
$ _
```

as explained in Chapter 7. Check again, and you'll find that you now have read/write/execute permissions:

```
$ ls -l dw
-rwx------ 1 stan other 13 Nov 13 13:40 dw
$ _
```

You may wish to extend execution rights to your group by changing the first chmod argument from u+x to ug+x. Or you can be generous and give everyone execution rights (whether they want them or not) by using a+x. (Just +x will also work since the default here is a). Of course, dw is currently in your home directory, so accessibility by others may be limited. Your new command may be more convenient in a more general directory, either /bin for everyone (if the system administrator agrees) or your own /bin directory (such as usr/stan/bin, or usr/mary/bin, the most natural place for personal executables). Some sites have a usr/local/bin for miscellaneous local commands.

Now you can test dw. It works like a simple command—just enter the script filename:

```
$ dw
Mon Nov 13 15:33:50 PDT 1995
root    tty02   Nov 13 11.08      . 168
stan    tty01   Nov 13 14:45      . 169
iwonka  tty06   Nov 13 12:32   0:02 170
$ _
```

In the above invocation, the login shell recognizes that dw is a shell script (because dw is an executable text file rather than a compiled binary file) and immediately spawns a subshell to read and execute the commands in the dw file. (The subshell does many other things that need not divert us just now.) The parent shell waits for the subshell to finish its work. The end-of-file signal, generated when dw has given its all, kills the subshell process, just as if you had keyed Ctrl-D. The parent shell now revives and shows the prompt. Quite a neat scenario!

NOTE

If dw doesn't run when you invoke it and you get a "file not found" message, then you will need to either add dw to your search path using the set path command or use mv to move dw to a directory in your search path. Or, if you don't intend to use it often, you can simply type in the full path when you enter it like this: $ /home/john/dw

Shell Script Summary

Let's pause to summarize the six basic shell-scripting steps:

1. Plan the command sequences and test them on the keyboard.

2. Choose a good, nonclashing name for your script.

3. Create the script file with your favorite editor.

4. Start the file with a colon and add pithy comments.

5. Make the file executable with chmod.

6. If necessary, mv the script to its proper directory or change your search path.

Script Debugging

One can scarcely talk about *debugging* at this early stage with such a minimal script as dw. But it is conceivably possible that your dw may not work! If you get a command not found or similar message, use pwd and ls to check that you are still in your home directory and that dw was created there. If you get an execute permission denied message, perhaps you forgot to chmod. Less common, but worth keeping in mind, is that another command of the same name exists in a directory listed ahead of your current directory in your PATH variable. Check your PATH with echo $PATH. For script testing, it is useful to have both the current and home directories in your PATH variable. Remember that date and who are in the /bin directory, so /bin must be in your PATH. Finally, make sure that dw contains the correct text. Recall that even if your PATH does not contain the directory holding a particular command (or script), you can still run it (permissions permitting!) by using the full path name /usr/stan/dw. The general rule is that when you invoke a command with a prefixed path starting with /, the shell does not bother to check the paths set in the PATH variable.

For more advanced debugging, you can include the command

```
set -v
```

in your script. This turns on the *verbose* mode in which each line of the script is echoed on the screen as it is read by the shell. The feature is turned off with

```
set +v
```

The verbose mode can also be switched on with

```
$ sh -v dw
```

which saves you editing the dw file. You can also use

```
set -xv
```

This reduces the verbosity by displaying only the executable lines—comments are not displayed.

Special Commands

The set command used above (not to be confused with the ex command of the same name that you saw in Chapter 11) is an example of a *special command* for the Bourne shell. Special commands are built into sh and can be executed efficiently without invoking a child process. (The C shell has its own set of special commands.) You have already met two special commands, echo and cd. In the interests of efficiency, these two common commands are implemented inside the shell. There's an added practical reason for executing cd within the shell without creating a new process. When a shell script changes a directory with the cd command, the new directory must prevail until the script encounters another cd or until the subshell terminates.

New Commands from Old

Meager though it is, dw is a *new* command that you've added to the hundreds that came from your Unix vendor. Some of the supplied utilities are, in fact, shell scripts, so dw need not have an inferiority complex. And, as you'll see, you can include dw in other scripts, and these scripts in other scripts, and so on, to produce more elaborate commands.

Since dw acts like a normal command, you can use all the tricks you've learned that are appropriate for a command that sends data to the standard output:

```
$ dw >datewho.dat
$ cat datewho.dat
Mon Nov 13 15:33:51 PDT 1995
root    tty02   Nov 13 11.08        . 168
stan    tty01   Nov 13 14:45        . 169
iwonka tty06    Nov 13 12:32    0:03 170
$ _
```

You could even generate a background process with

```
$ dw >datewho.dat &
44
$ _
```

The display of a process id (44 in my example) indicates that the & has worked in the usual way.

You can also filter the results of dw as follows:

```
$ dw | grep 'iwonka'
iwonka tty06   Nov 13 12:32 0:03 170
$ _
```

Here, we use grep (man section C) to search the output of dw for occurrences of the string "iwonka". grep means global-find regular expressions and print. grep <re> will display all lines containing the regular expression <re>. grep itself will be discussed in Chapter 14.

The single forward quotes around iwonka are optional here but recommended for safety: the grep family (grep, egrep, and fgrep) has many flags and options! When grepping for phrases or characters separated by spaces, by the way, the single quotes *are* essential:

```
$ dw | grep 'Nov 13'
root    tty02    Nov 13 11.08    . 168
stan    tty01    Nov 13 14:45    . 169
$ _
```

Even at this simple level, you can start to see how useful shell scripts can be developed by combining existing Unix tools. Let's write another shell script called prau (print active user):

```
:
# @(#)prau-print active user-SKB 11/13/95
#
dw | grep '.'
```

Here you see the script dw embedded in a new script. Once you have used chmod u+x prau, the new command is ready for testing:

```
$ prau
iwonka tty06   Nov 13 12:32    . 170
stan    tty01    Nov 13 14:45    . 169
$_
```

The prau command lists all lines with a dot in the output of dw. This will pick up all users who have been recently active, since the activity field from dw will be a dot. Of course, there *may* be other periods in the output of dw, and these will also be displayed. In Chapters 14 and 15, you'll see techniques for limiting the search to particular fields. The process can be continued: you could use prau inside a larger script to display other useful information about users.

The Dot Command

Yet another way of invoking dw exists using the Bourne shell *dot* command:

```
$ . dw
Mon Nov 13 15:33:53 PDT 1995
root    tty02   Nov 13 11.08    .    168
stan    tty01   Nov 13 14:45    .    169
iwonka  tty06   Nov 13 12:32    0:06 170
$ _
```

NOTE

The dot command is available in the Bourne and Korn shells, but not in the C shell.

Here the login shell itself reads and executes the commands found in the file dw—there is no subshell involved. Once again, the displayed results are the same as for sh <dw, sh dw, and dw. The technical differences will emerge later. Briefly, when a subshell runs a command, any changes that the command makes to your environment (variable assignments, changes of directory, and so on) affect only that subshell. When you return to the parent shell, the original environment is restored. Since the dot command executes its argument command in the current shell, any changes made are retained when the command exits.

As an illustration, your .profile file is (almost) a normal shell script (it has one nonstandard quirk: it can be run without execution permission) that is executed whenever you log in. If you edit your .profile file, the changes will have no effect until your *next* login. However, by running .profile with the dot command, you can immediately reinitialize the environmental variables in your current shell without having to log out and in again:

```
$ . .profile
$ _
```

SHELL AND SUBSHELL VARIABLES

You encountered shell variables (sometimes called shell parameters) in Chapter 6. They play a vital role in shell programming. You saw some of the many predefined *environment* variables such as TERM, PS1, PS2, HOME, and PATH, usually set in .profile:

```
TERM=ansi
HOME=/usr/$LOGNAME
```

```
PATH=:/bin:/usr/bin:$HOME:$HOME/bin
...
export TERM HOME LOGNAME PATH ...
```

The shell itself gives default values to PATH, PS1, PS2, and IFS. The defaults are usually as follows:

PATH   :/bin:/usr/bin:$HOME

PS1 $

PS2   >

IFS Space, tab, newline (These are the standard internal field separators, used by the shell when parsing the command line.)

IFS is not usually tampered with, but the other defaults are often overridden in .profile and other scripts. The HOME default is set by login (which reads the HOME field in /etc/passwd) to /usr/$LOGNAME—it can be reassigned but rarely is. An existing variable can be used when reassigning another variable, as indicated above. The $ prefix and the export special command will be explained soon.

The initial colon in PATH represents a difficult-to-see null path. A null path is interpreted by the shell as your current directory, so this is the first directory to be searched by the shell for the invoked command. You may sometimes see a PATH defined as

```
PATH=/bin::/usr/bin:$HOME:$HOME/bin
```

Here, the null path is more "visible" as the empty entry between two consecutive colons. Your current directory would now be the second place to be examined, after /bin, in the command search sequence.

The env command, with no arguments, will display all the environment variables with their current settings:

```
# env
HOME=/
HZ=100
LOGNAME=root
PATH=/bin:/usr/bin:/etc
SHELL=/bin/sh
TERM=ansi
TZ=PST8PDT
# _
```

For a change, I show you the values used by root. Run env in your home directory and note the settings. The variables HOME, LOGNAME,

PATH, and TERM are all obvious. The remaining variables are explained below.

HZ   Hertz: the number of clock interrupts per second. This hardware dependent value is stored in /etc/default/login and should not be tampered with.

SHELL   The path name of the default shell. In the absence of an explicit entry in the last field of /etc/passwd, SHELL provides your default shell. If there is an "r" in the file part of the name, the restricted form of the shell, for example /bin/rsh, will be used. rsh gives the system administrator more control over the commands available to a user.

TZ   Time zone information used by commands such as date to display the time appropriate to your zone, including automatic adjustment for summer daylight saving time. A special shell script called etc/tz is used by root during installation to set TZ, so you will not normally want to play with this value.

The importance of the environment (and other) variables is that your scripts can be more generic by accessing values that are not known when you write your scripts. If your script aims to write a file in the user's home directory, for example, the value $HOME is guaranteed to hold this value no matter who is running your script.

WARNING

No spaces are allowed between = and the adjacent expressions when assigning values to variables.

You also learned in Chapter 6 how to devise your own variable names (known as *user variables*) and assign useful values to them:

```
$ SKBLIB=/usr/stan/lib
$ echo SKBLIB
SKBLIB
$ echo $SKBLIB
/usr/stan/lib
$ echo "$SKBLIB"
/usr/stan/lib
$ cd $SKBLIB
$ _
```

The above sequence, performed at the keyboard, could equally be embedded in a shell script, of course. Note carefully the use of the $ character: it "converts" a variable name to the value contained in the variable. Forgetting this fact will cause you much grief, so don't forget! As the above example shows, SKBLIB without the $ echoes literally. I've also thrown in an example to show that $ retains its transforming power even when double-quoted. When I come to metacharacters and quoting, you'll see the importance of this property.

The rules for naming user variables are quite simple. They must start with a letter or an underscore. Following this can be any sequence of letters, digits, or underscores. Unix is case-sensitive. Upper- and lowercase letters are considered to be different: NEXT and NeXT are distinct variables! And, naturally, you should make your names usefully mnemonic and avoid incorporating any of the predefined environment variable names.

Variables can be combined in various ways. Consider the following examples:

```
$ CH="Chapter "
$ ch=1
$ echo $CH$ch
Chapter 1
$ echo $CHch

$ _
<newline only–CHch is an unknown variable>
$ echo ${CH}ch
Chapter ch
$ echo $CH{ch}
Chapter {ch}
$ echo ${CH}${ch}
Chapter 1
$ CH1=$CH$ch
$ echo $CH1
Chapter 1
$ echo CH1
CH1
$ echo "$CH"ch
Chapter ch
$ _
```

For convenience, I show these as keyboard conversations with the helpful echo command. Within a shell script, the combined names may well be arguments to other commands.

Note the use of braces and quotes to avoid a sequence that the shell might otherwise consider a valid variable name.

Setting and Unsetting Variables

The act of naming a variable in an assignment statement such as SKBLIB=
/usr/stan/lib serves both to define it and to give it a value. There are
occasions when you want to remove a variable name from the list. The
unset special command can do this. Alternatively, you can simply assign a
null value to a variable without actually removing it from the shell's list.

```
$ ANYVAR=
<assign nothing at all!>
$ echo $ANYVAR

$ _
<newline—null value>
$ unset SKBLIB
$ echo $ SKBLIB

$ _
<newline—not known>
$ _
```

The line ANYVAR= can equally be written ANYVAR=" " since the empty
string " " is as null as possible. Note that the environment variables PATH,
PS1, PS2, MAILCHECK, and IFS *cannot* be unset (and quite rightly so).
Although the two variables ANYVAR and SKBLIB echo in the same way,
there is a subtle but important technical difference between a variable
being unset (no longer defined) and a variable having a null value (but
still remaining defined). This may seem rather Zen, but some clever shell-
programming tricks depend on this difference.

Several expressions using $ and { } can be used to test whether a vari-
able is defined-but-null or simply undefined, and depending on the result
of the test, other values can be assigned. Table 13.1 later in this chapter
lists these expressions, but they will not be used until the next chapter.

In this and the next chapters, you'll also meet some special shell variables that are set *automatically* by the shell. Some of these specials cannot be changed by the user. Both types are tabulated below for reference,
with the $ prefixed, ready for action; their full significance will be clari-
fied as we proceed.

Variable	Meaning
$n	The *n*th positional parameter:
	$0 is the invoking command name.

Variable	Meaning
	$1 is the name of the first argument.
	$2 is the name of the second argument.
	$9 is the name of the ninth argument.
	The special command `shift` is used to access more than nine arguments. If only *M* arguments are used, $*n* is empty for values of *n* greater than *M*. The `set` command can be used to change the values of $1 to $9.
$*	Holds all the argument positional parameters (starting with $1 and separated by spaces) in the command line. Not limited to nine arguments.
$@	Same as $* except when quoted as `"$@"`. `"$@"` is `"$1"`, `"$2"`... but `"$*"` is `"$1  $2..."`.
$#	The total number of positional parameters excluding $0 (the command name).
$-	The option flags used in the command line.
$?	The exit value (decimal) returned by the command. Cannot be changed by user assignment. The usual convention followed by most commands is: a zero value indicates a successful command, a nonzero value indicates failure, and the nonzero value gives the reason for the failure. The exit values depend on how the command has been programmed, so there is no absolute guarantee that 0 means success.
$$	The process id of the current shell. Cannot be changed by user assignment. (Warning: the name of the variable is $, so you need $$ to access its value!) Since the process id is a unique number, $$ is often used to construct a unique name for temporary file. For example: `any_command>>$HOME/tmp/data.$$`
$!	The process id of the last background command (invoked with the & operator). Cannot be changed by user assignment.

Exporting Variables

Any variable "known" to a shell can be used in a shell script running under that shell. A variable can be inspected (to extract its value), compared with other variables, used in arithmetical operations, and (apart from the exceptions listed above) have new values reassigned or reset in a shell script; indeed, the use of variables is one of the features that makes the shell a "proper" programming language.

Unless you take specific steps, the names and values of variables are *local* (confined) to the shell in which they are declared. If a parent shell names a variable, that variable will not be known to any child processes (such as subshells) unless you *export* it using the `export` command.

```
$ GREET=Hello
$ echo $GREET
Hello
$ sh
<now running subshell>
$ echo $GREET

$ _ <newline response: GREET unknown in subshell>
<Ctrl-D back to parent shell>
$ export GREET
$ sh
<run a subshell again>
$ echo $GREET
Hello
<GREET is now known to subshell>
$ GREET=Saludos
<reassign GREET>
$ echo $GREET
Saludos
$ _
<Ctrl-D back to parent shell>
$ echo $GREET
Hello
<parent shell retains original value of GREET~TS>
```

There are two important lessons here. First, you need to export a variable name before the subshell knows of its existence. Second, even when the name is exported, any new assignments made within the subshell remain local to the child process. If you examine your `.profile` file, you'll find that the environmental and user variables are all exported so that they are available, with their assigned values, to all processes spawned by the login shell. If you assign new values to, say, HOME or PATH in a subshell, such changes will be temporary.

The set command you met earlier can be used to display all the variables known to the current shell, together with their values. Simply use set with no arguments:

```
$ set
PATH     :/bin:/usr/bin:/usr/stan
PS1      $
PS2      >
SKBLIB   /use/stan/lib
...
```

The rule that a subshell cannot alter the values of variables set in its parent shell is of fundamental importance. It is related to the concept of *local* and *global* variables found in most programming languages. In languages with global variables, nasty side effects are a constant danger, especially in large programs, because changes made in one module can unwittingly affect distant modules. Unix shell variables are global in the sense that their scope (or visibility) and initial values can be extended (via export) from parent to children. However, the side effect problem is solved by preventing child processes from affecting the parent environment. export simply provides *copies* of variables for child processes—the originals cannot be molested.

As you develop more complex shell scripts you'll come to appreciate this arrangement. Your script commands can be incorporated into other script commands, possibly by complete strangers many years from now, so there is no telling what variable names may be floating around at different process levels. Unrestricted global variables would greatly complicate the shell-programming process.

Another vital and related aspect of locality is that when you change a directory with a cd call in a shell script, you affect only the subshell environment. The current directory as seen by the parent is not changed. Consider the following skeleton script:

```
:
# @(#) tcd—test cd in a shell—SKB 11/27/95
#
SKBLIB=/usr/stan/lib
echo 'Starting directory='
pwd
cd $SKBLIB
echo 'After cd, subshell directory now='
pwd
```

Assuming tcd has been made executable with chmod, let's test it as follows:

```
$ cd
$ pwd
```

```
/usr/stan
$ tcd
Starting directory=
/usr/stan
After cd, subshell directory now=
/usr/stan/lib
$ pwd
/usr/stan
$ _
```

When we return to the parent shell, we are still in our starting directory in spite of the cd performed within the subshell.

How Shell Scripts Work

What really happens when you enter dw at the prompt? The full story is quite complex, but some of the subtleties need to be appreciated in order to master the art of shell scripting. Here's a brief walkthrough to give you a feel for the sequence and to establish some essential shell jargon.

The first hurdle for your parent sh shell (the login shell displaying the $) is *parsing* your command line. Parsing means that the command line is broken into *tokens* (or *words*) to determine the name(s) of the command(s) and the nature of the options and arguments, if any. During this parsing, certain special symbols (known as *metacharacters*) may trigger a variety of transformations to the arguments (such as command substitutions, parameter substitutions, blank interpretation, and filename generation, which we'll cover in more detail later).

To do all this, the shell must scan the environment to pick up the values assigned to environment variables. The shell also sets the special variables with useful values such as $#, the number of arguments, and the positional parameters ($0, $1, and so on), encountered during the parse. Next, the shell will set up any explicit redirections indicated by the > and < symbols.

Eventually, the dreaded moment of execution draws nigh. There may be several commands in the command line (you've met examples such as xxx | yyy and xxx;yyy), but let's concentrate on the situation where a single command such as dw has been invoked. The shell needs to locate the file dw (using the directory search sequence in PATH) and check the directory and file permissions. If the file is not found, the command is aborted.

This is a convenient point to introduce another vital chore performed by the shell. The shell always passes to the parent process a parameter $?

known as the *exit status* (also called the *condition code* or *return code*). By convention, a zero value indicates a successful command execution; a nonzero value indicates failure *and* its value tells you the reason for failure. All the standard commands follow this convention, but be aware that the values depend on the programmer following certain rules. Many shell-programming features make use of the exit status. When you test the result of certain operations in order to control the execution flow of the script, a zero exit status is taken as *true,* while a nonzero exit status is taken as *false.* I'll amplify this aspect of shell programming in subsequent chapters. You can perform commands conditionally as follows:

```
comm1 && comm2
comm3 || comm4
```

If comm1 executes successfully, returning an exit status of 0, then comm2 will be executed; if comm1 fails, returning a nonzero exit status, comm2 will be ignored. Actually, comm1 and comm2 can each be compound expressions representing a whole slew of commands such as x; y; z or x|y|z. The second line reverses the logic: comm4 will only execute if comm3 is unsuccessful.

Your script can actually force a command to fail! The special command exit *n* causes the processing shell to abort with an exit status of *n,* so that user-detected error conditions can be "passed on" to other shell scripts that include your script.

Having located dw and checked the permissions, the shell must analyze the type of the dw file. If it is a compiled, binary program, a dw process is spawned to execute it. If dw is an executable text file, a subshell is spawned that will read the commands from the file. During this process, further parsing and substitutions will occur depending on the text encountered. For example, occurrences of positional parameters will be replaced by the appropriate values. If $0 occurs in the shell script, it will be replaced by the invoking command name. Each occurrence of $0 to $9 is replaced with the corresponding command argument, and $* is set with a string representing all the command's arguments separated by spaces. Similarly, each occurrence of $# will be replaced with a value representing the number of arguments used in the command line.

As each line of the script "unfolds," further processes and subshells may be spawned to any number of levels down the process chain, depending on the type of commands encountered. Any special commands such as echo and cd will be executed "within" the current shell. It is not rewarding to dwell obsessively on all this activity. Eventually, child processes and subshells succeed and die, the script's end-of-file is reached, and control reverts back to the original login shell.

The Positional Parameters

So far, our dw script has been invoked without arguments. To endow your scripts with the same flexibility as normal Unix commands, you need to understand the positional parameters alluded to in the previous section. A simple, impractical example will illustrate the way a shell script "knows" how it was called: the number and names of its arguments. Consider the silly script called ssc:

```
:
# @(#) ssc: Silly Script-SKB 11/24/95
# This daft program illustrates the use of positional
# parameters and the shift command
# usage: enter ssc followed by at least one argument
echo 'Command='
echo $0
echo 'Number of args='
echo $#
echo 'The original arg list='
echo $*
shift
echo 'The arg list after a shift='
echo $*
```

Create and chmod this file as usual; then test it with various arguments:

```
$ ssc -a b cd efg
Command=
ssc
Number of args=
4
The original arg list=
-a b cd efg
The arg list after a shift=
b cd efg
$ _
```

The invoking command is ssc, as confirmed by the value echoed from $0. The number of arguments is 4, the value in $#. The first echo $* output displays each of the four arguments, $1, $2, $3, and $4. After the shift special command, $1 takes the value of the original $2, $2 takes the value of the original $3, and so on. Try ssc with ten or more arguments. Notice that $* holds all the arguments, even if their number exceeds nine. Since there is no positional parameter called $10, one of the applications of the shift command is to access the tenth or higher argument. Try quoting some or all of the arguments, and see how the shell strips the quotes. The number of arguments in

```
$ ssc "-a b" cd efg
```

is three, not four, because the space between -a and b has been *quoted,* that is to say *hidden,* from the shell.

Try ssc with no arguments. The first $* correctly reports an empty list of arguments, but you'll get an error on the shift command—there is nothing to shift!

An example that may puzzle you is

```
$ ssc x y x >misc.tmp
$ cat misc.tmp
Command=
ssc
Number of args=
3
The original arg list=
x y z
The arg list after a shift=
y z
$ _
```

No, the redirection expression >misc.tmp is *not* considered a command argument. Before we explore more complex scripts, let's spruce up dw to illustrate a few more basic principles. Use vi or ed to amend dw as follows:

```
:
# @(#)dw—show date and users—v 2.0 SKB 11/13/95
#
echo 'Today is:'
date
echo '
The following users have logged in:'
who -u
```

Running the new version produces the more legible display:

```
$ dw
Today is:
Mon Nov 13 17:33:50 PDT 1995
The following users have logged in:
stan    tty01   Nov 13 01:45   0:01   169
iwonka tty06   Nov 13 00:32     .    170
```

To help explain this enhanced script, a brief diversion on echo and quoted characters will be useful.

echo and the Shell Metacharacters

The echo command (introduced in Chapter 6) lets you display texts and variables so that you can annotate and tabulate the output of commands embedded in your scripts. echo by itself will give you a newline; otherwise it echoes each of its arguments. The arguments of echo are groups of characters separated by one or more spaces or tabs. It is vital to remember that these arguments are handled by the shell before being "echoed," so many strange transformations are possible: you do not always get back exactly the string of characters shown in the arguments.

After echoing the final (possibly transformed) argument, echo gives a concluding newline. You can suppress this newline in two ways: use the -n switch or the special '\c' escape sequence. (Not all versions support both of these features, but at least one of them should be available.) For example,

```
$ echo Enter your Name:
Enter your Name:
$ _
```

But,

```
$ echo  -n Enter your Name:
Enter your Name:$ _
```

and

```
$ echo Enter your Name:'\c'
Enter your name:$ _
```

The last variant can also be written as

```
$ echo 'Hear this:\c'
Hear this:$ _
```

or as

```
$ echo "Hear this:\c"
Hear this:$ _
```

WARNING

Don't confuse a single forward quote (') with a backquote (`).
Don't confuse two single forward quotes (' ') with a double quote (").
Don't confuse two backquotes (` `) with a double quote (").

The \c pair is known as an *escape sequence* since the character following the backslash "escapes" its normal interpretation by the shell. You met this concept in ed and vi, where regular expressions made use of \

as the escape character. In the case of \c, however, note that you must also use single or double quotes: '\c' or "\c" (more on quoting soon).

echo also allows the following useful escape sequences (your terminal may not recognize all of them, though):

'\b'	Backspace
'\f'	Formfeed
'\n'	Newline
'\r'	Carriage Return
'\t'	Tab
'\v'	Vertical Tab
'\oct'	The ASCII code represented by the octal number *oct*. For example, echo '\07' is equivalent to sending BELL (or Ctrl-G) to the terminal. Armed with a list of octal codes for special graphics symbols, you can give your scripts jazzy windows and boxes. Octal numbers must start with a zero.

Familiar Quotations

Going back to the enhanced dw example, note the use of single forward quotes around the legends. These *hide*, or *escape*, or *quote* the spaces, newlines, and other special characters from the shell. The three words are not quite synonymous, but they are often used to describe any of the various tricks available to modify the shell's normal actions. I'll use the verb "quote" to cover all such methods.

Space and tab, normally used as argument separators (or *delimiters*), can be quoted using single forward quotes. The two commands

```
$ echo Today is:
Today is:
$ _
```

and

```
$ echo 'Today is:'
Today is:
$ _
```

produce the same display, but for slightly different reasons. In the first version, echo has two arguments, Today and is:, which are echoed one after the other. In the second example, echo "sees" only one argument, the string 'Today is:'. In fact, the shell strips off the quotes and passes the sequence Today is: as one argument to echo. Try this with several spaces between Today and is: to confirm my story.

Similarly, in the entry,

```
echo '
The following users have logged in:'
```

we are quoting the newline after the first quote, so a newline will be echoed before the text (notice the extra line in the display). The following alternative achieves the same result:

```
echo
echo 'The following users have logged in:'
```

Even when not essential, using single forward quotes around text for display is a good habit to develop. The complete rules for forward quotes, double quotes, and backquotes are quite tricky. Here, and in the next section, I provide examples to give you a feel for the subject. I'll present the formal rules later. Note that for convenience I give the examples as direct keyboard interactions with the shell; they can, of course, also be translated as lines in a shell script.

```
$ echo 'What does "quote" mean?'
What does "quote" mean?
$ echo "What does 'quote' mean?"
What does 'quote' mean?
$ _
```

Backquotes

The backquotes play a leading role in shell programs. The general idea is that when the shell encounters `command`, it executes (or tries to execute) command and replaces the whole expression `command` with the output (if any) from that execution. The backquoted command expression can contain any legal switches, options or arguments—it may even be a compound expression holding several commands. Clearly, it is not usually fruitful to use backquotes with commands that do not produce any output. The term command substitution is used to describe the shell's action when a backquoted command (possibly with arguments) is found in a command line. Command substitution provides a powerful method for generating arguments, setting values in shell variables, and other tricks:

```
$ echo Today is `date`
Today is Tue Nov 14 17:33:50 PDT 1998$ _
```

The above provides an alternative way of creating the dw script file, by the way. The following example will come as no surprise:

```
$ echo 'Today is `date`
Today is `date`
$ _
```

Single quotes hide the backquotes from the shell, so no command substitution takes place. However, the following example *may* shock you:

```
$ echo "Today is `date`"
Today is Tue Nov 14 17:33:50 PDT 1998
$ _
```

What is going on? Well, rules are rules, and an important Unix shell rule is that double quotes do *not* hide backquotes. Double quotes (unlike single forward quotes) allow the shell to "see" backquotes, so the date command is invoked. You'll meet another double quote exception, the $ symbol. There are excellent reasons for these exceptions between single forward quote and double quote hiding. They allow you to control when and where the shell makes certain types of substitutions—you'll meet many such situations as the saga unfolds. Here's another use of backquotes:

```
$ pwd
/usr/stan/lib/misc
$ HERE=`pwd`
$ echo $HERE
/usr/stan/lib/misc
$ cd
<do things in /usr/stan>
$ cd $HERE
<return to /usr/stan/lib/misc>
```

The output from pwd is saved in the shell variable HERE. You can subsequently use $HERE to return to a previous directory. Examples like these are common in scripts where you may have no prior knowledge from which directory the script starts running.

In the following example, the backquoted command has an argument:

```
$ mail `cat mailshot` <memo
```

If mailshot contains a list of recipients, the cat command will "output" these names to provide an argument to the mail command. Each recipient will be sent the contents of the memo file. The mailshot file can be formatted as

```
stan
mary
boss
```

or as

```
stan mary boss
```

The first layout works because the command substitution mechanism interprets newlines as word delimiters and passes each name forward as a separate argument to mail.

MORE ON METACHARACTERS

As you've seen, the shell can treat a large number of *metacharacters* in a nonliteral sense. For instance, the shell will expand * to match filenames, so echo * will not display an asterisk! What you'll get is a list of filenames (all those in your current directory not starting with a dot, in fact). The shell action with *, ?, and regular expressions, is known as *name generation*. The full list of potential metacharacters (depending on the context) is quite daunting: < > ( ) { } [ ] ; | ? / \ $ " ' ` # & space, tab, and newline. You need to learn gradually when and where each symbol can have a special meaning, how the shell treats them, and how to inhibit (or delay) their special effects.

In the following sections I'll explain the more common metacharacters, glossing over some of the complexities until later. Since some of the metacharacters interact with each other, there will be some repetitions in these sections.

Escaping with \

The metacharacter \ (backslash) lets you quote any single metacharacter, including \ itself.

```
$ echo \*
*
$ echo \\\?
\?
$ echo `date`
Mon Nov 14 17:33:50 PDT 1994
$ echo \`date\`
`date`
$ echo "\`date\`"
`date`
$ _
```

The \ is also used to generate ASCII control codes, as explained earlier: '\t' for tab, '\0n' where n is the octal value of an ASCII character, and so on. The special sequence `'\c'` is used to suppress the newline you normally get from `echo`:

```
$ echo 'Enter Name: \c'
Enter Name: $ _
```

Note also the common use of \ at the end of a command line too long to fit on your screen.

```
:
# @(#): longline—show use of \ as line extension
#
echo This line seems to be far, far, far, far too long \
to fit on one line.
```

This script would display as follows:

```
$ longline
This line seems to be far, far, far, far too long to fit on
one line.
$ _
```

The layout would depend on the width and wraparound properties of your screen. The newline immediately after \ is hidden from the shell.

The Comment Character

is used to indicate comments in your shell script. Comments are annotations that appear in printed listings, telling you of such things as the author, revision dates, and reasons for certain lines. Such comments are ignored by the shell and are for human consumption only. As your scripts become more complex, pithy comments become essential both to you and your next of kin (i.e., those who may have to decipher and maintain your code when you have moved on).

Any word that starts with a # leads to the rest of the line being ignored. You can test the effect of # using `echo`:

```
$ echo Enter your Name: # added in version 2.0 11/14/95
Enter your Name:
$ echo Enter your Employee '#':
Enter your Employee #:
$ echo 'Enter your Employee #:'
Enter your Employee #:
$ echo abc#def
abc#def
$ echo abc #def
abc
$ _
```

In the first line, the # and all following characters are ignored. In the next two examples, the # is quoted so that its special meaning is lost: you get a literal # displayed. The previous examples illustrate the fact that # is also taken literally when it is not the first symbol of a word. You can also use the backslash:

```
$ echo abc \#def
abc #def
$ echo abc \\ #def
abc \
$ echo abc \\\#def
abc \#def
$ _
```

Note again the double \\ needed to display a single \.

Double Quotes

Double quotes can be used to quote *most* metacharacters: the exceptions are $ ` " and \. Apart from these, double quotes can be used in place of single forward quotes. The $ metacharacter is used for *parameter substitution;* the ` is used for *command substitution.* Both kinds of substitutions occur within double-quoted arguments encountered by the shell.

```
$ echo abc "#"def
abc #def
$ echo "abc #def"
abc #def
$ echo $HOME
/usr/stan
$ echo '$HOME'
$HOME
$ echo "$HOME"
/usr/stan
$ echo "\$HOME"
$HOME
$ echo "`date`"
Tue Nov 14 17:33:50 PDT 1995
$ echo ""

$ _
<empty string-newline response>
$ """
> Bye
> So long"
Bye
So long
```

```
<keeps prompting until matching " supplied>
$ echo "\""
"
$ echo "\\"
\
$ echo '\\'
\\
```

Before proceeding, make sure you understand why these examples work the way they do.

Metacharacter Sequences

To simplify the quoting of sequences of metacharacters, you can enclose them all in single forward quotes (or double quotes with the noted exceptions). For example, '$*' is equivalent to both '$'é*' and \$*. However, since $ is not quoted by double quotes, the shell would treat "$*" as $"*" with possibly peculiar results.

The double quotes and single forward quotes will not affect normal characters, so if a metacharacter occurs in the middle of normal text, you can quote the whole string:

```
$ echo The '*' in your eye
The * in your eye
$ _
```

can also be written as

```
$ echo 'The * in your eye'
The * in your eye
$ _
```

Care is needed to display ' and ", as you may have guessed. Look at the following:

```
$ echo Have you read "War and Peace?"
Have you read War and Peace?
$ echo 'Have you read "War and Peace?"'
Have you read "War and Peace?"
$ echo "Have you read 'War and Peace?'"
Have you read 'War and Peace?'
$ _
```

Now try the following examples, and see if you can explain the results:

```
$ echo \
> Hello
Hello
$ _
```

The \ has hidden the following newline from the shell, so you get the PS2 (secondary prompt), usually the symbol >. In other words, echo is still waiting for an argument. Once you enter Hello and newline, echo will echo as shown.

In the following exercises you'll see examples of *filename generation* and how it can be suppressed if not needed. Words containing unquoted occurrences of *, ?, and characters enclosed in the pair [] are treated by the shell as patterns. The shell generates a sorted list of filenames (including directory names) that match the pattern. If this list is empty, i.e., no matches are found, the word is left unchanged. Otherwise, the list of matching filenames *replaces* the word. The patterns recognized are not quite as complex as the regular expressions you met in ed and vi. The syntax is also just ever so slightly different. The Bourne and C shells also have minor differences. I'll concentrate on the Bourne shell here. (See Appendix A for shell variants.)

*	Matches any string including the empty (null) string, but excluding *dot* filenames, that is, filenames starting with a period. (In ed and vi, x* matches *zero* or more occurrences of *x*.)
?	Matches any single character except the initial period of a dot filename. (In ed and vi, the period is used for single-character matches, including the period itself but excluding newline.)
[xyz...]	Matches any one of the characters within the brackets.
[a-x]	Matches any character in the range.

A ! (pronounced *bang*) immediately following the [reverses the sense of the match. Thus:

[!xyz]	Matches any character *not* inside the brackets.
[!a-x]	Matches any character *not* in the range. (In ed and vi, the caret (^) rather than ! reverses the match.)

A key point that can mislead the unwary is that filename generation does *not* take place when no matches occur. Consider this example:

```
$ echo ?
?
```

You would normally expect to use '?' or "?" to echo a metacharacter such as ?. But here the shell happened to find no single-character filenames in the current directory! Hence the "word" ? was passed on unchanged. Obviously, the safest way to echo a literal ? is to escape or quote it since we can never be certain that no single-character filenames will be found.

```
$ echo \?
?
$ echo '?'
?
$ echo "?"
?
```

Compare these examples with the following:

```
$ echo /bin/??
/bin/ed /bin/dw /bin/vi
$ echo ???
bin tom tmp usr
$ echo \*
*
$ echo '*'
*
$ echo "*"
*
$ echo *
<lists all filenames except those with leading dot>
$ echo .*
<lists all filenames with leading dot>
# echo *+*
lost+found
$ echo wx*yz
wx*yz
<no matches were found>
$ echo 'wx*yz'
wx*yz
$ echo  'What's that? '
> OK
> OK'
What's that?
OK
OK
$ _
```

Notice the mismatched ' in the last example: with a missing ', the shell expects more input, and will keep prompting until you supply a final quote.

I conclude this section with a brief summary of the Bourne shell's meta-characters, shown in Table 12.1. Use quotes or \ to inhibit their action. Some of these metacharacters have already been discussed. Others are listed here for completeness and will be the subject of further elucidation in Chapter 15.

This is a good moment to recap some basic facts about the role of the shell. A clear picture of "who does what" is essential to good shell scripting. The correct use of shell variables, special commands, and metacharacters depends on a knowledge of how shells and subshells interact.

TABLE 12.1: Metacharacter Summary

SYMBOL	MEANING
>	*Command* >*file* redirects stdout to *file*.
>>	*Command* >>*file* appends stdout to *file*.
<	*Command* <*file* redirects stdin from *file*.
|	comm1 | comm2 pipeline: stdout from comm1 directed to stdin of comm2 asynchronously.
Delim	Takes data (known as a *here document*) embedded in a shell script and redirects it to a command's stdin. The data is redirected until the string specified in *delim* is reached.
*	Wildcard matches all strings including null but excluding dot filenames.
?	Wildcard matches all single characters except initial dot of a dot filename.
[char_list]	Matches any single character in *char_list*.
[!char_list]	Matches any single character *not* in *char_list*.
[r1-r2]	Matches any single character in range *r1* to *r2*.
[!r1-r2]	Matches any single character *not* in range *r1* to *r2*.
&	comm1 & comm2 executes comm1 in background. comm2 does not wait for comm1 to finish (asynchronous execution).
;	comm1;comm2 executes comm1 then comm2 (sequential execution).
;;	Used as command terminator in case commands.
\`commlist\`	The command(s) in *commlist* are executed and the output of the final command replaces the backquoted expression (command substitution).
(commlist)	The command(s) in *commlist* are run in a subshell.
{commlist}	The command(s) in *commlist* are run in the current shell.
$n	The parameter $0 is set to the command name; the parameters $1–$9 are set to the first nine arguments.
$*	Holds *all* the positional parameters starting with $1.

TABLE 12.1 continued: Metacharacter Summary

SYMBOL	MEANING
$@	Same as $* except when quoted as "$@". The parameter "$@" is "$1" "$2"... but "$*" is "$1 $2...".
$#	The total number of positional parameters excluding $0 (the command name).
$-	The option flags used in the command line.
$?	The exit status value (decimal). A zero value usually indicates a successful command. A nonzero value usually indicates failure.
$$	The process id of the current shell.
$!	The process id of the last background command.
$VAR	The value of the variable VAR. Empty if VAR not defined.
${VAR}str	The value of VAR is prepended to literal string str.
${VAR: -str}	$VAR if VAR is defined and non-null; otherwise str. $VAR remains unchanged.
${VAR:=str}	$VAR if VAR is defined and non-null; otherwise str. If VAR is undefined or null, str is assigned to $VAR.
${VAR:?mstr}	$VAR if VAR is defined and non-null; otherwise displays the message mstr and exits the shell. Default message if mstr empty is VAR: parameter null or not set.
${VAR:+str}	str if VAR is defined and non-null; otherwise makes no substitution. Without the :, the expressions work the same, but shell only checks whether VAR is defined (null or not).
\char	Takes char literally (escape).
'str'	Takes string str literally (single quote).
"str"	Takes string str literally *after* interpreting $, `commlist`, and \.
#	Comment character: ignores words starting with # and ignores all subsequent words up to next newline. (The Bourne shell also treats any line starting with a semicolon or space as a comment.)
VAR=str	Assigns str as new value of VAR.
VAR=	Assigns null value to VAR. Contrasts with unset VAR, which undefines VAR.
Commlist1 && commlist2	Executes commands in commlist2 only if the commands in commlist1 have executed successfully (i.e., have returned an exit status of zero).
Commlist1 || commlist2	Executes commands in commlist2 only if the commands in commlist1 have executed unsuccessfully (i.e., have returned a nonzero exit status).

The Shell Game

To put the traditional shell as a command interpreter in perspective, consider what happens when Unix first boots up. I'll simplify the details to avoid obscuring the key events. The sequence of events before your terminal is ready for action can be summarized as a succession of four major processes:

```
init-getty-login-shell
```

init acts as a general process spawner. (You may wish to reread Chapter 8 to refresh your understanding of how a parent process forks, or spawns child processes.) In the process hierarchy, the first init created during a Unix boot plays a similar role to that of root in the file hierarchy. Just as the root directory is mother to its subdirectories (and so on to other generations), the first init gives birth to offspring subprocesses (which in turn beget subsubprocesses). The big difference between processes and directories is that processes can spawn *subinstances* of themselves. In particular, init can spawn init children, which inherit fully their parent's procreative powers. root, however, cannot generate another root—it is the uniquely named parent of all subsequent subdirectories.

init works in conjunction with a file called /etc/initab (short for initialization table). Briefly, initab specifies which processes can be spawned by init in each of eight possible *run levels*. A run level represents a particular system configuration, for example, single-user mode or multiuser mode.

We often refer to process *paths* by analogy with directory paths. You can trace a path from the first init process down through a series of spawned child and grandchild processes. As each terminal logs off and each child terminates, Unix moves back up the path to the original init process.

After certain booting initialization phases are complete, and provided you are in multiuser mode, the original, Big Daddy init spawns separate child init processes for each connected terminal, then waits patiently for the drama to unfold. It is one of these init children that opens the standard input, output, and error files for your terminal, and then calls getty. getty sets the terminal type, speed and line protocol, and displays the login message seeking your login name. getty reads your login name and passes it as an argument to the login process.

login prompts for your password (if necessary) and checks it against the entry found in the /etc/passwd file. If this check fails, login will prompt you again. There may be limits to the number of login attempts or to the time allowed to complete them. Note that these prompts are being performed at system level by the login process—no shell is yet involved. If the login eventually fails for any reason, the process path will revert to the start-up init, which is aware of the fate of all its children. If you pass the password hurdle, login performs the following chores (not necessarily in the order indicated):

- ▶ Updates certain accounting files so that your presence as a logged-in user is known. Commands such as who and finger need to know who logged on, where, and when.

- ▶ Checks and notifies you if you have mail.

- ▶ Displays any motd (message of the day).

- ▶ Executes the start-up files, if any, (.profile for the Bourne shell, or .login for the C shell, as indicated in /etc/passwd), to set various environment variables, such as TERM (terminal type), PS1 (primary prompt symbol), and PS2 (secondary prompt symbol). You can also set up other tasks to be performed here (see later).

- ▶ Consults the file /etc/default/login (if present) to establish other environment variables, such as TZ (time zone), HZ (interrupt-clock frequency in Hertz [cycles per second]), and ALTSHELL (alternative shell).

- ▶ cd to your working directory (HOME).

- ▶ Gets the user and group ids from /etc/passwd. (These are needed by the shell to determine your access rights to directories and files ouside your HOME base.)

- ▶ Sets the permissions umask to octal 022. (This establishes default permissions for your own files and directories.)

- ▶ Executes the login shell named in the last field of /etc/passwd. (If the last field is empty, executes the default shell, usually /bin/sh, the Bourne shell.)

But, and this is a significant "but," the program name sitting at the end of /etc/passwd can represent any suitable executable filename your system administrator decrees. He or she can reduce you to a restricted shell (such as rsh), a nonstandard, vendor-supplied shell, or can even invoke a particular application with no direct shell access at all. Recall that only the superuser can edit the /etc/passwd file, so the start-up shell or program cannot be set or changed without suitable authority.

For the moment, though, let's assume that /etc/passwd gives you the Bourne shell, /bin/sh. Unless you have redefined the variable PS1 (the primary prompt symbol), you now see the $ prompt. The sh process now running and waiting to interpret your commands is your *parent* shell. You can picture the parent shell accepting input from your standard input (usually the keyboard unless redirected) until it receives an end-of-file sequence (Ctrl-D). Terminating the shell will normally wake up the process that spawned the shell, namely login. This explains why the login message reappears.

When you enter a command line, the shell has several jobs to do:

▶ Parse the command line to distinguish command names from options and arguments (remember that a command line may contain many commands together with redirections, pipes, and other operators).

▶ Expand any wildcard symbols.

▶ Convert any variable names encountered to their assigned values.

▶ Locate the file indicated by the first command name to be executed (using the PATH variable as explained in Chapter 6).

▶ Check that you have execute permission(s).

(There are a host of other details that I'll gloss over for the moment.)

If the file cannot be found, or if access and/or execute permissions are denied, the shell issues a warning message and redisplays the prompt. The shell will also reject your command line if the syntax is faulty.

If all is well, the next steps depend on the type of file located by the shell. You may recall the file command from Chapter 7, used to determine file types. The two file types of interest here are as follows:

▶ Executable program (also known as binary) files. These come in many flavors depending on the language and compiler used in their generation.

▶ Executable ASCII text or shell script (also known as *command text*).

In the first case, where the command file is a compiled, executable program, your login (or parent) sh process spawns a child process to execute the command. Any command arguments and options are passed to this process. What happens next depends on whether the & operator appears after the command entry. If the & operator has been used, the parent process (your login shell) will not wait for the child process to finish, so the prompt will appear immediately and the child process proceeds independently in the background. With no & operator, the parent waits for the child process to terminate, after which the process path returns to the login shell and the prompt reappears. You have seen both these variants in previous chapters. To avoid mental strain, you should, for the moment, ignore the fact that the process running the executable program can, and probably will, spawn its own child processes, and so on... but eventually, barring accidents, your login shell "regains" control.

The case where the file is a shell script (executable text file) has a very important difference. Your parent login shell has to spawn a fresh shell, known as a subshell, to handle the situation. The subshell is an sh process (the spitting image of its parent) but instead of reading commands from the keyboard, it reads and obeys the commands in the shell script.

With this background, you are getting nearer to understanding the Unix shell. In the next two chapters I introduce some of the most common tools used in shell scripts. Then we can start writing useful scripts to automate your daily chores.

WHAT'S NEXT?

In the next chapter, we'll examine some of the tools you can use to work with shells, such as sort, uniq, split, cut, and paste. With these tools, you'll be able to create Unix scripts of your own, so you can make your copy of Unix *your* Unix.

```
echo "2.        Show Date"
echo "3.        Display a file"
echo "4.        Change working directory
echo "5.        Return to original dir
echo "Q.        Quit
echo
echo -n "Enter choice: .\b"
read choice
case $choice in
1) who | more
   pause;;
2) date
   pause;;
3) echo "Enter file name: \c"
   read fil
   if [ -r "$fil" -a -f "$fil ]
   then
       clear
       more -d $fil
   else
       echo "Cannot d
   fi
   pause;;
4) echo "En
   read di
   if test      "$di        pwd`
   then
       cd $dir
   else
       echo "$dir: no such dir
   fi
   pause;;
5) if test "$dir" != "$p
   then
       cd $prevdir
   fi
   pause;;
```

Chapter 13

DIPPING INTO THE TOOLBOX

Before delving deeper into shell programming, I want to introduce a few commands that are particularly useful in shell scripts. I will confine the discussion to the most common options and applications for these commands. I suggest you skim through these commands at first reading to get a feel for their properties, then refer back to a command when it appears in the later shell script exercises.

THE SORT COMMAND

The sort command (in man section C) is a *filter* that sorts *lines* from your standard input and passes the sorted result to your standard output. By default, the sort will be in *ascending* order (usually determined by the ASCII code sequence, but there are local exceptions) and will sort by comparing whole lines. In most cases, sort is used to sort items in one or more files and pass the result to a file or to another filter for further processing. You'll also see examples where we sort the data emerging from other commands such as who and ls.

A rich fund of options exists to modify the sort ordering and/or to sort by selected fields (usually called *keys*) from each line. Let's start by sorting a naive file called staff containing employee names:

```
$ cat staff
Jones, A. P.
Amis, Q. K.
Brown, S.
Smith, E. M.
Smith, A. L.
$ sort staff
Amis, Q. K.
Brown, S.
Jones, A. P.
Smith, A. L.
Smith, E. M.
$ cat staff
Jones, A. P.
Amis, Q. K.
Brown, S.
Smith, E. M.
Smith, A. L.
$ _
```

Notice that you can use sort staff as well as sort <staff. If sort is followed by a valid filename, sort will read from that file without explicit redirection. In fact, you'll see later that sort can accept more than one input file, so that

```
sort staff temps
```

will read both files to give one sorted, composite output. Note that if you have used one or more spaces in your filename, you'll need to put single quotes around the filename or sort will treat the file as several files instead of one file with spaces in the name. Also, if you don't supply an input file-name, or if you name the file – (minus), sort will read and sort whatever you input from the keyboard after the command (remember to end your input with Ctrl+D). For example:

```
$ sort
John
Andrew
Magda
^D
Andrew
John
Magda
```

Notice also that sort does not alter the sequence in the file itself: the sorted output simply appears fleetingly on the screen. To obtain a sorted file, you can use redirection to save the sorted output in a separate file:

```
$ sort staff >s_staff
$ cat s_staff
Amis, Q. K.
Brown, S.
Jones, A. P.
Smith, A. L.
Smith, E. M.
$ _
```

You could now use mv s_staff staff to copy the sorted data over the original file. What you must *never* do is

```
$ sort staff >staff
```

This will destroy the staff file, since Unix has to overwrite the very file it is trying to sort. There is, however, a way to safely sort a file onto itself without using an intermediary file. You can use the -o (output) option with sort to redirect the output to the source file without destroying the input file. Instead, with -o the sorted data replaces the original data in the source file. Take a look at the following:

```
$ sort staff -o staff
$ cat staff
Amis, Q. K.
Brown, S.
Jones, A. P.
Smith, A. L.
Smith, E. M.
$ _
```

Incidentally, the -o option works with any output file, so it offers an alternative to redirection:

```
$ sort staff -o s_staff
$ _
```

or

```
$ sort -o s_staff staff
$ _
```

Both of the alternatives above give the same result as

```
sort staff >s_staff
```

Spaces after the -o are optional: sort staff -os_staff, and sort -os_staff staff work well enough, but I prefer to include spaces for legibility. The key point is that the filename following the -o is the output file regardless of its position in the argument list.

You can reverse the sort order by using the -r (reverse) option:

```
$ sort -r -o r_staff staff
$ cat r_staff
Smith, E. M.
Smith, A. L.
Jones, A. P.
Brown, S.
Amis, Q. K.
$ _
```

The output is now in descending ASCII sequence. Incidentally, if you are unfamiliar with the 7-bit ASCII code, you may encounter some surprises when using sort. If you refer to Appendix B (ASCII Tables), you'll see that the uppercase letters have lower numeric values than the lowercase letters! So, a strictly ASCII-ascending sort moves "Z" (value 90) ahead of "a" (value 97), and so on. The ASCII values of the control characters, numerals, tab, space, and punctuation symbols should also be noted: unless you take precautions, sort blindly follows these values, often with disconcerting results. Although sort usually makes sense only when applied to text files, Unix makes no attempt to enforce sensible usage. You can, for instance, sort binary files if you wish, though the results will not usually be meaningful.

Over There!

Since the sun never sets on Unix (or vice versa?), there are many foreign language variations that sort needs to support. Some languages need extended character sets for accented letters and diacritical marks. For example, Spanish lexicographers sort "czarina" ahead of "chabacano," while

Welsh dictionaries place "llabyddio" after "lwmp." The Cherokee syllabary, with 85 distinct single-case symbols, calls for a complete remapping of the ASCII character set, and still other languages, such as Chinese and Japanese, demand more dramatic extensions to 16 or higher bit encodings to accommodate their huge character sets. To overcome some of the shortcomings of the ASCII sequence, `sort` offers several order-overriding options, which are summarized in Table 13.1.

TABLE 13.1: Summary of sort Options

sort OPTION	ACTION
c	Check sort order. Used in conjunction with sort order options. No sort is performed but you get a warning message if the target file(s) are not in the specified sequence.
r	Reverse designated ordering.
f	Fold lowercase letters to uppercase.
d	Dictionary order.
i	Ignore nonprintable characters.
n	Numeric value order.
M	Month name order (JAN, FEB,<F128>£<F255%0>).
b	Leading blanks ignored (restricted sort keys only).
u	Removes duplicate values, so each value output is unique.
tx	Use x as the field separator symbol (the default is space and tab).

The sort f Option

`sort -f filename` treats lowercase letters as uppercase when sorting, so that "a" sorts ahead of "Z" in ascending order. (The f stands for "fold": we say that lowercase letters are *folded* into their uppercase equivalents.) Consider the following session:

```
$ cat staff
Jones, A. P.
Amis, Q. K.
deMoivre, Z.
Brown, S.
Smith, E. M.
Smith, A. L.
```

```
$ sort staff
Amis, Q. K.
Brown, S.
Jones, A. P.
Smith, A. L.
Smith, E. M.
deMoivre, Z.
$ sort -f staff
Amis, Q. K.
Brown, S.
deMoivre, Z.
Jones, A. P.
Smith, A. L.
Smith, E. M.
$ sort -fr staff
Smith, E. M.
Smith, A. L.
Jones, A. P.
deMoivre, Z.
Brown, S.
Amis, Q. K.
$ _
```

The concise -fr format is entirely equivalent to providing the two options -f and -r. Whenever a combination of sort options makes sense, you can save keystrokes by combining the option letters in any sequence after a single -.

The sort d Option

sort -d filename gives a "dictionary" sort. This means that sort will ignore any characters other than letters, digits, spaces, and tabs. Dictionary order, as I mentioned earlier, is a property that varies with language, and has to be defined in the locale setting.

The sort i Option

sort -i filename makes sort ignore nonprintable characters. (Recall that space and tab are considered to be "printable.") This option is primarily used to ignore control codes, which can cause undesirable results when sorting, since their ASCII values are lower than space. The definition of "nonprintable" also varies from language to language, and has to be defined in the locale setting.

The sort n Option

`sort -n` `filename` (the number option) lets you sort by arithmetical
value. Although the values of the ASCII numerals are in numeric order,
there are many situations where a string sort of numeric fields gives the
"wrong" result. Consider the following session:

```
$ cat nlist
90
100
200
080
$ sort nlist
080
100
200
90
$ _
```

You can guess why the string "90" comes in last (highest). The ASCII
sort simply compares all first characters, all second characters, and so on.
The "080" finds its rightful place because it has been padded with a leading zero (a leading space would also work). The -n option sorts by true
numeric value, ignoring leading spaces and spurious zeros:

```
$ sort -n nlist
080
90
100
200
$ _
```

The -n option goes even further by handling negative numbers and
decimals. Compare the following two sorts:

```
$ cat num
1.65
-.9
-2
.67
$ sort num
-.9
-2
.69
1.65
$ sort -n num
-2
```

```
-.9
.67
1.65
$ _
```

Multiple File Sorts

The sort command can also sort several files at the same time. Suppose you had two files, staff1 and staff2, giving names from different departments:

```
$ cat staff1
Herring, A.
Smith, E. M.
Ireland, J.
Jones, A. P.
Amis, Q. K.
$ cat staff2
Smith, E. M.
Smith, A. L.
Brown, S.
$ sort -o all_staff staff1 staff2
$ cat all_staff
Amis, Q. K.
Brown, S.
Herring, A.
Ireland, J.
Jones, A. P.
Smith, A. L.
Smith, E. M.
Smith, E. M.
$ _
```

Again, note that sort staff1 staff2 >all_staff would achieve the same results.

The sort u Option

In the previous example, the name *Smith, E. M.* appears in both files, and naturally shows twice in the sorted file. The sort command offers the -u (unique) option that automatically suppresses duplicates:

```
$ sort -u -o all_staff staff1 staff2
$ cat all_staff
Amis, Q. K.
Brown, S.
Herring, A.
```

```
Ireland, J.
Jones, A. P.
Smith, A. L.
Smith, E. M.
$ _
```

You'll shortly meet a related command called uniq that reports or hides duplicated fields in a sorted file.

The uniq Command

The uniq command (man section C) scans a file looking for any *adjacent* lines that happen to be identical. Options let you restrict the comparisons to certain fields and characters in each line. Other options let you select duplicates or nonduplicates. By default, uniq outputs nonduplicates together with one copy of each duplicate (hence the name uniq, pronounced *unique*). Consider the following sequence:

```
$ cat input_file
a
b
b
c
c
c
d
a
$ uniq input_file
a
b
c
d
a
$ _
```

The final "a" is not considered a duplicate since it is not adjacent to the previous occurrence of "a". To ensure that all duplicates are filtered out, you need to sort the file first. A single filename argument is always taken as the input to uniq, which then sends its output to the standard output (usually your screen). If you supply two filename arguments, the second argument is taken as the output file. So, the output from uniq can be sent to a file without the need for the redirection symbol >:

```
$ uniq input_file output_file
$ cat output_file
a
b
```

```
c
d
a
$ _
```

This gives rise to a slight quirk. What if you want to pass the output of a command to uniq and then send the output of uniq to a file? In this case, the > is needed. Take the following example:

```
$ sort input_file | uniq
a
b
c
d
$ sort input_file | uniq > output_file
$ cat output_file
a
b
c
d
$ _
```

Note first that "a" occurs only once in the output from uniq, since sort has brought the two "a's" together. Remember that uniq's idea of "duplicate" is "adjacent duplicate." Next, observe that if you omitted the >, uniq would "see" a single filename argument and would therefore consider output_file as its input source with much ensuing confusion.

The general syntax is

```
uniq [-udc [+n] [-n]] [input_file [output_file]]
```

The final four brackets indicate that you can omit both filename arguments or you can omit the output_file argument. You cannot, as I explained earlier, drop the input_file argument and retain the output_file argument.

The other options are explained briefly in the listing below, followed by detailed examples.

-u   Output only the nonduplicated lines.

-d   Output one copy of each adjacent duplicated line; do not output nonduplicates.

-c   Precede each line with a count number showing the number of duplicates found. Implies also -ud.

+n   Ignore the first n characters when testing for duplicates.

-n   Ignore the first n fields when testing for duplicates.

The default `uniq` with no options combines the actions of `-u` and `-d`. In other words, it displays the nonduplicated lines *and* one copy of each duplicate. The `-c` option implies and overrides `-u` and `-d` to give the default display plus a count on each line. In other words, `-cu`, `-cd`, `-cdu`, and `-cud` are all equivalent to `-c`.

```
$ cat input_file
a
b
b
c
c
c
d
a
$ cat -u input_file
a
d
a
$ cat -d input_file
b
c
$ uniq -c input_file
1 a
2 b
3 c
1 d
1 a
$ _
```

The proper use of *-n* requires an understanding of fields. As with the `sort` command, a field is any sequence of nonspace, nontab characters that has spaces or tabs (or a final newline) separating it from adjacent fields. The *-n* option tells `uniq` to skip the first *n* fields on each line together with any leading spaces or tabs before determining whether the rest of the line constitutes a duplicate. Here are some examples.

```
$ cat sales
Mar 96 230
Jan 98 178
Mar 98 178
Apr 99 178
Oct 99 780
Jan 99 780
Sep 99 780
$ uniq -1 sales
Mar 96 230
```

```
Jan 98 178
Oct 98 780
Jan 99 780
$ uniq -c -1 sales
1 Mar 96 230
3 Jan 98 178
1 Oct 98 780
2 Jan 99 780
$ uniq -2 sales
Mar 96 230
Jan 98 178
Oct 98 780
$ uniq -d -2 sales
Jan 98 178
Oct 98 780
$ _
```

Here, the -1 option tells uniq to ignore the first field, so that the month name takes no part in the process. Lines 2, 3, and 4 now appear as adjacent duplicates, and only the first copy, "Jan 98 178", is output. The other examples show how to combine several options.

The +n option skips n characters before the comparisons are made. You can combine -n and +m options. uniq skips the first n fields, then skips the first m characters of the (n+1)th field.

THE HEAD COMMAND

The head filter command (in man section C) lets you see the first few lines of one or more files. A similar command called tail that inspects the last few lines (10 by default) of a file is covered in the next section. Together they provide an easy way of answering such questions as "What on earth is this file called memo.misc?"

The head syntax is as follows:

```
head [-count] [file1 file2 <F128>£]
```

where count specifies the number of lines you wish to output from each of the filename arguments. The default count value is 10. Being a filter, head takes standard input and gives standard output. It is often used in pipelines. For example, to display the four best sales periods, you could use head with one of our earlier sort examples:

```
$ cat sales
Mar 98 -50
Jan 99 780
```

```
Oct 98 1206
Sep 99 340
Apr 98 -560
Jan 98 -50
Mar 96 230
Jun 96 -50
$ sort +2nr +1 -2 +0 -1M sales | head -4
Oct 98 1206
Jan 99 780
Sep 99 340
Mar 96 230
$ _
```

Note that if *count* exceeds the number of lines available, head simply does the best it can. Remember that if you supply a large enough value for *count* without redirecting output to a file, your display will run off the screen unless you pipe via the more filter:

```
$ head -40 mail_list | more
```

THE TAIL COMMAND

The tail filter command (in man section C) works like head but outputs the final *count* lines (or 10 by default), blocks, or characters from the argument file. The syntax is a tad more complex, though:

```
tail +|-[count][lbc] [-f] [filename]
```

The l, b, and c options designate lines, blocks, or characters. The default is l for lines. As with head, the default *count* is 10, so that

```
tail filename
```

simply displays the last ten lines of *filename*, while

```
tail -c filename
```

would display the last ten characters of the file.

The *count* argument determines the starting point in the file. If you specify a positive argument, *+count*, tail will start outputting *count* lines from the beginning of the file. A negative sign, *-count*, means start *count* lines from the end of the file. The default *count* is still 10 if you just supply the + or – with no number. So,

```
tail +b filename
```

displays *filename* from block 10 to the end. Similarly,

```
tail -c filename
```

outputs the last ten characters. The meaning of block, by the way, depends on the implementation, but is usually 512 bytes. tail is usually limited by buffer sizes to reporting about 300 lines, but in practice this is no impediment. `tail` and `head` are mainly used to check a few lines of a file to help identify its version and contents.

The `-f` (for "follow") option is used to check on the progress of a file being built by another process. For example,

```
tail -f filename
```

displays the final ten lines, then sleeps for a second before reading the file again. You can therefore see line by line as the file grows.

TIP

A really neat use for this command is `tail -f /var/adm/syslog` or any log file that you need to periodically check for new input.

Before leaving `head` and `tail`, note the quirk that `head` can take several filename arguments, whereas `tail` accepts only a single filename argument.

THE SPLIT COMMAND

The `split` command splits a given file into smaller files of a given size. You can specify the size and the names of the partial files created by `split`. The syntax is

```
split [-n] [filename [split_name]]
```

This will split `filename` into *n*-line pieces called `split_nameaa`, `split_nameab`, `split_nameac`,..., `split_nameaz`, `split_nameba`, and so on. The number of files produced depends entirely on the size of `filename` and the value of *n*. The last file may contain fewer than *n* lines, of course. The default *n* is 1000 lines, and the default `split_name` is x. So, if you had a 2001-line file called `hairs`, the command

```
$ split hairs
```

would create three files called `xaa`, `xab`, and `xac` as follows:

File	Contains
xaa	Lines 1–1000 from `hairs`
xab	Lines 1001–2000
xac	Line 2001

The command

```
$ split -1500 hairs gray
```

would create two files called grayaa and grayab:

File	Contains
grayaa	Lines 1–1500 from hairs
grayab	Lines 1501–2001

The split command needs some care when used with pipes. Consider

```
sort hairs | split gray
```

If your aim is to sort hairs before creating the grayaa, grayab split, this will not work! split would take gray as the filename argument, and would try to split it if such a file existed. To make split accept the output from sort (or any similar piped command) as its standard input, you can do one of two things: omit the gray argument and accept default splits called xaa, xab, and so on. Or, supply a dash (-) as follows:

```
sort hairs | split -gray
```

The dash warns split that the "file" to be split must be taken from the standard input, and that gray is really the *split_name* suffix.

There is a more sophisticated split command called csplit that splits a file into sections determined by markers in the text. You supply a sequence of arguments that locate the markers. These arguments can be line numbers or regular expressions with optional repetition factors. Consult man section C for more details. Splitting a large file into smaller files is useful in many e-mail situations.

THE CUT COMMAND

The cut command removes selected fields from each line of a set of files and sends the result to the standard output. The syntax is

```
cut -clist [file1 file2 <F128>£]
```

or

```
cut -flist [-dchar] [-s] [file1 file2 <F128>£]
```

WARNING

No spaces are allowed between the c (or f) and the list argument! Likewise, no spaces are allowed between d and *char*.

The list argument is a comma-separated sequence of ranges (*integer–integer*) indicating the fields. With the -c (for column) option, the ranges indicate the character (column) positions you wish to be retained in each line. (Some find the name cut confusing since the range arguments lead to *extraction* rather than elimination. You can alias cut as extract if you feel strongly about this.) Thus,

```
cut-c1-30,35-80filename
```

would display columns 1–30 inclusive and columns 35–80 inclusive from each line of filename. Characters outside these positions are ruthlessly suppressed. You can redirect the output, of course, with

```
>output_filename
```

The range can be a single number meaning "retain just that column position." The range *-n* means the same as *1-n*, while *n-* is equivalent to *n-last_column*. For example,

```
cut -c-30,35- filename
```

would simply suppress columns 31–34 inclusive.

With the -f option, the list represents field numbers and ranges. Fields are defined by the -d*char* argument. The *char* you supply is taken as the field separator (or delimiter, hence the -d). If you do not supply a -d argument, -f assumed that your fields are delimited by tabs, the most natural default. A common variant is to use -d: since many Unix files use the colon as a field delimiter. For instance,

```
$ cut -d: -f1,5 /etc/passwd
root: supervisor
daemon: system daemon
...
stan: Stan Kelly-Bootle
$ _
```

outputs the first and fifth fields of the password file, giving you a list of user id's and names.

The -d*char* trick works only with -f and is just like the -t*char* option for defining fields in the sort command. Sorry about the inconsistency! Also note that if your char is a character such as space or * that the shell treats specially, you should add single quotes: -d ' '.

Finally, the -s option, used only with -f, suppresses all lines that do not have the specified (or default) delimiter. This is useful when your file has headers or comment lines that are not really part of your database. Omitting the -s in such cases will lead to unwanted, nondelimited lines passing through.

THE PASTE COMMAND

The `paste` command works rather like the reverse of `cut` (whence the well-known text-editing collocation, "cut and paste"). `paste` merges (or concatenates) lines from a set of files and sends the result to your standard output. The syntax is

```
paste [-s] [-dchar] file1 file2 …
```

Take the simplest case (no options) first:

```
$ cat items
shoes
socks
pants
$ cat prices
12.90
3.45
19.95
$ paste items prices
shoes    12.90
socks    3.45
pants    19.95
$ cat deliveries
Jan 12 99
Feb  3 99
Dec 25 98
$ paste deliveries items
Jan 12 99    shoes
Feb  3 99    socks
Dec 25 98    pants
$ paste items prices deliveries
shoes    12.90    Jan 12 99
socks    3.45     Feb  3 99
pants    19.95    Dec 25 98
$ _
```

It is easier to see what is happening than to explain the process formally. The merge is done horizontally, treating each line in each file as a column. Corresponding lines from each file are pasted with a tab as the column separator. The effect with two file arguments is a two-column output, three files give three columns, and so on. Compare this with `cat` where files are merged vertically:

```
$ cat items prices deliveries
shoes
socks
pants
```

```
12.  90
3.   45
19.  95
Jan 12 99
Feb  3 99
Dec 25 98
$ _
```

What happens with the three-column paste shown earlier is that each newline in the items and prices file is translated to tabs, while the newlines in the final file, deliveries, are output without change. This is the general plan for all multifile pastings: the final file argument "retains" its newlines; the earlier files undergo the newline to tab translation. (Of course, the files themselves are unchanged by paste.)

The conversion to tab characters by paste is the default. You can set a different insertion character by using the -dchar option. For example:

```
$ paste -d: items prices
shoes:12.90
socks:3.45
pants:19.95
$ paste -d' ' items prices
shoes 12.90
socks 3.45
pants 19.95
$ _
```

Again, the final file's newlines get through, but the earlier file's newlines are converted to *char*. As with cut, the *char* argument may need to be quoted to prevent misinterpretation by the shell. If in doubt, quote!

The *char* argument can actually contain a sequence of column separator characters, so the option is often written as -d*list*. The *list* can include the familiar escape sequences: \n (newline), \t (tab, the default), \\ (backslash), and \0 (empty string, i.e., no column separation). paste will grab a separating code from your -d*list* for each column to be merged. If it runs out of separator codes before all the columns are processed, paste cycles around the list again. Consider

```
$ paste -d'\t:' items prices deliveries
shoes    12.90:Jan 12 99
socks    3.45:Feb  3 99
pants    19.95:Dec 25 98
$_
```

Note carefully that the final newlines of deliveries are *not* involved in the translation. The newlines in items pick up '\t' (tab); the newlines in prices pick up the colon.

The -s (for subsequent) option drastically changes the pasting action and can be used with one or more file arguments. Here are two examples:

```
$ paste -s items
shoes    socks     pants
$ paste -s items prices
shoes    socks     pants    12.90   3.45    19.95
$ _
```

The -s option says paste together the lines from the given file or files. By default, tabs replace every newline except for the final newline of the final line in the final file. That's my final word.

paste sends its results to the standard output so redirection *to* a file or filter is very popular. Redirection in the other direction needs some care. Using paste on the right hand of a filter raises the same problem you saw with split. To get paste to accept standard input rather than file input, you must use – (dash) in lieu of a file argument. Consider

```
$ ls | paste - - -
assets.1    basis     bible
crafts.x    dtd.skb   eric.mail
...
$ _
```

Each – invokes a line from the output of ls and pastes the result with the default tab. Recall that the normal output from ls is a single column listing of the current directory.

THE FIND COMMAND

The find command turns out to be more versatile and useful than its mundane name might suggest. It certainly finds files and directories that match the usual wildcards (*, ?, and []), just like ls and its relatives. But find can also search for files that match more complex criteria such as time of last access, ownerships, permission flags settings, and file type. You can also combine such tests using logical NOT, AND, and OR operators. find's other claim to fame is that it can be set to perform arbitrary commands depending on the results of its search. The full syntax is quite complex, but the basic scheme is simple enough:

```
find pathname expression
```

find searches first for files in the directory given by *pathname*. If any subdirectories are encountered, these will also be searched, and so on for any subdirectories found (rather like the ls -R recursive descent option).

In other words, the whole subtree from *pathname* downward is searched. For example,

```
find . expression
```

will search your current directory (represented by the famous dot) together with its subdirectories, and so on down the tree. Replacing the dot with your home directory ($HOME) gives a search over your own neck of the woods: your home directory and everything below it. Using / (root) as the *pathname* argument will invoke a search of the entire hierarchy. You can also list several directories in the *pathname* argument (separated by spaces), and find will do the same "in depth" search of each, one by one.

The *expression* argument tells find what to look for, and what to do when a match is made. The *expression* argument consists of one or more *primary* expressions. Each primary expression returns a Boolean value: *true* for a match, *false* for a mismatch. Some expressions provide "actions" rather than "matches" and always return *true*. The final expression usually represents the action to be taken if the preceding primary expressions combine to give *true*. There are many different primary expressions, each with its own *raison d'être* and syntax. Most of these expressions take arguments, so find combines flexibility and complexity in the true Unix tradition. Here's a simple example:

```
$ pwd
/usr
$ find . -name "poem.?" -print
./stan/poem.1
./stan/poem.3
$ _
```

Here, find is looking for files in (or below) the current directory (which happens to be /usr) that match poem.?. We quote this expression because of the wildcard character: we want find to "see" the ?. If unquoted, the shell would interpret it first. Remember to quote any file arguments that contain *,? or [. The expression -print says display (send to the standard output) the path names of all matching files. The expression -name *filename* returns *true* for those files matching *filename*. You can add any number of tests to the list. Each test is logically AND'd in sequence, so the final action is invoked only if all the tests return *true*. No explicit AND operator is needed; you simply use spaces between tests, as shown in the following example:

```
$ find . -name "poem.?" -size +2 -print
./stan/poem.3
$ _
```

This lists only the files matching poem.? that have more than two blocks (a block being 512 bytes on most systems). Here we apply the test -size +2 to each file matching poem.?. The -size expression takes a numerical argument as follows:

size argument	Meaning
n	*True* if file has exactly *n* blocks
+n	*True* if file has more than *n* blocks
-n	*True* if file has fewer than *n* blocks

Remember this syntax: many other "magnitude" tests use the same trick.

You can redirect or pipe the output of find in the usual way:

```
$ find . -name "poem.?" -size +2 -print >$HOME/temp
$ cat $HOME/temp
./stan/poem.3
$ _
```

Tests can be logically OR'd using the -o operator, or logically reversed with the ! (bang) operator. The three logical operators, OR (-o), AND (implied by space), and NOT (!), can be combined in any way required provided that you observe their built-in precedences. NOT has the highest precedence, followed by AND, followed by OR. (I'll cover the concept of operator precedence in detail in Chapter 14. Briefly: higher precedence operators are applied before lower precedence operators.) To override the precedence rules, or simply as an aid to legibility, you use the *escaped* parentheses \(and \). For example,

```
$ find . \( -name "poem.?" -o -name "ode.?" \) -size +2 -print
./usr/mary/ode.5
./usr/stan/poem.3
$ _
```

If you don't hide the parentheses, the shell will interpret them in its own fashion, with unexpected effects (usually a syntax error). Recall that (*command_list*) tells the shell to invoke a subshell to perform the commands in *command_list*. If you use unescaped parentheses with find, the shell will try to interpret your Boolean expressions as commands.

If I had run the last example from the /usr/stan directory, the output would have been ./poem.3. In other words, find produces a path name relative to the current directory.

So far, we have simply displayed the matching path names using the -print expression. The -exec *command* [*args*] \; expression lets you execute any command (with any relevant options and arguments)

whenever a match is found. The syntax of -exec is a tad quirky, but the power of -exec is ample reward:

▶ The command must be terminated with a space followed by an escaped semicolon: \;.

▶ A special argument {} (two braces) is recognized by find as the name of the currently matching filename.

Consider the following example:

```
find / -exec ls -ld {} \;
```

Here we pass each file and directory in the system as an argument to ls -ld to give a long listing of the entire hierarchy. The next example,

```
find / -name "*.junk" -exec rm {} \;
```

removes the entries for *every* file in the system (directory write permissions allowing, of course) that matches *.junk. Each matching file is passed via the symbol pair {} as an argument to the rm command. Note that you are free to supply any valid options for the given command. For example, you could write -exec rm -f {} \;.

A useful variant on -exec is -ok. The syntax and action are identical, but -ok displays the command followed by a query mark, ?, and pauses for confirmation. If you respond with y, the command is executed; otherwise find moves on to the next file match and again seeks confirmation. For example,

```
$ find / -name "*.junk" -ok rm {} \;
rm ./usr/joe/old.junk ? y
rm ./usr/stan/new.junk ? n
$ _
```

A common use for find is the selective backing up of files. I'll discuss the why's and how's of backing up in Chapter 17. For now, note that find offers the following primary expressions that let you select files that have been accessed, modified, or created since the last backup.

-atime *n*   *True* if the file was last accessed exactly *n* days ago

-mtime *n*   *True* if the file was last modified exactly *n* days ago

-ctime *n*   *True* if the file was last created or modified exactly *n* days ago

Each of these timing tests takes a numerical argument representing a number of days. As with -size *n*, you can add a + or - in front of the number to modify the test. +*n* means "more than *n* days ago"; -*n* means "fewer than *n* days ago." If you back up weekly, say, the following command tells you which of your files have been created or modified since the last backup:

```
find $HOME -ctime -7 -print
```

You can restrict this selection to regular files (excluding special files and directories) by adding a `-type` expression:

```
find $HOME -ctime -7 -type f -print
```

`-type` takes a single-letter argument, as shown in Table 14.2, later in this chapter. Rather than just list the files or pipe them into some copying command, you can perform the backup within `find` as follows:

```
find $HOME -ctime -7 -type f -cpio /dev/tape
```

The `-cpio` expression takes a device argument: the special file representing the backup device where your data and programs are to be saved. This is usually a tape or floppy-disk drive. In Chapter 17, you'll meet the `cpio` command upon which the `-cpio` expression is based.

Another expression that's useful when backing up (and in many other situations) is `-newer`. As the name suggests, this lets you select the more recent version of two files:

```
find . -name "poem.?" -newer "poem.index" -print
```

Any files matching `poem.?` that have been modified more recently than `poem.index` will be displayed.

`find` can also select files that belong to a given user or group:

```
find / -user "stan" -print
find / -user 25 -print
find / -group "sys" -print
```

These lines will display all files owned by `stan`; all files owned by user id 25; and all files belonging to the group `sys`. `-user` takes either a login name or a user id argument. `-group` takes either a group name or a group id argument. Since it is *possible* (but undesirable) that login and group names can be numeric, `find` checks all `-user` and `-group` arguments against the names stored in `/etc/passwd` and `/etc/group`, respectively. If the argument is numeric and not found as a name, `find` then checks for an id match.

The `-perm` expression lets you select files that have certain permissions set. The argument used is the octal permission mode that I explained in Chapter 7. The following line,

```
find / -type f -perm 0744 -print
```

will display all regular files that have `-rwxr--r--` set in the permissions field. Recall that octal 744 can be written in binary as

```
(111)(100)(100)
```

whence the mapping to

(rwx)(r–)(r–)

NOTE

A trick is available for testing the full internal mode used to encode the file type, the owner/group/others permissions, and several special modes such as setuid (set user id), setgid (set group id), and file locking and sticky bits. If you write –perm –*mode*, *mode* can include the following values:

```
0010000  fifo special
0020000  character special file
0040000  directory
0060000  block special file
0100000  regular file
0000000  regular file
0004000  set user id on execution
00020#0  set group id on execution if # is 7,
         5, 3, or 1;
         enable mandatory file/record lock if
         # is 6, 4, 2, or 0
0001000  set sticky bit (save text image after execution)
```

in addition to the usual 000 to 777 owner/group/others permissions.

Table 13.2 summarizes the more useful primary expressions available with find.

TABLE 13.2: Primary Expressions Available with find

Expression	Action or Return Value
-atime n	*True* if the file was last accessed exactly *n* days ago.
-atime +n	*True* if the file was last accessed more than *n* days ago.
-atime −n	*True* if the file was last accessed fewer than *n* days ago.
-cpio *dev*	Back up the current file to the device *dev*. Always returns *true*.
-ctime n	*True* if the file was last changed exactly *n* days ago.
-ctime +n	*True* if the file was last changed more than *n* days ago (changed means created or modified).
-ctime −n	*True* if the file was last changed fewer than *n* days ago (changed means created or modified).
-exec *command* \;	Executes command. Returns *true* if *command* returns a zero exit status (success); otherwise returns *false*.
-exec *command* {} \;	As above, but {} is replaced by the matching path name.

TABLE 13.2 continued Primary Expressions Available with find

EXPRESSION	ACTION OR RETURN VALUE
-links *n*	*True* if the file has exactly *n* links.
-links +*n*	*True* if the file has more than *n* links.
-links −*n*	*True* if the file has fewer than *n* links.
-mtime *n*	*True* if the file was last modified exactly *n* days ago.
-mtime +*n*	*True* if the file was last modified more than *n* days ago.
-mtime −*n*	*True* if the file was last modified fewer than *n* days ago.
-newer *file*	*True* if the current path name is newer (modified more recently) than *file*.
-name *file*	*True* if *file* matches a filename (wildcard characters must be quoted).
-ok *command* \;	Displays command followed by ?, and awaits confirming y before execution. Returns *true* if *command* returns a zero exit status (success); otherwise returns *false*.
-ok *command* { } \;	As above, but { } is replaced by the matching path name.
-perm *oct_mode*	*True* if the permission flags of the current file match the octal mode given by *oct_mode* (see Chapter 7).
-perm -*oct_mode*	*True* if the full internal mode of the current file matches *oct_mode*.
-print	Sends current matched path name to standard output. Always returns *true*.
-size *n*	*True* if the file is exactly *n* blocks long ($n \times 512$ bytes).
-size +*n*	*True* if the file is more than *n* blocks long ($n \times 512$ bytes).
-size −*n*	*True* if the file is fewer than *n* blocks long ($n \times 512$ bytes).
-type *t*	*True* if the file type matches the *t* argument. File types are: F regular file D directory B block I/O device file C character I/O device file P named pipe (Note that these letters match the first character in the permissions field, as shown by ls -l, apart from f. As you saw in Chapter 4, ls -l shows - for a regular file.)
-user *uname*	*True* if file is owned by *uname*. (If *uname* is numeric and does not match a login name in /etc/passwd, find treats it as a user id.)
-group *gname*	*True* if file belongs to group *gname*. (If *gname* is numeric and does not match a group name in /etc/group, find treats it as a group id.)

THE TR COMMAND

The tr (translate) command is a simple but worthwhile filter designed to replace one or more characters in your files with one or more other characters. The syntax is

```
tr [-cds] [in_string] [out_string]
```

The -s option substitutes all of the specified characters with another character specified character and displays the results. For example, initially the list in the file items looks like this:

```
$ cat items
shoes
socks
pants
```

To substitute "z"'s for all the "s"'s, for example, you would enter this:

```
$ tr s z <items
zhoez
zockz
pantz
```

The -d option deletes characters you specify from your file and displays the results. So, to delete all of the "s"'s, you'd enter this:

```
$ tr -d  s < items
hoe
ock
pant
```

The -c option tells tr not to match the specified characters. It is used with the -s and -d options to modify the way that those options operate. For example, in the list below (we'll use items once again) we want to delete all of the characters except the "s"'s:

```
$ tr -cd  s < items
ss
ss
s
```

Without any options, tr does a straight substitution. For example, using our laundry list, items, we can do a simple substitution like this:

```
$ tr o ' ' <items
sh es
s cks
pants
$ _
```

In this example, all of the "o"'s are replaced with spaces. Notice that you have to put single quotes around the space so tr recognizes the space as a substitution character, not just a delimiter. And, by the way, there are other characters that have actual meanings in Unix too, and these characters also need to be quoted if you want to use them as replacements:

; & () | ^ < >newline, and tab

You can also express both printable and nonprintable characters in either string using escape sequences with the octal ASCII value of the character. The table below shows the octal values of the most common control characters:

Character	Escape Sequence
Bell	'\07'
Backspace	'\010'
CR	'\015'
Escape	'\033'
Formfeed	'\014'
LF, Newline	'\012'
Tab	'\011'

The leading zeros are optional but recommended because of the C language rules for octal numbers that are also required in many Unix commands. For example, the expression [x*n] is used in tr to represent a string with *n* repetitions of x. If *n* is written as 10 you'll get ten x's, but if you write 010, only eight are formed because 010 is eight in octal!

For those characters that may confuse the shell, you must either quote or escape them with \: '&' '(' ')' '|' '^' '<' '>' '[' ']' and '\', or \& \(\) \| \^ \< \> \[\] and \\.

You can also use ranges of characters in your arguments for tr; for example, to change all of the lowercase characters to uppercase, you could enter:

```
$ tr '[a-z]' '[A-Z]' <items
SHOES
SOCKS
PANTS
```

THE dd COMMAND

The dd command is used for both copying and converting different files and media. The syntax is as follows:

    dd [option1=value1] [option2 =value2] …

For example, to convert all of the characters in items from lowercase to uppercase, you would enter:

    $ dd if=items of=itemsu conv=ucase
    SHOES
    SOCKS
    PANTS
    $

Table 13.3 lists many of the options available to you.

TABLE 13.3: Common dd Options

dd OPTION	VALUE
if= (input file)	Input filename (default is standard input).
of= (output file)	Output filename (default is standard output).
ibs= (i/p block size)	Number of bytes in input block:
	nk means $n \times 1024$ bytes.
	nb means $n \times 512$ bytes.
	nw means $n \times 2$ bytes.
obs= (o/p block size)	Number of bytes in output block.
bs= (i/p and o/p block size)	Number of bytes in input and output blocks.
skip=	Number of i/p records to be skipped before conversion or copying starts.
conv=	ascii converts EBCDIC to ASCII.
	ebcdic converts ASCII to EBCDIC.
	lcase converts to lowercase.
	ucase converts to uppercase.
	swab swaps pairs of bytes.
	Several conv values can be supplied separated by commas, e.g., conv=ascii,ucase.

PUTTING IT ALL TOGETHER

Perhaps we should pause here and take stock. I've thrown a whole slew of commands at you with short, illustrative examples. It might be helpful to see how these commands can be combined to perform more useful work. Unix, as you've seen, encourages you to combine simple commands by means of the filter and pipe mechanism. With these, the output of one command can be fed into another, and so on through a long chain of filters until the desired result emerges. Knowing which filters and options to use requires practice. Let's "walk through" a real problem so you can see how this might work.

In this exercise, we're going to determine the most frequently used words in a text file. To begin with, we need to separate the words so each word sits on its own line. What is a word? Consider the following text:

```
"What is Life?<tab>Perhaps,we will never know what life is!"
```

Certainly, spaces delimit words, but we do not want "Life?", "Perhaps,we", and "is!" to count as words. So first we need to convert any sequence of nonletters, such as spaces, tabs, and punctuation marks, into single newlines. To do this, we'll use the `tr` filter along with the `-s` option to squeeze out duplicates, and the `-c` (complement) option, since we are looking for *non*alphabetic characters:

```
tr -sc '[A-Z][a-z]' '[\012*]' <inf >outf1
```

The *in_string* (`[A-Z][a-z]`) selects all the alpha characters, both upper- and lowercase. The `-c` reverses the match to indicate all nonalpha characters.

The *out_string* is the newline, `'\012'` (the `*` tells the command to match every occurrence as necessary to match each character in the *in_string*). So, every nonalpha character in `inf` will be changed to a newline. The `-s` option ensures that multiple newlines are squeezed down to a single newline. Applying our `tr` filter will give us an `outf1` file like this:

```
What
is
Life
Perhaps
we
will
never
know
```

```
what
life
is
```

Are we going to treat "What" and "what", and "Life" and "life" as different words? If not, we'll need another tr pass to remove any case sensitivity:

```
tr '[A-Z]' '[a-z]' <outf1 >outf2
```

Now we have

```
what
is
life
perhaps
we
will
never
know
what
life
is
```

Later, of course, we aim to pipe these elements to avoid the intermediate files. The next step must be to sort outf2 to bring together occurrences of the same word:

```
sort <outf2 >outf3
```

outf3 now gives us:

```
is
is
know
life
life
never
perhaps
we
what
what
will
```

Next we bring in uniq -c to filter out multiple occurrences and give us a count of each word:

```
uniq -c <outf3 >outf4
```

outf4 now contains

```
2 is
1 know
2 life
```

```
1 never
1 perhaps
1 we
2 what
1 will
```

We can now sort again, reverse numerically on the first field, alphabetically (ascending) on the second field to give us a list by decreasing frequency:

```
sort +0 -1nr +1 -2 outf4 >outf5
```

We now have the required output in outf5:

```
2 is
2 life
2 what
1 know
1 never
1 perhaps
1 we
1 will
```

To limit the output to the *n* most frequently used words, we can tag on a final head filter:

```
head -n outf5 >outf6
```

Omitting the *n* option gives a default of the ten most frequent words. Putting all this together, and setting *n* to 20, we have the sequence,

```
tr -sc '[A-Z][a-z]' '[\012*]' <inf >outf1
tr '[A-Z]' '[a-z]' <outf1 >outf2
sort <outf2 >outf3
uniq -c <outf3 >outf4
sort +0 -1nr +1 -2 outf4 >outf5
head -20 outf5 >outf6
```

Piping the commands avoids the need for all the intermediate named files:

```
tr -sc '[A-Z][a-z]' '[\012*]' <inf |
tr '[A-Z]' '[a-z]' |
sort |
uniq -c |
sort +0 -1nr +1 -2 |
head -20 >outf
```

You can enter each line as shown. The final | on each line will invoke the secondary prompt >, at which point you enter the next command line. Alternatively, you can submit one long line via the keyboard. Long lines like this, exceeding the normal 80-character screen width, are rather awkward, so it's useful to break up the line with the continuation escape character \ followed by newline (Enter). The \ hides the newline from the shell, so you won't get a secondary prompt:

```
tr -sc '[A-Z][a-z]' '[\012*]' <inf | \
tr '[A-Z]' '[a-z]' | sort | uniq -c | \
sort +0 -1nr +1 -2 | head -20 >outf
```

Better still, you can save the whole sequence in a shell script. Let's call the script lwf (list word frequency) in keeping with the Unix penchant for obscure acronymy. lwf would be quite restrictive in the above listed format: it would work only on the files inf and outf for a fixed value of *n*! You can easily make lwf more popular by replacing inf with $1, -*n* by $2, and outf by $3:

```
$ cat lwf
:
# @(#)lwf-list word frequency-skb 3/16/95
#
# usage lwf in_file [-number] [out_file]
#
tr -sc '[A-Z][a-z]' '[\012*]' <$1 | \
tr '[A-Z]' '[a-z]' | sort | uniq -c | \
sort +0 -1nr +1 -2 | head $2 >$3
$ _
```

If you want to use this script, remember to set execution permission with chmod u+x lwf. You will recall that the positional parameters, $1, $2,..., are set by the arguments supplied to the script command. So,

```
$ lwf stan.poem -30 stan.lwf
```

would find the 30 most frequent words in stan.poem and record the list in stan.lwf.

What's Next?

In the next chapter, we'll look at three of the most useful utility programs that are standard in Unix: grep, sed and awk. grep is a file-finding program. If you are searching for a file but can't remember its name, grep is for you. sed and awk are text processing programs with their own special capabilities, but rather than go into that here, turn the page and read on....

```
echo "2.      Show Date"
echo "3.      Display a file"
echo "4.      Change working directo
echo "5.      Return to original dire
echo "Q.      Quit
echo
echo -n "Enter choice: .\b"
read choice
case $choice in
1) who | more
   pause;;
2) date
   pause;;
3) echo "Enter file name: \c"
   read fil
   if [ -r "$fil" -a -f "$fil" ]
   then
      clear
      more -d $fil
   else
      echo "Cannot di
   fi
   pause;;
4) echo "Enter target d
   read di
   if test      d "$(dir:  pwd`
   then
      cd $dir
   else
      echo "$dir: no such di
   fi
   pause;;
5) if test "$dir" != "$p
   then
      cd $prevdir
   fi
   pause;;
```

Chapter 14

GREPPING, SEDDING, AND A LITTLE AWKING

The three commands grep, sed, and awk have a common theme: they all scan text files. They differ greatly, however, in complexity. grep, the pattern searcher, is the simplest. Next comes sed, a stream editor that can search for patterns and edit files. Finally, awk is a fully-loaded pattern processing language with flow control and arithmetic operators. The fact is, you can use sed to perform nearly every grep operation, and you can use awk to do almost everything that grep and sed do. So why are grep and sed still around? Mostly it's because file searches for a given string or pattern are commonly needed and grep and sed offer a simpler syntax than awk, dedicated to accomplishing just those tasks.

THE GREP FAMILY

The grep command, originally devised by Doug McIlroy, stands for "**g**lobal **r**egular **e**xpression **p**rint." There are two variants, egrep and fgrep, hence my reference to the grep *family*. We'll describe the standard grep first, then list the family variations.

grep is the cure for those frustrating moments when you cannot recall which files contain what. For example, let's say you wrote several memos last month about office equipment maintenance. Which of them covered the copier contracts? All you need is the command

```
grep -l copier memo.*
```

and the names of all memo files in your current directory that contain the word "copier" will be displayed. Without the -l option, you also get the lines displayed that contain the target string.

grep searches for those files that contain matches for the given pattern. Options are available to control the amount of data that displays when a match is found. The basic syntax is

```
grep [options] [-e] 'pattern' [filenames] [>out_file]
```

The optional *filenames* argument is a list of files (separated by spaces) that grep will search for the given *pattern* argument. The *pattern* argument is usually quoted as shown—I'll explain when and why in a moment. If *filenames* is missing, grep will scan your standard input. Of course, it is rarely useful to grep your own keyboard input! What is common, though, is to pipe the output of other commands into grep. You can even grep the output from another grep.

The output from grep can be redirected, as indicated, or piped to other commands in the usual way. Remember that the shell will expand any wildcard characters (* and ?) in the *filenames* argument and apply grep to the resulting list of files.

Normally, if you are searching a single file, grep will output each line that contains a match with the given pattern:

```
$ cat hamlet
To be or not to be,
That is the question.
Or maybe not

$ grep 'or' hamlet
To be or not to be,
```

```
$ grep 'T' hamlet
To be or not to be,
That is the question.

$ grep Guildenstern hamlet
$ _
```

The search patterns `'or'` and `'T'` precede the filename hamlet. Note that a matching line appears once even if the pattern occurs more than once in that line.

NOTE

If you are grepping several files, the filename will be displayed before each match. You can suppress this filename display by using the -h option.

Quoting the Search Pattern

The single (forward) quotes around the search pattern are not essential in the previous example, but using them is a good idea since your patterns may contain symbols that would otherwise be interpreted as extra commands or options by the shell.

If your search pattern contains spaces or tabs, you must definitely quote the pattern like this:

```
$ grep or not hamlet
grep: cannot open not

$ grep 'or not' hamlet
To be or not to be,
```

In the first attempt, grep takes not as a filename. As luck would have it, no such file was found!

Word Searches and the -w Option

Matches are made without regard to word boundaries, so that `'or'` would match "for" and "oregano". To get a "word-only" search, you can try `' or '` with surrounding spaces, but this would miss the word "or" in some contexts. Some grep implementations provide the -w (word) option to overcome these problems. This is a good moment to warn you that implementations vary somewhat in the options provided with grep, so take care!

Case-Sensitive Searches

Note that the match is usually case-sensitive, so that 'or' did not match the "Or" in line 3 of hamlet. Similarly, 'T' did not match the "t" in the final "not". You can make the search case-insensitive with the -y or -i options. The -i (ignore case) option is the better one to use if you have it. The -y option on some older systems must be used with care. It takes lowercase letters in the pattern and matches them with lower- or upper-case versions of those letters. However, in some early versions of grep, uppercase letters in the pattern match only uppercase letters in the file even if you use -y. (There may also be problems using -y with range patterns such as [a-z].) The good news is that most current versions of grep have a -y option that works sensibly with uppercase characters in the pattern. More recent versions of grep offer the -i option, which gives completely case-insensitive matching: both 'Y' and 'y' will match both "Y" and "y". Experiment to see how your grep behaves. Here are some examples:

```
$ grep -y 'or' hamlet
To be or not to be,
Or maybe not
```

```
$ grep -i 'T' hamlet
To be or not to be,
That is the question.
Or maybe not
```

You can also use regular expressions to achieve case-insensitivity:

```
$ grep '[Oo]r' hamlet
To be or not to be,
Or maybe not
```

```
$ grep '[Tt]' hamlet
To be or not to be,
That is the question.
Or maybe not
```

The expression [Oo] matches either of the characters inside the brackets.

The -n Option

With the -n option, you also get the line number of the matching line:

```
$ grep -n 'or' hamlet
1:To be or not to be,
```

```
$ grep -in 'T' hamlet
1:To be or not to be,
2:That is the question.
3:Or maybe not
```

Note that options can be written separately: -i -n, or together, in any order: -ni.

The -h Option

You can grep several files with a single command,

```
$ grep 'or' hamlet lear
hamlet:To be or not to be,
lear: 'Faith, once or twice she heaved
```

by simply listing the filenames after the pattern. Note again that grep now helpfully reports the name of the file where the match was found. If you don't want the filenames displayed, the -h option will suppress them:

```
$ grep -h 'or' hamlet lear
To be or not to be,
'Faith, once or twice she heaved
```

If you call for line numbers, they appear after the filename:

```
$ grep -n 'or' hamlet lear
hamlet:1:To be or not to be,
lear:43: 'Faith, once or twice she heaved
```

You can also combine -h and -n if you wish:

```
$ grep -hn 'or' hamlet lear
1:To be or not to be,
43: 'Faith, once or twice she heaved
```

The -c Option

If you just want to count the number of matching lines without seeing them, use the -c option:

```
$ grep -ic 'T' hamlet
3
```

The -v Option

The -v option displays the lines that do *not* match the search pattern. For example, if the file payables has line entries with customer, amount, due date, and a string that either says Paid or " " (blank) depending on the status, you could run the following command:

```
$ grep -vi 'Paid' payables
```

```
Smith $450.12 09/12/95
Jones $ 78.89 08/12/95
```

The -b Option

The grep -b option has no immediate equivalent in sed or awk. It displays the disk block number of each matching line:

```
$ grep -b 'or' lear
3: 'Faith, once or twice she heaved
```

This is often useful for service and diagnostic work.

The -l Option

The -l option displays only the names of the files where matching lines are found; the lines themselves are suppressed:

```
$ grep -l 'or' hamlet lear
hamlet
lear
```

The -e Option

The -e option is useful when the search pattern begins with a hyphen. You can imagine the confusion if you want to search for the string "-n", say. Writing grep -n *file* is not going to do the job. And neither will grep '-n' *file* or grep "-n" *file* since '-n' and "-n" still look like an option to grep. The solution is grep -e -n *file*. The -e warns grep that the next string is to be taken as the pattern even though it looks like an option. The -e must come immediately before the pattern and after any other options. grep -e -ni -n *file* is an error (grep will look for a file named -n!). The correct form is grep -ni -e -n *file* (search for "-N" and "-n" and show line numbers).

The -s Option

The -s option suppresses the error messages that grep will normally display if the file arguments are faulty. For example, a file might not be found, or if found, you might not have read permission. In shell scripts, these messages are often a nuisance that the -s option can circumvent.

REGULAR EXPRESSIONS

Regular expressions are special strings of characters that you create in order to locate *matching* pieces of text. The principle extends (and modifies) the familiar idea of wildcard symbols to include quite complex matching possibilities.

A regular expression is a sequence of ordinary (or nonspecial) characters and special characters (also known as metacharacters).

You have already seen how the shell treats certain characters such as *, ?, and > as special. However, grep's special characters have their own flavor, so some care is needed. For example, some characters are special to grep only in certain contexts, and the meaning of a special character can vary according to its context!

The characters that grep's regular expressions may treat as special are \ ^ $. [ ] * and &, plus the pairs \(\) \{ \} and [: :].

You use these characters in combination with ordinary text strings in order to search your files for matches. When a match is found, grep allows you to perform any number of editing functions using the g (global) command. Before I show you the g command in action, I need to show you how to construct a regular expression. The best approach is to study some annotated examples:

Dear   Matches "Dear" anywhere in the file

^Dear   Matches "Dear" only at the *start* of any line

The ^ has two special meanings. As the first symbol inside [ ], it means NOT (that is, it reverses the sense of the match)—more on this usage later. If the ^ symbol appears anywhere after the first position inside [ ], it has no special meaning. Used outside [ ], ^ means "try to match the following text at the beginning of a line." If you need to search for a literal ^, you can "turn off" (or *escape*) the special meaning with the escape symbol \: \^Dear matches "^Dear" anywhere in the file. This is a general rule: a special symbol placed immediately after \ loses its special meaning. This rule is particularly important because of the large number of special characters used in grep. Later examples will clarify this point.

Similarly, $ means "match the preceding text at the end of line." For instance, sincerely$ matches "sincerely" only at the *end* of any line. Again, note that $ loses its special "end-of-line match" meaning when used inside [ ], or when escaped: sincerely\$ matches "sincerely$" anywhere in the file.

You can combine ^ and $ as follows: ^contents$ matches any line containing the string "contents" at both the start and end of a line. A useful variant is ^$, which matches any empty line (one with a newline only). There is, by the way, no regular expression that matches a newline character.

The next two examples show the escape mechanism at work:

\^\$ Matches "^$"

\\   Matches "\"

The period has yet another meaning in `grep`! In regular expressions, a period outside [ ] matches any single character:

i.m   Matches "iAm", "ibm", "i m", and so on, but NOT "i<newline>m"

i\.m   Matches "i.m" only

i?m   Matches "i?m" only

Note carefully that the wildcard, ?, used by the shell to match any single character, has a different application in `grep`'s regular expressions. The period in `grep`'s regular expressions works just like the ? in shell commands. `grep` uses the ? either as a normal character or to control backward searches (as you saw earlier).

The behavior of the wildcard asterisk, *, is also different when you move from shell commands to `grep`'s regular expressions. First, note that `grep`'s * is treated as a special character only when it is used outside [ ]. Second, recall that the shell matches a * with any string including the empty string (but excluding file names beginning with a period).

However, with `grep`, the regular expression x* (where x is any single-character regular expression) matches any number of occurrences of x including *none*. In other words, x* matches the empty string, x, xx, xxx, and so on. This takes some getting used to, especially if you've spent too many years with MS-DOS. Note the following example: HEL* matches "HE", "HEL", "HELL", "HELLL", and so on. The first match seems weird! But HEL* matches "HE" followed by *no* occurrences of "L". With MS-DOS, HEL* would not match "HE". DOS would certainly match "HEL", "HELL", and so on, but, unlike `grep`, it would also match "HELP", "HELxyz", and so on.

To obtain a DOS-like * match, you need the following combination:

.*

matches any string not containing a newline (so it also matches the empty string). The dot will match any single character, but with the modifying *, the match is with any number of any characters, including none. In this example, a.*S matches "aS", "aRubbishS", and so on. The only character between "a" and "S" that would escape a match is a newline. `grep`, recall, is a line-based editor, so a regular expression never "straddles" a line.

I've mentioned that ^ $. and * have special meanings only when used outside [ ] and without a preceding \. The reason is that characters inside [ ] are interpreted differently. Consider the following examples:

[35Z]	Matches "3", "5", or "Z"
X-[180]	Matches "X-1", "X-8", or "X-0"
Q[.21]p	Matches "Q.p", "Q2p", or "Q1p"
[m^*$]	Matches "m", "^", "*", or "$"

The idea is that a match is made with any *one* of the characters found inside the square brackets. A period or $ anywhere inside [ ] are taken as normal symbols. ^ and * are also taken literally *unless* they are the *first* characters after the [. When these two symbols occur first inside [ ], the search is logically inverted:

i[^b]m	Matches "iam", "i9m", and so on but does not match "ibm"
i[*b]m	Same as i[^b]m
i[^bc]m	Matches all "I-m" combinations except "ibm" and "icm"

If you are seeking a match with a range of ASCII characters, you can spell them out in full, or to save keystrokes, you can use the dash (-) to form a *range:*

[123456]	Matches "1", "2", <F128>£ <F255>or "6"
[1-6]	Matches "1", "2", <F128P255>£ <F255>or "6"

The dash trick only works with symbols in ascending ASCII sequence:

[a-z]	Matches any lowercase letter
[a-A]	Illegal, since "a" follows "A" in ASCII value
[9-<]	Matches "9", ":", "=", and "<"

You can include any number of ranges within [ ], and you can also combine ranges with the ^ symbol:

[A-C0-2]	Matches any string starting with "A", "B", "C", "0", "1", or "2"
[^0123456789]	Matches any nondigit
[^0-9]	Same as [^0123456789]

The next examples show how to find -, [, or] in a range of characters:

`[ ]0-2]`	Matches "]", "0", "1", or "2". (The first] immediately after the space [is treated as nonspecial.)
`A[-0-2]`	Matches "A-", "A0", "A1", or "A2". (The - immediately after [loses its special meaning.)
`A[^-0-2]`	Matches "A" followed by any character other than "-", "0", "1", "2", or newline. (The - immediately after [^ loses its special meaning.)
`array[02-4]\[[^0-3]\]`	Matches "array0[6]", "array4[Z]", and so on. (The second [and third] are taken literally because of \.)
`^["(][Tt].*["])]$`	Matches any line that starts with a quote mark or an open parenthesis followed by a "T" or "t", and ends with a quote mark or a close parenthesis.

Having seen how regular expressions are formed and how they match text strings, it's time to apply them in typical editing situations. First, let's look again at the s (substitute) command.

Substitute Command Revisited

Recall the syntax of the s command:

```
[s1_address,s2_address]s/find_exp/repl_exp/[g | N]
```

In our first explanation, find_exp was a simple piece of text that needed replacement; for instance, 1,$s/sun/moon/g replaces all occurrences of "sun" with "moon" in all lines.

I can now confirm that s works with regular expressions in the find_exp fields. The find string "sun" is in fact a very simple regular expression with no special effects. The replacement string, repl_exp, however, can not be a regular expression. repl_exp allows the special use of &, as explained earlier. Here's an example that should clarify this:

```
1,$s/sun/& and moon/g
```

The expression above replaces all occurrences of "sun" with "sun and moon" in all lines. The & in this command line is set to equal the matched find_exp. The &, of course, is not that useful in the above example, since we know in advance that it will set to "sun" if any matches occur. But suppose you had this command line:

```
1,$s/Ch[1-9]/& Appendix/g
```

This replaces "Ch*n*" with "Ch*n* Appendix" for *n* = 1–9. Here the & string assumes different (and appropriate) values for each match. The regular expression [1-9] matches any one numeral from 1 to 9. With this and similar tricks, you can make quite sophisticated, selective text substitutions.

Even more flexibility is available using the g and G (global) commands, and their "inverses" v and V. Read on.

Global Commands

The g (global) command has the following syntax:

```
[s1_address,s2_address]g/reg_exp/[command_list]
```

Briefly, the command means: "Find each line that contains a match for reg_exp, and perform command_list on it."

Unlike the s command (which defaults to . , .), the default address range argument for g is 1, $ —the whole buffer. The g command, like s, searches the address range (from low to high line numbers) seeking matches with the regular expression given in reg_exp. For each line providing a match, the dot value is set to that line; then g performs whatever grep commands are listed in the final argument, command_list. If you omit this list, a p (display) command is assumed.

The direction of search is controlled by the choice of the character (known as the *delimiter*) used to surround the reg_exp. In the last example, we used / to give us a *forward* search from the line following the current line toward the end of the file; if required by the address range, the search will wrap around to the start of the buffer and continue to the current line. This ensures that a 1, $ search, for example, will scan the whole buffer. For a backward search, you use ? in place of /:

```
[s1_address,s2_address]g? reg_exp?[ command_list]
```

Here, the search starts with the line preceding the current line, moves to the start of the buffer, then wraps around to the end (if necessary) to complete its scan at the current line.

In a typical application, the command_list would contain p, d, m, t, or s commands, so that displays, deletions, moves, transfers, and substitutions are made only on lines that meet certain criteria determined by reg_exp.

For example, g/^Para/s/;/:/gp will replace every ";" with ":" on every line that begins with "Para". The p ensures that you see what is going on.

A useful construct, similar to the & used in the repl_exp, is the special (and rather strange) *null* regular expression, //. As you saw briefly in the "Patterns and Searches" section, this is interpreted as the most recently "remembered" matching pattern. For complex regular expressions, this can be a great time-saver:

```
g/^Para[0-9]$/s//New Heading/p
```

The substitution find expression will be taken as /^Para[0-9]$/. You must not confuse the regular expression // with the empty replacement string //:

```
g/^Para[0-9]$/s///p
```

Here we are replacing the matched lines ("Para0", "Para1",<F128>£< F255%2>, or "Para9" on a single line) with empty lines.

The g command command_list can contain any number of grep commands, including a, i, and c but not !, g, G, v, or V. Each command except the last one has to end with a \ (here used as the traditional Unix command line "extender"—you can picture it as "escaping" the following newline character):

```
g/^Para[0-9]$/d\
```

deletes matching lines.

```
r file1\
```

reads in a file.

```
a\
```

appends text; then after text is entered, followed by a dot,

```
p
```

displays the last line read.

The G version of the global command works like g with one essential difference: after finding a match, the command waits for a command to be entered via the keyboard. G is therefore called the *interactive* global command. Only one manual command may be entered, but (unlike g) a, i, and c are not allowed. You can interrupt the G command with the Del key.

Inverse Global Commands

The v and V commands work like g and G but with the pattern-matching logic reversed. Let's look at an example:

```
v/^Para[0-9]$/s/Old Heading/New Heading/p
```

Here the substitution would be made on every line that did *not* match /^Para[0-9]$/. As you can guess, some care is needed with this one! Apart from the inverted matching search, the same rules and restrictions noted for g and G apply.

The dot

Outside a [*xxx*] pattern, the dot (period) matches any single character, so that .ust matches "dust", "must", and so on. Inside a [*xxx*] pattern, the dot loses its metacharacteristic and matches a literal ".".

^ and $

The metacharacters ^ and $ usually limit the matches to the beginning and end of a line. As with the dot, exceptions occur when ^ and $ appear inside [*xxx*] patterns; I'll cover these later.

```
$ grep -i '^or' hamlet
Or maybe not
$ grep 'not$' hamlet
Or maybe not
$ _
```

Here, '^or' matches only the leading "Or", and 'not$' matches only the final "not". Recall, too, the useful pattern '^xxx$', which will match a line containing the single string "xxx". The '^$' pattern matches only blank lines, characterized by successive newlines. As with grep, however, there is no regular expression that directly matches the newline character (so you cannot use grep '\n' *file*, for example).

The *

The pattern 'r*' matches zero or more occurrences of any regular expression r. The pattern '.*' therefore matches any sequence of characters, including the empty sequence. The pattern '..*' matches any nonempty string. These turn out to be more promising than might appear at first sight! Consider the following:

```
$ ls -1 | grep '^d..*stan. '
drwxrwxrwx   3 stan1 group   272 Nov 15 1995 stan1
drwxrwxrwx   3 stan2 accnt   678 Nov 25 1995 stan2
$ _
```

The output from ls -1 (namely the fully listed contents of the current directory—excluding dot files) is piped into grep. The ^d restricts the search to the subdirectories (all lines starting with "d"). grep then matches lines that contain "stan" followed by a single character followed by a space. The `..*` matches all the rubbish between "d" and "stan". (This is a rather artificial example, since you could use the `-ld` option to list just the subdirectories.)

You could achieve a similar goal with two `grep`s:

```
$ ls -l | grep '^d' | grep 'stan. '
drwxrwxrwx    3    stan1  group    272 Nov 15 1995 stan1
drwxrwxrwx    3    stan2  accnt    678 Nov 25 1995 stan2
$ _
```

Grepping the piped output from commands such as `ls` and `who` is quite common. The line

```
ls -l | grep '^-..*\.mail$'
```

will match all filenames (excluding dot files and directories) ending with `.mail`. The initial "-" in the permissions field matches `^-`, indicating a file. Note the essential `\` used to escape the final period. We want to match a *real* dot! Without the `\`, `grep` would treat the period as a metacharacter matching any single character. The final `$` returns matches at the end of the line. To check if Mary is logged in, you can `grep` the output of `who`:

```
$ who | grep 'mary'
mary     tty2      Oct 15 12:32
$ _
```

The absence of a response would indicate that Mary is not logged in.

Regular expressions with [ ]

The expression `'[abc]'` matches any one of "a", "b", or "c". Ranges are allowed: `'[0-5]'` matches any single digit from "0" to "5". You can combine regular expressions: `'[A-E]8[0-2]Z'` will match "B81Z", "D80Z", and so on.

Inside the brackets `[]` some metacharacters may have different meanings, and some resume their literal meanings! The dot and `$` are taken literally inside `[]`: `'[.*]'` matches "." and "*".

A `[` inside `[]` is also taken literally: So `'[a[]'` will match "a" and "[". To match a "]", however, you must escape it because `grep` will otherwise interpret the first closed brackets as the end of the expression. So `'[a\]]'` will match "a" and "]".

A leading `^` inside `[]` means reverse the sense of the match. Thus `'[a-m]'` matches any single character in the alphabetic range from "a" to "m", while `'[^a-m]'` matches any single character *not* in the range "a" to "m". The latter includes "n" to "z", of course, but also includes "A" to "Z" and many other characters! In other positions within [], the ^ is taken literally: '[a^]' will match "a" and "^".

Tagged Regular Expressions

Tagged regular expressions let you search for quite complex patterns that depend on parts of the text that have already been matched. You tag a regular expression by surrounding it with the symbols \(and \). Each such expression encountered in a pattern, from left to right, is assigned an internal register number, starting at 1 and increasing up to a maximum of 9. The characters matched with the nth tagged expression are stored in the nth register. Its contents can be referred to anywhere in the pattern using the sequence \n.

Consider the pattern '\([a-c]\)x\1', which has just one tagged expression, namely [a-c]. The sequence \1 will be replaced by whatever matches [a-c], so the whole pattern will match "axa", "bxb", and "cxc". In other words, the expression has the same function as [a-c] x [a-c].

The pattern

```
'\([a-c]\)\([d-f]\)x\2\1'
```

has two tagged expressions. \1 represents the [a-c] match, as before, and \2 represents the [d-f] match. This pattern therefore matches "adxda", "aexea", "afxfa", "bdxdb", "bexeb", and so on (a total of nine such strings). Replacing x with . and extending the ranges lets you search for five-letter palindromes (words like "radar" that are spelled the same in either direction):

```
grep -iw '\([a-z]\)\([a-z]\).\2\1' dictionary
```

A six-character palindrome would be detected by the following:

```
grep -iw '\(.\)\(.\)\(.\)\3\2\1' dictionary
```

Here we would match sequences such as "*&!!&*" as well as the more familiar palindromes.

A more practical example would be searching for any repeated adjacent strings to trap common typing errors such as "the the". Consider:

```
grep -i '\(..*\) \1' essay
```

The tagged expression ..* matches any string with at least one character. The whole pattern therefore matches "xxxx xxxx" and so on. Note that the expression \n can be used anywhere in the pattern, even before the nth tagged expression occurs. For example,

```
'\2\1\(.\)\)\(.\)'
```

is legal. This will match: "xyyx", "abba", and so on. The reason is that grep scans the whole pattern and knows in advance where all the tagged expressions are.

THE FGREP COMMAND

fgrep is a simplified version of grep that searches for fixed strings only. fgrep does not allow regular expressions but makes up for that deficiency in two ways: first, it is much faster than grep, especially with large files; second, you can have any number of search strings in the one fgrep command. These strings can either be entered on the command line (separated by newlines) or stored in an expression file (whence the name fgrep: file **grep**, though some say *fast* grep). You give the name of the expression file as an argument, and fgrep extracts pattern strings from it line by line. fgrep does a parallel search, so that each line is scanned in turn for matches with each of the given strings. Let's look at the syntax:

```
fgrep [options] 'strings' [-f expfile] [filenames]
[>out_file]
```

The fgrep options are slightly different from those of grep. The options –h, –b, –c, –i, –y, –l, –n, and –v all work the same as for grep. The –s option (suppress error messages) is *not* available with fgrep, but fgrep has a –x option not found with grep. The –x option restricts matches to exact, whole-line matches.

The –f option tells fgrep to open the named *expfile* (if possible) and take each line of this file as a search string. A good application is the simple, personalized spell checker. We all have "problem" words that we regularly misspell. You can make a file of such words, one per line, using the *bad* variations you usually employ. Then you let fgrep check your essays:

```
$ cat mywatch.words
supercede
abreviate
alimoney
allimony
allimoney
comittee
embarassment
logomarchy
overide
$ fgrep -in -f mywatch.words essay
```

```
12: which has been superceded by C++. This means
36: the Fortran/Algol logomarchy is over.
$ _
```

You can also enter multiple search strings directly in the command line:

```
$ fgrep -c 'Unix
> XENIX
> AIX' chap1
34
$ _
```

Notice that you must start with a quote (single or double would be fine here), enter a newline after each search string entry, and finally close the quote before typing the target filename.

Remember that `fgrep` does not allow fancy searches with regular expressions. Its main application is rapidly searching files for a number of key words. With a large expression file, there is an initial, noticeable pause while `fgrep` digests its contents, but the subsequent searching time is independent of the number of strings being hunted.

THE EGREP COMMAND

The final member of the `grep` family is `egrep` (*e* for exponential). `egrep` allows the `-f` *expfile* option of `fgrep`. Unlike `fgrep`, though, `egrep` can use regular expressions. It would be nice to report that `egrep` and `grep` support the *same* range of regular expressions, but alas, no. `egrep` has some additional search tricks, but does not support the tagged expressions of `grep` and `ed`.

Table 14.1 lists the additional regular expressions not found in `grep` or `ed`. The symbols `r`, `r1`, and so on stand for any `egrep` regular expression.

TABLE 14.1: Regular Expressions for egrep

REGULAR EXPRESSION	MATCHES
r+	One or more occurrences of *r*
r?	Zero or one occurrences of *r*
r1|r2	Either r1 or r2
(r1|r2)r3	Either r1r3 or r2r3
(r1|r2)*	Zero or more occurrences of *r1|r2* (e.g., *r1*, *r1r1*, *r2r1*, *r1r1r2r1*,...)

The | metacharacter means logical OR and is often pronounced as "or." This character has no special meaning to grep and fgrep, but if you were searching for a literal "|" with egrep, you would have to escape it with \|.

Who Takes Precedence?

With these new egrep tricks, you have to be aware of operator *precedence*. When you have a complex sequence of regular expressions joined end to end (*concatenated,* as we say in these parts), you need to know which metacharacters apply to which pieces of the pattern. To avoid ambiguities, there are rules governing the order in which the various regular expression operations are carried out. This is a standard problem in many areas of computing. Computer language designers must assign operator priorities so that the user (and the machine) know exactly how a complex expression will be handled. The rule is that higher precedence operations are carried out before the lower precedence operations. You may have met a similar problem in arithmetic and algebra: in the expression A + B × C, it matters greatly whether you add A + B first, then multiply by C, or whether you multiply B × C, then add A. In some languages, precedence simply goes left to right (or right to left) regardless of the operators involved. In others, multiplication has a higher precedence than addition, regardless of position. In some cases, different operators may have the same precedence, meaning that you can perform the operations in any sequence. For example, with A × B / C you can (in theory) do the multiplication or the division first and get the same answer. (In practice, the results may differ because of precision limitations.)

The point is that there are no absolute rules. You simply learn the man-made rules for a particular system, and break them at your own peril. Fortunately, most systems allow you to "override" the normal precedence rules by using parentheses. For example, since multiplication has a higher precedence than addition, you could write (A + B) × C if you want to ensure that C multiplies the sum A + B. Without the parentheses, you would be adding A to the product B × C. The following egrep examples include the use of parentheses.

```
$ egrep -n 'or|the' hamlet
1:To be or not to be,
2:That is the question.

$ cat qfile
question
maybe
```

```
$ egrep -f qfile hamlet
That is the question.
Or maybe not

$ cat ur.1
XENIX is a version of the
UNIX operating system
for the IBM PC range.
Usually, you will find that

$ egrep '(U|XE)NIX' ur.1
XENIX is a version of the
UNIX operating system

$ egrep 'U|XENIX' ur.1
XENIX is a version of the
UNIX operating system
Usually, you will find that
```

Notice how the parentheses are used to change the normal precedence of the metacharacters and other regular expression operations. 'U|XENIX' matches both "U" and "XENIX" because | has a *lower* precedence than concatenation. So, XENIX is "formed" before the OR operation with U. '(U|XE)NIX', on the other hand, forms NIX, does an OR with the result of (U|XE), and therefore matches "UNIX" and "XENIX" but not the "U" in "Usually".

With *r**, *r+*, and *r?*, the precedence works the other way round: these three metacharacters have a *higher* precedence than concatenation. So, for example,

'stan*'	Matches "sta", "stan", "stann", "stannn", …
'(stan)*'	Matches "", "stan", "stanstan", …
'stan+'	Matches "stan", "stann", "stannn", …
'(stan)+'	Matches "stan", "stanstan", "stanstanstan", …
'stan?'	Matches "sta" and "stan" only
'(stan)?'	Matches " " and "stan"

The matches shown as " " mean *zero* occurrences of the pattern. These must be used with care! The following example will serve as a warning:

```
$ egrep '(stan)*' ur.1
XENIX is a version of the
UNIX operating system
```

```
for the IBM PC range.
Usually, you will find that
```

Zero or more occurrences of "stan" occur in every line of ur.1!

Taking grep and egrep operations together, Table 14.2 shows them in decreasing order of precedence.

TABLE 14.2: Regular Expressions in Descending Precedence for grep and egrep

REGULAR EXPRESSION	MEANING
C	Normal (nonmeta) character
\m	Escape a character
^	Start of line
$	End of line
	Any single character (excluding newline)
[xyz...]	Any one of x, y, z, ...
[a-z]	Range
[^...]	Any single character not listed
\n	The nth tagged expression (grep only)
r*	Zero or more r's
r+	One or more r's (egrep only)
r?	Zero or one r's (egrep only)
r1r2	Concatenation: r1 followed by r2
r1|r2	r1 or r2 (egrep only)
\(\<MI>r\)	Tagged regular expression r (grep only)
(r)	Regular expression r: lowest precedence

THE GREP FAMILY SUMMARY

Table 14.3 summarizes the grep family options. All Unix systems provide at least the following options: -b, -l, -c, -n, -s, and -v. The others may not be present on older versions.

TABLE 14.3: GREP FAMILY OPTIONS

Option	Action
	fgrep ONLY
-x	Matches whole line exactly
	grep, fgrep, AND egrep
-h	Suppresses filename display
-b	Displays disk block number of matching line
-l	Displays only filenames where matches found
-c	Counts and displays number of matching lines
-n	Numbers each matching line
-v	Displays lines that do not match
-I	Ignores case when matching
-y	Older version of -i
-e	Matches following expression, usually one that starts with "-"; avoids clash with an option
	grep ONLY
-s	Suppresses error messages
-w	Matches whole words only
	egrep AND fgrep
-f *expfile*	Matches strings stored in *expfile*

The regular expressions supported by each of the grep family are summed up in Table 14.4 (see the earlier sections of this chapter for more details).

TABLE 14.4: grep Family Expressions

REGULAR EXPRESSION MATCHES	
grep, fgrep, AND egrep	
X	Ordinary characters match themselves (newlines and meta-characters are excluded)
Xyz	Ordinary strings match themselves
grep AND egrep:+	
\m	Matches literal metacharacter m
^	Start of line
$	End of line
.	Any single character
[xy^$z]	Any one of x, y, ^, $, or z
[^xy^$z]	Any one other than x, y, ^, $, or z
[a-z]	Any single character in given range
[^a-z]	Any single character not in given range
r*	Zero or more occurrences of r
r1r2	Matches r1 followed by r2 (concatenation)
grep ONLY	
\(r\)	Tagged regular expression: matches r
\n	Set to what matched the nth tagged expression (n = 1 to 9)
egrep ONLY	
r+	One or more occurrences of r
r?	Zero or one occurrences of r
r1|r2	Either r1 or r2
(r1|r2)r3	Either r1r3 or r2r3
(r1|r2)*	Zero or more occurrences of r1|r2 (e.g., r1, r1r1, r2r1, r1r1r2r1,...)

THE SED STREAM EDITOR

The picturesque word *stream* is widely used in computer science to represent a sequence of elements all with the same properties. This means that each element in a stream is of the same *data type* (bits in a bit stream, characters in a text stream, and so on). The number of elements is called the *length* of the stream. In a stream, you can read only one element at a time. When you read a stream, the computer sets a pointer that indicates which element is being read. After each read, the current position of the pointer usually advances to the next element in the stream. You can also write to the stream but you are limited to appending an element to the end of the stream. Streams that allow reading only are called input streams; those that allow writing only are called output streams; those that allow both reading and writing are called input/output streams (I/O streams for short).

In discussing `sed`, we will be concerned with text streams, namely sequences of ASCII characters. Input (read-only) streams are associated with `stdin` (the standard input, usually the keyboard); output (write-only) streams are associated with `stdout` (the standard output) and `stderr` (the standard error output). The I/O streams are usually represented by Unix text files (assuming that they have the appropriate read and write permissions). In other contexts, streams may be associated with special files representing various I/O devices such as modems or magnetic tape drives.

SED SYNTAX

Large tracts have been written covering all the tricks of `sed`. Here, I'll concentrate on the most common applications. There are two basic ways of using `sed`. You can either enter options directly into the command line like this:

```
sed [-n] [-e] 'edit_command' in_file
```

or you can control `sed` with an in-file script like this:

```
sed [-n] -fedit_script in_file
```

The two can also be combined, but let's take one gulp at a time.

The `in_file` represents the input stream that is to be edited. If you omit the `in_file` argument, `sed` will operate on your standard input. `sed` will output all the lines of `in_file`, whether changed by `sed` or not, excluding, of course, any lines deleted by your edit. This output is usually displayed (printed) on your standard output, as you might expect from a

Part I

well-behaved filter. You do have the option, however, to suppress some or all of the output. The −n option (think of it as no output) suppresses all output except for specific lines designated in the edit command. The trick with −n is to append the p (print) command to those edit commands for which the output is needed. You'll see how presently. *in_file* itself, of course, is not modified by sed. Whatever emerges from your sed operation can be written or appended to a file with the usual >*out_file* and >>*out_file* redirections, or piped to another command.

WARNING

It is unwise to redirect the output of sed to the same file that you are sedding!

The *edit_command* inside single quotes, such as 's/sun/moon/g' (change "sun" to "moon") or '1,5p' (with the −n option would print only lines 1 to 5). The surrounding single quotes are not always essential but are so highly recommended that beginners should treat them as mandatory. Two keystrokes can save you considerable concern. So many of the sed command characters have special meanings to the shell that it is easier to quote the whole edit command. You'll recall the similar caveats in force for the grep family.

You can have more than one *edit_command* in a single sed command. Simply enter −e before each *edit_command* and they will be processed in turn by sed.

The −f (file) option of sed is rather like the −f option in egrep and fgrep. The *edit_script*, following the −f, is the name of a file containing a set of ed-like commands (rather like a shell script). This allows some fancy operations. For example, suppose you need to keep several different versions of a large file, the results of various editing sessions. It is possible to save disk space by keeping just one version of the file, together with edit scripts that will generate the other versions. The edit scripts simply record the differences and are usually much shorter than the text files. In fact, Unix provides a command called diff that will generate an edit script. You give diff the two filenames, say A and B, as arguments.

The −e and −f options can be combined. The −e option is the default. If you have only one −e and no −f commands, you can omit the −e. In all other cases the −e is needed. The −f is never assumed, so

    sed scriptfile *in_file*

would default to

    sed -e scriptfile *in_file*

which is almost certainly an error, rather than the intended

```
sed -f scriptfile in_file
```

Likewise, it is wrong to write

```
sed 'command' -f scriptfile in_file
```

rather than

```
sed -e 'command' -f filename in_file
```

If an -f option is present, the -e is not assumed by default.

The edit_command

The *edit_command* works with line numbers, line number expressions, addresses, and regular expressions. You will usually be using sed with the pattern matching addresses rather than with line numbers, however. Here are some examples:

```
sed 's/sun/moon/' myfile
```

The above will replace the *first* occurrence of "sun" in each line of myfile with "moon". Without redirection, the output will appear on your screen. All lines will appear, whether changed or not.

```
sed 's/sun/moon/g' myfile
```

goes a bit further: the g (global) option will change *every* occurrence of "sun" in myfile to "moon".

```
sed -e 's/sun/moon/g' -e 's/day/night/g' myfile
```

Here you see two successive commands, requiring the -e option. sed operates by copying a line of myfile into a *pattern space*. It then applies each edit command in turn to the pattern space before outputting the result to the standard output. Of course, only those commands that "match" will affect the pattern space. There is one exception to this sequence: the q (quit) function will exit sed by branching to the end of the script:

```
sed '/sun/q' myfile
```

will output until a line containing "sun" is encountered. That line (if one exists) will be displayed; then sed terminates. As with ed, the full syntax for a command is

```
[address1 [,address2]] function [args]
```

WARNING

Watch! If you are sedding more than one file, the line numbers accumulate across these files. If your first file has 200 lines, the first line of the second file will be address 201.

The *function* argument is also referred to as a command or command letter. The addresses specify the range of lines to be edited. If both addresses are missing, sed assumes that every line is targeted. In other words, the default address arguments are 1,$ (from line 1 to the last line). If one address is given, the other defaults to the first or last line of the file. In the above s commands, for example, we gave no address arguments, so each line was a potential candidate for subsitution. Addresses can be supplied to narrow the editing, using either line numbers (or line symbols such as $ for last), or *context* addresses. The latter are our old friends, the regular expressions. Consider the following:

```
sed '1,4s/sun/moon/g' myfile
```

Here, the substitution will be limited to the first four lines of myfile. The rather daunting

```
sed '/^Example/,/QED$/s/sun/moon/g' myfile
```

will only substitute "moon" for "sun" in those lines in the inclusive range selected by the two context addresses. The first says: select the first line that begins with "Example"; the second says: select the first line that ends with "QED". If these selections happen to be the same line, just that line is selected. If the line with "QED" precedes the line with "Example", only the "Example" line is selected. Normally, though, the command would select a set of lines, and in each of these the substitution would be applied. This process is repeated throughout the file, so it might edit several sets of lines starting with "Example" up to and including lines ending with "QED".

Each function, designated by a single letter, expects a certain number of addresses (zero, one, or two), and a certain set of arguments (including none). The q function, for instance, takes a single address and no arguments. It simply stops sed when that address is matched. We'll now run through the more popular sed commands.

Substitution

The s (substitute) function has the following syntax:

```
[address1 [,address2 ]] s/regexp/replacement/flags
```

As you've seen, the regular expression matches are replaced by the replacement string within the given address ranges. The most common flag argument is g as shown earlier. The full set of flags is as follows:

n	A number 1–512 specifies that only the *n*th occurrence of *regexp* will be replaced.

g	Global substitution rather than just substituting the first occurrence on each line.
p	Displays (prints) the line if a replacement was made.
w *wfile*	Writes the line to the *wfile* if a replacement was made.

The w flag lets you write just the changes to a specified file while writing the whole, edited file elsewhere:

```
sed '/sun/moon/gw changes' myfile >tmp
```

The replacement string can be a new line, allowing you to insert extra line spacing:

```
sed 's/$/\
> /' myfile
```

This gives you double-line spacing since each end-of-line, indicated by $, is replaced by a newline. To get a newline in the replacement string, you have to enter \ followed by the Enter (↵) key. After the secondary prompt, you complete the entry with / '; then type the filename.

Reversals with a Bang!

A useful dodge to remember is that you can reverse the matching by placing! (pronounced "bang" or "not") before the function. Thus:

```
sed '1,4!s/sun/moon/g' myfile
```

says, do the substitution on all but the first four lines of myfile. Similarly,

```
sed '/^Example/,/QED$/!s/sun/moon/g' myfile
```

performs the substitution on each line outside the ranges discussed earlier.

A more practical application of ! is where you want to edit only nonempty lines. An empty line, remember, matches the regular expression '^$', so

```
sed '/^$/!s/^/     /' myfile
```

says "*Don't* substitute on empty lines." Hence this command will insert a tab at the beginning of each nonempty line. This is a useful operation known as *indenting*. The replacement string is a real tab that is hard to see on the printed page.

Deletion

The d (delete) function takes two addresses, and deletes the range of lines selected:

```
sed '4,5d' myfile
```

deletes lines 4 and 5, while

```
sed '/sun/d' myfile
```

will delete *every* line containing "sun". Note that the "missing" second address defaults to $, the last line. You can delete every line *except* the ones containing "sun":

```
sed '/sun/!d' myfile
```

I must stress again that myfile is not affected by this operation! The deletion affects only the output of sed. To effect a lasting edit, you must redirect and then copy:

```
$ sed '/sun/d' myfile >tmp
$ mv tmp myfile
$ _
```

Take the following variant:

```
sed '/sun/,/moon/d' myfile
```

What is deleted? Well, the range selected is, inclusively, from the first line holding a "sun" to the first line holding a "moon". If there are such lines, they will not appear on your standard output.

Appending and Inserting Text

As with ed, you can append and insert text using the a and i functions. The difference is that the added text must be part of the edit command (or script file), and care is needed if the text straddles more than one line. What you need is the escape character, \, to hide all but the final newline from the shell:

```
sed '3a\
Now is the hour'
myfile
```

This will add "Now is the hour" after line 3 of myfile. The i function inserts before the given address.

The y Function

The y function is simple but effective: it replaces characters on a one-to-one basis:

```
sed 'y/abc/ABC/' myfile
```

Here, each "a" is replaced by "A", each "b" by "B", and so on. You can set up any mapping of characters by listing the "from" and "to" strings as shown. The two strings must be of the same length to avoid error messages and embarrassment.

The p Function

This is the print (display) command with a few new wrinkles. Since sed already sends its output to the screen by default, p may seem to be a bit redundant. In fact, if you try the following command:

```
sed '/sun/p' myfile
```

you'll find that matching lines are displayed twice! Where p does earn its lunch is when used with the -n option. The -n option normally suppresses the standard output, but you can override this with a judicious p! (You can look on this as inhibiting the inhibition.) If you want to see only the matching lines, you can do the following:

```
sed -n '/sun/p' myfile
```

This is remarkably similar to grep 'sun'myfile. And you can display all lines except those with a "sun" by using

```
sed -n '/sun/!p' myfile
```

which is the same as grep -v 'sun'myfile. As I said earlier, sed will do almost everything that grep will do (however, the results of the grep -b option cannot be achieved by sed).

COME ALL YE TRAMPS AND 'AWKERS

awk, named for the triumvirate Aho, Weinberger, and Kernighan who designed it, is a complete language with its own band of dedicated enthusiasts. Some have described awk as a cult within a cult, and indeed awk does have its own bible: *The AWK Programming Language,* by Alfred Aho, Brian Kernighan, and Peter Weinberger (Addison-Wesley, 1988). Officially defined as a "pattern scanning and processing language," awk can be, and regularly is, coaxed into solving all manner of problems not immediately connected with patterns. awk uses a syntax that incorporates many features of the C language, so a knowledge of C is a great help if you wish to master awk (and conversely, of course). A useful rule of thumb is that if a job is too difficult for "normal" shell tools and scripts, try awk. If awk can't solve the problem, use C. Failing that, move up to C++ (Bjarne Stroustrup's object-oriented extension of C, which is rapidly gaining popularity).

In this section, I'll concentrate on some of the simpler features of awk that you can exploit without becoming a full-time hacker. The basic idea of awk is not unlike that of grep and sed: you scan one or more files, record by record (usually line by line), looking for pattern matches, and you perform some action whenever a match is found. The power of awk arises from the fact that the pattern-checking tools are more elaborate, and the actions you can trigger are more extensive than those of sed. In fact, you can initiate complete programs with conditional loops and arithmetic operations whenever a match is found. The general syntax is

```
awk [-F re] [parameter...] ['prog'] [-f progfile] [in_file...]
```

in_file... specifies the list of files to be processed. As with sed and grep, awk does not modify the input files. If no files are given, awk processes the standard input. The results of awk appear on your standard output, so all the familiar Unix filter operations are available: redirection with <, >, and >>, and piping with |. The prog argument is a string, single-quoted, as you would expect, to hide stuff from the shell. (Quoting is explained in the grep section.) The *parameter* options let you assign values to various variables. A typical prog argument looks like this:

```
'pattern { action }'
```

The *pattern* argument can be any of the egrep regular expressions, using the syntax /re/, plus a few more pattern-matching tricks as you'll see later. The *action* argument, always surrounded by braces, is a sequence of statements (separated by semicolons) that awk will interpret and execute for each *record* of the input file(s) that gives a pattern match. I'll explain records later. The default record for awk is the familiar line, so for the moment you can think of awk as processing the input files one line at a time. The *action* section can be quite long and complex, straddling many lines, or many pages even. As with shell scripts, you can insert comments using the # character:

```
'{ myaction }' # all mine!
```

Everything following # to the end of the line is ignored, so try to avoid `'{ myaction # all mine! }'`. This would generate a syntax error, since awk would not "see" the final brace. As I pointed out in Chapter 12, liberal use of comments is encouraged, especially where the program uses the kind of arcane tricks that Shakespeare warned us about:

> "Bloody instructions, that return to plague the inventor..."
> (Macbeth)

You can omit either the *pattern* or the *action* arguments (but not both). No *pattern* means match all records; the default *action* is to display on the standard output. A simple *action* is the print command:

```
awk '/sun/ { print }' myfile
```

This will display all lines of myfile that contain the string "sun". (In this example, you could actually omit the { print } argument, since this is the default action.) Of course,

```
grep 'sun' myfile
```

will do exactly the same job, so we have proved our earlier claim that awk can grep! Omitting the *pattern* argument means that all lines will match, so

```
awk '{ print }' myfile
```

displays each line of myfile. This example turns out to be less efficient than the equivalent cat myfile.

The following is legal but ineffective:

```
awk '{}' myfile # where's the beef?
```

The above empty action does nothing on every line of input!

As with sed, you can select a range of lines by using two patterns separated by a comma:

```
awk '/[Ss]un/,/[Mm]oon/ { print }' myfile
```

This would display the lines from the first one matching "sun" or "Sun" to the next one matching "moon" or "Moon". The selected output from print can be redirected or piped by using >, >>, or | within the action:

```
awk '/sun/,/moon/ { print >my.extract }' myfile
```

Before looking at more complex examples, note that the -f option works just like -f in sed and egrep. You can put all your awk commands and actions in a separate program file, and pass its name in the -f *progfile* argument.

awk Fields

One of the tricks of awk that gives it great power is the ability to isolate and process separate *fields* of the lines being scanned. You've met fields before in several contexts. For example, the sort command uses fields to achieve sorts over different parts of a line. Both grep and sed are pure "line-based" utilities and it is not so easy to manipulate subsections of a line. The fields in a line can be accessed by awk using the notation $1, $2, and so on, rather like, but not to be confused with, the positional variables in a shell script. Suppose you had a file called books:

```
$ cat books
Author     Title      Prices
Smith      Ants       $39.95
Jones      Cats       $29.95
Brown      Dogs       $19.95
$ _
```

The author field can be referenced as $1, the title as $2, and the price as $3. The symbol-pair $n is called a field variable, where n is the field number. The special symbol-pair $0 represents the whole line, that is, every field exactly as entered in the file. A built-in variable, NF, holds the number of fields, so $NF means the last field. NF and several other built-in variables can be accessed in your awk programs, rather like the predefined shell variables you first met in Chapter 6. (You'll encounter some important differences, though, so take care.)

By default, fields are defined as any contiguous set of nonwhite-space characters separated by white space (spaces or tabs, or newlines for the last field). Under the normal white-space separator regimen, any number of spaces/tabs serve to separate the fields and the fields themselves never contain white space. In the books file, $2 represents the title string with no leading or trailing spaces/tabs, no matter how much white space separates the columns.

The -F option lets you change the built-in variable FS (field separator) from spaces/tabs to any single nonspace character (including a single tab). Once you change the default separator, though, your fields *will* include any leading spaces. I'll return to the -F option soon.

awk Records

awk actually processes one *record* at a time. Records are determined by the character stored in the built-in variable, RS (record separator). The default RS is newline, so the standard awk record is one line of text, just like sed. awk, however, lets you change the RS, so your records can be parts of lines or multiple lines. This adds considerable flexibility in creating database applications. Before exploring these options, let's look at the default separators: white space for fields, newlines for records. The following examples show the field variables in action:

```
$ awk '{ print $0 }' books
Author     Title      Prices
Smith      Ants       $39.95
Jones      Cats       $29.95
Brown      Dogs       $19.95
$ awk '{ print $2 }' books
Title
Ants
Cats
Dogs
$ awk '{ print $3, $1, "Qty..." }' books
Prices    Author    Qty...
$39.95    Smith     Qty...
$29.95    Jones     Qty...
$19.95    Brown     Qty...
$ _
```

The first example is a long-winded version of awk { print } books, since print defaults to print $0. As you can see, the print command can take one or more field arguments in any order. You can even repeat a field if you want to:

```
$ awk '{ print $3, $1, $3 }' books
Prices Author Prices
$39.95 Smith $39.95
$29.95 Jones $39.95
$19.95 Brown $39.95
$ _
```

print allows fixed-string arguments such as "Qty…". You usually need a comma between each argument, as shown. If the comma is omitted, the fields will print as one. Note the spacing in the last example. Input field separators do not pass through to the output. Each comma in the print argument list simply generates a single OFS character (output field separator). By default, this is a space, but (as you've guessed), awk lets you change the OFS variable to any other character (tab being a common choice for pretty alignments). You can also tidy up the appearance using the tab character, \t, directly in the print arguments:

```
$ awk '{ print $3, $1, "\tQty…" }' books
Prices Author     Qty…
$39.95 Smith      Qty…
$29.95 Jones      Qty…
$19.95 Brown      Qty…
$ _
```

An interesting and useful aspect of awk's field variables is that they are *true* variables. Although $n starts life holding the nth field, you are free to assign new values to it during execution. For example:

```
$ awk '{ $1 = "O/S"; $3 = "N/A"; print $0 }' books
O/S        Title    N/A
O/S        Ants     N/A
O/S        Cats     N/A
O/S        Dogs     N/A
$ _
```

Remember that the input file is not changed, so you haven't lost the authors and prices from the books file.

You can use all the familiar egrep regular expressions to select lines from a file:

```
$ awk '/[Dd]|Smith/' books
Smith      Ants     $39.95
Brown      Dogs     $19.95
```

Here we match any line that has either "D", "d", or "Smith".

printf

For more complicated output formats, you can use the `printf` command (standing for print formatted). I won't go into all the `printf` tricks, but here's a typical example, showing how you can number each line of output. The built-in variable NR provides the line number. Unlike the shell variables you met in Chapter 6, the built-in awk variables like NR do not require a leading $ to reveal their values. ($NR would mean the NRth field, which is something else!)

```
$ awk '{ printf "%03d %s\n", NR, $1 }' books
001 Author
002 Smith
003 Jones
004 Brown
```

`printf` crawls out, almost intact, from the C language with a plethora of options for formatting numbers and strings in any conceivable layout. `printf` takes a format string, followed by the arguments to be printed. The format string, within double quotes, contains a set of formatting specifications, each starting with a %, one for each argument to be printed. In the above example, %03d formats the NR, and %s formats the field $1. d means format a decimal number; 03 means pad with leading zeros to a width of 3. s means format a string. The final \n should be familiar: this provides a newline. Unlike `print`, `printf` does not automatically generate a new line at the end of each display, so you have to provide one as shown (or suffer a messy layout). You can also insert \t in your format strings to generate a tab:

```
$ awk '{ printf "\t%03d \t%s\n", NR, $1 }' books
001     Author
002     Smith
003     Jones
004     Brown
```

A predefined variable, OFMT, determines the output format for numbers in the absence of an explicit % specifier. The default format is %.6g, which handles a decimal floating-point with a precision of 6 digits. (awk handles all numbers internally in floating-point format.)

The -F Option

The -F option lets you change the field separator character. You simply follow the -F with a single character (or regular expression). A typical application is -F: to set the separator to a colon. The /etc/passwd file, for example, uses colons to delimit fields:

```
$ cat /etc/passwd
root:gf54JQxxZ32Fd:0:1::/:/bin/sh
...
stan:oIg65rfRdffn8:24:12:Stan Kelly-Bootle:/usr/stan/:/bin/sh
fred:qEsgs3324Fcc2:25:12:Frederick Lemaitre:/usr/fred/:/bin/
csh
joe::27:14:Joseph Lussac:/usr/joe:
...
$ _
```

NOTE

For security reasons, many recent Unix implementations no longer hold the encrypted password in \etc\passwd. A ":*:" appears if the user has a password; otherwise an empty field, "::", indicates no password has been assigned. Some systems will always show ":*:" whether the user has a password or not.

awk can be used to investigate important properties of your system's password file. Consider the following:

```
$ awk -F: '$2 == ""' /etc/passwd # note: print is implied
joe::27:14:Joseph Lussac:/usr/joe:
$ _
```

This example may offer a quick method of uncovering those users who are not password protected! To see how it works, note first that -F: tells awk that fields will be defined in terms of : as separators. $2 now refers to the second field in /etc/passwd, namely the encrypted password field. The pattern-matching expression $2 == " " tests whether this field is null (empty) or not, that is, whether there is *anything* between the second and third colon. Remember that once FS is defined as :, any white space between the colons would "belong" to that field. I stress this because beginners often confuse spaces, nulls, and field separators. The == operator (also imported from C) is known as a *relational* operator since it tests for a relation between two expressions; in our case, it tests for equality between $2 and the empty string " ".

WARNING

Distinguish carefully between == (equality testing) and = (assignment). Confusing them is yet another common source for programming errors in awk and C.

The == operator gives you a neat way of selecting a range of line numbers:

```
$ awk 'NR == 5, NR == 20' myfile
```

will print from line 5 to line 20, inclusive. Recall that two patterns separated by a comma establish a range. You could list all lines except line 33:

```
$ awk 'NR != 33' myfile
```

The "not-equals" operator is !=. As in C, ! carries the hint of negation in several contexts. Let's look at awk's other relational operators.

awk Relational Operators

awk allows the tests shown in Table 14.5. These operators can be used in both the *pattern* and *action* sections. In the *pattern* section, the conditional test is implied: all you need write is, say, $2 == " ", and awk will seek a match. In the *action* section, however, you need explicit conditional and flow control operators such as if, else, and while that I'll explain later.

TABLE 14.5: Tests Allowed by awk

RELATIONAL OPERATOR	MEANING
x == y	x equals y?
x != y	x not equal to y?
x > y	x greater than y?
x >= y	x greater than or equal to y?
x < y	x less than y?
x <= y	x less than or equal to y?
x ~ re	x matches the regular expression re?
x !~ re	x does not match the regular expression re?

The exact meaning of a relational operator depends on the data type of the two variables or expressions being compared. With numbers and strings, equality and inequality tests obey the obvious rules. You can test x == 3 as well as str == "stan". With numbers, the comparisons >, >=, and so on, follow the usual arithmetic rules: 2 > 1, -1 > -2, etc. With strings, comparisons are made lexicographically (dictionary order), so that "b" > "a", "aa" > "a", and so on.

The test `$2 == " "` used in the previous example can also be expressed as follows:

```
$2 ~ /^$/
```

The ~ (tilde) is often pronounced "contains." The pattern test asks whether `$2` contains (or matches) the regular expression `/^$/`, which matches only an empty field. Note a subtle difference here between awk and `sed`: with awk, ^ and $ can designate the start and end of fields or lines. In `sed`, `/^$/` matches only an empty line. You can also write

```
$2 !~ /./
```

with the same result: `/./` matches any character, so we seek a `$2` field that does not contain any character. Only a null (empty) field can make this statement! Yet another version of this test uses `length`, one of many built-in awk functions that add to the fun:

```
length($2) == 0
```

The expression `length(str)` is set to the length (number of bytes) in the string *str*. A zero length means an empty string. A more common use of the `length` function is tracking overlong lines, which can be useful before printing a file:

```
$ awk 'length($0) > 80 { print NR }' myfile
367
569
$ _
```

This example displays the line numbers of all lines exceeding eighty characters.

Multiple Tests

awk's pattern checking powers are considerably enhanced by the provision of three logical operators: ! (NOT), || (OR), and && (AND). (Note especially the double symbols needed for OR and AND.) These operators let you test for complex combinations of matches:

```
'( length($1) >= 4 ) && ( NR % 2 != 0 )'
```

Here we are seeking lines that satisfy two conditions: the first field must contain at least four characters AND the line number must be odd. You never know, that could be useful one day. The test for oddness deserves study: NR % 2 gives the remainder after dividing the line number by 2. A nonzero remainder indicates an odd-numbered line.

The expression p||q is true if either p is true or q is true or both are true (we call this the inclusive OR). awk uses a shortcut when testing multiple conditions such as p | | q: if p is found to be true, no time is wasted evaluating q! awk already knows that p | | q is satisfied. Likewise when testing p&&q, if p is found to be false, the truth or falsehood of q is not explored. Here is | | in action. The pattern

```
( ($1*$2) > 0) || ($6 == "Late") '
```

will match any line where either Qty × Price (fields 1 and 2) is positive or Status (field 6) is "Late" (or both).

Notice the parentheses used to group each pattern. I recommend them for added legibility even if they are not essential for controlling precedence. You met the "precedence" problem in the egrep section, but in awk with its richer supply of operators, precedence is much more difficult. I'll list the precedence order in Table 14.6, but it is much safer to use parentheses. If you are seriously contemplating a career in programming, of course, you will need to master the AND (logical conjuction), the OR (logical inclusive disjunction), and the NOT (logical negation).

TABLE 14.6: Increasing Precedence of Operators for awk

Group	Operators
1	= += -= *= /= %=
2	||
3	&&
4	> >= < <= == != ~ !~
5	String concatenation: "x" "y" becomes "xy"
6	+ -
7	* / %
8	++ --

You've already met the NOT (or reverse) operator under several guises. In sed, the same symbol ! is used to reverse the sense of a match, but it is placed between the pattern and the action. In awk, the ! always goes before the expression to be negated: !x is pronounced "NOT-x." Any pattern, however complex, can be negated by a preceding bang (!).

Begin and End

Two special expressions, BEGIN and END, can be used in the *pattern* argument. Any action listed (within braces) after BEGIN will be performed before awk starts scanning the input, and any action listed after END will be performed after all the input has been scanned. BEGIN is used to display headings and to preset (initialize) variables. END is used to display any final results, such as field totals. Consider:

```
$ awk '
> BEGIN { FS = ":"; print "Security Check" }
> $2 == "" { count++ ; print }
> END { print count, "User(s) not passworded." }' /etc/passwd
Security Check
joe::27:14:Joseph Lussac:/usr/joe:
1 User(s) not passworded.
$ _
```

Let's examine some of the new awk constructs introduced here. First, I've given you a fresh way of setting the field separator. Rather than use -F:, you can assign ":" directly to the FS variable. Note the single = means "assign from the right to the left." We do this within a BEGIN section, so the assignment occurs only once before the real work starts. We've also sneaked in a print statement to display the heading "Security Check" (again, we need only one of these). When you the type the closing brace, }, you signal the end of the BEGIN section. The thrill of awk is that you can list as many action statements as you wish between the braces, as long as you remember the separating semicolons. Statements can also be separated by newlines. (C programmers will recognize the { } and ; as block and statement delimiters.)

The secondary prompt tells you that awk is waiting for more input. In fact, you could enter the whole command on one line, but for legibility I've divided it into three convenient sections. Long commands like these, of course, are eminently suitable for embedding in shell scripts (as discussed in Chapter 12), or in program files using the -f *progfile* option.

Next we have two action statements that will be triggered when the pattern $2 == "" tests true. The first action is count++, which increments (increases by 1) the variable count. count is your first encounter with *user-defined* variables. You can give your own variables any convenient, mnemonic names provided you avoid clashing with awk's predefined (built-in) variables such as NF, FS, OFS, and NR (the full list appears below in Table 14.7).

TABLE 14.7:

Predefined Variables for awk

Variable Name	Meaning
ARGC	Number of command-line arguments
ARGV	Array of command-line arguments
FILENAME	String = name of current input file
FNR	Current record number in the current file (starts at 1 for each input file)
FS	Input field separator character (default = space)
NF	Number of fields in current record
NR	Current record number (over all input files)
OFMT	Output format for numbers (default = %.6g)
OFS	Output field separator (default = space)
ORS	Output record separator (default = newline)
RS	Input record separator (default = newline)

awk variables differ from those used in C in several important respects. First, awk offers only strings, one numerical data type, and arrays of these, a much simpler choice than in C. Second, with C you have to *declare* variables, giving their names and data types (int, char, and so on), before they can be used (well, *nearly* always). In most cases, too, you also have to initialize C variables explicitly before they can be safely used. There are no explicit declarations with awk: it is sufficient to *use* a variable name. Upon its first appearance in an awk statement, a variable is data-typed as a string, number, or array according to its context. If you are adding numbers to a variable, for instance, awk will rightly conclude that the variable has numeric pretensions. Similarly, if you assign a string to a variable, or do some other string-like maneuver, awk data-types it as a string. (I'll cover arrays later.) When in doubt, awk assumes a string data type. awk then initializes the new variable: numbers to 0, and strings to " " (the null or empty string). awk is quite tolerant compared with strongly typed languages such as C and Modula-2. Strings and numbers are freely converted one to the other as demanded by the context. You can write X = "1" + 3, for example, without protest and X will be set to 4!

With this essential detour completed, let's return to the analysis of the last example. In the case of count++, the ++ (or postincrement) operator tells awk that count is to be treated as a number. count will therefore start off with the value 0, but each matching line triggers the statement count++, which adds 1 to count. count++ is a convenient shorthand for

```
count = count + 1
```

and is typical of C's economical syntax (a big reason for its popularity with programmers who hate typing). The postdecrement operator – works in the same way: count– decrements count by 1, as if you had written count = count -1. (C programmers should note that awk has no equivalent to C's preincrement or predecrement operators.)

When we reach the END section, count will hold the total number of matched lines. Our example prints this total with an explanatory legend. The print statement in the line

```
$2 == "" { count++ ; print }
```

displays the matching lines. Try omitting the print statement: you'll just get the final total and legend. You'll find this situation in many awk jobs: long files are scanned to give summaries, totals, averages, and the like, but the mass of detail is not usually displayed.

awk and Math

awk supports the usual arithmetical operations, a few fancy variants borrowed from C, and several useful mathematical functions. They are all listed below in Table 14.8.

TABLE 14.8: Mathematical Operations and Functions for awk

Operation	Function
x + y	Adds x to y
x–y	Subtracts y from x
x * y	Multiplies x and y
x / y	Divides x by y
x % y	Gives the remainder when x is divided by y
x = y	Assigns value of y to x
x++	Increments x by 1
x–	Decrements x by 1

TABLE 14.8 continued: Mathematical Operations and Functions for awk

OPERATION	FUNCTION
x += y	Same as x = x + y
x -= y	Same as x = x-y
x *= y	Same as x = x*y
x /= y	Same as x = x/t
x %= y	Same as x = x % y
int(x)	Truncates x to whole number
Rand	Gives a random number between 0 and 1
srand(x)	Sets x as new seed for rand
cos(x)	Gives the cosine of x
sin(x)	Gives the sine of x
atan2(x,y)	Gives the arc tangent of y/x
exp(x)	Gives e^x (e raised to the power x)
log(x)	Gives the logarithm of x (to base e)
sqrt(x)	Gives the nonnegative square root of x

Of special interest are the compound operators, +=, -=, and so on, which save a great deal of typing. Going back to the books file and modifying it slightly to help the arithmetic, let's calculate the average price of our meager catalog:

```
$ cat sbooks
Author    Title    Prices
Smith     Ants     39.95
Jones     Cats     29.95
Brown     Dogs     19.95
$ awk 'BEGIN { print "Summer Price List" }
> NR > 1 { sum += $3; print $2, "$" $3 }
END { print "Average price = $", sum/(NR-1) }' sbooks
Summer Price List
Ants $39.95
Cats $29.95
Dogs $19.95
Average price = $ 29.950
```

The NR > 1 pattern says, "Ignore the first line." NR gives the current line number, and we wish to avoid doing sums on the header line given by

NR equal to 1. On all subsequent lines, we accumulate the price in field $3 into the user-defined variable sum, since sum += $3 means sum = sum + $3. At the end NR will be equal to the total number of lines, which is one more than the number of prices. Hence the average price is sum/(NR-1). One little trick to note: awk automatically concatenates adjacent strings, so "$" $3 gives "$" followed by the price. If the variable X contains the string "this", then

```
'{ print "all" X "week" }'
```

would display "all this week". Even with numeric expressions, concatenation occurs: if X holds 1 and Y holds 2,

```
{ print X Y }'
```

will display "12". (print XY, of course, will display the contents of the variable XY, whatever *they* may be.)

Let's smarten up the previous example by displaying the current date on the price list. This will introduce a few more tools available in the awk toolbox.

```
$ awk 'BEGIN { print "Summer Price List";
> print "'"`date`"'" }
> NR > 1 { sum += $3; print $2, "$" $3 }
END { print "Average price = $", sum/(NR-1) }' sbooks
Summer Price List
Sun Jun 11 04:56:48 GMT 1995
Ants $39.95
Cats $29.95
Dogs $19.95
Average price = $ 29.950
```

The exuberance of quotes around date may have caught your attention! The inner expression `date` is our old friend the backquoted command, which the shell replaces with the output of date. Before awk can print it, though, this output has to be "stringized," and this is achieved by surrounding `date` with quotes. We can't get by with a simple '`date`', however, because we already have single (forward) quotes surrounding the awk program. So, we end up by double-quoting each single (forward) quote. The rest is history, as they say. You are not alone, by the way, if you find this expression weird and wondrous in equal parts. Even Brian Kernighan and Rob Pike (*The Unix Programming Environment*, Prentice-Hall, 1984) who devised it describe it as "remarkable."

But there is more to follow. Suppose you feel that the full date as issued by date is not appropriate to a commercial document. Perhaps you want just the day, month, and year as nature intended. In the following variant, we use one of awk's many string functions to create an *array* of strings from which we can select parts of the date. The function `split` works as follows:

```
split(string, array, fs )
```

takes a string and breaks it into fields according to the given field separator, `fs`. If you omit the `fs` argument, `split` takes the current value of FS as the separator. In our case, we'll just accept space as the current FS and omit the `fs` argument. If `string` is "Sun Jun 11 04:56:48 GMT 1995", `split` will form six fields and load them into `array`. Thereafter, you can access the fields by indexing as follows:

```
array[1] is "Sun"
array[2] is "Jun"
array[3] is "11"
array[4] is "04:56:48"
array[5] is "GMT"
array[6] is "1995"
```

The syntax should be clear: the numerical index is enclosed in brackets after the name of the array. Here's our latest price list example:

```
$ awk 'BEGIN { print "Summer Price List";
> split( "'"`date`"'", today);
> print today[3], today[2], today[6] }
> NR > 1 { sum += $3; print $2, "$" $3 }
END { print "Average price = $", sum/(NR-1) }' sbooks
Summer Price List
11 Jun 1995
Ants $39.95
Cats $29.95
Dogs $19.95
Average price = $ 29.950
```

awk Flow Control

No self-respecting language is complete without some form of execution flow control. The basic idea behind flow control is that a program can be written in a general way to cover a multitude of foreseen circumstances. Depending on values encountered in certain variables, the program will select a set of statements and bypass others. Flow control also lets you iterate a set of commands until a certain condition prevails. As a simple illustration, let's modify our `books` file to include stock levels:

```
$ cat books
Author     Title     Price      Stock
Smith      Ants      $39.95     3
```

```
Jones      Cats       $29.95     0
Brown      Dogs       $19.95     81
$ _
```

We can write a simple awk program that selects books with dangerously low stock levels:

```
$ awk 'BEGIN { lowlevel = 5 }     # establish warning level
> NR > 1 { if ($4 <= lowlevel)
>              { print $0; count++ }
>         }
> END { if (count == 0 ) print "No low stock"
>          else if (count == 1) print "1 book low"
>               else { print count, "books low" }
>      }' books
Smith      Ants       $39.95     3
Jones      Cats       $29.95     0
2 books low
$ _
```

I repeat an earlier caveat that once an awk program of more than one or two lines is debugged and proves useful, you would enter it into a file and use the -f *progfile* option, or develop a suitable shell script.

The if and else statements work in an obvious way:

```
if (expression)
 action1
else
 action2
```

If the *expression* tests true, *action1* is executed and *action2* is ignored; otherwise, if *expression* tests false, *action1* is ignored and *action2* is executed. The tested expression is known as a *Boolean* expression: it's either true or false (no fuzzy in-betweens). Thus, count == 0 is only true if awk found no books below the low stock level. Notice how I set this level in a variable and tested $3 <= lowlevel. I could have simply tested for $3 <= 5, but the given approach adds legibility and makes any future changes in the low level value much easier.

If *action1* involves several statements, they must be enclosed in braces to form a "single" action (known as a *block*). Even single actions, especially complex ones, are sometimes enclosed in braces to aid legibility. You can nest the if's and else's (with care) to set up sequences of actions to any degree of complexity.

There's nothing sacred about the layout of the given example. You can slap the code down on a single line without upsetting awk. All you need to remember is that an awk statement ends with either ;, newline, or }.

The parentheses around the expression to be tested *are* essential, but where you position the actions is a matter of taste. Certain rules have emerged over the years that give program texts a *structured* appearance. This is a great aid to the human reader in grasping the flow and logic of a program, but awk don't pay no mind.

There are two other flow control statements that I'll mention briefly: while and for. while lets you repeat an action until some condition tests false:

```
'BEGIN { i = 1 }
{
   while ( i <= NF ) {
   sum += $i
   i++
   }
}'
```

will add each field to sum. i starts at 1 and is incremented until it exceeds the number of fields, NF. Once it reaches NF+1, the while condition becomes false and the loop ends. If you are new to programming, you will almost certainly encounter the dreaded endless loop in your early coding attempts. Suppose, for example, that you omitted the i++ statement in the last snippet. The while loop would keep adding $1 to sum with no end in sight! Perhaps an overflow error condition might intervene, but the condition tested by while, namely i <= NF, is permanently true. Always make sure that some action inside the loop is going to (eventually) make the while condition false. Forewarned is forearmed.

The for loop equivalent to the while example looks like this:

```
'{
   for ( i = 1; i <= NF; i++ )
      sum += $i
}'
```

After for you supply three statements (some or all may be empty) inside parentheses:

1. The loop initializer

2. The loop condition

3. The loop modifier

If the loop condition is true, the loop action, sum += $i in our case, is executed followed by the loop modifier. The loop condition is then tested again, and so on. For any while loop there is an equivalent for loop, and vice versa, so the choice is up to you. Both loops allow you to exit "prematurely" by using the `break` statement:

```
'{
    for ( i = 1; i <= NF; i++ )
        if ($i == "STOP LOOP") break
    sum += $i
}'
```

A more spectacular exit right down to the END pattern is available with the appropriately named `exit` statement.

```
'{
    for ( i = 1; i <= NF; i++ )
        if ($i == "END PROG") exit
    sum += $i
}'
```

awk Round Up

With a complex utility like awk, you can expect to make many false starts and iterations before your program works correctly. awk is relatively helpful in reporting any programming errors: it will indicate which line or expression has a syntax violation. You will often encounter the colorful error message: awk bailing out at line so-and-so. In awk circles, there are many black parachute jokes. I hope this brief introduction to awk has whetted your appetite. There are many features such as associative arrays that I have not mentioned. Appendix C lists several resources for continued study. You'll also see more awk applications in the next chapter where I delve more deeply into shell scripts.

WHAT'S NEXT

In Chapter 15, we'll look at some of the functions in advanced shell scripting. We'll cover loops, test, reading data, and conditionals as well as error handling techniques.

```
echo "2.      Show Date"
echo "3.      Display a file"
echo "4.      Change working director
echo "5.      Return to original dir
echo "Q.      Quit
echo
echo -n "Enter choice: .\b"
read choice
case $choice in
1) who | more
   pause;;
2) date
   pause;;
3) echo "Enter file name: \c"
   read fil
   if [ -r "$fil" -a -f "$fil ]
   then
      clear
      more -d $fil
   else
      echo "Cannot d
   fi
   pause;;
4) echo "En
   read di
   if test   d "$(dir    pwd`
   then
      cd $dir
   else
      echo "$dir: no such di
   fi
   pause;;
5) if test "$dir" != "$p
   then
      cd $prevdir
   fi
   pause;;
```

Chapter 15

ADVANCED SHELL SCRIPTS

In this chapter, I'll build on the basic shell features introduced in Chapter 12 and the utilities covered in Chapters 13 and 14. The goal of this chapter is to provide a pratical introduction to the programming tools provided by the Bourne shell. I'll make the example scripts as useful as possible without becoming too complex. I'll analyze the scripts, show how they work, and offer suggestions on adapting them for your own applications. I'll also take the opportunity to revisit some of the trickier aspects of the shell: variables, assignments, and quoting.

THE MENU, PLEASE

Let's start by creating a simple menu from which you can select commands with a single keystroke. You've heard of painting-by-numbers: I now present Unix-by-numbers. Although quite simple, our first program (which is called a script in Unix) introduces several fundamental shell techniques and some new commands. Also, you can use this example as a template for almost any menu you may wish to create. Using ed , vi, or whatever text editor you like best, create this file called mymenu:

```
$ cat mymenu
:
# @(#)simple 3-choice menu–upd 1999
#
quit=n
clear
while test "$quit" = "n"
do
    echo "       Menu"
    echo "------------"
    echo
    echo "1.    List Users"
    echo "2.    Show Date"
    echo "3.    Quit"
    echo
    echo -n "Enter choice: .\b"
    read choice
    case $choice in
       1) who;;
       2) date;;
       3) quit=y;;
       *) echo "Invalid choice!\07\07"
       sleep 5;;
    esac
done
```

Then make it executable by entering this (remember the chmod command?)

```
$ chmod +x mymenu
```

To test this program, enter this:

```
$./mymenu
```

Wonder how it works? As the chapter proceeds, I'll explain how this script works. There will be several detours, however, so be patient. The layout of the mymenu script follows the guidelines for structured code that I discussed in the awk discourse (Chapter 14). Apart from the spacing between words (which the shell uses to parse commands), the shell ignores white space, so you are free to indent and align your code in any way you like. The aim is legibility, so you can see at a glance the overall flow structure of your script.

NOTE

The term *blanks* refers to the characters designated in the string $IFS (internal field separators). These are space, tab, and newline by default. The term *white space* (also written *whitespace*) refers to any combination of space, tab, and newline characters. So unless you alter the value of IFS, the terms blank(s) and white space are essentially the same.

Notice that you ran mymenu, the screen cleared, and the menu was displayed, followed by the "Enter choice" prompt, which allows you to enter your choice (1, 2, or 3). Entering a 1 runs the who command; 2 runs the date and 3 exits back to the shell prompt. Any other selection displays the message: Invalid choice, and rings the computer's bell. Then, after a five second pause, the program redisplays the menu.

Helpful Comments

Two general points that apply to all the scripts in this chapter: First, I will assume that you are working in your own directories, that your PATH is set to include your working directory, and that you have the appropriate default read/write permissions. Second, if you want to run your scripts in the usual way (simply typing the script name), you must remember to use chmod as shown to provide execution permission for your script files.

NOTE

Scripts can always be executed using sh *script_name*, but providing execution permission is usually more convenient. Executable scripts can be invoked directly by name just like any other Unix program. Also, you have *better* control over who gets to use your scripts.

If any of these conditions is overlooked, expect to get a "file not found" or similar message when you try to run a script.

The first three lines in mymenu establish good scripting habits. The leading : (null command) does nothing, but it does indicate to other programs that this is a Bourne shell script. For example, C shell users will be able to run mymenu without taking any special action. /bin/csh tests the first character of a shell program. If this is a # character, the program is assumed to be a C shell script and it will be executed by a spawned /bin/csh. On the other hand, when csh sees an initial non-# character (such as :), it invokes /bin/sh, the Bourne shell, to process the script. Bourne and C shell procedures have different syntaxes, of course, so /bin/csh will not always make much sense of a Bourne script, and vice versa.

The second line is a comment signaled by the leading # symbol. Any word *beginning* with # will be ignored, together with the rest of that line. You can write while #comment or while # comment, but # in the middle of a word will be taken literally: while#comment does not make a comment! The line continues with a special pattern, @(#), that is used by the what command.

```
$ what mymenu
# @(#)simple 3-choice menu—skb 1995
$ _
```

what *filename* looks for lines in *filename* containing the pattern @(#) and displays what follows until it meets a tilde (~), greater-than sign (>), newline, backslash (\), or null. You should use this feature to give each script a title/author/date legend, and, with more complex scripts, a syntax/usage message. You can have as many such @(#) lines as you wish. By following this entirely optional convention, you make it easier for you and your colleagues to check what a script is supposed to do. Filenames seldom reveal their full import.

The third line is also a comment, providing a blank line to improve legibility.

The while Loop

The script consists of a while loop that will execute relentlessly as long as the quit variable contains the value "n". The while construct is one of several *conditional* or *flow control* mechanisms that play a key role in all programming languages. Without them, a program would just roll on performing commands in the same fixed sequence. Allowing the execution to branch to alternative sequences, depending on user input or intermediate results, is the very heart of programming. The while shell command is conceptually the same as the while you met in awk (Chapter 14). The syntax, however, is rather different. The shell while follows this format:

```
while w_list
do
        d_list
done
…
```

w_list is called the *while list,* and consists of one or more commands, separated by semicolons or newlines. The commands inside the while list (which can contain arguments, redirections, pipes, other scripts, and all the other command mechanisms) are executed in order, one at a time as long as the conditions are specified by the loop. Once the while list has completed, the program continues with the command following the while list.

You will recall from Chapter 12 that each command returns an exit status (often known simply as the *return value*) to the current shell, which is a number used to indicate how the command performed. You can access this number via the special parameter $?. Although commands can be programmed to return any exit status number you wish, there are certain ground rules that you should follow to make your programs easier to troubleshoot. In general, for example, a zero exit status means *true* (the command was successful), while a nonzero exit status means *false* (the commands failed for some reason). This is contrary to the convention used in C (zero = false, nonzero = true), but has the merit that programmers can use different nonzero exit status numbers to indicate the *reason* for failure. For example, grep returns zero if a match was found (success), 1 if no match was found (failure), and 2 if there was an error in the arguments (another kind of failure).

In the example program, mymenu, the while command examines the exit status of the final command in *w_list*. If the exit status is *true,* the *d_list* of commands between do and done (known as the *do list*) is performed, and control then returns to the while command, which executes the *w_list* again. If the final exit status from *w_list* is *false,* the *d_list* commands are skipped and execution resumes with the command following done. In other words, the while loop repeats the *d_list* as long as the *w_list* returns an exit status of *true.* Once it returns a false, the loop ends and the program goes on to the command that follows the loop. The words do and done serve as block markers (the equivalent of braces in C and awk) for the do list. For clarity, you should indent the commands in the do list so they stand out as one "unit" that you can easily identify when you go back to make changes or troubleshoot your program later.

Oh, and by the way, the last command in the program is quite important. It tells the computer that it should end and return to the shell. That command is called done.

NOTE

If the do list ends with done &, the whole loop will be executed as a background process.

break and continue

There are two commands you can place in the do loop itself that alter the above scenario. The break command causes an exit from the while loop, sending control directly to the command following the loop. If you have nested while loops, you can use break n, where n is a number defaulting to 1, to "break" out of n loops. In other words, let's say you have a program that has eight nested loops (a loop inside a loop inside a loop, etc.). Giving the command break 8 will return you to the outermost loop. A break 6 will take you to the second nested loop.

The continue command in the do loop stops execution of the do loop and returns control to the enclosing while loop. If you have nested while loops, the continue n sends control to the nth enclosing while command. So after a break, the while loop is over; but after a continue, the while loop continues.

break is useful when a condition arises in the loop that prevents further action. continue is used when a particular item in the loop cannot be processed, but you want the loop to carry on processing further items. A typical example in *pseudocode* might be

```
while grab_next_item; any-left?
do
    if quota_full then break
    if item_empty then continue
done
```

We call this pseudocode because it does not have to follow the precise syntax of any computer (or natural) language. Rather, it can informally represent the logic and flow of an algorithm, and provide you with a useful guide for converting the algorithm into working code.

Endless Loops and the trap Command

Whenever you use loop commands such as while, you must guard against endless loops. Some action in the loop should eventually lead to an exit status when the while list is executed, or some condition in the do loop should invoke a break; otherwise the do loop will repeat forever. There are occasions when an intentionally endless loop is useful. But such programs should warn the user and indicate the appropriate action for terminating the loop. This is usually achieved with the key or Ctrl combination assigned to interrupt the program. The interrupt key is usually Rubout, Break, or Del but the default can be changed with the stty command:

```
stty intr ^a    # change interrupt key to Ctrl-a
```

Such changes are usually temporary and are intended to prevent "accidental" interruption during critical parts of a script. Your script can also trap (intercept) a user interrupt (and other unexpected signals) with the trap command and perform any set of actions before an eventual exit to the shell. trap is an internal shell command. The syntax is

```
trap ['commands'] [signals…]
```

The optional *signals* arguments are the same signal numbers you met with the kill command in Chapter 8. Each signal number represents a type of signal that one process can send to another (using kill) or respond to when received from another process (using trap). Signal number 9 is the unique "killer" signal that cannot be trapped or ignored. Zero represents the signal generated upon exit to the shell, 15 is the signal number for software termination (the default with the kill command), and 2 represents an interrupt signal generated by the currently assigned interrupt key. Another useful signal number to know is 1 for *hangup*. This is generated if the line is disconnected for any reason while a process is running. (The name comes from those occasions when someone hangs up the phone and cuts your link to the computer.) These signals represent a variety of "unexpected" calamities, and trap gives you a tool for ignoring them or handling them gracefully (except for the untrappable 9). When the specified signal numbers are trapped, the commands in the commands argument are executed. If commands is empty (" "or ' '), the signals are ignored by the shell.

Suppose your script generates a temporary file junk$$ in your home directory. $$ is the special shell parameter holding the process number for the current shell process. This is a useful trick for generating uniquely named files. Good housekeeping mandates that you erase this file before the program exits. A user interrupt or hangup could well frustrate this endeavor. The following line

```
trap "rm $HOME/junk$$; exit" 1 2
```

placed immediately after the file creation will trap signal types 1 and 2. Instead of an immediate exit, trap will run the command rm $HOME/junk$$ followed by an exit command. The latter, naturally, exits the current shell process. With no argument, exit will return an exit status equal to that of the last command executed. If the rm command failed (file not found), a nonzero exit code would be returned. By writing exit n, where n is a positive integer, you can set the exit status to n. You may recall my earlier statement that the exit status value is entirely a programming convention: successful operation should return zero, failure should return nonzero. You can now see how easy it is to break this convention. Unix relies on intelligent cooperation without heavy policing.

NOTE

If you enter exit at the prompt, you'll terminate your login shell process, which means you'll be logged off the system.

If the trap argument *commands* has more than one command, the whole argument must be quoted, since trap expects just one command argument (possibly empty). The double quotes are needed in the above example to allow $ substitution to occur. In the absence of any arguments, trap displays a list of the commands associated with each signal number.

The trap *commands* 0 command lets you invoke *commands* when the shell is exited. If you set this trap in your login shell, any desired set of actions can be triggered when you log off.

The until Loop

This is a good moment to mention a simple variant of the while loop called the until loop. It's kind of the opposite of the while loop. The until command will loop *until* a certain condition prevails rather than *while* a certain condition prevails. For example:

```
while X
do
  d_list
done
```

is equivalent to

```
until NOT-X
do
  d_list
done
```

Choosing between while and until really depends on the type of condition you are testing for. Sometimes the "positive" while condition is the natural (and easiest) one to test for; on other occasions, the "negative" until condition is more natural. Compare the following snippets:

```
while sleep 60
do
    who | grep stan
```

```
done
...
until who | grep stan
do
     sleep 60
done
...
```

Both versions will poll the list of users every 60 seconds to see if stan has logged in. The until version has the merit of exiting immediately if stan is already logged in; the while version sleeps for a minute before checking, and even after stan has logged in, it will continue to report the fact every minute until either stan logs off or you interrupt the process.

The do List

Before we explore the do list, let's study the anatomy of the while command in more detail.

With awk, while is followed by a single Boolean expression. With the shell, however, while can be followed by any number of commands, of which the last one provides a "Boolean" value as a side effect. I mention this because you may find awk commands embedded in a shell script and you must avoid confusion between the two sets of grammars. In practice, the shell while is usually followed by a single command intended to control the loop. The most common of these single commands is called test.

The test Command

The test command is not an internal shell command like while, although it is rarely used outside shell programs. (More recent Unix versions have made test a built-in command, but this does not affect the usage outlined here.) test exists solely to return an exit status depending on its options and arguments. It is used after the conditional commands, while, until, and if, to provide a Boolean value for flow control.

NOTE

You should resist the temptation to call any of your own programs test. Such programs could be looked at by the shell instead of the test command, making your scripts misbehave.

In mymenu, the while loop is controlled by the following test:

```
while test "$quit" = "n"
```

Here, test compares the two strings $quit and "n" and returns *true* (zero) if the strings are equal. If the two strings are unequal, test returns *false* (nonzero). The while loop will therefore iterate as long as $quit evaluates to "n". Remember that quit is a user-supplied variable, so $quit represents its current value.

NOTE

Note carefully the *essential* double quotes around each string and the *essential* spaces either side of the = sign.

The test command is so widely used that typing four characters proved irksome in the terse Unix environment. The following shorthand was therefore introduced:

```
while [ "$quit" = "n" ]
```

The character [must be treated like a command name (because it is!), so space is essential after the [. Further, since [invokes the test command in a certain way, it expects space before the closing]. This format for test is a more legible one in many contexts. Which version you use is a matter of personal taste, but you should be familiar with both in order to read and understand other programmers' code.

Variables, Values, and Quotes Revisited

The whole business of variables, values, and quotes, together with the syntax for assignment, substitution, and string comparison is a constant headache for beginners, so I'll digress a moment to clarify the situation.

When you assign a value to a variable, as in

```
quit=n
```

no white space (spaces, tabs, or newlines) is allowed on either side of the = sign. The right-hand side is interpreted by the shell as the string value, "n", to be stored in quit. You could write quit="n" or quit= 'n' with exactly the same effect. You need to quote the right-hand side expression only if (1) it contains white space that is truly part of the value to be assigned, or (2) it contains metacharacters that have special meanings to the shell.

There is no magical difference between assigning strings and numbers to a variable. quit=n and quit=45 are equally valid. In quit=45, quit simply receives two characters that happen to be digits. You'll see soon that there are arithmetical (integers only) operations on $quit that could exploit this numerical value, but quit itself is not data-typed in the way that C variables are. Shell variables are actually string variables. If the string represents a whole number (positive or negative), you can extract its value, perform sums, and store the result as a string.

After quit=n, we have the single character "n" sitting inside the variable called quit. But if you echo quit, you'll simply display the string "quit":

```
$ quit=n
$ echo quit
quit
$ _
```

The shell must be "teased" into revealing the value of the variable called quit, and this is done by prefixing quit with the substitution metacharacter $:

```
$ quit=n
$ echo $quit
n
$ _
```

The shell "gets to" $quit first, "sees" the $, unlocks the value of quit, and passes this value as the argument to echo.

Single (forward) quotes hide the $ from the shell:

```
$ quit=n
$ echo  '$quit'
$quit
$ _
```

so no substitution takes place. Double quotes do not hide the $:

```
$ quit=n
$ echo "$quit"
n
$ _
```

Here the shell performs the substitution and passes the value "n" to echo. Since $quit and "$quit" echo in the same way, you may wonder whether the double quotes are useful. The reason is that quit may be assigned a value such as "Now is   the hour" (note the extra spaces):

```
$ quit="Now is      the hour"
$ echo $quit
Now is the hour

$ echo "$quit"
Now is      the hour
$ _
```

In the first example, the shell passes four arguments to echo, namely the strings "Now", "is", "the", and "hour". The extra spaces between "is" and "the" are swallowed by the shell. echo displays the four arguments separated by single spaces.

In the second case, the double quotes around $quit preserve the embedded white space, and only *one* argument is passed to echo, namely the exact string stored in quit.

More test Options

With this in mind, let's return to the while loop test:

```
while test "$quit" = "n"
```

test has many applications, but here it is used to compare two strings. The test command syntax for string comparison calls for *three* distinct arguments: *string1*, =, and string2. This immediately alerts you that the spaces around the = *must* be present. "$quit=n", "$quit"="n", "$quit" ="n" or "$quit"= "n" are all wrong. The need for three arguments also implies that any white space in the strings being compared *must* be hidden from the shell. In the case of the fixed, literal right-hand string, either 'n' or "n" would be fine. On the left-hand side, only double quotes will work. As you saw earlier, "$quit" allows the $ to substitute and, equally importantly, passes the result as *one* argument to test.

But what if you need to compare strings containing a real, literal $? You would usually escape the $ with \ (backslash) since this hides the $ even within double quotes:

```
test "\$30" = "$val"
```

This would compare the string "$30" with the string stored in val. '$30' would also work. Table 15.1 summarizes how the different quoting methods work with each metacharacter.

NOTE
The syntax for string comparison with test uses a *single* = character (unlike the == equality test in awk and C).

TABLE 15.1: Quoting Methods

QUOTE	METACHARACTER					
	\	$	*	'	"	'
'	n	n	n	n	n	t
'	y	n	n	t	n	n
"	y	y	n	y	t	n

n = not interpreted (hidden from shell)

y = interpreted by shell

t = terminates the quote

Testing Empty Variables

In addition to testing variables and strings for equality and inequality, test can tell you if a variable is empty (null) or not. You've met the notations " " and ' ' for the empty string. There are several ways a defined variable (also known as a *set* variable) such as quit can become empty:

▶ Unless quit is assigned a value, it *is* empty

▶ The assignment quit= (no right-hand value)

▶ The assignments quit=" " or quit= ' '

NOTE

The terms *empty string*, *null string*, and *string of length zero* all mean the same in this book.

If quit is empty, echo $quit simply displays a blank line:

```
$ quit=
$ echo $quit
$ _
```

What happens here is that the substitution operation $ applied to a null variable returns no value whatsoever, so echo does not receive an argument. If you try

```
$ echo
$ _
```

you'll get the same result. (Kernighan and Pike quote Doug McIlroy's famous parable concerning the fair maid Unix and her dubiously crystal clear *echo*.)

NOTE

Variables are defined (or set) within a shell simply by being named without a preceding $. The occurrence of $quit, for example, does not define quit. If quit has not been defined, or has been defined without a value being assigned, $quit returns the empty string. Recall, also, that variables defined in a shell are not automatically defined in any of its subshells. You need an explicit export var_name statement in the parent shell in order that var_name will be known to its subshells.

The related operation unset quit actually removes quit from the shell's list of variables. quit is now undefined (unset), so asking if it is empty or not is a metaphysical question. echo will do its best:

```
$ unset quit
$ echo $quit

$ _
```

By the way, you can unset several variables in one fell swoop:

```
unset x y z
```

but, for obvious reasons, you cannot unset any of the predefined shell variables.

echo reacts to an empty, defined variable in the same way it reacts to an undefined variable. So, echo is not the ideal test for emptiness *or* existence! But worse follows:

```
$ quit=" "
$ echo $quit

$ echo "$quit"

$ _
```

quit now contains a space, so it's not empty in spite of appearances. In the second line, $quit produces a space which is immediately swallowed by the shell; echo gets an empty argument, hence the blank line. In line 4, a real space is passed to echo and is displayed, but you'll have to take my word for it.

Happily, test provides a more positive way of checking if a variable is empty or not. There are several options. Before I show them, recall that $?

is the special shell variable that holds the exit status value of the last executed command. I'll use this to show the exit status of `test` with different options and arguments. First, we have the simplest test for null strings:

```
test var
```

or, to remind you of the synonym:

```
[var ]
```

This returns true if `var` is not null, and false if `var` is null. For example,

```
$ quit=
$ test $quit
$ echo $?
1
$ test "$quit"
$ echo $?
1
$ quit=" "
$ test $quit
$ echo $?
1
$ test "$quit"
$ echo $?
0
$ _
```

When `quit` is empty, `test` returns 1 meaning *false*. When `quit` is nonempty, `test` returns 0 meaning *true*. So, `test` here is testing for "nonempty = true, empty = false." These negative queries are somewhat confusing, rather like the lawyer browbeating the witness: "Is it not the case that you have not denied that you refused to stop beating your spouse?"

The first two tests need careful attention. When you test the unquoted `$quit`, `test` receives no argument at all, yet it correctly reports an empty string. When you test the quoted `$quit`, `test` does receive an argument, namely `" "`. Again, the result is correct: `$quit` is empty. `test var` (like `echo`) treats no argument the same as a null-string argument. Many Unix commands, including some `test` variants, are less tolerant: if they expect an argument, they insist on one. The point is that in many contexts the empty string `" "` actually counts as a valid argument, as opposed to no argument at all!

The next examples use the −n and −z options for `test`. First the syntax:

```
test -n var
test -z var
```

The semantics here are less confusing. -n asks "Is the string length nonzero (string nonempty)?" and -z asks "Is the string length zero (string empty)?" Think of -n as "nonzero?", and -z as "zero?" Now the examples, and a little surprise:

```
$ quit=
$ test -z $quit
test: argument expected
$ echo $?
1
$ test -z "$quit"
$ echo $?
0
$ _
```

The lesson here is that text -z insists on precisely one argument. The unquoted $quit does not provide one, so you get an error message and a nonzero exit status (failure). When you quote $quit, test-z gets its argument, the null string, and returns *true:* quit is indeed empty. Similarly, test -n insists on an argument, but reverses the sense of the test:

```
$ test -n $quit
test: argument expected
$ echo $?
1
$ test -n "$quit"
$ echo $?
1
```

This time the test is for nonempty, so the answer is *false:* quit is not nonempty. See if you can follow the next examples, where quit contains a space:

```
$ quit=" "
$ test -z $quit
test: argument expected
$ echo $?
1
$ test -z "$quit"
$ echo $?
1
$ test -n $quit
test: argument expected
$ echo $?
1
$ test -n "$quit"
$ echo $?
0
$ _
```

I make no apologies for grinding on about `test`, empty variables, null strings, and their quirky symbiosis. It's one of those subjects that pervade Unix: you start with a bewildering set of apparently unconnected facts, then suddenly the light dawns, and everything becomes obvious and intuitive. In spite of the mystical overtones, an awareness of the differences between an empty argument and no argument turns out to be useful when writing robust programs. A robust program is one that survives rough treatment, such as unexpected input. Your scripts should always anticipate peculiar input (including no input) from the user, issue a polite, helpful warning, then reprompt for correct input. The unfriendly script is the one that exits with an untrapped error from the shell itself.

Testing Numbers

`test` also lets you compare two integers, although the syntax is rather ungainly:

```
test "$X" -eq "$Y"
```

returns *true* (zero) if X equals Y numerically. Note that you are no longer testing for string equality. Ponder the following:

```
$ X=9; Y="00009"
$ [ "$X" = 9 ]
$ echo $?
0                       <true>
$ [ "$X" -eq 9 ]
$ echo $?
0                       <true>
$ [ "$Y" = 9 ]
$ echo $?
1                       <false>
$ [ "$Y" -eq 9 ]
$ echo $?
0                       <true>
$ [ "$X" = "$Y" ]
$ echo $?
1                       <false>
$ [ "$X" -eq "$Y" ]
$ echo $?
0                       <true>
$ _
```

The string tests reveal "9" and "00009" as unequal, but the numerical tests treat them as equal. You should repeat these tests with strings such as " 9 " and "09 ".

In addition to testing for numerical equality, test allows the following comparisons:

"$X" -ne "$Y"	Tests true if X not equal to Y
"$X" -gt "$Y"	Tests true if X greater than Y
"$X" -ge "$Y"	Tests true if X greater than or equal to Y
"$X" -lt "$Y"	Tests true if X less than Y
"$X" -le "$Y"	Tests true if X less than or equal to Y

Testing Files

The test command can also be used to check the existence of files and directories and what permissions have been set for them. The syntax is

    test option file

The option is a single letter with some mnemonic significance, as shown below:

Option	test *option file* returns *true* if *file* exists and
-r	is readable (file or directory)
-w	is writeable (file or directory)
-x	is executable (file or directory)
-f	is a regular file (not a directory)
-d	is a directory
-c	is a character special file
-b	is a block special file
-u	its set-user-ID bit is set
-g	its set-group-ID bit is set
-k	its sticky bit is set
-s	has size greater than zero
-t[*fds*]	the open file with file descriptor *fds* is associated with a terminal device. (Default *fds* is 1.)

These provide considerable scope for checking on files before dangerous or illegal operations are attempted by your script. Recall my advice about averting abrupt program termination. A good example might be a script called `safecopy`. The user supplies two filename arguments, *source* and *dest*. The script can access these as $1 and $2. The number of arguments is stored in $#. We could test the following:

- ▶ `test "$#" -eq 2` to ensure we have two arguments.

- ▶ `test "$1" = "$2"` to prevent spurious copying. (A more refined test would look at implicit and explicit paths, since two distinct strings can represent the same file.)

- ▶ `test -r "$1"` to see if *source* exists and is readable.

- ▶ `test -f "$1"` to see if *source* is a file (not a directory).

- ▶ `test -w "$2"` and warn if *dest* exists and is in danger of being overwritten.

- ▶ `test -d "$2"` to see if *dest* is a directory.

Multiple Tests

As the previous example indicates, you often need to test for a set of conditions, and `test` allows you to do this. You can combine Boolean expressions with the logical operators NOT, AND, and OR as you saw in the awk syntax in Chapter 15. The way you do it with `test` is less elegant than awk but quite manageable, as shown in Table 15.2.

TABLE 15.2: Mathematical Operatons and Functions for test

OPERATOR	EXAMPLE	MEANING
!	[! expr]	NOT expr: *true* if expr tests *false*. *False* if expr tests *true*.
-a	[expr1 -a expr2]	expr1 AND expr2: *true* if both expressions *true*. *False* if either or both *false*.
-o	[expr1 -o expr2]	expr1 OR expr2: *true* if either or both expressions *true*. *False* if both *false*.

The [] notation here is much neater. The `test` versions would be `test ! expr`, `test expr1 -a expr2`, and `test expr1 -o expr2`. Here's a typical example:

```
filename=/usr/stan/richard.iii
if [ -r "$filename" -a -f "$filename" -a -s "filename" ]
```

```
then
    echo "$filename is a readable, regular, nonempty file"
    more -d "$filename"
else
    echo "Cannot display $filename"
fi
```

The if/else tests are quite obvious, but I'll cover them in detail later. We start by testing that filename meets three conditions before applying more to display its contents. It must be readable, a regular file (not a directory), and finally, it must have more than zero bytes. When combining logical operators, you need to watch the order in which they are applied. The test operators have built-in precedence rules that you can override by using parentheses. Before we examine these possibilities, let's review the basics. Just as

```
(x + y) x z
```

is not the same arithmetical expression as

```
x + (y x z)
```

the expression

```
(A OR B) AND C
```

is different from

```
A OR (B AND C)
```

In fact, George Boole's claim to fame was demonstrating the close affinity between arithmetical operators and the *Boolean* operators named for him.

The traditional way of evaluating complex Booleans is the *truth table*. The following truth table compares (A OR B) AND C and A OR (A AND C). We consider all the possibilities allowing A, B, and C to be true (T) or false (F). Let X = A OR (B AND C), Y = (A OR B) AND C.

A	B	C	X	Y
T	T	T	T	T
T	T	F	T	F
T	F	T	T	T
T	F	F	T	F
F	T	T	T	T
F	T	F	F	F
F	F	T	F	F
F	F	F	F	F

The differences in the X and Y columns establish that the two expressions are indeed distinct. Now consider the two expressions ! (A OR B) and (! A) AND (! B).

A	B	! A	! B	A OR B	! (A OR B)	(! A) AND (! B)
T	T	F	F	T	F	F
T	F	F	T	T	F	F
F	T	T	F	T	F	F
F	F	F	F	F	T	T

The last two columns are identical, so we have proved a useful identity:

```
! ( A OR B ) = ( ! A ) AND ( ! B )
```

It can be shown in the same way that

```
! ( A AND B ) = ( ! A ) OR ( ! B )
```

The built-in rules for test gives highest precedence to the string, file, and arithmetical operators (=, -eq, etc.), then comes -a (AND), and finally -o (OR). Higher precedence operations are evaluated before the lower precedence operations. This means that if you write

```
[ "$x" = "$y" -a "$n" -lt 0 -o "$m" -gt 30 ]
```

it will be interpreted, using conventional algebraic notation, as

```
if ( x=y AND n<0 ) OR ( m>30 )
```

If you wish to alter this interpretation, test lets you use parentheses (but they must be quoted):

```
[ "$x" = "$y" -a \( "$n" -lt 0 -o "$m" -gt 30 \) ]
```

You now have the distinct Boolean test:

```
if x=y AND ( n<0 OR m>30 )
```

Two vital facts about the parentheses: they must be quoted (the backslash offering the most convenient method) and they must have surrounding white space. The reason for quoting is that parentheses already have a meaning to the shell. You may recall that

```
(comm1; comm2 ) &
```

means run the two commands *together* as a background subshell process. The reason for the white space around \(and \) is that, like the operators, the parentheses represent real, separate arguments to test.

Back to the Menu

In mymenu, the quit variable is set to the literal string value "n" before the while loop, and retains this value until you select item 3 to quit the menu. Once `quit` is set to "y", the `while` loop terminates. To be exact, the `while` loop would terminate if `quit` received any value other than "n". So you could concoct any number of equivalents to the given test:

```
while [ "$quit" != "y" ]
```

This loops while `quit` does *not* equal "y". You could also use:

```
until test "$quit" = "y"
```

or even,

```
until [ "$quit" != "n" ]
```

Note that the `!` is the logical NOT operator, reversing the sense of the test. It can go in front of the = or in front of the whole expression. For instance, the last test could also be written as

```
until [ ! "$quit" = "n" ]
```

Of these five variants (and many more are available), the one used in `mymenu` seems the most "natural."

The read Command

The next element of our menu is the mechanism for inviting and receiving user input using the `read` command. The line

```
echo -n "Enter choice: .\b"
```

displays the argument string without a final newline because of the `-n` option. (The same effect can be obtained by adding `\c` at the end of the string.) The `\b` pair backspaces the cursor over the "." character. This is an optional trick; the idea is to display a dot for each input character expected. Typically, if a name of ten letters maximum was sought, the prompt would show

```
Enter Name: ..........
```

and ten backspaces would bring the cursor to the entry point. The next line is

```
read choice
```

This reads one line from the standard input and places it in the user-defined variable, `choice`. In other words, the `read` command waits for the user to type something and when a newline is detected, `read` transfers the input to the argument variable. In fact, `read` can do more than that. If you supply more than one argument to `read`, the first word of standard input goes into the first argument, the second word goes into the second argument, and so on. Any excess words end up in the last argument. For example, if you had

```
read x y z
```

and the user typed "To be or not to be", x would pick up "To", y would pick up "be" and z would pick up "or not to be".

The read command has a useful property. Its exit status will be *true* (zero) until an end-of-file condition occurs during input. Once the end-of-file is sensed, read returns *false*. If read is getting its input from the keyboard, it will return *true* until Ctrl-D is typed. If input is being redirected from a file, read returns *true* until the end of the file is reached. This can be exploited in while loops. If myscript contains the following:

```
while read line
do
    process_line
done
```

you can use myscript <data_file to read lines and process data from data_file until it runs out of lines to process. Without redirection, myscript would accept and process manually typed lines until Ctrl-D is keyed.

NOTE

From System V Release 2 onward, you can also redirect from a file to the read command: read line <data_file.

Sometimes read is used as a pause rather than as a way to invite useful data. The following snippet illustrates the familiar "Hit Enter to continue..." situation:

```
echo "Hit Enter to continue...\c"
read junk
```

The first line is informational only. It tells the computer operator to press Enter to continue. The second line tells the computer to read incoming data from the keyboard, so it just "sits there" and waits for input. When the read command receives a newline (from the Enter key) it terminates the pause.

By the way, it can be worthwhile to make this into a shell script, called pause. We can use it later to tidy up the menu.

if Only

In mymenu, choice will contain the item number selected by the user. Of course, there is no way of telling what the user may be inclined to type. Users are like that! The program must never assume that the value in choice contains only sensible responses to the prompt. Our script must now branch to the appropriate command depending on the value in choice, or warn if the value is unacceptable. We could proceed by testing the value of choice with a series of if/then/else statements. As with awk, the shell's if conditional statement is quite straightforward (but watch out for the inevitable syntax variations):

```
if command-list
then
    action1
[else
    action2]
fi
next-command
```

The command-list follows all the rules given for the while list. If the last simple command executed returns *true, action1* (any list of commands) will be executed followed by *next-command*. Otherwise, if *command-list* returns *false,* the else branch (if present) is taken and the *action2* commands are executed followed by *next-command*. Analogous to the do/done block markers, we have the if/fi pair.

NOTE

It's critical to match each if with an fi—otherwise, the shell will not know which sections of code to execute. Furthermore, you'll get a syntax error!

The else section is not essential: it all depends on the logic of your program:

```
if [ "$#" -ne 2 ]
then
    echo "This command needs 2 arguments"; exit
fi
...
```

Once the number-of-arguments test is passed, the rest of the script can roll on without a specific else clause.

The contrary situation can occur. Sometimes you may want to skip the if/then action and simply perform the else section (for example, it may be easier to test for the "negative" condition). The trick is to use the null command, : (colon), the subject of the next section.

Busy Doing Nothing

Whenever the Unix syntax demands a command argument but you don't have a command to perform, you can use :. The null command satisfies the syntactical demand for a command but does nothing. You've seen it in a rather passive role as the first character in a Bourne shell script. A more active application is the "while forever" loop:

```
while :
do
    process
    if [ "$x" -eq 0 ]
    then
        break
    fi
done
...
```

The command list after while must contain at least one command. In a "while forever" loop, the while condition is deliberately made permanently true, and you rely on a break command in the do list to end the loop. The null command returns a zero exit status (true), so it offers one solution as shown above. A more legible solution is the true command. This also does nothing except guarantee a zero exit status. So you'll often see while true, as well as while :. There is a corresponding false command, guaranteed to return a nonzero exit status without doing anything else of note. You can create an "until-hell-freezes" loop with until false. Again, you must create a break with the break command if you want your loop to end (other than by a user interrupt). Another common use for : is to provide an empty statement after then:

```
echo "Enter author's name : \c"
read author
if grep "^$author " /usr/stan/books >/dev/null
then
    :
else
    echo "$author not found" >&2    # redirect to standard
error
    exit 1
fi
...
```

If grep finds the target author (exit status 0, meaning *true*), we want to do nothing immediately. We are more interested in grep's failure. But if/then expects a command, so a blank line after then will invoke a syntax error. The : averts this tragedy.

Note the useful >/dev/null trick. You often meet a situation where a command in a shell script sends unwanted output to the screen. Here, we are using grep simply to see if a given pattern is matched, namely ^$author (the given author at the beginning of a line). Unless we take avoiding action, we risk the unnecessary distraction of matching lines on the standard output. The answer is to redirect unwanted output to /dev/null, a special "trash can" system file that takes everybody's rubbish without complaint. By the way, you cannot recover discarded data from /dev/null. If you read from /dev/null, you get an immediate end-of-file. In fact, that's a useful property of /dev/null: sometimes you need an immediate end-of-file!

Error Handling

The error message in the previous example introduces two important aspects of Unix commands:

```
echo "$author not found" >&2
exit 1
```

We exit with a nonzero status code so that if your script is incorporated in another script (by you or somebody else), other commands can check for failure and take appropriate action. The general idea is that if prog1 calls prog2 and prog2 exits with exit *n*, then prog1 can access *n* as $? to determine the cause of the exit. Since prog2 may have called prog3, and so on, this sequence of exit checks can be nested indefinitely.

Without an argument, exit returns the status of the last command executed. Often this will provide a suitable status value to the calling program. In the previous example, however, the last command performed before the error exit is a *successful* grep command! We must therefore use exit 1 (or any agreeable positive integer) to signal failure to any surrounding command.

The message from echo is redirected from the standard output to the standard error using the symbol & followed by 2, the file descriptor allocated to standard error (see below). You can write either >&2 or >& 2, but no spaces are allowed between > and &.

NOTE

Three standard files are opened automatically and have preassigned file descriptors as follows:

o   Standard input

1   Standard output

2   Standard error

Unix assigns a unique numerical fd (file descriptor) to each file that is opened for processing. C and other languages allow programmers to access files via their fd's (until the file is closed). At the shell script level, you will usually be concerned only with the three standard fd's listed above.

The syntax for accessing a file with fd (file descriptor) *n* is

command >& *n*	redirect output from *command* to file with fd *n*
command <& *n*	redirect input from file (with fd *n*) to *command*
command 2> file	redirect standard error output from *command* to *file*
<&-	close the standard input
>&-	close the standard output
n>&-	close the file with fd *n*
1>&2	send standard output to standard error
2>&1	send standard error to standard output

Most of the standard Unix commands use >&2 (or equivalent) to send error messages to standard error rather than to standard output. Your own scripts should follow the same strategy. Although standard output and standard error are both, by default, assigned to your screen, they are separate "files." If your error messages are sent to the standard output, there can be a problem. If you redirect the standard output to a real file, your error messages will also be redirected, usually with depressing consequences. If you send errors to standard error, of course, they will appear on the screen, by default, even if standard output has been redirected. You can redirect from standard error to a file, though, just as easily as you redirect standard output to a file. The syntax is either

```
command 2>file    # NO spaces allowed between 2 and >
```

or

```
command 2> file   # space OK here
```

The following examples may clarify the situation.

```
$ ls amelia
amelia not found
$ ls amelia >junk
amelia not found
$ _
```

The error message appears on the screen (standard error) in spite of the standard output being redirected.

```
$  ls amelia 2> errfile
$ _
```

Standard error is now redirected to errfile, so no error message appears. Look at the contents of errfile:

```
$ cat errfile
amelia not found
$ _
```

The elif Command

Nesting a sequence of if/then/else/fi conditions can become quite complicated:

```
if test "$choice" = 1
then
     who
else if test "$choice" = 2
     then
          date
     else if test "$choice" = 3
          then
               quit=y
          else echo "Invalid choice!\07\07"
               sleep 5
          fi
     fi
fi
...
```

To simplify such chains, the elif can be used in place of else if...fi:

```
if test "$choice" = 1
then
     who
elif test "$choice" = 2
then
     date
elif test "$choice" = 3
```

```
then
      quit=y
else echo "Invalid choice!\07\07"
      sleep 5
fi
…
```

This is still rather awkward. The `case` statement offers a simpler (and faster) solution.

The Best case Scenario

Most languages have a `case` multibranch flow control mechanism. (BASIC has ON X GOTO..., C and Pascal have `case`) In theory, `case` is not needed since there is always an equivalent sequence of `if`'s and `else`'s. In practice, the `case` mechanism offers safer, faster, and more legible coding. The `case` syntax is easier to use than to define exhaustively. Here is the overall scheme:

```
case word in
pattern1) command-list1 ;;
pattern2) command-list2 ;;
pattern3) command-list3 ;;
…
esac
next-command
```

The complete `case` statement starts with `case` and ends with `esac` (`case` spelled backwards). The *word* argument is an expression whose value will determine which branch to take. Each branch is "labeled" by a pattern, and whichever pattern first matches *word* will invoke its associated command list. After which, control moves to beyond `esac` to what I've called the *next-command*. The last command in each *command-list* must end with *two* semicolons.

NOTE

The pair of semicolons is in fact optional after the final command list, but it's safer to use them after every command list. If you ever need to add an extra pattern at the end of a `case` statement, the command list will not need changing!

Before I clarify the syntax, let's look at the menu example:

```
…
case $choice in
     1) who;;
```

```
        2) date;;
        3) quit=y;;
        *) echo "Invalid choice!\07\07"
           sleep 5;;
    esac
done
...
```

If `choice` receives 1 from the `read` command, a match is made with the first pattern: 1), so the `who` command is invoked. All the other patterns are then skipped, and control moves out of the `case` statement. Similarly choices 2 and 3 invoke just the commands associated with the 2) and 3) patterns. What if `choice` contains a 9? The first three patterns do not match, but the fourth pattern is * that matches zero or more occurrences of *anything*. In fact any `choice` other than 1, 2, or 3 gets "trapped" by the final * pattern (including null). For this reason, you'll find that most `case` statements end with this catch-all pattern. The patterns available in `case` are a special set of regular expressions, as tabulated below:

Pattern	Matches
*	Anything (including nothing)
?	Any single character
[abc]	Any one of "a", "b", "c"
[a-m]	Any one character in the range
pat1|pat2	Either `pat1` or `pat2`

These patterns borrow both from `ed` and the file substitution patterns used by the shell, with some private quirks thrown in to add to the fun. `ed` uses "." (period) rather than "?" to match any single character. `ed` also uses "*" differently. With `ed`, `r*` matches zero or more occurrences of `r`. With `case`, `r*` matches `r` and `r` followed by any character. In addition, you can quote metacharacters with double or single quotes, or with \, to match their literal values. The menu uses single character patterns, but it's common to find more complex patterns:

```
case $day in
[Mm]onday |[Ll]undi)        monday_wash;;
[Tt]uesday |[Mm]ardi)       tuesday_dry;;
...
[Ss]unday |[Dd]imanche)     sunday_school;;
*)                          echo "Not a day...";;
esac
```

It is quite legal for a pattern to have an empty command list, meaning ignore the matching cases. For example,

```
case $choice in
    0) ;;
    1) who;;
    2) date;;
    3) quit=y;;
    *) echo "Invalid choice!\07\07"
       sleep 5;;
esac
```

would take no action if 0 was entered as the choice.

Branching with && and ||

There's a neat alternative to the if/then branch. Rather than write

```
if command1
then
    command2
fi
```

you can achieve the same ends with

```
command1 && command2
```

In other words, if *command1* returns 0 (success), *command2* will be executed; if *command1* returns nonzero (failure), *command2* will be ignored. You can slot in *command1* && *command2* at any point in a script where a command is legal. Once you get used to this construct, it can save you the time spent laying out the if/then statements. For example,

```
grep "^$author " $fil >/dev/null && cat $fil >> biblio
```

will append the file $fil to biblio if the given author is found in $fil. If grep fails for any reason, the cat command is skipped.

The construct

```
command1 || command2
```

works the other way round: if *command1* fails, *command2* is executed; if *command1* succeeds, *command2* is ignored.

```
grep "^$author " $fil >dev/null || echo "$author not found"
```

You met the symbols && and || in a similar context in the awk section (Chapter 15). In awk they stand for the logical AND and OR operators used with Boolean expressions. In the shell, && and || have a slight affinity to AND and OR, but only in the context of two commands.

More Menu

To make use of some of the commands discussed so far, let's add a few choices to the menu:

```
$ cat newmenu
:
# @(#) simple 6-choice menu-skb 1995
#
quit=n
prevdir=`pwd`
dir=prevdir
clear
while test "$quit" = "n"
do
   echo "          Menu"
   echo "----------------"
   echo
   echo "Your current directory is `pwd`"
   echo
   echo "1.    List Users"
   echo "2.    Show Date"
   echo "3.    Display a file"
   echo "4.    Change working directory"
   echo "5.    Return to original directory"
   echo "Q.    Quit"
   echo
   echo -n "Enter choice: .\b"
   read choice
   case $choice in
   1) who | more
      pause;;
   2) date
      pause;;
   3) echo "Enter filenamefilename: \c"
      read fil
      if [ -r "$fil" -a -f "$fil" ]
      then
         clear
         more -d $fil
      else
         echo "Cannot display $fil"
      fi
      pause;;
   4) echo "Enter target directory: \c"
      read dir
      if test -d "${dir:=`pwd`}"
```

```
        then
            cd $dir
        else
            echo "$dir: no such directory"
        fi
            pause;;
        5) if test "$dir" != "$prevdir"
            then
                cd $prevdir
            fi
            pause;;
        Q|q) quit=y;;
         *) echo "Invalid choice!\07\07"
             sleep 5;;
     esac
  done
  $ _
```

In addition to the new items, we've made a few minor improvements. `who | more` will give page pauses if your system is busy (moral: always assume the worse case!). The original choice of 3 for the quit option left much to be desired. By making it "Q" or "q" we have less renumbering to do as we add new items, and, some would claim, it's a more natural choice. Note how we store the original directory:

```
prevdir=`pwd`
```

The backquoted pwd runs the pwd command *in situ* (right then and there) and returns the current working directory, which is then assigned to the variable `prevdir`. A quick test on your quota of "quote" understanding: do we need any additional quotes around the expression `` `pwd` ``? Single forward quotes would definitely be wrong. `` ' `pwd` ' `` would pass the literal five-character string `` `pwd` `` to `prevdir` since single forward quotes hide the command substitution meaning of the backquotes. Double quotes would work fine but they are not needed here. The pwd command returns a single, well-behaved value with no white space or metacharacters. We also store the initial working directory in `dir`. This value may change later if item 4 is selected.

The `pause` command is the small script I mentioned earlier, made executable with `chmod`.

```
$ cat pause
:
# #(@) pause til Enter key pressed...        skb 1995
#
echo "Hit Enter to continue...\c"
```

```
   read junk
$ chmod +x pause
$ _
```

Menu items 3 and 4 illustrate the file test commands used to avoid abrupt exits if illegal names are entered by the user. If we simply invited user input for dir and invoked cd $dir without testing, the shell might well intervene. Remember that read puts you at the mercy of Homo sapiens, a species capable of typing anything or nothing. So, we have to decide how to handle nondirectory input (test -d being the obvious ploy); we also need to cope with a null input. If the user presses Enter (or spaces followed by Enter) rather than typing a decent directory, dir will be empty or white space. cd $dir will give us cd with a null argument which is quite valid: it returns the user to his or her HOME directory. If this is what we want, we could write

```
if test ! "$dir"  -o  test -d "$dir"
then
    cd $dir
```

This says, if dir is null or a valid directory, invoke cd.

The new menu, though, takes a different tack. If the dir entered is null, we set it to the current directory. This means that a null entry leads to no change in the current directory. The code to achieve this uses one of the clever conditional parameter substitutions that I mentioned way back in Chapter 12:

```
if test -d "${dir:=`pwd`}"
```

The ${dir:=`pwd`} expression says: if dir is set and not null, replace the whole expression with $dir; otherwise, assign to dir the value given by `pwd`, and then replace the whole expression with the new $dir. We then test $dir to see if we have a valid directory. If so, we cd to $dir. To help you keep track of which directory you are in, we display `pwd` each time the menu is displayed.

Do I need to remind you that directory changes made within this script are *not* remembered when you exit back to the shell? What you can do with this menu is cd to the appropriate directory before selecting item 3 to display a file.

Positional Parameters

As a naive example of the use of positional parameters $n, suppose we allow the menu to take an item number argument. I'll call the new menu qmenu (q for quick). qmenu 1, for instance, would immediately invoke menu item

1. To reduce repetition, I'll limit qmenu to two choices. The example will illustrate some of the multiple tests I've been discussing. Testing that the right number of arguments has been supplied, as well as checking that the arguments are valid, is an essential part of safe scripting.

```
$ cat qmenu
:
# @(#) quick 2-choice menu—skb 1995
#
if [ "$#" -gt 1 ]
then
    echo "Usage: qmenu [1 |2]"; exit
fi
if [ "$#" -eq 1 -a \( "$1" -le 0 -o "$1" -gt 2 \) ]
then
    echo "Invalid argument: must be 1 or 2"; exit
fi
if [ "$#" -eq 0 ]
then
    quick=n
else
    quick=y
fi

quit=n
clear
while test "$quit" = "n"
do
  echo "        Menu"
  echo "----------------------"
  echo
  echo "Your current directory is `pwd`"
  echo
  echo "1.    List Users"
  echo "2.    Show Date"
  echo "Q.    Quit"
  echo

  if [ "$quick" = "n" ]
  then
      echo -n "Enter choice: .\b"
      read choice
  else
      choice=$1
      quick=n        # back to normal menu in next loop
  fi
```

```
case $choice in
    1) who | more
       pause;;
    2) date
       pause;;
 Q|q) quit=y;;
    *) echo "Invalid choice!\07\07"
       sleep 5;;
esac
done
$ _
```

The test shown below

```
if [ "$#" -eq 1 -a \( "$1" -le 0 -o "$1" -gt 2 \) ]
then
    echo "Invalid argument: must be 1 or 2"; exit
fi
```

illustrates the use of quoted parentheses to override the precedence of the Boolean operators. We are testing that

Number of arguments equals 1

AND

(argument is less than 0 OR greater than 2)

Since -a has a higher precedence than -o, the parentheses are needed. Without them, you would be testing

(Number of arguments equals 1 AND argument is less than 0)

OR

argument is greater than 2

Note the use of the variable quick. It is often helpful, both for execution speed and legibility, to use a variable to store the result of some complex test. Later on, you simply test the variable rather than repeat the original test (indeed, in many situations the original test may become impossible because other conditions and states have changed). There are no dogmatic rules in such cases: only constant practice and experiment will hone your skills.

The for Loop
The for loop has a do list between do/done keywords, just like while. The difference lies in how the do list is executed. With while, the do list can

iterate any number of times (or none at all), depending entirely on the return value of the command list. The for loop iterates a specified number of times, although, as with while, you can use the break command to exit the loop at any time. The key difference is that with a for loop, a given variable is successively assigned different, specified values each time round. Here's a simple example before we tackle the formal syntax:

```
for x in a b c
do
    echo $x
done
```

The do list is the single command echo $x, which will be executed just three times. In the first loop, x is set to "a"; for the second loop, x is set to "b"; in the third and final loop, x is set to "c". The output from this snippet will be:

```
a
b
c
```

The number of iterations is determined by the number of words occurring after in. Changing the for line to

```
for x in a b c d
```

for example, would produce one more loop with x set to "d". The output would be:

```
a
b
c
d
```

Now consider:

```
for x in "a b" c d
do
    echo $x
done
```

Yes, as you probably guessed, we only loop three times, since "a b" represents one word. The output will be

```
a b
c
d
```

The words after the in statement can be any expressions that can provide values (including null) to be assigned to the "roving" x variable. The shell will perform filename substitutions in such expressions before the for loop starts, so:

```
for filename in *
do
        process $filename
done
```

is a neat way of applying the command process to each file (excluding dot files) in the current directory. * will generate a list of all such files, and then assign each one in turn to the variable filename. Similarly,

```
for filename in poem.[1-3]
do
        process $filename
done
```

will process the three files poem.1, poem.2, and poem.3 if they exist.

The most common application for the for loop is scanning the command line and processing each command argument. Since $* represents all the arguments entered with a command, you can write

```
for arg in $*
do
    process arg
done
```

Here arg will assume, in turn, the value of each word produced by the sequence $1, $2, up to the final argument. Recall that $# represents the total number of arguments. There's a subtle *gotcha* here. If $1 is an argument containing white space, such as "a b", the for loop will see it as *two* words, and will loop twice, with arg set to "a" and then with arg set to "b". Even if you write

```
for arg in "$*"
```

the for loop will still see $1 as two words. The solution is to use

```
for arg in "$@"
```

I mentioned $@ briefly in Chapter 12. When $@ is unquoted, it behaves exactly like $*. You can picture $@, $*, and "$*" all producing the same sequence of positional parameters: $1 $2...$n, so that any spaces lurking within them provide unwanted words to the for loop. Once you double-quote $@, however, the shell provides the sequence "$1" "$2"..."$n". Each parameter is now double-quoted and each therefore presents a single word to the for loop, regardless of any internal white space. Unless you are absolutely certain of the contents of each $n, the safest way to scan an argument list is with "$@".

Here's a simple testbed for you to play with this mechanism.

```
$ cat teststar
```

```
:
# @(#) test 'for ' loops with $*
#
echo "We have $# arguments"
for arg in $*
do
    echo $arg
done
$ cat testat
:
# @(#) test 'for ' loops with "$@"
#
echo "We have $# arguments"
for arg in "$@"
do
    echo $arg
done
$ chmod +x teststar
$ chmod +x testat
$ teststar jim mary stan
We have 3 arguments
jim
mary
stan
$ testat jim mary stan
We have 3 arguments
jim
mary
stan
$ teststar "jim mary" stan
We have 2 arguments
jim
mary
stan
$ testat "jim mary" stan
We have 2 arguments
jim mary
stan
$ _
```

The crunch is that "jim mary" stan looks like two arguments to both test scripts, but teststar nevertheless passes three word arguments to for. testat behaves more reasonably: two arguments beget two words for the loop. Having belabored the importance of "$@", I can now announce that "$@" is the *default* if you have no in arguments at all! testat could be written as

```
:
# @(#) test  'for ' loops with "$@"
#
echo "We have $# arguments"
for arg
do
    echo $arg
done
```

The for provides a powerful tool for creating a host of useful scripts. The "roving" variable can assume values from a wide variety of sources, not just the positional parameters inherited from the command line. Consider a command such as date that produces six words. The following session shows how you can pass these six words to a for loop:

```
$ for x in `date`
> do
> echo $x
> done
Mon
Jul
5
09:15:32
GMT
1999
$ _
```

Yes, you can type this sequence directly. The secondary prompt will prompt you until done is entered. It's quite useful for experimenting with small loops prior to making scripts. Note the difference when you quote `date`:

```
$ for x in "`date`"
> do
> echo $x
> done
Mon Jul 5 09:15:32 GMT 1999
$ _
```

The set Command

There is a more powerful way of accessing the components of date's output, similar to the one you saw with awk. The set command, which is built into the shell, lets you assign your own values to $1, $2,... by breaking down the words in any expression. Remember that the positional parameters are not true variables, so you cannot directly reassign their values with $n=X. They start life with values dictated by the command's arguments, and only shift and set can alter them. set offers a simple way of assigning values to the positional parameters:

```
$ set `date`
$ echo $1
Wed
$ echo $5
GMT
$ echo $#
6
$ for x
> do
> echo $x
> done
Wed
Jul
5
09:15:32
GMT
1999
$ set
...
PATH=/bin:/usr/bin::/usr/stan/bin
PS1=$
PS2=>
SHELL=/bin/sh
TERM=ansi
x=1999
$ _
```

What magic is this? set has taken the words generated by date and passed their values, one by one, to the variables $1,...$6. The for loop with the default in "$@" argument proves that all six parameters have been set. It also sets $# to the number of parameters set.

set is often used to count the number of "words" in an expression, a "word" being any sequence of nonwhite-space characters surrounded by white space.

set is a rather overburdened command. As you can see from the previous session, if you enter set with no arguments, it displays the names and values of all variables defined in your environment, whether local or exported. set can also take options with or without an expression argument.

set takes many options from - to -x, and thereby lurks a little snag. If you try to set an expression that begins with -, set will interpret it as an option with weird results. So set - *expr* must be used to turn off the normal - action.

The two most useful options for budding script writers were mentioned in Chapter 12: -v and -x. These are used when debugging a shell script. With all but the most trivial scripts, it can be most frustrating when your program does not behave as intended. And programming being what it is, you must expect bugs. One debugging trick is to embed lots of temporary echo $x and echo "while loop reached" commands in your script in order to see whether values are being assigned as intended, and whether loops are looping correctly. set offers more help.

The -v (for verbose) option causes all shell input lines to display as they are read by the shell. The set -x (for execute) option puts the shell into *trace* mode until a set +x turns the trace mode off. You can enter set -x and set +x at the prompt while testing a script. While trace mode is on, you can see the executed commands displayed with a preceding + sign. Trace also shows you the variable assignments as they take place. The nice thing is that all the standard substitutions are made first (filename wildcards, variables, and backquoted commands). Tracing does not automatically extend to any subshell activity, but you can insert set -x and set +x directly in any script. You can combine the two options with set -vx.

Doing Sums

My final section will cover briefly the arithmetical tools available in the shell. First, the bad news. The shell offers only integer arithmetic. If you want floating point decimals, you must use awk, dc (a stack-based arithmetic package), or bc (an interactive calculator with a C-like syntax). See man section C for details.

The less-bad news is that shell sums are quite easy. I touched on the fact earlier that shell variables simply hold strings of characters. To convert a string such as "23" into a number, you use the command expr in man section C. expr is rather like the VAL function in BASIC. expr takes any sequence of "number strings" together with the five familiar arithmetical operators:

+   Plus

-    Minus

*   Multiply (must be backslash quoted!)

/   Divide

%   Modulus (also known as remainder)

The operators *, /, and % have higher precedence than + and -. expr evaluates its arguments and displays the result on the standard output. For example,

```
$ expr 2 + 3
5
$ expr 2 \* 3
6
$ a=4
$ a=`expr $a + 3`
$ echo $a
7
$ expr $a + 6
13
$ _
```

There are three quirks to remember. First, you must space between the numbers and operators (but you've met similar problems with other commands where the syntax demands distinct arguments):

```
$ expr 3+2
3+2
$ _
```

Second, you must backslash the * (multiply), or else the shell substitutes filenames! Lastly, when assigning the results of an expr operation, the command must be backquoted as shown.

Script Review

Our simple examples have introduced many of the constructions needed to craft more complex shell scripts. A common theme in all programming endeavors is putting together small "self-contained" chunks of code (called modules) to achieve a complex goal. In mymenu, we have a case statement embedded in a while loop. In the extended version, some of the case branches involve further input and tests.

WHAT'S NEXT

In Chapter 16, we'll cover connecting to and transferring data between remote computer systems. Some of the protocols we'll examine are UUCP and TCP/IP. We'll also take a first look at the Internet and e-mail.

```
echo "2.      Show Date"
echo "3.      Display a file"
echo "4.      Change working director
echo "5.      Return to original dir
echo "Q.      Quit
echo
echo -n "Enter choice: .\b"
read choice
case $choice in
1) who | more
   pause;;
2) date
   pause;;
3) echo "Enter file name: \c"
   read fil
   if [ -r "$fil" -a -f "$fil" ]
   then
      clear
      more -d $fil
   else
      echo "Cannot di
   fi
   pause;;
4) echo "En
   read di
   if test       "$dir        pwd`
   then
      cd $dir
   else
      echo "$dir: no such di
   fi
      pause;;
   5) if test "$dir" != "$p
      then
         cd $prevdir
      fi
      pause;;
```

Chapter 16

REACHING OUT TO REMOTE COMPUTERS

In Chapter 5, you saw the `mail` program in action, sending and receiving email to and from users on the same Unix system (computers that are physically connected to the same local area network). In this chapter, you'll see how easy it is to converse with other Unix (and non-Unix) sites beyond those computers in your own network. In addition to mailing text, you can send and receive files of almost any type to/from other systems. The other systems must cooperate, of course, and we will explain how their help is solicited.

We'll also explore some of the widely used commercial and noncommercial Unix networks and the services they offer. Telecommunications systems (like the Internet) are one of the most useful and rapidly growing areas of computing. Vast amounts of digital data pass each day through copper wire, optical fibers, and (more and more) over air waves via cellular modems. And this data exchange is not limited to our home cities or states: today we can communicate with computers that are sitting on the desks of people literally anywhere in the world at any time of the day. Analog voice data now takes second place compared to the volume of digital data being sent and received internationally. The applications are legion. Transactions on the Tokyo stock exchange are available within seconds on the Wall Street analyst's disk drive. Clusters of corporate PCs interact with mainframes, LANs (Local Area Networks), and WANs (Wide Area Networks). Weather and military satellites gather and transmit billions of bits each day to dedicated supercomputers.

Transmission speeds are also increasing from year to year. 56k bps modems are now available at prices that would have bought a now-laughable 2,400 bps device just a few years ago. And for those of you who are really hungry for speed, today you can get digital modems and cable modems that, when conditions are right, can attain transfer speeds approaching 10MB! That's 10 million bits per second! The software to support these advances has also escalated in size and sophistication. New protocols emerge regularly to improve accuracy, handle the connectivity jungle better, and simplify the user interface.

In the modern context, telecommunications and networking includes not only exchanging mail and files, but being able to access resources at a remote computer, for example, executing commands on a far distant Unix system.

I'll start this chapter by exploring the UUCP network and the collection of programs that underpin many of the Unix telecommunications tools, then introduce several important networking concepts, and then close the chapter with a look at the programs you can use to explore the wonderful world of the Internet.

UUCP

There is a specific command available on almost every Unix system called uucp (Unix-Unix copy in man section C) that you can use directly to send and receive files. It is just one element in the UUCP network software, a varied collection of programs and files that knits together Unix systems worldwide and beyond. Note the uppercase UUCP to distinguish the network and the complete family of commands from `uucp`, one particular program in that family. Most of the commands in UUCP start with the (lowercase) letters `uu` (thus, `uuname`, `uulog`, and so on), which makes them easy to spot in a crowd. There are many situations where UUCP commands will be invoked behind the scenes without your direct involvement. For example, when commands such as `mail` and `mailx` (described in Chapter 5) are used to send mail to remote UUCP sites, it is actually the UUCP family of programs that do the work.

UUCP is designed for use with standard serial cables, modems, and telephone service. If you have an Ethernet LAN, with or without a connection to the Internet, you do not have to use UUCP; you will usually need `ftp` instead. Most of the time, you won't have to make this choice, since a specific remote computer will only be accessible by one type of connection. More on `ftp`—and the Internet—later in this chapter.

Making Contact

There are some essential requirements before you can use UUCP. First, there must be a physical link between the two UUCP computers. In addition to the sites "directly" reachable from your system, there may be many more that can be accessed indirectly via other networks such as USENET or the Internet. Links with non-Unix commercial networks such as CompuServe and MCIMail are also available. The basic connectivity principle is simple: if site A has a link with site B, and B has a link with site C, B may be able to act as a bridge handling mail and file transfers between A and C. If A and C are nodes of distinct networks, and B is able and willing to act as a bridge, B is called a *gateway*. Your link with yet another site, say D, may call for a chain of connections, A to B, B to C, and C to D, involving a varied mix of machines and protocols. With the many thousands of UUCP and networked systems currently running, it is almost certain that a path exists between any two given sites. In fact, it is often the case that you have a choice of paths. Certain sites, known as *backbones*, are especially "well-connected," so once you find a path to a backbone, you can usually reach out and touch anybody!

Second, UUCP must be installed on *both* the local and remote sites. Installing UUCP is a fairly complex operation best left to your vendor or a knowledgeable system administrator, although menu-based tools, such as the SCO UNIX `sysadmsh`, are now available to simplify matters. This initial setup establishes various configuration files that determine how and when communications links are to be made: port numbers, dialup and security procedures, and so on. The system administrator also establishes a unique UUCP name, often called the *node name*, for the site and sets up a list with the name of each remote UUCP system that can be reached directly. You need to know your own node name as well as the names of any remote system you wish to contact via UUCP.

NOTE

It is also possible to set up one side of a UUCP link as a passive system—a system that can be called by other systems, but that will never originate calls of its own.

An important point that affects UUCP (and many other transmission protocols) operation is that UUCP is a "store and forward" system. Your commands are spooled (or queued or batched) by UUCP, just as you saw with the print services in Chapter 9. For example, mail to remote sites is stored locally and sent at convenient intervals. The timing of the transmissions is dictated by parameters set in various files by the system administrator. UUCP is very flexible. Sometimes, transmission will occur as soon as a link is established between the two sites. Often, the remote site is dialled during off-peak hours to reduce the telephone bill.

UUCP Applications

UUCP provides several important services:

- ▶ Determining your local node name
- ▶ Exchanging mail between Unix sites using `mail` or `mailx`
- ▶ Executing commands on a remote Unix system using the `uux` command and the non-uucp `cu` and `tip` commands
- ▶ Transferring files between Unix sites using the `uuto`, `uupick`, and `uucp`
- ▶ Commands
- ▶ Checking the status and progress of your UUCP jobs with the `uustat`,
- ▶ `uulog`, and similar commands

In the following sections, we will describe how you can use all of these commands.

The uuname Command

The uuname command is used to determine your local node name as well as the names of all UUCP systems that are immediately known to your system:

```
% uuname
basis2
ola
isis
mtxinu
beast
...
% _
```

uuname without an option lists the names of all the UUCP systems known to your site. uuname with the -l (local) option tells you your local system name. uuname with the -c option lists all the systems known to the cu command. This list is often the same as that given by uuname, but cu (call up) is not strictly speaking a UUCP command. I'll explain the differences in a moment.

Who You Gonna Call?

Suppose you know that Anne, with login name anne, is a valid user on the system called isis. uuname tells you that isis is "reachable" directly from your system, known as basis. Sending mail to Anne is as simple as mailing someone on your own system:

```
% mail isis\!anne
From:    basis!stan (Stan Kelly-Bootle)
To:      isis!anne (Anne B. Margaret)
Subject: This is a test!
Dear Anne: let me know if you don't receive this memo.
Stan
.
% _
```

Note that the recipient's login name is prefixed by the target system name and a bang (!). The general syntax for UUCP addresses is

system_name! user_name

With the C shell you must escape the bang with a backslash. This is because the C shell interprets ! as the history substitution prefix. With the Bourne shell you could simply mail isis!anne, since ! is not a Bourne shell metacharacter. I tend to use \! always, out of habit, regardless of which shell I am running. The bangs in the text of your mail are not "seen" by the shell and need not be escaped. You signal the end of your mail text in the usual way with either a period in the left-hand margin or with a Ctrl-D (end-of-file). (Try which of these works on your system.) If the mail has been wrongly addressed, you will get an error message, but not necessarily right away. Anne will eventually get a `You have mail` notice, and she can use `mail` on her machine to read something like this:

```
You have mail
$ mail
From uucp Sun Jul 9 10:31 PST 1995
>From stan Sat Jul 8 9:24 PST 1995 remote from basis
Status: R
From:    basis!stan (Stan Kelly-Bootle)
To:      isis!anne (Anne B. Margaret)
Subject: This is a test!
Dear Anne: let me know if you don't receive this memo.
Stan
? _
```

The header indicates the sender, the sender's system name, the time of the original composition, and the time of receipt. (Your header format may differ.)

If and when Anne responds, she would mail me at `basis\!stan`. All of your usual mail facilities are available, including the simple transmission of small (less than 64K bytes) files using redirection.

With `mail` you can only *send* files, and these files cannot exceed 64K bytes. For larger files, you must use `uuto` (send only) or `uucp` (send or receive), covered later in this chapter. Another disadvantage to using `mail` to send files is that the header `mail` attaches to the file can be a nuisance: your recipient may have to delete it before making use of the received file.

Mailing Binary Files

The only files you can physically transmit are pure ASCII text files. The reason is that many of the nontext control codes have special meanings to the telecommunications hardware and software. (Indeed, the control codes are so named because they are used to control devices such as modems!) In order to transmit binary coded files, they must first be translated to text format, then translated back again to binary by the receiver. UUCP offers the `uuencode` and `uudecode` commands to achieve this. To send a binary file called `prog` by mail, you could use the following command line:

```
% uuencode prog /usr/anne/prog | mail isis\!anne
% _
```

The first argument is the name of the file to be encoded. The second argument is the ultimate path name to be assigned when the file is decoded at the remote site. The output of uuencode is then piped through the usual mail *addressee* command. Anne at isis will receive a strange-looking encoded ASCII message in her mail. She then saves this message into a file called, say, prog.encoded. This file will be about 35% longer than the original binary prog file. prog.encode contains a header encoding the permissions field and the destination name, /usr/anne/prog. She can recover the binary data by entering

```
$ uudecode prog.encoded
```

uuencode creates a file called prog in the usr/anne directory. This will be a copy of the original prog with the same permissions. For those sites regularly exchanging binary files, the whole encoding and decoding process can be automated by creating a special "decode" user account to receive encoded files. You then set the sendmail environment variable in .mailrc (the local mail resource file) to a suitable shell command. The default sendmail is /bin/rmail, the standard tool for delivering mail. The replacement for rmail can invoke uudecode automatically on all messages arriving at the "decode" user.

Forward, Please!

Now suppose that Joe is on a system called scouse, a node name not known to my basis system. To reach Joe I need to find a willing backbone: an intercessory site that (1) is known to basis and (2) knows scouse. If, say, ucb fits the bill, I could mail Joe as follows:

```
% mail ucb\!scouse\!joe
Joe: whadya know?
sTaN (tm) (basis!stan)
% _
```

I can reach ucb, and ucb can reach scouse. Then Joe can reply to me using *system_name1! system_name2! system_name3..! user_name* where each system knows the following one, and the final system has your target user_name as a registered user. This mechanism is known as *forwarding*: each system forwards your mail to the next one named in the address chain (also known as the network path name).

The backbone sites are "better connected" than others and equipped to forward mail. You can soon build up a list of these to help establish network addresses.

Business cards often show net addresses: `research!skb, b!bison !dick`, and so on. The first node listed is usually a backbone site.

Several utilities exist to help you determine possible routes through the network. If you have `uuhosts` available, entering `uuhosts target_name` will list possible paths from your site to `target_name`. A path database managed by `pathalias` and a mailing program called `uumail` are available on some systems. These let you `uumail scouse!joe` without worrying about the routing. You can also use a command called `uupath` to query the path database.

The .mailrc File

As your address list grows in size and complexity, it is worth exploring the features available in the extended versions of `mail`. You can preset many parameters in a file called `$HOME/.mailrc`. This is your personal mail resource file, as opposed to the system-wide (or global) mail resource file called `/usr/lib/mail/mailrc`. At startup time `mail` will execute the global resource file (if present), then your personal resource file (if present). The idea is very similar to the profile files you saw in Chapter 6. You should first see if you have a `.mailrc` in your home directory. If not, create one with `ed` or `vi`. If you already have a personal mail resource file, list the contents to see what defaults are being set for you. The two commands that are relevant here are `alias` and `set`. `alias` lets you assign shorthand strings for lengthy addresses. `set` lets you assign values to the special `mail` environment variables. You can add lines to your `.mailrc` file, such as the following:

```
$ cd
$ cat .mailrc
alias dave beast\!uunet\!david
alias mark !scouse\!isis\!mkh
alias edd mary joan stan alf
set Sign="Your old pal, Stan Kelly-Bootle"
set sign="Contributing Editor, UNIX Review"
...
$ _
```

You can now use `dave` and `mark` in lieu of the longer addresses. You can `mail edd` rather than `mail mary joan stan alf`. The `Sign` variable is used as follows: whenever you enter ~A (tilde A) during mail input, the string value set in `Sign` will appear in your mail text. Similarly, ~a (tilde a) will cause the string assigned to `sign` to appear. The tilde must be entered at the beginning of a line. There are nearly thirty of these special tilde escape commands (see your `mail` or `mailx` manual).

Executing Commands on a Remote System

Running commands on a distant system takes several different forms. The `cu` command (and a Berkeley variant called `tip`) is not part of the UUCP family but is mentioned in this chapter since it offers related services. `cu` stands for *call up*; it lets you call a remote site (including non-Unix systems), log in (assuming you have a valid account and password), and perform interactive work. This may sound like normal remote operation from a dialup terminal, but with `cu` you are connected to both your local Unix system and the remote site. `cu` lets you "toggle" between the two systems, running commands locally and remotely as the mood takes.

The UUCP remote execution command, `uux`, is less flexible than `cu`. With `uux`, you set up commands that are batched and executed remotely at some future time. The scheduling, as with file transfer, is determined by configuration files established by the system administrator. Remote execution can also be delayed (or rejected) by the receiving system for obvious reasons: you may be trying to access protected directories, or the remote device requested may be offline. You are usually informed via `mail` if your requested command has been executed successfully. So `uux` only provides "interactive" computing if you are of a patient disposition! Commands sent by `uux` are usually background jobs that run non-interactively by specific permission of the remote site.

The most common use of `uux` is resource sharing. If another site has a fancy laser printer, for example, you may be allowed to print your local files on the remote laser. In return, you could perhaps share your expensive plotting device with the other site. `uux` can invoke the appropriate `lp` command on the remote system and also enlist the help of `uucp` to download the files (which may even be stored at a third site!) to be printed. Several batching operations are now involved. First, the local UUCP would queue the `lp` command and transmit it at some convenient time. Accessing the files might also invoke a batch process. Finally, the remote site would spool your print requests. If all goes well, your files will be printed and `mail` will advise you accordingly. With UUCP, however, you can track the progress of these operations without waiting for the mail to arrive. You'll meet the `uustat` and `uulog` tracking commands later on.

UUCP SECURITY

From the previous overview, it should be clear that security is a critical aspect of UUCP. Since each site has its own security awareness and protection schemes, it is hard (and possibly dangerous) to give you a definitive picture. You must find out what rules are imposed on your particular system and on the systems you wish to "talk" to. Most systems keep an extremely tight control over who can read and write files or execute commands from remote systems. Clearly, you must prevent intruders from reading sensitive files. You must also stop strangers from overwriting your files or depositing *Trojan Horses*. Trojan Horses are program files (often deviant versions of familiar commands) that can lurk unnoticed for long periods before wreaking havoc on your system. *Worms* and *viruses* are other threats that have been widely publicized. A common solution to such invasions is for each site to have a public directory called PUBDIR which holds subdirectories for incoming and outgoing files. This is often the *only* area that can be accessed from outside. Attempts to read or write files from/to directories outside this public area can be disallowed even if the target directories and files have the appropriate local permissions. PUBDIR insulates file transfers from the main file hierarchy and reduces the chances of accidental or deliberate corruption of your system.

PUBDIR usually represents the path name /usr/spool/uucppublic. This directory may have a general subdirectory called receive for holding incoming files. There may also be special subdirectories set up to handle file transfers for specific users or to/from specific sites.

It is important to realize that with UUCP there are two levels of access permissions at work. In addition to the usual file read/write/execute and directory read/write/search permissions that control access within your own system, UUCP allows the system administrator to place overriding restrictions for UUCP access to specific nonpublic directories.

Any directory to which UUCP sends files must have the read/write/search permissions set for "others." Further, files being transferred must be readable by "others" and must reside in directories that are readable/searchable by "others." For example, if you examine PUBDIR and its subdirectories with ls -ld you'll see that they all have rwx set for "others." The reason for this apparent contradiction is that UUCP as a *user* (called uucp and belonging to the group other or bin) needs to access directories and files that it does not *own* in order to transmit them! The pseudo user name uucp should not be confused with the uucp command, of course.

If the file to be sent is owned by you and has, say, `rw-rw--` permissions, a UUCP process running under the user `uucp` cannot read it. If you are `root`, UUCP must have "others" read permission. The file must have at least r– in the "others" permission field. Similarly, the directory holding the file to be transmitted must have "others" search permission (at least –x in the "others" field).

The converse problem can arise. Once a file or directory is copied by UUCP, the permissions of the originals are retained, *but* the copy is now owned by the user `uucp`! As the receiving user, you may well inherit files that you cannot delete because you lack write permission on the received directory. Another point that may confuse you: when I talk about UUCP *copying* a directory, this does not imply copying its files and subdirectories. UUCP simply *creates* the named directory on the target system: you need to specify (using wildcards, perhaps) the actual files to be copied into that directory. Later on, I'll show you methods that overcome this limitation. There are ways of creating special files that contain an entire directory together with its files, subdirectories, their files, and so on down the hierarchy.

A common solution to the permissions hazards is to set up your own public directory, such as `/usr/stan/public`, with full permissions (use `chmod 0777`). This can hold files (each set with `chmod 0666`) for UUCP operations without you having to relax the permissions on your normal working directories and files. For simplicity, from this point forward, I'm going to assume that the directories and files involved in all the following UUCP examples have the appropriate permissions set. Failing these, expect to see messages such as "remote access to path/file denied." And note that such rejections may take some time reaching you! So before you proceed with the examples in the rest of this chapter, make sure that you have set your permissions correctly.

In the next section, I'll show you the simplest way of exchanging files, using the `uuto` and `uupick` commands.

Using the uuto and uupick Commands

The `uuto` command is actually a Bourne shell script offering a simplified file-copying service based on `uucp`. (You can list `uuto` if you wish, and see how it works. Consult your colleagues, however, before making changes!) If you don't have `uuto` on your system, you'll have to learn the more complex syntax of `uucp` to be described later. `uuto` copies files to a public directory on a remote system and automatically advises the recipient by `mail` when they arrive. You need to know the remote system path name as explained in the `mail` section above. For example, to send the file memo to `anne` on the `isis` system, enter

```
$ uuto memo isis\!anne
$ _
```

If your recipient is not directly reachable, you need to go via a cooperating gateway:

```
$ uuto memo mtxinu\!scouse\!joe
$ _
```

You can send several files with `uuto` simply by listing them with white-space separators:

```
$ uuto memo poem ode isis\!anne
$ _
```

Where will the memo file to `isis\!anne` be written? For security reasons, `uuto` sends files to a subdirectory (typically called `receive`) of the public directory, PUBDIR. By default, the variable PUBDIR is set to `/usr/spool/uucppublic`. The full path name of the memo file as received at `isis` will be

```
/usr/spool/uucppublic/receive/anne/basis/memo
```

For this reason, `uuto` is known as the public Unix-to-Unix file copy utility. When the file arrives at `isis`, Anne will receive a mail message something like

```
From uucp Sat Aug 12 10:45 PST 1995
/usr/spool/uucppublic/receive/anne/basis/memo
from basis!stan arrived
```

This path name is quite an eyeful, but it turns out to be a rational and useful scheme. Breaking down the path, you can see that the general format is

```
$PUBDIR/receive/rec_user_id/send_system/filename
```

So the path name tells you the sender system, the target user, and the filename. On a busy system with hundreds of users receiving many files from different systems, you might find thousands of entries in the `$PUBDIR/receive` directory. Each recipient has his or her eponymous subdirectory, and each sending system has its own sub–subdirectory. When you think about it, any remote file transfer scheme has to guard against the inadvertent overwriting of files. If both `basis!stan` and `ucb!stan` (different Stans!) send different files called memo to `isis!anne`, chaos

can ensue if they hit the same directory on isis. Under the uuto protocol, Anne would receive two files:

```
$PUBDIR/receive/anne/basis/memo
```

and

```
$PUBDIR/receive/anne/ucb/memo
```

When Anne gets her UUCP mail, she knows which files have arrived
and where they are. Although she can use mv to move the files into her
own directory (the public area is accessible to all), the uupick command
is designed to simplify this operation. There are excellent reasons to move
received files from the public area as quickly as possible. First, of course,
is the obvious point that the files are vulnerable in PUBDIR. Second, the
public directories are considered as temporary abodes and are regularly
purged by the system administrator.

Here is a simple example of uupick in action:

```
$ cd /usr/ann/public
$ uupick
remote from system basis: file memo
?
m
10 blocks
remote from system scouse: file junk
?
d
?
q
$ _
```

First, Anne moves to her public directory. This has rwx permissions
for everyone and provides a convenient place to collect incoming directories and files. Like other UUCP programs, uupick will usually move files
only into directories that have read/write/search permissions for "others." uupick works rather like mail in receive mode, prompting with?
for your action. You then respond with either m for move, d for delete,
Enter to skip, q for quit, and so on.

When Anne enters uupick with no options, each subdirectory of
$PUBDIR/receive/anne is scanned, looking for files received from all
sender sites. You can limit this search to a specific sender site by using
the −ssender_name option. For example,

```
$ uupick -sbasis
```

would scan only the $PUBDIR/receive/anne/basis directory and report just the files sent by basis. If you already know the filename, you can add this as an argument:

```
$ uupick -sbasis poem
remote from system basis: file poem
?
...
```

For each file found, uupick displays the sending system name and filename followed by the ? prompt. If a directory has been received, uupick tells you:

```
$ uupick
remote from system basis: directory accounts
?
...
```

Your response after the ? prompt determines what happens next. You can move the file to your current directory with m or delete it with d. If you just press Enter at the prompt, nothing happens to the current file, and uupick passes on to display the next file (if any). uupick exits when it runs out of files, or you can quit at any time with a q. Table 17.1 lists all the interactive commands available with uupick.

TABLE 17.1: Interactive Commands Available with uupick

UUCP OPTION	ACTION
Enter	«Moves to next entry, if there is one; current file remains in public directory
*	Help: lists available commands
d	Deletes current file from public directory (no copy made); directories are deleted recursively using rm -rf
m[*dir*]	Moves current file to *dir* (default is the current directory)
a[*dir*]	«Moves all files received from current site to *dir* (default is the current directory)
p	Displays contents of current file
q or Ctrl-D	Quits uupick
! *command*	Escapes to shell and executes *command*

Returning to uuto, there are two useful options, -m and -p, you should know about:

```
$ uuto -m memo isis\!anne
$ uuto -p poem ucb\!joe
$ uuto -mp accounts scouse\!mary
```

The -m option tells UUCP to mail the *sender* when the file has been successfully transferred. Recall that the *recipient* is always mailed when the file arrives.

The -p (copy) option works as follows. The poem file you are sending will be copied into your local spool directory before uploading. It is this copy that will be transferred regardless of any changes you might make to the original poem. Without the -p option, UUCP will transfer the file from its particular directory. Since you never know exactly when the transfer will be scheduled, you may not be sure which version of a rapidly changing file is sent. (You may recall the same problem when passing files to the printer services.) A worse scenario is where you delete poem thinking that it has been safely uploaded! The -p option would have saved your bacon. Another point about -p concerns permissions. If poem is owner-only readable, -p will make an unprotected copy suitable for later UUCP transfer. (Some versions of UUCP will actually default to –C if the file to be sent lacks the proper permisssions; see Table 17.2 later in the chapter.)

uuto copies *to* public directories on remote systems. For more general file transfers, to and from public and nonpublic directories, you need the more powerful uucp command, the subject of my next section.

The uucp Command

The uucp command differs from uuto in several respects:

▶ uuto copies files only *to* a remote system. uucp copies *to* and *from* any two systems (local to/from remote or remote to/from remote).

▶ uuto copies files to the PUBDIR public directories. uucp can copy files to and from any directories that have appropriate permissions, including PUBDIR. Because of this difference, uucp requires that you supply full path names for the remote files.

▶ uuto lets you use uupick to automate the handling of received files. With uucp you must handle the files with mv, cp, and similar commands.

Here are some examples:

```
$ uucp memo isis\!/usr/spool/uucppublic/memo.anne
$ uucpisis\!/usr/spool/uucppublic/poem /usr/spool/uucppublic/
stan/
$ uucp chap.* isis\!/usr/mary/
$ uucp isis\!/usr/mary/prog.\* /usr/stan/
```

The first line copies the file memo in my current directory to the file memo.anne in the public directory at the isis system. The second line copies the file poem from a public directory on isis to the stan subdirectory of PUBDIR on my system. Here, we are copying files *from* a remote site, a feat that neither uuto nor mail can perform.

The third example sends all files matching chap.* in my current directory to Mary's home directory on isis. If all goes well, Mary will find the files chap.1, chap.2, and so on in /usr/mary/. The final / is vital! Without it, uucp would copy into a file called usr/mary. The wildcard * is *not* escaped since I want *my* shell to expand it.

The fourth and final example demands careful study. Here we are downloading files from the remote to the local site, a trick that uuto cannot do. The last line copies all prog.* files in Mary's home directory to my home directory. In this case, the wildcard * *must* be escaped. Can you see why? The reason is that this * has to be expanded by Mary's shell rather than by my shell. uucp must pass the * to the other site. Without the backslash, my shell would get to it first with chaotic results.

Of these four examples, only the first could be achieved with uuto. With the uuto command, the second transfer would only be possible if a user at isis undertook to send the file to me. Note that with uuto the PUBDIR paths are implied; with uucp, they must be explicitly stated. But before you go crazy typing these long path names, make note of a handy short cut: ~/ (tilde slash) can be used in place of /usr/spool/uucppublic/:

```
$ uucp memo isis\!~/memo.anne
$ uucp isis\!~/poem ~/stan/
$ _
```

TIP

Care is needed when using the tilde with the C shell. A leading tilde is expanded by the C shell to the path name of the user's home directory. Tildes embedded inside paths are ignored by the C shell and will therefore be expanded by UUCP to give PUBDIR. You can escape the tilde with a backslash to protect it from the C shell. On recent Unix versions, you can use uucp as the shorthand for the PUBDIR directory when using the uucp command regardless of which shell you are using.

In theory, you can use uucp to transfer files directly between ordinary user directories, as shown above. But recall my earlier warnings that such transfers will only work if the source and destination directories are readable, writable, and searchable by "others," and if the files are readable by "others." Further, the source and destination must be allowed by the appropriate read and write permissions in the Permissions files at each site. In most cases, unless you make special arrangements with both the local and remote sites' system administrators, you will be forced to use PUBDIR directories.

The basic uucp syntax is quite simple:

```
uucp [flags] from to
```

This syntax is very much like the cp (copy) command. You specify the source file(s) in the from argument, possibly with wildcards and paths, followed by the destination in the to argument. With uucp, the from and to arguments can also specify the system names of the sites involved, as explained in the mail and uuto commands. The defaults are quite natural. If you omit the system name, uucp assumes your local system name. (It's quite legal, but rarely useful, to send yourself files with uucp: from and to can both be the same system.) Directory defaults need some care. In the following example,

```
$ uucp chap.* isis\!/usr/mary/
```

the from path defaults to my current directory. Since I specify a directory in the to argument, the files copied will be in that directory with the filenames unchanged. If I specify a directory that does not exist in the target, uucp will create one (permissions allowing). Suppose I send

```
$ uucp chap.* isis\!/usr/mary/tmp/
```

If Mary had no tmp subdirectory, uucp would create one and then copy the chap.* files there. This can sometimes be a nuisance to Mary, so uucp has a useful -f option that says don't create the destination directory if it's not there:

```
$ uucp -f chap.* isis\!/usr/mary/tmp
```

As with uuto and its -p option, uucp has the -C option that lets you control whether a copy of the file being sent is spooled immediately, or whether uucp takes the current file when it is ready to transmit. The option letter is different, but the effect is the same. The -m option is the same for both uuto and uucp: the *sender* is notified by mail when the file transfer has succeeded. uucp also has the *-nuser* (notify) option to mail the named user when the file arrives. Table 17.2 summarizes the main uucp options.

TABLE 17.2: Common Options for uucp

uucp OPTION	ACTION
-f	Prevents creation of destination directories
-C	Copies source file to spool directory before transmission
-j	Displays UUCP job id
-m	mail sender when transfer succeeds
-nuser	mail *user* on remote system when transfer succeeds

Keeping Track with uustat and uulog

Since UUCP simply takes your requests and spools them, you need a method of checking the status of your commands. If your command is complete nonsense, of course, UUCP is able to reject it immediately:

```
$ uucp poem
usage uucp from ... to
uucp failed completely
$ _
```

The lack of instant error messages, however, does not imply success! Your command is floating around in the bowels of Unix, and various daemon processes will be prodding it from time to time beyond your immediate ken.

NOTE

Daemons (pronounced "daymons"), you will recall, are background processes that perform regular tasks for the Unix kernel. For example, cron is the clock daemon that can execute commands at dates and times specifies by the at, batch, and crontab commands. Other more specialized daemons, such as the printer daemon, are set to scan the status of queues and invoke the appropriate action.

Beginners have been known to panic at the apparent lack of response and repeat their UUCP command; this simply risks the future duplication of the job (not always a sound idea). The next section offers a solution to this problem.

Tracking UUCP Jobs

Each time you invoke a UUCP command, either directly with `uuto` and `uucp`, or indirectly with `mail`, the appropriate requests are queued and assigned a unique UUCP job id. The word *job* resists a precise definition: take it as identifying a group of tasks for achieving a certain UUCP command. The requests are stored in various files in subdirectories of the `/usr/spool/uucp` directory that make up the UUCP database. As jobs are processed, this database is updated, so tracking their progress is really a matter of interrogating the UUCP database. To protect you from long-winded files such as `/usr/spool/uucp/.Log/uucico`, UUCP supplies the `uustat` and `uulog` commands that pull out and list the relevant status information.

`uustat` lists the status of all (or selected) recent UUCP jobs. The word *recent* is relevant since UUCP's housekeeping process, known as the *cleanup daemon*, regularly (you can set the intervals) deletes old jobs (you can set the age) from the queue. Even incomplete jobs that for some reason have been lurking around too long will be expunged (although you can *rejuvenate* such jobs with the `-r` option). With no options, `uustat` lists the following data about each of your own UUCP pending jobs:

Job id	A unique id for this job
Submit time	The date and time your job entered the queue
Mode	S = send request; R = receive request
System	Name of target site
User id	Login name of user invoking the job
Job	For `uux`: name of program to be executed remotely
	For `uucp`: size and name of file being transferred

Table 17.3 summarizes the options that modify the action of `uustat`.

TABLE 17.3: Options Modifying Actions of uustat

uustat OPTION	ACTION
`-a`	Lists all jobs for all users in queue
`-uuser`	Lists jobs queued by given *user*
`-ssystem`	Lists jobs queued for the remote site given by *system*

TABLE 17.3 continued: Options Modifying Actions of uustat

uustat OPTION	ACTION
-m	Lists status of all connected sites (lists queue-count, last-action-date, and status)
-q	Lists jobs queued for each site (lists queue-count, last-action-date, and status)
-k*jobid*	Kills the UUCP request given by *jobid* (must be issued by owner of this job or by the superuser)
-r*jobid*	Rejuvenates the job given by *jobid* (sets the date-last-modified to the current date on all files associated with *jobid*)

Only uncompleted jobs can be killed with uustat -k*jobid*, and naturally you need to know their job ids. You should run uustat without options first to obtain the job id of the job you wish to cancel. Furthermore, you can kill only your own jobs unless you are the superuser (root). The superuser can kill any UUCP request. Of the uustat options, only the -u and -s options can be combined in the one uustat command. Together, they will select those jobs for a given user and a given remote site. For example:

```
$ uustat -sscouse -ustan
```

will list Stan's UUCP requests aimed at the remote system scouse.

uulog provides a more detailed account of what UUCP is doing by listing the various status messages saved (logged) by UUCP processes in various log files in subdirectories of the /usr/spool/uucp/.Log directory. As with uustat, you can use the -s and -u options to limit the listings to a given remote system or a given user id.

So far in this chapter, we have looked at a simple UUCP connection between two Unix computers. In the next few sections, we'll describe the position Unix occupies in the larger world of networking, and conclude the chapter with a discussion of the world's largest computer network, the Internet.

Unix and Networking; Reaching the Promised LAN

Networks allow users to share resources, such as file servers, printers, and communications hardware, as well as data. Networks are providing the basis for important business applications, often based on the client-server model, and in many corporate environments the network is seen as a cost-effective replacement for the large mainframe computer of days gone by.

In this section, we'll look at each of the major components of networking and examine the ways the Unix community has solved some of the complex problems associated with networking.

Introducing TCP/IP and Ethernet

One of the most common kinds of Unix system in use today is a group of workstations and servers connected together using Ethernet hardware and the TCP/IP protocols. TCP/IP (Transmission Control Protocol/Internet Protocol). TCP/IP is a set of communications protocols that define how computers communicate with each other remotely. The IP part of TCP/IP moves information between computers in the form of a packet, which is a message unit that contains the source and destination information as well as the data itself.

▶ TCP ensures that the datagrams that comprise a transmission are reassembled in the correct order at their final destination, and requests that any missing datagrams be resent until they are all received correctly.

Other protocols provided as part of TCP/IP include the following:

▶ Address Resolution Protocol (ARP) translates between Internet and Ethernet addresses.

▶ Internet Control Message Protocol (ICMP) is an error message and control protocol.

▶ Reverse Address Resolution Protocol (RARP) translates between Ethernet and Internet addresses; RARP is the reverse of ARP.

▶ Simple Mail Transport Protocol (SMTP) manages mail via TCP/IP.

▶ Simple Network Management Protocol (SNMP) performs distributed network management functions.

▶ User Datagram Protocol (UDP) provides an alternative delivery system, but without the guaranteed delivery features of TCP.

Users rarely have to deal directly with TCP/IP, but a system administrator may have to configure or even troubleshoot TCP/IP. In SCO UNIX, the `netconfig` program is used to install the device drivers, configure the kernel, and modify the startup files, and `ifconfig` is used to configure the network interface card.

Computers on the network can be connected in a variety of ways, including thick or thin Ethernet coaxial cable, twisted-pair wiring, or fiber-optic cable. The original Ethernet standard specified baseband transmission at 10 megabits (10 million bits) per second, but today most Ethernet networks operate at 100 megabits per second or faster.

Distributing Files over the Network

Several elegant systems exist in Unix that allow for *transparent* file sharing across the network. Transparent in this context means that you don't know or care where the files are physically located, because they always act as though they are on the local computer. The only time you might need to know where they are actually located is for reasons of efficiency, security, or disaster recovery. Sooner or later in your travels in the Unix world, you will encounter the Network File System (NFS) and the Network Information Service (NIS). Let's look at both of these facilities.

NFS

The Network File System was originally developed by Sun Microsystems. NFS allows a computer on the network to use the files and peripheral devices of another computer as if they were local.

NFS exports directories that are available for sharing, so clients can access the files in them. In this way, NFS avoids keeping copies of the same file on many computers, and lets all users access a single copy of a file on the server. This also means that you can use traditional Unix commands to access remote data. Any Unix system on the network can be an NFS server, an NFS client, or both at the same time. You can mount a remote file system by hand, which can reduce overhead by only having file systems mounted when they are needed, but the process is best accomplished by commands contained in the startup files.

NFS is platform-independent, and is available on mainframes, minicomputers, RISC-based workstations, and some personal computers. This means that NFS can be used to share files among computers running different operating systems. NFS has been licensed to and implemented by more than 300 vendors.

NIS

Network Information Service was formerly known as the Sun Yellow Pages (YP), and is used to make configuration information consistent on all machines across the network. It does this by specifying that one computer holds the master database of all the system administration information on the network, and then making this database available to all the other computers on the network. This arrangement makes it easier to maintain the database than it would be if there were several copies of the database kept in several locations, because it neatly avoids the problems of inconsistent updating.

NFS and NIS both use a session protocol known as RPC (Remote Procedure Call) which unfortunately is beyond the scope of this book. Suffice it to say that RPC allows a computer to make a procedure call that appears to be local, but which is actually executed remotely, on a different machine on the network.

Client-Server Computing

In the past, traditional computing was based on nonprogrammable "dumb" terminals connected to a mainframe or minicomputer. In this scheme, the database was on the same computer that was running the application.

A client-server architecture replaces this structure by using personal computers (PCs) or workstations for each individual in the network. Files are stored and managed by the server but each client computer shares in the processing of data by maintaining a local version of each relevant application and a temporary copy of the data file(s).

How does a client-server application differ from a network, and what benefits does it bring? Networks usually focus on sharing resources system-wide. In a client-server system, the emphasis is on processor sharing and application cooperation. This allows a mix-and-match approach to selecting the right level of computing power: workstation, minicomputer, or mainframe.

Typically, a client-server approach reduces network traffic, because relatively small amounts of data are moved over the network. This is in sharp contrast to the typical network, where entire files are constantly being transmitted between the workstation and the network file server (mainframe).

Database applications were some of the first to embrace this concept, particularly with Structured Query Language (SQL, usually pronounced "seekwell"). SQL has grown into an industry standard database language. It is relatively easy to implement, robust, powerful, and easy for users to learn.

Accessing the Internet

In this section, I will attempt the impossible: I will try to explain the Internet and show you how to access this vast wealth of information using just a few simple commands. No one person can understand all of the Internet; the resources available are just so vast that they are beyond comprehension. Something I *can* do within the confines of this chapter is tell you how to find out more about the Internet by actually using the Internet as a tool for information access, rather than concentrating on the mechanical components of the network.

I will explain how to transfer files from one system to another, and show you how to log on to a remote computer using common Unix commands. I will also quickly cover some of the other Internet utilities that are generally available, but which are not part of Unix.

What Is the Internet, Anyway?

The Internet is a "network of networks." It is, in fact, the world's largest network. The Internet was originally established more than 30 years ago to meet the research needs of the U. S. defense industry, but it has grown into a huge global network serving corporate needs, academic research, and millions of individuals. Astonishing as it sounds, no one "runs" the Internet, and no one organization pays the costs.

NOTE

While many Internet boosters are fond of quoting statistics, the most important thing to remember is that the Internet is a means to an end, a mechanism for accessing an incredible wealth of information.

Much of the work is done by volunteers, with some of these volunteers serving on the Internet's guiding committees. Millions of computers and users are connected to the Internet, and the rate of growth is still increasing rapidly with no end in sight. With all these computers and users connected to the Internet, there must be a way to identify each site in a unique way. To do this the Internet uses domain addressing.

UUCP Addressing versus Domain Addressing

So far in this chapter, we have used UUCP addressing for mail and mail routing, but there is another addressing scheme known as *domain* or *Internet* addressing. Domain addressing follows the pattern

    user_name@system_name.domain

Note that, unlike UUCP addressing, the user name comes before the system name, and that @ symbol (pronounced "at") is used rather than the bang. The domain, following a period, may consist of several subdomains also separated by periods. Table 17.4 lists the Internet top-level domains.

TABLE 17.4: Organizational Top-Level Domains

Domain	Category
com	Commercial organization
edu	Educational establishment
gov	U.S. government organization
int	International organization
mil	Branch of U.S. military
net	Networking organization
org	Nonprofit organization

In addition to these top-level domains, geographical domains are used to indicate the country in which a network is located. Usually, these geographical domains are the standard two-letter international abbreviation, such as ch for Switzerland or dk for Denmark. The exception to this rule is Great Britain. Its international abbreviation is GB, but its domain name is uk, for United Kingdom.

Underneath these domains and subdomains, and usually hidden from sight, the IP (Internet Protocol) address specifies the exact routing to the Internet host with a set of four numbers separated by periods, such as 116.37.10.30. These numbers work much like a telephone number, and you can use an IP address anywhere you would use a regular address. The part of the system that keeps track of addresses is called the *Domain Name System* or *DNS*. DNS is a TCP/IP service that translates domain addresses to and from IP addresses; this is all done out of sight, and there is little reason to delve further into the details.

Part i

You can find out about Internet domains with the whois and nslookup commands:

whois   Provides information about a domain such as its full name and location

nslookup   Provides the IP address of any domain, as well as information of interest to system administrators

Other programs that perform the same function that may be available on your system include dig and host.

If your system has the appropriate mail-forwarding software, the Internet format has the advantage that your mail can be routed to the remote site without the need to specify the intermediate gateways. Check with your vendor or local guru as to which addressing formats are viable for your system. In general, UUCP-style addresses are used within the UUCP network, while domain-style addresses are used for the Internet. For information on how to send mail to systems outside the Internet, such as CompuServe or MCIMail, see the section "Mailing Other Networks" near the end of this chapter.

Transferring Files with ftp

The ftp program allows you to transfer files to and from a remote computer, and work with files and directories on that remote computer. From a historical standpoint, ftp is part of the Berkeley heritage (while uucp originally comes from AT&T).

When you use ftp, you start a client program on your computer that connects to a server program running on the remote computer. You issue commands using ftp that are translated into instructions that the server program executes for you.

You start ftp as follows:

    ftp [options][hostname]

Most of the options are used for debugging ftp and are not used very often; hostname can either be a domain address or an IP address. Once the connection is complete, ftp enters command mode and is ready to receive your commands. If hostname is not specified, ftp enters the command mode immediately.

You can use ftp to connect to any computer on which you have an account and password, but most Internet users do not have accounts on all the machines from which they may want to copy files; the administration would just be a nightmare. To solve this problem, a particularly important application of `ftp`, known as *anonymous* `ftp`, is used instead; indeed, many people do not use `ftp` in any other way. You simply log in to the remote computer with the user name `anonymous` and your user id as a password. You cannot use anonymous `ftp` with every computer on the Internet; only those that have been set up to offer the service. The system administrator decides which files and directories will be open to public access, and the rest of the directories on the system are off limits, and cannot be accessed by anonymous `ftp` users. As an extra level of security, most anonymous `ftp` sites will only allow you to download files from them; you are not allowed to upload files to them. Having said all that, the world open to anonymous `ftp` is simply enormous; there are literally thousands of anonymous `ftp` computers on the Internet, and countless files you can download.

Once you have started `ftp` and established a connection to the remote computer, you will see the prompt

```
ftp>
```

meaning that `ftp` is ready for a command. Depending on the version of the `ftp` program you have, the number of commands may vary. Type `?` or `help` at the prompt to see the commands available on your system. You will notice that many of the `ftp` commands are very similar to Unix commands we covered in earlier chapters, such as `ls` to list files, `pwd` to display the name of the current directory, or `cd` to change to another directory. The most useful `ftp` commands are listed in Table 17.5.

TABLE 17.5: The Most Useful `ftp` Commands

Command	Action
BASIC COMMANDS	
`Quit`	Closes the connection to the remote computer and terminates ftp
`?`	Displays a list of the `ftp` commands
`?` *command*	Displays a short summary of the specified command
`Help`	Displays a list of the `ftp` commands
`help` *command*	Displays a short summary of the specified command
`!`	Pauses `ftp` and starts a shell on the local computer
`!` *command*	Executes the specified shell command on the local computer

TABLE 17.5 continued: The Most Useful ftp Commands

COMMAND	ACTION
CONNECTING COMMANDS	
open [*hostname*]	Establishes a connection to the specified remote computer
close [*hostname*]	Establishes a connection to the specified remote computer and continues to execute ftp
user [*name[password]*]	Identifies the user to the remote computer
DIRECTORY COMMANDS	
cd [*directory_name*]	Changes the working directory on the remote computer to that specified by *directory_name*
cdup	Changes the working directory on the remote computer to its parent directory
dir [*directory_name*]	Displays a listing of *directory_name* on the remote computer
lcd [*directory_name*]	Changes the working directory on the local computer
pwd	Displays the name of the current working directory on the remote computer
FILE TRANSFER COMMANDS	
get [*remote_filename[local_filename]*]	Downloads the file from the remote computer specified by *remote_filename*, and renames the file *local_filename* on the local computer
mget [*remote_filenames*]	Downloads the specified files from the remote computer
mput [*local_filenames*]	Uploads the specified files to the remote computer
Put [*local_filename[remote_filename]*]	Uploads the file specified by *local_filename* to the remote computer and renames the file *remote_filename*
OPTION SETTING COMMANDS	
Ascii	Sets the file transfer type to ASCII
Binary	Sets the file transfer type to binary
hash	Toggles the hash sign (#) printing for each block of data transferred
prompt	Toggles interactive prompting
status	Shows the current status of ftp

Once you have made a connection using `ftp`, and found your way to the right directory on the remote system, you only need a few commands to move files across the Internet to your local computer. You can become an `ftp` expert with just five commands: `ascii`, `binary`, `get`, `put`, and `quit`.

NOTE
Several file designations are common on the Internet: *filename*`.tar` indicates an archive created by `tar`; *filename*`.Z` indicates a file created by the Unix compress program and you must use the Unix uncompress program to restore the file to its original size before you can use it; *filename*`.tar.Z` indicates a compressed archive; *filename*`.zip` is a compressed file created by the PKZIP program; *filename*`.tar.gz` is a compressed file created by the GNU zip programs `gunzip` and `gzip`; *filename*`.txt` is a text file; *filename*`.1` is an nroff source file; and *filename*`.ps` is a PostScript file ready for printing on a PostScript printer.

The default file transfer type is `ascii`, but it makes good sense to set the mode before a transfer. Use the `ascii` command before transferring a purely text file, and use the `binary` command to create an exact byte-for-byte copy of a file.

The `get` command downloads a file from the remote computer to your local computer, and the `put` command uploads a file from your local computer to the remote computer (these commands are sometimes called `recv` and `send` instead of `get` and `put`). The `get` command must always include the name of the file you want to download, and it can also include the name you want to use for this file after it is on your system (you don't have to use the original name).

For example, to download a text file called `faq` (an Internet name for a file containing a set of frequently asked questions and their answers) located in the directory `/pub` on the remote computer, and name the file `faq.txt` on your local system, the sequence might look like the following:

```
ftp> cd pub
250 CWD command successful.
ftp> ascii
ftp> get faq faq.txt
200 PORT command successful.
150 Opening ASCII mode data connection for faq (50007 bytes).
226 Transfer complete.
```

After a `get` command, `ftp` reports the number of bytes transferred and the elapsed time that the transfer took to complete. If you have no more files to transfer, all that remains is to use the `quit` command to close the connection to the remote computer and terminate `ftp`.

Part i

Connecting to a Remote Computer with telnet

`telnet` is a remote access program that you can use to manually log in to a remote computer on the Internet. Unlike `ftp` (which makes a connection for the sole purpose of transferring files), a `telnet` connection is a general-purpose connection useful in three main ways:

▶ When you have a login on a remote computer and you want to do some work on that computer.

▶ When you want to use an Internet client-server program, but you do not have a client program installed on your usual machine.

▶ When you want to access an application that is only available on the remote machine.

The usual form of `telnet` is

```
telnet [host[port]]
```

where `host` may be a domain address or an IP address, and `port` specifies the port number on the remote computer you want to log into. Once a connection is established, anything you type on your keyboard is passed to the remote computer, and anything displayed by the remote computer appears on your screen. To pass a command to the `telnet` program itself (rather than to the remote computer), you can toggle into command mode by typing the `telnet` escape character, usually `Ctrl-]`, and you will see the prompt

```
telnet>
```

on your screen. Table 17.6 lists the most common `telnet` commands; type `man telnet` to see the on-line documentation available on your system.

TABLE 17.6: The Most Common `telnet` Commands

COMMAND	ACTION
?	Displays a list of the `telnet` commands
? [command]	Displays a short summary of the specified command
open hostname	Establishes a connection to the specified remote computer
close	Breaks the current connection and returns to the `telnet` command mode
quit	Breaks the current connection and terminates `telnet`

TABLE 17.6: The Most Common `telnet` Commands

COMMAND	ACTION
set *escape value*	Specifies the character to switch into `telnet` command mode
status	Displays the current status of `telnet`, including the name of the remote computer you are connected to

You can use `telnet` to perform any operation that you would normally do using a terminal connected directly to the remote computer; for example, you can even open a `telnet` connection to a third computer somewhere else on the network.

`telnet` does not have a file-transfer option; if you are using `telnet` and you want to transfer a file, you must exit `telnet` and use `ftp` to perform the transfer.

World-Wide Web

The World-Wide Web, also known as WWW or just the Web, is an information browser based on the concept of hypertext. Hypertext is a method of presenting information so it can be viewed by the user in a nonsequential way, regardless of how the original information was organized. Hypertext lets you browse through information, choosing to follow a new path (or link) each time the information is accessed.

There are many browsers available, both line and full-screen, for Unix, X Window, Microsoft Windows and other systems, via anonymous `ftp` from `info.cern.ch`. For information, look in the directory `/pub/www` for a file called `README.txt`.

The first widely available graphical browser for the Internet was the Mosaic browser. Mosaic was written at the National Center for Supercomputer Applications (NCSA) at the University of Illinois in Urbana. Today most systems include a selection of Internet browsers, including Netscape and Microsoft Explorer, the two most widely used browsers.

Talk, Talk, Talk

The Internet Relay Chat (IRC) is a 24-hours-a-day conversation where people from all over the world talk about anything and everything. IRC is difficult to explain in a short paragraph, so to learn more, use `ftp` to look

for a file called IRCprimer in any of the following places: the pub/
unix/irc/docs directory on nic.funet.fi, the irc/support
directory on cs.bu.edu, or the pub/irc/doc directory on coombs
.anu.edu.au. You may find several versions of the file: the extension
.txt indicates a text file, .ps indicates a PostScript file, and .Z indicates
a compressed file. Get the file using anonymous ftp. Be careful—IRC is
great fun and is known to be addictive.

Introducing USENET

USENET is an international, noncommercial, news-sharing network linking many thousands of Unix sites. USENET represents the best of the original Unix philosophy. It's a free-rolling, unmercenary, informal (almost
anarchic) affair developed by and for Unix users. USENET is more a way of
life than a traditional bulletin board. And USENET is easier to use than to
define. There are no enrollment or usage costs, apart from your CPU and
connect time. The latter is usually minimal since you'll probably connect
with a "local" call and exchange information during off-peak hours. If you
have one of the many versions of the Net News software (all available at no
charge) and a link, via UUCP or similar, to a USENET feeder, you can join in
the fun. The feeder sites are backbones or gateways, collecting and relaying
all or selected news to other USENET sites. You can post news items and
queries and browse through similar items posted by others. The items are
filed by category into many hundreds of newsgroups, ranging from abstruse
Unix technicalities to lonely hearts! Consult the list of contacts in Appendix C, "Unix Resources," if you are ready to risk USENET addiction.

Using News Readers

A *news reader* is a program that manages the newsgroups that you subscribe to and lets you read the USENET articles themselves. vnews, rn,
and nn are all screen-oriented news readers commonly available at many
sites. The tin and trn news readers are also screen-oriented, but they
can also organize news articles into threads, where a thread is an original
article followed by all the responses to that article. This makes it much
easier to follow a conversation and avoid redundant responses.

Many news readers are available via anonymous ftp, and you can get
more information from the USENET group news.software.readers.

What's Next?

In Chapter 17, you'll learn the basics of system administration. Some of the things we'll cover include backing up the system, setting up and maintaining accounts, and how all this helps to keep the system running.

Part i

```
echo "2.      Show Date"
echo "3.      Display a file"
echo "4.      Change working directo
echo "5.      Return to original di
echo "Q.      Quit
echo
echo -n "Enter choice: .\b"
read choice
case $choice in
1) who | more
   pause;;
2) date
   pause;;
3) echo "Enter file name: \c"
   read fil
   if [ -r "$fil" -a -f "$fil ]
   then
      clear
      more -d $fil
   else
      echo "Cannot di
   fi
   pause;;
4) echo "En
   read di
   if test -d `[dir= pwd`
   then
      cd $dir
   else
      echo "$dir: no such di
   fi
   pause;;
5) if test "$dir" != "$p
   then
      cd $prevdir
   fi
   pause;;
```

Chapter 17

BASIC SYSTEM ADMINISTRATION

Every computer system, large and small, needs "administration." Even the single-user PC running Windows, when you think about it, requires a host of miscellaneous activities to maintain smooth operation. These include mundane tasks such as the procurement, formatting, and filing of diskettes; regular and unplanned maintenance of the hardware; monitoring disk integrity; checking disk usage and purging old files; periodic backing up of programs and data; installing new hardware and applications software; upgrading; maintaining documentation; and so on. Less mundanely, one hopes, users may have to recover from disasters such as disk crashes. For PC users, these are do-it-yourself jobs that merge into the general pattern of computer operation and are seldom seen as formalized "administration."

With larger, multiuser systems, these and other tasks must be planned and scheduled with great care and delegated to specialists. Individual users are discouraged or prevented from performing the global operations associated with administration. Many maintenance and administration chores require the use of the whole system, so ordinary users must be warned that normal service is being interrupted. And, clearly, one needs a central authority for bug-fixing, for assigning user id's and priorities, allocating and policing disk and time quotas, and for smoothing out the inevitable resource conflicts between users.

UNIX SYSTEM ADMINISTRATION

In the Unix culture, system administration has always played an ambivalent role compared with the site-management strategies adopted for the proprietary operating systems of large commercial companies such as IBM or DEC. Unix, as you have seen, was developed by programmers for programmers, so for some time there was a certain laissez-faire indifference towards such apparently trivial and wimpish administrative tasks as backing up and assigning user id's. The early Unix manuals offered no specific guidance for administrators: there were lots of tools, and programmers were expected to use them or invent their own tools to fine-tune performance or perform backups. In the early days, if a programmer found bugs in the utilities, or even in the kernel itself, they would often be fixed on the spot without too much formality.

As Unix grew and entered the world of commerce, more attention was paid to having some central site authority, and the Unix system administrator was born. Compare the minute size of early System Administrator's (SA) documentation with the more current 300+ page *System Administrator's Reference Guide* and the equally voluminous *Operating System System Administrator's Guide* issued with SCO UNIX. Of great significance is SCO's `sysadmsh`, a system administration shell that presents clear menu selections for the most frequently used SA jobs. Similar shells are available from almost all Unix vendors which present an equally friendly interface for the smaller sites that cannot justify full-time supervision. You have to be logged in as `root` (or superuser) to use these admin shells. But once you acquire a basic understanding of the terminology and the rationale for the SA functions, the syntactical complexities of the commands are replaced by navigating plain English (or the language of your choice) menus. In this chapter, therefore, we'll focus on the basic logic of the commands that the menus offer. There are hundreds of commands dedicated to SA duties. I will concentrate on those that are needed to keep a Unix system running smoothly. The other duties that seem to go with the territory, such as being priest-confessor, patient font of wisdom, soother of frayed spirits, and shoulder-to-cry-on, must either come naturally, or be left to develop with time and experience.

Some of the essential jobs for a system administrator are the same whether the site supports 4 or 400 terminals, and whether it runs 2 or 24 hours a day. The large Unix mainframe systems, of course, will have highly trained, full-time SA's, often several on duty at all times, sharing the load. But I also have in mind the growing number of PC- and workstation-based Unix systems with a handful of users, one of whom is the designated part-time SA. Or possibly, the SA chores rotate, so everyone needs to know the standard procedures.

What's Involved

At the top of the list is the obvious task of ensuring satisfactory service to the users. This requires knowing how to perform the following tasks:

- ▶ Start up and shut down the system.
- ▶ Set up new accounts and remove old ones.
- ▶ Establish defaults for various user processes.
- ▶ Organize groups and assign group id's.
- ▶ Provide global defaults for various commands and files.
- ▶ Set up uucp and links to other sites.
- ▶ Maintain a central printer service.
- ▶ Establish crontab for regularly scheduled jobs.
- ▶ Cope with lost passwords.
- ▶ Handle security.
- ▶ Maintain a written log of system changes and other pertinent events.
- ▶ Maintain log files.
- ▶ Check the file system integrity.

- ▶ Back up data and systems files.

- ▶ Update the online and offline documentation.

- ▶ Disseminate the ground rules and read the Riot Act.

- ▶ Recover from miscellaneous disasters.

- ▶ Cope with hardware and software changes.

- ▶ Monitor performance, disk usage, and resource allocation.

- ▶ Provide help and guidance in person and via email.

I will not deal with the initial setup procedures when the units are unboxed and assembled. Most vendors will provide help for this, and in any case, it's hardly possible to give useful advice apart from RTFM (Unix slang for "Read the Manual!").

SUPERUSER RULES OK?

The first point to note, before I discuss these jobs in more detail, is that most system administration duties require the highest of privileges, namely *superuser* access to the system. The home directory of the superuser is /, the root directory, and the login name is therefore traditionally set as root (strictly speaking, the first user in /etc/passwd given user id 0 is the superuser. Many commands, though, rely on the fact that "root" is the superuser name, so it is unwise to change this). The token "root" has various meanings and parts of speech in Unix. When used as an adjective (root directory, root filesystem, root mode) or as a synonym for /, I'll use normal font. As a login name, you'll see root, as in root's password.

NOTE
The /etc directory usually has read/write permissions for root only. Run an ls to confirm this fact. As a reminder, I will usually give the full /etc/xxxx path name for commands and files in /etc.

At most sites, only the system administrator who administers the system regularly knows root's password. A common practice here to cope with sickness and death is to keep the current password for root in a secure place accessible only by a trusted nominee. As you saw in Chapter 7, root has the power not only to bypass the file and directory permissions set by any user, but can also change these permissions. root alone can add and remove users, and at any time (recall that `/etc/passwd` is writeable only by `root`). `root` alone can safely shut down the system or change its run level. For example, `root` can reduce the whole system to single-user mode (run level 1) for various maintenance chores. `root` alone can log in to any account without knowing its password. `root` alone can create special files with `/etc/mknod`, special filesystems with `/etc/mkfs`, and make filesystems available and unavailable with `/etc/mount` and `/etc/umount`.

NOTE

In Unix terminology, the file system consists of one or more filesystems. See "File Systems and Filesystems" later in this chapter.

Even simple jobs such as changing the system date with the `date` command can only be performed by `root`. `root` alone can `kill` any processes. And `root` alone can grant permission to employ certain commands such as `crontab` (see Chapter 8). I stress the omnipotence of `root` because even a brief, temporary access to `root` by the wrong person is highly dangerous, allowing deeper penetration. This *trapdoor* syndrome has been the source of many security breaches. A phoney superuser, of course, could shut down the system or change passwords (including `root`'s password) but is unlikely to attract attention so obviously. If the intention is unobtrusive long-term file peeking or snatching, the intruder may try to create an innocent-looking account. An important SA activity is maintaining security at the appropriate level and educating users about the possible loopholes. One aspect of this is maintaining both written *logs* and automated log files. For example, all attempts to log in as `root` via the `su` command (see later) can be automatically recorded in a designated SULOG file (usually `/usr/adm/ nsulog`) or displayed immediately on a designated terminal.

The whole concept of a single-passworded, all-powerful superuser is considered by some experts to be a major blemish in Unix security. Most of the large operating systems such as IBM's VM and DEC/Compaq VMS employ multilevel privileges to control access. This approach is gaining ground with some high-security versions of Unix. The DOD (Department of Defense) has a National Computer Security Center that issues the *Orange Book* guidelines for grading a system's security level. Unix systems can be submitted for testing. Achieving the proper grade is clearly a marketing advantage in many applications. There are also commercial packages that plug security breaches or warn the system administrator if they occur.

Many sites have "special users" such as `admin` or `backup` who can log in with less powerful privileges than `root` to perform certain administration duties. The general rule, to reduce the chances of catastrophic error, is to log in at the lowest possible privilege level for the task at hand.

Assuming Power

Having seen the power of a superuser, you will be anxious to know how to become one. There are several ways but they all require knowledge of root's password (sorry about that). First, note that even SA's do not spend all their time in root mode: they often have normal accounts named sys, sysop, or mary even, with normal file permissions for their nonprivileged duties, such as sending and receiving mail. At the login prompt, you can type root, followed by root's password, and everything works just like a normal login. If you are running as a normal user, you can log out then log in again as root. There's a shortcut, though: the su command.

If you are running as a nonroot user, know root's password, and have *su permission,* you can use the su (switch user or superuser) command to become root. If you are already running as root, su can be used to log in as any other user without knowing the user's password: powerful stuff! su has the following syntax:

```
su [-] [name [arg1 [arg2, …]]]…
```

The default *name* is root, so after entering su with no arguments, you will be asked for a password. Type the password for root and you become superuser with the # prompt. To return to your previous login, simply press Ctrl-D, and the $ or % prompt returns.

If, on the other hand, you are already logged in as root, you can enter su mary, for example, and you'll then be logged in with Mary's user id— no password is requested. There are a few subtle differences between su'ing to an account and logging into that account in the normal way. The differences concern the shell and its environment, and su has options to control these.

Whatever user you su to (root or mary), a new shell is spawned based on that user's /etc/password shell field (/bin/sh by default). However, you usually retain any previously exported environment variables from your earlier shell. You can alter this state of affairs with the - option. Provided that the new user's shell is /bin/sh (or similar), the - option sets up a new environment as though you had logged into the new account in the normal way. This is achieved by executing the appropriate profile files for the new user. The optional arg1, arg2,… arguments let you pass on commands to be executed by the new shell (see the su man pages for the grisly details). A Ctrl-D exits you back to your previous login state. System daemons regularly use su to "assume" other user identities.

Summing up, a superuser can su to root or any other account without logging out and in again.

PUTTING THE BOOT IN

Starting, or booting up, a Unix system is usually the easiest part of the whole exercise. Often, all you need to do is switch on the power and let the machine trigger the booting sequence. On some systems you are prompted first to name the boot device or program. This allows you to boot with different versions of the kernel, especially useful during experimental work. For example, before you can test new peripherals, their drivers have to be linked to the kernel, so there are occasions when you have several different kernels to choose from.

Cleanup Time

The boot program loads the Unix kernel (and maybe other things) into RAM. What happens next depends on the particular system. SCO UNIX, for instance, performs an integrity check on the *root filesystem* using the fsck command (filesystem check in man section ADM). I'll explain these terms soon when I discuss proper shutdown procedures. If the filesystem is "clean," normal startup proceeds; otherwise, you are prompted through an fsck cleanup session. If your system does not perform such a check automatically, fsck can be run manually (in single-user mode) as an insurance against corrupted files (rather like CHKDSK in DOS, only more so). Note that data can be lost when cleaning a corrupted filesystem. Furthermore, fsck is one of Unix's most complex commands (it keeps asking you questions). So, corrupted filesystems should be shunned if at all possible. The most common cause for filesystem corruption is the failure to follow the correct close down procedures, but a power surge or failure is also a possible candidate. Morals: (1) Read the next sections on how to turn off a Unix system correctly; (2) Invest in a UPS (uninterruptible power supply).

Next, again depending on your version, Unix may come up in multiuser (or *normal*) mode ready for action. Alternatively, you may be prompted to select a *run level,* usually a choice between multiuser mode and single-user mode (also known as *maintenance* mode). In the single-user case, you'll be prompted to enter root's password that I've been making such a fuss about.

Single-User Mode

Single-user mode gives you a bare-bones system and is usually reserved for emergencies or major scheduled maintenance operations. Emergencies would include restoring, rebuilding, and cleaning up the filesystem after some calamity. Typical cases of maintenance would include major hardware or software upgrades, normally performed at off-peak times to avoid inconvenience to users. Only root can run single-user mode, and, as the name implies, only one terminal is active (usually the system console): the rest of the system is dead to other users. Logging out of single-user mode (with Ctrl-D or logout) brings up multiuser mode.

Multiuser Mode

When you are in multiuser mode, any users who know root's password can play at superuser while the rest of the system supports ordinary users. Hopefully, only the privileged and responsible few will have that power.

Exactly how the system comes up depends on the contents of the /etc/inittab and /etc/rc2 (rc meaning "resource") files, both of which need root permission to edit. etc/rc2 is a longish sequence of scripts with names beginning with S*nn*, where *nn* runs from 00 to whatever. The number determines the order in which the scripts are obeyed. Thus, S00SYSINIT starts the ball rolling by initiating the kernel message logger; later comes S75cron to start the cron daemon, S80lp to start the printer scheduler, and so on. Note that single-user mode does not invoke /etc/rc2, so the features initiated by it are not immediately available.

THE HALTING PROBLEM

Multiuser systems such as Unix should never be just "shut off." Active users connected to the system are rightfully miffed if their terminals die without warning. Even if the users have all logged out and gone home, there may be background jobs and daemons ticking away. Daemons get mad if their processes are suddenly curtailed.

A less obvious danger lies in the way the Unix file system works. For improved performance, when a file is "changed," the disk version of that file is not always updated immediately. Usually, portions of the file to be changed are read into file buffers (a part of RAM memory). The changes may reside in memory for a while before being written to disk. Unix copies the data stored in memory to disk during periods of low processor activity to make the system more efficient. The price you pay for this more efficient use of processor time, however, is that a premature cessation of kernel activity may destroy the data before it is saved to disk. As you saw in the "Cleanup Time" section above, the `fsck` command tests for a corrupted file system, and helps you to repair the damage. But in mending the file structure, some data may be lost. For all these reasons, Unix provides several commands to the superuser for a graceful shutdown. If you are in single-user mode (and therefore already a superuser), there is no need to warn other users to terminate their jobs, but you still have to flush any pending file I/O to ensure the data is saved correctly. On SCO UNIX, the `/etc/haltsys` command achieves this. The syntax is simple:

```
/etc/haltsys [-d]
```

Typing `/etc/haltsys` will flush the file buffers, mark the file system as *clean,* then halt all kernel activity without any grace period or warning. Any background processes will die, of course, so it is your responsibility to kill them safely before using `/etc/haltsys`. A message then tells you that it is safe to power down or "Press any key to reboot." `/etc/haltsys` has only one option: `-d` withdraws the option to reboot, so all you can do is power down (you can read the `d` as *dead*). There is a variant of `/etc/haltsys` called `/etc/reboot` that does a `haltsys` followed by a reboot with no option to power down.

A much safer command is `/etc/shutdown`, (available only to superusers). `/etc/shutdown` is especially useful in multiuser mode, but can be used in place of `/etc/haltsys` in single-user mode. `shutdown` actually calls `haltsys` but not until all active users have been warned and all pending processes have been gracefully killed. `shutdown` also has options to switch the system to other `init` levels.

TIP

`/etc/haltsys` should only be used directly in multiuser mode if some weird system error prevents `shutdown` from working.

The `shutdown` command syntax is quite daunting, but you'll rarely need all the options—and if you do, a shell script should be created since typing errors in the `shutdown` command can be quite disconcerting.

```
shutdown [-y] [-g[hh:] mm] [-i[0156sS]] [-f"messg"] [-Ffile]
[su]
```

The -y option is *silent*: without it, `shutdown` asks you to confirm that you want to shut down the system. With the -y option, shutdown proceeds apace, no questions asked.

The -g option indicates the grace period in hours and minutes, or just minutes if you omit the *hh*: argument. The maximum grace period is 72 hours, and the default is one minute. Grace is the length of time before the shutdown begins. Users receive periodic messages that the system is going offline. The warnings are transmitted every hour if the grace period exceeds one hour; every 15 minutes if the grace period exceeds 15 minutes; otherwise every minute. Active users must save their files and finish up their work as best they can.

The -f option lets you vary the default warning message. Note that double quotes are needed around the *messg* string. -F is similar, except that you send the contents of the given *file*. The `wall` command can also be used for informing all users whenever you want to vary the periodic messages generated by the -g option.

The -i option specifies the *init level* (also known as the run level) to which the system will be brought. The default is 0 (safe-to-power-down state). Using either -i1, -is, or-iS will bring the system down to single-user state. `shutdown` actually calls `init` to change the run level. `init` (in man section M) is a general process spawner that takes an init level as argument. It plays a vital role in starting up a Unix system by creating the initial daemons and other processes under the guidance of the `etc/inittab` file.

`/etc/shutdown` also calls `/etc/sync`, a system primitive that updates the *super-block* to ensure synchronization. The super-block is the vital block 1 of every filesystem, holding the name and other essential information about the filesystem.

Yet another way to get from multi- to single-user mode is to use the `su` option. The `su` synonym exists to maintain compatibility with XENIX. The following command

```
/etc/shutdown -g10 -f"URGENT! Wind up and logout NOW!" su
```

starts sending the given warning ten minutes before switching to single-user mode. The message will be repeated every minute to all logged-in users. A common reason for a single-user shutdown is to back up files. It can clearly be counterproductive to start backing up files that users may be changing! Before I discuss the backup situation, though, a brief detour on filesystems is called for.

FILE SYSTEMS AND FILESYSTEMS

The Unix file system consists of one or more filesystems! The essential *root filesystem* is the familiar hierarchy of directories and files starting at /, the root. The root filesystem is *mounted* automatically when you boot, and must be present (it contains all the basics to run Unix). For smaller installations, root may be the only filesystem you need for both system and user files. To improve performance on larger systems, you can store user files in separate filesystems, the most common of which is known as the /u or *user filesystem*. When a Unix hard disk system is initially formatted and partitioned, decisions have to be made regarding the number and type of filesystems needed, since later changes require reinstallation of the whole system.

Similarly, the System Administrator will usually have to create partitions and new filesystems when new disk drives are added. This is, of course, a *big* subject that I can only touch on briefly. As Unix systems grow, more and more skills and tools are enlisted to optimize performance for different work loads and application mixes. For example, 50 biologists modeling DNA molecules present a different challenge from 50 users creating webpages. The filesystem organization is a vital factor here, as is the allocation of *swapping* areas. Swap spaces are disk partitions used to store processes that are temporarily swapped from RAM to disk. Clearly, the size of available RAM is a major part of the equation.

Filesystem names are stored in /dev along with other special files (device drivers and so on). The /mkfs command is used to name and create filesystems. The superuser can specify the type of files to be stored (ACER, UNIX, XENIX, even DOS), number of blocks, and various technical details. Before the system can access a filesystem, it must be "attached" to the root filesystem using the mount command that is also privileged. Thus:

```
# pwd
/
# mount /dev/u /u
# _
```

will mount the user filesystem /dev/u on the "directory" /u. The mounted filesystem looks rather like an ordinary directory under root, but the kernel knows better! Because of the low-level stuff associated with mount and /dev/u, commands accessing files in the /u filesystem will be correctly routed to the proper logical disk partition. Mounting nonroot filesystems is usually performed automatically by scripts in the /etc/rc2 file, but during maintenance and backups the System Administrator often has to mount filesystems "manually." The reason is that when you boot up in single-user mode, only the root filesystem is mounted and accessible (`/etc/rc2` is not invoked). In passing, note that `fsck` can be used to check any filesystem's integrity and clean up if necessary. Indeed, mounting a corrupt filesystem usually triggers a request to perform `fsck`.

Access to a filesystem can be removed, by `root` only, with the `umount` command meaning *unmount* (some talk of *demounting* or *dismounting* a filesystem):

```
# pwd
/
# umount /dev/u
# _
```

TIP

Unix spells "`creat`" with only one "e" and `umount` with only one "n"!

Notice that `umount` takes the *device* name as argument, not the filesystem directory. If you have a removable mass-storage device like a Zip™ drive , it should be unmounted *before* it is physically removed. If you don't, its "directory" under `root` will still be visible. There are several "gotchas" with `umount`. A common error is to attempt an unmount when you are logged into the target filesystem: you'll get a "device busy" message until you log into `root`.

The reason for the filesystem digression should now be clear: the System Administrator is intimately involved with filesystems even though the average user can function without any inkling that they exist. Both root and nonroot filesystems need to be backed up, of course, which leads me back to the mainstream of my dissertation.

BACKING UP

Even with proper shutdowns and regular `fsck` checks, the data and programs stored in your file system are subject to diverse catastrophes. Backing up means copying some or all of your fixed, hard disk files to an external medium (magnetic tape reels, cartridges, or cassettes; floppy disks; or removable hard disks) in such a way that the data can be copied back (restored) at some future date. The restoration, note, may have to be made on another machine of the same type, or possibly on an entirely different

Unix system. The latter situation requires special attention, being associated with a form of madness known as upgrading.

The need for regular backups will be so self-evident to those readers who have ever lost a vital file that we need say no more on the subject. To those of you with an "It can never happen to me" mentality, we can only say this: you have a painful lesson ahead. Apart from power fluctuations and outages, disk and related hardware failures, files can be deleted accidentally or as a result of software bugs. As Maxwell Smart used to say, "We've established the *why,* so let's consider the *when, what, who,* and *how.*" As you'll see, these four turn out to be cunningly interrelated.

When?

The optimal frequency for backing up is best decided by posing the following question: If the disks all crash *now,* how much work would be involved in restoring the system using the data from my previous backup? Only you can answer this risk-analytic conundrum. You need to balance the effort and cost of each backup against the effort and cost of redoing lost work. This clearly depends on the rate of change of your data and the degree to which you can automate the backup procedures. Not to be considered, nowadays, is the cost of the backup medium and the cost of storage. The obvious point of *where* it's stored is quickly answered: Any 100% safe place. And as far away from the point of origin as is compatible with easy accessibility. It is quite alarming how often fires, floods, and earthquakes destroy both the disk drives and their backups.

What?

The frequency of backup also depends on what you back up. We can distinguish several basic backup strategies:

- ▶ Low-level backups mean copying a complete filesystem to your external medium. Restoration is simple: just copy the backup to the filesystems.

- ▶ High-level or incremental backups mean copying only the files in the filesystem that have changed since the previous low-level backup. Restoration requires careful application of each incremental backup to the last total backup in the correct sequence.

A typical schedule might be a weekly total backup and a daily incremental backup. Clearly, different filesystems can require different schemes. At a small-to-medium business site, the systems and applications programs in the root filesystem can be quite static after the initial tribulations have subsided, justifying monthly total and weekly incremental backups. The database on filesystem /u, say, representing life-sustaining invoice, inventory, payroll, payables, and receivables (especially receivables) information, is throbbing with activity. The concept of incremental backup is hardly meaningful here, but it is often practical to maintain a smaller `trans-actions` filesystem for frequent backups throughout the day together with an overnight total backup. The backup tools are extremely flexible, allowing you to copy individual files, whole directories, or whole filesystems, or just those parts that have changed.

A related consideration is how long you should keep a particular backup copy. Total backups, since the effort is great and the medium cost trivial, should be kept for at least twelve cycles. If you do a monthly total backup, you would rotate twelve cartridges (or whatever) labeled Jan through Dec. You could keep four weekly and seven daily incremental backups. The main challenge is to log, label, and store the backups sensibly and consistently, shunning complacency during those inevitably uneventful periods when the whole exercise seems pointless. A further point is to have a verification strategy. This involves both checking that the backup is indeed a faithful copy, and occasionally rehearsing the restoration procedure.

The choice of backup medium involves the following considerations:

▶ Floppies are cheap but require human intervention (consider the number of 1.44Mb diskettes when backing up a modest 100Mb filesystem). On the plus side, for smaller systems which rely on floppies for system installation and emergency booting, no additional hardware is required.

▶ Some form of tape drive or removable cartridge disk is essential for medium-to-large filesystem backup. The higher capacity allows fully automated operation.

Who?

At those sites where users have PCs or workstations with local storage media, some or all of the backup responsibilities can be likewise distributed. More often, though, the bulk of the mass storage is centralized, and the backup lot must itself fall on the System Administrator. As you've seen, backing up a filesystem ideally requires single-user mode to ensure that the files are unchanged. This in turn requires superuser privilege.

Having said that, regularly scheduled backups can be scripted and automated to the point that they run unattended (with tape backups) or safely delegated to trusted nonsuperusers (with floppies). This is an area where admin shells such as SCO's `sysadmsh` earn their gravy. Both scheduled and unscheduled backups, as well as restorations, can be invoked with a few keystrokes. SCO's editable `schedule` file lists the various backup levels and even displays a color code for labeling the medium.

How?

I've saved the worst question for the last. Over the years, because of the importance rightfully accorded to backing up, a myriad of commands have evolved to do the dirty work. I will restrict myself to the three most common approaches: the `dump`, `cpio`, and `tar` commands. It is worth noting that many of the backup commands also serve a wider market: the distribution of software and databases to the wide world of Unix users, where the emphasis is on standard formats and portability. Here are some of the key points to be considered in choosing a backup utility:

▶ Does the backup allow easy restoration of individual files, or must you scan the entire backup?

▶ Does it allow *incremental* backups as an option? That is, is it smart enough to save only files that have changed since the previous backup?

▶ Can backed-up files be "split" across backup volumes?

▶ Are the backups portable to other systems in the event of prolonged downtime or the urge to upgrade?

The `/etc/dump` command and its sibling `/etc/restor` have been around a long time. `/etc/dump` copies a whole filesystem with a simple command syntax. For example,

```
# /etc/dump 0uf /dev/bak /dev/u
# _
```

copies everything in `/dev/u`, the user filesystem—files, directories, i-nodes, the lot—to the device called `bak` (which can be a floppy or tape drive of any sort). The `0uf` set of options translates as follows:

0   Dumps at level 0 (the whole filesystem).

u   Updates a file called `/etc/ddate` (used in subsequent incremental backups).

   f   Takes the following argument, /dev/bak, as the destination
       device to receive the backup.

Before restoring a complete dump'd backup, you must prepare a nice,
clean filesystem. /etc/restor simply dumps all the saved stuff back to
the new filesystem. /etc/dump and /etc/restor are not overly bright
(some device errors during copying are simply ignored) and you should
run fsck after each dump. Nor are they overly portable, since the i-node
information is filesystem-dependent. However, the simple syntax is an
advantage where portability is not a factor.

The cpio Command

You briefly met the cpio (copy file archives in and out) command during
the discussion on find in Chapter 13. cpio (in man section C) is not a
privileged command, so it is widely used (in conjunction with find) by
nonroot users to selectively back up personal files. root, of course, can
also use it, and it forms the backbone (sic) of many admin shell backup
procedures. cpio is extremely flexible and the syntax is correspondingly
horrendous. cpio can split big files across multiple volumes and can cope
with special files (device files and pipes) and empty directories (a good
backup should record such things, when you think about it). Another signal advantage is that cpio backups have a standard format which leads to
high portability. By changing the order of the arguments, cpio also performs the restore operation. On the downside, restoring an individual file
from a cpio backup can be painful: you need to read through all the previously saved volumes until you hit the target. If any corrupted files are
encountered *en route,* later files are inaccessible.

The tar Command

The versatile and popular tar (tape archive) command (in man section C),
like cpio, produces archived backups on floppies or tapes, restores such
backups, and can be used by nonroot users (read and write permissions
allowing). Whole directories (and their subdirectories) or individual files
can be backed up, and large files can split across volumes of the backup
medium. This splitting can save much time and frustration when backing
to floppies. tar also packs each floppy to the max, reducing the number
of floppies needed (not to mention all that inserting and removing nonsense). The tar syntax is a tad simpler than cpio's, but it does not copy
special files or empty directories. However, restoring individual files is
much easier than with cpio: you can start restoring from the volume that
contains your wanted file.

TIP

Before you back up to floppies, make sure you have enough formatted and labeled floppies (each one representing a separate *volume*) on hand. tar will prompt you as each floppy becomes full.

You can set up the name and characteristics of your default backup device in a file called /etc/default/tar. This file can hold several such devices, which you can select via the command line. Or, with the f option, you can supply a specific device name with the command, as in the following example:

```
$ assign /dev/floppy
$ tar cvfk /dev/floppy 720 chap*
$ _
```

Here, a nonroot user assigns the floppy drive for his or her exclusive use (see assign in man section C), then archives all files in the current directory that match chap*. The argument 720 specifies the capacity of the diskette in kilobytes. The cvfk options have the following meaning:

c   Creates a new archive file and starts writing at the beginning (see later for the r option, which appends to an existing non-tape archive).

f   Takes the /dev/floppy argument as the target archive name. Without this option, tar takes the default from a device name stored in /etc/default/tar. This file also stores defaults such as blocking factor and volume size. tar can also read and write from standard input and output, which is useful for piping.

v   The verbose option causes tar to display filenames as they are archived.

k   Tells tar to take the 720 argument as the device volume size in kilobytes.

The options for tar work differently from most Unix commands. The first *function* letter must be either r, x, t, u, or c with no hyphens. This first letter can be followed by one or more function modifiers (no intervening spaces or hyphens). Those function modifiers that take further arguments need their arguments listed after the group of option letters in the correct sequence. Thus in the above example, we have the function letter c followed by two modifiers f and k. f takes the argument /dev/floppy, and k takes the argument 720.

You cannot run `ls`, say, on a `tar` archive to see the files that you've saved, but `tar` itself has a display option:

```
$ tar tvf /dev/floppy
blocksize = 10
chap1
chap2
...
```

The `t` option says list the filenames. The `v` and `f` options are as described earlier. The following command restores the `tar` backup:

```
$ tar xvf /dev/floppy
$ _
```

The option `x` says *extract* (also known as *unarchive* or *de-archive*) *all* the files saved on the given floppy. To extract particular files, you can add filename arguments (including wildcards used with care) after the device. Where will the extracted files go to? Great question. The equally great answer is: It all depends! In the above example, I saved `chap*` without specifying an absolute path name, so when I restore, the `chap*` files will be written to my current directory (assuming I have proper write permissions). Internally, `tar` attached `./` to each `chap*` file. If I had written `/usr/stan/chap*` when backing up, using an absolute path name, `tar` would try to restore the files to the `/usr/stan` directory regardless of my current directory. And thereby hangs *two* dangers: I must have write permission, of course, but the more vexing problem is whether the target directory still exists! A `tar`'d backup might lie around for months, possibly years, so the original directories embedded in the archive might well have disappeared. To avoid this aggravation, it's wiser to use only relative path names. And, naturally, restore only into directories where you have write permission.

`tar` can also be used with both directory and filename arguments. Using wildcards when extracting can cause hardships. If I tried `tar xvf /dev /floppy chap*`, for instance, it is the *shell*, not `tar`, that expands the `*`, so only files in the current directory matching `chap*` will be extracted! It is therefore safer to spell out the files, or simply restore everything in a given directory.

Some other useful `tar` options follow:

r   Appends files (writes at end of an existing archive). NOT valid with mag tape archives.

u   Update option: archives only those files which are not already archived, or those files which have been modified since they were last backed up. NOT valid with mag tape archives.

w   Wait option: displays each filename and invites y/n response before the current action is performed (allows selective backup and selective restore).

b   Changes the default blocking factor to the following numerical argument (used with raw mag tape archives only).

m   Mod-time option: normally the modification time stamp on a file is set to the time when the file is extracted. m says do not change the modification time when extracting.

e   Prevents the split of a file across volumes: if the file about to be saved will not fit on the current volume, the e option prompts with an "Insert new floppy" (or similar). Without the e option, tar will save until the volume is full before prompting: a file might therefore be split across several volumes.

n   Tells tar that archive is not a mag tape. This can speed up certain operations.

p   Used with the x option: extracts the files and directories using their original permissions.

A   Suppresses absolute filenames by stripping any initial / characters.

NEW ACCOUNTS

The System Administrator has the important task of greeting new users and getting them online smoothly. Assuming that terminal or dial-in facilities are in place, the key steps are:

▶ Assign a user name and id. The traditional, friendly method of using first names is fine until the second Henry arrives! Several strategies are possible to avoid duplications: you can have smitha, smithjc, and so on, using surname and initials, or follow the Bard with henry1 through henry8.

▶ Change /etc/passwd to include the newcomer. You may need to assign an initial password. You will certainly advise the user as to your password philosophy.

▶ The /etc/passwd file also names a home directory (/usr/ henry) with the correct ownership (use mkdir and chown) and permissions (use chmod), and default shell (which might be a restricted shell initially, such as /bin/rsh).

▶ If necessary, assign the user to a login group by editing /etc/group and using chgrp.

▶ Establish the appropriate .profile or .login files for the user (and explain how it can be personalized).

▶ Assign the default CPU priority for use with the nice command.

▶ Set other parameters as required, such as number of login attempts, password change intervals, and auditing information.

Most of these jobs require superuser privileges. The admin shells such as SCO's sysadmsh, of course, also need you to be logged in as root to access the new user routines. Although the direct editing of /etc/passwd and /etc/group is still used at some sites by (one hopes) experienced SA's, the admin shells are far superior and much safer. sysadmsh lets you add and modify user accounts from easy-to-read screen forms.

Having settled in the new user, you will never hear from him or her again! If only. The truth is that you have simply added one more soul to wash, feed, and motherhen. I wish you well.

WHAT'S NEXT?

In Chapter 18, we'll take a look at Unix's graphical user interface(s) (GUIs) which are based upon a group of applications called X Windows. You'll learn how to use X Windows, and take a short look at X Windows programming using Open Look and Motif.

```
echo "2.      Show Date"
echo "3.      Display a file"
echo "4.      Change working director
echo "5.      Return to original dire
echo "Q.      Quit
echo
echo -n "Enter choice: .\b"
read choice
case $choice in
1) who | more
   pause;;
2) date
   pause;;
3) echo "Enter file name: \c"
   read fil
   if [ -r "$fil" -a -f "$fil ]
   then
      clear
      more -d $fil
   else
      echo "Cannot di
   fi
   pause;;
4) echo "En
   read di
   if test  -d  "$dir    pwd`]
   then
      cd $dir
   else
      echo "$dir: no such di
   fi
   pause;;
   5) if test "$dir" != "$p
      then
         cd $prevdir
      fi
      pause;;
```

Chapter 18

X Windows Exposed

Throughout this book, we have worked with a character-based shell, but in this chapter, we will take a look at Unix's graphical face, and describe the X Window System, usually known simply as *X*. X has become very popular in the modern Unix world, as it helps to overcome or avoid many of the limitations of the traditional Unix character-based interface.

In a graphical user interface (GUI), applications execute in windows, using a consistent set of menus and dialog boxes, along with other graphical elements such as scroll bars and icons. Instead of typing commands at the prompt, you use a mouse, trackball, or other pointing device to point to pictorial elements on the screen, then click, double-click, or drag one of the mouse buttons to make the desired action occur.

NOTE

The X Window System is complex enough that a whole book could easily be devoted to it. If you want to write X programs yourself, one publisher in particular, O'Reilly & Associates, has produced a library of technical books in its X Window System Series.

The use of graphical elements in the user interface was pioneered at Xerox Corporation's Palo Alto Research Center (PARC) in the early 1970s. Unfortunately, the computer required to support such an interface was very expensive. The early work at PARC greatly influenced Steve Jobs, cofounder of Apple Computer, and the design of the ill-fated Apple Lisa computer and the more successful Apple Macintosh (as well as Commodore's Amiga Computer, Atari's ST-series computers, and eventually, Microsoft's Windows operating system). Since then GUIs have emerged for most computing environments.

The fundamental idea behind using a windowing system with a consistent look and feel is that you do not have to learn new commands when you move to a new application. Instead, you take advantage of habit to perform similar tasks. You know that you will always find the Open command in the File menu, and the Resize command in the Window menu. Many Unix commands, on the other hand, use the same letter as an argument to produce completely different results. For example, -l when used with ls does one thing, but when used with who does something completely different. With a well-designed windowing system these kinds of inconsistencies disappear.

An Introduction to X

X development began in 1984 at the Massachusetts Institute of Technology (MIT) as a joint project between the Laboratory for Computer Science and Project Athena. Much of this early work was sponsored by DEC and IBM. By 1986, X was becoming a significant factor in computing. In 1988, MIT, Apple, AT&T, DEC, HP, and Sun contributed $150,000 each to form the X Consortium. Since then, X has been enhanced, mostly under the guidance of the X Consortium, which continually monitors standards for the system and ensures compatibility with earlier releases. But what is X, and how does it work?

Clients and Servers Revisited

X is a windowing system that provides for multiple resizable windows so that you can have many applications displayed on your screen at the same time. Unlike most windowing systems that have a specific built-in user interface, X is a foundation upon which almost any style of user interface can be constructed. The unique feature of X is that it is based upon a network protocol rather than on the more usual programming procedure calls.

NOTE

In the X Window System, the terms client and server do not have the same meaning as in the "Client-Server Computing" section in Chapter 16.

The X System consists of three main parts:

► The server software, which controls your display, keyboard, and mouse

► The client software, or applications programs, which are completely separate from the server

► A communications link that connects the client and the server

Figure 18.1 shows these three elements, and in the next section we'll look at these system components in more detail.

The Server

Under X, the server is the software that controls the display hardware. It accepts requests sent across the communications link from client application programs to open a window on the screen, to change the size or position of a window, and to draw graphics and display text in these windows. The server sends back events to the clients, telling them about keyboard or mouse input.

A server can manage simultaneous communications from many clients. This means you can run several applications at the same time, each with its own separate window on your screen.

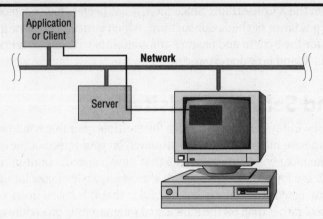

FIGURE 18.1:   The client represents the application while the server controls the display.

The Client

Under X, the client is the application program that, in addition to providing the code needed to support X and the graphical user interface, performs a specific function for the user, such as managing a database or sending e-mail. A client can work with any display, as long as there is a communications link to the server.

X is not limited to one server and one client, and in fact many combinations are possible. Several clients may interact with a single server when many different applications display on a single screen, or a single client can communicate with several servers and display the same information on many different screens.

The Communications Link

The third major element in X is the communications link. All communications between server and client must use this link, but it does not matter what form the link takes. There are two main implementations:

▶ Client and server execute on the same computer, for example, a workstation running X. In this situation, the link will be some form of interprocess communication (IP) such as shared memory (named pipes or streams).

▶ Client and server run on different computers, for example, across a network. X is independent from the network, so almost any physical link can be used: Ethernet, Token Ring, X.25, and serial lines have all been used. The two computers do not even need the same processor or operating system, because the information transmitted between the server and the client is always device independent.

How the X Protocol Works

The X Protocol is the real definition of the X System, and it defines just four types of message that can be transferred over the communications link. Requests are sent from the client to the server, and replies, events, and error messages are sent from the server to the client. This chapter is not the place to detail the decisions made and the trade-offs evaluated in defining what should be a client function and what should be a server function.

X Compared with Other Windowing Systems

Many other systems offer a windowed environment, but none of them can offer the combination of features that makes X such a powerful force.

`telnet` (see Chapter 16) lets you log in to a remote computer and then run programs as though they were executing on your own local computer. However, `telnet` cannot manage graphics or multiple applications.

The Macintosh interface is a consistent GUI and, ever since System 7, allows multitasking. But the interface is fixed and cannot be changed. Also, the interface is an integral part of the operating system—you can't run a Macintosh without its GUI.

Microsoft Windows is also a consistent GUI that allows multitasking, but again, the GUI is fixed and cannot be changed. Also, it can only be used with applications written for the PC; it cannot run a program on a VAX containing a built-in GUI and run the display to a PC.

What the Users See in X

The GUI that you see as a user consists of two separate X components:

▶ The application interface, which cannot be changed without changing the original program. This controls the flow of the program and what appears in the menus and the dialog boxes.

▶ A separate client program, known as the window manager, which controls how you move, resize, arrange, and close the windows on your screen.

This relationship is shown in Figure 18.2.

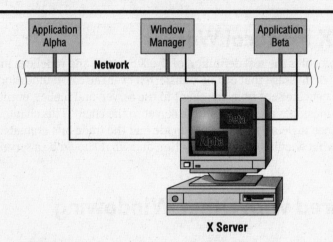

FIGURE 18.2:   A separate client program known as the window manager controls the windows on your screen

Because the window manager is not part of the application, you can change to a different window manager if one is available. However, at any given moment, all the applications windows on your screen work in the same way because they are all under the control of one window manager. See the section "X Window Managers: Open Look and Motif" later in this chapter for more information.

X-Terminals and PC X Servers

X-terminals are special terminals built to run X. An X-terminal consists of a simple and fast computer with a built-in X server, and includes a mouse, keyboard, graphics screen, and a network interface. The X server itself is usually stored in read-only memory (ROM) so that no disk storage is needed. In fact, a good way to think of an X server is to think of it in terms of a terminal.

Packages that allow an X server to run on a PC are also available, effectively transforming the PC into an X-terminal. These packages are available for the Macintosh and for PCs running Microsoft Windows, and Windows NT. Many of the packages also include the software necessary to add TCP/IP to the system.

X Benefits

In addition to the typical benefits of using a well-designed and consistent GUI (ease of use, short learning times for new applications, direct manipulation of individual interface elements, and multiple applications in overlapping windows), the X System offers many other important benefits. These are some of the most important:

- ▶ Once a network has been set up to use X, a user can access any application on any computer on that network. This can be particularly useful if an application must be run on a specific machine due to memory, disk space, or computational speed requirements, or if the network consists of a number of computers with different operating systems. By using X, anyone can access the application on the large computer and display the output on their own workstations. This is the most important X benefit.

- ▶ X can disguise the structure or architecture of a network, and can simplify subsequent growth of the system. Indeed, you may not even know that your application is running on a network.

- ▶ You can also run non-windowed applications with X by using a special X client called a *terminal emulator* (more on this in the section "Using the xterm Terminal Emulator" later in this chapter).

The code that implements X is widely available, and over time has shown itself to be extremely portable. Implementations are available for computers ranging from PCs to massive supercomputers. X is so completely independent of both the underlying computer hardware and the operating system, that carefully written software will compile and run on any system anywhere.

In the next section, we'll look at two popular X implementations, and then examine how to use X in more detail.

X WINDOW MANAGERS: OPEN LOOK AND MOTIF

The X Consortium controls the technical development of the X Window System, but not the implementation of the window manager. The window manager is just another X client (although it enjoys certain special privileges) that performs the following functions:

▶ Creates and removes windows

▶ Resizes and moves windows

▶ Converts windows into icons and icons into windows.

NOTE

An icon is a small image that represents an application that is not running or that is running in the background.

▶ Controls the management of overlapping windows, the top window always being completely visible, while only portions of other windows may be visible behind it.

The X System does not require you to run a specific window manager. You can use any window manager that performs the basic functions. Many X clients can run under any window manager, but some clients do depend on the facilities provided by a specific window manager.

NOTE

If you check the FAQ (frequently asked questions) in the comp.windows.x USENET newsgroup, you will find descriptions of well over 30 different window managers.

Window managers enforce the "look and feel" of the window system, usually as style guides. While many window managers do not have strict style guides, the two major, commercially available X standards that have emerged, Open Look (olwm) and Motif (mwm), most certainly do.

A style guide usually specifies more than the simple objects that form the user interface; it also describes the ways in which these objects can be configured in an interface. For example, the Motif style guide specifies that a pull-down menu should be in a menu bar located at the top of the main window, while Open Look interfaces quite often have menus and command buttons distributed throughout the interface. Open Look lets you pin up a menu on your screen, even if the menu's parent window is buried and out of sight. Motif counters this with the tear-off menu.

Open Look was developed by AT&T and Sun Microsystems, and is derived from user interface work performed at Xerox in the early 1980s. Sun was chiefly responsible for the design of the interface. Open Look was also included in AT&T's release of SVR4.2.

Motif was developed by the Open Software Foundation (OSF), a collaboration of hardware and software vendors including DEC, IBM, and Hewlett-Packard. The OSF released the first version of Motif in 1989, along with a style guide and a plan for application certification—two elements required for a consistent user interface. In appearance and function, Motif is similar to Microsoft Windows, and this may be important for users who want to integrate their X applications with existing Windows software.

The Common Open Software Environment (COSE) has now established OSF/Motif as the standard look and feel for Unix user interfaces, which leaves a large body of Open Look-based software that will probably be converted to Motif sometime in the future.

Using X

To use X, you will need the following:

- ▶ An X server for your system, a PC running X, or, if you are not using a workstation, an X-terminal instead.

- ▶ Client application programs X software can run directly; older, non-X applications can run under X by using a terminal emulator such as `xterm`. See the section headed "Using the `xterm` Terminal Emulator" later in this chapter for more information.

- ▶ A window manager to manage your application windows.

- ▶ Certain standard default files, usually supplied as part of the application that define font usage, colors, and layout.

- ▶ If your system supports shared libraries and your application uses them, these libraries must be present on each computer that runs the applications.

If you work in a networked environment and run the applications on a remote computer, you will also need access to the appropriate network hardware and software.

Logging In

Many systems start X automatically, and you log in under X in the same way you normally would. The xdm (X Display Manager) program handles logins and manages X sessions, and is normally called as part of the system initialization. After you have logged in, xdm runs xterm by default, or an application you specify. You can also run, xdm remotely with X-terminals and PC X servers to provide a login window; one copy can manage multiple terminals or PCs.

If X was not started automatically, you can start it with the xinit program, usually located in the main X directory; /usr/bin/X11 on many systems. Either way, you can use an initialization file that contains commands executed when X starts; the location of the file and the filename depend on whether X was started manually or automatically:

- ▶ If X was started automatically, the initialization file is usually located in your home directory and called .xsession. The contents of .xsession are executed before the initialization files associated with your shell.

- ▶ If X was started manually, the initialization file is called .xinitrc (on SCO's Open Desktop, the .xinitrc file is usually called .startxr). As a minimum, this file should contain commands to call xterm in the background and a window manager in the foreground. If .xinitrc does not exist, xinit starts the X session by running an xterm window.

If you do not use an initialization file, you will just be accepting system-specific default values for the more than 30 environmental variables.

X Resources

It is possible to specify X resources at the command line, but the commands are long and there are many options. People entering the X resources by hand are likely to make errors. It is generally better to put these options in shell scripts. You will find details on how to do this in an X client's man pages. Many clients follow the naming conventions used with xterm options, and we will get to xterm in the next section. You can also use a resource database file, usually called .Xdefaults in your home directory if it is a local database. If it is a system-wide file, look in /usr/lib /Xlib. You will have to see your system administrator for information on configuring these files, because this is a subject well beyond the scope of this book.

NOTE

Two terms you will hear sooner or later in connection with X are *toolkit* and *widget*. The X toolkit is a set of predefined functions that an applications programmer uses to create the user interface, and a widget is a user interface element created within X guidelines. Widgets actually provide the look and feel of an interface, in terms of the appearance of the menu, scroll bar, and push-button widgets.

There are other ways you can adjust the look and feel of an application. SCO's Open Desktop provides the Controls window so you can select your own color scheme, configure the mouse, select fonts, or choose a background pattern or image. SunSoft's OpenWindows Workspace Properties window lets you alter window frames, change colors, configure your mouse, and even create your own icons. Even individual application programs will often give you a way to configure their own resources.

But what do you do when you want to use X with a program that is not an X program? The answer is straightforward enough: use X and the xterm terminal emulator.

Using the xterm Terminal Emulator

The xterm terminal emulator program provides an X window that behaves just like a terminal, sometimes known as a virtual terminal, under the control of the shell specified by the SHELL environment variable, with /bin/sh as the default. xterm emulates two ancient terminals, the DEC VT102 text terminal and the Tektronix 4015 graphics terminal. You are unlikely to have either, but that is not important. What is important is that you understand what this emulation gives you.

NOTE

The name of the X-terminal emulator may vary depending on the Unix you use. In SCO Open Desktop, xterm is known as scoterm, and in Hewlett-Packard systems, as hpterm; in Sun systems you will find cmdterm, and shelltool in addition to xterm, and in UnixWare you will find a Terminal window.

Put simply, a terminal emulator program pretends to be a real terminal, and so gives you a window that acts just like a physical terminal running your shell. It can display any input you type at the keyboard, as well as run programs just like any normal shell. Therefore, you can still run all the old character-based programs and utilities described in the first part of this book such as ls, pwd, and even vi, all without leaving X.

Running your character-based applications in this way gives you several other advantages, too:

▶ You can cut and paste between xterm and other X windows, giving a degree of communication between the older programs and your X clients.

▶ You can customize your keyboard and map function keys separately for each window.

▶ You can scroll text output or log your session to a file.

▶ You can connect each xterm window to a different host computer so you can perform work on several different computers, all from one physical terminal.

▶ By using telnet from an xterm window, you can run applications on computers that do not have any X Window support of any kind.

▶ You can open multiple terminals at once in different windows, and you can run several copies of the same program if you wish.

The form of the xterm command line is

```
xterm [options]
```

The command line options can be long and complex. A – usually turns on an option, while a + usually turns it off—just the opposite of what you might expect. You can also abbreviate an option to its shortest unique form, so you can use -bg for -background, or -fn for -font. Table 18.1 lists the most frequently used xterm command line options; remember that you can use many of these options with other X clients.

TABLE 18.1: Common xterm Command Line Options

Option	Description
-bd color	Specifies color as the window border color.
-bg color	Specifies color as the window background color.
-bw width	Specifies a window border of width pixels.
-e program	Executes program and uses program as the window title (unless you also use the -title option).

TABLE 18.1 continued: Common xterm Command Line Options

Option	Description
-fg *color*	Specifies *color* as the window foreground color.
-fn *font*	Specifies the name of the fixed-width font to use.
-help	Displays a list of command options.
-j or +j	Turns jump scrolling, also known as speed scrolling, on or off, which makes xterm much faster when you are scanning through long text files.
-l	Sends xterm input and output to the default log file called XtermLog.*n*, where *n* is the five-digit decimal number that represents the process id number.
-lf *filename*	Specifies *filename* as the log file.
-ms *color*	Specifies *color* for the mouse pointer.
-rv	Simulates reverse video by swapping the foreground and background colors. +rv prevents this swapping when reverse video is set as the default.
-sb or +sb	Displays a scroll bar on the xterm window, and saves text that is scrolled out of the top of the window in a text buffer for later viewing.
-sl *number*	Specifies the number of lines in the text buffer.
-title *string*	Specifes *string* as the title of the window if the window manager requests a title.

When using xterm or any other X client, it is always a good idea to spell the command out in full, as most of them use long English-language names. You should also remember to keep commands standard; you can always expect foreground, background, and so on.

NOTE
You will always see two separate independent cursors in an xterm window; the mouse cursor and the text cursor.

You can open an xterm window with scroll bars if you enter

    xterm -sb &

Remember that the & starts the program running in the background. See Chapter 8 for more on background and foreground processes. To store commands and output from those commands into a logfile called foocmds, use

    xterm -l -lf foocmds &

When you start an `xterm` window in this way, it runs another instance of the shell specified by the `SHELL` environment variable. If you would rather create an `xterm` window that runs a program and then disappears when that program terminates, use

`xterm -e program`

If you are using several command line options, be sure that the `-e` option is the last one you type. Everything after the `-e` is treated as a command. In this case, the `xterm` window title will also show the name of the command that followed the `-e`, unless you also used the `-title` option to specify that something else is to be used instead.

`xterm` has menus you can activate if you press the Ctrl key on the keyboard at the same time you press a mouse button:

▶ Ctrl and the left mouse button open the `xterm` menu. This contains selections you can use to start logging and to send signals of various kinds to the current foreground process.

▶ Ctrl and the middle mouse button open a menu containing options to set various terminal modes.

▶ Ctrl and the right mouse button may open a menu containing font selections. On some systems, however, Ctrl and the right mouse button do not open a menu.

There are also several more advanced systems available. While they are still basically terminal emulators, they also allow you to add an X front end to a character-based application without changing the original application. Such systems are occasionally termed *frontware*. The simplest systems add a set of pushbuttons to the side of the `xterm` window; these buttons are configured by a script file. More advanced systems are completely programmable, and can provide much more complex front ends, to the point where the original character-based interface is no longer visible, and the user sees a fully functioning graphical user interface. The advantage of this approach is that the original application has not changed. You don't care what language it was originally written in because you don't even need the source code.

Using Other X Clients

Many other X clients are commonly available. Some you use as utility programs and others as configuration programs. There is, however, some variation between different X systems. These are some of the more useful clients:

Client	Description
bitmap	Lets you create and edit bitmap images
xbiff	Raises a flag on the mailbox icon to let you know that the mail has arrived
xcalc	Provides a scientific calculator
xcalendar	Displays a monthly calendar and lets you mark appointments
xclock	Provides a clock display with either analog or digital form
xcolors	Displays a color chart of available colors
xdpr	Runs xwd to make a screen capture and send the output to the printer
xfd	Displays font selections or the font specified by the -fn option
xfontsel	Displays fonts and lets you choose a new font
xkill	Kills an X client
xload	Displays a graphical image of system load
xlsfonts	Lists the fonts supported on your system
xman	Provides an X version of the regular man command
xrefresh	Refreshes the whole screen
xset	Allows you to specify screen and keyboard options
xsetroot	Sets the background of the root window to the color or bitmap you specify
xwd	Makes a partial or complete screen capture to a file
xwud	Displays images made using xwd

xclock and xbiff are often run in the background, so that their windows are always visible on the screen. The form of the xclock command is

    xclock [*options*] &

The `options` include `-analog` for a conventional clock face, `-digital` for a 24-hour digital face, and `-chime` to chime once on the half hour and twice on the hour.

The form of the `xbiff` command is

```
xbiff [options] &
```

The flag on the `xbiff` mailbox is raised if you have mail and lowered when the mail has been retrieved. Both `xclock` and `xbiff` respond to X command line options; see Table 18.1 for a list of the common options and your system manual for others specific to your X implementation.

Common public domain tools include `xloadimage`, which displays various graphics files, and `pbm`, which converts graphics files from one file format to another.

Killing an X Client

One of the X clients listed in the previous section is worth a closer look. The `xkill` program forces the X server to close the connection to a client and is useful for removing unwanted windows, although in some cases the client may not always terminate cleanly. The command has the form

```
xkill [options]
```

The `options` depend on the particular implementation of X on your system.

X Marks the Spot: The Future of X

Some of the formal standard-producing organizations are developing X standards. For example, the ANSI task group X3H3 is working on the X Window data stream definition (in other words, the X protocol), including how it should operate over OSI networks, and the IEEE P1201.1 group is developing standards for the user interface. The European Commission has specified X and Motif as standards for its own use, and X has been specified as a standard for many U.S. government systems.

The religious wars between those who favor Motif over Open Look may also be drawing to a close. Sun has agreed to support Motif as part of the Common Open Software Environment OSE) initiative, but it may be a long time before all the existing Sun and AT&T Open Look users switch over. Because there is often a fairly close mapping between Open Look and Motif interface objects, automatic conversion tools may make this transition less painful for those software developers concerned with porting X applications.

NOTE

You can obtain the X System files over the Internet using anonymous `ftp` from `ftp.x.org.mit.edu`, from `gatekeeper.dec.com`, from `x11r5.b.uu.net`, or from several third-party vendors. You can get information about X from the USENET `comp.windows.x` newsgroup; to join, send an e-mail message to `xpert-request@expo.lcs.mit.edu`. You can also access a set of programs and documentation by sending email with the single word `help` as the message to `xstuff@expo.lcs.mit.edu`. You might also consider joining the local chapter of the X User's Group by sending an email message to `xug@ics.come`.

The X version number (X11) refers to the protocol, and the version number changes when the protocol changes. The new version becomes incompatible with the old version and existing programs will no longer work. For this reason I don't think there will be a version 12, because that would require too much conversion of existing software. But that does not mean that X cannot change and add new functions.

Every so often MIT releases a collection of sample programs and programming libraries; these represent the release level. New releases might contain bug fixes, performance improvements, and improvements or enhancements to programming libraries.

The original designers of X went out of their way to ensure that X would never be limiting. An extension mechanism allows new features to be built into the server without producing a performance penalty. In fact, extensions are often used by system manufacturers to take advantage of hardware features. They are also used by the X Consortium to implement and agree on new features.

Even with the wide acceptance of X11, new developments continue. Works in progress include extensions to support various input devices, X for Japanese use, a multithreaded X server, and 3-D graphics.

Other interesting developments on the GUI front concern the evolution of the graphical desktop, a screen-based metaphor for a real desktop that contains icons representing applications and other accessories. The DeskSet bundled with Solaris, SCO's Open Desktop, and Hewlett-Packard's VUE (Visual User Environment) are all good examples. The only question is, can these desktop managers replace the shell command line, and will the evolution of the desktop give rise to the same kind of religious wars we have endured between the C shell and the Korn shell, and between Open Look and Motif?

WHAT'S NEXT

Although it would be easier to operate in a world in which everyone used the same data standards and all files moved seamlessly from one computer system to another, in fact, computers do not yet operate this way. In Chapter 19, we'll take a look at several ways in which Unix can communicate with all the other computers in the world.

```
echo "2.      Show Date"
echo "3.      Display a file"
echo "4.      Change working directo
echo "5.      Return to original di
echo "Q.      Quit
echo
echo -n "Enter choice: .\b"
read choice
case $choice in
1) who | more
   pause;;
2) date
   pause;;
3) echo "Enter file name: \c"
   read fil
   if [ -r "$fil" -a -f "$fil ]
   then
      clear
      more -d $fil
   else
      echo "Cannot di
   fi
   pause;;
4) echo "E
   read di
   if test    "$dir    pwd`
   then
      cd $dir
   else
      echo "$dir: no such di
   fi
      pause;;
   5) if test "$dir" != "$p
      then
         cd $prevdir
      fi
      pause;;
```

Chapter 19

OUT OF A VACUUM:
THE DOOR TO MAINSTREAM
APPLICATIONS

Although the Unix operating system offers both users and system administrators incredible reliability and configurability, the fact is, Unix cannot operate in a vacuum. The vast majority of computer users today use another operating system—Microsoft Windows, which currently claims in excess of 90% of all the computers in the world. While it might be interesting to examine some of the reasons for Microsoft's dominance, we'll leave that for another day. Here, we shall simply note the net result, which is that virtually every important application program produced today runs under Windows. As such, it's important for Unix to allow its users access to Windows data files. So in this chapter, we'll look at how a Unix system can manage Windows (and while we're at it, DOS) files and applications.

Although there are a number of approaches available to exchange data between these otherwise incompatible systems, in this chapter, we'll focus on just two, which operate under almost any Unix or Linux system.

Samba A set of programs used to provide DOS and Windows users access to files on a Unix file server using the SMB (Server Message Block) protocol. The SMB protocol was originally defined by Microsoft and Intel for their Open/NET-FILE SHARING PROTOCOL.

mtools Consists of a number of public-domain utilities designed to allow Unix users direct access to MS-DOS files.

SAMBA

Samba consists of a series of utilities that allow Windows and DOS users access to files on a Unix file server. The interface resembles a DOS window if you're in Windows, or a pretty standard DOS file session if you're using DOS. The difference is that you're accessing a drive that's on a Unix server. To use Samba, you need to set it up on your server first. Once it's set up, it will appear more or less like another drive on your network. The following utilities are included with Samba.

smbd

smbd provides file and print services to users running Windows 95, Windows 98, Windows NT, Windows for Workgroups, and Lan Manager. It may be run on demand or it may be set up to operate in the background as a daemon. The syntax for smbd is:

```
smbd [-D][-a][-o][-d debuglevel][-l loglevel][-p port number]
[-O socket options][-s configuration file][-I scope][-P][-h
```

Table 19.1 describes the parameters in more detail.

TABLE 19.1: Parameters used with smbd.

OPTION	DESCRIPTION
-D	This parameter causes smbd to run independently in the background as a daemon. In this mode, it monitors the activity on a specified port and services the file and print service for that port. By default, smbd will *not* operate as a daemon.

TABLE 19.1 continued: Parameters used with smbd.

OPTION	DESCRIPTION
-a	Instructs smbd to append log messages to the log file. Note: This is the default mode for smbd.
-o	Overrides -a causing each new connection to overwrite the log file.
-d debuglevel	The options for this parameter are integers between 0 and 15. Note: If no debuglevel is specified, the command defaults to 0.
	Level 0: Only critical errors and serious warnings are entered into the log file.
	Level 1: At level 1, debuglevel will generate short reports about most daily communications activites at the specified port. (This is the most commonly used level.)
	Beyond level 1, the debuglevels are used only for debugging system errors.
-l log file	The filename of the log file used by smbd to store debug messages and other information generated by the communications port.
-p port number	This parameter is not generally specified. It defaults to 139, which is the number that connecting systems will look for when they communicate with your system. If, for some reason you wish to use another value here, which is not generally recommended, be sure to redirect the services to the port number you specify.
-s configuration file	smbd will look to the file named here for configuration information, such as which printcap file to use. The name specified here is determined by the system at compile time.
-h	This parameter will print the help information for smbd.
-P	Passive mode. In this mode, smbd does not transfer any data to the network; it is only used for system administration/debugging.

smb.conf & swat

The smb.conf file is used to provide configuration data for all of the utilities within Samba. It tells your system how to communicate with the network. The list of configurable parameters in smb.conf is huge and the options are numerous. As such, these parameters are not generally set manually unless you are simply making one or two changes to an existing file or you are *really* enthusiastic. The best way to create and/or manage smb.conf is with a program called swat.

nmbd

nmbd operates a lot like smbd in that it has many of the same options. The difference, of course, is that nmbd provides NetBIOS connectivity for IP name service requests, while smbd provides file and print services. Additionally, nmbs can be used as a WINS (Windows Internet Name Server) and a WINS proxy server for systems that do not utilize WINS. The syntax for nmbd is:

nmbd [-D][-o][-a][-H lmhosts][-d debuglevel][-l loglevel]
[-nprimary NetBIOS name][-p port number][-s configuration
file][-I NetBIOS scope][-h]

Table 19.2 describes the parameters in more detail.

TABLE 19.2: nmbd parameters

OPTION	DESCRIPTION
-D	This parameter causes smbd to run independently in the background as a daemon. In this mode, it monitors the activity on a specified port. The default for nmbs is to *not* run as a daemon.
-a	Instructs nmbd to append log messages to the log file. Note: This is the default mode for nmbd.
-o	Overrides -a causing each new connection to overwrite the log file.
-H filename	The name of NetBIOS's lmhosts file. This file is a list of NetBIOS names and their corresponding IP addresses.
-d debuglevel	The options for this parameter are integers between 0 and 10. Note: If no debuglevel is specified, the command defaults to 0.
	Level 0: Lists only critical errors and serious warnings.
	Level 1: At level 1, debuglevel will generate short reports about most daily communications activites at the specified port. (This is the most commonly used level.)
	Beyond level 1, the debuglevels are used only for debugging system errors.
-l log file	The filename of the log file used by nmbd to store debug messages and other information generated by nmbd.
-n primary NetBIOS name	This option allows you to override the NetBIOS name parameter that is specified in smb.conf.
-p UPD port number	This parameter is not generally specified. It defaults to 139, which is the number that connecting systems will look for when they communicate with your system.

TABLE 19.2 continued: nmbd parameters

Option	Description
-s configuration file	nmbd will look to the file named here for configuration information, such as which printcap file to use. The name specified here is determined by the system at compile time.
-i scope	A rarely used function. Only set by the system administrator who controls all of the NetBIOS systems that are communicating with each other.
-h	This parameter will print the help information for nmbd.

smbclient

smbclient operates a lot like ftp. It's designed to to move files between a local computer and a server. It also allows the local computer to retrieve directory names and filenames from the server. The syntax for smbclient is:

smbclient servicename [password][-s smb conf][-B IP addr][-O
socket options][-R name resolve order][-M NetBIOS names][-I
scope][-N][-n NetBIOS name][-d debuglevel][-P][-p port][-l log
basename][-h][-l dest IP][-E][-U username][-L NetBIOS name][-t
terminal code][-m max protocol][-W workgroup][-T tar options][-
D directory][-c command string]

Table 19.3 describes the parameters in more detail.

TABLE 19.3: smbclient parameters

Option	Description
servicename	This parameter specifies the name of the service you want access to on the server. The syntax for a requested service is:
	//server/service
	Server is the NetBIOS name of the server; service is the requested service on the server.
password	As you might guess, this is the password you need to access the the server. Note that if you embed the password here, then Samba will supress the password prompt by default. This is the same as entering the –N parameter. If you don't embed the password here, then you will be prompted for a password even if none is required. To enter an empty password, just press the Enter key.

TABLE 19.3 continued: smbclient parameters

Option	Description
-s smb.conf	This parameter tells Samba where it can find its configuration file: smb.conf. It should contain the full path name.
-B IP addr	Broadcast packet address
-0 socket options	This parameter defines the socket options for the client side of a TCP connection. The following options take a 1 or 0 argument (the default is 1): SO_KEEPALIVE SO_REUSEADDR SO_BROADCAST TCP_NODELAY IPTOS_LOWDELAY IPTOS_THROUGHPUT These options take an integer argument: SO_SNDBUF SO_RCVBUF SO_SNDLOWAT SO_RCVLOWAT
-R name resolve order	This parameter is used to determine which name resolution service will be used to look up the NetBIOS name of the host system. The options are: lmhosts Uses the lmhosts file in the smb.conf directory. host Standard host name to IP address matching using /etc/hosts NIS or DNS lookup tables. wins Searches for IP address match in wins.server in the smb.conf file. bcast Broadcast to each of the connected local interfaces listed in smb.conf.
-M NetBIOS names	The –M option of smbclient sends messages from one computer to another on the network using the WinPopup protocol. To send a message, you simply establish the connection, type in your message, and press Ctrl-D to end the message. Note: There is a 1600 character limit to this protocol. To get around this limitation, you can create a message using your text editor and then send the file as a unit, using this syntax: cat <yourmessage.txt> | smbclient –M <recipient>
-i scope	A rarely used option that determines the NetBIOS scope the smbclient uses to generate NetNIOS names.
-N	Supresses the password prompt to the user.

TABLE 19.3 continued: smbclient parameters

OPTION	DESCRIPTION
-n NetBIOS name	This supresses the default hostname (usually the hostname in UPPERCASE), replacing it with the hostname you specify.
-d debuglevel	The options for this parameter are integers between 0 and 10. Note: If no debuglevel is specified, the command defaults to 0. Level 0: Lists only critical errors and serious warnings. Level 1: At level 1, debuglevel will generate short reports about most daily communications activites at the specified port. (This is the most commonly used level.) Beyond level 1, the debuglevels are used only for debugging system errors. Level A prints all debug messages.
-P	No longer used.
-p port	The TCP port number. Note: The default value is 139.
-l log basename	The base name of the file that will hold all of the client log data. This is the name used to generate the log filenames. For example, if the specified base name is magda then the debug filename would be magda.client.
-h	The help option. When specified, displays a brief listing of the smbclient arguments and their functions.
-l dest IP	The IP address of the server you want to connect to.
-E	Redirects messages from the standard output (usually the video display) to the standard error stream.
-U username	The user's name.
-L NetBIOS name	The look option. This argument displays a list of the services that are available on the server.
-t terminal code	Tells smbclient how to translate filenames. Used with foreign language systems using multibyte characters like Japanese or Chinese.
-m max protocol	Samba 2.0 always tries to connect at the higest protocol level that the server supports. Older versions had to have this level specified. The -m option is included for backward compatibility.
-W workgroup	Used to temporarily select a different workgroup than the one specified in the configuration file for the current connection.
-T tar options	This argument allows you to use the server as a backup device. The options for tar are: c [filename] Creates a new tar file with the specified filename.

TABLE 19.3 continued: smbclient parameters

Option	Description
	x [filename] Restores and reads the specified tar file.
	I Specifies the files to include in tar.
	X Specifies files to exclude in tar.
	b Defines the block size to be used by tar.
	g Sets archive backup mode. Backs up only files that have their archive bit set (have not been backed up since the last backup).
	q (Quiet Mode) Supresses output of diagnostic data while it is operating.
	r This argument tells smbclient to use a regular expression to include or exclude files.
	N This argument must be followed by a filename. The date of the specified file is used by tar to determine which files to backup. Only files newer than the specified file will be backed up.
	a Sets the archive bit on the files being backed up.
-D directory	Tells smbclient to change to the initial directory—operates like an automatic cd.
-c command string	Tells smbclient that what follows is a string of commands. Each command must be separated by a semicolon. The commands operate as if they were entered one at a time from the keyboard.

Running Samba

After you have set up Samba and are connected to the server, running Samba is a lot like reading and writing DOS files on a local drive. For example, in DOS, the normal prompt from the local processor consists of the drive name, the path (if you're logged on to a directory other than root) and a greater-than symbol like this:

```
C:\>
```

In Samba, the prompt you'll see looks like this:

```
smb:\>
```

Like the C: prompt in DOS, this prompt tells you that the server is awaiting your command. The commands available to you are as follows:

cd

The cd command means "change directory" just as it does in DOS. It's syntax is:

```
cd [directoryname]
or cd [full path]
```

If the directory you're changing to is down a level from where you are (is listed in the current directory) then you can simply enter its name. If you want to go up a directory level or down several levels, then you'll need to enter the full path for Samba to find it. If the directory is not found or is left blank, then you'll get an error message.

del

Like the DOS command, del is used to delete files. To delete a file, just enter the command:

```
del [filename]
```

and it's gone! Actually, depending upon how you've set up smb.conf, you may be prompted for a confirmation before it's tossed into the virtual furnace.

To delete several files, you can enter a few characters along with wildcards (also called a mask) instead of just a filename. The wildcards at your disposal are * and ?. For example, if you wanted to delete all of the files in the current directory that ended in .txt, you'd enter:

```
del *.txt
```

dir

The directory command, dir, is used to display a list of files and/or directories. To display all of the files in your current directory, simply enter:

```
dir
```

To list the files in another directory, enter dir with the full path name, like this:

```
dir \somedirectory\anotherone
```

exit (quit)

The exit (and quit) commands simply disconnect you from the server and end Samba.

get

The get command is similar to the DOS copy command. It is used to make a duplicate of a file that's on the server in the local computer. The syntax for get is:

```
get <file to copy> [name of new copy]
```

So, if you wanted to copy a file named blivet.doc from the server and you wanted to call it blivet2.doc on your own system, you'd enter this:

```
get blivet.doc blivet2.doc
```

By the way, if you just enter the name of the file to copy, leaving off the new name, get will give the copy the same name as the original.

help

The help command, as you may have guessed, accesses a help database containing information on how to use Samba. The shortcut for the help command is ?. So, if you want to get information on using get, for example, you could enter:

```
help get
```

or

```
? get
```

This will display a short description of the command and how to use it.

lcd

No, this doesn't mean "liquid crystal display." It's a local version of the cd (change directory) command. The command has the same options as cd except that it operates on your computer instead of the server. Note that like cd, if the directory you're changing to is not in the specified path or doesn't exist, the command will return an error.

ls

This command is basically the same as dir. It's included in Samba for the "Unix-ites" in the system, since ls is the Unix equivalent of the DOS command, dir.

md (mkdir)

This is an alternative command name for mkdir. It makes a new directory on the server, assuming that the user has the privilege. To make a new directory, you'd enter this:

```
md <new directoryname>
```

print

This prints a file from the local computer on a printer connected through the server.

put

This is the other half of the get command. It makes a copy of a file that's on the local machine on the server. For example:

```
put <file to copy on local computer> [name of new copy on server]
```

So, if you wanted to copy a file named blivet.doc from the server and you wanted to call it blivet2.doc on your own system, you'd enter this:

```
put blivet.doc blivet2.doc
```

And like get, if you just enter the name of the file to copy, leaving off the new name, put will give the copy the same name as the original.

queue

This command displays a list of the files that are waiting to be printed, the size of the files, and their current status.

rd (rmdir) (rm)

These commands (rd is a shortened form of the rmdir command) remove a directory from the server, if the user has such privileges. rm is similar to rd, but deletes several directories at once, based upon the mask entered.

setmode

Similar to the DOS attrib command, the setmode command changes the file attributes (read/write/archived, etc.)

tar, blocksize, tarmode

Used to backup files (for more details, see the previous section).

MTOOLS

mtools is the complement to Samba. It allows Unix systems to read, write, copy, and delete files on a DOS computer or separate DOS filesystem on the same computer. Although mtools is designed to access DOS files, there are some significant differences between the way mtools and DOS operate. For example, while DOS uses *.* to match all files, mtools uses the Unix convention, in which * matches all files. Additionally, mtools ignores the file attributes archive, hidden, and read-only when matching the filespec for multiple files. Also, options to commands in mtools follow the Unix convention of being prefaced by − (dash) instead of the DOS / (slash).

Configuring mtools

Like Samba, mtools has a configuration file that is read before mtools is started. On most systems, the default location of the mtools' global configuration file is called:

```
/usr/local/etc/mtools.conf
```

On some other systems, the global configuration file is:

```
/etc/defaults/mtools.conf
/etc/mtools.conf [FHS 2.0 / Linux]
```

and in either case, the user's configuration file is:

```
~/.mtoolsrc
```

Most of the following options are either set or not set. To set them, set them to 1. To clear them, set them to 0. For example:

```
option=1
```

The options you can configure in the global configuration file are as follows.

MTOOLS_FAT_COMPATIBILITY

Set to 1, this option allows mtools to read disks with file allocation tables that are larger than mtools would ordinarily accept.

MTOOLS_LOWER_CASE

If set to 1, mtools displays all uppercase, short filenames as lowercase. This is included for backward compatibility; older versions did not look at the case bits of filenames.

MTOOLS_NO_VFAT

If you set this option to 1, mtools will not create VFAT entries for upper/lower-case filenames. This is included for compatibility with versions of DOS that can't handle long filenames.

MTOOLS_DOTTED_DIR

When set to 1, this option converts long filenames to short form with a dot separating the filename from it's extension.

MTOOLS_NAME_NUMERIC_TAIL

When set to 1, this option adds numeric tails (ie: ~3) to the end of all long filenames. If it's set to 0, it only adds them if two filenames would be displayed using the same name in the directory listing.

MTOOLS_TWENTY_FOUR_HOUR_CLOCK

If set to 1, this option causes mtools to display time in 24 (military) time. If set to 0, it uses the US convention (12 hours +am or pm).

MTOOLS_DATE_STRING

This option takes a string variable as its argument instead of a 1 or 0. It determines how the date is formatted. Default is: dd-mm-yyyy. To change it, set this with:

```
option=new string
```

SETTING DRIVE PARAMETERS

To be able to read or write to DOS floppies, you need to set up the drive parameters for each drive on your system. Unlike Unix, which requires you to mount/unmount disks each time you insert or remove one in or from a drive, mtools is able to operate much like DOS. To do this, however, you need to set up the following parameters for the drive(s) first. Drive configuration information begins by designating which drive is being defined, like this:

```
drive a:
    file="/dev/fd1" use_xdf=1
```

NOTE

Some floppy drives support more than one type of diskette. For example, most 5 1/4", 1.2M drives can read and write to both 1.2MB diskettes and to 360K diskettes. Similarly, most 3 1/2" floppy drives can read and write to 720KB diskettes as well as 1.44MB floppies. mtools, however, will not be able to use this capability unless you include the specific drive geometry to accomplish the task. To do this, you can specify multiple drive geometries in the configuration file.

Drive Geometries

The specifications for most floppy drives are included in the default values in the mtools configuration file. You can, however, add or change the properties of the drives in the configuration file. If you choose to do this, you'll need to define the following.

Cylinders   These used to be called tracks, as they pertained to floppy diskettes. Each diskette has concentric, circular, magnetic "tracks" that determine where the data will be written. Since virtually all diskettes are now double-sided, the two tracks on each diskette, which are stacked one on top of the other, are called cylinders.

Heads   Today, floppy drives have two heads: One facing downward to read the top side of the media and one facing upward to read the bottom of the media. Since you can use this parameter to define hard drives, too (and they can have many more than two heads), you need to define this here.

Sectors   Each cylinder (track) is divided into crescent-shaped sections called sectors. Each addressable sector holds a block of data containing information about the location of the sector as well as "link" information. Since files can be much larger than the capacity of a single data block, the computer will link the data blocks together via information stored in the track. The link information tells the computer if there are additional tracks, and if there are, what the address of the next block (and the previous block, if present) are.

The sectors argument tells mtools how many sectors the diskette has per track. So, for example, to specify a 360KB, double-density floppy drive, you could enter:

```
drive b:
        file="/dev/fd1H360"
        fat_bits=12
```

```
cylinders=40 heads=2 sectors=9
mformat_only
```

Before we continue, you may be asking yourself, "what's that `mfor-mat...`" specification? The reason for this is that without this argument, the computer will attempt to find the drive geometry in the diskette's boot sector. In fact, however, most systems today can determine what kind of diskette is present and automatically read the boot sector. So by adding the `mformat...` argument, you avoid the possibility of reading incorrrect data from an unformatted diskette.

Multiple Drive Geometries

As you certainly know, for each drive size there are a few different diskette capacities available. To make your system check for more than one drive/ diskette type, all you need to do is enter all of the geometries you want to check, one after the other, in the drive parameter section for that drive. If the first one fails, mtools will check the second, and so on. Here's an example:

```
drive a: file="/dev/fd0H1440" 1.44m
drive a: file="/dev/fd0H720" 720k
```

With the above configuration, mtools will first try reading diskettes in drive 0 in 1.44MB format. If they do not read correctly, mtools will try 720KB format. If it's still unsuccessful, mtools will generate an error.

Running mtools

The following commands available in mtools allow users on Unix systems to read and write to DOS systems.

floppyd

`floppyd` authenticates users wishing to access a drive on the server. It's syntax is:

```
floppyd [-d][-l][-s port][-r user][-b
ipaddr]devicename[displayname]
```

-d	This specifies daemonmode. In this mode, `floppyd` runs its own server loop. You should not use this argument if you start `floppyd` from `inetd.conf`.
-s port	This is the port number to be used in daemon mode (the default is 5703 + the display number).
-b ipaddr	The bind address (used only in daemon mode).

-r user	Tells mtools to run the server using the named user.
l	Tells mtools not to generate any local display names.

mattrib

mattrib allows you to change the attribute bits of files and flags. The options are listed below.

-a / +a	This sets or clears the archive bit. If the archive bit is set to (1), the file will not be backed up the next time an intermediate backup is performed.
-r / +r	This sets or clears the read-only bit. If this bit is set to (1), the file can be neither changed nor deleted.
-s / +s	Indicates whether a file is part of DOS or not. If the bit is set, the file is a system file and should not be tampered with.
-h / +h	Determines if a filename will be hidden from the dir command or not. If it is set, the file will not be listed using dir.

mcat

This command performs a disk image copy of an entire diskette. This is its format:

```
mcat [-w] drive:
```

mcd

Similar to cd, mcd is used to change the directory of a remote DOS disk.

```
mcat [dos_directory]
```

mcopy

Similar to the copy command, this command is used to copy files to and from Unix. Its syntax is:

```
mcopy [-b/ptnvmoQOsSra] sourcefile targetfile
```

The options with mcopy have these effects:

-b	Batch mode. Copies many files at once.
-/	Recursive copy. Copies whole directories at once (including all subdirectories).
-p	Preserves the attributes of the copied file(s)—all file copies will have the same attributes as the original.

-Q   Causes mcopy to quit if it receives any filecopy errors.

-t   Text file copy only. Will not translate graphics files correctly.

-n   Prevents mtools from reporting file overwrites.

-m   Preserves the file modification time on the copies of files so the copies will have the same file modification date as the originals.

mdel

Similar to the del command, this command is used to delete files from MS-DOS. Its syntax is:

```
mdel [-v] dosfilename [more dosfilenames… ]
```

NOTE

The –v attribute asks for verification before deleting files.

mdeltree

Similar to the rd command, this command is used to delete directories from MS-DOS. Its syntax is:

```
mdeltree [-v] dosdirectoryname [more dosdirecotorynames… ]
```

NOTE

The –v attribute asks for verification before deleting files.

mdir

Similar to the dir command, this command is used to read the directories from MS-DOS. Its syntax is:

```
mdir [-/]][-f][-w][-a][-x] dosfilename [dosfilenames]
```

These are the parameters that may be used with mdir:

-/   Recursive mode—reads all lower subdirectories (similar to the /s option in DOS).

-w   Wide output. Just like /w in DOS. Leaves out file details; only prints filenames.

-a   List all files, including hidden files.

-f   Fast mode. Prevents mtools from checking the free space.

-x   Brief mode. Lists files and pathnames without any additional formatting or details.

mdu

This command lists the space used up by a specified directory, it's subdirectories, and files.

mformat

This command formats a floppy diskette. For details on this command, check the man pages on mtools.

mmd

Similar to the md (mkdir) command. This is used to create a new directory on the MS-DOS system.

mmove

Similar to the DOS move command, this is used to move or rename an existing DOS file or directory.

mren

Similar to the ren (rename) command in DOS, this command is used to rename a file or directory on the MS-DOS system. Unlike DOS, mren can be used to rename a directory.

mtype

Similar to the type command in DOS, this command displays the contents of a file on display. It's used mostly to view text files. For example:

```
mtype myaddress_list
Mommy 1234 Somewhere Pl
Uncle Sloprag 98765 Middle Rd
```

If you try to look at a non-text file (like a program, for example), you'll get a lot of garbage on screen instead.

AND ONE MORE THING: SCO, VISIONFS, AND MERGE

VisionFS and Merge are programs that are specific to SCO Unix. VisionFS allows Windows users on a SCO network to access files on Unix servers as if they were Windows servers via the Network Neighborhood. Unlike Samba, which can be a bit complex to set up, VisionFS includes an automatic setup program that runs on the Unix server. Once set up, any number of Windows users can access files on the Unix server just as they do any files on another Windows server. The whole thing is transparent to the Windows users.

Merge is a standalone version of Windows 95 that actually runs inside a Unix X-Window. Installation of Merge is automatic if you specify it when configuring the Unix server. Installing it on an existing system requires little more than loading the initialization files from a CD and then loading Windows 95 from a standard Windows 95 CD. The initial Merge files create a DOS emulation that allows Windows 95 to install just as if it were running on a dedicated PC.

Once installed, the emulation operates exactly as you would expect, like Windows 95—only a bit slower.

WHAT'S NEXT

The complete Unix Desk Reference—a comprehensive guide to Unix terms, utilities, and commands with examples, syntax, and options for the most important Unix products.

```
echo "2.      Show Dat
echo "3.      Display f
echo             Wo   dire
echo             n t    inal
echo "Q.      Quit
echo
echo -n "Enter choice:  \
read choice
case $choice in
1) who | more
   pause;;
2) date
   pause;;
3) echo "Enter file name: \c"
   read fil
   if [ -r "$fil" -a -f "$fil
   then
      clear
      more -d $fil
   else
      echo "Cannot d
   fi
   pause;;
4) echo "En
   read di
   if test            pwd
   then
      cd $dir
   else
      echo "$dir: no such
   fi
      pause;;
5) if test "$dir" !
   then
      cd $prevdir
   fi
   pause;;
```

PART II

UNIX DESKTOP REFERENCE

```
echo "2.      Show Date"
echo "3.      Display a file"
echo "4.      Change working director
echo "5.      Return to original d
echo "Q.      Quit
echo
echo -n "Enter choice: .\b"
read choice
case $choice in
1) who | more
   pause;;
2) date
   pause;;
3) echo "Enter file name: \c"
   read fil
   if [ -r "$fil" -a -f "$fil ]
   then
      clear
      more -d $fil
   else
      echo "Cannot d
   fi
   pause;;
4) echo "En
   read di
   if test       "(dir:= pwd`
   then
      cd $dir
   else
      echo "$dir: no such di
   fi
      pause;;
   5) if test "$dir" != "$p
      then
         cd $prevdir
      fi
      pause;;
```

Chapter 20

The Complete Unix Desk Reference

A

ABI

Abbreviation for Application Binary Interface. A specification that aims to ensure binary compatibility between applications running on the same family of processors or CPUs using Unix System V Release 4.

Applications developed using ABI can run on hardware from different manufacturers without the need for recompilation; any system calls needed for specific hardware are maintained in libraries.

The specification was originally developed by AT&T and Sun Microsystems and includes a test and verification suite used to determine if a system complies with the standard.

absolute pathname

A pathname that starts with the root directory (/) and specifies the full name of every directory to the actual file. An absolute pathname locates a file with no reference to the current working directory and always refers to the same file no matter where you are in the filesystem.

See also relative pathname

account

On a local area network or multiuser operating system, an account is set up for each user. Before you can use Unix, your system administrator must establish an account and a user identifier for you.

Accounts were originally maintained for security or administrative reasons, although in some systems, particularly in online services, they are used as a method of identifying a user for billing purposes.

Your account keeps track of certain system resources, such as disk space.

See also user, username

acct

An SVR4 command used by the system administrator to turn system accounting on or off.

ACK

Abbreviation for acknowledgment. In communications, a control code, ASCII 06, is sent by the receiving computer to indicate that data has been received without error and that the next part of the transmission may be sent.

See also NAK

active window

In a GUI capable of displaying more than one window on the screen at a time, the active window is the window that contains the cursor. Only one window is usually active at any one time.

See also focus

adb

The oldest of the Unix debuggers, adb is a general-purpose debugger, used to examine executable files and provide a controlled environment within which the programmer can examine the program as it executes. Extensive discussion of adb is beyond the scope of this book; see the man pages on your system for more details.

See also gdb, sdb

adding a new user

One of the essential tasks a system administrator must be able to tackle is that of adding a new user to the system. Some systems, such as SCO and HP-UX, have special applications that automate this process, while on other systems it is more of a manual process using `adduser` or `useradd`. See your man pages for more information.

A new user needs more than a login name to be able to access the system. A user must also have the necessary files, directories, and permissions, as well as a password and a home directory.

To add a new user, follow these steps (which must be performed with superuser privileges):

1. Add an entry for the new user in `/etc/passwd`.

2. Create a password for the new account.

3. Create a home directory for the new account with `mkdir`, and change the ownership to that of the new user with `chown`.

4. Add any dot files to the new home directory, and make sure to change the ownership of these files to that of the new account. Users of the C shell will need `.login` and `.cshrc`; Bourne shell users will need `.profile`, and Korn shell users will need `.kshrc`. Default versions of many of these files are usually maintained by the system administrator for this very purpose.

See also `passwd`

admin

See SCCS

AFS

Abbreviation for Andrews File System. A protocol developed at Carnegie Mellon University used to share remote files across systems using TCP/IP.

AFS has certain advantages over NFS in that it only allows users to access files linked to AFS rather than giving access to all files, it has a built-in cache that helps to reduce the demands made on the system, and system administrators can allocate disk space on the fly as required.

AIX

Acronym for Advanced Interactive Executive. A version of Unix from IBM that runs on its RISC/6000 work-stations, minicomputers, and mainframes.

Although AIX is derived from System V Release 3, it contains many of the features available in System V Release 4, is POSIX-compliant, and meets the Trusted Computer Base (TCB) Level C2 security.

One of the major enhancements AIX offers is Visual Systems Management (VSM), a graphical interface into the older System Management Interface Tool (SMIT). VSM contains four main elements: Print Manager, Device Manager, Storage Manager, and Users and Groups Manager.

alias

A built-in command in the Korn and C shells that lets you define new commands. In this way, an alias becomes an alternative name for a script, program, or command.

There are three reasons to use an alias:

▶ To reduce the amount of typing that you do. If you are in the habit of always using a command with the same options, you can create a one-character alias and use that instead.

▶ To automate a complex procedure you use only infrequently and find difficult to remember.

▶ To avoid long path searches. A command starts up more quickly when it is aliased to its full pathname.

The syntax you use for this command depends on which shell you use.

Korn Shell Syntax

In the Korn shell, the syntax is:

```
alias[options][name[='command']]
```

which assigns a shorthand name to command. If you leave out ='command', you can print the alias for name, *and if you leave out* name, you can print all the aliases. In the Korn shell, alias has two options, as Table A.1 shows.

If you use the ls command with the -alt options in the Korn shell, you can alias this to a single letter by typing:

```
alias l='ls -alt'
```

Now you can just type l when you want to see a long directory listing showing all files sorted by the time they were last modified.

TABLE A.1: Options to Use with alias

Option	Description
-t	Allows the Korn shell to remember the full pathname for the aliased command, which allows it to be found quickly and to be issued from any directory. Tracked aliases are the same as hashed commands in the Bourne shell.
-x	Exports the alias so that you can use it in shell scripts.

C Shell Syntax

The alias syntax in the C shell is even easier to remember:

    alias [name][command]

where name is the shorthand name or alias you want to use with command. As in the Korn shell, if you leave out command, alias prints the alias for name, and if you leave out name, alias prints all the current aliases. In the C shell, you can define an alias on the command line, but aliases are usually stored in .cshrc so that they are available as soon as you log in. To bypass the alias and use the original command name, type \name.

See also unalias

alloc

A built-in C shell command that displays information on dynamic memory used by the system. When you provide a memory address (8, or any multiple of 8) with this command, alloc displays the status of each memory block as either busy or in use.

ambiguous file reference

Any reference to a file that does not specify one particular file but can be expanded by the shell to specify a list of filenames.

Special characters representing one character (?), zero or more characters (*), and character classes ([]) can all be used in an ambiguous file reference.

See also regular expressions

anonymous ftp

A method used to access an Internet host with ftp, which does not require you to have an account on the target computer system. Just log in to the Internet computer with the username "anonymous" and use your e-mail address as your password. This information was originally provided as a courtesy so that system administrators could see who had accessed their systems, but now it is often required to gain access to their systems.

You cannot use anonymous `ftp` with every computer on the Internet; just those that have been set up to offer the service. The system administrator decides which files and directories will be open to public access, and the rest of the system is considered to be off limits and cannot be accessed by anonymous `ftp` users. Some sites only allow you to download files from them; as a security precaution, you are not allowed to upload files to them. All this aside, the world open to anonymous `ftp` users is enormous; you can access tens of thousands of computers, and you can download hundreds of thousands of files.

See also archive, `ftp`, `telnet`

anonymous server

A special Internet service that removes from a USENET post all information that could be used to identify the original sender and then forwards the message to its destination. If you ever use an anonymous server, don't forget to remove your signature from the bottom of your post; not all anonymous servers look for and strip off signatures.

ANSI

Acronym for American National Standards Institute, pronounced "an-see." A nonprofit organization of business and industry groups, founded in 1918, devoted to the development of voluntary standards. ANSI represents the U.S. on the International Organization for Standardization (ISO).

ANSI committees have developed many important standards, including the following:

- ▶ ANSI C Transition Guide: System V Release 4 guidelines on writing new or upgrading existing C programs so that they conform to the ANSI C standard.

- ▶ ANSI X3J11: Standard for the C programming language, including language semantics, syntax, execution environment, and definition of the library and header files.

- ▶ ANSI X3J16: Standard for the C++ programming language.

- ▶ ANSI X3J3: Definition of the Fortran programming language compiler.

- ▶ ANSI X3.131-1986: Definition of the SCSI (Small Computer System Interface) standard. The X3T9.2 standard contains the extensions to SCSI-2.

▸ ANSI X3T9.5: The working group for the Fiber Distributed Data Interface (FDDI) definition.

▸ ANSI X3H3.6: The standard for X Window systems.

ANSI C

That version of the C programming language standardized by the ANSI-authorized C Programming Language Committee X3J11 and the ISO-authorized Committee JTC1 SC22 WG14. Sometimes called *Standard C*.

ANSI C is designed to codify existing practices but also adds new features, such as function prototypes to correct deficiencies in the language. The standard resolves the different rules for declaring data objects, and clarifies certain long-standing ambiguous areas.

See also **C++, K&R, POSIX**

ansitape

A command provided with BSD that reads and writes files to and from ANSI-standard magnetic tapes.

Syntax

The syntax for `ansitape` is:

```
ansitape [option][arguments]filenames
```

Options and Arguments

The `ansitape` options are listed in Table A.2.

Once you have chosen an option, you can use one of the `arguments` listed in Table A.3 to modify that option.

`ansitape` will not copy certain kinds of files, including directories, character or special block files, or binary executables; if you try, you are rewarded with a warning message, and the file is skipped.

TABLE A.2: Options to Use with ansitape

Option	Description
c	Creates a new tape.
r	Files are written to the end of the tape.
t	Lists the specified files each time they occur on tape.
x	Extracts the specified files from the tape.

TABLE A.3: Arguments to Use with ansitape

ARGUMENT	DESCRIPTION
b	Allows the user to specify the block size to use.
f	Allows the selection of a different tape drive.
F	Creates an ANSI D-type fixed record length tape.
l[*label*]	Creates the specified label on the tape.
n[*filename*]	Uses the specified file as a control file containing the names of the files to store on tape.
v	Turns on verbose mode.

a.out

The default name of the executable file produced by the Unix assembler, link editor, and C compiler.

You can use a.out just as you would use other programs by typing its name on the command line, but you should change its name to something more descriptive; otherwise, you may accidentally overwrite it during a later compilation.

To create an executable file with a more meaningful name of your choice, use the compiler's -o option and specify the filename you want to use.

See also as, cc, gcc, ld

API

Abbreviation for application programming interface. A set of callable functions provided by an operating system or a third-party application that a program can use to perform tasks such as managing files, displaying information, and performing tasks specific to the application area.

An API provides a standard interface along with documentation on how the functions that wake up the interface should be used.

append

- ▶ In the C or Bourne shells, to add the standard output from a command to the end of an existing file using the >> redirection symbols.
- ▶ In Unix text editors, to place one block of text immediately after an existing block of text.

See also greater than symbol

Application Programming Interface

See API

apropros

A command used to look up keywords in the online manual pages.

Syntax

The apropros syntax is:

```
apropros [options]keyword...
```

apropro shows which manual pages contain any of the keywords in their names or title lines. Each keyword is considered separately, and part words are located; for example, if you search for "edit", you will also find "editor", and if you search for "compile", you will also find "compiler." Case is ignored.

Options and Arguments

apropros options are shown in Table A.4.

TABLE A.4: Options to Use with apropros

Option	Description
-M	Overrides the standard list of directories and uses *path*. The *path* must be a list of directories separated by colons. This search path may also be set using the environment variable MANPATH.
-m	Adds a list of colon-separated directories to the beginning of the standard apropro path. These directories are searched first.

Examples

To find all the manual pages that have "compile" in their name lines, type:

```
apropros compile
```

and to find all the manual pages with "editor" in their name lines, type:

```
apropros editor
```

Notes

Using apropro produces the same result as using man -k.

See also man, whatis

ar

A command used to create and manage archive libraries, combining several files into one and allowing files to be added to or removed from the archive. ar does not compress text, so there are no savings in disk space, although there are savings in file accounting because only one i-node is needed instead of several. The most common use of ar is to create and maintain library files used by ld, the link editor.

Syntax
The syntax for ar is as follows:

```
ar [-V] key [key_modifier][position]archive[files]
```

Only one key letter may be used at a time, but several key_modifiers may be combined (with no separating spaces). The position argument is a filename used to specify a position within the archive, archive is the name of the archive file itself, and files represents the names of the files that you want to add or remove. -V prints the ar version number.

Options and Arguments
The key argument is one of the characters from Table A.5, combined with one or more of the optional key_modifiers listed in Table A.6. The key can include a hyphen prefix.

Two other Unix commands are available for archive services; tar provides tape-oriented facilities, while cpio is oriented toward the directory system and inter-system copying. ar, tar, and cpio all use different archive formats.

TABLE A.5: Options to Use with ar key

Option	Description
d	Deletes the named files from the *archive*.
m	Moves the named file to the end of the *archive*. If one of the *key_modifier* options a, b, or i is specified, the files are placed before or after the *position* file in the archive.
o	In 4.4BSD, sets the access and modification times of all extracted files to the modification time of the file when it was entered into the archive. You must be the owner of the extracted file or be the superuser; otherwise, this option fails.
p	Displays the named files to the standard output.
q	Quickly appends the named files to the end of the *archive* without checking to see if the file has been archived previously. If the *archive* does not exist, it is created.
r	Adds or replaces the named file in the *archive*. New files are written at the end of the *archive* unless the a, b, or i *key_modifier* is used.
t	Displays a table of contents for the *archive*.
x	Extracts the named files into the current directory, or extracts all files if no names are specified. The archive remains unaltered.

TABLE A.6: Options to Use with ar key_*modifier*

OPTION	DESCRIPTION
a	Combine with r or m to place *files* in the *archive* after *position*.
b, i	Use with r or m to place *files* in the *archive* before *position*.
c	Suppresses messages and creates the *archive* in silence.
l	In System V Release 3 only, places temporary files in the current directory rather than in /tmp.
s	Forces a regeneration of the archive symbol table. This may become necessary if an *archive* has been operated upon by another program.
T	In 4.4BSD, limits archived filenames to the first 15 characters; if names are truncated, a warning message is printed to the standard error output.
u	When combined with r, replaces only files that have been modified since they were last archived.
v	Prints a verbose, file-by-file, description. When combined with t, it gives a long listing of file information, and when combined with x, it displays the name of each extracted file.

Examples

To add myfile to the library.a archive, type:

```
ar -q library.a myfile
```

This command adds myfile to the end of the archive even though the archive may already contain the file. To delete a file from an archive, type:

```
ar -d library.a yourfile
```

This command removes yourfile from the archive library.a. To list the contents of the archive file library.a, type:

```
ar -t library.a
```

See also ansitape

archive

- ▶ A collection of related files kept in storage for backup; the files may have been compressed to save hard disk or magnetic tape space.
- ▶ To make a copy of a set of files for long-term storage.
- ▶ On the Internet, a site containing files available via anonymous ftp.

See also ar, cpio, compact, compress, compressed file, gzip, pack, tar

argument

Any letter, number, filename, option, or other string that gives additional information to a command at the time the command is used. When a shell script is called, the arguments of the call become available as parameters within the script.

See also command-line argument, option

argument list

The set of filenames that can be accessed by either the ex or the vi text editors.

argv

A C shell variable that contains the command-line arguments from the command invoked by the shell. argv is used to manipulate positional parameters without requiring a shift mechanism. For example, argv[0] contains the name of the calling program, argv[1] contains the first command-line argument, and so on. You can change any element of this array with the exception of argv[0], and you can use argv[*] to reference all of the arguments together.

A similar variable, ARGV, is used in awk to get information from the command line. The first element ARGV[0] contains the name of the command itself, normally awk; the following elements, ARGV[1], ARGV[2], and so on, contain the actual arguments. The related variable, ARGC, contains the number of command-line arguments used.

array

An ordered collection of data items arranged in one or more dimensions. Each item in an array is known as an *element* or a *member*. Both the C and Korn shells can store and process arrays. For example, the C shell stores its command search path in an array called path. The first array element is called path[1], the second path[2], and so on.

as

The Unix command that runs the assembler, creating an object file from an assembly language source file.

Syntax
The syntax for as is as follows:

```
as [options] files
```

Object files have the same name as their source equivalents, except the .s suffix is replaced by .o.

Options and Arguments

Table A.7 lists the options available with as.

See also dis

TABLE A.7: Options to Use with as

Option	Description
-m	Runs the m4 macroprocessor on *file*.
-n	Turns off the optimization of long/short addresses.
-o *object-file*	Places the output in the object file *object-file*; the default filename is *file*.o.
-Qc	When *c* is set to y, places the version number of the assembler in the object file; when *c* is set to n, does not.
-R	Removes *file* on completion.
-V	Displays the version number of the assembler.
-Y[*key*]*dir*	When *key* is set to m, searches the *dir* directory for the m4 macroprocessor; when set to d, searches for a file containing predefined macros. as searches for both if *key* is omitted.

asterisk

A metacharacter used as a wildcard in filename expansion that can be used as a substitute for any unknown number of characters, including one or more blank spaces. When you use a wildcard, the shell interprets the pattern and replaces it with the appropriate file names; you must always specify a / (slash), you cannot match it using a wildcard.

For example, when you type:

```
ls q*
```

the shell replaces q* with all the filenames that begin with the letter q.

This process of using a wildcard to specify filenames is called *filename substitution* in the C shell and in Tcsh; in the Bourne shell and Korn shell, it is known as *filename generation*; and in the Bash shell, it is called *pathname expansion*.

You will hear different terms used to identify the asterisk character: "star," "splat," or even "glob."

The asterisk is used as a metacharacter within regular expressions in the ed, ex, vi, sed, grep, and awk programs.

See also globbing, question mark, square brackets

at

The Unix at command takes the list of commands that you type at the keyboard and runs them at the time you specify; you do not have to be logged in to the system at the time the command is scheduled to run. at allows you to run certain kinds of jobs unattended when system load is low, for example, printing long documents in the middle of the night.

Syntax
The syntax for at is as follows:

```
at options1 time [date][+increment]commands
at options2[jobs]
```

You can use two sets of options with at: options1 controls setting the time and date, and options2 lets you make changes to jobs you have already scheduled.

In options1, you type the information needed by at, followed by the command you want to run, and then terminate the whole sequence by typing **Ctrl-D** on the following line.

Because at takes its input from standard input, you can enter the commands you want to execute from the keyboard, pipe them in from another program, or use input redirection to use an existing file of commands. at returns a job ID when it is invoked, and you use this ID number with the second syntax described above.

Many systems restrict the use of at. Only those users specified in the file /usr/lib/cron/at.allow can schedule jobs; if this file doesn't exist, the file /usr/lib/cron/at.deny holds a list of users who cannot use at. If this file exists but is empty, everyone can use at. If neither file exists, only the *superuser* can use at.

When Unix executes commands using at, it uses e-mail to send you any output from the resulting process; you can redirect this mail if you want to.

Options and Arguments
In the first line of syntax, time is the time of day when you want at to run your job, and you can specify time in one of several different ways:

▶ A one or two-digit number specifying the hour.

▶ A four-digit number specifying the hour and minute.

▶ Two numbers separated by a colon to specify hours and minutes.

▶ noon, midnight, or now.

Any of these first three forms can be followed by am, pm, or zulu (for Greenwich mean time) to make the time specification more precise.

You can specify the date you want at to use as:

▶ A three-letter month name followed by the day number, an optional comma, and an optional year number.

▶ A day of the week, abbreviated to the first three letters.

▶ today or tomorrow.

If you omit date, at defaults to today if the hour you specify in time is later than the current time; if not, at runs the job at the same time tomorrow.

The final argument, increment, is a positive number followed by minutes, hours, days, weeks, months, or years, or their singular form. at adds this increment to the time and date you specify. In place of increment, you can use the word next to specify next week, or next year.

In the second line of syntax shown above, jobs is a list of one or more at job numbers.

You can use the options shown in Table A.8 to report or remove jobs.

SCO adds one more option, q letter, which places a job in the queue specified by letter. Three letters have special significance: a (the default) represents the at queue, b the batch queue, and c, the cron queue.

TABLE A.8: Options to Use with at

Option	Description
Options1	
-f filename	Executes the commands contained in filename.
-m	Sends any mail to the user when the job is complete.
Options2	
-l[jobs]	Reports all jobs, or if jobs is specified, reports on those.
-r[jobs]	Removes the specified jobs. To remove a job, you must be the owner of the job or the superuser.

Examples

To run the spell program on a file called bigfile at 4 a.m. tomorrow and send any output to a file called wordout, use:

```
at 04 tomorrowspell bigfile > wordoutCtrl-D
job 424765800.a at Tue Oct 30 04:00:00 1996
```

The last line above contains the job number and the time at will run the job.

See also atq, atrm, batch

atq

A command that displays a list of the jobs waiting in the at job queue.

Syntax

The syntax for atq is as follows:

```
atq [options][users]
```

Ordinarily, atq lists jobs in the order in which they will execute; if users is specified, those jobs are listed. If you are the superuser, all jobs are listed; otherwise, only those jobs that you own are shown.

Options and Arguments

The options available with atq are shown in Table A.9.

See also at, atrm

TABLE A.9: Options to Use with atq

OPTION	DESCRIPTION
-c	Sorts the jobs in the queue by the time that the at command was originally given.
-n	Displays the total number of jobs in the queue.

atrm

A command used to remove jobs from the at job queue.

Syntax

The syntax for atrm is as follows:

```
atrm [options][jobs][users]
```

Options and Arguments

When users is specified, all jobs belonging to that user are removed. This argument can be specified only by the superuser.

If a jobs number is specified, only that job is removed from the queue. The options available with atrm are shown in Table A.10.

See also at, atq

TABLE A.10: Options to Use with atrm

Option	Description
-a	Removes all jobs that belong to the current user; the superuser can remove all jobs.
-f	Operates quietly. Suppresses all information related to the removal of the specified jobs.
i	Prompts for a y to remove all *jobs*; or for n.
-	In 4.4BSD, removes all *jobs* belonging to the user who invoked atrm.

autoload

A Korn shell alias used to define or load functions when they are first used. autoload is an alias for typeset -fu.

See also typeset

automounter

A feature that allows resources (both local and remote) to be activated as they are needed and unmounted when no longer needed. All this takes place without intervention from the system administrator.

awk

A Unix programming language used to manipulate text files. awk scans text files for patterns or simple relationships and then performs specified actions on matching lines. awk is named after the program creators, Alfred Aho, Peter Weinberger, and Brian Kernighan.

During the 1980s, the authors made several enhancements to awk and called this enhanced version nawk for new awk. This program was released as part of System V Release 3.1 and is still found on many systems. The GNU Project's version of awk is known as gawk; in the 4.4BSD release, it is installed as awk. In most cases, you can assume that gawk implements all features of awk and nawk.

Using a programming language to manipulate text files may sound a bit daunting, but awk is straight-forward to use; you can even write simple awk scripts at the command line. awk scans a set of input lines contained in a text file, searching for lines that match a pattern you have specified. For each pattern, you can specify an action; when awk recognizes the pattern, the action is performed on each line that matches the pattern. Many of the constructs found in awk were taken from the C programming language, including:

▶ A flexible format

▶ Regular expressions

▶ String and numeric variables

▶ Conditional execution

▶ Looping statements

▶ C's printf statement

Syntax

awk can be invoked as follows:

```
awk [options]'script' var=value files
awk [options] -f program_file var=value files
```

You can specify s script direct from the command line, or you can store a script in program_file and specify it using -f. You can assign the variable var a value from the command line; the value can be a literal, a shell variable, or a command substitution, but the value is only available after the BEGIN block of the awk program has been processed.

Options and Arguments

The options available with awk are shown in Table A.11.

TABLE A.11: Options to Use with awk

OPTION	DESCRIPTION
-Fc	Sets the field separator character to the single character c, rather than the default Space or Tab.
-fprogram_file	Uses the program_file rather than command-line instructions.

Patterns and Procedures

An awk program consists of one or more program statements in the form:

```
pattern {procedure}
```

If pattern is missing, then {procedure} is performed for all lines in the text file; if {procedure} is missing, then the matched line is printed.

A `pattern` can be one of the following:

- ▶ A quoted string, number, operator, function, defined variable, or any of the predefined variables listed in Table A.11.
- ▶ A regular expression.
- ▶ A relational expression using one of the relational operators listed in Table A.12.
- ▶ A pattern-matching operator, such as ~ (match) or !~ (don't match).
- ▶ The BEGIN pattern lets you specify procedures (such as setting global variables) that take place before the first line of input is processed.
- ▶ The END pattern lets you specify what happens after the last line of input has been read.

A `procedure` can be made up of one or more commands or functions, separated by newlines, and contained within curly braces. Commands are of four types:

- ▶ Variable or array assignments
- ▶ Printing commands
- ▶ Flow-control commands
- ▶ Built-in awk functions

Table A.12 lists all the operators available in awk, in order of increasing precedence, Table A.13 lists the predefined functions available in awk, and Table A.14 lists the system variables in awk, nawk, and gawk.

Of the commands in Table A.13, `atan2`, `close`, `delete`, `do/while`, `function`, `getline`, `gsub`, `match`, `next`, `rand`, `return`, `srand`, `sub`, and `system` are not available in the original awk but are available in later versions of nawk and gawk; `tolower` and `toupper` were not available in awk or nawk but appeared in gawk. All other commands are available in all versions.

TABLE A.12: Operators to Use with awk

Operator	Description
= += -= *= /= %= ^=	Assignment.
?:	The C programming language conditional expression or the ternary operator.
||	Logical OR.

TABLE A.12 continued: Operators to Use with awk

OPERATOR	DESCRIPTION
&&	Logical AND.
~ !~	Match regular expression and negated match.
< <= > >= != ==	Relational operators.
(blank)	String concatenation.
+ -	Addition and subtraction.
*/ %	Multiplication, division, and modulus.
+ - !	Unary plus, unary minus, and logical negation.
^	Exponentiation.
++ --	Increment and decrement, either prefix or postfix.
$	Field reference.

TABLE A.13: Predefined Commands Available in awk

COMMAND	DESCRIPTION
atan2(y,x)	Returns the arctangent of y/x in radians.
break	Exits from a for or while loop.
close(*filename-expr*) close (*command-expr*)	Closes a file or pipe using the same expression that opened the file or pipe. Most versions of awk let you open up to 10 files and one pipe at a time.
continue	Begins the next iteration of a for or while loop.
cos(x)	Returns the cosine of x radians.
delete(*array* [*element*])	Deletes an *element* of *array*.
Do *body* while(expr)	Performs a looping statement, executing the statements in *body*, then evaluating *expr*. If *expr* is true, the loop repeats, and *body* executes again.
exit	Ignores remaining instructions, does not read more input, but branches directly to the END procedures.
exp(*arg*)	Returns the exponent of *arg*.
for(*i=lower*; *i<=upper*;*i++*) *command*	Performs *command* while *i* is between the valuesof *lower* and *upper*. If you use a series of *commands*, they must be contained within curly braces ({ }).
for(*item* in *array*) *command*	Performs *command* for each *item* in *array*. If you use a series of *commands*, they must be contained within curly braces ({ }).
function *name* (*parameter-list*){ statements }	Allows you to specify your own user-defined functions.The parameter-list is a comma- separated list of variables passed as arguments to the function when the function is called. The body of the function can contain one or more statements and usually contains a return statement to pass control back to the point that called the function.

TABLE A.13 continued: Predefined Commands Available in awk

COMMAND	DESCRIPTION
`getline[var][<file]` or `command |` `getline[var]`	Reads the next line of input. The first syntax reads input from `file`, and the second form reads the output from `command`. Both forms read just one line at a time, which is assigned to $0 and is parsed into fields setting NF, NR, and FNR.
`gsub(r,s,t)`	Substitutes *s* for each match of the regular expression *r* in the string *t*. If *t* is not specified, it is taken to be $0. The substitution is made globally. The value returned by gsub is the number of substitutions made.
`if(condition)` command `[else]`	If *condition* is true, execute *command*, otherwise execute the *command* in the `else` clause. A series of commands must be enclosed within curly braces ({ }).
`index(substr,str)`	Returns the position of the first place within the string *str* where the substring *substr* occurs. If *substr* does not occur within *str*, index returns 0.
`int(arg)`	Returns the integer value of *arg*.
`length(str)`	Returns the number of characters in the string *str*; if *str* is not supplied, S0 is assumed.
`log(x)`	Returns the natural logarithm of *x*.
`match(s,r)`	Tests whether the string *s* contains a match for the regular expression *r*, and returns either the position where the match begins or 0 if no match is found. Sets both RSTART and RLENGTH.
`next`	Reads the next line of input and starts a new pass through all the pattern/procedure statements in the awk program or script.
`print[args]` `[destination]`	Prints *args* on the appropriate output device. Literal strings must be quoted, and successive values separated by commas are separated by the predefined variable OFS; successive values separated by spaces are concatenated. You can use redirection with the default output.
`printf[format][,` `expressions].`	Produces a formatted print following the conventions of the C programming language `printf` statement, including %s to print a string, %d to print a decimal number, and %*n.m*f to print a floating-point number, where *n* represents the total number of digits and *m* represents the number of digits after the decimal point.
`rand()`	Returns a random number between 0 and 1. This command returns the same random number each time it is run, unless the random number generator is seeded using `srand()`.
`return[expr].`	Returns the value *expr* at the end of a user-defined function.
`sin(x)`	Returns the sine of *x*.
`split(string,array` `[,sep]`	Splits the string *string* into fields using the separator *sep* and then puts those fields into the array *array*. If *sep* is not specified, then FS is used.
`sprintf[format` `[,expression]]`	Returns the value of *expression* using the *format*. Nothing is actually printed; data is only formatted.
`sqrt(arg)`	Returns the square root of *arg*.

TABLE A.13 continued: Predefined Commands Available in awk

COMMAND	DESCRIPTION
srand(*expr*)	Sets a new seed value for the random number generator using *expr*. If *expr* is not specified, the time of day is used as the default.
sub(*r*,*s*,[*t*])	If the string *t* is specified, substitute the string *s* for the first occurrence of the regular expression *r* in *t*. If *t* is not specified, $0 is assumed; returns 1 if successful, 0 if not.
substr(*string*,*m*,[*n*])	Returns the substring of *string* beginning at character number *m* and consisting of the next *n* characters. If *n* is not specified, includes all characters to the end of the string.
system(*command*)	Executes the Unix *command* and returns an exit value.
tolower(*str*)	Converts all uppercase characters in *str* to lowercase, and returns the new string.
toupper(*str*)	Converts all lowercase characters in *str* to uppercase, and returns the new string.
while(*condition*)	Executes *command* while *condition* is true.
command	A series of commands must be contained within curly braces ({ }).

TABLE A.14: System Variables to Use with awk, nawk, and gawk

VARIABLE	DESCRIPTION
awk	
FILENAME	Current filename.
FS	Field separator; the default is a blank.
NF	The number of fields in the current record.
NR	The number of the current record.
OFS	The output field separator; the default is a blank.
ORS	The output record separator; the default is a newline.
RS	The record separator; the default is a newline.
$0	The entire input record.
$*n*	The *n*th field in the current record; the fields are separated by FS.
nawk	
ARGC	The number of arguments on the command line.
ARGV	An array that contains the command-line arguments.
awk	
FNR	The input record number in the current input file.
OFMT	The output format for numbers; the default is %.6g.
RSTART	The first position in the string matched by the match function, or 0 if no match.
RLENGTH	The length of the string matched by match, or -1 if no match.

TABLE A.14 continued: System Variables to Use with awk, nawk, and gawk

Variable	Description
SUBSEP	The separator character used for multiple subscripts in array elements; the default is \034.
gawk	
ENVIRON	An array containing environment variables.
IGNORECASE	When non-zero, all regular expression matches are made independent of case. The default is 0, so that all regular expression operations are normally case-sensitive.

Examples

An awk program, or script, can be as simple as one command entered at the command line or as complex as any C language program. Here are two simple examples.

```
awk '/waffle/{print FILENAME": "$0}' myfile
```

This command extracts all lines in the file myfile that contain the word "waffle." It then prints the filename and the complete line of text for each line found. You don't need to place a $ in front of the built-in awk variable FILENAME, and the $0 references all fields in the record.

```
awk '{print $1+$2, subtotal +=$1+$2}' myfile.db
```

This example uses the C language increment operator += to accumulate a subtotal; as this example processes each line in myfile, it adds the value of $1+$2 to subtotal.

See also icon, perl

B

background

A processing environment in which programs or shells operate at a low priority and without input from the user.

In traditional Unix systems, a process spends its entire existence in either the background or the foreground. In newer systems with job control, you can change the processing environment and move a foreground process into the background and vice versa. When a background operation ends, a message appears on the screen.

See also **background processing,** bg, fg, **foreground processing**

background processing

A mechanism used to run a program in the background, without input from a terminal or from the user. Also called *detached processing*.

To start a background process, end the command line with the ampersand (&); you do not have to wait for this background process to run to completion before giving additional shell commands.

Both the Bourne shell and the C shell allow background processing, and on Unix systems with job control, the C and Korn shells provide additional commands for manipulating background processing.

If you forget to run a program in the background, you can stop it by typing **Ctrl-Z** and use the bg command to put the program into the background and to restart it. You can bring the current background job to the foreground with the fg command, and if you have lots of jobs running at the same time, use the jobs command to list them by job number.

The best candidates for background processing are programs that do not require input from you, and those that do not write to the screen. If a program running in the background needs input from the keyboard, it stops and waits for that input, and it will wait and wait until you finally provide the input. A program that writes to the screen will do so even from the background, and if you are in the middle of doing something else, you may not be able to make sense of the output. With this category of program, you can always redirect the output to a file and look at it later.

When putting several programs separated by semicolons into the background using the Bourne shell, remember to group them using parentheses; the Bourne shell puts the last command on the line into the background but always waits for the first. Use this syntax, and you won't have any problems:

```
(command; command)&
```

Also, any background processes you have running are usually terminated when you log out. Use the nohup command to avoid this, or set up the job using cron and at.

See also at, cron, **foreground processing**

backquote

The backquote (`), also known as *accent grave* or just *grave*, is not the same as the single quote (').

When you enclose a part of a shell command line in backquotes, that portion is executed as a command, and the output of the command is inserted into the command line. This is also known as command substitution and sounds complex, but it isn't really. Here's an example:

```
now = 'date'
```

In this command line, the shell variable now is being set to a value. Without backquotes, now would be set to the word date; with backquotes, now is set to the output of the date command.

backslash

The backslash (\) is sometimes called the *reverse slash* or *backslant*. This character changes the meaning of the next character in some important ways; in the shell, in many standard editors, as well as in awk, sed, and grep.

It is also used to extend a shell command over more than one line. When you reach the end of the line, use the \ to continue the command onto the next line. The \ quotes the newline character that follows it, and the shell does not treat it as a command terminator.

See also **metacharacter, regular expressions, slash**

backspace

A key on most keyboards used to move the cursor one space or one column to the left, erasing the character or characters in those spaces or columns.

bang

The exclamation point character (!), also known as *pling* in the U.K. and in other parts of the world.

bang path

An old-style UUCP e-mail address that uses exclamation points to separate the sequence of host computer names to get to the addressee.

Bang paths list the addresses—general to specific—from left to right, which is the reverse of the sequence used by many other addressing schemes.

See also **DNS, Internet address**

banner

An SVR4 utility that prints the specified message as very large characters on the standard output. These characters are formed from asterisks (*) or pound signs (#) depending on your system. Each line in the banner output can be up to 10 uppercase or lowercase characters for an 80-column display; other hardware can support more characters.

Syntax

Here is the syntax to use:

```
banner string
```

Depending on the capability of your hardware, all characters appear in uppercase; lowercase input characters appear as small uppercase letters. To make all the words stay on the same line, enclose them in quotes.

Examples

You can use banner to create flashy title pages for your reports, signs for birthdays or other celebrations, or page separators for long printouts. This example:

```
banner "NO PARKING" "" "AT ANY TIME" | lp
```

makes a sign with NO PARKING printed on the first line, then a blank line, followed by the words AT ANY TIME.

See also echo

banner page

An extra title page added to printouts or listings by most of the print spoolers. The banner page often includes user or account ID information in large character-graphics letters that are formed by rows and columns of letters. (The letter *A*, for example, is formed by rows and columns of *A*s.) Also called a *burst page*, because it indicates the place where fan-folded paper should be separated or burst apart.

See also banner

basename

The name of a file after the filename extension (the period and anything following the period) has been removed.

See also basename, dirname, **pathname**

basename

A utility used to extract a filename from a path statement; the filename is then printed on the standard output. You can also remove the filename extension from the filename using this command.

Syntax

The syntax for basename is as follows:

```
basename pathname [extension]
```

Options and Arguments

Given a pathname, this command removes the whole path prefix, leaving just the filename. If you also specify the optional extension, it is removed. basename is often used with command substitution using backquote characters to generate a filename; this allows the filename to be used rather than simply displayed.

Examples

To extract the basename of a file, use:

```
basename /pwd/myfile.txt
```

and the result is myfile.txt. You can strip off the filename extension if you use:

```
basename /pwd/myfile.txt.txt
```

This gets you simply myfile with no extension.

To assign the basename of a file to a shell variable, use:

```
FILENAME='basename /pwd/myfile.txt'
```

If you then execute:

```
echo $FILENAME
```

you will see the result:

```
myfile.txt
```

See also dirname, **pathname**

Bash

The Bourne-Again Shell (bash), first released in 1989 by Brian Fox and Chet Ramey as part of the Free Software Foundation GNU Project. Bash extends the features found in earlier shells and is a popular addition to systems such as Linux.

Bash provides features found in the Bourne shell, the C shell, the Korn shell, and Tcsh, including Bourne shell syntax, redirection and quoting, C shell command-line editing and tilde expansion, job control, and command history. Bash also includes built-in commands and variables, shell syntax, and aliases from the Korn shell.

When Bash first starts a login shell, commands in /etc/profile are executed, followed by commands in /.bash_profile, /.bash_login, and /.profile, assuming all these files exist on your system. And when you log out, the commands in /.bash_logout are executed.

For more information on Bash, see the bash manual and Info pages or one of the excellent books now available on Bash.

See also Bourne shell family, rbash

basic regular expressions

See regular expressions

batch

An SVR4 utility that runs jobs one after the other, as system load allows, even after you log out. The batch utility accepts commands from the standard input and executes these commands, one after the other, waiting for each one to complete before starting the next.

Syntax
To use batch:

    batch commands

and then terminate the sequence with an end-of-file (EOF) character, Ctrl-D. If you prefer, you can use re-direction and use a file containing the commands instead of typing them at the command prompt. batch is best for long sequences of commands that do not need much attention from you; you can even log out before they are complete.

Using batch is similar to using the at command, but at executes commands at a specific time; it is also similar to using background processing, except that the job continues after you log out.

Examples
To run a set of commands contained in a file, use:

    batch < myfile

This places all the commands contained in myfile in the job queue.

See also at, background, cron, crontab

batch queue

A mechanism used to schedule and sequence large jobs. The batch queue receives job requests from users and then schedules the jobs to run one at a time.

SVR4 and Solaris both have a simple batch queue facility similar to the at command, except with `batch`, you cannot specify the time you want your job to run. To delete jobs from the queue on Solaris systems, use `atq` and `atrm`; on SVR4, use `at -l`, or `at -r`.

bc

An interactive, programmable scientific calculator that can also be used to convert numbers from one system to another. bc is also a language and a compiler quite like the C programming language. Input can be from a file or from the standard input. To exit bc, you can type **quit**, or press Ctrl-D.

Syntax
To use bc:

```
bc options filelist
```

where `filelist` contains a set of bc functions you want to execute. For a complete list of operators and keywords available in bc, see Table B.1.

bc uses single-character, lowercase identifiers (a, b, c, and so on) as names for variables, arrays, and functions; the same letter may be used for all three simultaneously. The letters A through F are treated as hexadecimal digits whose values are from 10 to 15. Separate statements one from another with newlines; braces are needed only when grouping multiple statements.

You can choose the base for numerical input and output, and these bases can both be different. This means that you can enter numbers in decimal and display them in binary if you wish. Common bases used in computer-related calculations are base 16 (hexadecimal), base 8 (octal), and base 2 (binary), but bc works in any base from base 2 to base 16.

TABLE B.1: Operators and Keywords Available in bc

Operator	Description
STATEMENT KEYWORDS	
for (expr1;rel-expr;expr2) {statements}	Repeats one or more statements as long as rel-expr is true; similar to while with the exception that a for statement must contain all three expressions.
if (rel-expr){statements}	Executes one or more statements if rel-expr is true.
while(rel-expr){statements}	Repeats one or more statements as long as rel-expr is true; similar to for.

TABLE B.1 continued: Operators and Keywords Available in bc

OPERATOR	DESCRIPTION
FUNCTION KEYWORDS	
auto x,y	Establishes x and y as variables local to a function definition initialized to zero. x and y have no meaning outside the function.
define $j(k)${	Begins the definition of the function j, which has a single argument k. You use additional arguments separated by commas. The statements of the function follow on separate lines, and the whole function is terminated with a closing brace (}).
length(expr)	Calculates the number of decimals in expr.
return(expr)	Passes the value of expr back to the program; returns zero if expr is omitted.
scale(expr)	Calculates the number of digits to the right of the decimal in expr.
sqrt(expr)	Calculates the square root of expr.
INPUT/OUTPUT KEYWORDS	
ibase=n	Sets bc to read numbers input in the base n; the default is base 10. Once ibase has been changed to something other than 10, type **A** to restore decimal.
obase=n	Sets bc to display output in the base n; the default is base 10. Once obase has been changed to something other than 10, type **A** to restore decimal.
scale=n	Sets the number of decimal places for calculations; the default is zero, which truncates all results to integers. scale has meaning only for calculations performed in decimal; the maximum value of scale is 100.
MATH LIBRARY KEYWORDS	
a(n)	Calculates the arctangent of n.
c(angle)	Calculates the cosine of angle.
e(expr)	Calculates e to the power of expr.
l(expr)	Calculates the natural log of expr.
MATH LIBRARY KEYWORDS	
j(n,x)	Calculates the Bessel function of integer order n.
s(angle)	Calculates the sine of angle.

TABLE B.1 continued: Operators and Keywords Available in bc

OPERATOR	DESCRIPTION
COMMON OPERATORS	
+	Addition
-	Subtraction
/	Division
*	Multiplication
%	Modulo or remainder after a division
^	Exponentiation
++	Increment, both prefix and postfix
-	Decrement, both prefix and postfix
=+ =- =* =/ =^ =	Assignment
< <= > >= == !=	Relational
- ++ -	Unary
MISCELLANEOUS SYMBOLS	
/* */	Encloses comment lines.
()	Controls evaluation of precedence.
{}	Used to group statements.
[]	Used as an array index.
"text"	Prints the text within the quotes.

Options and Arguments

Two options are available with bc, and they are shown in Table B.2.

TABLE B.2: Options to Use with bc

OPTION	DESCRIPTION
-c	Invokes the compile only option. bc is a preprocessor for dc, the desk calculator. With this option, bc sends the compiled output from bc to the standard output instead of dc.
-l	Loads the math library containing the trigonometric and logarithmic functions.

Examples

To convert the octal number 20 into decimal:

```
$ bc
ibase=8
20
```

```
16
quit
```

To find the square root of 11 to seven decimal places:

```
$ bc
scale=7
sqrt(11)
3.3166247
quit
```

When you enter an expression or number such as `sqrt(11)`, it is evaluated and then printed; assignment statements such as `scale=7` are not printed.

These examples are just a hint of what `bc` can do; you can use it to work up some very complex functions.

See also dc, expr, xcalc

bcc

See blind courtesy copy

BCD

Abbreviation for binary coded decimal. A simple system for converting decimal numbers into binary form, in which each decimal digit is converted into binary and then stored as a single character.

In binary, the largest number that can be stored in 8 bits is 255, and this obviously represents a severe limitation to storing larger numbers. BCD is a way around this limitation that stays within the 8-bit storage format. For example, the decimal number 765 can be broken down so that the numbers 7, 6, and 5 are represented by one byte each. In BCD, each decimal digit occupies a byte, so 3 bytes are needed for a 3-digit decimal number.

bdes

A BSD utility used to encrypt and decrypt information using Data Encryption Standard (DES) algorithms.

Syntax
Use this syntax with `bdes`:

```
bdes [options]
```

`bdes` implements all aspects of the DES as defined in the "Data Encryption Standard," FIPS #46, National Bureau of Standards, U.S. Department of Commerce, January 1977. `bdes` reads from the standard input and writes to the standard output. If you don't specify an encryption key on the command line, bdes prompts you to enter one.

Options and Arguments

The options shown in Table B.3 are available with bdes.

The key and the vector described in Table B.3 are taken to be ASCII characters that are then mapped onto their bit representations. If either begins with the sequence 0X or 0x, they are assumed to be hexadecimal numbers indicating the bit pattern, and if they begin with 0B or 0b, they are assumed to be a sequence of binary digits indicating the bit pattern. Only the first 64 bits of the key and the vector are used; if too few bits are supplied, zero bits are added to pad the key out to 64 bits.

See also crypt, **DES**

TABLE B.3: Options to Use with bdes

Option	Description
-a	Forces both the *key* and the *vector* to ASCII.
-b	Uses electronic code book mode.
-d	Decrypts the input.
-F*n*	Uses *n*-bit alternative cipher feedback mode. *n* must be a multiple of 7, between 7 and 56.
-f*n*	Uses *n*-bit cipher feedback mode. *n* must be a multiple of 8, between 8 and 64.
-k *key*	Uses *key* as the encryption key.
-m*n*	Calculates a message authentication code (MAC) of *n* bits on the input; *n* must be a multiple of 8.
-o*n*	Uses *n*-bit output feedback mode. *n* must be a multiple of 8, between 8 and 64.
-p	Disables resetting the parity bit; only used when the *key* is in ASCII.
-v *vector*	Sets the initialization vector to *vector*.

bdiff

An SVR4 utility that compares two very long files and reports on the differences. bdiff divides the two comparison files into smaller pieces and then runs the diff utility on them, thus allowing diff to act on files that would normally be too large for it to manage.

Syntax

The syntax for bdiff is as follows:

```
bdiff file1 file2 [options]
```

Options and Arguments

bdiff compares file1 with file2 and lists every line that is different. If a hyphen (-) is used instead of one of these filenames, bdiff reads from the standard input instead.

bdiff takes the two options shown in Table B.4.

TABLE B.4: Options to Use with bdiff

OPTION	DESCRIPTION
n	Splits each of the comparison files into segments each *n* lines long; the default is 3500 lines. If you use this option, you must use it first.
-s	Suppresses error messages from bdiff; does not suppress error messages that come from diff.

Examples

To compare two large files, use:

```
bdiff page1.txt page2.txt
```

See also cmp, diff, diff3, sdiff, split

bg

A shell command that resumes a stopped job and runs it in the background. It is useful if you forgot to add an ampersand (&) at the end of the command line when you first started the job, or you have since changed your mind and decided to do something else while the current job is running.

This command runs in all the popular shells with one or two minor differences. In the C shell:

```
bg %
```

executes the current job in the background, or:

```
bg %1
```

executes job number 1 in the background. To do the same in the Bourne and Korn shells, use:

```
bg 1
```

See also background processing, fg, percent sign

bib

A BSD preprocessor for nroff or troff that formats a bibliography from a bibliographic database.

Syntax

The syntax for bib is straightforward:

    bib [options]

The input files are copied to the standard output, except for text between [. and .] pairs, which are assumed to be keywords used in searching the bibliographic database; when a matching reference is found, a citation is created. References are collected, sorted, and written out as specified by the user.

Options and Arguments

The options listed in Table B.5 are available with bib; if you select one of the standard formal styles (see the -t option), you do not usually have to specify any more options for most documents.

You may also encounter other bibliographic-manipulation programs, such as listrefs, bibinc, or bib2tib. The options listed in Table B.5 also work with listrefs.

bib was designed to work with ms macros; to use it with the me macros, you must add a special header to your nroff/troff file.

See also invert, me **macros,** ms **macros,** nroff, troff

TABLE B.5: Options to Use with bib

Option	Description
-aa	Substitutes initials for authors' first names.
-ar*number*	Reverses the first *number* authors' names, last names appearing first.
-ax	Prints authors' last names in capitals-small capitals format.
-c*string*	Creates citations according to the template *string*.
-d	Changes the default search directory for style files; defaults to /usr/new/lib/bmac.
-ea	Substitutes initials for editors' first names.
-ex	Prints editors' last names in capitals–small capitals format.
-er*number*	Reverses the first *number* editors' names, last names appearing first.
-f	Creates footnote references.
-i*file*	Processes *file*, which may be a file of definitions.
-h	Changes form of three or more references so that 1,2,3,4 becomes 1–4. Used with -o.
-n*string*	Turns off the options indicated by *string*.
-o	Contiguous citations are ordered according to the reference list before they are printed; this is the default.
-p*file*	Searches *file* instead of searching the INDEX file, where *file* is a comma-separated list of indices, created by the invert utility.
-s*string*	Sorts references according to the template *string*.

TABLE B.5 continued: Options to Use with bib

OPTION	DESCRIPTION
-t*type*	Uses the standard macros and switch settings indicated by *type* to create citations and references.
-Tib	Use the TiB style macro where the name is enclosed in vertical bars.
-Tibx	Writes a special format file used when converting to TiB-style macros.

biff

A BSD utility used to tell the system if you want to be notified when new mail arrives for you during your current session.

biff operates asynchronously and requires that sendmail and lmail are running; for synchronous notification, use the MAIL variable of the Bourne shell or the mail variable of the C shell.

The command:

    biff y

enables mail notification, and the command:

    biff n

turns it off again. When mail notification is turned on and mail arrives for you, the header and the first few lines of the message are printed on your screen.

It makes sense to include the biff y command in your .login or .profile file, so that the command is run automatically each time you log in.

biff was named for a dog that belonged to a graduate student working at Berkeley during the summer of 1980. The story that Biff barked at the mailman is apparently a fiction, although legend has it that Biff once got a B in a compiler class.

See also mail, mailx, xbiff

/bin

A Unix root directory used to contain executable software. Many systems have at least two such directories, /bin and /usr/bin, although you may find many more. The name is derived from the word *binary* because most of the files in /bin are binaries.

binary coded decimal

See BCD

binary file

A program or data file that contains binary information in a machine-readable form, rather than in human-readable ASCII form. Because a binary file uses all eight bits in a byte, but an ASCII file only uses seven, you must tell programs such as ftp which type of file you are transferring.

binary numbers

Numbers stored in binary form. All the values from 0 to 255 can be stored in a single eight-bit byte, while a 16-bit word can store all the values from 0 to 65,535.

See also BCD

bind

An emacs feature that lets you associate a specific key combination with a particular command.

See also emacs

BISON

The Free Software Foundation's version of yacc (yet another compiler compiler), a part of the GNU project.

bit

Contraction of binary digit, a bit is the basic unit of information in the binary numbering system, representing either 0 for off or 1 for on. Bits are grouped together to make larger storage units such as the eight-bit byte.

bitwise operator

An operator that manipulates data as a series of bits. In the C programming language, bitwise operators include bitwise AND (&), inclusive OR (|), exclusive OR (^), shift left (<), shift right (>), and NOT (~).

See also Boolean

blank character

A space or a tab character, also called *whitespace*. In certain contexts, a newline and each of the nonprinting ASCII characters may also be considered blank characters.

blind courtesy copy

Abbreviated bcc. A list of recipients of an e-mail message whose names do not appear in the To: message header, so that the original recipient does not know that copies have been forwarded to other locations.

blocks

Sections of a disk or tape that are read or written at the same time; units of storage allocation that are transferred as single units.

In some systems a block is 512 bytes, in others it is 1024 bytes, and the BSD fast file system uses 8192-byte blocks. Most block devices always use the same block size when transferring data, although some tape drives can write variable-length blocks on the same tape. The block size may be specified when reading and writing to a device; for example, when you use the `tar -b` option.

See also `tar`

block device

A peripheral capable of storing a Unix filesystem; in other words a disk or a tape drive. A block device is accessed via a block special file and transfers data one block at a time using a specific block size. A block device may also use a cache to speed up reading and writing data.

See also character device, device file, raw device

/boot

An SVR4 root directory containing files used to load and configure a new operating system installation.

See also root filesystem

Bourne shell

The oldest Unix shell still in popular use, originally developed by Dr. Steven Bourne of AT&T Bell Labs. The Bourne shell is a command interpreter with a built-in programming language.

The Bourne shell offers the following features:

▶ A built-in command set for writing shell scripts

▶ Background execution of commands

▶ Input and output redirection

▶ Wildcard or metacharacters for filename abbreviation

- ▶ Job control (starting with the Bourne shell in SVR4)
- ▶ A set of shell variables to customize your environment
- ▶ Exportation of specified variables to a child process

Startup Files

The Bourne shell program, started by the `sh` command, executes the statements in the `/etc/profile` and `$HOME/.profile` files, if they exist. The commands in `/etc/profile` are likely to be general commands applying to all users of the Bourne shell on your system, while the commands in `$HOME/.profile` can be modified to suit each user. The normal shell prompt is a dollar sign, and you can log out with Ctrl-D or by typing **exit** at this prompt.

Using Commands

The Bourne shell allows you to use and group commands on the command line in several different ways, which are shown in Table B.6.

TABLE B.6: Using Bourne Shell Commands

COMMAND	DESCRIPTION
cmd &	Executes cmd in the background.
cmd1 ; cmd2	Executes cmd1 and cmd2 consecutively, with the semicolon acting as a command separator.
(cmd1 ; cmd2)	Creates a subshell to execute cmd1 and cmd2 as a group.
cmd1 | cmd2	Creates a pipe, and uses the output from cmd1 as input to cmd2.
cmd1 'cmd2'	Performs command substitution; uses the output from cmd2 as arguments to cmd1.
cmd1 && cmd2	Executes cmd1, and if cmd1 completes successfully, then executes cmd2.
cmd1 || cmd2	Executes either cmd1, or if it fails, executes cmd2.
{ cmd1 ; cmd2 }	Executes commands in the current shell.

Filename Metacharacters

You can use any of the patterns shown in Table B.7 to generate filenames.

TABLE B.7: Bourne Shell Filename Metacharacters

METACHARACTER	DESCRIPTION
*	Matches any string or zero or more characters; for example, w*n matches wn, win, won, when, worn, and many other filenames.
?	Matches any single character; for example, myfile.? matches myfile._, myfile.1, myfile.a, and so on.

TABLE B.7 continued: Bourne Shell Filename Metacharacters

METACHARACTER	DESCRIPTION
[abc...]	Matches any single character from the list, and you can use a hyphen to indicate a range, as in a-z,0-9, and so on.
[!abc...]	Matches any single character not on the list, and you can use a hyphen to indicate a range.

Redirection

When you execute a command, the shell opens three files known as the standard input, the standard output, and the standard error. By default, the standard input is the keyboard, and the standard output and standard error are the terminal or screen. Redirection is the process of directing input to or output from a different file from that used normally.

In simple redirection, you can change the input source or output destination in any of the ways listed in Table B.8.

The shell assigns a file descriptor to each standard file, using 0 for standard input, 1 for standard output, and 2 for standard error; it may also use higher numbers, starting at 3 for any other files required to complete the process. You can use the file descriptors listed in Table B.9 in redirection.

In multiple redirection, you can use the file descriptors listed in Table B.10.

TABLE B.8: Simple Redirection in the Bourne Shell

COMMAND	DESCRIPTION
cmd > *filename*	Sends output from *cmd* to *filename*, overwriting the file if it already exists.
cmd >> *filename*	Appends output from *cmd* to *filename*.
cmd < *filename*	Takes input for *cmd* from *filename*.
cmd << *text*	Reads standard input as far as a line identical to *text*.

TABLE B.9: Redirection Using File Descriptors in the Bourne Shell

FILE DESCRIPTOR	DESCRIPTION
cmd >&n	Sends output from *cmd* to file descriptor *n*.
cmd m>&n	Same as above, except that output that would normally go to the file descriptor *m* is sent to file descriptor *n* instead.

TABLE B.9 continued: Redirection Using File Descriptors in the
Bourne Shell

FILE DESCRIPTOR	DESCRIPTION
cmd >&–	Closes standard output.
cmd <&n	Takes input for *cmd* from file descriptor *n*.
cmd m<&n	Same as above, except that output that would normally have come from the file descriptor *m* comes from the file descriptor *n* instead.
cmd <&–	Closes standard input.

TABLE B.10: Multiple Redirection in the Bourne Shell

FILE DESCRIPTOR	DESCRIPTION
cmd 2>filename	Sends standard error to *filename* while standard output remains on the screen.
cmd > filename 2>&1	Sends both standard error and standard output to *filename*.
(cmd > filename1) 2>filename2	Sends standard output to *filename1* and standard error to *filename2*.
cmd | tee filenames	Sends output from *cmd* to standard output and also to *filename*.

Quoting

Quoting disables the special meaning of a character and allows you to use
it literally. The characters listed in Table B.11 have special meaning in the
Bourne shell.

TABLE B.11: Quoting in the Bourne Shell

CHARACTER	DESCRIPTION
;	Command separator.
&	Runs a command in the background.
( )	Command grouping.
|	Creates a pipe.
*? [ ] !	Filename metacharacters.
< > & |	Redirection symbols.
" " ' ' \	Used when quoting other characters. Anything placed between the double quotes is interpreted symbolically; anything placed between the single quotes is interpreted literally, and the backslash is used to quote a single character.

Predefined Variables

The Bourne shell includes a large set of built-in variables as Table B.12 shows; many of these variables are not set by the shell but are used in .profile where you can define them to meet your individual needs. You assign value to a variable with the command:

```
$ variable=value
```

If you do not specify values, the Bourne shell applies defaults to certain environment variables, including PATH, PS1, PS2, and IFS, and the HOME variable is set when you log in to the system.

TABLE B.12: Built-in Bourne Shell Variables

Variable	Description
$#	Contains the number of arguments on the command line.
$?	Contains the return code for the last command executed.
$$	Contains the PID of the current process.
$!	Contains the PID of the most recent background process.
$-	Displays the options currently in effect for sh.
$0	The first word on the command line, the command name.
$n	Individual arguments on the command line; you can reference up to 9, where n = 1–9.
$*	All the arguments on the command line, quoted as a single string ("$1 $2 $3...").
"$@"	All the arguments on the command line, quoted as individual strings ("$1" "$2" "$3...").
CDPATH=dirs	Specifies the search path for the cd command, with individual directory names separated by colons.
HOME=dir	Specifies the home directory; set by login. If you use the cd command without an argument, the shell makes this directory the current directory.
IFS='chars'	Sets the internal field separator to chars; the defaults are space, tab, and newline.
MAIL=filename	Sets the default name of your mail file; the shell tells you when you receive mail via the mail or mailx commands.
MAILCHECK=n	Specifies the frequency n with which the shell checks for new mail; the default is 600 seconds, or 10 minutes.
MAILPATH=filename	Indicates one or more files, separated by a colon, in which to receive mail.
PATH=dir	Sets one or more pathnames, separated by colons, that the shell should search for commands to execute; the default is /usr/bin.
PS1=string	Specifies the primary shell prompt; the default is $.
PS2=string	Specifies the secondary shell prompt for use in multiline commands; the default is >. The appearance of this prompt indicates that the shell expects more input.

TABLE B.12 continued: Built-in Bourne Shell Variables

Variable	Description
SHACCT=*filename*	Specifies the shell accounting file used to log records for all executed shell scripts.
SHELL=*filename*	Specifies the shell to be used by commands when you escape to a sub-shell; of special interest to ed and vi.
TERM=*string*	Specifies your terminal type; required by some commands that use the whole screen for output.

Built-in Commands

The Bourne shell offers a set of built-in commands as Table B.13 shows; many of these commands are also available in the Korn shell.

Because the Bourne shell was the only significant shell when it was first introduced, you may find that older Unix documentation refers to "the shell" when it really means the Bourne shell; some of these references apply only to the Bourne shell and are not appropriate for newer shells such as the C or Korn shells.

See also csh, C shell, Bash, Bourne shell family, Korn shell, ksh, sh, Tcsh, Unix shell, Zsh

TABLE B.13: Built-in Bourne Shell Commands

Command	Description
:	Null command. The shell performs no action and returns an exit status of 0.
.*filename*	Reads and executes lines in *filename* as part of the current process.
break [*n*]	Exits from *n* levels in a for or while loop; the default is 1.
cd [*directory*]	Changes to the specified *directory*; the default is the home directory.
continue [*n*]	Skips any remaining commands in a for or while loop, resuming with the next iteration of the loop or skipping *n* loops.
echo *args*	Writes *args* to the screen.
eval [*args*]	Executes the specified *args*, allowing evaluation and substitution of shell variables.
exec [*command*]	Executes *command* without starting a new process.
exit [*n*]	Exits from the current shell procedure with an exit status of *n*.
export [*names*]	Exports the value of one or more shell variables, making them global in scope rather than local, which is the default.
getopts *string var* [*args*]	Checks command options, including *args* if provided, for legal choices.

TABLE B.13 continued: Built-in Bourne Shell Commands

COMMAND	DESCRIPTION
hash [-r][commands]	Establishes a tracked alias for commands to speed execution; the -r option clears tracked aliases.
newgrp [-][group]	Switches to group, or returns to your login group.
Pwd	Displays the pathname of the current working directory.
read var1 [var2...]	Reads one line from standard input, and assigns each word to a named variable; all leftovers are assigned to the last variable.
Readonly [var1...]	Makes the specified variables read-only so that they cannot be changed.
return [n]	Exits from a function with the exit status n, and returns to the shell.
set [option arg1 arg2...]	Without arguments, set prints the names and values of all shell variables. option can be turned on by using a minus sign or turned off with a plus sign, and arguments are assigned in order to the parameters $1, $2, and so on. The options are listed in Table B.14.
shift [n]	Shifts positional arguments n places (by default 1 place) to the left.
Test	Tests a condition, and if true, returns a zero exit status.
Times	Displays cumulative system and user time for all processes run by the shell.
trap [[commands] signals]	Executes commands if any signals are received.
type [names]	Shows whether names are Unix commands, built-in commands, or a defined shell function.
ulimit [-f n]	Sets a limit of n hard disk blocks for files created by the shell and child processes. Without n, displays the current limit.
umask [nnn]	Sets the user file creation mask to octal value nnn; if nnn is omitted, displays the current user creation mask.
unset [names]	Removes definitions of the specified functions or variables in names.
wait [n]	Waits for the process with ID of n to complete execution in the background and display its exit status.

TABLE B.14: Options to Use with the set Bourne Shell Command

OPTION	DESCRIPTION
-/+a	Export/do not export defined or modified variables.
-/+e	Exit/do not exit if a command yields a non-zero exit status.
-/+f	Disable/enable filename metacharacters.
-/+h	Enable/disable quick access to commands.
-/+k	Provide/do not provide all environment variable assignments.

TABLE B.14 continued: Options to Use with the set Bourne Shell Command

Option	Description
-/+n	Read but do not execute/execute commands.
-/+t	Execute/do not execute one command, and exit.
-/+u	Consider/do not consider unset variables as errors.
-/+v	Show/do not show each shell command line when read.
-/+x	Display/do not display commands and arguments when executed.

Bourne-again shell

See Bash

braces

The two left { and right } characters also known as *curly braces* but never called *brackets*. Braces are used in several different ways:

- ▶ In the Bourne shell, they are used to surround commands that you want to execute as a group.

- ▶ In the C shell, they are used to surround variable names and also to force the expansion of items in a comma-separated list.

- ▶ In the C language, they are used to indicate the beginning and end of blocks of code.

break

A Bourne, C, and Korn shell command that stops or exits from a looping construct such as for, while, select, until, or continue. In most cases, break is combined with some sort of test condition, and execution continues at the next statement following the end of the loop.

breaksw

Abbreviation for break switch. breaksw is a C shell command used to indicate the end of a set of commands in a case string search.

See also case, endsw, switch

built-in command

Any command that is actually a part of the shell and is executed directly by the shell, rather than by forking a new process. This allows built-in commands to execute quickly and lets them affect the environment of the current shell.

Each of the three major shells—the Bourne shell, the C shell, and the Korn shell—have their own distinctive set of commands. Because most of the built-in commands work in the same way as the normal Unix utilities work, you may not always be aware of whether the command is a utility or a built-in command. Table B.15 indicates the number of built-in commands in each of the popular shells.

A built-in command is also known as an *internal command*.

TABLE B.15: The Number of Built-in Commands in Each Shell

SHELL NAME	NUMBER OF BUILT-IN COMMANDS
Bourne shell	32
Bash	50
C shell	52
Korn shell	43
Tcsh	56
Zsh	73

bzip

`bzip` is a block-sorting compression program with somewhat better compression than the older `gzip` program. Unfortunately, it is also quite a bit slower than `gzip`, taking about twice as long to compress a typical text file. `bzip` uses the Burrows-Wheeler-Fenwick block-sorting text compression process. `bzip` includes the reverse function, `bunzip`, which is used to decompress bzipped files.

C

CAE

Abbreviation for Common Application Environment. A set of standards developed by X/Open for application development, including standards for the operating system, compilers, software development tools, data management, networking, and the graphical user interface (GUI).

See also CDE

cal

A command that prints a simple calendar for the current month on the standard output.

Syntax

The syntax for cal is straightforward:

```
cal [month][year]
```

Options and Arguments

cal prints a 12-month calendar beginning in January for any given year (ranging from 1 to 9999), in full, as in 1996. If you enter cal 96, a calendar for the year 96 is displayed, which is probably not what you want. cal displays a one-month calendar for the specified month (ranging from 1 to 12) and year.

Examples

To print a calendar for October 1996, use:

```
cal 10 1996
```

This calendar contains more lines than one screen can display, so you might pipe the output through pg and view it one screen at a time:

```
cal 10 1996 | pg
```

And to see a really odd-looking calendar, take a look at the year 1752 when the Gregorian calendar came into being.

See also calendar, date

calendar

A utility that reads your /home/calendar file and displays all the lines that contain certain dates. You can use this as a to-do list or as a reminder service.

On weekdays, calendar displays items with today's and tomorrow's dates; on Fridays and Saturdays, calendar shows items through Monday; and on Sunday, it displays items for both Sunday and Monday.

Syntax

The syntax for calendar is:

```
calendar [option]
```

In BSD, entries in the calendar text file must contain a reference to a date as the first item; in other systems, the date can appear anywhere on the line. You can enter the date in one of several ways; you can use 05/08, May 8, or 05/08/99. If you use an asterisk (*) in the month position, the associated reminder is posted on that day every month. A day without a month matches that day every week, and a month without a day matches the first day of that month. Your `calendar` file must be readable by everybody.

Options and Arguments

`calendar` takes one option, a - in System V and -a in BSD, for superuser use only, which tells `calendar` to send reminders for today and tomorrow to all users on the system by e-mail.

Examples

You can add entries like these to your `calendar` file:

```
May 6      Meet VP Eng 2pm
05/08      Buy flowers
```

`calendar` can be automated by using at or crontab, or by including it in your startup file, `.profile`, `.login`, or `.cshrc`.

On some systems, certain default `calendar` files are provided, including `calendar.birthday`, a file of birthdays of famous and infamous people; `calendar.computer`, a list of important dates in computer history; and `calendar.music`, a list of musical births, deaths, and other important events.

See also `cal`, `cron`, `date`

call

In programming, a statement that refers to an independent subroutine or function. A call is turned into a branch instruction by the assembler, compiler or interpreter, and the function that is called is responsible for returning to the original program in an appropriate way.

In most programming languages, it is possible to pass information in the form of arguments to a called function and to receive return values back from the function when it finishes executing. Such function-calling protocols are known as *calling conventions* and allow standardized function calls across object code originating from different languages and different compilers.

See also call by reference, call by value

call by reference

A feature found in many programming languages that allows you to pass a reference to a variable to a called function. During execution of the function, the value of the referenced variable can change.

See also call, call by value

call by value

A feature found in many programming languages, including C, that allows you to pass a value to a called function. During execution of the function, the value of the referenced variable can change, but this does not affect the original information.

See also call, call by reference

calling environment

That list of variables and their values made available to a program; also called the *environment.* In the C shell, you can use the env command to display the current environment.

See also Bourne shell, environment variables, export

cancel

An SVR4 utility that cancels a print request made by the lp spooler. You can also stop a print job that has already started printing.

Syntax
The syntax for cancel is:

```
cancel [options][printer]
```

Unless you are a superuser, you can cancel only the print jobs that you have requested. And if a job is in the middle of printing when you try to cancel it, a message is added to the printout to this effect; the next print job in the queue will start printing.

Options and Arguments
cancel has three options shown in Table C.1.

TABLE C.1: Options to Use with cancel

Option	Description
request-id	Cancels print request request-id.
printer	Cancels the print request currently printing on printer.
-uuser	Cancels the print request associated with user.

Examples
To cancel print request number 10 on the default printer, use:

```
cancel 10
```

To find out the `request-id` or the name of the `printer` to cancel, use the `lpstat` command. Each `request-id` contains the name of the printer, followed by a hyphen, followed by a sequence number.

To cancel two jobs at once, use:

```
cancel laser-10 laser-15
```

caret symbol

- ▶ A metacharacter with many meanings and uses within Unix. Do not use a caret in a filename, because to access the file you will always have to turn off the special meaning of this character—more trouble than it is worth.

- ▶ One representation of a control character; for example, Ctrl-D can also be written as ^D.

- ▶ A metacharacter used in regular expressions in the awk, ed, egrep, ex, grep, sed, and vi programs. The caret matches character strings located only at the beginning of a line. It is also used to invert a match; for example, the sequence ^[^a] means select all lines not starting with a.

- ▶ An indicator in the C shell that shows a command substitution has been made in command-line input. To replace some of the characters in the previous command, type ^, followed by those characters you want to replace, then another ^, followed by the new characters.

See also history, history substitution, regular expressions

carriage return

A control character (Ctrl-J) that signals the print head or display cursor to return to the first position of the current line.

See also EBCDIC, linefeed, newline

case

- ▶ A conditional statement in the Bourne and Korn shells; each alternative in the case statement begins with a case label.

- ▶ A C shell keyword used to mark each label in a switch statement; this usage is the same as that found in the C programming language.

See also esac, if, switch.

case-insensitive

Any situation that ignores the case of letters and accepts input in both upper- and lowercase letters. DOS is an example of an operating system that is case-insensitive.

case-sensitive

Any situation in which the case of letters is important. Unix is case-sensitive in most areas, and the C programming language is always case-sensitive. For example, unless you set the ignorecase parameter, vi always performs case-sensitive searches; similarly, unless you use the -i option with grep, searches are always case-sensitive.

cat

A common Unix command used to concatenate (join end-to-end) and display files on the standard output.

Syntax

The syntax for cat is:

```
cat [options][-][filename...]
```

The cat utility reads the specified files in sequence, writing them to standard out; the single hyphen represents standard input.

Options and Arguments

The options available with cat are shown in Table C.2.

TABLE C.2: Options to Use with cat

Option	Description
-b	In the BSD version, implies the -n option but does not number the lines.
-e	Prints a $ at the end of each line; must be used with the -v option.
-n	In the BSD version, numbers all output lines, starting at 1.
-s	Suppresses messages when cat cannot find nonexistent files. In the BSD version, this option squeezes out multiple adjacent lines, making output single spaced.
-t	Displays each tab as Ctrl-I and each formfeed as Ctrl-L; must be used with the -v option.
-u	Prints the output as unbuffered; the default mode is buffered in blocks or screen lines.
-v	Displays control characters and other nonprinting characters found in binary files. Control characters are displayed as ^n where n is the corresponding octal character in the range octal 100 to octal 137. The del character is shown as ^? .

Examples

To display the contents of a file, use:

```
cat /etc/passwd
```

You can use `cat` to create short text files without bothering to open an editor. To send input from the keyboard to a file, use the following redirection instruction:

```
cat > myfile.txt
```

In this mode, you can use the basic editing keys on the keyboard, but you cannot rework an existing line. Use Ctrl-D on a line by itself to end your input and return to the shell.

If you want to empty a file, but leave the file in place, use:

```
cat /dev/null > myfile.txt
```

The /dev/null file is a system file 0 bytes long used to consume unwanted output; you can also use `cp` with /dev/null to create a new, empty file.

Notes

Because of the way the shell language mechanism works when performing redirection, the command:

```
cat filename1 filename2 > filename1
```

overwrites and destroys the original data in `filename1`. If you are using the C shell or the Korn shell, you can prevent this kind of problem by setting the `noclobber` variable.

See also cp, echo, od, pg, pr

catenate

To join end-to-end or sequentially. The Unix `cat` utility catenates files—it displays them one after the other.

See also concatenate

cb

The C programming language beautifier; a utility that formats C language source code files using proper C programming structure, making the content of the files look neat and more readable.

See also cc, gcc, C compiler

cbreak mode

An operational mode of the BSD terminal handler that allows a terminal to receive each character as it is typed, but still lets you use the interrupt and quit characters as you normally would. `cbreak` mode is a compromise between cooked mode and raw mode.

cc

The Unix C programming language compiler. The compiler processes a source-code file through the four stages of preprocessing, compiling, assembling, and linking. This entry describes the SVR4 compiler with notes on Solaris and SCO implementations. BSD includes the GNU C compiler, `gcc`, which is also used on many other systems including Linux; see `gcc`.

Syntax

You can invoke the C compiler using:

```
cc [options][filename...]
```

This command runs the ANSI C compiler; to use the compiler for Kernighan and Ritchie's C, use:

```
/usr/bin/cc
```

Options and Arguments

You can use the options listed in Table C.3 with `cc`. Table C.4 describes options available for use with the SVR4 C compiler and includes comments specific to the Solaris compiler. Options for use with the SCO C compiler are given in Table C.5.

TABLE C.3: Options for Use with cc

Option	Description
-#	A Solaris-only option that indicates when each separate compiler stage is invoked.
-A name[tokens]	Supplies an assert directive, assigning *name* with any optional *tokens* as parameters.
-A-	Ignores predefined assertions and macros.
-B mode	When *mode* is dynamic, libraries are shared, and library files ending in both .so and .a are searched. When *mode* is static, only .a files are searched.
-c	Creates a linkable object file for each file compiled, but does not call the link editor.
-C	Keeps comments during preprocessing.
-dc	Tells the link editor to link dynamically when *c* is y (the default), or to link statically when *c* is n.
-D name[=def]	Supplies a define directive, specifying *name* to be *def*, or if no *def* is given, the value of 1.

TABLE C.3 continued: Options for Use with cc

Option	Description
-dalign	Produces double load/store instructions to improve performance—Solaris only.
-E	Runs just the macro processor, sending the output to standard out.
-fast	A Solaris-only option that uses the cc options that give the fastest compilation.
-flags	A Solaris-only option that briefly describes the available options.
-fnonstd	Produces a special Solaris format.
-fsingle	A Solaris-only option that evaluates float expressions as single-precision.
-g	Generates extra symbol table information for the dbx and sdb debuggers.
-G	Produces a shared object file instead of a linked executable.
-H	Lists the pathnames of the header files on standard out.
-I *dir*	Searches for include files in the specified *dir*. You must use a separate -I option for each new *dir* you want searched.
-K *word*	When *word* is PIC, produces position-independent code; when *word* is minabi, cc compiles with minimum dynamic linking to keep ABI compliance.
-keeptmp	A Solaris-only option that preserves temporary files.
-L *dir*	Searches for library archive files in the specified *dir*. You must use a separate -L option for each new *dir* you want searched.
-o *filename*	Creates an object file with the name of *filename* rather than the default a.out.
-O	Makes the compiler optimize the object code.
-p	Generates profile information that counts each time a routine is called. Results are stored in the file mon.out, and you can use the profiler prof to analyze the results and create an execution profile.
-P	Runs just the preprocessor, and stores the result in the file *filename*.i.
-Qc	When *c* is y, lists information about the compilation tools invoked; when *c* is n, no list is created.
-ql	Produces code to count the number of times each source line is executed. Use lprof to list the counts.
-qp	Same as -p.
-S	Compiles only (and optimizes if -O is supplied), but does not assemble or link.
-U *name*	Removes the definition of *name* as in an #undef directive.
-v	Checks C language semantics strictly.
-V	Prints the version numbers of the compiler tools.

TABLE C.3 continued: Options for Use with cc

OPTION	DESCRIPTION
-W[p0ab1]arg1 [,arg2...]	Sends a particular cc option arg1, arg2... to a specific compiler tool. The p or 0 specifies the compiler, 2 the optimizer, b the basic block analyzer, and 1 specifies the link editor.
-Xc	Specifies c as the level of ANSI C compliance. When c is set to a, specifies ANSI compliance; to c, specifies conformance, which is stricter than ANSI; to t, specifies pre-ANSI features; and the Solaris-only s setting is for a Sun C setting.
-xpg	A Solaris-only option used like -p to create a file gmon.out for analysis by gprof.
-xsb	A Solaris-only option that creates symbol-table data for the Solaris Source Code Browser.
-xsbfast	A Solaris-only option, the same as xsb but does not compile.
-xstconst	A Solaris-only option that adds string literals to the text segment rather than to the data segment.
-Yc,dir	Specifies that item c is searched in dir, where c can be p, 0, 2, a, b, or 1 as in -W above. With this option, c can also be I (see -I), P (see -L), or S for startup object files.

TABLE C.4: Options for Use with the SCO UNIX C Compiler

OPTION	DESCRIPTION
-ansi	Enforces full ANSI compliance.
-B1 path/filename	Defines alternate first pass for compiler.
-B2 path/filename	Defines alternate second pass for compiler.
-B3 path/filename	Defines alternate third pass for compiler.
-c	Creates a linkable object file for each file compiled, but does not call the link editor.
-C	Keeps comments during preprocessing.
-compat	Creates an executable file that is binary-compatible across 386 UNIX System V Release 3.2, UNIX-286 System V, UNIX-386 System V, UNIX-286 3.0, and UNIX-8086 System V. Uses XENIX libraries, and creates OMF object files.
-CSON, -CSOFF	Enables or disables common subexpression optimization when the -O option is specified.
-d	Displays compiler passes and their arguments before execution.
-dos	Creates a DOS executable.
-Dname[=string}	Defines name to the preprocessor in the same way as a #define statement in the source file.
-E	Preprocesses each source file as described for -P, sending the results to standard out.

TABLE C.4 continued: Options for Use with the SCO UNIX C Compiler

Option	Description
-EP	Preprocesses each source file as described for -P, sending the results to standard out and to a file.
-F*number*	Sets the stack size to *number* in hexadecimal.
-Fa, -Fa*filename*	Creates a masm assembly source listing in source.asm or in *filename*.
-Fc, -Fc*filename*	Creates a merged assembly and C source listing in source.L or in *filename*.
-Fe*filename*	Creates an executable file *filename*.
-Fl, -Fl*filename*	Creates a listing file in source.L or *filename* with assembly source and object code.
-Fm, -Fm*filename*	Creates a map file called a.map or *filename*.
-Fo*object-filename*	Creates an object file called *object-filename*.
-FPa, -FPc, -FPc87, -FPi, -FPi87	These options are used with -dos or -os2 to specify the type of floating-point code generated and the library support to use.
-g	Generates symbol table information needed by the sdb, dbxtra, and Code View debuggers.
-Gc	Specifies calling sequences and naming conventions used with System V 386 Pascal and Fortran.
-Gs	Removes stack probe routines. This option can make the binary file smaller and can increase execution speed somewhat.
-H*length*	Sets the maximum length of internal symbols to *length*.
-help, -HELP	Prints a help menu.
-i	Creates separate code and data spaces for small model programs in 8086/186/286 compilations only.
-I *dir*	Searches for include files in the specified *dir*. You must use a separate -I option for each new *dir* you want searched.
-iBCS2	Enforces strict Intel Binary Compatibility Standard 2 compliance.
-J	Changes the default char mode from signed to unsigned.
-K	Removes the stack probes from a program.
-L	Creates an assembler listing that contains assembled code and assembly source code in the file source.L.
-l *name*	Searches library *name*.a for unresolved function references.
-LARGE	Invokes the compiler's large model mode.
-link	Passes all options that follow this option directly to the link editor.
-m *filename*	Creates a map file called *filename*.
-M *string*	Sets program configuration to *string*, where *string* can be any of those listed in Table C.5.
-n	Sets pure text model.
-nl *length*	Sets maximum length of external symbols to *length*.
-nointl	Creates an executable file without international functions.

TABLE C.4 continued: Options for Use with the SCO UNIX C Compiler

Option	Description
-ND *name*	Sets the data segment for each assembled or compiled source file to *name*.
-NM *name*	Sets the module name for each assembled or compiled source file to *name*.
-NT *name*	Sets the text segment name for each assembled or compiled source file to *name*.
-0	Makes the compiler optimize the object code.
-o *filename*	Creates an object file with the name of *filename* rather than the default a.out.
-O *string*	Invokes the object code optimizer; *string* can contain one or more of the items listed in Table C.6.
-os2	Creates an OS/2 executable, using OS/2 libraries.
-p	Generates profile information that counts each time a routine is called. Results are stored in the file mon.out, and you can use the profiler prof to analyze the results and create an execution profile.
-P	Runs just the preprocessor, and stores the result in the file *filename*.i.
-pack	Packs structures.
-posix	Enforces strict POSIX compliance.
-ql	Invokes the basic block analyzer to count the number of times each source line is executed. Use lprof to list counts.
-qp	Same as -p.
-quiet	Turns off echoing of source filenames during compilation.
-r	Performs an incremental link.
-s	Tells the linker to remove symbol table information from the executable file.
-S	Creates an assembly listing in masm format.
-Sl *linewidth*	Specifies the maximum characters per line for the source file.
-Sp *pagelength*	Specifies the number of lines per page in the source file.
-Ss *string*, -St *string*	Sets the subtitle (-Ss *string*) and title (-St *string*) for source listings, and bypasses cc's linking operation.
-strict	Restricts language to ANSI C.
-svid	Enforces SVID compliance.
-Tc *filename*	Tells cc that *filename* is a C source file.
-u	Removes all manifest defines.
-U *definition*	Removes or undefines the *definition* manifest define.
-unix	Generates Unix COFF files, the default mode.
-V *string*	Places *string* in the object file.
-w	Suppresses compiler error messages.

TABLE C.4 continued: Options for Use with the SCO UNIX C Compiler

OPTION	DESCRIPTION
-W *number*	Sets the level for compiler error messages, from 0 (no warnings issued) to 3 (all warning messages are issued).
-WX	Turns all errors into fatal errors.
-xenix	Creates a XENIX program using XENIX libraries and #include files.
-x2.3	Same as -xenix, but adds extended functions available with XENIX System V 386 Release 2.3.
-xout	Same as -x2.3, but adds functions from SCO UNIX 3.2.
-xpg3	Enforces XPG3 compliance.
-xpg3plus	Enforces XPG3 compliance with SCO added value.
-X	Removes standard directories from list of directories to search for #include files.
-z	Displays compiler passes and arguments, but does not execute them.
-Za	Confines language to ANSI specifications.
-Zd	Includes line numbers in the object file.
-Ze	Enables near, far, huge, pascal, and fortran keywords.
-Zg	Generates function declarations from function definitions and writes declarations to standard out.
-Zi	Includes information for the sdb, dbxtra, and Code View debuggers.
-Zl	Removes the default library information from the object file.
-Zp*n*	Packs structure members in memory. *n* can be 1 for the 8086 processor, 2 for the 80286 processor, or 4 for the 80386 processor.
-Zs	Performs only a syntax check.

TABLE C.5: Values to Use with the -M Option in the SCO Unix C Compiler

VALUE	DESCRIPTION
0	8086 code generation.
1	80186 code generation.
2	80286 code generation.
3	80386 code generation.
b	Reverses word order for long data types.
c	Creates a compact model program for 80186/80286 compilations only.
d	Tells cc not to assume register SS equates to register DS.
e	Enables near, far, huge, pascal and fortran keywords.
f	Enables software floating point.
h	Creates a huge model program for 80186/80286 compilations only.

TABLE C.5 continued: Values to Use with the -M Option in the SCO Unix C Compiler

VALUE	DESCRIPTION
l	Creates a large model program for 8086/80186/80286 compilations only.
m	Creates a medium model program for 8086/80186/80286 compilations only.
s	Creates a small model program; the default setting.
t *number*	Sets largest size of a data item to *number*; default is 32,767.

TABLE C.6: Values to Use with the -O Option in the SCO Unix C Compiler

VALUE	DESCRIPTION
3	DISABLES PASS 3 OPTIMIZATION.
a	Relaxes alias checking.
c	Enables default local common expressions.
d	Turns off all the following optimization options; a, c, e, g, i, l, s, t.
e	Enables global register allocation.
g	Enables global optimization.
h	Optimizes code for functions returning short or char.
i	Generates intrinsics.
l	Performs loop optimizations.
n	Disables unsafe loop optimizations.
p	Improves floating-point calculations.
r	Disables inline returns from functions.
s	Optimizes code for size.
t	Optimizes code for speed, the default setting.
x	Performs maximum optimization.
z	Enables maximum loop- and global-register allocation.

Examples

To compile the source file myprog.c into an executable file called skinny, use:

```
cc -o skinny myprog.c
```

See also C, C++, cb, C compiler, C library, compiling a C program, gcc, libc, makefile

ccat

A BSD shell script used to cat files compressed by the compact command.

Syntax

The syntax to use with `ccat` is:

```
ccat [-v][filename...]
```

The `compact` command compresses the specified `filename` using adaptive Huffman coding into a file called `filename.C`, and you can use `ccat` to cat the file without uncompressing it first. If you use the `-v` option, `ccat` provides the names of the compressed files.

See also `compact`, `compress`, `makefile`, `pack`, `uncompact`

cd

A built-in shell command used to change from one working directory to another. When used without arguments, `cd` changes directories to your home directory1; otherwise, it changes to the specified directory. If the specified directory is a relative pathname, the CDPATH (Bourne and Korn shells) or `cdpath` (C shell) variable is searched.

In the Korn shell, you can also use:

```
cd -
```

where `-` indicates the name of the previous directory, or:

```
cd [old-dir new-dir]
```

where the shell replaces the string `old-dir` *with* `new-dir` and changes to the resulting directory.

See also `cdpath`, CDPATH, `chdir`, pwd

cdc

See SCCS

CDE

Abbreviation for Common Desktop Environment. A set of specifications developed by the Common Open Software Environment (COSE) that define an API for a common Unix graphical user interface (GUI). The specifications cover the interoperability of applications across different hardware platforms, multimedia and networking operations, as well as object-oriented technology and system administration issues.

cdpath

A C shell variable used to specify the paths to be checked when the `cd` or `chdir` commands are used. If this variable is not set, you can execute a file only by specifying its complete pathname.

CDPATH

A Bourne and Korn shell variable used to specify the paths to be checked when the `cd` or `chdir` commands are used.

This variable is usually defined in your `.profile` file and contains shorthand names for commonly used directories. If this variable is not set, you can execute a file only by specifying its complete pathname.

character class

A group of characters in a regular expression, usually surrounded by square brackets, that define which characters can occupy a single character position. For example, the character class defined by:

    [abcd]

represents a single character that can by occupied by an a, a b, a c, or a d.

See also **caret symbol, regular expressions**

character special file

A Unix special file that provides an interface definition to a character device such as a terminal or printer. This interface is used with devices that cannot support a filesystem and as an alternative interface for those devices that can.

You can find these files in the `/dev` directory; some of the more important are `/dev/console`, the system console; `/dev/tty`, your terminal; and `/dev/null`, the null device.

See also **block device, device file**

chdir

A built-in C shell command used to change the current working directory. The `cd` command is a much more popular way of achieving the same end, but `chdir` can be useful if you want to redefine `cd`.

checkmail

A SCO command that reports on the status of mail you have sent but has not yet been delivered.

Syntax
The syntax for `checkmail` is:

    checkmail [options]

Options and Arguments

If you use `checkmail` without arguments, the `Subject:` of each message is displayed along with a list of addressees who have yet to receive this message. The `checkmail` options are listed in Table C.7.

If mail consistently remains in the queue, it may mean that a host computer is down somewhere in the network.

See also **CRC,** `mail,` `Mail,` `mailx`

TABLE C.7: Options for Use with checkmail

Option	Description
-a	Shows all addresses, both delivered and undelivered.
-f	Suppresses display of the Subject: line.
-m	Checks all the mail in the mail queue; not just your mail.

checknr

A BSD command that checks `nroff` or `troff` input files for certain types of errors and unknown commands.

Syntax

The syntax for `checknr` is:

```
checknr [options] filename
```

If no files are specified, `checknr` checks standard input.

Options and Arguments

You can use the options listed in Table C.8 with `checknr`.

`checknr` is intended for use on files prepared with `checknr` originally in mind, and certain document style standards; `checknr` also understands the me and ms macro packages.

See also me **macros,** ms **macros,** `nroff,` `troff`

TABLE C.8: Options for Use with checknr

Option	Description
-a.x1.y1...xn.yn	Adds additional pairs of macros to the list of known macros. This option must take the form of a period, the first macro name, another period, and the second macro name. For example, to define the macros .BS and .BT, use -a.BS.BT.
-c.x1.x2...xn	Adds new command definitions.

TABLE C.8 continued: Options for Use with checknr

Option	Description
-f	Ignores \f font changes.
-s	Ignores \s size changes.

chflags

A BSD command used to change file flags.

Syntax

The syntax for chflags is as follows:

```
chflags [-R[-H|-L]-P] flags filename...
```

flags represents a comma-separated list of keywords, which are listed in Table C.9.

To turn a flag off, add no before an option, so that dump becomes nodump, for example.

TABLE C.9: Keywords for Use with chflags

Keyword	Description
dump	Sets the dump flag.
sappnd	Sets the system append-only flag; superuser only.
schg	Sets the system-immutable flag; superuser only.
uappnd	Sets the user append-only flag; owner or superuser only.
uchg	Sets the user-immutable flag; owner or superuser only.

Options and Arguments

The options for chflags are listed in Table C.10.

TABLE C.10: Options for Use with chflags

Option	Description
-H	When the -R option is used, symbolic links on the command line are followed.
-L	When the -R option is used, all symbolic links are followed.
-P	When the -R option is used, no symbolic links are followed.
-R	Changes the file flags for the file hierarchies rooted in the files, instead of just the files themselves.

chgrp

A command that changes the group associated with a file or a set of files. You must be the superuser or the owner of a file before you can change the group association of a file; if you are the owner, you must also belong to the specified group.

Syntax
The syntax for chgrp is as follows:

```
chgrp [options] group filenames
```

where group is the name or numeric ID of the new group, and filenames represents the file or files whose group association you want to change.

Options and Arguments
Table C.11 lists the options that are available with this command.

SCO supports no options for this command, SVR4 supports the -R option, while BSD supports several more, as shown in Table C.11; see the man pages for more information about the options available on your system.

TABLE C.11: Options to Use with chgrp

Option	Description
-f	Invokes force option that ignores errors.
-h	Changes a symbolic link, not the file referenced by a symbolic link. This option is not available on all systems.
-H	When the -R option is used, symbolic links on the command line are followed.
-L	When the -R option is used, all symbolic links are followed.
-P	When the -R option is used, no symbolic links are followed.
-R	Changes the group ID for files, subdirectories, and symbolic links.

Examples
To change the group that the file myfile.doc is associated with to that of pub, use:

```
chgrp pub myfile.doc
```

See also chmod, chown

chkey

A BSD command used to change your encryption key. chkey first prompts you for your login password and then uses your password to encrypt a new encryption key for storage in the public key database.

See also keylogin

chmod

A command that changes the access mode of one or more files. Only the owner of the file or the superuser can change the access mode, or permissions, of a file.

The mode of a file controls the access permissions associated with that file. There are three levels of security: ownership, group access, and everyone else; and within these levels there are three permissions: read, write, and execute. Read permission means that you can look at the contents of the file, write permission means that you can change the file, and execute permission means that you can execute the file; the permissions for directories behave only slightly differently. You can use the `ls -l` command to display these file access privileges.

Syntax

The syntax for chmod is as follows:

```
chmod [options] mode filename
```

You can specify the new access mode either absolutely, by specifying an octal number representing the mode, or symbolically, by specifying individual modes. The latter is a more incremental method because you can add and remove permissions.

Options and Arguments

The mode argument can contain either:

An absolute mode   An octal number that sets all the permissions for this file for all levels. Each number sets the appropriate bit in the file's mode field.

A symbolic mode   A set of arguments that specify the class of user, the operation to be performed, and the access permission you want to change.

Absolute modes are listed in Table C.12. Build up the number you need by ORing the values from the table together; this is equivalent to adding them together. Some of the more common modes are listed in Table C.13 for your convenience; for example, 0644 is combined from 0400 (owner-read) plus 0200 (owner-write) plus 0040 (group-read) plus 0004 (all other-read).

To use a symbolic mode, you must select a class of user, an operation, and the access permission you want to change or modify from each part of Table C.14. These three elements are then combined into a string that is applied to the file or files you are working with.

TABLE C.12: Absolute Modes Used with chmod

OCTAL NUMBER	DESCRIPTION
4000	Sets user ID when the program executes.
2000	Sets group ID when the program executes.
1000	Sets the "sticky bit"; superuser only.
0400	Allows the owner to read the file.
0200	Allows the owner to write to the file.
0100	Allows the owner to execute the file.
0040	Allows the group to read the file.
0020	Allows the group to write to the file.
0010	Allows the group to execute the file.
0004	Allows others to read the file.
0002	Allows others to write to the file.
0001	Allows others to execute the file.

TABLE C.13: Common Absolute Modes Used with chmod

OCTAL NUMBER	DESCRIPTION
0777	Allows the owner, group, and public to read, write, and execute the file.
0755	Lets the owner read, write, and execute the file; lets the group and public read and execute the file.
0711	Lets the owner read, write, and execute the file; allows the group and public to execute the file.
0644	Lets the owner read and write the file; lets the group and public read the file.

TABLE C.14: Symbolic Modes Used with chmod

SYMBOLIC MODE	DESCRIPTION
Select a Class of User	
u	Selects user or owner of a file.
g	Selects group to which the owner belongs.
o	Selects all other users.
a	Selects all users, which is the default. This option can be used in place of u, g, and o listed above.
Select an Operation	
+	Adds permission for the specified class of user.
-	Removes permission from the specified class of user.
=	Sets the permission for the specified user, and resets all other unspecified permissions for that user class.

TABLE C.14 continued: Symbolic Modes Used with chmod

Symbolic Mode	Description
Select an Access Permission	
r	Sets read permission.
w	Sets write permission.
x	Sets execute permission.
s	Sets user ID or group ID to that of the owner of the file while the file is being executed.
t	Sets the sticky bit; superuser only.

Examples

All three examples in this section assign read-only permission to everyone for the file myfile.doc:

```
chmod 444 myfile.doc
chmod =r myfile.doc
chmod a-wx,a+r myfile.doc
```

The symbolic mode is more useful when you want to tweak individual modes, while the absolute mode method is better if you want to set all permissions at the same time.

See also ls

chown

A command that changes the ownership of a file or files.

Syntax

The syntax for chown is:

```
chown [option] owner filename
```

Options and Arguments

The owner is the name or the numeric user ID of the new owner, and filename is a list of files whose ownership you want to change. Some systems are configured so that only the superuser can change file ownerships.

Examples

To change the ownership of the file myfile/chapter1.doc to that of Brenda, use:

```
chown brenda myfile/chapter1.doc
```

See also chgrp

chpass

A BSD command used to change user database information.

Syntax

Syntax for chpass is as follows:

```
chpass [-a list][-s newshell][username]
```

chpass allows you to edit information contained in the user database associated with your username; the information is formatted and supplied to vi for changes unless you specify a different editor.

Options and Arguments

Two options are available with chpass, as shown in Table C.15.

Possible display items are taken from the list in Table C.16.

See also finger, login, passwd

TABLE C.15: Options Available with chpass

Option	Description
-a *list*	As superuser, you can specify items directly to the database without using an editor. *list* must be a colon-separated list of all the user database fields, although some fields may be left empty.
-s *newshell*	Changes the user's shell to *newshell*.

TABLE C.16: Display Items for Use with chpass

Item	Description
Login:	User's login name.
Password:	User's login password in encrypted form.
Uid:	The number associated with the user's login field.
Gid:	The number associated with the user's login group.
Change:	The date by which the password must be changed.
Expire:	The date on which the account expires.
Class:	Unused.
Home Directory:	The absolute pathname where the user will be placed at login.
Shell:	The name of the user's shell; if this field is empty, the Bourne shell is assumed.
Full Name:	User's full name.
Location:	User's office location.
Home Phone:	User's home phone number.
Office Phone:	User's office phone number.

cksum

A BSD command that displays a file's checksum cyclic redundancy check, size of the file, and the filename.

Syntax
The syntax for cksum is:

```
cksum [-o[1|2]][filename ...]
```

where the -o option specifies that different checksum calculation be used rather than the default. Algorithm 1 is the algorithm traditionally used by BSD sum and by AT&T System V sum -r. Algorithm 2 is that used by the default sum algorithm.

clear

An SVR4 command that clears the terminal screen and leaves the prompt in the upper left corner of the screen. This command has no options.

click

A SunOS command used to control the keyboard click. click with no arguments turns off the key click. To turn it on again, use click -y.

cmchk

An SCO command that reports hard disk block size.

cmdedit

A special version of the C shell written by Digital Equipment Corporation (DEC), which includes command-line editing.

cmp

A command used to compare two files. cmp is often used to identify copies of files so that duplicates can be removed.

Syntax
The syntax for cmp is as follows:

```
cmp [options] file1 file2
```

cmp reports the first difference between file1 and file2 but reports nothing if the two files are identical.

If you replace file1 with a hyphen (-), cmp uses standard input instead.

Options and Arguments

The cmp options let you list differences between the files or suppress all output. This can be useful if you use cmp in a shell script in which you are interested only in the exit value returned by cmp rather than any other output. Options are listed in Table C.17. Bytes and line numbers are numbered beginning at 1.

TABLE C.17: Options to Use with cmp

Option	Description
-l	For each difference found, prints the byte number (in decimal) and the values of the differing bytes (in octal).
-s	Suppresses all output and works silently. This is the form to use in your shell scripts; returns the following exit codes: 0 files are identical; 1 files are different; 2 files are missing or inaccessible.

Examples

The two files brenda and brenda1 can be compared using:

```
cmp brenda brenda1
brenda brenda1 differ: char  20, line 1
```

This output shows that the first difference between the two files is at the 20th byte or character in the first line. If you are performing some file housekeeping, you can use the shell's && AND operator to delete a file once a comparison is complete:

```
cmp -s brenda brenda1 && rm brenda1
```

If cmp finds that the two files are identical, the rm command is used to delete the second file. If the two files are not identical, the && operator cannot pass control to the rm command. The -s options runs cmp in quiet mode.

See also comm, diff, diff3

cof2elf

An SVR4 command that converts one or more COFF files to ELF format, overwriting the originals in the process.

Syntax

The command-line syntax for cof2elf is:

```
cof2elf [options][filename]
```

Input files can be object files or archives.

Options and Arguments

You can use the options listed in Table C.18 with `cof2elf`.

TABLE C.18: Options for Use with cof2elf

Option	Description
-i	Ignores any unrecognized data, and continues with the conversion.
-q	Runs in quiet mode; suppresses all output.
-Qc	Prints information when *c* is set to y, and prints nothing when *c* is set to n, the default.
-s*dir*	Saves the original file into the existing directory specified by *dir*.
-V	Prints the version number of cof2elf on standard error.

COFF

Abbreviation for common object file format. A revision to the format of executable and object files to provide support for dynamically linked libraries. The COFF definition was replaced by the Executable and Link Format (ELF) in System V Release 4.

col

A command that filters out reverse linefeeds and escape characters so that output from `nroff` and `tbl` can be shown on the screen; these characters cannot be displayed on an ordinary terminal or printer.

Syntax

The syntax to use with `col` is straightforward:

```
col [options]
```

`col` reads from the standard input and writes to the standard output; this means that you use redirection to examine a file or create a new output file.

Options and Arguments

The options listed in Table C.19 are available when using `col`.

TABLE C.19: Options for Use with col

Option	Description
-b	Ignores backspace characters; useful when printing man pages.
-f	Print forward half linefeeds on the following line.
-l*number*	In BSD, buffers *number* of lines in memory; the default is to buffer 128 lines.

TABLE C.19 continued: Options for Use with col

OPTION	DESCRIPTION
-p	In SVR4, prints any unknown escape characters as regular characters; this can garble the output and is not usually recommended.
-x	Replaces tabs with spaces.

Examples
To display a file on your terminal that contains reverse linefeeds, use:

```
col < document1
```

If you then decide you want to print this file, pipe the output from col to your printer like this:

```
col < document1 | lp
```

See also colcrt, expand, nroff, tbl

colcrt

A BSD command that filters out reverse linefeeds and underline characters so that output from nroff and tbl can be shown on the screen. These characters cannot usually be displayed on an ordinary terminal or printer.

Syntax
Syntax for use with colcrt is:

```
colcrt [-][-2][filename...]
```

Half linefeeds and underlines are placed on new lines, and underlines are converted to hyphens.

Options and Arguments
Two options are available for use with colcrt, and they are shown in Table C.20.

TABLE C.20: Options for Use with colcrt

OPTION	DESCRIPTION
-	Suppresses all underlining; this can be useful when looking at output from tbl.
-2	Prints all half lines, effectively double-spacing the screen output.

Examples

`colcrt` reads from standard in and writes to standard out, so you can use input redirection or pipes to control the input and output to this command. For example, to pipe output from an `nroff` file called `jenny.doc` to the screen, you can use:

```
nroff jenny.doc|colcrt| more
```

The `more` filter sends output to the screen one page at a time.

See also `col`, `nroff`, `tbl`, `troff`, `ul`

colon

The null shell command; sometimes used as the first character in a file to signify a Bourne shell script. In the Korn shell, you can place shell variables after the : to expand them to their values.

colrm

A BSD command that removes specified columns from the lines in a text file.

Syntax

The syntax to use with `colrm` is:

```
colrm [start[stop]]
```

`colrm` reads from the standard input and writes to the standard output, so you can use pipes or input redirection with this command.

Options and Arguments

A column is defined as a single character in a file, and columns can be removed beginning with `start` and continuing as far as `stop`.

Columns are numbered from 1, not from 0, and a tab character increments the counter to the next multiple of eight, while a backspace character decreases the count by one.

Examples

To extract all the characters from the file `tyler.doc` between columns 10 and 30 and then display these characters on the screen page by page, use:

```
colrm 10 30 tyler.doc | more
```

See also `cat`, `less`, `more`, `pg`

column

A BSD command that forms its input into multiple columns.

Syntax

The syntax to use with `column` is:

```
column [-tx][-c columns][-s sep][filename...]
```

Input comes from `filename` or from standard input, and empty lines are ignored.

Options and Arguments

The `column` options are shown in Table C.21.

TABLE C.21: Options for Use with column

OPTION	DESCRIPTION
-c	Formats output in a display *columns* wide.
-s	Specifies a set of characters to be used as delimiters with the -t option.
-t	Creates a table from the input.
-x	Fills columns before filling rows.

Examples

To form a small table from the output of the `ls` command, use:

```
ls -l | column -t
```

See also `colrm`, `paste`

comm

A command that finds common lines in sorted files.

Syntax

The syntax to use with this command is:

```
comm [options]file1 file2
```

`comm` creates a three-column output, consisting of lines unique to `file1`, lines unique to `file2`, and lines that are common to both files. Lines in the second column are preceded by a tab character, while lines in the third column are preceded by two tabs.

Options and Arguments

`comm` compares `file1` and `file2`; you can use a hypen in place of either one (but not both) to make `comm` use standard input instead.

The options available with `comm` are listed in Table C.22.

TABLE C.22: Options for Use with comm

Option	Description
-1	Suppresses display of column 1; suppresses the lines it finds only in *file1*.
-2	Suppresses display of column 2; suppresses the lines it finds only in *file2*.
-3	Suppresses display of column 3; suppresses the lines it finds in both files.
-12	Displays only the lines common to both files; column 3.
-13	Displays only the lines unique to *file2*; column 2.
-23	Displays only the lines unique to *file1*; column 1.

Examples

If you want to extract the lines common to both files and store the results in a third file called newlist, use:

```
comm -12 list.one list.two > newlist
```

See also cmp, diff, diff3, dircmp, sdiff, sort, uniq

command directories

That collection of directories in Unix that contain commands, including /bin, /usr/bin, /etc, and /usr/lib. You may also find that other directories are specifically configured for your system by your system administrator.

command file

An ordinary text file containing a list of executable commands, usually shell commands. Also known as a *shell program* or, more commonly, a *shell script*. These files exist throughout the Unix system and are responsible for many of the system functions.

command line

The commands you enter at the shell command prompt; a line of instructions and related command-line arguments used to execute a shell command or Unix utility. In Unix, a command line may have more than one command joined by operators such as semicolons (;), pipes (|), or ampersands (&).

Usually, the elements found on the command line are the command name, followed by any appropriate command-line arguments you want to use with the command. You can also use options, usually preceded by a hyphen, to modify the operation of the command itself.

In the vi editor, the command line is the bottom line of the screen, where certain commands are echoed as you type them.

command-line argument

When you type a command at a shell prompt, the first word you type is the name of the command; anything that follows is considered to be an argument to that command.

Arguments provide more information to the command and are often filenames, directory names, options, or parameters. Options come right after the command name and consist of a hyphen (-) and one or more letters, while parameters follow the command name and provide additional information to the command.

command mode

A mode in many applications that allows you to enter commands. In the vi editor, command mode interprets anything you type as a command to act upon the text rather than new text to be added to the buffer.

See also input mode

command substitution

A feature of the shell in which the output of one command is passed to another command, which is then executed.

A command substitution is always enclosed in backquotes ('), and the shell replaces the command, and the backquotes, with the output from the command. Here is an example:

```
now = 'date'
```

In this example, the shell variable now is being set to a value. Without backquotes, now is set to the word date; with backquotes, now is set to the output of the date command—in other words, the actual calendar date.

Command substitution is often used within shell scripts. For example, you can add a timestamp to a specific operation such as backing up a file, as in this next example:

```
echo $0 utility used 'date' >> transaction.log
```

If this line is in a shell script called backit, the variable $0 contains the name of the shell script and so is set to backit. Then, the echo command creates the message:

```
backit utility used Wed May 8 1996 02:22:25 PST
```

and appends this message to the end of a file called transaction.log.

If you use the Korn shell, these examples will work, but you can use another syntax. Rather than enclosing the command in backquotes, you can use a dollar sign followed by the command in parentheses, as in this example:

```
print The time is $(date)
```

In the Korn shell, the `print` command usually replaces the `echo` command.

comment

Any part of a program or shell script that is intended to convey information to the user but should be ignored by the language compiler or interpreter. Comments are useful to annotate complex or seldom-used operations or to add other information of use to the user. In the C programming language, comments must be enclosed between /* */ pairs; in C++, comments start with //, and in the C shell, a comment must start with the pound sign (#).

compact

A BSD command used to compress files so that they occupy less hard disk space.

Syntax
The syntax to use with `compact` is:

```
compact [-v][filename...]
```

`compact` compresses the specified `filename` using adaptive Huffman coding; if no filenames are supplied, the standard input is compacted to the standard output. Files are compacted to a file called `filename.C`. Usually `compact` does its job in silence, but if you use the -v option, `compact` reports the compression percentage for each file. Typical compression values for text are 38 percent; Pascal source code, 43 percent; C source code, 36 percent; and binary files, 19 percent; however, the `compress` and `pack` commands can both achieve better compression ratios than this and take less time to compute.

See also `ccat`, `compress`, `gzip`, `pack`, `uncompact`, `uncompress`, `unpack`, `zcat`

compile

The process of converting a set of program language source code statements into a machine-readable form suitable for execution by a computer.

See also `compiler`

compiler

A program that converts a set of program language source code statements into a machine-readable form suitable for execution by a computer.

Most compilers do much more than this, however; they translate the entire program into machine language, while at the same time they check your source code syntax for errors and post messages or warnings as appropriate.

In the Unix world, the machine language output from the compiler is known as an *object file,* which must be linked with other files by the link editor before it can execute. The compiler usually invokes the link editor automatically.

See also C compiler, compile

compiler compiler

A program capable of transforming a tabular description of a compiler, including all the syntax rules, into an actual compiler. The Unix system's compiler compiler is called `yacc`, for "yet another compiler compiler."

compress

A command used to compress files so that they occupy less hard disk space.

Syntax
The syntax to use with `compress` is:

```
compress [options][filename...]
```

`compress` uses adaptive Lempel-Ziv coding to compress `filename` to `filename.Z`, but if compression would not decrease the size of `filename`, then `filename` is simply ignored.

Options and Arguments
Several options are available for use with `compress`, as Table C.23 shows. SVR4 and BSD provide a basic set of options, while other systems add more.

One of the options lets you force compression, so if you are creating an archive, you can use this option to be sure that all files in the archive are in the same format.

Compression ratios of up to 50 to 60 percent can be achieved when compressing text files or C source code files with `compress`. The `compress` utility consistently outperforms both the `pack` and `compact` commands in this respect.

TABLE C.23: Options for Use with compress

OPTION	DESCRIPTION
-b*n*	Limits the number of bits in coding to *n*, where *n* is between 9 and 16, with 16 as the default. Making *n* smaller produces a larger, less compact file.
-c	Writes compressed files to standard out, leaving the original files unchanged.
-d	On SCO and UnixWare, decompresses a compressed file.
-F	On SCO and UnixWare, forces compression of *filename* even if the size of the file won't be reduced.
-f	Forces compression of *filename* even if the size of the file won't be reduced, and overwrites files without prompting for confirmation.
-H	On SCO and UnixWare, uses a slightly different compression algorithm to achieve approximately 20 percent greater compression.
-P *fd*	On SCO and UnixWare, reads a list of filenames from a pipe associated with the file descriptor *fd*.
-q	On SCO and UnixWare, runs in quiet mode, suppressing all messages except error messages.
-v	Shows the percentage reduction for each *filename*.

Examples

To compress the file `lonestar.doc` and display the compression percentage, use the following command:

```
compress -v lonestar.doc
lonestar.doc: Compression: 52.44% - replaced with lonestar.Z
```

To compress all the files in the current directory, use:

```
compress *
```

See also ccat, compact, gzip, pack, uncompact, uncompress, unpack, zcat

concatenate

To combine two or more sets of characters or files into one single sequence. The cat program serves this function; it concatenates two or more input files. If you concatenate the character strings "Hello" and " world", the result is one string containing "Hello world".

See also catenate

/config

An SVR4 root file system directory that contains the files used to create a new operating system.

continue

▶ In the Bourne and Korn shells, the `continue` command resumes the next iteration of the loop containing the `continue` statement; this may be a `while`, `for`, or `until` statement.

▶ In the C shell, the `continue` statement resumes the next iteration only when used with the `while` and `foreach` statements.

control character

A nonprinting character with a special meaning. Control characters, such as carriage return, linefeed, and the bell, perform a specific operation on a terminal, printer, or communications line. Control characters are represented by the ASCII codes below 32 decimal.

You can type a control character from the keyboard by pressing and holding the Ctrl key while simultaneously pressing another key. For example, if you press and hold the Ctrl key and then press D, you create Ctrl-D, an end-of-file character used to tell a program that it has reached the end of its input. Control characters are sometimes represented by the caret symbol; you may find that Ctrl-D is written as ^D. By convention, control key combinations are always shown with capital letters as they are easier to read; compare Ctrl-L with Ctrl-l, for example.

See also `stty`. `copy`

copy

A SCO command used to copy the contents of one directory to another directory.

Syntax

The syntax for the `copy` command is as follows:

```
copy [options] source destination
```

Options and Arguments

`source` may be an existing file, a special file, or a directory, and `destination` must be a file-name or directory different from `source`. If the `destination` files or directories do not exist, they are created with the same owner and permissions as their source equivalents; if they already exist, the owner and permissions are not changed. You can use several options with `copy`; they are listed in Table C.24.

TABLE C.24: Options for Use with copy

Option	Description
-a	Asks permission before starting a copy. A response starting with y is assumed to be a yes; anything else is assumed to be no.
-ad	Asks you if the -r option applies (recursively copies directories) when copy encounters a directory; if the answer does not begin with y, the directory is ignored and not copied.
-l	Uses links when possible; otherwise, a copy is made. If links are possible, this makes for a very fast copy because no data is actually copied; this option cannot be used with directories.
-m	Sets modification time and access time to be same as the source. Without this option, modification time is set to the time of the copy.
-n	Creates a new destination file; if the destination file already exists, no copy is made. This option applies only to files, not to directories.
-o	Sets the owner and group to be the same as the source. Without this option, the owner is set to the user who invoked.
copy-r	Recursively examines directories as they are located, copying each file and directory as they are encountered. When this option is not set, directories are ignored.
-v	Verbose mode. When used with -a, messages are not displayed.

Examples

To copy all the files in the current directory to the /usr/recipe directory, use:

```
copy -v * /usr/recipe
```

If the current directory contains subdirectories you also want to copy, remember to use the -r option:

```
copy -r * /usr/recipe
```

See also cp

copyleft

The copyright statement or General Public License of the Free Software Foundation (FSF), which states that any of the software developed using free software from the FSF must be distributed to others without charge.

COSE

Acronym for Common Open Software Environment, pronounced "cosy." An industry group consisting of almost 100 members, organized to develop a standard graphical user interface (GUI) for Unix, known as the Common Desktop Environment, or CDE. Original members included Hewlett-Packard, IBM, SCO, Sun, and the UNIX Systems Group.

cp

A command used to copy one or more files to another file, a list of files, or a directory.

Syntax

There are two forms of the cp command:

```
cp [options] source destination
cp [options] source directory
```

In the first case, source is copied to destination, and in the second, the files contained in source are all copied to directory using the same names. If the destination is an existing file, the file is overwritten, so take care; if the destination is an existing directory, the file or files are copied into the directory. You cannot use the cp command to copy a file onto itself.

Options and Arguments

You can use several different options with cp, depending on the version of Unix you use. Table C.25 lists the options available with SVR4 and BSD.

TABLE C.25: Options Available with cp

Option	Description
-f	In BSD, forces cp to overwrite existing files without asking for confirmation, regardless of the existing permissions. This option also ignores the -i option, if specified.
-H	In BSD, when the -R option is specified, symbolic links are allowed on the command line.
-i	Asks for confirmation before overwriting an existing file.
-L	In BSD, when the -R option is specified, all symbolic links are followed.
-p	Preserves the modification time and as many of the file permissions as possible. Without this option, cp provides the permissions of the user who invoked cp.
-P	In BSD, when the -R option is specified, no symbolic links are followed.
-r	Copies directories, files, and subdirectories to *directory*.
-R	In BSD, if *source* is a directory, cp copies that directory and all subdirectories, duplicating the original form of the directory tree.

Examples

To copy one file to another, use:

```
cp lonestar texas
```

This command copies the contents of lonestar to texas. If texas does not exist, it is created; if it does exist, the original contents are overwritten and lost.

To copy complete directories, across different file-systems if necessary, use:

```
cp -pR /usr/tom /usr/peter
```

The -p option preserves the modification time and permissions of the original files, and the -R option makes cp copy symbolic links, block and character device files, as well as regular data files.

See also copy, ln, mv, rcp, rm

cpio

A command used to copy files and directories into and out of archive files; cpio is also useful when you want to move files around the filesystem.

Syntax

There are three major forms of syntax for cpio; they are as follows:

```
cpio -i [options][pattern]
```

The -i or copy in mode extracts specified files whose names match pattern from an archive of files and places the copies in the current directory. A pattern can include filename metacharacters and should be quoted or escaped so that they are interpreted by cpio rather than the shell. If you don't use a pattern, all files are copied in. During extraction, existing files are not overwritten by older versions in the archive, unless you use the -u option.

```
cpio -o [options]
```

The -o or copy out mode copies a specified list of files from a directory into an archive file.

```
cpio -p [options] directory
```

Finally, the -p or pass mode copies files from one directory tree to another without creating an archive.

Options and Arguments

The cpio command can use many different options in each of the three modes as Table C.26 illustrates; the hyphen in front of each option has been omitted from this table for the sake of clarity.

The options themselves are listed in Table C.27. Some of these options may be used in slightly different ways in different versions of cpio; check the man pages on your system for details.

TABLE C.26: Comparison of cpio Options

CPIO MODE	VALID OPTIONS
-i	6 b B c C d E f H I k m M r R s S t u v V ..
-o	a A B c C H L M O v V ..
-p	a d l L m R u v V ..

TABLE C.27: Options to Use with cpio

OPTION	DESCRIPTION
-a	Resets the access times of input files to those values before cpio was used; by default, the access times are updated. Appends files to an existing archive; must be used with –O.
-b	Swaps bytes and half-words; this option assumes 4-byte words.
-B	Uses 5120-byte blocks; used only with files representing character devices such as raw tape drives. The default is 512-byte blocks.
-c	Reads or writes header information as ASCII for increased portability between different systems.
-Cn	Specifies a block size of any positive integer, n, in multiples of 1024 bytes or 1 KB.
-d	Creates directories as needed; this is useful if you are copying a mixture of files and directories.
-E filename	Extracts the files listed in filename from an archive.
-f	Reverses the sense of the cpio syntax by copying all those files except those that match pattern.
-H format	Reads or writes header information according to format, which can be crc (ASCII header containing expanded device numbers), odc (ASCII header information containing small device numbers), ustar (IEEE/P1003 Data Interchange Standard header), or tar (tar header). Solaris adds another type, bar (bar header and format). Not available in SCO.
-I filename	Reads filename as input.
-k	Skips corrupted file headers, ignores input/output errors, and extracts as much good information as possible. You should use this option only when you know that an archive has been damaged by a disk or tape error and would otherwise be unreadable.
-Kvolume-size	Specifies volume-size as the size of the media volume; only available in SCO.
-l	Links files instead of copying them.
-L	Follows symbolic links.
-m	Keeps the previous file modification time; does not apply to directories.
-M message	Prints message when switching between media. You can use %d in your message to indicate the number of the next tape or disk. This option can be used only with –O and –I.
-O filename	Directs output to filename.

TABLE C.27 continued: Options to Use with cpio

OPTION	DESCRIPTION
-r	Allows you to rename files interactively. When cpio copies a file, it prompts you with the old filename and waits for you to enter a new one. If you press Enter (or Return), the file will be skipped. If you type a period (.), the original path and filename will be used.
-R ID	Reassigns file ownership and group information to the user's login ID; available to the superuser only.
-s	Swaps bytes within each half-word; assumes four bytes per word.
-S	Swaps half-words within each word; assumes four bytes per word.
-t	Prints a table of contents of the input but creates no files. When used with the –v option, this list includes file-access permissions, ownership, and access time, along with the name of each file. Looks like output from ls -l.
-u	Copies unconditionally and allows old files to overwrite newer ones with the same name; without this option, cpio does not overwrite these newer files.
-v	Prints a list of filenames.
-V	Indicates that cpio is working by printing a dot on the screen for every file read or written.
-6	Processes a file in the old Unix Sixth Edition archive file format. Not available in Solaris.

Examples

To copy all the files in the current working directory to the tape mounted on /dev/rmt/1, use:

```
ls | cpio -o > /dev/rmt/114 blocks
```

This command does not copy any subdirectories since ls does not list them. When cpio finishes, the number of 512-byte blocks used is displayed.

To restore all txt files from a tape archive and place them in the current directory on the hard disk, use:

```
cpio -iv "*.txt" </dev/rmt/1
```

The -v option tells cpio to list all the files as they are restored.

Notes

Archives created by cpio are not compatible with those made by tar or ar.

See also ar, find, ls, tar

cpp

A command used to invoke the GNU C compiler preprocessor; sometimes cccp is used instead. You automatically invoke the preprocessor as part of a C program compilation cycle, but there might be an occasion when it is appropriate to call the preprocessor individually. For a complete description of the GNU C preprocessor and the available options, see the file `cpp` `.info` or the manual *The C Preprocessor* created from the documentation source file called `cpp.texinfo`, which accompanied the preprocessor.

See also cc

CRC

Abbreviation for Cyclic Redundancy Check. A complex calculation method used to check the accuracy of a digital transmission over a communications link or to ensure the integrity of a file stored on disk.

The sending computer calculates a 1- or 2-byte CRC from the bits contained in the data, and this field is appended to the message before it is sent. The receiving computer performs the same calculation on the same data and compares this result with the received CRC. If the two CRCs do not match, indicating a transmission error, the receiving computer asks the sending computer to retransmit the data. This procedure is known as a redundancy check because each transmission includes extra or redundant error-checking values as well as the data itself.

As a security check, a CRC may be used to compare the current size of an executable file against the original size of the file to determine if the file has been tampered with or changed in some way.

See also Kermit, RZSZ

creation mask

A three-digit octal code that sets file-access permissions when a file is first created.

Use the `umask` command to set the file creation mask when you first create a file, or use the `chmod` command to change it later.

cron

A Unix background program or daemon that runs continuously, starting other programs at specified times. These programs are identified and scheduled by `crontab`.

`cron` is normally started automatically, so you never have to type this command.

crontab

A utility that specifies jobs to be run at regularly scheduled times.

Syntax

The syntax for `crontab` takes two forms as follows:

```
crontab [filename]
crontab [options][username]
```

`crontab` lets you specify a list of jobs that the system will run for you at the times you choose. This information is stored in a file known as a `crontab` file; the system daemon `cron` reads this file and executes the commands it contains at the appropriate times.

Options and Arguments

In the first line of syntax shown above, `filename` is the name of a `crontab` file; if you don't specify a filename, you can enter commands at the command prompt, terminating them with Ctrl-D.

Each `crontab` entry starts with five fields that specify the time when the command should run, followed by the command itself. An entry must be in the form:

```
M H D m d command
```

where:

M	Minute, from 0 to 59
H	Hour, from 0 to 23
D	Day of the month, from 1 to 31
m	Month, from 1 to 12
d	Day of the week, starting with 0 for Sunday
command	The command you want to execute at the specified time

If you place an asterisk (*) in one of these fields instead of a number, `crontab` interprets that as a wildcard for all possible values. Use a comma to separate multiple values and a hyphen to indicate a range; you can also include comments by preceding them with the pound (#) character.

In the second line of example syntax, `username` can be specified only by the superuser to change the contents of a specific user's `crontab` file.

Table C.28 lists the options available with `crontab`.

TABLE C.28: Options to Use with crontab

Option	Description
-e	Opens an editor on your crontab file so you can create, add, delete, or change entries.
-l	Lists the contents of your crontab file.
-r	Removes your crontab file.

Examples

To set up your crontab file, use:

```
crontab mytodo_file
```

With this command you copy the contents of the mytodo_file into your crontab file; you can have only one crontab file at a time.

Notes

On some systems, not all users can use crontab. The cron.allow file in the /etc/cron.d directory (or /usr/lib/cron on some systems) lists the login names of users who can use crontab, and a file called cron.deny lists those users not allowed to use crontab.

See also at, batch

crypt

A utility used to encrypt and decrypt a file.

Syntax

The syntax for crypt is as follows:

```
crypt [password]
```

crypt uses the same password to encrypt and decrypt a file; if you don't provide a password, crypt asks you to supply one. crypt uses a one-rotor encryption machine similar to the German Enigma but with a 256-element rotor.

Examples

crypt reads from the standard input and writes to standard output, so you must use redirection, as in this example of file encryption:

```
crypt megalith < secrets.txt > secrets.enc
```

which uses the password megalith to encrypt the file secrets.txt; the encrypted file is named secrets.enc.

Notes

Although this utility is documented in many Unix systems, it is available only in the United States due to export restrictions. crypt generates files compatible with the Unix editors ed, edit, ex, and vi when in encryption mode.

See also bdes, DES

cscope

An SVR4 interactive utility that builds a symbol cross-reference from one or more C, lex, or yacc source files and then lets you search for functions, macros, variables, and so on.

csh

A command used to invoke the C shell or interactive command interpreter.

Syntax

The syntax to use with csh is:

```
csh [options][arguments]
```

csh uses syntax that resembles the *C* programming language and can execute commands from the keyboard or from a file.

Options and Arguments

The C shell is usually available on all Unix systems; you may find some small differences in options between these different systems, but in general, usage is very consistent.

Table C.29 lists the options available with csh.

TABLE C.29: Options Available with csh, the C Shell

OPTION	DESCRIPTION
-b	Allows the remaining command-line options to be interpreted as options to a command, rather than as options to csh. Not available in SCO.
-c	Executes commands or scripts contained in the first *filename* argument.
-e	Exits the shell if a command produces an error or a non-zero exit status.
-f	Starts csh without searching for or executing commands found in the file .cshrc or .login.
-i	Invokes interactive shell.
-l	Makes the shell a login shell when only the -l option is specified. Available in BSD only.
-n	Parses and checks commands, but does not execute them. You can use this mode to check your shell scripts.
-s	Reads commands from standard input.

TABLE C.29 continued: Options Available with csh, the C Shell

Option	Description
-t	Exits from csh after executing just one command; you can use a \ to escape the newline at the end of this line and continue on to the next.
-v	Sets verbose mode, which displays commands before executing them.
-V	Same as -v, but sets verbose mode before executing .cshrc. This means that the contents of .cshrc are displayed.
-x	Displays commands before executing them, and expands all substitutions; often used with -v. This option has the same effect as setting the C shell echo variable.
-X	Same as -x, but sets the mode before executing .cshrc. This means that the contents of .cshrc are displayed.

Examples

If you want to launch a new shell temporarily, use:

    csh

This command works no matter which shell you were using. When you exit from the C shell, you are returned to your previous working environment.

To execute a command or shell script contained in a file, use:

    csh -c mystuff.txt

This is a good way of ensuring that a C shell script is executed properly.

See also **Bourne shell, C shell, Korn shell,** ksh, sh

C shell

Pronounced "sea shell." The C shell has been the favorite shell of many users since it was developed by Bill Joy at the University of California at Berkeley between 1979 and 1981 as part of the BSD development and an alternative to the Bourne shell. It was first included in standard System V with SVR4, although several manufacturers included it in their earlier implementations, and is the standard shell on many Unix systems, particularly those derived from BSD.

The C shell offers the following features, which are also found in the Bourne shell:

► Input and output redirection

► Wildcard or metacharacters for filename abbreviation

► A set of shell variables to customize your environment

The C shell adds the following new features:

► Integer arithmetic

- ▶ A history mechanism allowing you to recall previous commands in whole or in part
- ▶ Aliasing for abbreviating frequently used commands without using a shell script
- ▶ More flexible forms of command substitution
- ▶ Job control—the ability to switch between several processes and control their progress
- ▶ A built-in set of operators based on the C programming language for writing shell scripts

Startup Files

The C shell program, started by the `csh` command, first executes the statements in the file `.cshrc` in your home directory; if you invoked `csh` as your login shell, the C shell then executes the contents of `.login` and also executes the commands contained in `.logout` when it terminates. Every time you start a new shell or run a shell script, the commands in `.cshrc` are executed; the commands in `.login` are executed only once, when you log in.

The normal prompt in the C shell is the percent symbol (%), and you can use `exit` or `logout` at any prompt to leave the C shell.

Using Commands

The C shell allows you to use and group commands on the command-line in several ways. Table C.30 lists the ways you can use C shell commands.

TABLE C.30: Using C Shell Commands

COMMAND	DESCRIPTION
cmd &	Executes *cmd* in the background.
cmd1 ; cmd2	Executes *cmd1* and *cmd2* consecutively, with the semicolon acting as a command separator.
(cmd1 ; cmd2)	Creates a subshell to execute *cmd1* and *cmd2* as a group.
cmd1 | cmd2	Creates a pipe and uses the output from *cmd1* as input to *cmd2*.
cmd1 'cmd2'	Performs command substitution; uses the output from *cmd2* as arguments to *cmd1*.
cmd1 && cmd2	Executes *cmd1*, and if *cmd1* completes successfully, then executes *cmd2*.
cmd1 || cmd2	Executes either *cmd1*, or if it fails, executes *cmd2*.

Filename Metacharacters

You can use any of the patterns shown in Table C.31 to generate filenames.

You can also combine these metacharacters into more complex expressions.

TABLE C.31: C Shell Filename Metacharacters

META-CHARACTER	DESCRIPTION
`*`	Matches any string or zero or more characters; for example, `w*n` matches `wn`, `win`, won, `when`, worn, and many other filenames.
`?`	Matches any single character; for example, `myfile.?` matches `myfile._`, `myfile.1`, `myfile.a`, and so on.
`[abc...]`	Matches any single character from the list, and you can use a hyphen to indicate a range, as in `a-z`, `0-9`, and so on.
`~`	Current user's home directory.
`~ name`	Home directory for user *name*.

Redirection

When you execute a command, the shell opens three files known as the standard input, the standard output, and the standard error. By default, the standard input is the keyboard, and the standard output and standard error are the terminal or screen. Redirection is the process of directing input to or output from a file other than the default file.

In simple redirection, you can change the input source or output destination in any of the ways shown in Table C.32.

In more complex multiple redirection, you can use any of the ways shown in Table C.33.

TABLE C.32: Simple Redirection in the C Shell

COMMAND	DESCRIPTION
`cmd > filename`	Sends output from *cmd* to `filename`, overwriting the file if it already exists.
`cmd >! filename`	Same as above, even if the `noclobber` shell variable is set; see the section "Predefined Variables" for more information.
`cmd >> filename`	Adds or appends output from *cmd* to the end of `filename`.
`cmd >>! filename`	Same as above, even if the `noclobber` shell variable is set.
`cmd < filename`	Takes input for *cmd* from `filename`.
`cmd << text`	Reads standard input as far as a line identical to *text*.
`<&-`	Closes the standard input.
`>&-`	Closes the standard output.

TABLE C.33: Multiple Redirection in the C Shell

FILE DESCRIPTOR	DESCRIPTION
cmd >& filename	Sends both standard output and standard error to filename.
cmd >&! Filename	Same as above, even if noclobber is set.
cmd >>& filename	Appends both standard output and standard error to the end of filename.
cmd >>&! Filename	Same as above, but creates filename even if noclobber is set.
cmd1 |& cmd2	Pipes standard error together with standard output.
(cmd > filename1) >& filename2	Sends standard output to filename1 and standard error to filename2.
cmd	tee filename	Sends the output from cmd to standard output and to filename by creating a tee.

Quoting

Quoting disables the special meaning of a character, and allows you to use it literally. These characters, listed in Table C.34, have special meaning in the C shell.

Also, the newline, space, and tab are used as word separators.

TABLE C.34: Quoting in the C Shell

CHARACTER	DESCRIPTION
;	Separates commands
&	Runs commands in the background
( )	Groups commands
		Creates a pipe
*? [ ] ~	Filename metacharacters
{ }	String expansion characters; they don't usually require quoting.
< > & !	Redirection symbols
! ^	Characters used for history substitution and quick substitution
" " ' ' \	Used when quoting other characters. Anything placed between double quotes is interpreted symbolically; anything placed between single quotes is interpreted literally, and the backslash is used to quote a single character.
`	Command substitution
$	Variable substitution

Predefined Variables

The C shell includes a large set of predefined variables, as shown in Table C.35. You can set a variable in one of two ways:

```
set variable=value
```

or by simply turning them on:

```
set variable
```

The C shell automatically sets the `argv`, `cwd`, `home`, `path`, `prompt`, `shell`, `status`, `term`, and `user` variables.

TABLE C.35: C Shell Variables

VARIABLE	DESCRIPTION
0	The name of the current shell script.
?*variable*	Contains 1 if the *variable* is set; zero if it is not set.
$	Contains the PID of the current process.
argv=*arguments*	List of arguments passed to the current command.
cdpath=*directories*	Contains the list of directories to search when locating arguments for cd, popd, or pushd.
cwd=*directory*	Contains the complete pathname of the current directory.
Echo	Redisplays each command before executing it; same as using csh -x.
fignore=*characters*	Contains a list of filename suffixes to ignore during filename completion.
Filec	Enables filename completion, using two special key combinations: Ctrl-D displays filenames that begin with the string you just entered, and Esc replaces the string you just entered with the longest possible extension.
Hardpaths	Forces the dirs C shell command to display the actual pathnames of directories without their symbolic links.
Histchars=*ab*	Specifies the two-character string to use in history substitution (!) and quick substitution (^); this makes the default !^.
history=*n*	Specifies the number of commands you want to save in the history list—typically between 100 and 200.
home=*directory*	Contains the name of your home directory, initialized from the environment variable HOME; the ~ character is shorthand for this directory.
Ignoreeof	Ignores end-of-file (EOF) Ctrl-D characters when typed at the keyboard to avoid accidental logouts.
mail=*n filename*	Contains a list of mail files checked for new mail every five minutes; if the list begins with a number, this specifies a check every *n* seconds.
Nobeep	Turns off the ambiguous filename completion beep.
Noclobber	Does not allow redirection to an existing file; prevents accidental overwriting of files.
Noglob	Turns off filename expansion; this is sometimes a good idea in shell scripts.
Nonomatch	Treats filename metacharacters as normal characters, and does not generate an error if the filename expansion does not match anything.

TABLE C.35 continued: C Shell Variables

VARIABLE	DESCRIPTION
Notify	Forces the shell to tell you as soon as a job has completed, rather than waiting for the next prompt.
path=*directories*	Lists the pathnames to search for commands to execute prompt='*string*'.
savehist=*n*	Specifies the number of commands you want to save in the .history file when you log out; the higher this number gets, the longer the C shell takes to log you in next time.
shell=*filename*	Specifies the name of the shell you are currently using; the default is /bin/csh.
status=*n*	Contains the exit status of the last command; built-in commands return 0 indicating success or 1 indicating failure.
term=*ID*	Contains a terminal type, initialized to /etc/ttytype.
time='n %c'	If a command execution takes longer than *n* CPU seconds, reports user time, elapsed time, system time, and CPU percentage.
user=*name*	Contains your login name; initialized from USER.
verbose.	Displays commands after history substitution; same as invoking csh -v.

Environment Variables

The C shell also maintains a set of environment variables, which are distinct from shell variables and are not really part of the C shell. Shell variables only have meaning within the current shell, but environment variables are exported automatically, which means they act globally and can be accessed by mail systems, your favorite editor, and your shell scripts. Environment variables are listed in Table C.36.

In the cases where the shell variable and the environment variable have the same name (the shell variable in lowercase and the environment variable in uppercase letters), you can change the value of the shell variable and the appropriate environment variable value will also change automatically. This is a one-way street, however, changing the environment variable does not change the shell variable.

TABLE C.36: C Shell Environment Variables

VARIABLE	DESCRIPTION
EXINIT	Contains a string of startup commands for ex or vi; similar to .exrc.
HOME	Home directory, same as home.
LOGNAME	Contains your username; another name for the USER variable.
MAIL	Specifies the file that holds mail; this is not the same as the C shell mail variable, which only checks for mail.

TABLE C.36 continued: C Shell Environment Variables

VARIABLE	DESCRIPTION
PATH	Contains the search path used when executing commands.
PWD	Contains the name of the current directory; initialized from cwd.
SHELL	Contains the pathname of the shell in current use.
TERM	Contains your terminal type; same as term.
TERMCAP	Contains the filename that holds the cursor-positioning codes for use with your terminal.
USER	Contains your username, same as user.

Built-in Commands

The C shell offers a rich set of built-in commands, as shown in Table C.37. Built-in shell commands are executed as part of the current shell process; there is no need to fork or spawn a new process to execute them.

The C shell is a huge, complex topic and has been the subject of many excellent books and articles over the years. To make sure you get the best out of the C shell, consult the reference material that comes with your system, or seek out a book that deals exclusively with csh.

See also **Bash, Bourne shell, Bourne shell family,** csh**, Korn shell,** ksh, sh**, Tcsh, Zsh**

TABLE C.37: Built-in C Shell Commands

OPTION	DESCRIPTION
#	The comment character in a C shell script; any script that begins with this character is interpreted as a C shell script.
#!*shell*	Often used as the first line in a shell script to invoke the named *shell*.
:	Null command; returns an exit status of zero.
@ *variable = expression*	Assigns the value of *variable* to *expression*; if none is specified, prints the values of all the shell variables
alias [*name*[*command*]]	Assigns *name* as the shorthand name for *command*.
Alloc	Displays a report on the amount of used and free memory.
bg [*jobIDs*]	Places the current or the specified job in the background.
break	Skips to the next end command from the enclosing while or foreach statement.
breaksw	Breaks from a switch statement, and continues execution after the endsw statement.
case [*pattern*]	Identifies a *pattern* in a switch statement.

TABLE C.37 continued: Built-in C Shell Commands

OPTION	DESCRIPTION
cd [*directory*]	Changes to the specified directory; the default directory is your home directory.
chdir	Same as cd.
continue	Resumes execution of the enclosing while or foreach statement.
default:	Labels the default case, usually the final case in a switch statement.
dirs [-1]	Prints the directory stack, with the current directory first; use -1 to expand the ~ symbol to the complete home directory name.
echo [-n] *string*	Writes the specified *string* to the standard output; specify -n to remove the newline character from the end of the *string*. This command, unlike the Unix and the Bourne shell echo, does not accept escape sequences.
end	Terminates a foreach or while statement.
endif	Terminates an if statement.
eval *arguments*	Scans and evaluates the command-line; often used in shell scripts.
exec *command*	Executes *command* in the place of the current shell, terminating the current shell, rather than creating a new process.
exit [*expr*]	Exits a shell script with the status provided by *expr*.
fg [*jobIDs*]	Moves the current or specified job into the foreground.
foreach *name* (*wordlist*) commands	Assigns *name* to each value in *wordlist*, and executes the *commands*.
glob *wordlist*	Similar to echo, but does not display spaces between its arguments and does not place a newline at the end.
goto *string*	Skips to the line labeled *string* followed by a colon, and continues execution there.
hashstat	Displays statistics on the C shell's hash mechanism; hash speeds up the process of searching through the directories in your search path.
history [*options*]	Displays the history list of commands. Options are listed in Table C.38.
if	Begins a conditional statement.
jobs [-1]	Lists all running or stopped jobs; use the -1 option to display PIDs.
kill [*options*] *ID*	Terminates the specified process; use the -1 option to list all the signal names, and use -*signal* for the signal number or name.
limit [-h][*resource* [*limit*]]	Limits the number of resources that can be used by the current process and by any processes it creates. By default, the current limits are listed; use the -h option to set a hard limit.
login [*user*| -p]	Logs in a user; -p preserves the environment variables.
nice[+/-n]*commands*	Changes the execution priority for *command*, or if no parameters are given, changes the priority of the current shell. This is a useful command if you want to run a job that makes large demands on the system, but you can wait a while for the final output. Priority range for *n* is from +20 to -20, with a default of 4; -20 gives the highest priority.

TABLE C.37 continued: Built-in C Shell Commands

OPTION	DESCRIPTION
nohup [*command*]	Lets you log off without terminating background processes; some systems are set up to do this automatically.
notify [*jobID*]	Reports any change in job status to you immediately.
popd [*+n*]	Removes a directory from the directory stack, or removes the *n*th entry.
pushd [*name*]	Changes the working directory to *name* and adds it to the directory stack.
rehash	Forces the shell to recreate its internal hash tables. You should always use rehash if you add or create a new command during the current session; otherwise, the shell may not be able to find it.
repeat *n command*	Executes the *command n* times.
set	Sets, initializes, and displays the values of local variables.
setenv [*name*[*value*]]	Sets, initializes, and displays the values of environment variables; assigns the *value* to the variable *name*.
shift [*variable*]	When *variable* is specified, shifts the elements in an array; without *variable*, shifts the command-line arguments. Often used in a while loop.
source [-h] *script*	Reads and executes the commands in a C shell *script*; with -h, the commands are added to the history list but are not executed.
stop [*jobIDs*]	Stops the specified background job.
suspend	Suspends the current foreground job.
switch	Runs specified commands depending on the value of a variable, which is useful when you have to manage more than three choices.
time *command*	Executes the specified *command*, and displays how much time it uses.
umask [*nnn*]	Displays the file creation mask, or sets the file creation mask to the octal number *nnn*.
unalias *name*	Removes *name* from the alias list.
unhash	Turns off the hash mechanism.
unlimit [*resources*]	Removes the imposed limits on *resources*.
unset *variables*	Removes a variable declaration.
unsetenv *variable*	Removes an environment variable.
Wait	Makes the shell wait for all child processes to complete.
while (*expression*) commands	As long as *expression* is true, executes *commands*.

TABLE C.38: Options to Use with the history C Shell Command

Option	Description
-h	Prints history list without event numbers.
-r	Prints history list in reverse order.
n	Prints the last *n* history commands, rather than the number specified by the history variable.

.cshrc

A file in your home directory that the C shell reads and executes each time you invoke a new copy of the C shell. You can customize your environment by setting variables and aliases that you define in this file.

csplit

A utility used to separate a file into smaller pieces, breaking each file at a point specified by the user.

Syntax

The syntax used with csplit is as follows:

    csplit [options] filename arguments

This utility splits a named file into smaller files called **xx00** *through* **xxnnn**, *where* nnn is less than 100, breaking the original file at locations specified by arguments.

Options and Arguments

arguments can be any one or any combination of those listed in Table C.39.

Several options are also available for use with csplit; see Table C.40 for details.

TABLE C.39: Arguments for Use with csplit

Argument	Description
/expression/	Creates a file f to the line containing the regular expression *expression*. You can also use an optional suffix +*n* or -*n*, where *n* specifies a number of lines above or below *expression*.
%expression	Same as the previous argument, except that no file is created for lines before the line containing *expression*.
number	Creates a file from the current line up to the line number specified by *number*.
{n}	Repeats any of the above arguments *n* times.

TABLE C.40: Options for Use with csplit

Option	Description
-f *filename*	Names the new files *filename*00 through *filename*nnn (where *nnn* must be less than 100) rather than using the default filenames.
-k	Keeps any newly created files, even in the case of an error that would normally cause them to be destroyed.
-s	Suppresses all character counts.

Examples

To divide a file into sections, each 200 lines long, use:

```
csplit myreport 200 {50}
```

The argument 200 specifies each file will be 200 lines in length, while the {50} repeats this argument 50 times. Any lines remaining will appear in the last file.

See also split

ct

A SCO utility that dials a phone number and issues a login prompt on a terminal accessed by modems and a telephone line.

Syntax

The syntax for ct is as follows:

```
ct [options] number
```

ct actually works by spawning a getty to a remote terminal.

Options and Arguments

You can use the following to specify the telephone number number to use; 0–9, - (one-second delays), = (secondary dial tones), *, and #. There are several important communications parameters you must set using the options listed in Table C.41 before you can use ct.

TABLE C.41: Communications Options for Use with ct

Option	Description
-h	Prevents a hangup.
-s*speed*	Sets the modem baud rate; the default is 1200.
-v	Sends comments and error messages to standard error; useful for debugging difficult or new connections.

TABLE C.41 continued: Communications Options for Use with ct

OPTION	DESCRIPTION
-w*minutes*	Specifies the number of minutes to wait for a dial tone before hanging up.
-x*n*	Sends a detailed copy of program comments and error messages to standard error; useful for debugging difficult or new connections.

Examples

To dial out on a 9600-baud modem to the number 111-1212, waiting one minute for a dial tone, use:

```
ct -s9600 -w1 111-1212
```

See also cu, stty, uucp

ctags

A Unix software development command that creates a list of macro and function names from the specified C, Pascal, Fortran, yacc, or lex source file. This list contains three sets of entries: name, which represents the macro or function name, filename, which represents the name of the source file containing name, and context, which shows the line of code containing name.

ctrace

A Unix software development command used to debug a C language program. This command reads the C source file and sends a modified version (depending on the options you choose) to standard output.

Ctrl-\

The control character used as the quit key. This key combination sends a quit signal to your program to halt it immediately and also generates a core dump of memory at that instant. Mostly used by programmers testing software, Ctrl-\ is not intended for casual use.

Ctrl-C

The default control character used to interrupt a running program; on some systems, you can use Del or Delete instead. Also known as the *break key*.

Ctrl-D

The default control character used to indicate an end-of-file character. Control-C is used to tell a program that it has come to the end of its input. You can also use Ctrl-D in response to a Bourne or Korn shell prompt to log out from your system.

Ctrl-H

The default control character used on some systems to indicate back-space or erase. On Sun systems, use the Delete key (the one on top).

Ctrl key

A key on the keyboard that, when pressed in conjunction with another key, generates a nonprinting control character. On some keyboards, the key is labeled Control rather than Ctrl; both perform the same function.

See also stty

Ctrl-L

The default control character used to redraw the screen in vi and other full-screen display applications.

Ctrl-Q

The control character used to restart screen output after it has been paused temporarily.

See also Ctrl-S

Ctrl-R

An alternative control character used to redraw the screen in vi.

See also Ctrl-L

Ctrl-S

The control character used to pause screen output temporarily.

See also Ctrl-Q

Ctrl-U

The control character used to erase the entire line of input. On some systems, Ctrl-X performs this function.

Ctrl-W

The control character used to erase the last word you typed from the input.

Ctrl-X

The control character used to erase the entire line of input. On some systems, Ctrl-U performs this function.

Ctrl-Z

The control character used to suspend, but not kill, the currently active process.

cu

A command used to call up a remote Unix system or terminal using a direct line or a modem.

Syntax

The syntax for cu is:

```
cu [options][destination]
```

cu connects you to a remote system. Since you have to log in to be able to use the system, it makes sense to use cu to call systems on which you have an account.

The cu command actually runs as two separate processes; a transmit process reads lines from your keyboard (standard input) and transmits them to the remote system; any lines that begin with a tilde (˜) are treated as local commands rather than information that should be transmitted to the remote system. A receive process takes input from the remote system and passes it to your screen (standard output). These tilde commands are listed in Table C.42.

TABLE C.42: Tilde Commands Used with cu

Command	Description
˜.	Terminates the connection.
˜!	Escapes to the shell on the local system.
˜!command	Runs command on the local system.
˜$command	Runs command on the local system, and sends output to the remote system as a command to be run there.

TABLE C.42 continued: Tilde Commands Used with cu

Command	Description
~+*command*	Runs *command* on the local system, but takes input from the remote system. Available on SCO only.
~%cd	Changes directory on the local system.
~%take *filename* [*target*]	Copies *filename* from the remote system to *target* on the local system. If you omit *target*, *filename* is used, or in other words, the new file will have the same name as the original.
~%put *filename* [*target*]	Copies *filename* from the local system to *target* on the remote system. If you omit *target*, *filename* is used, or in other words, the new file will have the same name as the original.
~~*line*	Allows you to pass a *line* that begins with a tilde to a remote system, so that you can issue commands to more than one system in a chain; you need to enter a tilde for every system you want the command to pass through.
~%b	Sends a Break sequence to the remote system. This command may appear as ~%break on some systems.
~%d	Toggles debug mode on or off.
~t	Prints information for the local terminal.
~l	Prints information about the communications line.
~%ifc	Toggles between XON/XOFF flow control and no flow control.
~%ofc	Toggles output flow control.
~%divert	Toggles diversions not specified by ~%take.
~%old	Toggles old-style syntax for diversions received.
~%nostop	Toggles between XON/XOFF flow control and no flow control.

Options and Arguments

The arguments for cu are listed in Table C.43.

There are several options you can use with cu, as shown in Table C.44.

TABLE C.43: Arguments Used with cu

Argument	Description
number	The telephone number of the modem you want to connect to.
system	The name of the system to call.
address	The address of the system to call.

TABLE C.44: Options for Use with cu

OPTION	DESCRIPTION
-b*n*	Sets the character size in bits, where *n* is either 7 or 8.
-c*name*	Searches UUCP's devices file for a system called *name*.
-d	Prints diagnostics.
-e	Uses even parity; this option is the opposite of -o.
-h	Emulates a local echo to support connections to remote systems that expect to see half-duplex terminals.
-l*device*	Communicates using *device*, e.g., /dev/tty002; not used when *destination* is set to *address*.
-n	Prompts you to enter a phone number to call.
-o	Uses odd parity; this option is the opposite of -e.
-s*number*	Sets the transmission rate to *number*; not used when *destination* is set to *address*.
T	Dials an ASCII terminal that has auto-answer set. Carriage return is mapped to carriage return/linefeed. Used only when *destination* is set to *number*.

Examples
To connect to the system called sausage, use:

```
cu sausage
```

To connect to the phone number 111-1212 at 9600 baud, use:

```
cu -s9600 111-1212
```

See also anonymous ftp, ftp, telnet, tn3270, uucp, uux

curses

A C library of screen-handling routines written by Mark Horton, which allows you to control the location of the cursor on the screen. curses can interact with either SVR4's termcap or BSD's terminfo files so that the software can run on any terminal, even creating windows on simple ASCII terminals.

cut

A command that extracts a list of columns or fields from one or more files.

Syntax
The syntax for cut is:

```
cut options [filename]
```

You can use cut to print certain columns from a table or to select certain fields from a data file. Fields may be defined by specific integer character positions, or relatively by using a comma as a field separator, or by using a hyphen to specify a range. You can also combine all three methods if you wish. The notation 23- specifies from column 23 to the end of the line.

Options and Arguments

Several options are available for use with cut; see Table C.45. However, you must specify either -c or -f, as they are mutually exclusive.

TABLE C.45: Options for Use with cut

Option	Description
-c*list*	Cuts the column positions specified by *list*.
-d*char*	Specifies the field separator character as *char*; use with the -f option. The default is a tab; if you plan to use a special character such as a space, make sure that it is quoted.
-f*list*	Cuts the fields specified in *list*.
-s	Suppresses lines without delimiters; use with the -f option.

Examples

To extract the user ID and names from the password file, use:

```
cut -f1,5 -d: /etc/passwd
```

The /etc/passwd file uses a colon to separate fields, and the -d: option makes the colon the field delimiter.

See also join, newform, paste

cut

To remove a marked portion of a document into a temporary storage area. This material can then be pasted into a different place in the original document or even into an entirely different document. Cutting moves the marked text, it does not copy the marked text.

See also cut-and-paste

cut-and-paste

To remove a marked portion of a document into temporary storage and then insert it into either a different document or a new place in the original document.

Cut-and-paste allows compatible application programs to share text and graphics.

See also cut

cxref

A Unix software development command that builds a cross-reference table for each C language source code file. The table lists all symbols, giving the name, associated function, filename, and line number.

cyclic redundancy check

See CRC

D

daemon

Pronounced "dee-mon," or "day-mon." A Unix program that runs unattended and is usually invisible to the user, providing important system services.

Daemons manage all sorts of tasks, including mail management, networking, Internet services, ftp sessions, and NFS services. Some daemons are triggered automatically by events to perform their work; others operate at set time intervals. Because they spend most of their time inactive, waiting for something to do, daemons do not consume large amounts of system resources. Table D.1 lists some of the common daemons and their areas of responsibility, although some of their names may differ on different versions of Unix.

See also cron, init, kernel

TABLE D.1: Common Unix Daemons

DAEMON	DESCRIPTION
ftpd	File transfer protocol daemon
inetd	Internet daemon
lockd	Network lock daemon
lpd	Line Printer daemon
named	Internet domain name server daemon

TABLE D.1 continued: Common Unix Daemons

DAEMON	DESCRIPTION
nfsd	NFS daemon
pppd	Point-to-point protocol daemon
uucpd	UUCP daemon

DARPA

Abbreviation for Defense Advanced Research Projects Agency, a U.S. military research funding agency that funded the ARPANET, the predecessor to the Internet.

date

A command that displays the system time and date. Only the superuser can use it to change the date.

Syntax

The syntax for date is:

```
date [options][+format]
date [options] string
```

When used without arguments, date displays the current system time and date in the form:

```
Sat Oct 30 16:18:20 PDT 1999
```

Options and Arguments

When the superuser specifies a new date in the form of string, it must have the following form:

```
nnddhhmm[cc[yy]]
```

where nn is the number of the month (from 1 to 12), dd is the day of the month (from 1 to 31), hh is the hour (from 00 to 23), and mm is the minutes (from 00 to 59). The final four digits are optional and are only used when changing the year; cc specifies the first two digits of the year and yy the last two.

If you specify +format, a string normally enclosed in single quotes, you can specify the format of date output by using field descriptors preceded by percent signs. Anything in the string that is not a field descriptor or a percent sign is copied directly to the output. You can use this feature to add text or punctuation to the date. Table D.2 lists some of the common field descriptors used with `date`.

The options for use with `date` are shown in Table D.3.

TABLE D.2: Common date Field Descriptors

FIELD DESCRIPTOR	DESCRIPTION
%a	The abbreviated weekday name, Sun to Sat
%A	The full weekday name, Sunday to Saturday
%b	The abbreviated month name, Jan to Dec
%B	The full month name, January to December
%c	The time and date representation
%C	The century
%d	Day of the month, 01 to 31
%D	Date in mm/dd/ty format
%h	The abbreviated month name, Jan to Dec; same as %b
%H	Hour in 24-hour format, 00 to 23
%I	Hour in 12-hour format, 01 to 12
%j	Julian day of the year, 001 to 366
%m	Month of the year, 01 to 12
%M	Minutes, 00 to 59
%n	Inserts a newline character
%p	String to indicate a.m. or p.m.; the default is AM or PM
%r	Uses AM/PM notation, the default
%R	Time in HH:MM format
%S	Seconds, 00 to 61; 61 permits up to two leap seconds
%t	Inserts a tab character
%T	Time in HH:MM:SS format, 24-hour clock
%U	Week number, starting on Sunday, 0 to 53
%w	Day of the week, 0 (Sunday) to 6
%W	Week number, starting on Monday, 0 to 53
%x	Country-specific date format
%X	Same as %x
%y	Last two digits of the year, 00 to 99
%Y	Four-digit year
%Z	The time zone name

TABLE D.3: Options Used with date

Option	Description
-a s.f	Allows the superuser to adjust the current time by s seconds in increments of f fractional seconds; this lets the clock be adjusted slowly while the system is still running. By default, time increases; use -s.f to slow the clock down.
-r	In 4.4BSD, use this option to print time in elapsed seconds since the beginning of Unix time at 00:00:00 GMT, January 1st, 1970.
-u	Displays or sets time in GMT (Greenwich mean time).

Examples

To set the date to 3:46 p.m. on 30th October, 1996, use:

```
date 10301546
Wed Oct 30 15:46 PDT 1996
```

If you use the following command:

```
date '+%h %d, 19%y'
```

the date is displayed as:

```
Oct 30, 1996
```

See also time

dbx

A Solaris source code debugger for programs written in C, C++, Fortran, or Pascal. dbx offers a large number of commands which you can store in a file called .dbxinit in your home directory. This file is read and the commands executed just before the symbol table is read. See the dbx man pages for more information.

See also adb, sdb

dc

A command that starts an interactive desk calculator that uses reverse polish, or postfix, notation. You don't normally run dc directly because it is usually called automatically when you start bc.

Because dc uses reverse polish notation, you enter operators and commands after the numbers they apply to; if you are not comfortable in reverse polish, just use bc instead.

See also xcalc

dd

A command used to copy and convert files. dd is different from the normal Unix copy command cp in that dd can access the raw devices, such as floppy disks. You can also use dd to convert files from one format to another so that you can swap them between different computer systems.

Syntax
The syntax for dd is as follows:

```
dd [option=value]
```

You can use any number of options with dd, but if and of are two very common options and are often specified first; if lets you specify an input filename, of lets you specify the name of an output file.

Options and Arguments
All the options available with dd are listed in Table D.4.

You can multiply the size values indicated by n in Table D.4 by a factor of 2, 512, or 1024 by appending the letter w, b, or k. If you separate these arguments with an x indicating multiplication, the product of the numbers is used as the argument.

You can also string the conversion types together, separated by a comma, although ascii, ebcdic, ibm, block, and unblock are all mutually exclusive.

TABLE D.4: Options for Use with dd

Option	Description
bs=*n*	Sets the input and output block size to *n*, superseding the ibs and obs options.
cbs=*n*	Sets the conversion record size to *n* bytes; used only when the conversion *type* is ascii, ebcdic, ibm, block, or unblock.
conv=*type*	Converts the input according to one or more of the *types* listed in Table D.5.
count=*n*	Copies only *n* input blocks before terminating.
files=*n*	Copies only *n* files before terminating.
ibs=*n*	Sets the input block size to *n* bytes, the default is 512 bytes.
if=*filename*	Reads input from *filename* rather than from the standard input.
obs=*n*	Sets the output block size to *n* bytes, the default is 512 bytes.
of=*filename*	Writes output to *filename* rather than to the standard output.
iseek=*n*	Seeks *n* blocks from the start of the input file.
oseek=*n*	Seeks *n* blocks from the start of the output file.

TABLE D.4 continued: Options for Use with dd

Option	Description
seek=*n*	Seeks *n* blocks from the start of the output file before copying; same as oseek and retained for compatibility.
skip=*n*	Skips the first *n* input blocks before copying.

TABLE D.5: Conversion Types Available with the conv=type Option in dd

Type	Description
ascii	From EBCDIC to ASCII
block	From variable-length records to fixed-length records
ebcdic	From ASCII to EBCDIC
ibm	From ASCII to EBCDIC with IBM conventions
lcase	From uppercase to lowercase, multibyte characters are not converted
noerror	Continues processing after an input error
swab	Swaps all pairs of bytes
sync	Pads the input blocks to the size specified by ibs
unblock	From fixed-length records to variable-length records
ucase	From lowercase to uppercase, multibyte characters are not converted

Examples

The dd swap option lets you swap each byte as it is processed, which is useful when moving from a big-endian system to a little-endian system. You can also use dd to convert from ASCII to EBCDIC and back again:

```
dd if=myfile.ascii of=mtfile.ebcdic conv=ebcdic
```

This command converts the ASCII file myfile.ascii into the EBCDIC file myfile.ebsdic using the conversion ebcdic.

To read from a tape using one block size and output to a file using a different block size, use a command like this:

```
dd if=/dev/rmt02 of=/usr/myfiles/wally ibs=1024 obs=512
```

This command reads input from a tape with 1024-byte blocks and writes this data into a file called wally that is written with 512-byte blocks.

See also cp, cpio, copy, hd, mt, tar, tr

DDI

Abbreviation for Device Driver Interface, an SVR4 definition for device drivers and hardware interfaces intended to improve system compatibility.

DDRM

Abbreviation for Device Driver Interface/Driver Kernel Interface Reference Manual. An SVR4 system document aimed at programmers who create or maintain device drivers.

default

A standard value or action that is used if you do not explicitly choose a different option.

A default is usually a relatively safe course of action to try first; many programs provide defaults you can use until you know enough about the program to specify your own settings. For example, `ls` lists the files in the working directory by default when you use it without arguments.

delimiter

A special symbol used to separate one element from another; the Unix command line uses space characters as delimiters between words.

In a C program, comments are delimited by `/* */` pairs; in a tab-delimited file, data items are separated by tabs, and in a comma-delimited file, the comma is the separator.

delta

See SCCS

deroff

A command used to remove all `nroff/troff` dot requests, macros, escape sequences, and `eqn` and `tbl` formatting commands from a file.

Syntax
The syntax used with `deroff` is as follows:

```
deroff [options][filename]
```

If you don't specify an input `filename`, `deroff` reads from the standard input.

Options and Arguments
There are several options you can use with `deroff`, and they are listed in Table D.6. In BSD, only the `-w` option is available.

TABLE D.6: Options for Use with deroff

Option	Description
-mm	Suppresses any text that appears on macro lines; paragraphs will print, but the headings may have been stripped away.
-ml	Same as -mm, but also removes lines created by mm macros.
-w	Outputs the text as a list with one word on each line.

Examples

To remove all nroff/troff formatting and macro commands from the file myfile.doc and write the resulting text into a file called burke.txt, use a command like the following:

```
deroff -mm myfile.doc > burke.txt
```

See also eqn, nroff, tbl, troff

DES

The abbreviation for Data Encryption Standard. A standard method of data encryption and decryption developed by the United States National Bureau of Standards.

DES works by a combination of transposition and substitution and is used by the federal government and most banks and money-transfer systems to protect all sensitive transactions.

See also **Pretty Good Privacy**

des

A Solaris command used to encrypt and decrypt a file according to the DES. Some Sun SPARCstations have an encryption chip installed, and you can direct des to use it; encryption using software is only about 50 times slower.

descriptor table

A list created for every process running on a system that identifies all input and output functions.

/dev

A root directory that contains the files needed to manage device drivers for terminals, printers, and other hardware devices used on the system. Table D.7 lists some of the entries you can find in /dev and explains what they are.

In SVR4, the /dev directory is divided into subdirectories named after the type of device it supports; dsk and rdsk for disks accessed in block mode and raw mode, term for terminals, and pts and ptc for pseudo-terminals.

See also **major device number, minor device number**

TABLE D.7: Typical /dev Entries

Entry	Description
/dev/console	The character special file for the system console.
/dev/null	The null device; any output sent here is discarded, and any attempt to read from /dev/null produces an immediate end-of-file. Also known as the bit bucket.
/dev/tty	Files used to manage the generic terminal management, such as the handling of erase and kill characters, tabs, and so on. You will also find files used to access specific communications lines or terminals, which might be called /dev/tty10 for the tenth serial port. These numbers are specific to each Unix installation.
/dev/mem	A device that corresponds to the system's memory, through which certain authorized programs can read or modify virtual memory; used only for debugging. A similar device, /dev/kmem, is used to read or modify the kernel's memory.

devconfig

A file in SVR4 Basic Network Utilities used in streams-based communications.

device-dependent

Any software system designed to run only with specific input or output hardware. Device-dependent software is often very difficult to port, or move, to another computer system due to this reliance on specific hardware.

See also **device-independent, hardware-dependent, hardware-independent**

device driver

The part of the Unix kernel that controls a specific hardware device such as a tape drive, printer, or terminal. Selecting the appropriate device drivers is one of the main tasks for the system administrator during Unix system generation.

See also **/dev, major device number, minor device number**

device driver calls

A set of standard calls used with device drivers, including those listed in Table D.8.

TABLE D.8: Device Driver Calls

CALL	DESCRIPTION
close	Indicates the end of a transmission of data, and terminates the connection to the device.
ioctl	Establishes input/output control for the device.
open	Readies the device to receive commands.
read	Requests data from a device.
write	Transmits data or control information to the device.

device file

A file in the /dev directory that represents a device; also known as a *special file*. There are two types of device files: character special files and block special files. Many versions of Unix also support named pipes and sockets. Device files identify the type and location of a particular piece of hardware so that information can be sent to or received from that device.

See also major device number, minor device number

device filename

The pathname of a device file. Device files are usually found in the /dev directory.

device-independent

Any software system designed to run without requiring the presence of specific input or output hardware but can run on a range of hardware systems.

See also device-dependent, hardware-dependent, hardware-independent

device number

An address or path used to access a particular device.

See also major device number, minor device number

df

A command that reports the amount of free disk space on a mounted device.

Syntax

The syntax for df is:

```
df [options][name]
```

If you use df with no arguments, it reports the amount of free disk space on all of the currently mounted devices; otherwise, it reports on name, where name can be a device name, the directory name of a file-system mounting point, a directory, or an RFS or NFS resource name.

Options and Arguments

The df command has a wide range of different options on different versions of Unix. Apart from those listed in Table D.9, many additional options relate specifically to different types of filesystems; see your man pages for more details.

TABLE D.9:   Options for Use with df

OPTION	DESCRIPTION
-b	Reports the amount of free disk space in kilobytes.
-e	Reports only the number of free files.
-f	An SVR3 option that reports the number of free blocks but not the free i-nodes.
-F type	Reports on the unmounted filesystem type. A list of the available types is in /etc/vfstab.
-g	Reports the amount of occupied and free disk space, type of filesystem and the filesystem ID, filename length, block size, and fragment size.
-i	In BSD and SCO, this option includes statistics on the number of used and free i-nodes.
-k	Reports the allocation in kilobytes. In some versions of Unix, this option reports the amount of occupied and free space in kilobytes, as well as the percentage of used disk capacity.
-l	Reports only on the local filesystem.
-n	Prints the filesystem type name. When you use this option by itself, it lists the types for all mounted filesystems. On BSD systems, this option prints out statistics obtained previously, to avoid a potentially long delay in reporting. Some of this information may be out-of-date by the time you see it.
-o suboptions	Lets you specify a comma-separated list of options specific to type.
-t	Reports the total allocated space as well as the amount of free space.
-v	On some systems, including SCO, this option reports the free percentage of blocks and number of free and used blocks.
-V	Echoes the command line but does not run the command.

Examples

To see how full each mounted filesystem is and to print that information on the default printer, you can use;

```
df -t | lpr
```

You will see a listing of all the mounted filesystems and the number of free blocks and i-nodes.

Notes

In the BSD version of df, the -n and -t options are ignored when you specify a filename or filesystem name as name in the syntax given above.

See also dfspace

DFS

Abbreviation for Distributed File System. A standard set of commands used with NFS and RFS to manage a distributed network environment and provide users with easy and transparent access to all files they have the appropriate permissions to use.

See also mount

dfspace

A SCO shell script similar to the df command that reports free disk space. When used with no arguments, dfspace reports the total amount and percentage of disk space used, and the space available on each mounted filesystem.

See also df

/dgn

An SVR4 root directory that contains the programs used for system diagnostics.

diction

A BSD command used to find poorly written or unnecessarily wordy text.

Syntax

The syntax for diction is as follows:

```
diction [options] filename
```

The diction command prints all sentences in a document containing phrases that are either frequently misused or unnecessarily wordy. The document is compared against a database containing several hundred phrases; if you prefer you can provide your own version of this file.

`diction` uses the `deroff` command to prepare the text for comparison; use the `-ml` option if your document contains many lists of items that you want `diction` to skip.

Options and Arguments

Table D.10 lists the options you can use with `diction`.

TABLE D.10: Options Used with diction

Option	Description
-f *filename*	Uses *filename* in addition to the default pattern file; this option lets you add your own phrases to those used by `diction`.
-ml	Makes `deroff` skip all lists; use this option if your document contains many lists that do not consist of sentences.
-mm	Overrides the default -ms macro package.
-n	Turns off usage of the default pattern file.

Examples

To check the text contained in `myfile.doc`, use:

```
diction myfile.txt | lpr
```

All the errors that `diction` finds are displayed in square brackets; in this example, the file is piped to the default printer.

See also deroff, `explain`, `style`

diff

A command that displays the differences between two text files, line by line.

Syntax

The syntax for `diff` can take several forms:

```
diff [options] file1 file2
diff [options] file1 directory
diff [options] directory file2
diff [options] directory1 directory2
```

You can use `diff` to find the differences between two files; if one of the filenames is replaced by a hyphen (-), `diff` uses the standard input. By carefully choosing options, you can also use `diff` to create an ed script you can use to re-create the second file from the first.

In the Unix tradition, no output is created if the two files are identical.

Options and Arguments

When you use two filenames as arguments to diff, the files are compared. If you use directory rather than file1, diff looks for a file in directory with the same name as file2, and if you use directory rather than file2, diff looks for a file in directory with the same name as file1. When two directory arguments are used, diff sorts the contents of each directory by name and then compares all files in directory1 with files in directory2 that have the same filenames. Binary files, common subdirectories, and files that appear in only one of the directories are noted.

In Table D.11, the options you can use with diff are arranged under three headings: Output Options, Comparison Options, and Directory Comparison Options.

diff always assumes that you want to change file1 into file2, and when you use it without any options, the output is a series of lines containing add (a), delete (d), or change (c) instructions. Each of these lines is followed by the lines from the file that you need to modify. A less than symbol (<) precedes lines from file1, and a greater than symbol (>) precedes lines from file2. If you want to know how to change file2 into file1, just run diff again, but this time reverse the order of the file arguments.

TABLE D.11: Options Available with diff

OPTION	DESCRIPTION
OUTPUT OPTIONS	
-cn	Presents three lines of content, although you can optionally specify *n* lines of context.
-Dstring	Merges the two files into one file containing conditional C preprocessor statements so that compiling while defining *string* yields *file2* and compiling without defining *string* yields *file1*.
-e	Creates output in a form suitable as input to ed, which can then be used to convert *file1* into *file2*.
-f	Produces output reversed from that produced by the -e option; this output cannot be used with ed.
-h	Uses a different comparison algorithm capable of managing very long files. The algorithm requires that changes are well defined and brief; otherwise, it gets confused.
-n	Produces similar output to the -f option, but counts the changed lines. This option is useful with the RCS command rcsdiff.

TABLE D.11 continued: Options Available with diff

OPTION	DESCRIPTION
COMPARISON OPTIONS	
-b	Causes leading and trailing blanks and tabs to be ignored.
-i	Ignores uppercase and lowercase distinctions.
-t	Expands tabs in output lines.
-w	Similar to –b, but ignores all blanks and tabs.
DIRECTORY COMPARISON OPTIONS	
-l	Produces a long output format; each file compared is passed through pr so that it is paginated, and other differences are summarized at the end.
-r	Runs diff recursively through common subdirectories.
-s	Reports on identical files, which would otherwise receive no report.
-S*filename*	Restarts a directory diff beginning with *filename*. This option skips all files whose names begin with letters before the first letter of *filename*.

Examples
You can create an ed script that converts document1.doc into document2.doc by using:

```
diff -e document1.doc document2.doc > edscript.doc
```

Redirection captures the output from this comparison in the file called edscript.doc.

Notes
The Unix commands comm, diff (and diff3), and cmp all compare files; comm is limited to sorted text files, and diff to text files. You can use cmp with both text and non-text files, including binary files, but the output is rather less informative.

See also bdiff, cmp, comm, diff3, ed, **RCS**, sdiff

diff3

A command that compares three versions of a file and reports the differences to the standard output.

Syntax
The syntax for diff3 is:

```
diff3 [options] filename1 filename2 filename3
```

Differences are reported using the following indicators:

====   Lines below this indicator are different in all three files.

====1   `filename1` is different.

====2   `filename2` is different.

====3   `filename3` is different.

Changes are described in terms of the `ed` commands, add (a), delete (d), or change (c), needed to create the target from the different versions.

Options and Arguments

You can use several options with `diff3`, as Table D.12 shows, allowing you to merge the different versions into a new file.

See also `bdiff`, `cmp`, `comm`, `diff`, `ed`, **RCS**, `sdiff`

TABLE D.12: Options Available with diff3

OPTION	DESCRIPTION
-e	Creates output suitable as input to ed to add to *file1* all the differences between *file2* and *file3*.
-E	Same as option -e, but lines that differ between all three files are marked with a line of <<<<<< and >>>>>> symbols.
-x	Creates an ed script that incorporates into *file1* all differences among all three files.
-X	Same as -x, but lines that differ between all three files are marked with a line of <<<<<< and >>>>>> symbols.
-3	Creates an ed script that incorporates into *file1* any differences between *file1* and *file3*.

diffmk

A command used to compare revisions or changes made between drafts of a document.

Syntax

The syntax for `diffmk` is as follows:

```
diffmk oldfile newfile changes
```

Options and Arguments

The `diffmk` command compares the two versions of the document contained in `oldfile` and `newfile` and creates a third file, `changes`, that contains `troff` change mark requests.

When you format changes using either nroff or troff, differences between the two files are marked in the margin, even if the changes are trivial, such as extra spaces or different line lengths. A | marks changed lines and a * marks deleted lines.

See also bdiff, cmp, comm, diff, sdiff

dig

A BSD command used to query DNS name servers.

Syntax
The syntax for use with dig is:

```
dig @server domain query-type query-class
```

dig is an abbreviation for domain information groper, which is used to collect information from the DNS servers.

Options and Arguments
In the syntax given above, server can be either the name or the dotted decimal IP address; if your system does not support DNS, you have to use the dotted decimal address. domain is the domain name you are requesting information about. query-type *is the type of information or DNS query type you are requesting; if you leave it out, the default is* a *for network address.* query-class *is the network class requested by the query; if you omit this argument, the default is* in *for Internet class domain. Several other very complex options are available with this command; see the man pages on your system for more information.

See also nslookup

dircmp

An SVR4 command that compares the contents of two directories, listing the files unique to each directory.

Syntax
The syntax to use with dircmp is:

```
dircmp [options] directory1 directory2
```

Options and Arguments
The dircmp command compares the contents of directory1 and directory2 and lists information on the files unique to each directory. This list is made up of two columns, with the word same before all files

that are the same in both directories. A period (.) indicates that one of the directories for comparison is the current directory.

You can use the options listed in Table D.13 with the dircmp command.

See also cmp, diff

TABLE D.13: Options Available with dircmp

Option	Description
-d	Runs diff on files with the same name.
-s	Suppresses all messages about identical filenames.
-w*width*	Sets the width of the output to *width*; the default is 72 characters.

directory

An abbreviation for directory file. In Unix a directory is considered to be a special kind of file that lists the filenames and corresponding i-nodes for all the files and directories it contains. A directory may be empty, it may contain a number of other files, or it may contain other directories.

Unix uses a hierarchical system of directories to organize the thousands of files required by a typical installation, beginning at the root directory (/). Other directories branch from the root, including /dev, /usr, /etc, and /bin, for example, and other directories (often called subdirectories) branch in turn from these directories.

See also cd, **current working directory, dot, dot dot, file type, home directory,** ls, **ordinary file,** pwd, **special file**

dirname

An SVR4 command used to extract a directory name from a complete pathname.

Syntax
Here is the syntax to use for dirname:

    dirname pathname

This command removes a filename from a pathname and sends the resulting directory name to the standard output. dirname is often used in shell scripts that create a new file in a specific directory. There are no options for dirname.

Examples

When you provide this command with a complete pathname, it returns the pathname without the final component:

```
dirname /usr/pmd/wally
/usr/pmd
```

See also basename

dirs

A C shell command that lists the current working directory. When in your home directory, this command lists the tilde (~), and you can use dirs -l to expand this symbol to the actual name of your home directory.

See also popd, pushd

dis

The Unix software development command that runs the disassembler on an executable, object, or archive file.

Syntax

The disassembler is a programmer's tool used to look at executable or object files in hexadecimal machine instructions. Here's the syntax:

```
dis [options] filename
```

Options and Arguments

dis disassembles the executable or object file specified by filename. Several options are available with this command, and they are listed in Table D.14.

See also as

TABLE D.14: Options for Use with dis

Option	Description
-d *section*	Disassembles the specified *section* of data, printing the offset.
-D *section*	Same as -d, but also prints the data's actual address.
-F *function*	Disassembles the specified *function*; repeat the option for additional functions.
-l *string*	Disassembles the library file *string*.
-L	Looks for C source labels in files compiled using cc -g.
-o	Prints the output in octal rather than the default hexadecimal.
-t *section*	Same as -d, but prints text output.
-V	Prints the dis version number on the standard output.

disable

A command that temporarily turns off terminals or printers.

Syntax

Here's the syntax for `disable`:

```
disable tty...
disable [options] printer
```

The `disable` command is often used when clearing up paper jams in printers or when swapping out printers or terminals for maintenance.

When you disable a printer, the current print job stops; when you enable the printer once again, this print job starts from the beginning unless you use the `-c` option described in the next section.

Options and Arguments

In the first line of syntax shown above, `disable` will not allow logins on `tty`, and in the second line, `disable` stops print jobs from being sent to the named `printer`. Table D.15 lists the options you can use with `disable`.

TABLE D.15: Options Available with disable

OPTION	DESCRIPTION
`-c`	Cancels the print job currently printing.
`-r[reason]`	Associates *reason* with the specified *printer*. This *reason* is reported by `lpstat`. To use more than one word in *reason*, be sure to enclose the text in double quotes (as in `"a message"`).
`-W`	Waits for the current print job to complete before disabling *printer*.

Examples

To prevent logins on the tenth terminal on your system, use:

```
disable tty10
```

To let everyone know that you are clearing out a paper jam on the department printer, use a message such as:

```
disable -c -r"Paper Jam! Printer back up in 5 minutes."
deptptr
```

See also `enable`, `lp`, `lpstat`

disassembler

A software development tool used to convert a machine language program back into the assembly language source code from which it was originally created.

See also assembler, dis.

diskcmp

An SCO command that compares the contents of two floppy disks, using the cmp utility.

Syntax
Here's the syntax for diskcmp:

```
diskcmp [options]
```

The diskcmp command presents self-explanatory prompts for its use.

Options and Arguments
Most of the options available with the diskcmp command are used to specify the type of floppy disk for the comparison, as Table D.16 shows.

See also diskcp

TABLE D.16: Options to Use with diskcmp

OPTION	DESCRIPTION
-d	Specifies your computer has two floppy disk drives; ordinarily the contents of the source floppy disk are copied to the hard disk, and then the comparison is made.
-s	Runs a checksum to verify the accuracy of the comparison.
-48ds9	Specifies a 360 KB floppy.
-96ds9	Specifies a 720 KB 51/4 floppy.
-96ds15	Specifies a 1.2 MB 51/4 floppy.
-135ds9	Specifies a 720 KB 31/2 floppy.
-135ds18	Specifies a 1.44 MB 31/2 floppy.

diskcp

An SCO command that copies floppy disks.

Syntax
Here's the syntax for diskcp:

```
diskcp [options]
```

The diskcp command presents self-explanatory prompts for its use, telling you when to insert and remove the source and target floppy disks.

Options and Arguments

Most of the options available with the diskcp command are used to specify the type of floppy disk for the comparison, as Table D.17 shows.

See also diskcmp

TABLE D.17: Options to Use with diskcp

OPTION	DESCRIPTION
-d	Specifies your computer has two floppy disk drives; ordinarily the contents of the source floppy disk are copied to the hard disk, and then the comparison is made.
-f	Formats the target floppy disk before starting the copy.
-r	Uses the second floppy disk drive as the source drive.
-s	Runs a checksum to verify the accuracy of the comparison.
-u	Prints out a usage message.
-48ds9	Specifies a 360 KB floppy.
-96ds9	Specifies a 720 KB 51/4 floppy.
-96ds15	Specifies a 1.2 MB 51/4 floppy.
-135ds9	Specifies a 720 KB 31/2 floppy.
-135ds18	Specifies a 1.44 MB 31/2 floppy.

ditroff

A version of the troff command, known as the *device-independent* troff. The original version of troff was designed to run with one specific typesetter. The program was modified by Brian Kernighan to be hardware independent and run with a variety of typesetters, terminals, and printers. Most modern versions of troff are really ditroff.

See also nroff, troff

do

A Bourne and Korn shell programming command that indicates the beginning of a block of commands following a for, while, select, or until loop.

document instance

In SGML (Standard Generalized Markup Language), the text component of a document as distinct from the structure of the document.

See also DTD

document type definition

See DTD

dollar sign

- ▶ The default system prompt used in the Bourne shell.
- ▶ A metacharacter used to match characters at the end of a line by vi, ed, ex, sed, grep, and awk.
- ▶ A character used when accessing shell variables in both the Bourne shell and the Korn shell.

See also **regular expression**

domain

A unique name that identifies a computer system. The most common high-level domains on the Internet include:

.com   a commercial organization

.edu   an educational establishment such as a university

.gov   a branch of the U.S. government

.int   an international organization

.mil   a branch of the U.S. military

.net   a network

.org   a nonprofit organization

Most countries also have unique domains based on their international abbreviations—for example, .uk for the United Kingdom and .ca for Canada.

domain address

A unique name that identifies a computer within a network. For example, wally.my.iberia defines a computer called wally within the subdomain my, which in turn is part of the larger iberia domain.

domain member list

A file maintained by the primary name server in an RFS system that contains a list of all hosts within the domain and their passwords.

domain name

In DNS, a unique name that identifies an Internet host.

See also domain address

domain name server

A host computer in an RFS system acting as the network's primary name server, maintaining and monitoring the network's file-sharing environment.

Domain Name Service

See DNS

domainname

A Solaris command that sets or displays the name of the current Network Information Service (NIS) domain.

Syntax
The syntax for domainname is:

```
domainname name
```

Only the superuser can set the domain name, and this is usually done during system installation. Using the domainname command without arguments displays the current domain name. There are no options for this command.

done

A Bourne and Korn shell programming command that indicates the end of a for, while, select, or until statement.

DOS

Acronym for disk operating system. An operating system originally developed by Microsoft for the IBM PC.

DOS exists in two similar versions: MS-DOS, developed and marketed by Microsoft for use with IBM-compatible computers, and PC-DOS, supported and sold by IBM for use on computers manufactured by IBM.

Many important Unix concepts have been copied in DOS, including the hierarchical file structure, redirection, pipes, and filters, but DOS remains a poorly featured operating system when compared to Unix.

Several DOS emulators are available for the Unix world so that you can run DOS and Windows applications on Unix workstations. SCO and UnixWare both use Merge from Locus Computing Corporation, and Linux uses a program called `dosemu` or an X Window version called `xdos`. A Windows emulation package for Linux is under development.

See also DOS commands

DOS commands

Certain versions of Unix include a set of commands you can use to access files and disks created by the DOS filesystem to run your DOS and Microsoft Windows applications. SCO and UnixWare both use an emulation package called Merge from Locus Computing Corporation. Linux uses a program called `dosemu` or an X Window version called `xdos`.

These programs create a DOS environment within Unix, and let you run as many DOS and Windows sessions as your computer's memory allows. Table D.18 lists the common commands used when accessing DOS disks and files from Unix.

Unfortunately, DOS and Unix use very different file-naming conventions, and so Merge changes Unix filenames that do not conform to the DOS rules. These changed names are only for display purposes; the actual filenames on disk are not changed. When you use a DOS application or a Merge command, you see the changed name; at all other times, you see the full Unix name.

The UnixWare desktop contains commands you can use to convert DOS files to Unix format, and vice versa.

See also dtox, xtod

TABLE D.18: Commands Used to Access DOS Disks and Files

COMMAND	DESCRIPTION
doscat	Displays a DOS file by copying it to the standard output.
doscp	Copies files between a DOS disk and the Unix filesystem.
dosdir	Lists DOS files in the DOS-style directory listing.
dosformat	Formats a DOS floppy disk; cannot be used to format a hard disk.
dosls	Lists DOS files in a Unix format.
dosmkdir	Creates a directory on a DOS disk.
dosrm	Deletes files from a DOS disk.
dosrmdir	Deletes directories from a DOS disk.

dosemu

A DOS emulation program often used with Linux. dosemu requires that you own a licensed copy of DOS and creates a virtual machine allowing you to run DOS and DOS applications in real mode. The virtual machine emulates the BIOS, XMS, and EMS memory, keyboard, serial ports, printer, and disk services ordinarily found on a PC.

The dosemu package is still in development, but you can obtain a copy of the source code from the anonymous ftp sites tsx-11.mit.edu or dspsun.eas.asu.edu. The files are in the /pub/linux/ALPHA/dosemu directory; the ALPHA in the pathname refers to the status of the software release, not to the microprocessor.

See also xdos

dot

A synonym for the name of the current directory. The Unix mkdir command places this entry in every directory, but it is usually invisible because its name begins with a period. If you use the ls -i command (the -i option shows i-node numbers), you see that the name is a link to the same i-node as the directory's name in the parent directory.

See also dot dot, dot file

dot command

A Bourne shell and Korn shell command that reads a file and executes its contents as though they were input from the command line.

dot dot

A synonym for the name of the parent directory of the current directory. The Unix mkdir command places this entry in every directory, but it is usually invisible because its name begins with a period.

See also dot, dot file

dot file

A file whose name begins with a period and so is not usually displayed in an ordinary directory listing. Also known as a *hidden file*.

Many programs, including the Unix shells, use one or more dot files to store configuration information; you can customize your environment by creating the appropriate dot file in the current directory or in your home directory.

Table D.18 contains a list of common dot files and their uses.

TABLE D.18: Common Dot Files and Their Uses

FILENAME	CONTENTS
.bash_logout	Bash logout commands
.bash_profile	Bash login initialization commands
.bashrc	Bash initialization commands
.cshrc	C shell initialization commands
.elm	Directory of elm configuration files
.emacs	emacs editor initialization commands
.exrc	vi editor initialization commands
.gopherrc	Gopher initialization commands
.history	History file
.login	C shell login commands
.logout	C shell logout commands
.netrc	ftp autologin information
.newsrc	List of USENET newsgroups you can access
.mailrc	List of mail initialization commands
.pinerc	Pine configuration information
.plan	Information displayed by finger
.project	Additional finger information
.profile	Bourne shell initialization commands
.rcrc	rc shell initialization commands
.signature	Signature file used in postings to USENET newsgroups
.tcshrc	Tcsh shell initialization commands
.xsession	X Window start-up commands
.xinitrc	X Window initialization commands
.zshenv	Zsh shell initialization commands
.zshrc	Zsh shell initialization commands
.zlogin	Zsh shell login initialization commands
.zlogout	Zsh shell logout initialization commands
.zprofile	Zsh shell login initialization commands

dot requests

Formatting commands in the nroff family of text-processing programs. Each command that begins with a dot (or period) tells the program to format the document in a specific way; for example, the .bp (for break page) command produces a new page.

double quote

The " character; used to enclose that part of the command line in which you want the shell to perform command and variable substitution and, in the C shell, history substitution. Double quotes allow specific characters, the dollar sign ($), the backquote (`), and the backslash (\) to keep their special meanings.

See also single quote symbol

dpost

A postprocessor command used to translate `troff`-formatted files into PostScript for printing.

Syntax

The syntax for `dpost` follows:

    dpost [options][filename]

Options and Arguments

If you do not specify `filename`, `dpost` reads from the standard input. Table D.19 lists the options available with this command.

TABLE D.19: Options Available with dpost

Option	Description
-c *n*	Prints *n* copies of each page; the default is one copy.
-e *n*	Sets text encoding to *n*, where *n* can be 0 (the default), 1, or 2; higher numbers speed processing and reduce output size but may be less reliable.
-F *directory*	Specifies *directory* as the font directory; the default is /usr/lib/font.
-H *directory*	Sets the host-resident font directory to *directory*. Files contained in *directory* must describe PostScript fonts and must have filenames corresponding to a two-letter troff font.
-L *filename*	Specifies *filename* as the PostScript prolog; the default is /usr/lib/postscript/dpost.ps.
-m *scale*	Increases the size of each logical page by a factor of *scale*; the default is 1.0.
-n *n*	Prints *n* pages of output on each page; the default is 1.
-o *list*	Prints the pages specified in the comma-separated *list*.
-O	Removes PostScript pictures from the output.
-p *layout*	Sets *layout* to p for portrait or 1 for landscape.
-w *n*	Draws troff graphics (pic or tbl) using a line *n* points wide; the default is 0.3.
-x *n*	Offsets the x coordinate of the origin *n* inches to the right when *n* is a positive number—otherwise, to the left when *n* is negative.
-y *n*	Offsets the y coordinate of the origin *n* inches down when *n* is a positive number—otherwise, to the left when *n* is negative.

Examples

If you want to print five copies of each page of the file `trevor.eon` to the default printer, use:

```
dpost -c5 trevor.eon | lpr
```

See also `lp`, `lpr`, `nroff`, `troff`

DTD

Abbreviation for document type definition. In SGML, the structural component of a document as distinct from the actual data or text contained within the document.

See also document instance

dtox

A command that converts a DOS text file into a Unix text file.

Syntax

The syntax for `dtox` is:

```
dtox filename > output-filename
```

Unix uses a single newline character to indicate the end of a line, while DOS uses two characters, a linefeed followed by a carriage return. DOS also uses Ctrl-Z as an end-of-file marker. `dtox` removes the carriage return and the Ctrl-Z characters so that Unix can read the file successfully.

Options and Arguments

The `filename` argument contains the name of the DOS file you want to convert; if you leave it out, `dtox` reads from standard input. Because `dtox` always writes to standard output, you must use redirection to capture the converted output in a file `output-filename`.

Examples

To convert the DOS file `norman.dos` into a Unix file called `norman.unix`, use:

```
dtox norman.dos > norman.unix
```

See also `xtod`

dtype

An SCO command used to determine the type of a floppy disk, print a report to the standard output, and then exit with an exit code related to the disk type.

Syntax

Here's the syntax for `dtype`:

```
dtype [options] devices
```

Options and Arguments

The `dtype` command has just one option, `-s`, which suppresses the report to standard output. With this option, `dtype` will return only the exit code, and the exit code will refer only to the last disk specified by `devices`. Table D.20 lists all the `dtype` exit codes.

TABLE D.20: dtype Exit Codes

Exit Code	Description
60	Error
61	Unrecognized data or empty disk
70	Backup format
71	tar format
72	cpio format
73	cpio character format
80	DOS 1.x; 8 sectors/track, single-sided
81	DOS 1.x; 8 sectors/track, double-sided
90	DOS 2.x; 8 sectors/track, single-sided
91	DOS 2.x; 8 sectors/track, double-sided
92	DOS 2.x; 9 sectors/track, single-sided
93	DOS 2.x; 9 sectors/track, double-sided
94	DOS 2.x; hard disk
100–103	DOS data disk
110	DOS 3.x; 9 or 15 sectors/track, double-sided
111	DOS 3.x; 18 sectors/track, double-sided
112	DOS 3.x; 8 sectors/track, single-sided
113	DOS 3.x; 8 sectors/track, double-sided
120	XENIX 2.x filesystem
130	XENIX 3.x filesystem
140	Unix 1K filesystem

Examples

To create a report on the high-density drive:

```
dtype /dev/rfd096 > lpr
```

Notes

This command is reliable only when used with floppy disks; it may not recognize `tar` or `cpio` formats created on a foreign system.

du

A command that reports on the amount of disk space used by a specific directory and its subdirectories; the information is reported as a number of 512-byte blocks. Partial blocks are rounded up.

Syntax

Here's the syntax for the du command:

    du [options] [directories]

If no `directories` are specified, the `du` command reports on the current directory and all of its subdirectories and files.

Options and Arguments

This command has different options on different versions of Unix; check the man pages on your system for more details. Table D.21 lists the major options you can use with the `du` command.

TABLE D.21: Options to Use with du

Option	Description
-a	Displays totals for all files and subdirectories.
-f	Displays totals for files and directories in the current filesystem only; other filesystems are ignored. Not available on all Unix systems.
-k	On Solaris, reports totals in kilobytes.
-L	In BSD, all symbolic links are followed.
-P	In BSD, no symbolic links are followed.
-r	Displays the message "cannot open" for directories it cannot access and files it cannot read; normally du does not report the information.
-s	Displays a summary total for each specified filename and directory name.
-u	Ignores files with more than one link. Not available on all Unix systems.
-x	In BSD, displays totals for files and directories in the current filesystem only; other filesystems are ignored.

Examples

To find out the total number of blocks used by the `trainspotter` directory, its files, and subdirectories, use:

    du -s /trainspotter3462 ./trainspotter

See also df, dfspace

duplex

In asynchronous transmissions, the ability to transmit and receive on the same channel at the same time; also referred to as *full duplex*. Half-duplex channels can transmit only or receive only.

See also **communications parameters**

E

e

▶ A system-level alias for the Unix editor **ed**, a line editor included with almost all Unix systems.

▶ On AIX systems, the **e** command starts the INed editor, a multi-window editor with a built-in file manager.

eb

Abbreviation for error bells; a variable in the **ex** and **vi** editors that sounds the bell to alert you to an impending error message.

EBCDIC

Acronym for Extended Binary Coded Decimal Inter-change Code, pronounced "eb-se-dic." EBCDIC is the character set commonly used on large IBM mainframe computers, most IBM minicomputers, and computers from many other manufacturers. It is an 8-bit code, allowing 256 different characters. Unlike with ASCII, the placement of the letters of the alphabet in EBCDIC is discontinuous. Also, there is no direct character-to-character match when converting from EBCDIC to ASCII; some characters exist in one set but not in the other, and several slightly different versions exist.

echo

The ability of the Unix tty driver to display typed characters on the screen. Characters may come from a program or may be typed on the keyboard.

See also **echoing**

echo

A command that writes arguments to the standard output. **echo** is also a built-in command in the C shell and Bourne shell.

Syntax

The syntax for echo is:

```
echo [-n] [string]
```

echo is particularly useful in shell scripts to prompt the user for input or report on the status of a process.

Options and Arguments

The echo command normally follows any output with a newline character; the -n option turns the newline off. string represents any characters that you want echo to output; enclose them in quotes. The sequences listed in Table E.1 create special effects when you include them in string.

TABLE E.1: Special echo Sequences

Sequence	Description
\b	Backspace
\c	Suppress final newline, same as −n option
\f	Formfeed
\n	Newline
\r	Carriage return
\t	Tab
\v	Vertical tab
\\	Backslash
\0n	An octal number, specified by n

Examples

To display the current setting of the path variable, use:

echo $PATH

To prompt the user for a yes or no answer without a newline, use:

echo "Please enter Y or N \c"

You would then use the read command to obtain the user's input, followed by an if statement to decode the input.

You can also use echo in creative ways. The spell command accepts input only from a file, not from the command line, so you can use:

echo trainsptter | spell

to pipe a single word into spell. If the word is misspelled, spell redisplays the word; if you just get the command prompt back, you know the word is spelled correctly.

See also cat, sh

echo area

The bottom line on the screen in emacs, used to echo the commands that you type and to display error messages. The echo area shares this screen line with the minibuffer.

See also emacs

echoing

Displaying characters on a screen as a result of input from the user and keyboard, or from a program. Echoing may be turned off occasionally, for example, when you enter your password.

See also echo

ed

Pronounced "ee-dee." The oldest and the simplest of the Unix text editors; ed is a line editor.

Syntax
The syntax for ed is:

```
ed [options] filename
```

ed is not much used these days; it has been superseded by more capable and easier to use screen editors such as ex, vi, and emacs. Some of the older commands, such as diff continue to use ed.

Options and Arguments
If the specified filename does not exist, ed creates it; if it does exist, ed opens the file for editing. The options you can use with ed are listed in Table E.2.

See also emacs, ex, sed, vi

TABLE E.2: Options for Use with ed

OPTION	DESCRIPTION
-p *string*	Specifies *string* as the ed command prompt; there is no default ed prompt.
-s	Suppresses the ed character count and other explanatory messages.
-v	In 4.4BSD, displays the ed mode, either BSD or POSIX.
-x	Specifies a key to encrypt or decrypt *filename* using the crypt command; crypt encryption is available only in the U.S. because it is illegal to export certain encryption schemes.

edit

A simplified version of the ed line editor, often used by people new to Unix text processing.

See also ed

egrep

A command that searches one or more files for text strings that match a specified regular expression. This command, along with the related fgrep command, is considered to be obsolete.

See also grep

eject

A Solaris command used to eject a disk from a drive without an eject button.

Syntax
Here is the syntax to use with eject:

```
eject [options][device]
```

Options and Arguments
You can specify device as a name, but if no device is specified, eject uses the default device /dev/rdiskette. The eject command automatically checks for any mounted filesystems on the device and attempts to umount them before ejecting them. The options for eject are listed in Table E.3.

TABLE E.3: Options for Use with eject

Option	Description
-d	Displays the name of the default drive.
-f	Forces an eject, even if the device contains a currently mounted partition.
-n	Displays the system nickname for the device.
-q	Checks if media is present in the drive.

Examples
Use this command on a Sun system to eject a floppy disk from the default disk drive:

```
eject /dev/fd0
```

You can use this command to eject a CD from a CD-ROM drive:

```
eject /dev/sr0
```

See also fdformat, mount

ELF

ELF (Executable and Linking Format) is the binary format produced by current gcc compilers. ELF replaces the older a.out format produced by the older Unix C compilers. A.out was replaced by ELF primarily because a.out files were difficult to adapt for use as shared libraries. ELF files are designed for just that purpose. The default output from most gcc compilers is still named a.out and older a.out format files can be recompiled by gcc as well.

See also C, C++

elif

A Bourne shell and Korn shell programming command used to mark the beginning of the else part of an if then else construct. If the commands that follow the if statement fail, the commands that follow the elif statement are executed.

See also else, fi, if, then

elm

A screen-oriented mailer written by Dave Taylor, and now in the public domain.

Like other modern e-mail programs, elm lets you reply to or forward a message, delete messages, and create aliases for groups of addresses that you use frequently. elm is easy to use and simple to learn.

The elm mailer is bundled with some versions of Unix, including Linux, or you can ftp to ftp.dsi.com and retrieve elm from the /pub/elm directory. You can get a list of other sites where elm is available by sending the message:

```
send elm elm.ftp
```

to archive-server@dsi.com. You can also consult the USENET newsgroup comp.mail.elm. The elm distribution contains several useful documents, including a reference guide and a user's guide.

See also mail, mailx, mush

else

A Bourne shell and Korn shell programming command that is part of an
`if then else` conditional statement.

See also `elif`, `fi`, `if`, `then`

emacs

A popular Unix screen editor, written by Richard Stallman, founder of the
Free Software Foundation (FSF) and author of much of the GNU software. `emacs` is a contraction of "editing macros." There are many versions
of `emacs`; this entry covers GNU `emacs`.

`emacs` is much more than a simple text editor, however, and includes
extensions for all sorts of tasks, ranging from compiling and debugging
programs, to reading and sending e-mail, to X Window system support.
You can even extend `emacs` yourself because the editing commands are
written in the Lisp programming language.

Syntax

The syntax for `emacs` is as follows:

    emacs [options][filename]

You can also simply specify `filename` on the command line, and
`emacs` will open the file for editing.

Options and Arguments

You can use several options with `emacs`, and they are listed in Table E.4.

You can also use a large number of X Window configuration switches
when you start `emacs`; see the *GNU Emacs Manual* from the FSF for
more details.

TABLE E.4: emacs Options

OPTION	DESCRIPTION
`+n filename`	Goes to the line number specified by *n* in `filename`.
`-batch command-file`	Opens emacs in batch mode using the commands in `command-file`; the text is not displayed. If you use this option, it must be the first argument on the command line; usually combined with `-f` or `-l`.
`-f function`	Executes the Lisp function without arguments.
`-kill`	Performs all initialization operations, then exits from emacs batch mode.
`-l filename`	Loads the Lisp code contained in `filename`.
`-q`	Does not load the `.emacs` initialization file from your home directory.

TABLE E.4 continued: emacs Options

OPTION	DESCRIPTION
-t *filename*	Uses *filename* as the terminal rather than standard in and standard out; if you use this option, it must be the first argument on the command line.
-u *user-name*	Loads the specified user's .emacs initialization file.

Major and Minor Modes

The emacs editor has a large number of major and minor modes you can choose between. Your editing needs when entering C source code are different from those when you are working with straightforward text, and emacs has a major mode to suit everyone, as Table E.5 shows. Major modes are mutually exclusive; only one can be active at any time. Minor modes add variations that you can turn on or off as you wish; minor modes are independent of each other.

If you are in doubt about which of these modes you should use, try fundamental-mode, it is fairly safe.

TABLE E.5: Major and Minor Modes

MODE	DESCRIPTION
MAJOR MODES	
asm-mode	Assembly language programming
awk-mode	awk scripts
bibtex-mode	BibTEX files
c++-mode	C++ programming
c-mode	C programming
change-log-mode	For working with change logs
command-history-mode	For working with command history files
completion-list-mode	For working with lists of possible completions
edit-abbrevs-mode	For working with abbreviation definitions
emacs-lisp-mode	emacs Lisp programming
forms-mode	For working with field-structured data using a form
fortran-mode	Fortran programming
fundamental-mode	Unspecialized, nonspecific mode (when in doubt, use this mode)
hexl-mode	For working with hexadecimal and ASCII data
indented-text-mode	For working with indented paragraphs
latex-mode	For working with LATEX formatted files

TABLE E.5 continued: Major and Minor Modes

Mode	Description
MAJOR MODES	
lisp-interaction-mode	For evaluating and entering Lisp forms
lisp-mode	Non-emacs Lisp programming
mail-mode	For sending outgoing mail messages
makefile-mode	Used with make
mh-letter-mode	For managing MH mail messages
nroff-mode	For working with nroff and troff-formatted text files
outline-mode	For working with outlines and a selective display
pascal-mode	For Pascal programming
perl-mode	For Perl programming
picture-mode	For working with text-based drawings
plain-tex-mode	For working with TEX-formatted files
prolog-mode	Prolog programming
rmail-mode	For managing mail with rmail
scheme-mode	Scheme programming
scribe-mode	For working with Scribe-formatted text files
sgml-mode	For working with Standard Generalized Markup Language files
slitex-mode	For working with SliTEX-formatted files
tcl-mode	For working with Tool Command Language files
tex-mode	For working with TEX, LATEX, or SliTEX-formatted files
texinfo-mode	For working with TEXinfo files
text-mode	Used with normal text
tpu-edt-mode	TPU/EDT emulation of a DEC-style editor
vi-mode	Makes emacs work like vi
wordstar-mode	Makes emacs use WordStar keystrokes
MINOR MODES	
abbrev-mode	For working with abbreviations
auto-fill-mode	Uses automatic filling
auto-save-mode	Uses automatic saving
binary-overwrite-mode	For editing and overwriting binary files
compilation-minor-mode	For compiling programs
delete-selection-mode	Replaces typed text with selected text
double-mode	Makes certain keys work differently when you press them twice
font-lock-mode	Shows text in the selected font as you enter it

TABLE E.5 continued: Major and Minor Modes

MODE	DESCRIPTION
MINOR MODES	
hide-ifdef-mode	C programming, hides certain constructs
indent-according-to-mode	Indents for the major mode
iso-accents-mode	Uses ISO accents
ledit-mode	Lisp programming
outline-minor-mode	Variation on the major outline mode
overwrite-mode	Overwrites/inserts text
pending-delete-mode	Same as delete-selection-mode
resize-minibuffer-mode	Dynamically changes the mini-buffer
tpu-edt-mode	TPU/edt emulation
toggle-read-mode	Opens emacs in read-only mode
transient-mark-mode	Highlights defined regions
vip-mode	VIP emulation of vi
vt100-wide-mode	Uses 132 columns for a VT100 terminal

Key Combinations in emacs

The emacs editor does not use modes like the vi editor; anything you type in emacs appears as text, unless you use special key combinations to indicate you are invoking a command rather than entering text.

There are a lot of key combinations in emacs, and most of them use either the Ctrl key or the Meta key:

Ctrl key The Ctrl key is used as you would expect; hold down the Ctrl key and press another key, but some commands consist of more than one Ctrl combination in a row, or a Ctrl combination followed by another letter. To quit emacs, you press Ctrl-X Ctrl-C—that is, Ctrl-X immediately followed by Ctrl-C. And to open the emacs tutorial, you press Ctrl-H t—Ctrl-H followed by t. In emacs, the Ctrl key is often represented by a letter *C* followed by a lowercase letter, so instead of writing *Ctrl-X*, you would write *C-x* or *C-h t*.

Meta key The Meta key is used in the same way as the Ctrl key; you hold it down while you press another key. The Meta key is a virtual key; a key that acts as the Meta key. Sun workstations often use the keys with the small diamonds close to the spacebar; PCs often use the Alt keys, and Macintoshes use the Command or Option keys. You may also be able to use the Escape (Esc) key as the Meta key; however, don't hold it down, press it, release it, and then press the appropriate letter. The Meta key is abbreviated as M, and key combinations are written as M-f, for example.

Other important keys include the Delete (Del) key and the Enter (or Return) key. To display information about all the key combinations used in emacs, you have to know how to use the built-in help system.

How to Get Help

Unlike many other Unix programs, a great deal of excellent help material is built right into emacs; you just have to know how to get to it. Table E.6 lists the most common ways you can access emacs help information.

TABLE E.6: Help Commands in emacs

COMMAND	DESCRIPTION
Ctrl-H ?	Displays a summary of all the help options.
Ctrl-H a	Prompts you for a string, then lists all the commands that contain the string.
Ctrl-H b	Displays a very long list of all the key combinations.
Ctrl-H c	You specify a key, and emacs briefly tells you what it does.
Ctrl-H f	Prompts you for the name of a function, then tells you what that function does.
Ctrl-H i	Starts the Info documentation browser.
Ctrl-H k	You specify a key, and emacs tells you its function.
Ctrl-H m	Describes the current major mode.
Ctrl-H t	Starts the emacs tutorial.
Ctrl-H v	Prompts you for a Lisp variable name, and then displays the documentation for that function.
Ctrl-H w	Prompts you for a command name, and shows you the key combination for that command.

Using Point, Cursor, Mark, and Region

Point, cursor, mark and region are basic emacs concepts:

Point   Point (just "point", never "the point") is the place between two characters where the editing commands actually take effect. Point can also be at the very beginning or end of the buffer.

Cursor   The cursor is always on the character to the right of point. Even though you may have several emacs windows open at the same time, there is always only one cursor.

Mark   The mark is a location in the buffer, which, like point, is either at the beginning or the end of the buffer or between two characters. The mark stays in one place until you explicitly move it to a new location.

Region   The region is the area between point and the mark. Many emacs commands operate in the region.

Yanking Killed Text or Cutting and Pasting

When you delete (or kill in emacs terminology) text in emacs, it is not deleted immediately but is kept in a special area called the *kill ring*, which can hold the last 30 deletions. You can retrieve (or yank) text from the kill ring back into your editing buffer. So in emacs, killing and yanking are roughly the same as cutting and pasting in other applications, and you can use them to move and to copy text in much the same way.

Editing Commands

The heart of any editor is the set of commands used to manipulate text. The most common editing commands are listed in Table E.7 under several important subheadings. For more information, see the help system.

In Table E.7, commands are shown as Ctrl-x Ctrl-y, which means press Ctrl-x followed by Ctrl-y, or as Ctrl-x y, which means press and release Ctrl-x and then press y. You can use the Escape key or the Alt key as the Meta key depending on your configuration.

TABLE E.7: Editing Commands

Command	Description
WORKING WITH FILES	
Ctrl-X Ctrl-F	Prompts you for a filename you want to create or open for editing.
Ctrl-X I	Inserts a file at the current point in the buffer.
Ctrl-X Ctrl-W	Saves the file, and allows you to specify a new filename.
Ctrl-X Ctrl-S	Saves the file to the original filename.
Ctrl-X Ctrl-C	Terminates emacs, and gives you a chance to save your file
MOVING THE CURSOR	
Ctrl-F	Moves the cursor one character to the right.
Ctrl-B	Moves the cursor one character to the left.
Meta-f	Moves the cursor forward one word.
Meta-b	Moves the cursor backward one word.

TABLE E.7 continued: Editing Commands

COMMAND	DESCRIPTION
MOVING THE CURSOR	
Ctrl-A	Moves the cursor to the beginning of the line.
Ctrl-E	Moves the cursor to the end of the line.
Ctrl-P	Moves the cursor up to the previous line.
Ctrl-N	Moves the cursor down to the next line.
Meta-{	Moves the cursor to the previous paragraph.
Meta-}	Moves the cursor to the next paragraph.
Ctrl-X {	Moves to the previous page.
Ctrl-X }	Moves to the next page.
Ctrl-V	Moves one screen forward.
Meta-V	Moves one screen backward.
Meta->	Moves the cursor to the end of the buffer.
Meta-<	Moves the cursor to the beginning of the buffer.
Ctrl-L	Clears and redraws the screen with the current line placed in the center of the screen.
EDITING TEXT	
Del	Deletes the character to the left of the cursor.
Ctrl-D	Deletes the character under the cursor.
Meta-d	Deletes from the cursor to the end of the word.
Meta-Del	Deletes from the cursor backward to the beginning of the previous word.
Meta-k	Deletes to the end of the sentence.
Ctrl-X Del	Deletes to the beginning of the sentence.
Ctrl-K	Deletes to the end of the line.
Ctrl-@	Sets the mark to the current location of point.
Meta-@	Sets the mark after the next word without moving point.
Ctrl-X Ctrl-X	Swaps the locations of the mark and point.
Meta-h	Places a region around the current paragraph.
Ctrl-X h	Places a region around the entire buffer.
Ctrl-W	Deletes (or "kills") a marked region.
Ctrl-Y	Restores (or "yanks") the most recently deleted region at point; sets the mark at the beginning of this text, and sets the cursor and point at the end.
Meta-w	Copies the region to the kill ring without deleting text from the buffer.
Ctrl-X Ctrl-U	Converts the region to uppercase.
Ctrl-X Ctrl-L	Converts the region to lowercase.
Ctrl-G	Aborts the current command.

TABLE E.7 continued: Editing Commands

COMMAND	DESCRIPTION
WORKING WITH BUFFERS AND WINDOWS	
Ctrl-X Ctrl-B	Displays the buffers you are using in a new window.
Ctrl-X b	Prompts you for a buffer name, and then changes to that buffer.
Ctrl-X k	Prompts you for a buffer name, and then deletes the buffer.
Ctrl-X o	Selects the other window.
Ctrl-X 0	Deletes the current window.
Ctrl-X 1	Deletes all windows except the current window.
Ctrl-X 2	Splits the current window into two, vertically.
Ctrl-X 3	Splits the current window into two, horizontally; in older versions of emacs, this command was Ctrl-X 5.
Ctrl-X }	Widens the current window.
Ctrl-X {	Narrows the current window.
Ctrl-X ^	Enlarges the current window.
SEARCHING	
Ctrl-S	Incrementally prompts for a string; as soon as you type the first character, immediately starts searching forward. Type Meta-P or Meta-N to cycle through previous search strings. Enter terminates the search; mark is set to point, which is at the end of the matched string.
Ctrl-R	Incrementally prompts for a string; as soon as you type the first character, immediately starts searching backward. Type Meta-P or Meta-N to cycle through previous search strings. Enter terminates the search; mark is set to point, which is at the end of the matched string.
Ctrl-S Enter	Prompts you for a string, and searches forward for that string.
Ctrl-R Enter	Prompts you for a string, and searches backward for that string.
Ctrl-S Enter Ctrl-W	Prompts you to enter a word, and searches forward for that word.
Ctrl-R Enter Ctrl-W	Prompts you to enter a word, and searches backward for that word.
Meta Ctrl-S	Searches incrementally forward for a regular expression.
Meta Ctrl-R	Searches incrementally backward for a regular expression.

Notes

You can get GNU emacs from the Free Software Foundation at:

675 Massachusetts Ave.
Cambridge MA 02139, U.S.A.
617-876-3296

or by anonymous `ftp` from `prep.ai.mit.edu` in the `/gnu/emacs` directory; `emacs` is free, although there may be a small charge for the distribution media.

An excellent `emacs` FAQ file can be found in the USENET newsgroups `gnu.emacs.help`, `comp.emacs`, and `news.answers`. The FAQ contains answers to over 100 common `emacs` questions.

There is no doubt that `emacs` is a broad subject. As well as the extensive online help and the printed `emacs` manual, several good books have been written on how to get the most out of `emacs`; if you want to know more, check them out.

See also `vi`

e-mail

The use of a network to transmit text messages, memos, and reports; also called *electronic mail* or *messaging* and sometimes just *mail*.

Users can send a message to one or more individuals, a predefined group, or all users on the system. When you receive a message, you can read, print, forward, answer, or delete it. E-mail is, by far, the most popular Internet application, with well over 80 percent of Internet users taking advantage of the service.

E-mail has several advantages over conventional mail systems, including:

▶ E-mail is fast when compared to conventional mail.

▶ If something exists on your computer as a file—text, graphical images, even program files and video segments—you can usually send it as an e-mail attachment.

E-mail's problems are similar to those associated with online communications in general, such as security, privacy (always assume that your e-mail is not private), and the legal status of documents exchanged electronically.

See also `elm`, `mail`, **mailbox, mailer,** `mailx`, **MIME,** `talk`, `wall`, `write`

e-mail address

The addressing information required for an e-mail message to reach the correct recipient.

See also **bang path, mailbox**

embedded command

An `nroff` or `troff` dot command placed in a text file and used in formatting the document. For example, the command `.c3` is used to center text, and the `.pl` command sets the page length.

See also `nroff, troff`

enable

A SCO Unix command that enables terminals and printers.

Syntax
The syntax for `enable` is:

```
enable name
```

where `name` is a particular terminal or printer. `enable` allows logins from the specified terminal and lets the specified printer process print requests made by `lp`.

No command-line options are available with `enable`.

See also `disable`

encryption

The process of encoding information in an attempt to make it secure from unauthorized access. The reverse of this process is known as *decryption*.

Two main encryption schemes are in common use:

Private (Symmetrical) Key Schemes   An encryption algorithm based on a private encryption key known to both the sender and the recipient of the information. The encrypted message is unreadable and can be transmitted over non-secure systems.

Public (Asymmetrical) Key Schemes   An encryption scheme based on using the two halves of a long bit sequence as encryption keys. Either half of the bit sequence can be used to encrypt the data, but the other half is required to decrypt the data.

See also crypt, des, DES, Pretty Good Privacy, rot13

end

A C shell programming command used to terminate a `foreach` or `switch` statement; `end` must always appear on a line by itself.

end-of-file character

Abbreviated EOF. A special code placed after the last byte in a file that indicates to the operating system that no more data follows. An end-of-file code is needed because disk space is assigned to a file in blocks, and the file may not always terminate at the end of a block. In the ASCII system, an EOF is represented by the decimal value 4 or by the Ctrl-D control character.

You can also type Ctrl-D to signal the end of data entry from the keyboard.

end-of-text character

Abbreviated ETX. A character used in computer communications to indicate the end of a text file. In the ASCII system, an ETX is represented by the decimal value 3 or by the Ctrl-C control character. A different symbol, end-of-transmission (EOT, ASCII 4 or Ctrl-D), is used to indicate the end of a complete transmission.

end-of-transmission

Abbreviated EOT. A character used in computer communications to indicate the end of a transmission. In the ASCII system, an EOT is represented by the decimal value 4 or by the Ctrl-D control character.

endif

A C shell programming command used to terminate an if statement.

See also fi, if

endsw

A C shell programming command used to terminate a switch statement.

enhanced C shell

See Tsch

Enter key

Also known as the *Return key*. The key that indicates the end of a command or the end of user input from the keyboard.

env

A command that displays or changes environment variables.

Syntax

The syntax for the env command is as follows:

```
env [option] [variable=value ...] [command]
```

When used without options or arguments, the env command displays all the global environment variables.

Options and Arguments

The env command has a single option, hyphen (-), which instructs it to ignore the current environment and restricts the environment for command to just those variables specified by variable=value. The variable =value argument sets the specified variable to value and adds it to the environment before executing command.

Examples

To display your current environment, enter:

```
env
```

To change your home directory before starting a subshell, use:

```
env HOME=/usr/user/pmd bash
```

See also printenv, set, setenv

ENV

A Korn shell environment variable that sets the path to the environment file you want to execute when you start the shell. This environment file is used to establish user variables, aliases, and other configuration options.

environment

The set of environment variables that are passed to a program when it is started by the shell.

environment file

A Korn shell file used along with the .profile file to set up and run your environment. These initialization commands are executed every time you start a new copy of the shell.

environment variables

In the Unix shell, a variable accessible to any program. Environment variables are exported so that they are available to any command executed by the shell. A Unix process automatically gets its own copy of its parent's environment, and any changes it makes to those variables it keeps to itself; a process cannot change its parent's environment.

The C shell has three commands for managing environment variables: `setenv` marks a variable for export, `unsetenv` removes a variable from the environment, and `printenv` prints the environment variables.

In the Korn shell, environment variables are often called *shell variables*.

See also child process

EOF

See end-of-file character

EOT

See end-of-transmission

epoch

The date used as the beginning of time in Unix.   In most Unix systems, the epoch is 00:00:00 GMT (Greenwich mean time), January 1, 1970, and system time is measured in seconds (or ticks) past the epoch. This means that a Unix day is 86,400 seconds long.

See also date, Julian date, `time`

e protocol

One of the three common UUCP protocols, along with the g and the G protocols.

The e protocol assumes data is being transferred without errors. It does no error checking or flow control and is most often used over TCP/IP links. It should not be used over serial lines or modem connections.

The protocol sends an initial packet containing details of the file to be transferred, including size information, and then sends the rest of the file in 4096-byte packets until everything has been sent.

See also f protocol, g protocol, G protocol, t protocol, x protocol

eqn

A preprocessor for `troff` designed to manage the typesetting of mathematical formulas and equations.

Syntax
The syntax for eqn is:

```
eqn [options][filename]
```

eqn reads a `troff` file that contains pairs of special codes: `.EQ` starts special typesetting, and `.EN` ends special typesetting. The mathematical formula for typesetting is located between these two directives. The output from eqn is a `troff` input file in which this mathematical formula has been replaced by `troff` instructions for creating the formula on the printed page, normally on a line by itself, although you can force a formula within a line by using special delimiters. eqn manages:

- ▶ Special mathematical symbols and Greek letters
- ▶ Superscripts and subscripts
- ▶ Summations, products, integrals, and limits
- ▶ Fractions, matrices, and arrays
- ▶ Specialized commands for spacing parts of formulas

Options and Arguments

The options you can use with eqn are listed in Table E.8.

TABLE E.8: Options Available with eqn

Option	Description
-dxy	Uses x and y as start and stop delimiters.
-fn	Changes the font to the font specified by n.
-pn	Reduces the superscript and subscript size by n points.
-sn	Reduces the point size by n points.
-T$name$	Formats the output to the device specified by $name$.

Notes

The eqn command is often used in a pipeline containing several commands to format a file:

```
myfile.doc | eqn | troff | lpr
```

In this example, `myfile.doc` is piped into eqn, and output from that command is passed to `troff` for final output to the default printer.

See also groff, **LATEX**, nroff, pic, tbl, **TEX**, troff

error handling

The way that a program copes with errors that occur as the program is running. Good error handling manages unexpected events or wrongly entered data gracefully, usually by prompting the user to take the appropriate action or enter the correct information. Badly written programs

may simply stop running when the wrong data is entered or when an
unanticipated disk error occurs.

esac

A Bourne shell and Korn shell programming command that ends a `case`
statement (`esac` is `case` spelled backwards). Leaving out the `esac`
statement is a very common shell programming error.

See also `case`

escape

▶ A feature of the shell that lets you suspend an operation, start
a new copy of the shell, and run commands. For example, many
interactive programs let you temporarily leave the program to
enter shell commands by entering the `!` command.

▶ To disable the special meaning that certain characters have for
the shell, for example, the asterisk (*) or question mark (?). This
is done by preceding the special character by a backslash (\) or
by enclosing the character inside single or double quotes. Sometimes called *quoting*.

See also escaped character

escape character

A character that tells the shell to ignore the special meaning of the following character or characters and to use the literal meaning. Escape characters vary from application to application; in the shell, an escape character
is preceded by a backslash (\) or enclosed inside single or double
quotes.

See also escaped character

escape commands

A command used in the `mailx` program when in input mode. The `mailx`
program distinguishes between ordinary text input and commands by
requiring that you type a tilde (~) to signal that what follows is a command rather than message text.

See also tilde escape commands

escaped character

A character that follows an escape character. The escape character removes
any special meaning that the character may have had.

escape sequence

A sequence of characters, beginning with Escape (ASCII 027 in decimal, 033 in octal) and followed by one or more characters, that performs a specific function. Escape sequences are often used to control printers or monitors, which treat them as commands and act upon them rather than process them as characters that should be printed or displayed.

/etc

The root directory where the system administration and configuration commands are located. Table E.9 lists some of the files and directories you might expect to find in /etc.

You may also find some administrative commands in the /usr/etc directory on some systems.

TABLE E.9: Files and Directories Located in /etc

ENTRY	DESCRIPTION
/etc/bkup	Files used to backup and restore the system.
/etc/checklist	Filesystems to be mounted.
/etc/cron.d	File used to manage the cron daemon.
/etc/default	Contains default parameter values for many commands.
/etc/dfs	Contains system files for DFS.
/etc/ethers	Database used to match Ethernet addresses with computer host names.
/etc/ff	Command that displays filenames and filesystem statistics.
/etc/ffstat	Command that displays filesystem statistics.
/etc/fstypes	Command that displays filesystem type.
/etc/fuser	Command that displays processes using a file.
/etc/gettydefs	SVR4 file used to control serial interfaces, equivalent to 4.4BSD /etc/gettytab.
/etc/gettytab	4.4BSD file used to control serial interfaces, equivalent to /etc/gettydefs in SVR4.
/etc/group	Lists all the groups on the system along with which users belong to which group.
/etc/hosts	Lists Internet hosts, including host names, addresses, and aliases.
/etc/hosts.equiv	Lists trusted hosts; checked by the system for access authorization when a rsh or rlogin attempt occurs.
/etc/inetd.conf	Lists hosts available once the inetd Internet daemon is started.
/etc/init.d	File used during system state changes.
/etc/inittab	SVR4 file used to initialize serial interfaces; equivalent to 4.4BSD /ect/ttys.
/etc/login	Login file read by the C shell.

TABLE E.9 continued: Files and Directories Located in /etc

Entry	Description
/etc/lp	Contains printer configuration information.
/etc/mail	Contains files for the mail system.
/etc/mnttab	Contains currently mounted local and remote filesystems.
/etc/motd	Contains the message of the day; often used by administrators as a way of posting important information to users as they log in.
/etc/netmasks	Contains configuration information for the Internet Protocol.
/etc/passwd	Lists login information for each user on the system. Each line gives information for one user, including encrypted password, login name, full name, user ID, group ID, home directory, and the name of the login shell.
/etc/profile	Contains the profile file read by the Bourne and Korn shells.
/etc/shadow	Contains secure password information.
/etc/shutdown	Contains the system shutdown command.
/etc/ttys	Contains the 4.4BSD file used to initialize serial interfaces; equivalent to /etc/inittab in SVR4.
/etc/uucp	Contains UUCP configuration information.
/etc/vfstab	Contains default parameters for DFS.

euid

Abbreviation for Effective User Identifier. A part of the Unix system security, the euid is used to identify the user who owns a program. This euid is then checked for the appropriate permissions before the program can access specific files and directories.

eval

A Bourne shell and Korn shell command used to evaluate shell variables and then run the output as arguments to other shell variables.

ex

The line editor, found on almost all Unix systems, was written by Bill Joy while at University College Berkeley. The ex or extended editor was so called because it extended the original ed editor.

Syntax
The syntax used with ex is as follows:

```
ex [options] filename
```

The file you are editing is kept in a buffer, and a typical editing sequence would be to read the file into the buffer, make the required editing changes, and then write the buffer back out to the same file.

Options and Arguments

The options available for use with ex are listed in Table E.10.

TABLE E.10: Options for Use with ex

OPTION	DESCRIPTION
-c*command*	Starts an editing session by executing the specified ex *commands*.
-C	Same as -c but assumes that *filename* was in encrypted form.
-L	Lists filenames that were saved due to an editor or system crash.
-r*filename*	Recovers *filename* after an editor or system crash.
-R	Sets read-only mode to prevent accidental editing.
-s	Turns off error messages; used when running an ex script.
-t *tag*	Edits the file containing *tag*.
-v	Invokes the vi editor.
-x	Requires a key to encrypt or decrypt *filename*.

Line Addressing in ex

Most of the ex commands operate on a line or range of lines, and you must know how to specify a particular line. The most useful methods of specifying a line or range are listed in Table E.11.

TABLE E.11: Line Addressing in ex

COMMAND	DESCRIPTION
0	Adds a line before the first line.
.	Specifies the current line.
1,$	Specifies all lines in the file.
$	Specifies the last line of the file.
n	Specifies the nth line in the file.
-*n*	Specifies *n* lines previous.
-	Specifies the previous line.
+*n*	Specifies *n* lines ahead.
'1	Specifies the line marked by the letter 1.
''	Specifies the previous mark.
/*pattern*/	Specifies the next line matching regular expression *pattern*.
?*pattern*?	Specifies the previous line matching regular expression *pattern*.

Useful ex Commands

ex uses about 50 commands, many of which you will never need; the most often used commands are listed in Table E.12.

TABLE E.12: Useful ex Commands

COMMAND	ABBREVIATION	DESCRIPTION
append	[address]a text	Appends the specified text at address.
change	[address]c text	Replaces the specified lines with text.
copy	[address]co destination	Copies the lines in address to destination.
delete	[address]d [buffer]	Deletes the specified lines; if buffer is specified, saves the text to the buffer.
global	[address]g/pattern/ [commands]	Executes commands on all lines containing pattern or, if address is specified, on the lines in that range.
insert	[address]i text	Inserts text before the specified address.
move	[address]m destination	Moves the specified lines to destination.
print	[address]p count	Prints the lines given by address; count specifies the number of lines to print, beginning with address.
quit	q	Ends the current editing session.
read	[address]r filename	Copies in the text from filename to the line after address.
source	so filename	Reads and executes the ex commands contained in filename.
substitute	[address]s ➥[/pattern/replacement/]	Replaces each instance of pattern with replacement.
write	[address]w[filename]	Writes the lines specified by address to filename.

Notes

Encryption options are only available in the U.S.

See also ed, emacs, .exrc, **regular expressions**, vi

exa-

Abbreviated E. A prefix meaning one quintillion or 1018. In computing, 1,152,921,504,606,846,976, or the power of 2 closest to one quintillion (1060).

exabyte

Abbreviated EB. 1 quadrillion kilobytes, or 1,152,921,504,606,846,976 bytes.

exclamation point

The ! character, often called *bang* or *pling*.

▸ In UUCP, a character used as a host name delimiter, as in: yoursystem!mysystem!myname.

▸ In the C shell, repeats a command. For example, ! ! repeats the last command you entered, and ! 3 means repeat the third command.

▸ The exclamation point is used in some interactive programs to execute a shell command; when using ftp, you can use !date to run the date command without leaving your ftp session. When date exits, you return to the ftp prompt once again.

▸ An exclamation point is sometimes used to override an automatic check. For example, if you set the noclobber variable, the shell will not let you overwrite an existing file when redirecting the standard output. To override this, you can use >! instead.

See also **bang path, shell escape**

exec

A Unix system call that replaces the current process with another using the same process ID number (PID) as the original process. This means that you cannot return to the original program when the new one has done its job, but it saves the overhead of creating a new process space.

See also **fork**

exec

A built-in Bourne shell and C shell command that causes the current shell to be replaced by another program.

execute permission

An access permission on a file or directory that gives you permission to execute the file or access the contents of the directory.

You cannot change to a directory or include that directory in your path unless you have execute permission in that directory. When you use the ls -l command to make a long file and directory listing, an x indicates you have execute permission for that file or directory; r indicates read permission, and w indicates write permission.

executing remote commands

Several Unix commands allow you to access a remote system. These commands include rcmd in SCO UNIX and rsh in Solaris and UnixWare, both used over a TCP/IP link. You can also use the UUCP command uux in a UUCP communications session or telnet over a modem and telephone line.

See also ftp, rlogin, telnet

exit

- ▸ A built-in shell command that terminates the current process and returns control to the previous shell.

- ▸ A shell programming command that terminates the current shell script.

- ▸ In an X Window system, a command that closes an xterm window.

- ▸ A command used to exit the shell and log out of the system; same as pressing Ctrl-D.

exit status

Sometimes called *exit value* or *return value*. A value returned by a process or command that indicates a successful (usually 0) or unsuccessful (usually 1) conclusion.

In a Bourne shell script, the exit status of the previous command is stored in the built-in $? variable, and in the C shell the exit status of the previous command is stored in the $status variable.

A few commands such as grep return a different non-zero exit value for different kinds of problems; see the grep man pages for more details.

expand

A command that converts tab characters to spaces or blanks.

Syntax
The syntax to use with expand is:

```
expand [-tabstop][-tab1, tab2,...]filename
```

expand processes the specified `filename`, or the standard input, writing the results to the standard output, and all tab characters are converted to space characters.

Options and Arguments

If you use a single `tabstop` argument, tabs are set at `tabstop` spaces apart, the default being eight spaces. If you specify several `tab` settings, these are used instead to set tabs. The expand command has no options.

Examples

To convert the tabs in a file called `myphonelist` to 4 spaces, use:

```
expand -4 myphonelist > myphonelist.notabs
```

See also unexpand

explain

A BSD interactive program that looks up words in a thesaurus file and displays synonyms you can use instead. You can also use `explain` with the output from the `diction` program.

See also diction

export

A Bourne shell and Korn shell command that gives global meaning to one or more shell variables. For example, a variable defined in one shell script must be exported before it can be used by another program called by the script.

See also global variable, local variable

/export

An SVR4 root directory used by the NFS as the root of the export filesystem tree.

exportfs

An NFS command used to make resources on a computer available to all users on the network.

expr

A command that evaluates its arguments as an arithmetic expression and prints the results.

Syntax

Here's the syntax to use with `expr`:

```
expr arg1 operator arg2 ...
```

All `args` and `operators` must be separated by spaces on the command line. `expr` accepts three kinds of operators: arithmetic, comparison, and logical, and they are listed in Table E.13.

Several of the symbols in Table E.13 have special meaning to the shell and so must be escaped before they can be used. Always escape the symbols *, (,), >, <, |, and &.

The `expr` command provides three different exit status values: 0 indicates that the expression is non-zero and non-null, 1 indicates that the expression is 0 or null, and 2 indicates that the expression is invalid.

TABLE E.13: Operators Used with expr

OPERATOR	DESCRIPTION
ARITHMETIC OPERATORS	
+	Adds the arguments.
-	Subtracts *arg2* from *arg1*.
*	Multiplies the arguments.
/	Divides *arg1* by *arg2*.
%	Modulus when *arg1* is divided by *arg2*.
COMPARISON OPERATORS	
=	Is *arg1* equal to *arg2*?
!=	Is *arg1* not equal to *arg2*?
>	Is *arg1* greater than *arg2*?
>=	Is *arg1* greater than or equal to *arg2*?
<	Is *arg1* less than *arg2*?
<=	Is *arg1* less than or equal to *arg2*?
LOGICAL OPERATORS	
|	Logical OR.
&	Logical AND.
:	Matching operator.

Examples

To use `expr` in a shell script as a loop counter, use:

```
i='expr $i + 1'
```

The spaces before and after the addition operator are required.

You can also use `expr` as a fast integer calculator from the command line. To add two numbers, use:

```
expr 20 + 277
```

Notes

The `expr` command cannot manipulate floating point numbers, just integers; decimals are truncated so that an answer of 9.3 appears as 9.

See also bc, dc

expressions

See regular expressions

.exrc

An initialization file located in the user's home directory for the `ed`, `ex`, and `vi` editors. When you start one of these editors, the configuration commands contained in `.exrc` are executed first, so you can automatically initialize your own custom environment.

exstr

A software development command used to extract strings from C language source code. These strings are stored in a database and retrieved by a Unix system call when the compiled application program is run. This process is often used when preparing an application for international use.

See also mkmsgs, mksrt, srchtxt

ext2fs

Abbreviation for Second Extended Filesystem; a popular Linux filesystem that allows filenames of up to 256 characters and filesystems of up to 4 terabytes in size.

eyacc

Another version of `yacc` (yet another compiler compiler), called *extended* yacc. `eyacc` is based on the original `yacc` but provides better error recovery.

See also yacc

F

f

A frequently used system alias for the `finger` command.

See also `finger`, `w`, `who`

face

The command that starts the Framed Access Command Environment (FACE), a window and menu-based user interface released with SVR4.

Syntax
The syntax to use with `face` is:

```
face [options][filenames]
```

This command invokes FACE and opens `filename`. Each `filename` must have the form `menu.string`, or `text.string`, or `form.string`, depending on the kind of object you are opening.

If no `filenames` are specified, this command opens the FACE menu and default objects as specified by the environment variable `LOGINWIN`.

Options and Arguments
You can use three configuration-related options with `face`, as shown in Table F.1.

TABLE F.1: Options to Use with face

OPTION	DESCRIPTION
`-a afilename`	Loads the list of pathname aliases from *afilename*. Entries in this file have the form *alias=pathname*.
`-c cfilename`	Loads the list of command aliases from *cfilename*.
`-i ifilename`	Loads *ifilename*, which specifies startup features.

FACE

Abbreviation for Framed Access Command Environment, a window and menu-based graphical user interface (GUI) released with SVR4. FACE gives ASCII terminals the capability of displaying windows and pop-up menus. You can also use function keys and menus in certain system administration and file and printer management tasks.

factor

A command used to produce the prime factors of a specified number. If you don't specify a number on the command line, factor waits for input and then factors the number you enter.

false

▶ A shell programming command used to return an unsuccessful (non-zero) exit status from a shell script. Often used in Bourne shell scripts.

▶ A Korn shell alias for let 0.

See also true

FAQ

Abbreviation for frequently asked questions, pronounced "fack." A document that contains answers to questions.

fc

A Korn shell command used to display or edit the command history list.

Syntax

There are two ways to use the fc command:

```
fc [options][first[last]]
fc -e -[old=new][command]
```

Options and Arguments

In the first form above, first and last are numbers or strings used to specify the range of commands you want to display or edit; use first alone if you just want to work with a single command. If you leave out both these arguments, fc edits the last command or edits the last 16 commands.

In the second form above, fc replaces the string old with the string new in command and then executes the modified command. If you don't specify these strings, command is re-executed, and if you leave out command, the previous command is re-executed.

Table F.2 lists the options you can use with the fc command.

TABLE F.2: Options for Use with fc

Option	Description
-e [*editor*]	Opens the specified *editor* to edit the history commands; the default name is specified by the FCEDIT shell variable.
-e -	Executes a history command.
-l [*n*]	Lists the specified command *n*, the range of commands, or the last 16 commands if *n* is not specified.
-n	Turns off command numbering from the -l listing.
-r	Reverses the order of the -l listing.

Examples

To list commands 25 through 35, use:

```
(fc -l 25 35
```

To list the last command beginning with ls:

```
(fc -l ls
```

If you want to edit a series of commands, say commands 5 through 25 inclusive, with emacs, use:

```
(fc -e emacs 5 25
```

See also history, r

FCEDIT

A Korn shell environment variable that contains the name of the default text editor, usually either emacs or vi. This information is used by the built-in command fc unless overridden by the -e option.

fdformat

A Solaris command used to format a floppy disk.

Syntax

The syntax for fdformat is as follows:

```
fdformat [options]
```

The fdformat command formats and verifies all the tracks on the floppy disk and terminates if it finds any bad sectors. Any previous data on the floppy is destroyed during the formatting process. You can also use fdformat to create a DOS-compatible disk.

Options and Arguments

Table F.3 lists the options for use with fdformat.

TABLE F.3: Options Available with fdformat

Option	Description
-d	Installs a DOS filesystem and boot sector on the disk once formatting is complete.
-D	Formats a 720 KB disk under Solaris 2 for x86.
-e	Ejects the disk when the formatting is complete. This option only works with disk drives without manual eject buttons.
-f	Starts formatting immediately without asking you to confirm the format operation.
-l	Formats a 720 KB disk on a Sun workstation.
-m	Formats a 1.2 MB disk.
-v	Verifies the disk when the formatting is complete.
-b *label*	Writes the DOS *label* on the disk when formatting is complete; use only with the -d option.

Examples

If you want to format a 1.44 MB floppy disk for use with a Unix filesystem, use:

```
(fdformat /dev/rfd0c
```

To format a floppy disk using a DOS-compatible format, and to install a DOS filesystem and boot sector, use:

```
(fdformat -d /dev/rfd0c
```

fg

A Korn shell and C shell command used to bring the current or specified job to the foreground.

See also **background processing,** bg, **job control, percent sign**

fgrep

A command that searches one or more files for text strings that match a specified regular expression. This command, along with the related egrep command, is considered to be obsolete.

See also grep

fi

A Bourne shell and Korn shell programming command used to terminate an if statement.

See also if

FIFO file

Abbreviation for first in first out file. In SVR4, a named pipe.

A special type of temporary file that exists independently of any process and allows unrelated processes to exchange information; normal pipes work only between related processes. Any number of processes can read or write to a FIFO file.

See also mkfifo, mknod

fignore

A C shell predefined variable that contains a list of filename suffixes. The C shell ignores the specified suffixes when it performs filename completion.

file

A command that determines file type and then lists each filename followed by a brief description.

Syntax
Here's the syntax for the file command:

```
file [options]filename
```

This command can recognize a file by type, such as a 286 executable, 386 executable, ASCII text file, or C source code. Many of the Unix commands are shell scripts, and you can use this command to tell those files apart from the utilities that are executable files.

Options and Arguments
The file command looks in the so-called magic file, /etc/magic (or another file that you specify), for information on how to determine a specific file's type. file looks at the first part of a file, looking for keywords and special numbers placed there by the link editor and other software development programs. file also looks at the file permissions associated with the file.

The options you can use with file are listed in Table F.4.

TABLE F.4: Options to Use with file

OPTION	DESCRIPTION
-c	Checks the format of the magic file.
-f*list*	Runs file on the filenames contained in *list*.

TABLE F.4 continued: Options to Use with file

OPTION	DESCRIPTION
-h	Does not follow symbolic links.
-m*filename*	Specifies *filename* instead of /etc/magic.

Examples
To determine the type of a file, use:

```
file myfile.doc
myfile.doc        ascii text
```

The `file` classifications include the following:

```
ascii text
commands text
c program text
c-shell commands
data
English text
empty
executable
iAPX 386 executable
directory
sccs
shell commands
symbolic link to
```

Notes
Because of all the possible combinations of file types, the results from `file` are not always correct.

file attributes

A collection of general information concerning a file, including the type of file, its i-node, its size, the name of the device the file is on, and information about the owner of the file.

file commands

That group of Unix commands related to file operations, including `cat`, `cp`, `ln`, `ls`, `mv`, `rm`, `touch`, and `umask`.

file locking

A method of controlling file access in a multiuser environment, in which there is always a possibility that two users may attempt to update the same file at the same time but with different information. The first user to access the file locks out all the other users, preventing them from opening the file. After the file is updated and closed again, the next user can gain access.

File locking is a simple way to prevent simultaneous updates, but it can seriously degrade system performance if many users attempt to access the same files time after time. To prevent this slowdown, many database management systems use record locking instead. Record locking limits access to individual records within the database file.

file permissions

A special binary number associated with a file that specifies who can access the file and in what way.

There are three independent permissions: read, write, and execute.

- ▶ Read permission lets you read the file.
- ▶ Write permission lets you write to the file and change it if you wish.
- ▶ Execute permission means that you can execute the file.

You can set and change the file permissions for your own files, and the main reasons for doing this are to prevent others from accessing your files and to protect yourself against accidental changes or deletions to important files.

Directories also have these same three permissions, but they work in a slightly different way:

- ▶ Read permission lets you read the filenames in the directory.
- ▶ Write permission lets you make changes to the directory; you can create, rename, move, or delete files.
- ▶ Execute permission means that you can search the directory; to include a directory in your path, you must have execute permission for that directory.

There are also three sets of file permissions: one set for the user or owner of a file, one set for the group of the file, and one set for everyone else.

See also chmod, ls, umask

file server

A networked computer used to store files for access by other client computers on the network. This allows computers without local storage to access filesystems from the server.

See also NFS, RFS

file type

There are several types of files in the Unix system, including:

Ordinary files   hold user data and programs; most files are of this type. An ordinary file may be a text file or a binary file. Sometimes known as *regular files*.

Directories   hold files or other directories.

Block special files   represent a specific kind of device driver that communicates with the hardware in units known as *blocks*.

Character special files   represent a specific kind of device driver that communicates with the hardware character by character.

FIFO special files   allow unrelated programs to exchange information; sometimes called *named pipes*.

Sockets   allow unrelated programs on the same or different computers to exchange information.

Symbolic links   let you link files that are in different filesystems.

The type of each file is displayed in the first column of the long format `ls` listing.

See also Internet file types

filec

A C shell environment variable that allows filename completion. When this variable is set, an input line followed by Ctrl-D prints all the filenames that begin with the contents of the input line. You can also enter an input line followed by an Escape keystroke to replace the line with the longest non-ambiguous filename extension.

filename

The name of a file within a directory; sometimes written as two words, *file name*.

In some cases, filename refers to the full absolute pathname for a file; in others, just to the filename itself.

Within a directory, filenames must be unique, although files with the same name may exist in different directories.

You can use almost any character you like in a Unix filename. Table F.5 lists some of the characters you should avoid because they have a special meaning in Unix.

You should also avoid the space, backspace, and tab characters, and you cannot create a file named . (dot) or . . (dot dot) because these two names are reserved for the names of the current and the parent directories.

See also **filename extension**

TABLE F.5: Characters to Avoid in Unix Filenames

CHARACTER	DESCRIPTION
!	Exclamation point
#	Pound sign
&	Ampersand
( )	Parentheses
'	Single quote
"	Double quote
`	Backquote
;	Semicolon
< >	Redirection symbols
\	Backslash
@	At sign
$	Dollar sign
^	Caret
{ }	Braces
~	Tilde
?	Question mark

filename completion

The automatic completion (or best guess) of filenames and usernames after you specify a unique prefix.

See also filename substitution

filename expansion

The process that the shell uses to convert the contents of the command line, including any metacharacters, into real filenames.

See also asterisk, filename substitution

filename extension

That part of a filename that follows a period. Unix, unlike DOS, doesn't have any rules about filename extensions; the period has no special significance as a separating character, and extensions can be any length.

Some Unix software development programs, such as the C compiler, do use specific one-character extensions such as .c for a C language source file, while others use extensions as indicators of their contents, such as .txt to indicate a text file. Table F.6 lists common Unix filename extensions and their associations.

See also Internet file types

TABLE F.6: Common Unix Filename Extensions

Extension	Description
.a	Archived file or assembler code
.au	Audio file
.c	C language source code
.csh	C shell script
.enc	Encrypted file
.f	Fortran source code
.F	Fortran source code before preprocessing
.gif	Graphics Interchange Format file
.gl	Animation file
.gz	File compressed with the gzip command
.h	C program header file
.jpg or jpeg	Joint Photographic Experts Group format still image
.mm	Text file containing troff mm macros
.mpg or .mpeg	Motion Picture Experts Group format video file

TABLE F.6 continued: Common Unix Filename Extensions

Extension	Description
.ms	Text file containing troff ms macros
.o	Object file
.ps	PostScript source file
.s	Assembly language source code
.sh	Bourne shell script
.shar	Shell archive
.tar	tar archive file
.tex	Text file formatted with TEX commands
.txt	ASCII text file
.uu	A uuencode file
.xx	Text file formatted with LATEX commands
.z	File compressed by the pack command
.Z	File compressed by the compress command
.1 to .8	Online manual source files

filename generation

A term used in the Bourne shell, Korn shell, and Zsh as a synonym for *filename substitution*.

filename substitution

In the C shell, replacing a pattern that is a part of a command with all the filenames that match that pattern. The pattern may also contain metacharacters or wildcards with special meanings.

See also asterisk

filesystem

A complex collection of files, directories, and management information, usually located on a hard disk or other mass storage device such as a compact disc. Sometimes written as two words, *file system*.

All Unix systems have at least a root filesystem, with additional filesystems, as requirements dictate. Each filesystem is controlled by a superblock containing information about the filesystem and consists of i-nodes, which contain information about individual files, and data blocks, which contain the information in the files.

See also /etc, NFS, RFS, standard directories

filter

A Unix command that can take its input from the standard input, perform an operation on the data, and send the result to the standard output. A filter usually does just one operation on the data but does it well. Table F.7 contains a list of useful Unix filters.

An important aspect of filters is that they can be used with redirection and with pipes. This means that you can combine filters with input from a file or from the keyboard or with the output of another command.

TABLE F.7: A List of Useful Unix Filters

Filter Name	Description
cat	Copies standard input to standard output; combines files.
colrm	Removes the specified columns from each line.
crypt	Encrypts or decrypts data using a specified key.
cut	Extracts specified columns from each line.
fmt	Formats text.
grep	Extracts lines that contain a specified pattern.
head	Displays the first few lines of data.
less	Displays data one screen at a time.
look	Extracts lines that begin with a specified pattern.
more	Displays data one screen at a time.
nl	Creates line numbers.
paste	Combines columns of data.
pg	Displays data one screen at a time.
pr	Formats data for printing.
rev	Reverses the order of thecharacters in each line.
sort	Sorts data.
spell	Checks for spelling errors.
tail	Displays the last few lines of data.
tr	Translates selected characters.
uniq	Locates repeated lines.
wc	Counts characters, words, or lines.

find

A command that searches for files meeting specified criteria, descending the Unix directory tree as it goes.

Syntax

The syntax to use with find is as follows:

    find pathname expression

Files can be matched according to name, size, creation date, modification time, or other criteria.

You can also execute a command on the files each time a match is found.

Options and Arguments

The find command is an extremely useful, adaptable, and powerful tool; it may seem difficult to master, but it is well worth the effort. find searches pathname, a space-separated list of directory names that you want to search for a file or files, and expression contains the matching specification or description of the files that you want to find. expression may also contain a list of actions to be taken on each match.

The expression list is evaluated from left to right, and as long as the test in expression evaluates to true, the next test is performed; the expression is evaluated as though connected by a logical AND. If the test is not met, processing on the current file ends, and the next file is checked. You can group conditions by enclosing them in escaped parentheses \(expression\), negate them by !expression (you must use \!expression in the C shell), or separate alternatives with expression -o expression (this acts as a logical OR).

Table F.8 lists the options that you can use with the find command. You can also use a + or – with any of the n *arguments in Table F.8 to indicate either more than or less than, respectively.*

The most useful options are -print, which you must use if you want to see any output from find, -name, and -type. More advanced users will want to experiment with -exec and -size, too. Most of the others are best left to system administrators.

TABLE F.8: Options for Use with find

Option	Description
-atime *n*	Finds files accessed more than, less than, or exactly *n* days ago.
-cpio *dev*	An SVR3 option that writes matching filenames on the device *dev*.
-ctime *n*	Finds files that were changed more than, less than, or exactly *n* days ago; includes files whose permissions have changed.
-depth	This option indicates an action to follow rather than a check that must be made, and so is always true. Makes find act on entries within a directory before acting on the directory itself; often used with cpio.

TABLE F.8 continued: Options for Use with find

OPTION	DESCRIPTION
-exec *command*{}\;	Runs *command* on each matched file. The specified *command* must be followed by an escaped semicolon (\;), and when the *command* runs, the {} argument substitutes the name of the current file.
-follow	Follows symbolic links.
-fstype *type*	Finds files on filesystem *type*.
-group *groupname*	Finds files belonging to *groupname*.
-inum *n*	Finds files with the I-node number *n*.
-links *n*	Finds files with *n* links.
-local	Finds files on the local filesystem.
-mount	Searches for files on the same filesystem as specified by *pathname*.
-mtime *n*	Finds files modified or written to more than, less than, or exactly *n* days ago.
-name *pattern*	Finds files whose names match *pattern*; you can use an *, ?, or [and], but they must be escaped within quotes or preceded by a backslash.
-newer *filename*	Finds files modified more recently than *filename*.
-nogroup	Finds files that belong to a group not found in /etc/passwd.
-nouser	Finds files that belong to a user not found in /etc/passwd.
-ok *command*{}/;	Same as -exec, but you must respond (with a y) before *command* is executed.
-perm *nnn*	Finds files whose permissions match the octal number *nnn*.
-print	Prints matching filenames, along with their full pathnames; this option is always true because it is an option to perform rather than a check to be made.
-prune	This option is always true because it is an option to perform rather than a check to be made. Makes find skip unwanted directory searches.
-size *n*	Finds files of *n* 512-byte blocks; if *n* is followed by a c, the size is in characters not in blocks.
-type *c*	Finds files of type *c*, where *c* can be one of the types listed in Table F.9.
-user *username*	Finds files belonging to *username*; you can use a numeric user ID.

TABLE F.9: File Types Converted by the -type Option in find

FILE TYPE	DESCRIPTION
b	block special file
c	character special file
d	directory
f	ordinary file
l	symbolic link

TABLE F.9 continued: File Types Converted by the -type Option in find

FILE TYPE	DESCRIPTION
p	named pipe
s	socket

Examples

To list all filenames and directories, starting in the current directory and continuing through all subdirectories, use:

```
find . -print
```

To print the names of all the files in the current directory whose names end in .txt, use:

```
find . -name \*.txt -print
```

To find all files accessed more recently than 10 days ago, use:

```
find / -atime +10 -print
```

To find those files not accessed in the last 10 days, substitute -atime -10 instead.

If you want to delete all files that you have not accessed within the last 30 days, use:

```
find . -type f -size +1000c  -atime +30 -ok rm {} \;
```

This command finds ordinary files of larger than 1000 characters that have not been accessed within the last 30 days and then asks if you want to delete them. It actually uses the rm utility to perform the deletion.

Notes

The find command changes the access time of directories provided as pathname; this may be important if you plan on repeating several find commands.

See also chgrp, chmod, ln, ls

finger

A command that displays information about users logged on to the system.

Syntax

To use finger, here's the syntax you need:

```
finger [options]username
```

If you don't specify a `username`, `finger` displays information about each user logged on to the system, including:

- ► Login name
- ► Full name
- ► Terminal name (You will see a * by the name if write permission is denied.)
- ► Idle time—time since the user typed a key
- ► Login time
- ► Location, taken from the comment field in `/etc/ttytab`.

When you specify a `username` as a first name, last name, or login name, `finger` also displays:

- ► User's home directory and login shell
- ► Time the user logged in
- ► Terminal information from `/etc/ttytab`
- ► Time the user received and read mail
- ► Contents of the user's `.plan` file, if it exists, from his or her home directory
- ► Contents of the user's `.profile` file, if it exists, from his or her home directory

Options and Arguments

The options you can use with `finger` are listed in Table F.10.

If you work in a networked environment or have access to the Internet, `finger` also recognizes `username` in the form:

```
user@host
```

TABLE F.10: Options for Use with finger

OPTION	DESCRIPTION
-b	Omits user's home directory and shell from the display.
-f	When used with -s, removes display heading.
-h	Does not display contents of .profile.
-i	Displays information in a condensed format.
-l	Outputs a long format. This option is the only option you can use over a network link.
-m	Matches only the username.
-p	Does not display contents of .plan.
-q	Displays the shortest format.

TABLE F.10 continued: Options for Use with finger

Option	Description
-s	Displays the short format.
-w	When used with -s, omits the user's full name.

Examples

Several Internet users use finger in a rather novel way. The University of Wisconsin has a computerized soft drink vending machine. To buy a drink, you log in to a terminal next to the machine and use the appropriate commands; you must pay in advance to have credit in your account. The command:

```
finger coke@cs.wisc.edu
```

displays the instructions for the system.

Other non-traditional uses include the baseball scores displayed by:

```
finger
```

or the recent earthquake activity displayed by:

```
finger quake@geophys.washington.edu
```

See also finger entry, w, who

finger entry

Information contained in the /etc/passwd file that identifies the user and location to the finger command.

See also finger

firewall

A computer that sits between a trusted in-house network and the Internet to protect the internal network against unauthorized access by restricting the type of information that can pass between them.

A firewall provides controlled access to authorized users and should be configured to block all services by default, except those that you specifically intend to allow.

flex

The GNU version of the lex software development tool, often available on Linux and other systems.

FMLI

Abbreviation for Forms and Menu Language Interpreter. An SVR4 addition to aid programmers in writing windowed applications.

See also FACE, fmli

fmli

A command used to invoke the Form and Menu Language Interpreter (FMLI).

Syntax
The syntax to use with fmli is as follows:

```
fmli [options][filenames]
```

This command invokes FMLI and opens filename. Each filename must have the form menu.string, text.string, or form.string, depending on the kind of object you are opening.

Options and Arguments
You can use three configuration-related options with fmli as Table F.11 shows.

TABLE F.11: Options for Use with fmli

OPTION	DESCRIPTION
-a *afilename*	Loads the list of pathname aliases from *afilename*. Entries in this file have the form *alias=pathname*.
-c *cfilename*	Loads the list of command aliases from *cfilename*.
-i *ifilename*	Loads *ifilename*, which specifies startup features.

fmt

A command that starts a simple text formatter.

Syntax
The usual syntax for fmt is:

```
fmt [options][filenames]
```

fmt breaks long lines of text into lines of roughly the same length; lines are not justified, and blank lines or lines starting with a period are ignored.

In 4.4BSD, the fmt command is slightly different:

    fmt [goal[maximum]]filename

where goal is the required line length, and maximum is the longest allowable line length. Spacing at the beginning of lines is preserved, as are blank lines.

Options and Arguments

The SVR4 fmt command has the three options shown in Table F.12.

TABLE F.12: Command Options to Use with fmt

Option	Description
-c	Leave the first two lines in a paragraph alone; used when paragraphs have a hanging indent.
-s	Splits long lines but leaves short lines intact.
-w n	Creates lines of up to n characters long; the default is 72 characters.

Examples

In the emacs editor, you can use Esc-q to join paragraphs, but in vi the following command reformats a paragraph, evening up the lines:

    !]fmt

This next command shortens long lines to 80 characters but leaves short lines intact. When the formatting is complete, the resulting text is written to a new file:

    fmt -w 80 -s myfile.txt > myfile80.txt

See also fold, nroff

fmtmsg

An SVR4 command used in shell scripts to print messages.

Syntax

The syntax to use with fmtmsg is as follows:

    fmtmsg [options] text

The text is printed on standard error as part of a formatted error message and must be quoted as a single argument.

Options and Arguments

You will find the options available with fmtmsg listed in Table F.13.

TABLE F.13: Options for Use with fmtmsg

Option	Description
-a *action*	A string describing the action to be taken; preceded by the words TO FIX when output.
-c *source*	The source of the problem; can be hard, soft, or firm, for hardware, software, or firmware.
-l *label*	A string used to identify the source of the message.
-s *severity*	An indication of importance; one of halt, error, warn, or info.
-t *tag*	An additional string identifier for the message.
-u *types*	Message type. Can be one of appl (application), util (utility), or opsys (operating system), either recov or nrecov (recovery is possible or not possible), print (message displays on standard error), or console (the message displays on the system console).

Examples
Messages display in this format:

```
label:     severity:   text
TO FIX:    action      tag
```

focus

In an X Window environment, a term used to describe which window is active. Once the right window has the focus, anything you type at the keyboard is used as input for the program running within that window.

fold

A command that breaks long lines in text files into shorter segments.

Syntax
The syntax for fold is:

```
fold [option]filename
```

Options and Arguments
The fold command has one option, -w width, that specifies the length of the lines in characters; the default is 80 characters. If the file contains tabs, make width a multiple of 8 or use the expand command on the file before you use fold.

Examples
To reformat myfile80.txt so that lines are 30 characters or less in length, use:

```
fold -w 30 myfile80.txt > myfile30.txt
```

See also fmt, nroff

for

A Bourne shell and Korn shell keyword used to start a loop or repetitive process. A typical example might look like this:

```
for n [in list]do        commandsdone
```

In other words, for the variable n in the optional list *of values, execute all the* commands.

See also do, done, foreach

foreach

A C shell keyword used to start a loop or repetitive process. An example might look like this:

```
foreach name (wordlist)       commandsend
```

In other words, assign the variable name to each of the values in wordlist, and execute all the commands.

See also do, done, for

foreground

A processing environment in which one program or shell is directly controlled by input from a terminal.

In traditional Unix systems, a process spends its whole existence in either the background or the foreground; in newer systems with job control, you can change the processing environment and move a foreground process into the background, and vice versa.

See also background processing, bg, fg, foreground processing

foreground processing

A mechanism used to run a program in the foreground, with direct input from a terminal or from the user.

When you enter a command to run a program in the foreground, the shell waits for the program to finish before displaying the system prompt so you can enter the next command.

If your Unix system has job control, you can move a foreground process to the background, and vice versa.

See also background processing

fork

To create a new process. When a process starts another identical process by making a copy of itself, it is said to fork the process.

See also child process, exec

format

An SCO UNIX command that formats floppy disks for use with Unix.

Syntax
The syntax to use with format is:

```
format [options]device[-i interleave]
```

The format command formats floppy disks for use with Unix (not with DOS) and can be used interactively or as a command-line utility.

Options and Arguments
The name of the floppy disk drive to use is specified by device; the default device is specified in /etc/default/format. The available options are listed in Table F.14.

See also DOS commands, fdformat.

TABLE F.14: Options to Use with format

Option	Description
-f	Forces format into command-line mode.
-iinterleave	Specifies the interleave factor to use while formatting. This option should be placed after the device argument.
-n	Turns off disk verification.
-q	Turns off track and head display; combine with -f to suppress all output.
-v	Verifies the floppy disk once formatting is complete.

formfeed

Abbreviated FF. A command that advances the paper in a printer by one whole page. In the ASCII character set, a linefeed has the decimal value of 12.

See also linefeed, newline

4.4BSD Lite

A version of the 4.4BSD source code from which all the AT&T code has been removed in an attempt to avoid licensing conflicts. It is not possible to compile and then run 4.4BSD Lite without a pre-existing system because several important files (including several utilities and some important files from the operating system) are missing from the distribution.

4.4BSD Lite has served as the basis for several other important Unix implementations, including FreeBSD and NetBSD.

FPATH

A Korn shell environment variable that specifies search paths for function definitions; these paths are searched after those specified by the PATH variable.

fpr

A BSD filter that translates a Fortran file into a file formatted according to the normal Unix conventions.

f protocol

One of the UUCP protocols, developed for use on X.25 communications links as part of the Berkeley Software Distribution (BSD). Not available in all versions of Unix.

The f protocol is a simple protocol that assumes data is being transferred without errors; it has one checksum for the entire file.

See also e protocol, g protocol, G protocol, t protocol, x protocol

fragment

A small part, usually one quarter, of a filesystem data block. Originally developed as a feature in the Berkeley Software Distribution (BSD) filesystems.

If the last part of a file doesn't completely occupy all of the last disk block, the filesystem can allocate that space to another file; fragments allow the BSD filesystem to use large block sizes without leaving too much unusable space. Do not confuse fragments with fragmentation.

fragmentation

The storage of files in small pieces scattered on a disk. As files grow on a hard disk, they can be divided into several small pieces. By fragmenting files, the operating system makes reasonable use of the disk space available. The problem with file fragmentation is that the disk heads must move to different locations on the disk to read or write to a fragmented file. This process takes more time than reading the file as a single piece. Do not confuse fragmentation with fragments, a useful feature of the BSD filesystem.

free blocks

Unused data blocks on a disk, which are available for use by a file.

Free Software Foundation

See FSF

FreeBSD

A free implementation of Unix for the Intel series of microprocessors, derived from the 4.4BSD Lite releases. The distribution is free, but there may be a small charge to cover the distribution media and packaging. FreeBSD also includes XFree86, a port of the X Window system to the Intel architecture, which supports a large number of graphics adapters.

A complete distribution is available over the Internet from ftp
.FreeBSD.org, and information is available from info@FreeBSD.org.

Most of FreeBSD is covered by a license that allows redistribution as long as the code acknowledges the copyright of the Regents of the University of California and the FreeBSD Project. Those parts of FreeBSD that include GNU software, the C compiler, emacs, and so on, are all covered separately by the FSF license.

See also Linux, NetBSD

freeware

A form of software distribution in which the author retains copyright of the software but makes the program available to others at no cost.

See also copyleft

frequently asked questions

See FAQ

from

A BSD command that prints the names of those who have sent mail to you.

Syntax
The syntax to use with from is:

```
from [options][username]
```

The from command prints out the mail headers from your mailbox.

Options and Arguments
You can use two options with the from command, as Table F.15 shows.

If you specify username, that user's mailbox is examined, but you must have the appropriate privileges and permissions.

See also biff, mail.

TABLE F.15: Options to Use with from

Option	Description
-f *filename*	Examines *filename* instead of the mailbox; if you use this option, do not use the *username* argument.
-s *sender*	Examines mail from mail addresses specified in the string *sender*.

fsck

The Unix filesystem check command, pronounced "fisk." fsck is used by a system administrator logged in as the superuser to check for and repair hard-disk-related problems.

When fsck is run on a filesystem, the filesystem must not be mounted; often the best way of running fsck is to bring the system into single-user mode, check the filesystem, and then reboot and restore normal operations.

For each problem fsck finds, it asks whether you want to try to fix the problem or to ignore it. If you choose to repair the problem, which is usually the most reasonable approach, you may lose some data. The best insurance against data loss is not fsck but is a comprehensive backup program.

See also /lost+found

f77

A Fortran 77 compiler supplied with many Unix systems. This version of Fortran is popular among scientists and engineers for technical programming.

FSF

Abbreviation for Free Software Foundation, an organization founded by Richard Stallman that develops the GNU software.

The FSF philosophy is that all software should be free for everyone to use, and source code should accompany the software. That way, if you make a modification to or fix an error in the software, that change can be sent out to all the other users, saving everyone time and preventing duplication of effort. Also, any software developed under the FSF General Public License (GPL) must also be covered by the same terms of the GPL.

Their address is:

> 59 Temple Place - Suite 330,
> Boston, MA 02111, USA

See also copyleft

fsplit

A 4.4BSD software development command used to split a multiroutine Fortran source code file into files containing individual routines.

fstat

A BSD command that identifies and reports on open files. Because `fstat` takes a snapshot of the system, the results it reports are valid only for a very short period of time. This command is of most interest to system administrators.

ftp

A command used to transfer files to and from remote hosts using the File Transfer Protocol (FTP). You can use `ftp` to log in to an Internet computer and transfer ASCII or binary files during your Internet connection.

Syntax

The syntax to use with `ftp` is as follows:

```
ftp [options] [hostname]
```

When you use ftp, you start a client program on your computer that connects to a server program running on the remote host. The commands that you give to ftp are translated into instructions that the server program executes for you.

Options and Arguments

You can use the options listed in Table F.16 on the command line when you start ftp. hostname can be either a domain address or an IP address. Many computers, not just Unix systems, support the File Transfer Protocol (FTP) and allow file transfers using ftp.

TABLE F.16: Options to Use with ftp

Option	Description
-d	Enables debugging.
-g	Turns off filename expansion so that filenames are read literally.
-i	Turns off interactive prompting during multifile transfers.
-n	Does not try to log in to the remote system automatically on initial connection; unless you specify this option, ftp assumes that your login name of the remote system is the same as on your local system.
-v	Displays all responses from the remote host and all file transfer statistics.

Using the ftp Interpreter

If you do not specify any command-line arguments, ftp starts its command interpreter and waits for you to enter commands. The normal prompt is ftp>. Table F.17 lists the commands commonly used during an ftp session. On most systems other commands are available, but they are mostly concerned with trouble-shooting transfers; see the man pages if you want to know more.

Once you have made a connection using ftp and found your way to the right directory on the remote system, you need only a few commands to move files across the Internet to your own computer. You can become an ftp expert with just five commands: ascii, binary, get, put, and quit.

Depending on the level of security in place on the remote computer, you may find that you are not allowed to use many of those ftp commands that create or delete files and directories, and you may find that your ability to transfer files to a remote computer is also limited.

TABLE F.17: ftp Commands

COMMAND	DESCRIPTION
BASIC COMMANDS	
?	Displays a list of the ftp interpreter commands.
? *command*	Displays information on *command*.
!	Pauses ftp, and starts a shell on the local computer.
! *command*	Executes the specified *command* on the local computer.
bye	Terminates ftp.
help	Displays a list of the ftp interpreter commands.
quit	Closes the connection to the remote computer, and terminates ftp.
CONNECTING COMMANDS	
account [*passwd*]	Supplies a password required by the remote system.
open [*hostname*]	Establishes a connection to the specified remote computer.
close [*hostname*]	Terminates the connection to the specified remote computer, but continues to execute ftp.
disconnect	Same as close.
user [*name*[*password*]]	Identifies the user to the remote computer.
DIRECTORY COMMANDS	
cd [*directory*]	Changes to *directory* on the remote computer.
cdup	Changes the current directory on the remote computer to its parent directory.
delete [*remote_filename*]	Deletes the specified file from the remote system.
dir [*directory*]	Displays a listing of *directory* on the remote computer.
lcd [*directory*]	Changes the current directory on the local computer to *directory*.
ls	Displays a listing of the current directory on the remote computer.
mkdir [*directory*]	Creates the specified directory on the remote computer.
pwd	Displays the name of the current directory on the remote computer.
rmdir [*directory*]	Deletes the specified directory on the remote computer.
FILE TRANSFER COMMANDS	
append [*local_filename*] [*remote_filename*] cr	Toggles stripping of Return characters during the transfer of an ASCII file. Appends a local file to a file on the remote system.
get [*remote_filename* [*local_filename*]]	Transfers *remote_filename* from the remote computer and renames the file *local_filename* on the local computer.

TABLE F.17 continued: ftp Commands

COMMAND	DESCRIPTION
FILE TRANSFER COMMANDS	
mget [*remote_filenames*]	Transfers the specified files from the remote computer.
mput [*local_filenames*]	Transfers the specified files to the remote computer.
put [*local_filename* [*remote_filename*]]	Transfers the file specified by *local_filename* to the remote computer, and renames the file *remote_filename*.
OPTION SETTING COMMANDS	
ascii	Sets the file transfer type to ASCII.
bell	Sounds the terminal bell after each command is complete; a very irritating option and rarely used.
binary	Sets the file transfer type to binary.
hash	Toggles printing of a pound sign (#) for each block of data transferred. This can be a useful indicator that the transfer is continuing as you expect, especially when transferring large files.
prompt	Toggles interactive prompting.
status	Shows the current status of ftp.

Examples

To transfer a text file called faq from the /pub directory on the remote computer and rename the file faq.txt on the local computer, the ftp dialog might look like this:

```
ftp> cd pub
250 CWD command successful.
ftp> ascii
ftp> get faq faq.txt
200 PORT command successful.
150 Opening ASCII mode data  connection for faq  (50007
bytes)
226 Transfer complete.
ftp>
```

The original ftp program started as a Unix utility, but versions are now available for all popular operating systems. The traditional ftp program starts a text-based command processor; the newer versions use a graphical user interface (GUI) with pull-down menus. The consensus seems to be that the GUI versions may be easier to use, but once you get the hang of things, the text-based versions, while not as pretty, are usually faster.

See also anonymous ftp, ftpmail, telnet

FTP

Abbreviation for File Transfer Protocol, the TCP/IP Internet protocol used when transferring single or multiple files from one computer system to another.

FTP uses a client/server model, in which a small client program runs on your computer and accesses a larger FTP server running on the Internet host. FTP provides all the tools needed to look at directories and files, change to other directories, and transfer ASCII or binary files from one computer to the other.

See also ftp

full regular expressions

See also regular expressions

full-screen editor

Any text editor capable of using the whole screen.

See also emacs, **line editor,** vi

fvwm

An X Window window manager specifically developed for use with Linux.

G

g++

A shell script used instead of the gcc command when compiling C++ code with the GNU C language compiler from the Free Software Foundation (FSF).

See also gcc

gadgets

In the X Window system programming toolkit, this is a graphical object, not directly associated with a window, that is used to create graphical applications.

See also widget

gawk

The GNU version of the awk command, available from the Free Software Foundation (FSF) and standard on some Unix systems.

See also awk, nawk, perl

gcc

The GNU C compiler available from the Free Software Foundation (FSF) and standard on some Unix systems, including 4.4BSD and Linux. gcc also compiles C++ source code, as well as source code written in other dialects of the C language.

Syntax
The syntax for use with gcc is as follows:

```
gcc [options] filename
```

Options and Arguments
Many of the options you can use with gcc are very complex and have to do with subtle distinctions between different versions of the C language and machine-dependent options; they are not discussed in this book. See the man pages or the Info files for complete details. Table G.1 lists some of the general-purpose options used when compiling either C or C++ source code with gcc.

See also adb, as, cc, cpp, dbx, g++, gdb, ld, sdb

TABLE G.1: Options for Use with gcc

OPTION	DESCRIPTION
-c	Compiles source code, but does not link.
-E	Stops when the preprocessor is complete, but does not compile the source code.
-g	Turns on debugging information.
-I *directory*	Appends *directory* to the list of directories searched for include files.
-l *library*	Uses the specified *library* when linking.
-L *directory*	Adds the specified *directory* to the list to be searched for libraries used for linking.
-O	Turns on optimization; the compiler attempts to reduce code size and execution time.
-o *filename*	Names the compiler output *filename*. If this option is not specified, output is placed in the file a.out.
-S	Halts after compiling, does not assemble.
-traditional	Attempts to support aspects of traditional C compilers.

TABLE G.1 continued: Options for Use with gcc

OPTION	DESCRIPTION
-v	Prints the commands executed to run the various stages of compilation.
-w	Turns off all warning messages.

gcore

A troubleshooting command used to obtain a core image of a running process. The core image can then be examined using a debugger such as gdb or sdb.

gdb

The GNU debugger, available from the Free Software Foundation (FSF) and standard on some Unix systems, including 4.4BSD. You can use gdb to debug a running program or to examine the cause of a program crash with a core dump.

Syntax

To use gdb, here's the syntax:

```
gdb [options][program[core|PID]]
```

You can use gdb in four main ways to help locate programming errors:

▶ Start the program with gdb specifying anything that might affect its behavior.

▶ Make your program stop on certain specified conditions.

▶ Examine a stopped program.

▶ Make changes to a stopped program and continue execution.

You can use gdb to debug programs written in C and C++. You can start gdb with a specified *program* name, with both a *program* and a core file, or with a *program* name and a process ID (PID) number.

Options and Arguments

The options available for use with gdb are listed in Table G.2.

Table G.3 lists some of the common gdb commands you might use during the course of a debugging session.

See also adb, sdb

TABLE G.2: Options for Use with gdb

Option	Description
-b *bps*	Sets the baud rate of a serial connection used for remote debugging to *bps*.
-batch	Runs gdb in batch mode.
-c *filename*	Uses the specified file as a core dump to examine.
-cd *directory*	Uses the specified *directory*, rather than the current directory.
-command *filename*	Executes the gdb commands contained in *filename*.
-d *directory*	Adds *directory* to the path to search for source files.
-e *filename*	Specifies *filename* as an executable file.
-f	Set by emacs when it runs gdb as a subprocess.
-h	Lists help information.
-n, -nx	Does not execute commands from the .gdbibit file.
-q	Turns off initial copyright messages.
-s *filename*	Reads the symbol table from *filename*.
-se *filename*	Reads the symbol table from *filename*, and uses it as the executable file.
-tty=*device*	Specifies *device* as your program's standard input and standard output.
-x *filename*	Executes the gdb commands contained in *filename*.

TABLE G.3: Common gdb Commands

Command	Description
break [*filename*:]*function*	Sets a breakpoint at *function* within *filename*.
Bt	Backtrace; displays the program stack.
C	Continues execution after a breakpoint.
Help	Displays help information.
help *command*	Displays help information for *command*.
Next	Executes the next program line, stepping over any function calls in the line.
print *expression*	Displays the value of *expression*.
Quit	Terminates gdb.
Step	Executes the next program line, executing any function calls in the line.

GDS

Abbreviation for Global Directory Service, an implementation of the X.500 directory service for managing remote users and addresses.

gencat

A command used to append or merge message files into a message file database.

The syntax to use for gencat is:

```
gencat [option] database messagefile
```

This command merges or appends one (or more) *messagefile* into the formatted *database* file; if the file does not exist, it is created. Every message in *messagefile* is numbered, and you can add comment lines by placing a dollar sign at the beginning of a line, followed by a space or a tab.

gencat has only one option, -n, used to ensure that the *database* is compatible with previous versions of the command.

get

See sccs

getoptcvt

An SCO command used to convert old-style shell scripts that use the obsolete getopt command into scripts that use getopts. getoptcvt reads the shell script, converts it to use getopts, and writes the result to the standard output. A single option, -b, ensures that the results of getoptcvt are portable to earlier UNIX releases.

getopts

A built-in Bourne shell command used to parse command-line options and check for legal options. getopts is often used in shell script loops to ensure a standard syntax for command-line options.

The syntax to use for getopts is as follows:

```
getopts string name [arguments]
```

string contains the option letters to be recognized by getopts, which are processed in turn and then placed in *name*.

The getopts command is also available in SCO Unix as an ordinary utility and is available to many non-Bourne shell users as /usr/bin/getopts.

gettxt

An SVR4 command used to manage message files. The syntax to use for gettxt is:

```
gettxt messagefile:n[default]
```

Extracts the message identified by *n* from the `messagefile`. If the command fails, it displays the contents of the `default` string, or if the string is not specified, it displays Message not found!!

See also `exstr`, `mkmsgs`, `srchtxt`

Ghostview

A GNU application for viewing PostScript files on the X Window system. The document is displayed with a vertical scrollbar on the right side of the screen and a horizontal scrollbar across the bottom; menu options are shown on the left side of the window.

GID

See group ID

glob

A built-in C shell command often used in shell scripts to set a value so that it remains constant for the rest of the script.

The syntax is:

```
glob wordlist
```

and the command performs filename, variable, and history substitution on *wordlist*.

See also global variable, local variable

global variable

Any variable whose value is available to the shell as well as any other programs you run. In the C shell, a global variable is known as an environment variable; in the Korn shell, a global variable is often called a *shell variable*.

See also `export`

globbing

In the shell, the process of performing filename substitution. The shell globs when it replaces a pattern in a command with all the filenames that match that pattern.

See also wildcard

GNU

Pronounced "ga-noo." A Free Software Foundation (FSF) project devoted to developing a complete, freely available Unix system that contains no

AT&T code. The name GNU is a recursive acronym standing for "GNU's not Unix!"

Most of the tools designed for this project have been released and are very popular with users of 4.4BSD, Linux, and many other systems.

See also Hurd

goto

A C shell keyword used to change the flow in a shell script. goto skips to a line in the script labeled by a string ending in a colon (:). This string cannot be located within a foreach or while construct.

gprof

A BSD and Solaris software development tool used to create an execution profile of a C, Pascal, or Fortran program.

See also lprof, prof

G protocol

An enhanced version of the UUCP g protocol, released with SVR4, which increased the packet size from 64 bytes to 256 bytes. A clear 8-bit channel between the two ends of the connection is required.

See also e protocol, f protocol, t protocol, x protocol

graph

A BSD and SCO command that draws a graph.

Syntax
The syntax is:

```
graph [options]
```

graph takes pairs of numbers from the standard input as abscissas and ordinates of the graph, and entered data points are connected by straight lines.

If the coordinates of a point are followed by a non-numeric string, the string is printed as a label at that point.

Options and Arguments
The options you can use with graph are listed in Table G.4.

TABLE G.4: Options for Use with graph

OPTION	DESCRIPTION
-a	Supplies abscissa automatically; spacing is given by the next argument, and the default is 1.
-b	Disconnects the graph following each label in the input.
-c	Specifies the character string given by the next argument as the default label for each data point.
-g	Specifies grid style; 0 for no grid, 1 for a frame with no ticks, 2 (the default) for a full grid.
-h	Specifies a fraction of space for height.
-l	Specifies a graph label.
-m	Specifies line style; 0 for disconnected data points, 1 (the default) for connected points.
-r	Specifies a fraction of space to the right.
-s	Saves the screen.
-t	Swaps horizontal and vertical axes.
-u	Specifies a fraction of space up.
-w	Specifies a fraction of space for width.
-x [1]	If 1 is specified, the x axis is logarithmic; the next two arguments specify the lower and upper axis limits, and the third argument specifies the grid spacing.
-y [1]	If 1 is specified, the y axis is logarithmic; the next two arguments specify the lower and upper axis limits, and the third argument specifies the grid spacing.

grave

See backquote

greater than symbol

The greater than symbol (>) is used in redirection of the standard output from a command to a file or other device. If the file already exists, it is overwritten by this operation.

By using two greater than symbols together (>>), the output from the command is added or appended to the end of an existing file.

Some command interpreters, including programs such as ftp, use the greater than symbol as part of their command prompt.

See also less than symbol

grep

A command used to search for patterns in files.

Syntax

The syntax to use with grep is:

    grep [*options*]*pattern*[*filename*]

grep searches one or more files, line by line, for a *pattern*, which can be a simple string or a regular expression, and then takes actions, specified by the command-line options, on each line that contains a match for *pattern*.

If you use grep to search a file for the word moth, it will also find mother and motherhood; to restrict the search to moth, surround moth in single quotes, ' moth ' with spaces at the start and end of the word. Use the caret (^) to specify the beginning of a line and a dollar sign ($) to specify the end. To specify several characters, enclose them in square brackets; [Ee]vis matches elvis or Elvis, and [A-Z]lvis matches any uppercase letter followed by lvis.

Use a period to match any single character, and in a range enclosed in square brackets, a caret indicates any character except those in the brackets, so [^0-9] matches any non-numeric character.

If you have to specify any of the special Unix characters, escape it with a backslash.

Options and Arguments

The grep utility takes input from the standard input or from *filename* specified on the command line. The options available for use with grep are listed in Table G.5.

grep's exit status is 0 if any lines in the file match the specified *pattern*, 1 if none match, and 2 if a syntax error occurred or the file is unreadable.

TABLE G.5: Options Available with grep

Option	Description
-b	Preceeds each line with its hard disk block number.
-c	Counts the matched lines found in each file.
-h	Prints matched lines but omits filenames; the reverse of the −1 option.
-i	Ignores any distinctions between uppercase and lowercase letters. A good option to use when searching for a word that sometimes begins a sentence and other times occurs in the middle of a sentence.
-1	Prints filenames but omits matched lines; the reverse of the −h option. Lists each filename only once , even if the file contains more than one match.
-n	Precedes each matched line with its line number, even if the file does not contain line numbers.

TABLE G.5 continued: Options Available with grep

Option	Description
-o	In 4.4BSD grep, always prints filename headers with output lines.
-s	Turns off error messages for nonexistent or unreadable files. In 4.4BSD, this option turns everything off except error messages.
-v	Inverts the search; prints all the lines that don't match *pattern*.
-w	In 4.4BSD, limits the search to whole words.

Examples

To list all files in the current directory that contain the word SYBEX, use:

```
grep SYBEX *
```

To search for lines in files in the current directory that contain numbers, use:

```
grep '[0-9]' *
```

Notes

The grep command is a very useful Unix tool, and there have been many variations on this theme:

▸ Extended grep, or egrep, handles extended regular expressions.

▸ Fast grep, or fgrep, is not particularly fast but can be used to find expressions containing literal backslashes, asterisks, and other characters that you ordinarily have to escape.

▸ Approximate grep, or agrep, a public domain grep that locates lines that more or less match your specified search string.

▸ The Free Software Foundation's fast version of grep, called egrep.

▸ A version of grep called rcsgrep, which is used to search through Revision Control System (RCS) files.

grodvi

See groff

groff

The Free Software Foundation's implementation of the Unix text processing commands nroff and troff. groff is distributed with many systems, including 4.4BSD and Linux.

Syntax
The syntax to use is:

```
groff [options][filename...]
```

The groff command is the front end to the groff document formatting system, and it normally runs troff followed by the appropriate postprocessor.

Options and Arguments
If you omit *filename* and use – instead, groff reads from the standard input. The options for use with groff are listed in Table G.6.

TABLE G.6: Options for Use with groff

OPTION	DESCRIPTION
-e	Uses eqn as preprocessor.
-h	Prints help information.
-l	Sends the output to a printer.
-L *argument*	Passes *argument* to the spooler.
-p	Uses pic as preprocessor.
-P *argument*	Passes *argument* to the postprocessor.
-R	Uses refer as preprocessor.
-s	Uses soelim as preprocessor.
-t	Uses tbl as preprocessor.
-T *device*	Prepares output for *device*.
-v	Forces the programs run by groff to print their version numbers.
-z	Suppresses troff output; only error messages are printed.
-Z	Does not use troff as the postprocessor.

Notes
You might encounter several other members of the groff family, including:

- grodvi converts groff output into TEX format
- grog guesses the correct options to use with groff
- grops is a PostScript driver for groff
- grotty is a tty driver for groff

See also eqn, **LATEX**, nroff, pic, soelim, tbl, **TEX**, **Texinfo**, troff

grog
See groff

grops

See groff

grotty

See groff

group

A collection of users; the basis for establishing file permissions.

Each file in the filesystem has a group identifier associated with it, and members of the group are given permissions to use the file, which are not available to other users. Group access permissions for files are displayed as the middle three characters of the nine-character access mode in a long ls listing.

In most Unix systems, you can belong to several different groups simultaneously; on older systems, you could only belong to one group at any time.

See also chgrp, chmod, groups, newgrp

group ID

A number defined in the password database when a user is assigned a group number. Each group is identified by a number that defines the permissions assigned to members of the group. Sometimes abbreviated as group GID.

See also chgrp, newgrp

groups

A command that lists all groups to which a user belongs. The syntax is:

```
groups [username]
```

Groups are listed in /etc/passwd and /etc/groups. With no arguments, this command lists the groups that the current user belongs to; with a username, the command lists the groups to which the username belongs.

See also chgrp, newgrp

groupware

Network software designed for use by a group of people all working on the same project or using the same data.

Groupware can range from relatively simple programs designed to do one thing well, to enhanced e-mail products (such as Corel Perfect Office, Lotus Notes, or Novell Groupwise).

See also workflow software, workgroup

gunzip

See also gzip

gwm

The name of the X Window system generic window manager; a very flexible window manager able to emulate either the Open Look or the Motif window managers.

gzexe

A BSD command that compresses executable files in place and then automatically uncompresses them when they are run. There is a performance penalty for this convenience, however, and gzexe is most often used on systems with small hard disks.

The syntax is:

```
gzexe filename...
```

The only option is -d, used when you want to decompress the executable without running it.

See also gzip

gzip

A set of file compression utilities from the Free Software Foundation's GNU Project and included with many systems, such as 4.4BSD and Linux. It is also available free of charge for almost every brand of Unix.

The gzip family has three members; gzip compresses the file, gunzip uncompresses the file, and zcat cats the file.

Syntax
The syntax to use is:

```
gzip [options] filename...
```

The gzip command compresses the specified *filename* using a Lempel-Zif compression method. It keeps the original filename and timestamp, and adds the filename extension .gz whenever possible, while preserving ownership modes, modification times, and so on. The original uncompressed file is removed when gzip completes the compression process – it is very difficult to delete files accidentally using gzip.

The gunzip command uncompresses files that were compressed using gzip, zip, compress, or pack. The compressed file is removed once the decompression process is complete.

Using zcat is identical to using gunzip -c.

Options and Arguments

The options available with these utilities are listed in Table G.7.

You can use all of these options with gzip and gunzip; you can only use -f, -h, -L, and -V with zcat.

TABLE G.7: Options Available with gzip, gunzip, and zcat

Option	Description
-a	ASCII mode, supported on some non-Unix systems. For DOS, carriage return–linefeed pairs are converted to linefeeds when compressing a file, and the reverse translation is performed when decompressing a file.
-c	Leaves the original files intact, and writes the output to the standard output.
-d	Decompresses the specified file.
-f	Forces a compression or decompression even if the file has multiple links or a corresponding file already exists.
-h	Displays help information.
-l	Lists information on compressed files, including compressed size, uncompressed size, compression ratio percentage, and name of the original file.
-L	Displays license information and terminates.
-n	When compressing, saves the original filename and timestamp; when decompressing, restores the original name and timestamp.
-q	Turns off all warnings.
-r	Compresses (or uncompresses) files in the specified directories.
-S.*suffix*	Uses .*suffix*, rather than .gz.
-t	Tests the compressed file's integrity.
-v	Displays the version number and then terminates.
-*n*	Specifies the speed of compression, where -1 indicates the fastest method with the least compression, and -9 indicates the slowest compression with the most compression; the default is -6. This option is not available with gunzip.

Examples

To compress the file `allmine.doc`, use:

```
gzip allmine.doc
```

The file will be replaced by a compressed file called `allmine.doc.gz`.

To decompress this file, use:

```
gunzip allmine.doc.gz
```

The file is decompressed and restored to its former name of `allmine.doc`.

Notes

The `gzip` command uses the same Lempel-Zif method used in the other familiar file-compression programs `zip` and PKZIP. The amount of compression you see depends on the original file type; ASCII text files and program source code files may show a 60 to 70 percent reduction in size. If the file is already in a compressed form, such as JPEG files, `gzip` will have little or no effect.

See also `compress`, `gzexe`, `pack`

H

hard link

A directory entry containing the filename and i-node for a file. The i-node identifies the location of the file's control information, which, in turn, defines the location of the file's contents on the hard disk. Hard links are always confined to the same filesystem; they cannot cross into another filesystem, and you cannot create a hard link to a directory.

See also link, soft link, symbolic links

hardware interrupt

An interrupt or request for service generated by a hardware device, such as a keystroke from the keyboard or a tick from the clock. Because the processor may receive several such signals simultaneously, hardware interrupts are usually assigned a priority level and processed according to that priority.

See also interrupt handler

hard-wired

Describes a system designed in a way that does not allow for flexibility or future expansion. May also refer to a device that is connected directly to an individual computer system, such as a printer.

See also hard-coded

hash

A built-in Bourne shell command that reports the path associated with the previous command or with commands running in the background.

Used with no arguments, hash displays hits (the number of times that the shell has previously run the command) and cost (a relative indicator of the amount of work needed to find the command); the output looks like this:

```
hash
hits    cost    command
0       1       /bin/eric
```

hashing

The process of creating or rebuilding a hash table by recalculating the search index code assigned to each piece of data in the table.

In the C shell, hashing involves creating a table of commands in your path and then searching that table (rather than the full path) when you ask for a command to be executed. Without hashing, every directory specified in your path must be searched on every new command.

hash table

A method of representing data so that it can be found again very quickly.

A hash table assigns a special index code to each piece of data, and specially designed software uses this code to locate the data, rather than repeating what might be a lengthy search each time the data is requested.

The C shell uses a hash table to locate commands quickly, and the rehash command is used to rebuild this hash table after you add a new command. Hash tables are also used by many database products.

hashstat

A built-in C shell command that displays statistics indicating the hash tables' success rate at locating commands via the path variable.

hd

An SCO command used to display files in character, decimal, hexadecimal, and octal formats.

Syntax

The syntax for this command is:

```
hd [-format][options][filename]
```

Options and Arguments

The -format argument specifies what information is displayed and in what form. This information is provided in Table H.1.

The default is -abx -A, for addresses and bytes displayed in hexadecimal. The default also specifies that characters are printed.

If no *filename* is specified, hd reads from the standard input. The options listed in Table H.2 are available with the hd command.

TABLE H.1: hd format Flags

Flags	Description
AcbwlA	Specifiers for addresses, characters, bytes, words (2 bytes), long words (4 bytes), and ASCII.
Xdo	Specifiers for hexadecimal, decimal, or octal.
T	Specifies that the text file be printed with each line numbered.

TABLE H.2: Options Available with hd

Option	Description
-n *count*	Specifies the number of bytes to process.
-s *offset*	Specifies the offset from the beginning of the file where you want printing to start, as a decimal number, a hexadecimal number (prefaced by 0x), or an octal number (prefaced by 0). *offset* can be followed by an optional multiplier: w for words (2 bytes), 1 for long words (4 bytes), b for half kilobytes (512 bytes), or k for kilobytes (1024 bytes).

Examples

To list the contents of the file allmine.txt in octal, starting 100 bytes (in decimal) into the file, use:

```
hd -Ao -s 100 allmine.txt
```

See also cat, hexdump, more, od, pg

HDB

See HoneyDanBer UUCP

head

A command that prints the first few lines of one or more text files.

The head command sends the beginning of a file (or the standard input) to the screen (or to the standard output). The syntax to use is:

```
head -n filename...
```

where -n specifies the number of lines of the file you want to display; if you don't specify a value, head prints the first 10 lines.

If you specify multiple files, each file is separated by the header:

```
==> filename <==
```

where *filename is the name of the file.*

There are no options for the head command.

See also cat, less, more, pg, tail

hello

An SCO command that sends a message to a terminal.

The syntax is:

```
hello user [tty]
```

When you first start hello, the following message is displayed:

```
Message from sending-system! sender's-name sender's-tty
```

Communication continues between the two terminals until one user terminates the session with Ctrl-C or Del, and hello outputs:

```
(end of message)
```

hexdump

A BSD filter command that displays a file in a specified format—as ASCII, decimal, hexadecimal, or octal.

Syntax

The syntax for hexdump is as follows:

```
hexdump [options]filename...
```

The hexdump command reads from the specified file or files, or if none are specified, it reads from the standard input.

Options and Arguments

Several options are available with hexdump, as Table H.3 shows.

See also cat, hd, more, od, pg

TABLE H.3: Options to Use with hexdump

OPTION	DESCRIPTION
-b	Displays the input offset in hexadecimal, followed by the data displayed in one-byte octal.
-c	Displays the input offset in hexadecimal, followed by the data displayed in hexadecimal.
-d	Displays the input offset in hexadecimal, followed by the data displayed in unsigned decimal.
-e *format-string*	Specifies a *format-string* for displaying the data.
-f *format-file*	Specifies a *format-file* for displaying the data.
-n *length*	Displays only *length* bytes of data from the file.
-o	Displays the input offset in hexadecimal, followed by the data displayed in two-byte octal.
-s *offset*	Skips *offset* from the beginning of the file; by default a decimal number, a leading 0x is interpreted as a hexadecimal number, and a leading 0 as an octal number. You can also specify *offset* as b (multiples of 512 bytes), k (multiples of 1024 bytes), or m (multiples of 1,048,576 bytes).
-v	Forces the display of all data.
-x	Displays the input offset in hexadecimal, followed by the data displayed in two-byte hexadecimal.

hidden character

Any nonprinting character that performs a special function, such as backspace or erase.

hidden file

See dot file

hierarchical file structure

The organizational system used by Unix to keep track of files and directories on a disk.

The Unix file structure resembles an inverted tree, with the root directory (/) as the starting point. Files and directories are contained within directories that branch off from the root. A directory is usually devoted to files relating to a specific subject or purpose and may or may not contain subdirectories.

One of the strengths of the Unix filesystem is its ability to adapt to the needs of different users. In a standard Unix system, users start with one directory, and within this directory, they can create as many subdirectories as they like, expanding the structure according to their needs. This hierarchical structure has been adopted in many other operating systems, including the Macintosh, DOS, Windows, and OS/2.

See also **current working directory, directory tree, home directory**

histchars

A C shell environment variable that contains the two characters used to replace ! and ^, respectively, in history substitution commands.

history

A mechanism found in the Bourne Again shell, C shell, and Korn shells, which allows you to modify and re-execute recent commands without having to retype them.

All your previously executed commands are stored in the history file, even your mistakes, and the shell lets you access this list so that you can repeat commands or re-issue them in a modified form. Each command is assigned a number, beginning with 1, so you can refer to command number 5 or command number 20, and so on.

By default, the shell saves the last 128 commands; if you want to save more, increase the value of the HISTSIZE variable in the Korn shell or the history variable in the C shell.

See also fc, history, **history substitution**

history

A built-in C shell command that lists recent keyboard commands. The syntax is:

```
history [options]
```

The options available with this command are listed in Table H.4.

history also is a Korn shell command that lists the last 16 commands; history is a Korn shell alias for fc -1.

See also fc, **history,** .history, **history file**

TABLE H.4: Options to Use with history

Option	Description
-h	Prints the history list without event numbers.
-r	Prints the history list in reverse order, oldest commands first.
n	Displays only the last *n* commands, rather than the number set by the shell variable.

.history

The name of the history file, which is the file that holds all the commands entered by a user while that user was logged on to the system; the file is deleted or cleared when the user logs off at the end of a session.

See also history

HISTSIZE

A Korn shell environment variable that specifies how many past commands are accessible; the default is 128 commands.

See also history

home

The initial cursor location at the top left corner of the screen.

home

A C shell variable containing the full path of your home directory. The ~ character is a shorthand notation for the name of your home directory.

See also HOME

HOME

A Bourne shell and Korn shell variable containing the full path of your home directory. The tilde character (~) is a shorthand notation for the name of your home directory.

/home

An SVR4 root directory that contains user home directories and files.

home directory

A directory that contains the files for a specific user ID. The name of your home directory is kept in the passwd file, and when you log in, your current directory is always set to be your home directory. The home directory is usually the starting point for your own directory structure, which you can make as austere or as complex as you like.

As a shortcut, you can use the tilde character (~) as a symbol for the name of your home directory. The complete path for your home directory is stored in the home or HOME variable, depending on which shell you use.

See also cd, pwd

home page

On the World Wide Web, an initial starting page. A home page may be prepared by an individual, a nonprofit group, or a corporation and is a convenient jumping-off point to other Web pages or Internet resources.

See also HTML, HTTP, SGML, URL

HoneyDanBer UUCP

A version of UUCP developed by Peter Honeyman, David Nowitz, and Brian D. Redman, which replaced the original AT&T version. Also known as the *Basic Networking Utilities*, sometimes abbreviated *BNU*.

host

The central or controlling computer in a networked or distributed processing environment, providing services that other computers or terminals can access via the network.

A large system accessible on the Internet is also known as a host. Sometimes known as a *host system* or a *host computer*.

hostid

A command that prints the hexadecimal ID number for the host system. The command is found in /usr/uch/hostid.

See also hostname.

hostname

A command that sets or prints the name of the current host. The syntax is:

```
hostname [newhost]
```

where *newhost* is the new name to use for the host; you must be the superuser to change this name.

See also hostid.

hp

An SCO command that handles special functions found on Hewlett-Packard's 2640 series of terminals so that accurate `nroff` output can be displayed on them.

HP-UX

A version of Unix for Hewlett-Packard computers. HP-UX includes BSD extensions, including the networking commands, the Korn shell, and a version of `emacs`. VUE (Visual User Environment) is HP's GUI, with individual workspaces for different tasks, drag-and-drop functions, a text editor, color icon editor, as well as other productivity tools.

HP-UX also includes SAM (System Administration Manager) for common administration tasks, such as adding new users, installing and configuring peripherals, managing processes and scheduling jobs. Diskless computers, either clients or servers, can boot from the server and can support locally mounted filesystems, so that each client has access to its own data files as well as being able to share files with others.

HTML

Abbreviation for Hypertext Markup Language. A standard hypertext language used to create World Wide Web pages and other hypertext documents.

When you access an HTML document, you see a mixture of text, graphics, and links to other documents or to other Internet resources. When you select a link, the related document opens automatically, no matter where that document is located. Hypertext documents often have the filename extension `.html` or `.htm`.

HTML has been vital in the development of the World Wide Web; however, the functions that it can provide via the Web browser are becoming restrictive. This has led to other developments such as Java, which can provide 3D interactive applications.

See also home page, HTTP, SGML, URL

HTTP

Abbreviation for Hypertext Transfer Protocol. The protocol used to manage the links between hypertext documents.

HTTP is the mechanism that opens the related document when you select a hypertext link, no matter where that related document happens to be.

See also home page, HTML, SGML, URL

Hurd

A project from the Free Software Foundation (FSF) to develop and distribute a free version of Unix for many different hardware platforms. Still in the early stages of development, Hurd (or sometimes HURD) is considered to be a collection of all the GNU software, compilers, editors, utilities, as well as the operating system.

hwconfig

An SCO command that lists configuration information contained in /usr/adm/hwconfig.

Syntax
The syntax for this command is:

```
hwconfig [options]
```

Information is displayed in the following columns:

- magic_char
- device_name
- base+finish
- vec
- dma
- rest

where magic_char is a percent sign (%), device_name is the name of the device driver, base+finish are the starting and ending addresses of the driver working space, vec is the interrupt vector number (in decimal), dma is the number of the DMA channel, and rest is a list of *parameter* =*value* pairs. rest may also be empty.

Options and Arguments
Options for use with hwconfig are listed in Table H.5.

TABLE H.5: Options for Use with hwconfig

OPTION	DESCRIPTION
-c	Checks for device conflicts.
-f *filename*	Uses information from *filename* rather than from /usr/adm/hwconfig.
-h	Uses long format with headers.
-l	Uses long format, the default setting.
-n	Forces the output of the device name.
Param	Shows values for *param*. Valid system *param* include name, base, offset, vec, dma, unit, type, nports, hds, cyls, secs, and drvr.
param=value	Shows information from the entry where *param* is equal to *value*.
-q	Quiet mode; when used with -c displays conflicts only.

hypermedia

A term used to describe nonsequential applications that have interactive hypertext linkages between different multimedia elements of graphics, sound, text, animation, and video.

If an application relies heavily on text-based information, it is known as hypertext; however, if full-motion video, animation, graphics, and sound are used, it is considered to be hypermedia.

hypertext

A method of presenting information so that it can be viewed by the user in a non-sequential way, regardless of how the topics were originally organized.

Hypertext was designed to make a computer respond to the nonlinear way that humans think and access information—by association, rather than the linear organization of film, books, and speech.

In a hypertext application such as the World Wide Web, you can browse through the information with considerable flexibility, choosing to follow a new path each time you access the information. When you click on a highlighted word, you activate a link to another hypertext document, which may be located on the same Internet host or can be on a completely different system thousands of miles away. These links depend on the care that the document originator used when assembling the document; unfortunately, many links turn into dead ends.

See also home page, HTML, HTTP, SGML

Hypertext Markup Language

See HTML

Hypertext Transfer Protocol

See HTTP

I

iconv

A command used to convert a file from one character set into another. The syntax is:

```
iconv -f char-set1 -t char-set2 filename
```

where *filename* is converted from *char-set1* to *char-set2*; if there is no equivalent for a character in *char-set2*, that character is translated into an underscore (_). You will find supported conversions listed in /usr/lib/conv.

id

A command that displays a user's login name, ID, and group ID. When used with the -a option, the id command lists all the groups to which you belong.

See also finger, users, w, who

ident

See RCS

if

A shell programming command used to provide a conditional branching statement.

An if statement in the C shell is used in a different way from an if statement in the Bourne and Korn shells:

▶ In the C shell, you don't need brackets around the test part of the statement.

▶ The C shell uses == for an equality statement rather than a single = as in the Bourne and Korn shells.

▸ In the C shell, a semicolon must follow then.

▸ The C shell uses endif to terminate the if statement rather than fi.

See also elif, else

IFS

A Bourne shell and Korn shell variable used to specify the characters used as the shell's default field separators, which are the space, tab, and newline.

ignoreeof

A C shell environment variable that ignores end-of-file (EOF) characters typed from the keyboard and prevents an accidental logout.

image copy

A term used to describe an exact, byte-for-byte copy of a file.

imake

An extension to the make software development command used when compiling source files into an application.

Creating makefiles by hand can be a long complex process; imake automates the process from a template of cpp macro functions, reading an input file called Imakefile and then converting the two into a makefile. imake provides an excellent solution to the long-standing problem of how to maintain a set of hierarchical makefiles when an application's source files exist in several different directories.

inactive window

In an interface capable of displaying multiple windows on the screen, all open windows except the currently active window, the window that contains the cursor. If you click on an inactive window with the cursor, it becomes the active window.

include file

A source code file that contains code needed by several different program modules. Also called a *header file*. These files are normally given characteristic filename extensions such as .h, .hpp, .hxx, and so on.

incremental backup

A backup of a hard disk that consists of only those files created or modified since the last backup was performed.

incremental search

A search that starts as soon as you type the first letter of the search string and is modified as you enter subsequent letters.

indent

A BSD software development command used to reformat C language source code. This is a complex utility, with more options than the `ls` command; there are in fact over 50 different options.

See also cb, cc

index node

See i-node

indxbib

A command used to create an inverted index file for bibliographic databases.

Syntax

The syntax for this command is:

```
indxbib [options][filename...]
```

If you don't specify an output filename, the index file is stored as /usr/ share/dict/papers/Ind.i.

Options and Arguments

The options available with `indxbib` are listed in Table I.1.

See also invert, lkbib, lookbib, refer.

TABLE I.1: Options Available with indxbib

OPTION	DESCRIPTION
-c*filename*	Reads a list of common words from *filename*.
-d*directory*	Specifies that the index is stored in *directory*.
-f*filename*	Reads *filename* as the input file.
-h*n*	Specifies the size of the hash table; the default is 997.
-i*string*	Doesn't index the fields specified in *string*.

TABLE I.1: Options Available with indxbib

Option	Description
-k*n*	Uses *n* keys per input record; the default is 100.
-l*n*	Throws away keys shorter than *n*; the default is 3.
-n*n*	Throws away the *n* most common words; the default is 100.
-o*basename*	Specifies the base filename for the output file.
-t*n*	Truncates key to *n*; the default is 6.
-v	Prints the program version number.
-w	Indexes entire files; each file is a separate record.

info

The command used to start the InfoExplorer application on an IBM Unix system. InfoExplorer is a large hypertext help system with both an ASCII terminal and an X Window system interface.

inheritance

In object-oriented programming, the ability of one class of objects to pass on properties to a lower class of objects. Inheritance can even include features of the parent's environment, such as open files. Multiple inheritance lets you create a new class with properties of more than one previously defined class.

See also encapsulation, polymorphism

init

The first process created by the Unix kernel as the system boots up; an abbreviation for initialize. The init process always has the process ID number (PID) of 1. init creates all subsequent processes and additional init processes for new users as they log on to the system. init also controls the level or state in which Unix runs, as Table I.2 shows.

On BSD systems, init starts the system but then relies on instructions generated by the kill command to change run levels or to shut down the system.

TABLE I.2: Unix System States

STATE	DESCRIPTION
0	Shutdown state; used before turning the computer off.
1	Administrative state; starts Unix so that the filesystem is available to the system administrator but not to other users. Used when troubleshooting corrupted files or changing hardware configuration information.
2	Multiuser state; the normal operating mode, in which filesystems are mounted and available to all users.
3	Remote File Sharing (RFS) state; used to start the RFS, and to mount and share resources over the network.
5	Firmware state; used to run special commands and system diagnostics.
6	Stop and reboot state; used to restart in the mode specified by the `initdefault` entry in `/etc/inittab`.
S or s	Single-user state; used by the system administrator for maintenance. Only a limited number of kernel processes are running, and only the root filesystem is available.

initialization file

A file executed by a program as it starts running, before it begins its main purpose. Most initialization files are found in your home directory, and so you can customize them to your exact needs. For example, the `emacs` editor loads the contents of the `.emacs` file as it starts up; `vi` loads `.exrc`, and so on.

See also dot file

initialization string

A string of characters sent to your terminal as you log on to configure it to your specific needs.

i-node

Pronounced "eye-node"; the abbreviation for information node, sometimes written *inode*. A data structure on the disk that describes a file. Each directory entry associates a filename with an i-node; although a single file may have several filenames (one for each link), a file has only one i-node. Within a filesystem, the number of i-nodes (and therefore the number of files) is defined when the filesystem is first initialized.

An i-node contains all the information Unix needs to be able to access the file, including the file's length, the times that the file was last accessed and modified, the time that the i-node was last modified, owner and group ID information, access permissions, the number of links to the file, the type of the file, and the disk addresses of the data blocks that contain the actual file.

See also i-number

i-node table

A list of all the i-nodes in a filesystem. Within the i-node table, each i-node is known by a number, the i-number or index number. If a file is defined by i-node #300, has an i-number of 300.

integer

A built-in Bourne shell and Korn shell command used to specify integer variables.

interactive

Any program that allows a dialog with the user to take place; most modern programs are interactive.

Interactive UNIX

A version of Unix from Sun Microsystems based on AT&T's System V Release 3.2 kernel.

See also Solaris

internet

Abbreviation for internetwork. Two or more networks using different networking protocols, usually connected by means of a router. Users on an internetwork can access the resources of all the connected networks as though they were local.

Internet

The world's largest computer network, consisting of millions of computers supporting billions of users in every country. The Internet is growing at a phenomenal rate—between 10 and 15 percent per month—so any size estimates are quickly out of date.

The Internet was originally established to meet the research needs of the U.S. defense industry, but it has grown into a huge global network serving universities, academic researchers, commercial interests, and government agencies. The Internet uses TCP/IP protocols and many of the Internet hosts run Unix.

See also IAB, Internet address, ftp, PPP, SLIP, telnet, USENET

Internet address

An absolute address on the Internet. An Internet address takes the form *someone@abc.def.xyz*, where *someone* is a user's account name , *@abc* is the network computer of the user, and *def* is the name of the host organization. The last three letters, *xyz*, denote the kind of institution the user belongs to: in the U.S. you will find edu for educational, com for commercial, gov for a branch of the government, mil for the military, org for nonprofit organizations, and net for Internet administrative organizations. In other countries, other identifiers are used, and outside the U.S., you will also find an identifier for the specific country. For example, ca for Canada or uk for Great Britain.

See also **bang path, domain, domain address, dotted decimal, IP address**

Internet file types

The Internet offers many opportunities for downloading files from a huge number of Internet hosts. These files may have been generated on different computer systems, and so before you download a file, it is important that you understand the type of file you are dealing with. Many files are compressed to minimize the time the file takes to download. Table I.3 lists many of the common file types you may encounter on your Internet travels.

See also compress, gzip, pack, tar, uudecode, uuencode

TABLE I.3: Internet and Unix File Types

FILENAME EXTENSION	DESCRIPTION
tar	A tape archive file created by the tar utility.
Z	A file created by the compress utility. You must use the uncompress utility to restore the file before you can use it.
tar.Z	A compressed tape archive file.
z	A compressed file created using pack. You must use unpack to restore the file before you can use it.
ls-1R.Z	A file listing sorted by time, showing the most recent files first. The file is also compressed.
ls-1tR.Z	A file listing sorted into alphabetical order; the file is also compressed.
ZIP	A compressed file created using PKZIP that must be uncompressed with PKUNZIP before you can use it.

TABLE I.3 continued: Internet and Unix File Types

FILENAME EXTENSION	DESCRIPTION
gz	A Unix file compressed by the GNU gzip utility. This file must be decompressed before you can use it.
HQX	A compressed Macintosh file.
SIT	A Macintosh file compressed by StuffIt.
TIF or TIFF	A graphics file in TIFF format.
GIF	A graphics file in GIF format.
JPG or JPEG	A graphics file in JPEG format.
MPG or MPEG	A video file in MPEG format.
TXT	A text file.
1	An nroff source file.
ps	A PostScript file ready for printing on a PostScript printer.
uue	A uuencoded file. You must use uudecode before you can use the file.
uue.z	Compressed uuencoded file.
shar	A USENET newsgroup archive file created by the shar program.
shar.Z	Compressed shar file.

interpreter

A programming language translator that converts high-level program source code into machine language statements one line at a time.

Unlike a compiler, which must translate the whole program before execution can start, an interpreter translates and then executes each line one at a time; this usually means that an interpreted program runs more slowly than a compiled program.

BASIC was often an interpreted language, although recent releases of the language have used a compiler, and C, C++, and Pascal are always compiled.

See also command interpreter

interprocess communications

Abbreviated IPC. A term that describes all the methods used to pass information between two programs running on the same computer or between two programs running on a network, including pipes, shared memory, message queues, sockets, and semaphores.

See also ipcrm, ipcs

interrupt

A signal to the processor generated by a device under its control (such as the system clock) or by software, which interrupts normal processing.

An interrupt indicates that an event requiring the processor's attention has occurred, causing the processor to suspend and save its current activity, block out any lower priority interrupts, and then branch to an interrupt handler or service routine. This service routine processes the interrupt, whether it was generated by the system clock, a keystroke, or a mouse click; and when it's complete, returns control to the original suspended process.

interrupt handler

Software in the Unix kernel that manages and processes system interrupts. The actual task performed by the interrupt handler depends on the nature of the interrupt itself. Also known as an *interrupt service routine.*

i-number

Contraction of index number. A number used to identify an i-node; part of the file control information that Unix keeps in an i-node. Sometimes written as *inumber.*

See also i-node table

invert

A BSD command that creates an inverted index intended for use with bib.

Syntax
The syntax for this command is:

    invert [options]filename...

Options and Arguments
Table I.4 lists the options you can use with invert.

See also bib, lookup

TABLE I.4: Options to Use with invert

OPTION	DESCRIPTION
-c *filename*	Specifies that the words listed in *filename* will not be used as keys.
-k *i*	Specifies the maximum number of keys per record; the default is 100.
-l *i*	Specifies the maximum length of keys; the default is 6.

TABLE I.4 continued: Options to Use with invert

Option	Description
-p *filename*	Specifies *filename* as the name of the output file.
-s	Turns off statistics, silent mode.
-%*string*	Ignores lines that begin with % followed by any characters defined in *string*.

invisible character

Any nonprinting character such as backspace, erase, or any of the control characters.

invisible file

Any file whose name begins with a period. Such files are known as invisible files because the ls command does not list them in the normal file and directory display, although you can see them when you use the -a option. It is also worth noting that the shell will not expand an asterisk (*) to match the names of invisible files.

See also dot file

IP

Abbreviation for Internet Protocol. The TCP/IP network-layer protocol that regulates packet forwarding by tracking Internet addresses, routing outgoing messages, and recognizing incoming messages.

See also TCP, UDP

ipcrm

A command used by the system administrator to clean up after a program has failed to de-allocate space for message queues, semaphores, or shared memory.

Syntax

The syntax for the ipcrm command is as follows:

```
ipcrm [options]
```

Options and Arguments

Table I.5 lists the options you can use with ipcrm.

See also ipcs.

TABLE I.5: Options to Use with icprm

Option	Description
-m *shmemid*	Removes the shared memory identifier *shmemid*.
-M *shmemkey*	Removes the shared memory identifier created with the key *shmemkey*.
-q *msgqid*	Removes the message queue identifier *msgqid*.
-Q *msgkey*	Removes the message queue identifier created with the key *msgkey*.
-s *semid*	Removes the semaphore identifier *semid*.
-S *semkey*	Removes the semaphore identifier created with the key *semkey*.

ipcs

A command that prints interprocess communications (IPC) information.

Syntax

The syntax to use with this command is:

    ipcs [*options*]

This command provides information on waiting processes, shared memory segments, and message queues.

Options and Arguments

You can use the options listed in Table I.6 with the ipcs command. When you use the -m, -q, or -s options, only information about the specific interprocess communications facility is given; otherwise, information is displayed about all three.

The default display produced when you use this command with no options lists the IPC type, associated ID, key, mode, owner, and group.

See also ipcrm

TABLE I.6: Options for Use with ipcs

Option	Description
-a	Combines all the display options; equivalent to -bcopt.
-b	Displays the maximum number of message bytes, segment sizes, and number of semaphores allowed.
-c	Displays login name and group.
-C *filename*	Reads status from the specified *filename*, rather than from /dev/kmem.
-m	Reports only on active shared memory segments.
-N *list*	Uses the arguments contained in *list*.
-o	Displays outstanding usage.

TABLE I.6 continued: Options for Use with ipcs

OPTION	DESCRIPTION
-p	Displays process numbers.
-q	Reports only on active message queues.
-s	Reports only on semaphores.
-t	Displays time information.

IPX

Abbreviation for Internet Packet Exchange. Part of Novell NetWare's protocol stack, used to transfer data between the server and workstations on the network. IPX packets are compatible with multiple types of media including Ethernet and Token Ring.

See also SPX

IRC

Abbreviation for Internet Relay Chat. An Internet client/server application that allows large groups of users to communicate with each other interactively, developed by Jarkko Oikarinen in Finland. Specific channels are devoted to one particular topic, from the sacred to the profane, and topics come and go regularly as interest levels change. Each channel has its own name, usually prefaced by the pound sign (#), as in #hottub.

When you join a channel, you can see what others have already typed; when you type a line and press the Enter key, your text is seen by everyone else. Table I.7 lists a summary of basic IRC commands.

Most but not all the conversations are in English. If somebody asks you for your password during an IRC session, don't be tempted to give it; somebody is trying to trick you into giving away important information about your system that he or she might be able to use against it.

TABLE I.7: Summary of Basic IRC Commands

COMMAND	DESCRIPTION
/flush	Discards remaining output for the current command.
/help	Displays a list of all IRC commands.
/help *command*	Displays help information about the specified *command*.
/help intro	Displays an introduction to IRC.
/help newuser	Displays information for new users.

TABLE I.7 continued: Summary of Basic IRC Commands

COMMAND	DESCRIPTION
/join *channel*	Lets you join the specified *channel*.
/leave *channel*	Lets you leave the specified *channel*.
/list	Lists information about all channels.
/list *channel*	Lists information about a specific *channel*.
/mode * +pi	Makes the current channel completely private.
/msg *nicknames text*	Sends a private message, *text*, to *nicknames*.
/msg , *text*	Sends a message back to the last person who sent a message to you.
/msg . *text*	Sends a message to the last person you sent a message to.
/nick	Displays your own nickname.
/nick *nickname*	Changes your current nickname to *nickname*.
/query	Stops sending private messages.
/set novice off	Allows more advanced options, such as joining multiple channels.
/who *channel*	Shows who is on the specified *channel*.
/who *nickname*	Displays information about the specified person.
/who *	Shows who is joined to the current channel.
/whois *nickname*	Displays complete information about the person.
/whois *	Displays all information about everyone.

ismpx

An SVR4 command that tests whether the standard input is running under layers software. Output is either yes (exit status 0) if the terminal is running under layers, or no (exit status 1) if it is not. The main use for this command is in shell scripts that use a windowing terminal or require a certain screen size.

See also jterm

ISO

Abbreviation for International Organization for Standardization. An international standard-making body, based in Geneva, that establishes global standards for communications and information exchange. ANSI is the United States member of ISO.

The seven-layer International Organization for Standardization's Open Systems Interconnection (ISO/OSI) model for computer-to-computer communications is one of the ISO's most widely accepted recommendations.

See also ISO/OSI model

ISO/OSI model

Abbreviation for International Organization for Standardization/Open System Interconnection model. A networking reference model defined by the ISO that divides computer-to-computer communications into seven connected layers. Such layers are known as a protocol stack.

Each successively higher layer builds on the functions of the layers below, as follows:

Application layer 7   The highest level of the model. It defines the way that applications interact with the network, including database management, e-mail, and terminal-emulation protocols.

Presentation layer 6   Defines the way that data is formatted, presented, converted, and encoded.

Session layer 5   Coordinates communications and maintains the session for as long as it is needed, performing logging, and administrative functions. Note: Security is implemented in the Presentation Layer.

Transport layer 4   Defines protocols for structuring messages and supervises the validity of the transmission by performing some error checking.

Network layer 3   Defines protocols for data routing to ensure that the information arrives at the correct destination node.

Data-link layer 2   Validates the integrity of the flow of data from one node to another by synchronizing blocks of data and controlling the flow of data.

Physical layer 1   Defines the mechanism for communicating with the transmission medium and interface hardware.

isochronous

A communications mode used to transmit real-time data over a preallocated bandwidth, allowing time-synchronized transmissions with very little delay.

Isochronous service is needed for real-time data such as synchronized voice and video and multimedia presentations, in which delays in delivery would be unacceptable and very easy to detect with the human eye or ear.

J

Java

A programming language developed by Sun Microsystems. Java technology has been licensed by Microsoft, IBM, Abode Systems, Oracle, Borland, and many other companies developing World Wide Web applications.

See also World Wide Web

job

A command or group of commands that exists as a single unit. A job can be moved from the foreground to the background (and vice versa) on any Unix system with job control. It is easy to use the terms *process*, *program*, and *job* as though they are interchangeable, but strictly speaking, *job* refers to one command line. That command line may be very complex and consists of several processes (for example, you can use pipes and redirection to link several processes together on a single command line), but as far as Unix is concerned, it is still just one job.

job control

A Unix mechanism that manages jobs, allowing them to be started, stopped, killed, and moved between the background and foreground. Job control lets you run several jobs at the same time, with different priorities, and was first included in the 4.0BSD Unix releases from the University of California, Berkeley.

The Bourne shell and Korn shell provide several commands for job control as Table J.1 shows.

There are other ways in Unix that you can run several jobs at a time. The X Window system allows you to run multiple processes, running each one in its own window. Certain versions of Unix, such as Linux and UnixWare, support virtual terminals that you can switch between, each acting as an independent connection to your computer but sharing the same physical keyboard and screen.

See also ampersand, bg, Ctrl-Z, fg, jobs, jsh, kill

TABLE J.1: Bourne and Korn Shell Job Control Commands

COMMAND	DESCRIPTION
bg	Places a job in the background.
fg	Places a job in the foreground.
jobs	Lists all the active jobs.
kill	Terminates a job.
stop	Suspends a background job.
stty tostop	Stops a background job if it attempts to write to the terminal.
suspend	Suspends a foreground job.
wait	Waits for a background job to finish.
Ctrl-Z	Suspends a foreground job.

job number

Those shells with job control assign a number to every command that is stopped or running in the background.

Job numbers are easier to use than PIDs, because they are smaller, usually between 1 and 10, and you can use them with several Unix utilities such as at and atrm.

See also ampersand, bg, **Ctrl-Z,** fg, jobs, kill

jobs

▶ A built-in C shell command that lists all running or stopped jobs that were started with the current instance of the C shell. If you use the -l option (the only option available), this command also includes the process IDs (PIDs).

▶ A built-in Korn shell command that lists all running and stopped jobs or lists those jobs specified by the jobID command-line argument. This command recognizes three options: -l, which lists the process IDs (PIDs); -n, which displays jobs that have stopped or whose status has changed in some way; and -p, which lists just the process group IDs.

See also bg, fg, kill, ps

joe

A text editor based on wordstar.

See also jove, pico

join

A command that extracts common lines from two sorted files.

Syntax

The syntax for the join command is as follows:

```
join [options] filename1 filename2
```

One line of output is created for each line in the two files that match, based on the information you specify.

Options and Arguments

This command joins the common lines found in *filename1* and *filename2*; if you don't specify *filename1*, join reads from the standard input. You can use the options listed in Table J.2 with join.

In the options shown in Table J.2, the argument *n* can be either 1 or 2, referring to *filename1* or to *filename2*. In join, all field numbering starts at 1 rather than at zero.

See also comm, sort, uniq

TABLE J.2: Options to Use with join

Option	Description
-a *n*	Lists unmatched lines from file *n* or from both if *n* is omitted.
-e *string*	Replaces any empty field with *string*.
-j*n m*	Joins the two files on the *m*th field of file *n*; if *n* is not specified, the files are joined on the *m*th field of both files.
-o*n.m*	Specifies the fields to output from each file for each line with matching join fields, where *n* specifies the file number and *m* specifies the field number.
-t*char*	Uses character *char* as a field separator for input and output.

Joint Photographic Expert Group

See JPEG

jot

A BSD command used to print sequential or random data, usually numbers, one per line.

Syntax

The syntax for this command is:

```
jot [options][repetitions[begin[end[increment]]]]
```

jot is used to print increasing, decreasing, or random numbers, or specific words, a specified number of times.

Options and Arguments

In the syntax given above, *repetitions* defines the number of data items; *begin*, the starting point or lower bound; *end*, the ending point or upper bound; and *increment*, the step size, or for random data, the seed. The default values are 100, 1, 100, and 1, respectively, and when random numbers are used, the seed is based on the time of day. You can also use the options listed in Table J.3 with jot.

TABLE J.3: Options Available with jot

OPTION	DESCRIPTION
-b *word*	Prints *word*.
-c	Prints character data.
-n	Suppresses newlines.
-p *precision*	Specifies how many digits of data to print.
-r	Specifies random data.
-s *string*	Separates data by *string*.
-w *word*	Prints *word* with the generated data appended to it. You can specify octal, hexadecimal, exponential, ASCII, zero padded, or right justified formats by using the appropriate C language printf convention inside *word*.

jove

A popular text editor, based on emacs written by Jonathon Payne. The name is an abbreviation for Jonathon's Own Version of emacs.

JPEG (.jpg)

Abbreviated JPEG, pronounced "jay-peg." An image-compression standard and file format developed as a joint effort of CCITT and ISO.

Since image files can often be very large, JPEG was developed to define a set of compression methods for high-quality still images such as photographs, single video frames, or scanned pictures; compressed images occupy much less memory or disk space. JPEG does not work very well when compressing line art, text documents, or vector graphics.

JPEG uses lossy compression methods that result in some loss of original data; when you decompress the image, you don't get exactly the same image you originally compressed, although JPEG was specifically designed to discard information not easily perceived by the human eye. We can detect small changes in brightness much easier than we can see small changes in color. JPEG can store 24-bit color images in up to 16 million colors; by comparison, files in GIF (Graphics Interchange Format) format can only store up to 256 colors. JPEG can achieve a compression ratio as high as 20 to 1, and files usually have the filename extension `.jpg` or `.jpeg`.

See also **data compression, lossless compression, MPEG**

jsh

In some versions of SVR4 you can use the Bourne shell with job control features by executing `jsh` rather than `sh`. The job control features are similar to those found in the C shell and Korn shell. Jobs are tracked by number, starting at 1 for the first job.

See also `bg`, `fg`, `kill`

jterm

A command that resets a windowing terminal after a program changes the attributes of the layer. This command is only used with `layers`.

See also `ismpx`, `jwin`

jukebox

A high-capacity storage device that uses an autochanger mechanism to automatically mount or dismount optical disks. A jukebox typically contains one to four disks and a mechanism that picks up disks from a bay and loads them into the drives as they are needed.

Julian date

A method of representing the date often used in computer systems. The first digit, from 0 to 9, represents the year, and the remaining three digits represent the day of the year, counting from January 1st. In some systems, two digits are used to represent the year, from 00 to 99. This error (using two digits for the year) is the primary cause of the Y2K problem.

See also **epoch**

jwin

A command used with `layers` that prints the size of the current window, in bytes.

See also `ismpx`, `jterm`

K

K&R

A reference to the hugely influential book, *The C Programming Language*, written by Brian Kernighan and Dennis Ritchie and published in 1978. The book is sometimes referred to as *Kernighan & Ritchie* or *The C Bible* or, simply, *The White Book* because of the white cover used on the original edition. Dennis Ritchie was the original designer of the C language.

kdestroy

A BSD command that destroys Kerberos tickets by writing zeros to the file that contains them and then removing the file. If kdestroy cannot wipe out the ticket file, it beeps your terminal.

This command has two options; -f runs kdestroy without displaying any status messages, and -q turns off terminal beeping.

See also **Kerberos**, kinit, klist, register

kdump

A BSD command that displays kernel trace information in the file ktrace .out. This file is created by ktrace.

Syntax

The syntax to use for this command is:

```
kdump [options]
```

Options and Arguments

You can use the options listed in Table K.1 with kdump.

See also ktrace

TABLE K.1: Options for Use with kdump

Option	Description
-d	Displays all information in decimal.
-f *filename*	Displays *filename* rather than the default file, ktrace.out.
-l	Loops trace reading.
-m *maxdata*	Displays up to *maxdata* when decoding input/output.
-n	Turns off certain translations.
-R	Displays relative timestamp.
-T	Displays absolute timestamp.

TABLE K.1 continued: Options for Use with kdump

OPTION	DESCRIPTION
-t *cnis*	Sets tracepoints; *c* traces system calls, *n* traces namei translations, *i* traces input/output, *s* traces signal processing.

Kerberos

A network security system developed as part of Project Athena at MIT. Kerberos is used to authenticate a user who is asking to use a particular network service.

Kerberos can be used to control the initial connection to a server or can be used to authenticate every single request and message passed between the client and the server. It grants tickets to a client to allow the use of a specific service and is secure even on a nonsecure network.

Kerberos takes the following precautions:

▶ Passwords are never sent unencrypted over the network. This means that network snoopers cannot easily capture passwords.

▶ All Kerberos messages are timestamped so that they cannot be captured and replayed later; Kerberos does not accept old messages.

▶ When you request access to a service—to access a file server, for example—Kerberos gives you a "ticket," which is valid for access to the file server but not valid for any other service. When you try to connect to the server, you send your ticket with the request. Once the server knows who you are, the server decides whether to grant you access. Tickets also expire, and if your session lasts longer than the predefined time limit, you will have to re-authenticate yourself to Kerberos to get a new ticket.

Kerberos is named after the three-headed dog Cerberus, who guards the gates of the underworld in Greek mythology.

You can obtain the files for Kerberos by anonymous `ftp` from `athena-dist.mit.edu`, and you can get the source code, documentation, and articles on Kerberos from MIT Software Center:

W32-300
20 Carlton Street
Cambridge, MA 02139 U.S.A.

See also `kdestroy`, `kinit`, `klist`, `ksrvtgt`, `register`

kernel

The central, memory resident part of the Unix operating system that allocates resources, manages memory, and controls processes.

The design strategy behind Unix has always been to keep the kernel as small as possible (when compared to other similar operating systems) and to add functions as small, separate utility programs.

See also **mach, rebuilding the kernel, shell, system call**

kernel address space

That part of memory used to store data and programs that can only be accessed by the kernel.

key binding

In emacs, the connection between a specific key on the keyboard and the command that it invokes.

kernel description file

A standard file describing devices attached to the system and the different kernel settings. Only the superuser can look at or change this information.

keylogin

A command that prompts the user for a login password and then uses it to decrypt the user's secret key. This key can then be used by secure network services. If the user is always prompted for a password when logging in to the system, there is no need for this command to be used.

See also chkey, keylogout

keylogout

A command that revokes the secret key used in secure network services. If used with the -f option, keylogout can remove the root key that, if invoked on a file server, can compromise network security.

See also chkey, keylogin

keyword

Those words in a programming language that have a special reserved meaning and so cannot be used as variable names.

Most languages have keywords for conditional statements (`if`, `while`), for defining data and functions (`int`, `float`, `static`, `extern`), and for input and output (`scanf`, `printf`, `putchar`, `getchar`). Some specialized languages also have keywords relating to their particular function.

kill

A command used to terminate one or more process IDs (PIDs). This command is similar to the `kill` command built into the C shell and Korn shell.

Syntax

The syntax for the `kill` command is:

```
kill [options]IDs
```

The `kill` command terminates a process, as defined by its PID, by sending it a signal. A signal is a kind of message, and `kill` usually sends a signal -15 to a process to request that the process shut down; if the process is harder to terminate, a -9 may be needed instead. A process may ignore a -15, but it cannot ignore a -9. Some of the more commonly used signals are listed in Table K.2.

TABLE K.2: Common Unix Signals

SIGNAL	DESCRIPTION
-1	Hangup, sent when you log out or hang up the modem
-2	Interrupt, sent when you type Ctrl-C
-3	Quit, sent when you type Ctrl-\
-4	Illegal instruction
-5	Trace trap
-6	IOT instruction
-7	EMT instruction
-8	Floating point exception
-9	Kill, stops the process immediately
-10	Bus error
-11	Segment violation, indicates you have tried to access memory illegally
-12	Bad argument to a system call
-13	Write to a pipe, but no reading process
-14	Alarm clock
-15	Default software termination
-16 and -17	User-defined
-18	Child process died
-19	Restart after a power failure

Options and Arguments

You can use two options with `kill`; both are listed in Table K.3.

Only the superuser can kill other users' processes. To determine the appropriate PID number, use the `ps` command first.

TABLE K.3: Options for Use with kill

OPTION	DESCRIPTION
-1	Lists all the signal names.
-signal	Specifies either the signal number (determined by ps -f) or the signal name (from kill -1).

Examples

To kill process ID 100, use:

    kill 100

The default signal is -15. If this doesn't work, try:

    kill -1 100

As a last resort, use:

    kill -9 100

Although a -9 is a sure bet, it is always better to try -15 or -1 first. These signals are caught by the application and give it a chance to halt in an orderly fashion, closing files as it does so. When you use -9, the application must terminate immediately, and you will inevitably be left with some cleaning up to do.

Notes

If you are logged on as the superuser and you execute the command:

    kill -9 0

you will bring down the system.

See also ps

kill character

A character that when typed, deletes the contents of the current line so you can retype your command or entry. The default is Ctrl-U or the at sign (@) but can be changed by the user. Also called the *line erase* character. This character has nothing to do with, and should not be confused with, sending a kill signal to a process.

kill file

A file maintained by your USENET newsreader that excludes articles that match certain criteria, such as subject, author, or other header lines. The articles identified in this way are abandoned and not presented for reading in the normal way; it is as though they are not there at all. They do not appear in thread or subject lists.

Using a kill file is the proper defense against those subjects or people that you find give offense, and many newsreaders let you kill at two different levels, one within a particular newsgroup, and one for all newsgroups. This means that you can ignore one person in a specific newsgroup and one subject in all newsgroups.

See also **flame, flame war**

kill signal

A signal sent to a process to terminate it immediately.

Unlike other Unix signals, a kill signal (number 9, also known as SIGKILL) cannot be intercepted or ignored.

Sending a kill signal to a process should only be used as a last resort when all else fails; because the process cannot ignore the signal, it cannot close open files and terminate in a tidy fashion, and there is a very good chance that you will lose data.

See also `kill`

`kinit`

A BSD command used to log in to the Kerberos authentication and authorization system.

Syntax
The syntax for this command is:

```
kinit [options]
```

You only need to use `kinit` after your initial Kerberos tickets have expired.

Options and Arguments
When you use `kinit` without options, you are prompted for your username and Kerberos password, and `kinit` then attempts to authenticate your login with the Kerberos server. You can use the options listed in Table K.4 with `kinit`.

See also **Kerberos,** `kdestroy`, `klist`, `ksrvtgt`, `register`

TABLE K.4: Options for Use with kinit

OPTION	DESCRIPTION
-i	Prompts for a Kerberos instance.
-l	Prompts for a ticket lifetime in minutes; this value must be between 5 and 1275 minutes.
-r	Prompts for the name of a Kerberos realm; not fully implemented.
-v	Prints the name of the ticket file used, along with various status messages.

klist

A BSD command that lists currently held Kerberos tickets.

Syntax

The syntax for this command is as follows:

    klist [options]

klist prints the name of the tickets file, as well as the principal names of all the Kerberos tickets held by the user along with the issue and expiration dates for each authenticator.

Options and Arguments

You can use the options listed in Table K.5 with klist.

See also **Kerberos,** kdestroy, kinit, ksrvtgt, register

TABLE K.5: Options to Use with klist

OPTION	DESCRIPTION
-t	Checks for unexpired tickets in the ticket file. The exit status is set to 0 if one is present; otherwise, the exit status is 1. No other output is displayed.
-file *name*	Specifies *name* as the ticket file.
-srvtab	The ticket file is treated as a key file, and the names of the keys it contains are printed.

Korn shell

Pronounced "corn shell." The Korn shell is a very popular upward-compatible extension of the original Unix shell (the Bourne shell), written by David Korn of AT&T Bell Labs and first released as part of System V in 1982. Major improvements were made in 1986, 1988, and 1993. The Korn shell is the default shell on many Unix systems, particularly those based on System V, including UnixWare and many others.

Because the Korn shell is an upward-compatible extension of the Bourne shell, everything that works with the Bourne shell also works in the Korn shell; however, the Korn shell can do a lot more, and adds:

- ▸ Interactive editing of the command line with either emacs or vi.
- ▸ Better function definitions providing local variables and the ability to create recursive functions.
- ▸ Extensive pattern matching for filenames, similar to regular expressions.

Several features were also adapted from the C shell, including:

- ▸ Command history for retrieval and reuse of previously typed commands.
- ▸ Job control, and the mechanism for moving jobs between the background and the foreground.
- ▸ Aliases for abbreviated command names.
- ▸ The tilde (~) used as shorthand for the name of the home directory.

Startup Files

The Korn shell program, started by the ksh command, first executes the statements in the environment file .kshrc in your home directory. If you invoked ksh as your login shell, then the commands found in /etc/profile and /HOME/.profile are executed first, when you log in, just before the environment file is processed.

The default prompt for the Korn shell is the dollar sign ($).

Using Commands

The Korn shell allows you to use and group commands on the command line in several different ways, which are shown in Table K.6.

TABLE K.6: Using Korn Shell Commands

Command	Description
cmd &	Executes cmd in the background.
cmd1 ; cmd2	Executes cmd1 and cmd2 consecutively, with the semicolon acting as a command separator.
(cmd1 ; cmd2)	Creates a subshell to execute cmd1 and cmd2 as a group.
cmd1 | cmd2	Creates a pipe and uses the output from cmd1 as input to cmd2.
cmd1 `cmd2`	Performs command substitution; uses the output from cmd2 as arguments to cmd1.
cmd1 $(cmd2)	Command substitution; nesting of commands is allowed.

TABLE K.6 continued: Using Korn Shell Commands

COMMAND	DESCRIPTION
cmd1 && cmd2	Executes cmd1, and if cmd1 completes successfully, then executes cmd2.
cmd1 || cmd2	Executes either cmd1 or if it fails, executes cmd2.
{ cmd1 ; cmd2 }	Executes commands in the current shell.

Filename Metacharacters

You can use any of the patterns listed in Table K.7 to generate filenames.

TABLE K.7: Korn Shell Filename Metacharacters

METACHARACTER	DESCRIPTION
*	Matches any string or zero or more characters; for example, w*n matches wn, win, won, when, worn, and many other filenames.
?	Matches any single character; for example, myfile.? matches myfile._, myfile.1, myfile.a, and so on.
[abc...]	Matches any single character from the list, and you can use a hyphen to indicate a range, as in a-z, 0-9, and so on.
[!abc...]	Matches any single character not on the list, and you can use a hyphen to indicate a range.
?(pattern)	Matches zero or one instance of pattern.
*(pattern)	Matches zero or more instance of pattern.
+(pattern)	Matches one or more instance of pattern.
@(pattern)	Matches just one instance of pattern.
!(pattern)	Matches strings that don't contain pattern.
~	Home directory of the current user.
~name	Home directory of the user specified by name.
~+	Current working directory.
~-	Previous working directory.

Redirection

When you execute a command, the shell opens three files known as the standard input, the standard output, and the standard error. By default, standard input is the keyboard, and standard output and standard error are the terminal or screen. Redirection is the process of directing input to or output from a different file from that normally used.

In simple redirection, you can change the input source or output destination in the ways listed in Table K.8.

The shell assigns a file descriptor to each standard file, using 0 for standard input, 1 for standard output, and 2 for standard error; it may also use higher numbers, starting at 3 for any other files required to complete the process. You can use the file descriptors listed in Table K.9 in redirection.

In multiple redirection, you can use the file descriptors listed in Table K.10.

Don't use a space between the redirection symbol and a file descriptor; in the other cases, spacing is less strict, and you can space characters as you wish.

TABLE K.8: Simple Redirection in the Korn Shell

COMMAND	DESCRIPTION
cmd > filename	Sends output from cmd to filename, overwriting the file if it already exists.
cmd >> filename	Appends output from cmd to filename.
cmd < filename	Takes input for cmd from filename.
cmd << text	Reads standard input as far as a line identical to text.

TABLE K.9: Redirection Using File Descriptors in the Bourne Shell

FILE DESCRIPTOR	DESCRIPTION
cmd >&n	Sends output from cmd to file descriptor n.
cmd m>&n	Same as above, except that output that would normally go to the file descriptor m is sent to file descriptor n instead.
cmd >&–	Closes standard output.
cmd <&n	Takes input for cmd from file descriptor n.
cmd m<&n	Same as above, except that output that would normally have come from the file descriptor m comes from the file descriptor n instead.
cmd <&–	Closes standard input.

TABLE K.10: Multiple Redirection in the Korn Shell

FILE DESCRIPTOR	DESCRIPTION
cmd 2>filename	Sends standard error to filename while standard out remains the screen.
cmd > filename 2>&1	Sends both standard error and standard output to filename.

TABLE K.10 continued: Multiple Redirection in the Korn Shell

FILE DESCRIPTOR	DESCRIPTION
(cmd > filename1) 2>filename2	Sends standard output to *filename1* and standard error to *filename2*.
*cmd	tee filenames*	Sends output from *cmd* to standard output and also to *filenames*.

Quoting

Quoting disables the special meaning of a character and allows you to use it literally. The characters listed in Table K.11 have special meaning in the Korn shell.

TABLE K.11: Quoting in the Korn Shell

CHARACTER	DESCRIPTION
;	Command separator.
&	Runs a command in the background.
( )	Command grouping.
|	Creates a pipe.
*? [ ] !	Filename metacharacters.
< > & |	Redirection symbols.
" " ' ' \	Used when quoting other characters. Anything placed between the double quotes is interpreted symbolically; anything placed between the single quotes is interpreted literally, and the backslash is used to quote a single character.

Korn Shell Options

You can customize your shell with the shell options listed in Table K.12. These options are like on/off switches; when you use the `set` command to turn on an option, you tell it to act in a certain way, and when you unset an option, it stops. To display all current shell options and their settings, use:

```
set -o
```

To turn an option on, use:

```
set -o option
```

and to turn an option off, use:

```
set +o option
```

Not all of the options listed in Table K.12 are available in all versions of the Korn shell; your list may be slightly different.

TABLE K.12: Korn Shell Options

Option	Description
allexport	Sets the export attribute for each shell variable as it is assigned a value.
bgnice	Runs all background jobs at a lower priority.
emacs	Uses the emacs built-in editor for command-line and history editing.
errexit	Executes the ERR trap after a command fails with a non-zero exit status.
gmacs	Uses the gmacs built-in editor for command-line and history editing.
ignoreeof	Does not exit when you type an EOF (Ctrl-D); when this option is set, you must use exit.
keyword	Uses Bourne shell syntax for assignments on the command line.
markdirs	Adds a / character to directory names created using wildcard expansion.
monitor	Runs background jobs in a separate process group; the default on all systems with job control.
noclobber	Does not allow redirection to overwrite an existing file.
noexec	Reads commands and checks their syntax, but does not execute them.
noglob	Turns off expansion of filenames.
nolog	Does not store function definitions in the history file.
nounset	Treats unset variable names as errors.
physical	Makes the built-in cd and pwd commands use physical mode; they will not track symbolic links.
privileged	Disables $HOME/.profile, and uses /etc/suid_profile instead.
protected	The old version of the privileged setting.
trackall	Tracks all aliases.
verbose	Displays each command before running it.
vi	Uses the vi built-in editor for command-line and history editing.
viraw	Like vi but uses character input rather than line input.
xtrace	Turns on trace debugging.

Built-in Shell Variables

The Korn shell automatically sets built-in variables, and they are often used in shell scripts. In Table K.13, which lists the built-in shell variables, the dollar sign character ($) is not part of the variable name, although the variable is always referred to in this way.

TABLE K.13: Built-in Shell Variables

VARIABLE	DESCRIPTION
$#	Contains the number of arguments on the command line.
$?	Contains the return code for the last command executed.
$$	Contains the PID of the current process.
$!	Contains the PID of the most recent background process.
$-	Displays the options currently in effect for sh.
$0	The first word on the command line; the command name.
${n}	Individual positional parameters on the command line specified by n.
$*	All the arguments on the command line, quoted as a single string ("$1 $2 $3...").
"$@"	All the arguments on the command line, quoted as individual strings ("$1" "$2" "$3...").
$_	A temporary variable; stores the pathname of the script being executed, the last argument of the previous command, or the name of the MAIL file during mail checks.
$ERRNO	Error number of the most recent system call, listed in /etc/include/sys/errno.h.
$LINENO	Current line number in the current shell script or function.
$OLDPWD	The name of the previous working directory, the directory before the most recent cd command.
$OPTARG	The name of the last option processed by getopts.
$OPTIND	The numerical index of the option that getopts processes next, the index of $OPTARG.
$PPID	The PID number of this shell's parent.
$PWD	The current working directory.
$RANDOM[=n]	Generates a new random number with each reference, beginning with n, if specified.
$REPLY	The default reply used by select and read.
$SECONDS[=n]	The number of elapsed seconds since this shell was started; if n is specified, number of seconds since the shell started plus the value n.

Other Shell Variables

The shell variables described in this section are not set by the shell but are usually set by commands in your .profile file, where you can configure them to your exact needs. Use the following form to set them:

```
$ variable=value
```

Table K.14 lists the Korn shell variables.

TABLE K.14: Korn Shell Variables

VARIABLE	DESCRIPTION
CDPATH=*dirs*	Specifies the search path for the cd command, with individual directory names separated by colons (:).
COLUMNS=*n*	Specifies the number of columns or characters across your screen or window; the default is 80.
EDITOR=*filename*	Specifies the editor to use, usually emacs or vi; used when VISUAL is not set.
ENV=*filename*	Name of the shell script to execute at startup, usually $HOME/.ksrc.
FCEDIT=*filename*	Editor used by the fc command; the default is /bin/ed.
FPATH=*directories*	Directories to search for function definitions.
HISTFILE=*filename*	Name of the file used to store command history; the default is $HOME/.sh_history.
HISTORY=*n*	Number of lines to keep in the history file; the default is 128.
HOME=*directory*	Specifies the home directory; set by login. If you use the cd command without an argument, the shell makes this directory the current directory.
IFS='*chars*'	Sets the internal field separator to *chars*; the defaults are space, tab, and newline.
LANG=*directory*	Directory to use for certain language-dependent functions.
LINES=*n*	Specifies the number of rows or characters down your screen or window.
MAIL=*filename*	Sets the default name of your mail file; the shell tells you when you receive mail via the mail or mailx commands.
MAILCHECK=*n*	Specifies the frequency *n* with which the shell checks for new mail; the default is 600 seconds, or 10 minutes.
MAILPATH=*filename*	Specifies one or more files, separated by a colon, in which to receive mail.
PATH=*dir*	Sets one or more pathnames, separated by colons, that the shell should search for commands to execute; the default is /usr/bin.
PS1=*string*	Specifies the primary shell prompt; the default is $.
PS2=*string*	Specifies the secondary shell prompt for use in multiline commands; the default is >. The appearance of this prompt indicates that the shell expects more input.
PS3=*string*	The prompt used by the select command; the default is #?.
PS4=*string*	The prompt used with the trace option; the default is +.
SHELL=*filename*	Specifies the shell to be used by commands when you escape to a subshell; of special interest to ed and vi.
TERM=*string*	Specifies your terminal type; required by some commands that use the whole screen for output.
TMOUT=*n*	Specifies the timeout to wait after the last command before logging you out automatically.
VISUAL=*filename*	Sets the name of the default editor to use, emacs or vi; overrides the EDITOR variable.

Built-in Commands

The Korn shell offers a rich set of built-in commands, as shown in Table K.15.

TABLE K.15: Built-in Korn Shell Commands

COMMAND	DESCRIPTION
:	Null command. The shell performs no action and returns an exit status of 0.
.filename	Reads and executes lines in filename as part of the current process.
Alias[options] [name[='cmd']]	Establishes the shorthand name as an alias for cmd. If ='cmd' is omitted, prints the alias for name, and if name is also omitted, prints all aliases.
Autoload	Korn shell alias for typeset -fu.
Bg [JobIDs]	Places the current job or the jobs specified by JobIDs into the background.
Break [n]	Exits from n levels in a for or while loop; default is 1.
Case	Starts a case statement.
Cd [directory]	Changes to the specified directory; the default is the home directory. You can also use cd -, where - stands for the name of the previous directory, or cd old new, which replaces the string old with the string new and changes to the resulting directory.
Continue [n]	Skips any remaining commands in a for or while loop, resuming with the next iteration of the loop, or skipping n loops.
Do	Keyword used in a for, while, until, or select statement.
Echo args	Writes args to the screen.
Esac	Keyword that ends a case statement.
Eval [args]	Executes the specified args, allowing evaluation and substitution of shell variables.
Exec [command]	Executes command without starting a new process.
Exit [n]	Exits from the current shell procedure with an exit status of n.
export [names]	Exports the value of one or more shell variables, making them global in scope rather than local, which is the default.
Fg [JobIDs]	Places the current job or the jobs specified by JobIDs into the foreground.
Fi	Keyword that ends an if statement.
For	Keyword used in a looping construct.
Function name {commands;}	Korn shell alias for typeset -f.
getopts string var [args]	Checks command options, including args if provided, for legal choices.
Hash	Korn shell alias for alias -t; creates a tracked alias for the named command.
History	Displays the last 16 commands; a Korn shell alias for fc -1.
if	Keyword used in an if/then/else/fi conditional statement.
Integer	Korn shell alias for typeset -i.
Jobs [options] [jobIDs]	Lists all running or stopped jobs, or lists those specified by jobIDs.

TABLE K.15 continued: Built-in Korn Shell Commands

COMMAND	DESCRIPTION
Kill [options] IDs	Terminates the specified process; to do this you must be either the owner of the process or the superuser.
Let expressions	Keyword that performs the arithmetic specified by one or more expressions.
Newgrp [group]	Switches to group, or returns to your login group.
Nohup	Prevents termination of a command after the owner logs out.
Print [options] [string]	Prints the specified string on the standard output; used instead of echo on most systems.
Pwd	Displays the pathname of the current working directory.
R	Korn shell alias for fc -e-; repeats the previous command.
read var1 [var2...]	Reads one line from standard in, and assigns each word to a named variable; all leftovers are assigned to the last variable.
Readonly [var1...]	Makes the specified variables read-only so that they cannot be changed.
Return [n]	Exits *{*t*}* from a function with the exit status n, and returns to the shell.
Select x [in list]	Displays a list of menu items on the standard output in the order specified in list.
Set [option arg1 arg2...]	Without arguments, set prints the names and values of all shell variables. option can be turned on by using a minus sign or turned off with a plus sign, and arguments are assigned in order to the parameters $1, $2, and so on. The options are listed in Table K.16.
shift [n]	Shifts positional arguments n places (by default 1 place) to the left.
test	Tests a condition and, if true, returns a zero exit status.
time command	Executes command and prints the total number of elapsed seconds.
times	Displays cumulative system and user time for all processes run by the shell.
Trap [[commands] signals]	Executes commands if any of signals are received.
type [names]	Shows whether names are Unix commands, built-in commands, or a defined shell function; an alias for whence -v.
typeset[options] [variable[=value...]]	Assigns a type (function, integer, flush-left, or flush-right string) to each variable and an optional value.
ulimit [options][n]	Prints the value of one or more resource limits, or when n is specified, sets the limit to n.
umask [nnn]	Sets the user file creation mask to octal value nnn; if nnn is omitted, displays the current user creation mask.
unalias names	Removes the specified aliases.
unset [-f]names	Removes definitions of the specified functions or variables in names.
until	Starts an until/do/done construct.
wait [n]	Waits for the process with ID of n to complete execution in the background and display its exit status.

TABLE K.15 continued: Built-in Korn Shell Commands

COMMAND	DESCRIPTION
Whence [options]commands	Shows whether a command is a Unix command, a built-in shell command, an alias, or a defined shell function.
while	Starts a while/do/done construct.

TABLE K.16: Options to Use with the set Korn Shell Command

OPTION	DESCRIPTION
-/+a	Export/do not export defined or modified variables.
-/+Aname	Assign the remaining arguments as elements of the array *name*.
-/+e	Exit/do not exit if a command yields a non-zero exit status.
-/+f	Disable/enable filename metacharacters.
-/+h	Enable/disable quick access to commands.
-/+k	Provide/do not provide all environment variable assignments.
-/+m	Enable/disable job control; –m is usually set automatically.
-/+n	Read but do not execute/execute commands.
-/+o *options*	Turn on/off the Korn shell options listed in Table K.12.
-/+p	Start up as a privileged user, don't process $HOME/.profile.
-/+s	Sort/do not sort the positional parameters.
-/+t	Execute/do not execute one command and exit.
-/+u	Consider/do not consider unset variables as errors.
-/+v	Show/do not show each shell command line when read.
-/+x	Display/do not display commands and arguments when executed.

Command History

The Korn shell lets you change and re-enter previous commands without having to retype them, even commands from a previous session. The shell saves everything you type (including your mistakes) into the history file, giving each command a number starting at 1; this means that you can refer to command 6 or command 126, using this number. By default the shell stores the last 128 commands you typed, but by changing the value of the HISTSIZE variable, you can change that number if you wish. The Korn shell also stores all lines of a multiline command, whereas the C shell does not; it only stores the first line.

You can modify commands in your history file by using one of the two built-in editors, emacs or vi, or by using the fc command. When you use one of the editors, you use the normal editing commands to find and then revise a command from the history file, you then press Return to execute the command. The vi editor starts in input mode; remember to press the Escape key before you type a vi command.

Two options in the fc command are very handy; use fc -l to list commands and fc -e to edit them. You can also use the r command (really an alias for fc -e-) to re-execute the previous command.

Arrays and Arithmetic Expressions

The Korn shell supports a wide range of arithmetic expressions, including integer arithmetic and array manipulation. Some later versions of the Korn shell also support floating point as well as integer arithmetic.

The arithmetic operators used in the Korn shell are those used by the C programming language, and they are most often used in combination with the let command.

Coprocesses

The Korn shell supports a feature called a *coprocess*, which lets you start a process in the background that can communicate directly with the parent shell. You invoke a coprocess by ending the command line with |&.

There are restrictions on coprocesses; they must be filters and must process their input line by line, rather than processing several lines at the same time. When you start a coprocess, it is connected to the current shell by a two-way pipe. You can use read -p to read its standard input or print -p to write to its standard output. You can also use *command* <&p to take input for *command* from the coprocess and *command*>&p to send the output from *command* to a coprocess.

ksh

Command used to invoke the Korn shell or interactive command interpreter.

Syntax

When starting the Korn shell, the syntax to use is:

```
ksh [options][arguments]
```

If you use ksh without options or arguments, you will start a new instance of the Korn shell, even if you are already running the C shell or the Bourne shell.

Options and Arguments

ksh can execute commands from a terminal when the -i option is specified, from a file when the first argument on the command line is a shell

script filename, or from the keyboard (standard input) if you specify the
-s options. All the options you can use with ksh are listed in Table K.17.

See also **Bash,** csh, sh, **Tcsh, Zsh**

TABLE K.17: Options for Use with ksh

Option	Description
-c *string*	Reads commands from *string*.
-i	Starts an interactive shell that prompts for input.
-p	Starts the shell without executing the commands in /$HOME/.profile.
-r	Starts a restricted shell; same as executing rksh or rsh.
-s	Reads commands from the standard input.

.kshrc

The Korn shell environment file, executed each time a new instance of the
shell is started. The .kshrc file defines shell-specific information and is
usually located in your home directory. You can set ENV=$HOME/.kshrc
in your .profile file and then create a .kshrc file in your home directory for these commands.

ksrvtgt

A BSD Kerberos utility that retrieves and stores a ticket-granting ticket
using a service key. The syntax to use is:

    ksrvtgt *name.instance* [[*realm*[*srvtab*]]]

This command retrieves a ticket-granting ticket valid for five minutes for
the principal who can be identified as *name.instance@realm,* decrypts
the response with the service key *srvtab,* and stores the ticket in the
standard ticket cache.

See also **Kerberos,** kdestroy, kinit, klist, register

ktrace

A BSD command that turns on kernel process tracing.

Syntax
Here's the syntax:

    ktrace [*options*]

Kernel trace data is written into the file ktrace.out, and you must
use the kdump command to examine the contents of the file.

Options and Arguments

You can use the options listed in Table K.18 with the `ktrace` command.

The `-g`, `-p`, and *command* options are all mutually exclusive.

See also kdump

TABLE K.18: Options to Use with ktrace

OPTION	DESCRIPTION
command	Executes *command* with the specified trace options.
-a	Appends output to the `ktrace.out` file.
-c	Clears all trace points.
-C	Disables all tracing.
-d	Performs the trace operation on all children of the specified process.
-f *filename*	Specifies *filename* as the log file rather than `ktrace.out`.
-g *pgid*	Enables or disables tracing on all processes in the process group.
-i	Uses the trace options on all future children of the specified process.
-p *pid*	Enables or disables tracing on the specified process.
-t *cnis*	Sets tracepoints; *c* trace system calls, *n* trace namei translations, *i* trace input/output, and *s* trace signal processing.

L

l

A common alias for the `ls` command, used to list files and directories.

See also ls

lam

A BSD command that displays files side by side on the standard output.

Syntax

The syntax for this command is:

```
lam [options]filename...
```

The `lam` command can also read from the standard input if you use -.

Options and Arguments

Each option usually affects the following filename, unless the option letter is an uppercase letter; then the option affects all files until the option is respecified as a lowercase letter. Table L.1 lists the options available.

TABLE L.1: Options Available with lam

Option	Description
-f *min.max*	Prints lines according to the format *min.max* where *min* is the minimum field width and *max* is the maximum field width.
-p *min.max*	Pads the file when the end-of-file is reached and other files are still active.
-s *separator*	Prints *separator* before printing information from the next file.
-t *char*	Terminates lines with *char* rather than with a newline.

Examples

To join four files together along each line, use:

```
lam file.a file.b file.c file.d > file.out
```

See also join, pr

LAN

Abbreviation for local area network. A group of computers and peripheral devices connected by a communications channel, capable of sharing files and other resources between several users. Usually restricted to a relatively small area, a single company or campus department.

last

A Solaris and BSD command that reports the last logins by a user or a terminal.

Syntax

The syntax for this command is:

```
last [options] user...
```

This command is useful as a fast accounting log of which users are accessing which systems.

Options and Arguments

This command has several options, as Table L.2 shows.

TABLE L.2: Options for Use with last

Option	Description
-f *filename*	Reads the specified file instead of the default /var/log/wtmp (on BSD systems), /etc/wtmp (on SCO systems), or /var/adm/wtmp.
-h *host*	Specifies the name *host*, which can be either a name or a number.

TABLE L.2 continued: Options for Use with last

OPTION	DESCRIPTION
-n *n*	Limits the display to *n* entries.
-t *tty*	Specifies the *tty*.

Examples

To see a list of the last 10 logins, use:

    last -n 10

On some systems, this can be expressed as:

    last -10

To see the names of everyone who has logged in to the system console, use:

    last console

See also lastcomm, login

lastcomm

A BSD command that displays information on previously executed commands. Commands are listed in reverse order. The syntax is:

    lastcomm [option][command...][username...][terminal...]

When used with no arguments, lastcomm displays information on all commands stored in the current accounting file. When you use the -f *filename* option, information is read from *filename* rather than from the default accounting file. And when you specify an argument, only those commands with a matching *command* name, *username*, or *terminal* name are displayed. For each entry in the file, this command displays the command name, the name of the user executing the command, the associated terminal port, the execution time of the command, and the date and time the command was executed.

See also last

LATEX

A set of extensions to TEX, the text processing system developed by Leslie Lamport of DEC. LATEX commands are really TEX macros, and they greatly simplify the use of TEX, hiding almost all the low-level functions from the view of the writer.

For more details, see *LATEX; A Document Preparation System* by Leslie Lamport, published in 1994.

A large collection of public domain LATEX (and TEX) material is available from the Comprehensive TEX Archive Network (CTAN) via anonymous `ftp` from `ftp.shsu.edu`, or from `ftp.tex.ac.uk`, or `ftp.dante.de`. You will also find a useful collection of TEX-related material developed by Karl Berry via anonymous `ftp` from `ftp.cs.umb.edu` in the `pub/tex` directory.

layers

The command used to start the ASCII windowing system in SVR4.

Syntax

The syntax for this command is:

```
layers [options][program]
```

Options and Arguments

program is the name of a file containing configuration information that *layers* downloads to the terminal as it starts running.

Table L.3 lists the options available with this command.

See also `ismpx`, `jterm`, `jwin`

TABLE L.3: Options to Use with `layers`

Option	Description
-d	Prints information on the downloaded file on standard error.
-D	Prints debugging information on standard error.
-f *filename*	Loads *filename* as a configuration file.
-h *list*	Supplies *list* of modules for `layers`.
-m *size*	Sets the data packet size; range is 32 to 252.
-p	Prints downloading statistics on the standard error.
-s	Exits `layers` and creates a protocol statistics report on the standard error.
-t	Exits `layers` and then creates a trace dump on the standard error.

LBX

Abbreviation for low-bandwidth X. A protocol included in the X11 Release 6 (X11R6) X Window system designed to improve the performance of X Window terminals operating at 9600 baud or less over dial-up connections. The performance boost is achieved by removing a certain amount of the X Window system handshaking and information swapping usually found on networks.

ld

The Unix command that starts the link editor. The link editor is a software development tool used to combine several object files into a single executable. Ordinarily, you invoke the link editor automatically as part of a C program compilation cycle, but there might be an occasion when it is appropriate to call the linker individually. For a complete description of the link editor and the many options available, see the man pages on your system.

See also cc, C compiler, cpp, **compiling a C program**

ldd

A utility that lists any dynamic dependencies or shared objects that would be loaded if the specified file were executed; if the file has no such shared objects, the utility does not display any output. The syntax is:

```
ldd [options]filename
```

The command has two options. The -d option checks references to data objects, and the -r option checks references to both data objects and functions.

See also lorder, lprof

leaf

In an hierarchical filesystem, the last node on the end of a branch. In Unix, a file that is not a directory is considered to be a leaf.

See also **node**

learn

A BSD command that starts a computer aided instruction course on the use of Unix and several important subjects, including the C programming language, files, and the vi editor.

When you first start learn, the program asks you questions to decide what subject to begin with; you can specify a subject or even a lesson to bypass some of these questions. If you are restarting a previous session, learn uses information stored in $HOME/.learnrc to start at the place you left off last time. To end a session, type **bye**.

leave

A BSD command that reminds you when it is time to go home.

Syntax

The syntax for this command is:

```
leave [+[hhmm]]
```

Options and Arguments

If you use leave with no arguments, you see the prompt:

```
When do you have to leave?
```

You can enter the appropriate time; if you press Enter, leave exits. You can also specify a time on the command line in the form of *hhmm*. If you precede the time with a + sign, leave sets the alarm for that many hours and minutes from the current time.

leave reminds you 5 minutes and 1 minute before the designated time, at the time, and then every minute afterward. When you log off to go home, leave terminates.

See also calendar

less

A popular and flexible pager utility generally available as part of the GNU package. less contains all the features found in more, and adds backwards scrolling, bookmarks, searching, and many other useful features.

Syntax

Here's the syntax to use with less:

```
less [options][filename...]
```

Options and Arguments

You can use the command-line options listed in Table L.4 with less.

less displays the contents of the file you specify one screenful at a time. After each screen, you see a prompt at the bottom left corner of your screen, where you can enter any of the commands listed in Table L.5.

TABLE L.4: Options to Use with less

OPTION	DESCRIPTION
-c	Displays new information from the top of the screen down.
-C	Clears the screen before displaying new information.
-e	Exits from less at the end of the file.
-f*filename*	Opens the specified binary file.
-h*n*	Scroll backwards *n* lines.
-I	Ignores case when searching through a file.

TABLE L.4 continued: Options to Use with less

OPTION	DESCRIPTION
-m	Displays the percentage of the file that has been displayed.
-M	Displays the name of the file being viewed, the current line number, and the percentage of the file that has been displayed.
-N	Adds line numbers to the display.
-s	Replaces multiple blank lines with a single blank.
-S	Turns off word wrap.

TABLE L.5: Commands Available to Use with less

COMMAND	DESCRIPTION
Q	Quits the program.
Space	Displays the next screenful.
Return	Displays the next line.
[n]Return	Displays the next n lines.
B	Displays previous screenful.
Y	Displays previous line.
[n]y	Displays previous n lines.
D	Displays next half screenful.
U	Displays previous half screenful.
G	Goes to the first line.
Ng	Goes to line n.
G	Goes to the last line.
/[pattern]	Searches forward for the specified pattern.
?[pattern]	Searches backward for the specified pattern.
N	Repeats the previous search command.

Examples

The simplest way to use less is with a single file:

    less letter

This command displays the file, one screen at a time, with a prompt in the bottom left corner of your screen.

Notes

You can get less by anonymous ftp from prep.ai.mit.edu in the /pub/gnu directory or from any other site that carries GNU software.

See also more, **pager,** pg

less than symbol

The less than symbol (<) is used in redirection of the standard input to a command from a file rather than input from a terminal; in other words, the shell reads the input from the file instead of the keyboard.

See also **greater than symbol**

let

A Korn shell keyword used when performing arithmetic or conversions between different number bases.

See also expr

lex

A command that generates a lexical analysis program created from regular expressions and C language statements contained in specified source files. The lexical analyzer searches for strings and expressions and then executes the C routines when they are found. You can use lex to create classic Unix filters that read from the standard input, perform a function on the data, and send the results to the standard output.

See also flex, yacc

lexical analysis

Any analysis of programs or commands to find patterns of symbols, such as numbers, operators, keywords, and variable names.

See also flex, lex, **parse**

/lib

A root directory that contains program libraries.

See also **library**

library

A collection of routines stored in executable files available for use by several different programs. Using libraries saves programmers time and effort (as well as minimizing the potential for making mistakes) as they don't have to rewrite common routines every time they are needed.

Libraries can include standard routines for a particular programming language (such as the Unix stdio library or a math library) or can consist of custom routines prepared by the programmer.

See also ar, **archive**, makefile

library function

In programming, a routine or collection of routines stored in a library that can be used by any program that can link into the library.

See also system call

LILO

▶ Abbreviation for Linux loader, a general-purpose boot manager program used to load Linux. You can use LILO to boot Linux in the usual way from your hard disk, or you can also use it to boot from a floppy disk.

▶ LILO is also an abbreviation for "last in last out," an alternative to the FIFO data management method.

limit

A built-in C shell command used to display or set limits on system resources used by the current process.

Syntax

The syntax is:

```
limit [-h] [resource[value]]
```

If you don't specify a *value*, the current value is displayed, and if you don't specify a *resource*, all values are printed. When you use the –h option, a hard limit is set that can only be changed by the super-user. Table L.6 lists the resources you can control with this command.

You can specify the *value* as a number followed by an optional units specifier. For cputime, use *n*h for hours, *n*m for minutes, or *mm:ss* for minutes and seconds, and for the other resources, use *n*k for kilobytes (the default) or *n*m for megabytes.

See also ulimit

TABLE L.6: Resource Names to Use with limit

RESOURCE	DESCRIPTION
Cputime	Maximum number of processor seconds.
Filesize	Maximum size of any file.
Stacksize	Maximum size of the stack.
Coredumpsize	Maximum size of a core dump file

---

limited regular expressions

See regular expressions

line

A command that reads a line from the standard input and writes that same line to the standard output. This command is often used in shell scripts that read input from the terminal.

line editor

A text editor that displays and manipulates just one line of text at a time. The Unix editors ed and ex are both line editors.

See also screen editor

linefeed

Abbreviated LF. A command that advances the cursor on a terminal or the paper in a printer by one line. In the ASCII character set, a linefeed has the decimal value of 10.

See also formfeed, newline

line printer

Any high-volume printer that prints a complete line at a time, rather than printing one character at a time (as a dot matrix or daisy wheel printer does) or one page at a time (as a laser printer does). Line printers are very high-speed printers and are common in the corporate environment where they are used with mainframe computers, minicomputers, and networked systems.

LINENO

A Korn shell variable that contains the line number of the command currently executing in a shell script.

link

▶ The last stage in creating a program—the process of combining object files into a single executable.

▶ A connection between a filename and the corresponding i-node. There are two kinds of links—hard links and symbolic links. A hard link associates a filename with the place on the hard disk where the contents of the file are located. A symbolic link associates the filename with the pathname of a hard link to a file.

See also ln

link editor

A software development tool used to combine separately compiled source programs into a single executable program.

The Unix link editor is called ld.

linker

See link editor

lint

A software development tool that carefully checks C source code for syntax errors, portability problems, and fragments of code that are never used or are unreachable, even though the source code may have compiled correctly. Use lint before you use the C compiler, and you will avoid all sorts of problems.

See also cb, cc

Linux

A free Unix-compatible operating system for Intel-based PCs developed by Linus Torvalds at the University of Helsinki in Finland.

Strictly speaking, Linux is the name of the operating system kernel, the central part of the system that manages the basic operating system services, but many people use the name to refer to a complete operating system package, including utilities, editor and compilers, and games. Many of these important elements are actually part of the GNU Project, particularly the C compiler and other software development tools, while others have been written and released by volunteers.

Linux is a complete Unix clone and supports the X Window system, TCP/IP (including PPP, SLIP, support for many Ethernet cards, ftp, and telnet), emacs, UUCP, mail, newsreaders, NFS, a DOS emulation, and a complete set of GNU software development tools.

Linux is available free, although there may be a charge for the distribution media and additional printed documentation. You can get Linux on CD from Yggdrasil or from Slackware at:

Walnut Creek CDROM
4041 Pike Ln Suite D-386
Concord, CA 94520

or by calling 1-800-786-9907.

It is even bundled with several books, including Dan Tauber's *The Complete Linux Kit* from SYBEX. A huge number of Linux and Linux-related documents are available from many sites by anonymous ftp, and you can reach the Linux documentation home page at http://sunsite.unc .edu/pub/Linux. And as you might imagine, there are Linux newsgroups on USENET, too, including:

► comp.os.linux.admin

Linux system administration topics.

► comp.os.linux.advocacy

Merits and demerits of various operating systems.

► comp.os.linux.announce

New announcements for Linux users, moderated.

► comp.os.linux.answers

Linux HOWTO documents, moderated.

► comp.os.linux.development

Discussions on kernel development.

► comp.os.linux.development.apps

Information on porting applications to Linux.

► comp.os.linux.development.system

Discussions on software development tools.

► comp.os.linux.hardware

Supported hardware.

► comp.os.linux.help

General questions and answers on running Linux.

► comp.os.linux.misc

Other Linux topics.

▶ comp.os.linux.networking

Networking with Linux.

▶ comp.os.linux.setup

Discussions on setup problems.

▶ comp.os.linux.x

X Window and X Window applications and Linux.

You can also subscribe to the *Linux Journal*, published by Specialized System Consultants, at:

SSC
7723 24th NW,
Seattle, WA 98117, U.S.A.

See also dosemu, XFree86

listserver

An automatic mailing system available on the Internet.

Rather than sending e-mail on a particular topic to a long list of people, you send it instead to a special e-mail address, where a program automatically distributes the e-mail to all the people who subscribe to the mailing list.

Several programs have been written to automate a mailing list; the most common is called listserv, but you may also encounter mailserv, majordomo, or almanac. Table L.7 summarizes the most important listserv commands. To issue one of these commands, send an e-mail to the listserver address, leaving the subject line blank, and include one command as the body of the message; do not add a signature file. For example, if I wanted to subscribe to the listserv mailing list called writers, my e-mail message would look like this:

```
subscribe writers peter dyson
```

Many listservers require your real name; they will not let you sign up otherwise. And finally, remember that almost all these mailing list services are run by volunteers in their spare time; be nice to them.

Mailing lists are usually devoted to a very specific subject, such as training dogs or wearing panty hose, rather than for general interest communications.

See also digest, distribution, newsgroup, USENET

TABLE L.7: Summary of Important listserv Commands

COMMAND	DESCRIPTION
Help	Sends back a summary of basic commands.
info ?	Sends back a list of available topics.
info *topic*	Sends back information on the specified *topic*.
review *list*	Sends back information about the specified *list*.
set *list* ack	Sends a confirmation message for the specified *list*.
set *list* noack	Does not send a confirmation message for the specified *list*.
set *list* mail	Begins mail deliveries from *list*.
set *list* nomail	Stops mail deliveries from *list*.
set *list* repro	Sends copies of your own messages.
set *list* norepro	Does not send copies of your own messages.
subscribe *list your-name*	Opens a subscription to *list*.
signup *list your-name*	Opens a subscription to *list*.
unsubscribe *list your-name*	Cancels a subscription to *list*.
signoff *list*	Cancels a subscription to *list*.

listusers

A command found on UnixWare and some other systems that displays a list of usernames and IDs. This command has two options; the -g *groupname* option lists members of *groupname*, and the -1 *login* lists the users with the name *login*.

lkbib

A BSD command used to search bibliographic databases.

Syntax
Here's the syntax to use with lkbib:

```
lkbib [options] key...
```

Options and Arguments
The lkbib command searches bibliographic databases for references containing *key* and prints matching references to the standard output. This command has the options listed in Table L.8.

See also bib, indxbib, lookbib, refer

TABLE L.8: Options for Use with lkbib

Option	Description
-i *string*	If no index exists for the search file, ignore any fields whose names appear in *string*.
-p *filename*	Searches *filename*.
-t*n*	Requires only the first *n* characters of a *key*; the default is 6.
-v	Prints the version number.

ln

A command that creates both symbolic (soft) and physical (hard) links, allowing a file to have more than one name.

Syntax

There are two syntax forms you can use with the ln command:

```
ln [options] filename1 filename2
ln [options] filenames directory
```

In the first form above, *filename1* is linked to *filename2*, which is usually a new name; if *filename2* exists, it is overwritten.

In the second form, ln creates a link in *directory* to *filenames*. The new links will have the same filenames as the originals but different full pathnames.

Options and Arguments

You can use the options listed in Table L.9 with the ln command.

TABLE L.9: Options for the ln Command

Option	Description
-f	Forces the link to be created without asking for overwrite permission.
-n	Does not overwrite existing files.
-s	Creates a symbolic link rather than a hard link.

Examples

If you and a coworker insist on using different names for the same file, ln can solve the dilemma. To create a link, use something like this:

```
ln little large
```

which creates a link to little called large.

Notes

A hard link to a file behaves just like the original filename; you can use the original filename or the name assigned by the ln command, and the result is always the same. All hard links to a file must be in the same filesystem as the original file.

There is a very important difference between creating a link with ln and simply copying the file to another location. With linked files, when one copy is updated, all the links to that file are also updated simultaneously and automatically. With a copy, you must update each copy individually.

See also cp, link, rm, **symbolic links**

local variable

A variable in a program or in the shell, which is not visible or available to any other program.

See also exec, **global variable**, typeset

locate

A BSD command that finds files by searching a database for all pathnames that match the specified pattern; locate *pattern*. The database, located in the file locate.*database*, is updated from time to time and contains the pathnames of all publicly accessible files.

See also **find**

lock

A BSD and SCO command that locks a terminal. The lock command asks the user to enter and then verify a password and then locks the terminal until the password is re-entered.

In BSD, the -p option does not ask for a password but uses the user's current login password, and the -t *timeout* option changes the default 15 minute time out to the value specified by *timeout*.

In the SCO version, the -*timeout* option does not have an initial -t, and the -v option sets verbose mode.

logger

A BSD command that provides a shell command interface to the syslog system log module and creates entries in the system log; see the man pages for more details.

logging in

The process of establishing a connection to a Unix system by responding appropriately to the `login:` and `Password:` prompts. Sometimes written as *log in* or *login*.

logging off

The process of terminating a Unix session. Sometimes written *log off* or *log out*.

login

A command used to identify yourself and gain access to the system. By requiring users to log in, the system can be customized for each user, and the system itself can be protected against unwelcome intruders.

See also `exit`, `logout`, `passwd`

.login

A C shell initialization file executed when you first log in. You can use `.login` to set environment variables and to run any commands that you want to execute at the beginning of each new login session.

See also `.cshrc`, `.logout`

;login

The name of the newsletter provided to all members of the USENIX Association, containing articles and technical papers.

login name

The name that you type in response to the `login:` prompt on a Unix system. Every login name has a corresponding user ID number, and both are established in the password database or `/etc/passwd` file.

login shell

The shell that is available immediately when you log in to a Unix system. The login shell can fork other processes to run a different shell, utilities, or other programs. The name of your login shell is kept in the `/etc/passwd` file.

logname

A command that displays your login name. There are no arguments or options available for use with this command.

See also login, who, whoami

logout

A built-in C shell command that terminates the current login shell.

.logout

A C shell file executed when you logout from the system. You can place commands in .logout that you want to execute automatically every time that you logout from the system.

See also .cshrc, .login

long filename

Long filenames that may contain spaces, more than one period, and mixed upper- and lowercase letters.

look

A Solaris and BSD command that finds words in the system dictionary (/usr/dict/words or /usr/share/dict/words) or lines in a sorted file that start with a specified string.

Syntax

The syntax to use with look is as follows:

```
look [options]string filename
```

Options and Arguments

The look command displays the lines in *filename* that contain *string* as the first word. If you don't specify *filename*, the system dictionary is used instead, the case of letters is ignored, and only alphanumeric characters are compared. You can use the options listed in Table L.10 with look.

See also grep, sort

TABLE L.10: Options for Use with `look`

Option	Description
-d	Compares only alphanumeric characters.
-f	Ignores case.
-t *termchar*	Specifies a string termination character *termchar*; only the characters in *string* up to and including *termchar* are compared.

lookbib

A BSD command that searches a bibliographic database for a specified keyword.

Syntax
The syntax for this command is as follows:

    lookbib [options] filename...

Options and Arguments
The `lookbib` command displays a prompt and reads a line from the standard input containing a set of keywords. `lookbib` searches the specified *filename* for references containing those keywords and prints the matches it finds on the standard output. You can use the options in Table L.11 with this command.

See also bib, indxbib, lkbib

TABLE L.11: Options for Use with `lookbib`

Option	Description
-i *string*	When searching files for which no index exists, ignore those fields whose names are specified in *string*.
-t*n*	Requires only the first *n* characters of a key; the default is 6.
-v	Prints the program version number.

lorder

A utility that lists dependencies for a group of object files specified on the command line. Output from `lorder` is usually used with `tsort` when a library is created to determine the optimum ordering of the object modules so that the loader can resolve all references in a single pass.

See also ldd, lprof

lossless compression

Any data compression method that compresses a file by rearranging or recoding the data that it contains in a more compact fashion. With lossless compression, none of the original data is lost when the file is decompressed again. Lossless compression methods must be used on program files and images such as medical X-rays, in which data loss cannot be tolerated.

Many lossless compression programs use a method known as the Lempel-Ziv (LZ) algorithm, which searches a file for redundant strings of data and converts them to smaller tokens; when the compressed file is decompressed, this process is reversed.

See also JPEG, lossy compression, MPEG

lossy compression

Any data compression method that compresses a file by throwing away any data that the compression mechanism decides is unnecessary. Original data is lost when the file is decompressed again. Lossy compression methods may be used for shrinking audio or image files in which absolute accuracy is not required and the loss of data will never be noticed, but it is unsuitable for more critical applications in which data loss cannot be tolerated, such as medical images or program files.

See also JPEG, lossless compression, MPEG

/lost+found

A root directory found in most filesystems, which is used as a collection point for damaged files identified by the `fsck` command. Once the files have been copied into this directory, the system administrator can decide on an appropriate fate for the files.

See also `fsck`

lp

An SVR4 command that sends files to the print queue for printing.

Syntax
The syntax used with the `lp` command is:

```
lp [options][files]
```

The `lp` command also allows you to print several files, one after the other.

Options and Arguments

The *files* argument specifies one or more pathnames of ordinary text files that you want lp to print. Specify - if you want to use the standard input rather than a file. The options available with this command are listed in Table L.12; check with your system administrator for details on the many printer-dependent options available with this command.

TABLE L.12: Options Available with lp

OPTION	DESCRIPTION
-c	Copies the files before printing so that they cannot be changed. If you don't use this option, any changes you make to the file after the print request is made but before it is completed will be reflected in the printed output.
-d *destination*	Specifies *destination* as the printer; may be the name of an individual printer or a class of printers.
-m	Sends you a mail message to let you know that the files have been printed.
-n *number*	Prints the specified *number* of copies.
-o *option*	Specifies printer-dependent options; see your system administrator for details.
-P *list*	Prints only the pages specified in *list*.
-q *priority*	Assigns this print request the specified *priority*. Values for *priority* range from 0, the highest priority, to 39, the lowest.
-s	Suppresses messages including the request ID message you would otherwise see on submitting a print job.
-w	Displays a message on your terminal when all the files have been printed. If you have logged off, you will get a mail message instead.

Examples

To print a text file to the default printer, use:

```
lp text.file
```

Notes

In BSD systems, the lpr command is equivalent to SVR4's lp command.

See also cancel, lpstat, pr

lpq

A BSD command that displays the printer queue status.

Syntax

Here's the syntax to use with the lpq command:

```
lpq [options][jobID...][user...]
```

For each print job, lpq displays the username, rank in the queue, file-names, the job ID, and the total size in bytes.

Options and Arguments

When you use lpq with no arguments, the command reports on all jobs currently in the queue. You can request information by specifying a *jobID* or *user*. The options for lpq are listed in Table L.13.

TABLE L.13: Options for Use with lpq

OPTION	DESCRIPTION
-l	Displays all available information; ordinarily, only one line is displayed for each print job.
-P *printer*	Specifies a particular *printer*.

Notes

In SVR4 systems, the lpstat command is equivalent to BSD's lpq command.

See also lpr, lprm, lpstat

lpr

A BSD command that sends text files to the print queue for printing.

Syntax

The syntax to use with lpr is as follows:

    lpr [*options*]*filename*...

The lpr command also allows you to print several files, one after the other.

Options and Arguments

The lpr command uses the print spooler to output the print jobs to the printer; if no *filename* is specified, lpr prints from the standard input. Table L.14 lists the options available with this command.

TABLE L.14: Options Available with lpr

OPTION	DESCRIPTION
PRINT JOB OPTIONS	
-h	Does not print a burst page.
-m	Sends the user a mail message when the print job is complete.
-P *printer*	Specifies a particular *printer*.

TABLE L.14 continued: Options Available with lpr

Option	Description
	PRINT JOB OPTIONS
-r	Removes the file when printing is complete.
-s	Uses symbolic links rather than copying files; used to save disk space when printing very large files.
	PRINTING OPTIONS
-# *number*	Prints the specified *number* of copies of each file.
-i *font*	Specifies a particular font.
-C *class*	Prints the job classification on the burst page.
-J *job*	Prints the job name on the burst page, usually the filename.
-T *title*	Prints the *title* rather than the filename on the burst page.
-U *user*	Prints the username on the burst page.
-i *columns*	Sets the number of leading blank characters, usually 8.
-w *number*	Specifies the page width.
	FILTER OPTIONS
-c	File was created by cifplot.
-d	File contains TEX data.
-f	File contains Fortran source code.
-g	File contains plot data.
-l	File contains control characters.
-n	File contains ditroff data.
-p	Use pr to print the file.
-t	File contains troff data.
-v	File contains raster data.

Examples

To print three copies of the text files my.txt and your.txt, use:

```
lpr -#3 my.txt your.txt
```

Notes

In SVR4, the lp command is equivalent to BSD's lpr command. On some systems, such as SCO, the lpr command is a link to the lp command, and so the two names can be used interchangeably.

See also lpq, lprm, pr

lprint

An SCO command that prints a text file on a local printer rather than using the print spooler and the default system printer.

Syntax
The syntax is:

```
lprint [option] filename...
```

The only option you can use with this command is a hyphen (-), which prints from the standard input rather than from a file.

lprm

A BSD command that removes jobs from the print spooler.

Syntax
The syntax to use with lprm is:

```
lprm [options][jobID...][user...]
```

Since the spooling directory is protected from users, this command is the only way to remove a job from the print spooler.

Options and Arguments
You can remove a print job by specifying the appropriate *jobID* (obtained from the lpq command), and the superuser can remove a print job belonging to a specified *user*. The other two options are listed in Table L.15.

TABLE L.15: Options for Use with lprm

OPTION	DESCRIPTION
-	Removes all jobs owned by the current user; if this option is invoked by the superuser, the print queue is emptied completely.
-P *printer*	Selects the print queue associated with a particular *printer*.

Notes
In SVR4, the cancel command is equivalent to BSD's lprm command.

See also lpq, lpr, pr

lprof

A command that displays a program's profile data, line by line. Information displayed includes a list of the source code files, each source code line, and the number of times each line executes.

See also gprof, ldd, lorder, prof

lpstat

A command used to display status information for the lp print spooler.

Syntax

Here's the syntax to use with lpstat:

```
lpstat [options]
```

For each of the jobs in the queue, lpstat displays the name of the user requesting the print job, the job's current location in the queue, the name of the file being printed, the print request number (the number you need to remove the job from the queue), and the size of the print job in bytes.

Options and Arguments

Table L.16 lists the options you can use with lpstat.

Some of the options in Table L.16 take a list argument, and if you leave out the list, all the information available for that option is displayed. Items in list can be separated by commas or, if enclosed in double quotes, by spaces.

If you specify the print request number, lpstat reports on just that print job; if you specify a userID, lpstat reports on all jobs associated with that user.

TABLE L.16: Options Available with lpstat

Option	Description
-a list	Shows whether the printers specified in list are accepting print requests.
-c list	Displays class names for the printers specified in list.
-d	Reports the default system printer.
-D	Used with -p to display a short printer description.
-f list	Verifies that the list of forms are defined by the lp spooler.
-l	Used with -f to display the available forms; after -p to show printer configuration and after -S to display print wheel information.
-o list	Reports the status of all output requests, including printer names and print request ID numbers.
-p list	Reports the status of printers in list; used to see if the printer is enabled, and if not, why not.
-r	Indicates whether the print spooler is on or off; if the spooler is not running, no print jobs can be scheduled, and no printing can take place.
-R	Displays the job's position in the print queue.
-s	Displays a status summary of the spooler, including whether the spooler is running, the default printer, and the printer names and the devices associated with them.
-S list	Verifies that the list of print wheels and character sets is known to lp.

TABLE L.16 continued: Options Available with lpstat

OPTION	DESCRIPTION
-t	Displays all information; equivalent to using -acdusr. If you have several printers on your system, this option provides more information than will fit on one screen; use more to prevent the information from scrolling off your screen.
-u *list*	Similar to -o but for *list* of users.
-v *list*	Displays a list of printers and the devices associated with them.

Notes

In BSD systems, the lpq command is equivalent to SVR4's lpstat command.

See also cancel, lp

lptest

A command that sends a ripple test to the standard output. Originally developed to test printers, the ripple test outputs all 96 printable ASCII characters in all positions, taking 96 lines to complete the test.

Syntax

The syntax is:

```
lptest [length][count]
```

where *length* specifies the line length (the default is 79 characters), and *count* sets the number of lines to output (the default is 200 lines). This test is also used with terminals.

ls

The command is used to list the contents of a directory.

Syntax

The syntax to use with this command is:

```
ls [options] pathname ...
```

The ls command lists the files and subdirectories in a directory, sorted in alphabetical order, and adds additional information about each file, depending on the options you choose. If you do not specify *pathname*, the contents of the current directory are displayed.

Options and Arguments

The ls command has a large number of options that determine the type of information that ls displays; see Table L.17 for details. If you use ls without an option, you see a short listing that contains just filenames.

TABLE L.17: Options for Use with ls

OPTION	DESCRIPTION
-1	Lists one file per line.
-a	Lists all files, including those whose names begin with a dot.
-A	Lists entries, including those whose names begin with a dot, except for . and .. (BSD only).
-b	Displays nonprinting characters in octal (SVR4 only).
-c	Lists files sorted by creation/modification time.
-C	Lists files in columns, sorted down each column.
-d	Lists only directory names, not their contents.
-f	Lists the files within directories, but not the directories themselves.
-F	Places / after listed directories, * after executable files, and @ after symbolic links.
-g	Lists files in the -1 long format, but without owner names (SVR4 only).
-i	Displays the i-node for each file.
-1	Lists files in the long format; see the section "Using the Long Option" in this entry for more details.
-L	Lists the file or directory referenced by a symbolic link rather than the link itself.
-m	Lists the files separated by commas (SVR4 only).
-n	Lists files in the -1 long format, with user and group numbers rather than names (SVR4 only).
-o	Lists files in the -1 long format, but without group name.
-p	Places a / after directory names (SVR4 only).
-q	Displays nonprinting characters as ?.
-r	Lists files in reverse order.
-R	Lists subdirectories recursively.
-s	Displays the file size in blocks.
-t	Lists files according to modification time, with the newest first.
-T	Displays complete time information, including year, month, day, hour, minute, and second (BSD only).
-u	Lists files according to file access time.
-x	Displays files sorted in rows across the screen (SVR4 only).

Examples
To display a list of all the files in the current directory and its subdirectories, sorted by their modification time, enter:

```
ls -altR
```

See also chmod, **file permissions**

Lynx

A text-based World Wide Web browser for VT100 (non-graphic) terminals, developed by Lou Montoulli of the University of Kansas. Lynx is very easy to use and is available on a variety of different Unix systems. Lynx includes keyword searches and also stores a history list of the sites you have visited.

LZ

Abbreviation for Lempel-Ziv, an algorithm used in data compression developed by Abraham Lempel and Jacob Ziv in the late 1970s.

M

Mach

An operating system created at Carnegie Mellon University, designed to support advanced features such as multiprocessing and multitasking.

Mach has its roots in the Unix world and was originally based on BSD 4.2; however, its most notable feature is that it employs a relatively small microkernel rather than a conventional monolithic kernel.

The microkernel is designed to manage only the most fundamental operating system operations, including interrupts, task scheduling, messaging, and virtual memory; other modules can be added as necessary for file management, network support, and other tasks.

The NeXT operating system and OSF/1 are both based on Mach.

machid

An SCO command that determines the type of Intel microprocessor on which the system is running. The machid command is used with one of the following options, and returns a true value if the machine is of this type: i286, iAPX286, i386, i486.

On certain other systems this command is replaced by the mach or the machine command.

mail

In the Unix world, when someone talks about mail, they mean e-mail, rather than the U.S. Postal Service. Unix has supported some form of e-mail since the very beginning, and perhaps as a result, there are several different kinds of mail programs. You may find that more than one of them is available on your system. Some programs developed from the AT&T branch of Unix, others from BSD, and then there are some programs that are in the public domain. Here's a look at the more popular mail programs:

mail   The original, rather primitive, AT&T e-mail program.

Mail   A much enhanced BSD version of `mail`.

mailx   An SVR4 version of `Mail` known as extended `mail`, hence `mailx`.

MH   The MH (Message Handling) system is different from the standard mail programs, in that it consists of a large set of commands rather than one single large program. MH was originally developed at the Rand Corporation and then adopted as part of the BSD releases; it is now in the public domain. An X Window interface to MH called `xmh` is also available.

elm   `elm` is a menu-driven program designed as a replacement for the `mail` program. `elm` combines power and ease of use with advanced features you can use to create your own customized mail-handling system.

Pine   An easy-to-use program well-suited to new or occasional users, Pine comes with its own built-in editor called `pico` for creating messages and a paging program used to read messages.

mush   An abbreviation for mail user's shell. A public domain program with two modes; you can use it with a line-oriented interface or with a full-screen interface.

emacs   The `emacs` editor includes a large number of commands for handling e-mail. `emacs` uses its own mail format, called Rmail format for mail files, which is not compatible with the standard Unix mail-file format but does provide commands for converting between the two formats.

Both `mailx` and `Mail` are upwardly compatible with `mail` and are quite similar to each other. Nowadays, most systems are set up so that when you type the word `mail`, either `mailx` or `Mail` starts, whichever is appropriate on your system. Also, many versions of Unix include graphical mailers as a part of their desktop environment; these mailers are often very easy to use and extremely powerful.

The mail programs that you work with as a user are known as mail user agents, and most of them use other mailers to manage the actual transmission of your message. These mailers are known as *mail transport agents,* and it is unlikely that you will ever have to deal with them directly; delivermail, sendmail, and rmail are all mail transport agents.

mail

The original Unix e-mail program; also used on many systems as an alias to one of the modern mail programs, either mailx or Mail.

Syntax

The syntax to use with mail is as follows:

```
mail [options][users]
```

Options and Arguments

The mail command reads incoming e-mail or sends mail to one or more *users*. The options for use with mail are listed in Table M.1; you can also type a question mark to see a summary of commands.

See also elm, **mail,** Mail, mailx, MH, mush, **Pine**

TABLE M.1: Options for Use with mail

Option	Description
OPTIONS FOR SENDING MAIL	
-m *type*	Prints Message-type: *type* in the message header.
-t	Prints To: in the message header, listing the names of the recipients.
-w	Forces mail to be sent.
OPTIONS FOR RETRIEVING MAIL	
-e	Test to see if mail exists without displaying anything; the exit status is zero if mail exists, 1 if there is no mail.
-f *filename*	Reads mail from the mailbox specified by *filename*.
-F *Names*	Forwards all incoming mail to *Names*.
-h	Displays several messages.
-p	Prints all messages.
-P	Prints all messages and all message headers.
-q	Terminates on an interrupt.
-r	Reverses the message order and prints the oldest messages first.

Mail

The BSD e-mail program; sometimes called `mail`.

Syntax

The syntax to use with `Mail` is:

    Mail [options]address

Used without options, `Mail` checks for new mail, then displays a one-line header for each message found. You can move up and down through the message list using + and -, and you can print messages using the `print` command, often abbreviated to simply p.

To send a message, use `Mail` with the appropriate *address*, then type the message, and press Ctrl-D.

When you have read all your mail, you can delete or reply to individual messages, and then end your session by pressing either e for exit or q for quit.

The section "Command Summary" below lists the commands you can use in your `Mail` session.

Options and Arguments

You can use the options listed in Table M.2 when you first start `Mail`.

TABLE M.2: Options for Use with Mail

Option	Description
-b *list*	Sends blind carbon copies to *list* of users.
-c *list*	Sends carbon copies to *list* of users.
-f *filename*	Reads mail from the mailbox specified by *filename*.
-i	Ignores interrupts.
-I	Forces interactive mode.
-n	Prevents reading `mail.rc` on startup.
-N	Turns off initial display of message headers.
-s *subject*	Specifies *subject*.
-u *username*	Reads mail from the mailbox specified by *username*.
-v	Displays delivery details.

Command Summary

The `Mail` program also has a large number of commands, each typed on a line by itself, followed by any appropriate arguments. You don't have to type many of these commands in full; they can be abbreviated. In Table M.3, which lists these commands, the abbreviation is shown in the left column before the full command name.

When you are in input mode composing your message, you can use tilde (~) escape commands to perform special functions; the tilde is only recognized when it is the first character on a line.

See also biff, elm, **mail**, mail.rc, .mailrc-, mailx, MH, mush, **Pine, tilde escape commands**, xbiff

TABLE M.3: Mail Command Summary

COMMAND	DESCRIPTION
-	Displays the previous message.
?	Displays a summary of commands.
! *command*	Executes the shell *command*.
a or alias	Displays, creates, or changes an alias.
alt or alternate	Avoids message duplication if you have accounts on several different systems.
c or chdir	Changes the directory.
co or copy	Saves the message file.
d or delete	Deletes a message.
dp or dt	Deletes the current message and prints the next message.
e or edit	Edits the message.
ex, x, xit or exit	Exits immediately, without making any changes.
fi or file	Lists all files.
fo or folder	Changes to a new mail folder.
folders	Lists all your folders.
f or from	Prints the message headers from a list of messages.
h or headers	Lists headers in groups of 18 messages.
help	Displays a summary of commands.
ho or hold	Saves messages in the user's system mailbox; opposite of mbox.
ignore	Adds header fields to your ignore list, a list of fields that are not displayed when you look at a message.
m or mail	Sends mail to the specified names.
mbox	Saves messages in mbox in your home directory; opposite of hold.
n or next	Displays the next or the next matching message.
pre or preserve	Saves messages in the user's system mailbox; opposite of mbox.
p or print	Displays messages on your terminal without ignore fields.
P or Print	Displays messages on your terminal including ignore fields.
q or quit	Quits after saving all unsaved messages in mbox.
r or reply	Replies to the sender and all recipients of a message.
R or Reply	Replies only to the sender of a message.

TABLE M.3 continued: Mail Command Summary

COMMAND	DESCRIPTION
respond	Replies to the sender and all recipients of a message.
Retain	Adds header fields to your retain list, a list of fields that are displayed when you look at a message.
s or save	Saves the message in the specified file.
se or set	With no options, prints all variable values; otherwise, sets variables.
Saveignore	When saving messages, does not save ignored list fields.
Saveretain	When saving messages, saves ignored list fields.
sh or shell	Invokes an interactive version of the shell.
Size	Displays the size of each message.
Top	Displays the first few lines of each message.
t or type	Same as print.
T or Type	Same as Print.
Unalias	Removes aliases.
u or undelete	Recovers a deleted message.
U or unread	Marks a message you have read as unread.
Unset	Discards variable values; reverse of set.
v or visual	Opens the editor on each message.
w or write	Saves just the message text without the header information.

mailalias

An SVR4 command that displays the e-mail address associated with one or more *names*. The syntax is:

```
mailalias [options]names
```

This command takes two options; -s displays the address associated with *names*, and -v turns on debug mode.

mailq

A BSD command that prints a short summary of the messages waiting for delivery in the mail queue. A single option, -v prints extra information, including the priority of the message.

mail.rc

A file located in the /usr/lib/mailx directory that establishes the system-wide e-mail variables.

See also .mailrc, mailx

.mailrc

A file used to establish your own e-mail configuration, containing commands that configure the mail system to your own liking and establish groups of mail recipients as aliases. This file is located in your home directory.

See also mail.rc

mailx

The SVR4 e-mail program; sometimes called mail.

Syntax

The syntax for the mailx command is as follows:

    mailx [options][users]

Options and Arguments

The command-line options you can use with mailx are listed in Table M.4.

TABLE M.4: Options for Use with mailx

Option	Description
OPTIONS FOR SENDING MAIL	
-F	Saves messages in a file named after the first recipient.
-i	Ignores interrupts.
-n	Prevents reading mail.rc on startup.
-s *string*	Sets the message subject to *string*.
OPTIONS FOR RETRIEVING MAIL	
-e	Tests for presence of mail without printing anything.
-f *filename*	Reads mail from *filename* rather than mbox.
-h *n*	Stops sending after *n* network hops.
-H	Displays only message headers.
-I	Assumes the first newsgroup in the Newsgroups field is the sender; use only with the -f option.
-N	Don't display initial header summary.
-r *address*	Passes the *address* to network delivery software.
-T *filename*	Saves the list of article-id fields in *filename*.
-u *user*	Reads mail from *user* mailbox.
-U	Converts UUCP addresses into Internet addresses.

Command Summary

The `mailx` program also has a large number of commands, each typed on a line by itself, followed by any appropriate arguments. You don't have to type many of these commands in full; they can be abbreviated. In Table M.5, which lists these commands, the abbreviation is shown in the left column before the full command name.

When you are in input mode composing your message, you can use tilde (~) escape commands to perform special functions; the tilde is only recognized when it is the first character on a line.

See also `biff`, `elm`, **mail,** `Mail`, `mail.rc`, `.mailrc`, MH, `mush`, **Pine,** `xbiff`

TABLE M.5: mailx Command Summary

COMMAND	DESCRIPTION
n	Displays message number *n*.
-	Displays the previous message.
. or =	Displays the current message number.
#	Treats the rest of the line as a comment.
?	Displays a summary of commands.
! *command*	Executes the shell *command*.
a or alias	Displays, creates, or changes an alias.
alt or alternate	Avoids message duplication if you have accounts on several different systems.
cd	Changes to the specified directory.
ch or chdir	Changes the directory.
c or copy	Saves the message file.
C or Copy	Saves each message in a file named for the message's author.
d or delete	Deletes a message.
di or discard	Does not display the specified header fields when displaying messages.
dp or dt	Deletes the current message and prints the next message.
ec or echo	Echoes the specified string.
e or edit	Edits the message.
ex, x, xit, or exit	Exits immediately, without making any changes.
fi or file	Lists all files.
fold or folder	Changes to a new mail folder.
folders	Lists all your folders.
fo or followup	Replies to a message, and stores the reply in a file named for the message's author.
F or Followup	Replies to the first specified message, and sends the reply to all the originators of the list of messages.

TABLE M.5 continued: mailx Command Summary

Command	Description
f or from	Prints the message headers from a list of messages.
g or group	Creates a group alias.
h or headers	Lists headers in groups of 18 messages.
help	Displays a summary of commands.
ho or hold	Saves messages in the user's system mailbox; opposite of mbox.
ignore	Adds header fields to your ignore list, a list of fields that are not displayed when you look at a message.
l or list	Lists available commands without explanations.
m or mail	Sends mail to the specified names.
M or Mail	Sends mail to the specified name, and stores the message in a file named for the recipient.
mb or mbox	Saves messages in mbox in your home directory; opposite of hold.
n or next	Displays the next or the next matching message.
pi or pipe	Passes the specified messages to a command.
pre or preserve	Saves messages in the user's system mailbox; opposite of mbox.
p or print	Displays messages on your terminal without ignore fields.
P or Print	Displays messages on your terminal including ignore fields.
q or quit	Quits after saving all unsaved messages in mbox.
r or reply	Replies to the sender and all recipients of a message.
R or Reply	Replies only to the sender of a message.
respond	Replies to the sender and all recipients of a message.
s or save	Saves the message in the specified file.
se or set	With no options, prints all variable values; otherwise, sets variables.
sh or shell	Invokes an interactive version of the shell.
size	Displays the size of each message.
source	Reads and executes commands from a specified file.
top	Displays the first few lines of each message.
tou or touch	"Touches" each message so it appears to have been read.
t or type	Same as print.
T or Type	Same as Print.
u or undelete	Recovers a deleted message.
unset	Discards variable values; reverse of set.
ve or version	Displays the version number and release date of mailx.
v or visual	Opens the editor on each message.
w or write	Saves just the message text without the header information.
z or z+	Scrolls the header summary one screen forward.
z-	Scrolls the header summary one screen backward.

mailx.rc

A file used to establish the system-wide e-mail configuration, containing commands that should be appropriate for all users. It is named either `/usr/lib/mailx/mailx.rc` or `/usr/lib/Mail.rc` depending on your system.

See also `.mailrc`

major device number

A number assigned to a class of devices such as disk drives, tape drives, printers, or terminals.

If you use the `ls -l` command to list the contents of the `/dev` directory, you will see the major and minor device numbers, separated by commas, listed where you would expect to see the file sizes in bytes in a normal listing. The rest of the information is the same as that shown by any `ls -l` listing.

major mode

Within `emacs`, one of many modes in which aspects of `emacs` operation are tailored to suit the needs of a particular common type of text processing. Major modes include those specially designed for C programming, normal text processing, `awk` scripts, `nroff` and `troff`-formatted files, and so on.

See also minor mode

make

A software development utility used to maintain a set of source code file dependencies so that changes to these files can be managed with the minimum of effort, and the resulting executables can be kept up-to-date.

The time dependency rules used by `make` utilities can be used on any project in which dependencies between files must be explicitly controlled.

Almost every commercially offered compiler and assembler includes some form of `make` utility these days.

See also `imake`, `makefile`, **RCS, SCCS**

makefile

A file, created by the `make` utility, that lists the source code files, object files, and their dependencies for a specific software development project. Using information from this makefile, `make` keeps track of the sequences needed to create certain files and can perform updating tasks automatically for the programmer. This means that when a program is changed in some way, make can recreate the proper files with the minimum of input from the programmer.

See also SCCS

makekey

A utility that creates a complex encryption key; due to export restrictions, makekey is only available in the U.S.

man

A utility that displays the Unix online reference manuals.

Syntax
Here's the syntax to use with man:

```
man [options][[section]subject]
```

Options and Arguments
The man command displays information from the Unix online reference manual, where *subject* is normally the name of a command or system call and *section* is a section number between 1 and 8. Some of the online reference material is terse and difficult to understand, but it does contain a wealth of information that it is difficult to find elsewhere. See Table M.6 for a list of the command-line options you can use with man.

Because the command-line options for man differ from system to system, check the man pages on your system for details by entering:

```
man man
```

TABLE M.6: Options for Use with man

Option	Description
-a	Displays all specified *section* and *name* combinations.
-c	Copies the specified page to the standard output rather than using the more command to break it up into pages (4.4BSD only).
-C *filename*	Uses the specified *filename* rather than the default configuration file man.conf (4.4BSD only).
-d	Enters debug mode (Solaris only).
-f *filenames*	Displays a one-line summary of one or more reference *filenames*.
-h	Displays just the "SYNOPSIS" section of the page (4.4BSD only).
-k *keywords*	Displays any header line containing the specified *keywords*.

TABLE M.6 continued: Options for Use with man

Option	Description
-l	Displays all page references for the specified *section* and *name* combinations (Solaris only).
-m *pathname*	Adds *pathname* to the list of directories searched by man; *pathname* contains a comma-separated list of directory names.
-M *pathname*	Replaces the standard list of directories with *pathname*, which contains a comma-separated list of directory names.
-t	Formats the pages with troff.
-T *macro*	Displays information using the specified *macro* package.
-w	Lists the pathnames for the specified *section* and *name* combinations.

Examples

To display the manual page for the vi editor, use:

    man vi

If you want to know if a particular word occurs in a specific manual page but don't want to read through the page yourself, you can use grep with the man command. For example, to see if the word alias appears in the csh page, use:

    man csh | grep alias

See also man **pages,** whatis, whereis, xman

man pages

The man (manual) utility displays pages from the system documentation stored on disk on your terminal screen. Type the man command, followed by the name of the command that you want information about and Unix displays the documentation for that command.

The Unix system manual is divided into eight sections, as follows:

1. User Commands

2. System Calls

3. C Library Functions

4. Devices and Network Interfaces in BSD; Administrative Files in SVR4

5. File Formats in BSD; Miscellaneous Information in SVR4

6. Games and Demos

7. Environments, Tables, and Macros in BSD; I/O and Special Files in SVR4

8. System Maintenance Commands

Most users find everything they want to know (and more) in sections 1 and 6; system administrators and programmers may have to consult the other sections. On some versions of Unix, you will find that these major categories have been further subdivided into even more categories; for example, UnixWare includes networking commands in Section 1C and X Window commands in Section 1X.

A command name followed by a number in parentheses–ls (1), for example, – means that information on the ls command is in Section 1 of the online manual. You can use this form of the man command to look at that entry:

```
man 1 ls
```

Each man page treats a single topic; some are short, while others are much longer, but they are all organized according to a standard format using the headings described in Table M.7.

Not all man pages have all of these headings, and some versions of Unix use slightly different names for these headings.

```
man man
```

TABLE M.7: Organization of man Pages

Heading	Description
NAME:	The name and main purpose of the command.
SYNOPSIS:	The syntax to use with the command.
DESCRIPTION:	A complete description of the command; in some cases, such as the C shell (man csh), this description is very long.
FILES:	A list of the important files related to this command.
See also:	Places to look for related information.
DIAGNOSTICS:	A list of warning and error messages.
BUGS:	Details of programming errors, and shortcomings of the command.

managing processes

Every process running under Unix has several important pieces of information associated with it, including:

▶ The process ID (PID) is a number assigned when a process starts; no two processes can have the same PID at the same time.

- ▶ The user ID tells Unix to whom the process belongs and so determines the files and directories that the process is allowed to read from and write to.

- ▶ The group ID tells Unix to which group the process belongs.

- ▶ The environment is a list of variables and their values, often customized for each user.

See also **background processing,** bg, fg, **foreground processing, job control,** kill, nice, ps

map

- ▶ An NFS term describing a file containing the mount points and their resources.

- ▶ The process of relating a piece of data, for example, a network address, with a physical location such as a network interface card (NIC).

- ▶ In vi, a command used to create a macro

mask

A binary number, usually written in octal, which is used to remove bits from another binary number. Masks are often used when manipulating file permissions.

See also chmod, **creation mask,** umask

master map

A file that contains the names and configurations of systems using the NFS.

mbox

A default system file that contains e-mail messages from other users that have been read and saved.

mcs

An SVR4 command used to add to, delete from, compress, or print one or more comments sections from an ELF object file.

Syntax
The syntax for mcs is:

```
mcs [options]filenames
```

Options and Arguments

Table M.8 lists the options you can use with this command; at least one option must be specified. The name of the default comments section is `.comment`.

TABLE M.8: Options to Use with mcs

Option	Description
-a *string*	Appends *string* to the comment area of *filenames*.
-c	Compresses the comment section of *filenames*.
-d	Deletes the comments section from *filenames*.
-n *name*	Specifies *name* as the comments section rather than .comment.
-p	Prints the comments on the standard output.
-V	Displays the version

See also face, **FACE,** fmli

me macros

A set of over 80 nroff and troff macros distributed with BSD systems, originally created by Eric Allman while at Berkeley. The me macro package is equivalent to the ms and mm macro packages on SVR4 systems and supports all common preprocessors such as eqn, tbl, and refer. Macros are used to provide complex formatting options such as automatic numbering of lists, running head control, and font changes.

See also mm **macros,** ms **macros**

menu

A list of the commands or options available in the program displayed on the screen.

You select a menu item by typing a letter or number corresponding to the item, by clicking it with the mouse, or by highlighting it and pressing the Enter key.

merge

An operation that combines two ordered lists or files in such a way that the resulting list is still in order.

See also merge, sort

merge

A BSD command that combines separate sets of changes from two files into one.

Syntax
Here's the syntax for merge:

```
merge [options] filename1 filename2 filename3
```

Options and Arguments
The merge command is very useful for combining the separate sets of changes into one file. For example, if *filename2* contains the original text, and *filename1* and *filename3* include modifications, you can use merge to create one file that contains all the modifications.

To send the results of the merge to the standard output rather than to *filename1*, use the -p option, and to suppress all messages, use the -q option.

See also diff3

merge

See RCS

mesg

A command used to control message posting on your terminal. To stop other users from sending you messages with the write command, use:

```
mesg -n
```

and use

```
mesg -y
```

when you are ready to start receiving messages once again.

See also write, talk

metacharacter

A character with a special meaning in certain specific situations. Metacharacters are used in ambiguous file references in the shell and in regular expressions in other programs. You must always quote a metacharacter with a backslash (\) or single quotes if you want to use the ordinary meaning of the character. Sometimes called a *wild card*.

See also asterisk, question mark, regular character

metafile

A file that contains both data and output control information. For example, a graphics metafile contains not only a graphical image of some kind but also information on how the image should be displayed. This allows one single version of a file to be output to a variety of different display devices.

Meta key

A key used extensively in emacs. Some keyboards have a Meta key, while others map the function of this key onto the Alt or other suitable key on the keyboard. The Meta key is used in the same way as the Ctrl key, in combination with other keys to create unique commands.

m4

A macro language preprocessor for Ratfor (a version of Fortran), Pascal, or other languages that do not have a built-in macro processing feature.

MH

A message handling system, originally developed by the Rand Corporation and now in the public domain; sometimes written as mh.

MH is different from Mail or mailx in that it consists of a large set of individual commands rather than one single program; this makes it easy to combine mail-handling tasks with other chores, and you can combine MH commands with shell features such as pipes, redirection, aliases, and command history if you wish.

MH stores each message as a separate file with a numerical name, and you can use all the usual Unix file-management commands with these files. Table M.9 lists the MH commands.

You can get MH from a variety of sites including ftp.ics.uci.edu in mh/mh-6.8tar.Z; consult the USENET newsgroup comp.mail.mh for more information.

See also mail, Mail, mailx

TABLE M.9: MH Commands

COMMAND	DESCRIPTION
ali	Lists mail aliases.
anno	Annotates a message.
bbc	Checks on electronic bulletin boards (BBSs), a form of newsgroup.

TABLE M.9 continued: MH Commands

COMMAND	DESCRIPTION
burst	Separates a digest into individual messages.
comp	Creates a message.
dist	Distributes a message to additional recipients.
folder	Sets the current folder or directory.
folders	Lists all folders or directories.
forw	Forwards a message.
inc	Incorporates new mail.
mark	Marks a message.
mhl	Creates formatted listings of messages.
mhmail	Sends or receives mail.
mhn	Manages multimedia mail, including audio and video.
mhook	Runs a program automatically when you receive mail.
mhparam	Prints MH parameters.
mhpath	Displays all MH folder pathnames.
msgchk	Checks for mail.
msh	Invokes the msh shell on a file in packf format, a program that combines the most often used MH commands into one single program.
next	Displays the next message.
packf	Compresses a folder into a single file.
pick	Selects a message by content.
prev	Displays the previous message.
prompter	Opens an editor so you can create a new message.
rcvstore	Stores a message entered at the keyboard (standard input) into a message file.
refile	Files messages in other folders.
repl	Replies to a message.
rmf	Removes a folder.
rmm	Removes a message.
scan	Creates a one-line summary of each message.
send	Sends a message.
show	Lists messages.
slocal	Creates a message for special local mail delivery.
sortm	Sorts messages.
vmh	Opens an MH windowing interface.
whatnow	Prompts for send information.
whom	Expands a message header.

MIME

Abbreviation for Multipurpose Internet Mail Extensions. A set of extensions that allows Internet e-mail users to add non-ASCII or binary elements such as graphics, PostScript files, audio, or video to their e-mail. Most of the common e-mail client programs such as elm, Z-mail, and MH include MIME capabilities. (mail, however, does not support MIME.)

You can obtain metamail, a public domain MIME implementation from thumper.bellcore.com in /pub/nsb/mm.2.6.tar.Z. For more information on MIME, consult the USENET newsgroup comp .mail.mime or the FAQs posted in news.answers.

See also uudecode, uuencode

minibuffer

In emacs, the line at the bottom of the screen, used to ask you questions and to display your replies. The minibuffer shares this screen line with the echo area.

minor device number

A number assigned to a specific device within a class of devices.

If you use the ls -l command to list the contents of the /dev directory, you see the major and minor device numbers, separated by commas, listed where you would expect to see the file sizes in bytes in an ordinary listing. The rest of the information is the same as that shown by any ls -l listing.

See also major device number

minor mode

Within emacs, an optional feature that you can turn on or off as you work, including inset mode or overstrike mode, automatic file saving, automatic indenting, and so on.

See also major mode

mkdep

A BSD software development command that creates a makefile dependency list.

See also make

mkdir

A command that creates one or more new directories in the filesystem.

Syntax

Here's the syntax for mkdir:

    mkdir [options]directory ...

You must have write permission in the parent directory to be able to create a new directory.

Options and Arguments

The mkdir command has two options, as shown in Table M.10. The *directory* argument contains the name or names of the directories that you want to create, and mkdir automatically includes the two invisible entries . (representing the directory itself) and .. (representing the parent directory) in the newly created directory.

TABLE M.10: Options to Use with mkdir

OPTION	DESCRIPTION
-m *mode*	Specifies the access mode for the new directories; see the chmod entry for details.
-p	Creates the specified intermediate directories if they do not exist.

Examples

To create a new directory called accounts in the current directory, use:

    mkdir accounts

To create a directory as a subdirectory of another directory, use:

    mkdir -p /home/julia/cookbook/part1

See also cd, chdir, chmod, rm, rmdir, umask

mkfifo

A BSD and SCO command that creates a FIFO file. The syntax is:

    mkfifo name ...

The FIFO is created with access mode 0777 in BSD and 0666 in SCO; you must have write permission in the parent directory before you can create a FIFO.

See also mknod

mklocale

A BSD command that reads a LC_CTYPE source file from the standard input and creates a binary file on the standard output suitable for use in /usr/share/locale/LC_CTYPE.

mkmsgs

An SVR4 command that converts a list of text strings contained in *string_file* into a message file *message_file* in a format readable by several other commands. The syntax is:

    mkmsgs [options] string_file message_file

The -i option creates the *message_file* in the specified directory, and the -o option lets you overwrite an existing *message_file*.

mknod

An SCO command that creates a directory entry and an i-node for a special file.

Syntax

The syntax for mknod is:

    mknod name [options] major minor

Options and Arguments

In the syntax line above, *name* specifies the name of the entry, *major* specifies the major device number, and *minor* the minor device number.

Only the superuser can use all the options listed in Table M.11; ordinary users can use only -p.

See also mkdep

TABLE M.11: Options to Use with mknod

OPTION	DESCRIPTION
-b *major minor*	Indicates that the special file is a block special file with specified *major* and *minor* device numbers.
-c *major minor*	Indicates that the special file is a character special file with specified *major* and *minor* device numbers.
-m	Creates shared memory.
-p	Creates a pipe.
-s	Creates a semaphore.

mksrt

A BSD command that creates an error message file from C source code.

See also xstr

mm macros

Abbreviation for manuscript macros. A set of almost 100 nroff and troff macros distributed with SVR4 systems. The mm macro package is equivalent to the me macro package on BSD systems. Macros are used to provide complex formatting options such as automatic numbering of lists, running head control, and font changes. The mm macros also support the eqn and tbl preprocessors.

See also me **macros,** ms **macros**

/mnt

An SVR4 root directory often used as the mount point where filesystems are mounted.

mode

An octal number that specifies what access a file's owner, group, and others have to the file.

See also chmod, **file permissions,** mkdir

mode line

In emacs, a line at the bottom of each window in which emacs displays information about the contents of the window.

See also **echo area, minibuffer**

modulo

The remainder after an integer division; sometimes called *modulus* or *mod*.

You may also find that modulo is used in expressions such as "modulo wildcards," which just means "everything but wildcards."

more

A Unix filter program that displays the contents of a text file one screenful at a time.

Syntax

Here's the syntax to use with more:

```
more [options] filenames
```

The command displays the contents of *filenames* and waits for you to press the Return key to view the next line, or the spacebar to see the next screenful.

When the more command pauses, it interprets several keystrokes as commands; you can press h for help information, q to quit, even / followed by a regular expression to search. Table M.12 lists the most common more commands.

TABLE M.12: Commands to Use with more

COMMAND	DESCRIPTION
=	Displays the current line number.
/pattern	Searches for the next occurrence of *pattern*.
h	Displays help information.
*n*b	Skips back *n* screenfuls; b alone skips back one screenful.
*n*f	Skips forward *n* screenfuls; f alone skips forward one screenful.
*n*s	Skips *n* lines and displays the next screenful; s alone skips one line.
q or Q	Quits the more command.
v	Starts the vi editor on the current file at the current line.

Options and Arguments

You can use the options listed in Table M.13 with the more command.

TABLE M.13: Options to Use with more

OPTION	DESCRIPTION
-c	Clears the screen before displaying the file's contents.
-d	Displays the prompt Press space to continue, 'q' to quit.
-f	Counts logical lines rather than screen lines; useful when a file contains very long lines.
-l	Ignores formfeed characters.
-r	Displays control characters as ^x.
-s	Displays multiple blank lines as one blank.
-u	Turns off display of backspace and underline.
-w	Waits for a keystroke before exiting more.
-*n*	Sets the display window to *n* lines; the default is to use the whole screen.
+*number*	Starts the display at line *number*.
+/*pattern*	Starts the display two lines before *pattern*.

Examples

To look at the contents of your `.profile` file, use:

```
more .profile
```

You can also use more with a pipe on the command line; this is a good way to slow down the display of a long listing so that you can read it before it flashes past:

```
ls -R | more
```

This command displays all files in all directories and so can be a very long listing. Using more lets you read each screenful; press the spacebar to see the next screenful, and press q when you are ready to quit.

See also cat, less, MORE, pg, pr

MORE

An environment variable used by the more command to determine the line options available to the user. Users of the Bourne shell and Korn shell set MORE in their `.profile` files, while C shell users set it in their `.cshrc` files.

See also more

Motif

A widely adopted X Window-based graphical user interface (GUI) developed by the Open Software Foundation (OSF). The first version was released in 1989, along with a style guide and a plan for application certification—two important elements for a consistent user interface.

See also mwm, **Open Look**

mount

▶ To make a filesystem available to other users. A filesystem must first be mounted before you can read or write to the files that it contains.

▶ To physically place a tape on a tape drive.

See also **mounting a filesystem, mount point**

mount

An NFS command that mounts or adds a filesystem. Only the superuser can use this command. Using mount you can add filesystems contained on floppy disks, CD-ROMs, or hard disks.

To track filesystems, mount keeps a table in /etc/mtab on BSD systems or in /etc/mnttab on SVR4 systems; you may also find additional filesystem information in /etc/fstab (BSD) or /etc/vfstab (SVR4). The list of filesystems that can be mounted is defined in /etc/mnttab, while the list of filesystems that are actually physically mounted is maintained in /etc/vfstab.

See also mounting a filesystem, mount point, umount

mounting a filesystem

To be able to access any filesystem under Unix, you must first mount it on a certain directory known as the mount point. This directory must already exist, and it becomes the root directory of the newly mounted filesystem. Once this is done, the files in the filesystem appear to be located in the mount point directory, and you can read and write to them just like any other files on the system. If the mount point directory contained files or directories prior to the new filesystem being mounted, they are hidden until the file system is unmounted again.

The reverse of this process is known as "unmounting" a filesystem and is done with the umount command. Unmounting a filesystem does two things: first, it synchronizes the system buffers with the filesystem on the disk, and second, it makes the filesystem inaccessible from its mount point. You are now free to mount a different file system on that mount point.

See also mount, umount

mount point

Any directory in which a filesystem is mounted. You can mount a filesystem on any directory you like; it does not have to be directly off the root directory.

See also mounting a filesystem

mscreen

An SCO command, normally invoked from your .profile or .login file, that allows a terminal to have multiple login screens.

mset

A BSD command used with IBM 3270 systems that retrieves an ASCII-to-3270 keyboard map.

See also tn3270

msgs

A BSD command used to read system messages.

Syntax
The syntax for msgs is as follows:

    msgs [options]number

This command is used to read short system messages that you only need to read once. It is normally invoked from your .login or .profile file.

Options and Arguments
You can specify a message *number* from the command line, or if you use *-number*, you can start *number* messages back from the current message; you can also use the options listed in Table M.14 with the msgs command.

See also mail, more

TABLE M.14: Options to Use with msgs

OPTION	DESCRIPTION
-c *days*	Removes all messages over *days* old; the default is 21 days.
-f	Turns off No new messages display.
-h	Prints just the first part of each message.
-l	Displays only local messages.
-q	Checks for new messages; msgs -q is often used in login scripts.
-s	Enables posting of messages.

ms macros

Consists of the original set of approximately fifty nroff and troff macros. The ms macro package is no longer supported but is often found on many systems. Macros are used to provide complex formatting options such as automatic numbering of lists, controlling running heads, and changing fonts.

See also me **macros,** mm **macros**

mt

A BSD utility used to manipulate a magnetic tape drive.

Syntax
The syntax for mt is:

```
mt [tape_name]command[count]
```

Options and Arguments
The *tape_name* argument refers to a raw device. The commands you can use with mt are listed in Table M.15; you have to enter only enough characters to make the command unique; you don't have to type them all. You can repeat the command by specifying a *count*.

TABLE M.15: Commands to Use with mt

COMMAND	DESCRIPTION
eof *count* or weof *count*	Writes *count* end-of-file marks at the current location on tape.
fsf *count*	Forward space for *count* files.
fsr *count*	Forward space for *count* records.
bsf *count*	Backward space for *count* files.
bsr *count*	Backward space for *count* records.
offline or rewoffl	Rewinds the tape, and places the unit offline.
Rewind	Rewinds the tape.
Status	Displays tape drive status information.

mush

Abbreviation for mail user's shell. A public-domain e-mail program with two modes: you can use it with a line-oriented interface (rather like mail) or with a full-screen interface (such as Pine or elm).

You can get mush by anonymous ftp from many sites, including ftp.uu .net in /usenet/comp.sources.misc, and ftp.waseda.ac.jp in /pub/archives/comp.sources.misc. For more information, you can read the postings in the USENET newsgroup comp.mail.mush.

An enhanced version of mush is commercially available as Z-mail.

See also elm, **mail**, Mail, mailx, MH, **Pine**

mv

A command used to rename or move files.

Syntax
Here's the mv syntax:

```
mv [options] source target
```

There are three ways you can use mv:

- ▶ To change the name of a file.
- ▶ To change the name of a directory.
- ▶ To move a file or directory to a different directory.

Remember, when moving a file, mv copies the file to its new location and then deletes the original.

Options and Arguments

The mv command moves or renames the files or directories specified in *source* to *target*; if the *target* directory does not exist, mv creates it for you. Table M.16 lists the two mutually exclusive options for this command.

If you use mv with no arguments, you will only see a usage message.

TABLE M.16: Options to Use with mv

Option	Description
-f	Forces removal, even if the file and directory permissions do not allow it.
-i	Asks for confirmation beforereplacing an existing file or directory.

Examples

To move all the files from the current directory to the /home/pmd/new directory, use:

```
mv -i * /home/pmd/new
```

The -i option tells mv not to overwrite any existing files without asking for confirmation.

The mv command just returns to the system prompt if the command completed without problems, and with new users, this lack of communication may lead to accidentally deleted files. It is a good idea to use mv-i until you are sure about the results of your mv commands.

Notes

You cannot use mv to move directories across NFS file systems.

Because mv first removes the *target* file, if one exists, before completing the move, any links on the *target* file are lost. To preserve those links, you should copy the file to the *target* name and then remove the original file.

See also chmod, copy, cp, cpio, rm, rmdir, tar, umask

mwm

Abbreviation for Motif window manager, a window manager developed by the Open Software Foundation.

N

\n

See newline

NAK

Acronym for negative acknowledgment. In communications, a control character, ASCII 21, sent by the receiving computer to indicate that the data was not properly received and should be sent again.

See also ACK

named pipe

A special type of temporary file that exists independently of any process and allows unrelated processes to exchange information; ordinary pipes only work between related processes. Any number of processes can read or write to a named pipe. Also known as a *FIFO* (first in, first out) *special file*.

See also interprocess communications

nawk

Acronym for new awk, an updated version of the awk pattern-matching language, used to scan text files for patterns or simple relationships and then perform specified actions on matching lines.

The original awk is named after the program creators, Alfred Aho, Peter Weinberger, and Brian Kernighan. During the 1980s, they made several enhancements to awk and called this enhanced version nawk for new awk. This program was released as part of System V Release 3.1 and is still found on many systems.

Syntax

The syntax for nawk is as follows:

```
nawk [options]['program'][files][var=value]
```

You can specify a script direct from the command line, or you can store a script in *program* and specify it using -f. You can assign the variable *var* a value from the command line; the value can be a literal, a shell variable, or a command substitution, but the value is only available after the BEGIN block of the awk program has been processed.

Options and Arguments

Table N.1 lists the options you can use with nawk.

Table N.2 lists the predefined commands available in nawk; some of these commands are available in awk, but many are new in nawk.

See also awk, gawk, **icon,** perl

TABLE N.1: Options to Use with nawk

OPTION	DESCRIPTION
-f *filename*	Reads instructions from *filename* instead of providing instructions on the command line.
-F *regular-expression*	Separates fields using *regular-expression*.
-v *variable=value*	Assigns *value* to *variable* before starting '*program*'.

TABLE N.2: Predefined Commands Available in nawk

OPTION	DESCRIPTION
atan2(*y*,*x*)	Returns the arctangent of *y*/*x* in radians.
break	Exits from a for or while loop.
close(*filename-expr*) close (*command-expr*)	Closes a file or pipe using the same expression that opened the file or pipe.
continue	Begins the next iteration of a for or while loop.
cos(*x*)	Returns the cosine of *x* radians.
delete(*array*[*element*])	Deletes an *element* of *array*.
Do *body* while(*expr*)	Performs a looping statement, executing the statements in *body*, then evaluating *expr*. If *exr* is true, the loop repeats, and *body* executes again.
exit	Ignores remaining instructions, does not read more input, but branches directly to the END procedures.
exp(*arg*)	Returns the exponent of *arg*.
for(*i=lower*; *i<=upper*;*i++*) *command*	Performs *command* while *i* is between the values of *lower* and *upper*. If you use a series of *commands*, they must be contained within curly braces ({ }).
for(*item* in *array*) *command*	Performs *command* for each *item* in *array*. If you use a series of *commands*, they must be contained within curly braces ({ }).

TABLE N.2 continued: Predefined Commands Available in nawk

Option	Description
Function *name* (*parameter-list*) { *statements*}	Allows you to specify your own user-defined functions. The *parameter-list* is a comma-separated list of variables passed as arguments to the function when the function is called. The body of the function can contain one or more statements and usually contains a return statement to pass control back to the point that called the function.
getline[*var*][<*file*] or *command* | getline[*var*]	Reads the next line of input. The first syntax reads input from *file*, and the second form reads the output from *command*. Both forms read just one line at a time, which is assigned to $0 and is parsed into fields setting NF, NR, and FNR.
gsub(*r,s,t*)	Substitutes *s* for each match of the regular expression *r* in the string *t*. If *t* is not specified, it is taken to be $0. The substitution is made globally. The value returned by gsub is the number of substitutions made.
if(*condition*) *command* [else] [*command*]	If *condition* is true, execute *command*; otherwise, execute the *command* in the else clause. A series of commands must be enclosed within curly braces ({ }).
index(*substr,str*)	Returns the position of the first place within the string *str* where the substring *substr* occurs. If *substr* does not occur within *str*, index returns 0.
int(*arg*)	Returns the integer value of *arg*.
length(*str*)	Returns the number of characters in the string *str*; if *str* is not supplied, S0 is assumed.
log(*x*)	Returns the natural logarithm of *x*.
match(*s,r*)	Tests whether the string *s* contains a match for the regular expression *r*, and returns either the position where the match begins or 0 if no match is found. Sets both RSTART and RLENGTH.
next	Reads the next line of input and starts a new pass through all the pattern/procedure statements in the nawk program or script.
print[*args*][*destination*]	Prints *args* on the appropriate output device. Literal strings must be quoted, and successive values separated by commas are separated by the predefined variable OFS; successive values separated by spaces are concatenated. You can use redirection with the default output.
printf[*format*] [, *expressions*]	Produces a formatted print following the conventions of the C programming language printf statement, including %s to print a string, %d to print a decimal number, and %n.mf to print a floating point number, where *n* represents the total number of digits and *m* represents the number of digits after the decimal point.
rand()	Returns a random number between 0 and 1. This command returns the same random number each time it is run, unless the random number generator is seeded using srand().
return[*expr*]	Returns the value *expr* at the end of a user-defined function.
sin(*x*)	Returns the sine of *x*.

TABLE N.2 continued: Predefined Commands Available in nawk

Option	Description
split(*string*,*array*[,*sep*]	Splits the string *string* into fields using the separator *sep*, and then puts those fields into the array *array*. If *sep* is not specified, then FS is used.
Sprintf [*format*[, *expression*]]	Returns the value of *expression* using the *format*. Nothing is actually printed; data is only formatted.
sqrt(*arg*)	Returns the square root of *arg*.
srand(*expr*)	Sets a new seed value for the random number generator using *expr*. If *expr* is not specified, the time of day is used as the default.
sub(*r*,*s*,[*t*])	If the string *t* is specified, substitute the string *s* for the first occurrence of the regular expression *r* in *t*. If *t* is not specified, $0 is assumed; returns 1 if successful, 0 if not.
substr(*string*,*m*,[*n*])	Returns the substring of *string* beginning at character number *m* and consisting of the next *n* characters. If *n* is not specified, includes all characters to the end of the string.
system(*command*)	Executes the Unix *command*, and returns an exit value.
tolower(*str*)	Converts all uppercase characters in *str* to lowercase and returns the new string.
toupper(*str*)	Converts all lowercase characters in *str* to uppercase and returns the new string.
while(*condition*) *command*	Executes *command* while *condition* is true. A series of commands must be contained within curly braces ({ }).

neqn

A version of eqn used with nroff to format text containing mathematical symbols and equations.

See also eqn, nroff

NetBSD

A free implementation of Unix derived from the BSD series of releases, designed to run on Intel microprocessors. The distribution is usually free but there may be a small charge to cover the distribution media and the packaging.

NetBSD emphasizes multiple platform support, and so has been ported to several non-Intel systems. You can get the system from ftp .netbsd.org.

See also FreeBSD, Linux

.netrc

A file located in your home directory that contains the configuration information required to make an FTP connection to a remote computer system or to the Internet.

See also anonymous ftp

network filesystem

See NFS

newalias

A command used to recreate the database for the mail alias file /etc/ aliases. This command must be run each time the file changes so that the changes take effect. There are no options or arguments used with this command.

newform

An SVR4 command that acts as a text file formatter.

Syntax

The syntax to use with newform is as follows:

```
newform [options]filename
```

Options and Arguments

The newform command formats the specified *filename* according to the options listed in Table N.3.

You can combine options with this command, and you can intersperse them (with the exception of -s, which must always appear first), between different filenames on the command line.

TABLE N.3: Options to Use with newform

Option	Description
-a*n*	Appends *n* characters to the end of each line; if you don't specify *n*, each line is expanded to the length specified by -1.
-b*n*	Deletes *n* characters from the beginning of each line; if you don't specify *n*, each line is shortened to the length specified by -1.
-c*m*	Uses the character specified by *m* when padding lines with -a or -p; -c must appear before -a or -p.
-e*n*	Deletes *n* characters from the end of each line; if you don't specify *n*, each line is shortened to the length specified by -1.

TABLE N.3 continued: Options to Use with newform

Option	Description
-f	Displays the *tabspec* format used by the last -o option used.
-i '*tabspec*'	Expands tabs to spaces using *tabspec*.
-1*n*	Sets the line length to *n*; the default is 72 characters. This option usually appears before any other options that modify the line length.
-o '*tabspec*'	Converts spaces into tabs using *tabspec*.
-p	Appends *n* characters to the beginning of each line; if you don't specify *n*, each line is expanded to the length specified by -1.
-s	Strips the leading characters from each line up to and including the first tab.

Examples

To convert all tabs in a file to eight spaces, set the output to 80 characters wide, and truncate any lines longer than 80 characters, use:

```
newform -i -180 -e september.sales >> yearly.sales
```

This example also appends the results of processing the file `september.sales` to the end of the file `yearly.sales` using redirection.

See also cut, paste

newgrp

A Unix command as well as a built-in Bourne and Korn shell command that changes your current group so that you can work with the new group's files. Only the group ID is changed; you are still a member of your previous group. If you don't specify a new group name (and this new group must already exist), your original group as specified in /etc/passwd is reinstated. The newgrp command has no options.

See also chgrp, chmod, chown, id, passwd

newline

The character that by convention marks the end of a line of text in most Unix files; a combination of a carriage return and a linefeed, represented by \n.

news

A command used to read the news items posted in /usr/news (/var/news on certain systems). This command is for a local network news system and is not a USENET newsreader.

Syntax
The syntax for this command is:

    news [options][filenames]

news reads simple text files placed in the publicly accessible /usr/news (or /var/news) directory by other users. To create a news item, you just copy a text file into this directory.

Options and Arguments
With no arguments, the news command displays all the current *filenames* in /usr/news. You can use the options listed in Table N.4 with news.

TABLE N.4: Options for Use with news

OPTION	DESCRIPTION
-a	Displays all *filenames*, current or not.
-n	Displays the names of news items, but not the contents.
-s	Reports the number of news items.

Examples
Some news items are long so it makes sense to pipe them through a pager such as more, like this:

    news -a | more

Notes
The news command places a zero-length file called .news_time in your home directory and compares the time and date from this file to the articles in the /usr/news directory to determine if you have read an article.

See also Mail, mailx, write

NFS

Abbreviation for network filesystem. A distributed file-sharing system developed almost a decade ago by Sun Microsystems. NFS allows a computer on a network to use the files and peripheral devices of another networked computer as if they were local, subject to certain security restrictions. The physical location of files is usually unimportant to you; all of the standard Unix utilities work with NFS files in just the same way that they work with local files stored on your computer. Using NFS, you can share files on your system with other computers running DOS, the Macintosh operating system, Unix, VMS, or many other operating systems.

NFS is platform-independent and runs on mainframes, minicomputers, RISC-based workstations, diskless workstations, and personal computers. NFS has been licensed and implemented by more than three hundred vendors.

nice

A command that lowers a process's scheduling priority. nice is also a built-in C shell command.

The syntax for this command is:

```
nice [-n]command
```

The *-n* argument tells nice just how nice to be; the larger the number, the lower the priority that *command* gets and the slower it runs. You can use a number in the range of 1 (highest priority) to 19 (lowest priority), with the default being 10. On certain BSD systems, this range is 0 to 39, with a default of 20.

Only the superuser can increase the priority; entering *-n* as a negative number such as -10 increases the scheduling priority of the command.

When using the C shell's nice command, a plus sign followed by a number decreases the priority (this means that you are being nice to other users by taking fewer system resources for your command); the range is from -20 (highest priority) to +20 (lowest priority), with a default of 4.

NIS

Abbreviation for Network Information Service, formerly known as the *Yellow Pages* or *YP*; a part of NFS.

A program used to manage password and group files, host address information, access permissions, and data for a system running NFS. NIS makes configuration information consistent across all the systems using NFS by locating a master database on one system, and making this database available to all the other computers on the network, so avoiding the problem of inconsistent updating.

nl

A command that adds line numbers to a text file.

Syntax
Here's the syntax to use:

```
nl [options][filename]
```

The nl command is a filter, reading input from the standard input if you do not specify a *filename*, and writing output to the standard output. nl adds numbers to each line in a text file, with numbering reset to 1 at the top of each page. A page consists of three elements:

- ▸ Header: defined by one line containing only \:\:\:
- ▸ Body: defined by one line containing only \:\:
- ▸ Footer: defined by one line containing only \:

Different line-numbering options are available within each section.

Options and Arguments
You can use the options listed in Table N.5 with the nl command.

TABLE N.5: Options to Use with nl

OPTION	DESCRIPTION
-b *type*	Numbers the lines in the file according to *type*, where *type* is one of the following:
	a All lines
	n No numbering
	p *string* Only those lines containing *string*
	t Printable text, the default
-d *xy*	Specifies the characters *xy* as logical page delimiters; the default is \:.
-f *type*	Same as –b, but controls numbering for the file footer. Numbers the lines in the file according to *type*; the default *type* is n.
-h *type*	Same as –b, but controls numbering for the file header. Numbers the lines in the file according to *type*; the default *type* is n.
-i *n*	Increments the line count by *n*; the default is 1.
-l*n*	Counts *n* consecutive blank lines as one line.
-n *format*	Sets the format for the line numbers; *format* is one of the following:
	ln Left justified with no leading zero
	rn Right justified with no leading zero, the default
	rz Right justified
-p	Continues line numbering across page breaks without a reset.
-s*c*	Specifies the character *c* used as a separator between the line number and the text.
-v*n*	Starts the numbering on each page at *n*; the default is 1.
-w*n*	Uses *n* columns to show line numbers; the default is 6.

Examples
To number all the lines in a file called first-draft and send the results to the printer, use:

```
nl first-draft | lp
```

If you want to number those lines that contain text and display the results on your terminal, one screenful at a time, use:

```
nl -bt first-draft | more
```

See also pr, wc

nm

A software development command that prints the symbol table from one or more object files in alphabetical order.

The output includes each symbol's name, value, type, size, and so on. The nm command is most often used with ELF or COFF files; see the man pages on your system for more details.

noclobber

A C shell environment variable that is used for safer redirection processing by preventing accidental destruction of existing files. When set, noclobber allows redirection (>) to be used only to create new files, not to overwrite existing files, and appending (>>) can be used only with existing files.

node

- ► In the Unix hierarchical filesystem, a directory is considered to be a node, the end of a branch capable of supporting other branches.

- ► Any device attached to the network capable of communicating with other network devices.

See also leaf

noglob

A C shell environment variable that disables filename expansion.

nohup

A command that lets you continue to execute a command in the background after you log out. Normally, when you log out, Unix kills all the processes that you started during your session.

The syntax for this command is:

```
nohup command [arguments...] &
```

If you don't redirect the output from a process you execute with nohup, both the standard output and the standard error are sent to a file called nohup.out in the current directory; if you don't have write permission in the current directory, the file is created in your home directory instead.

The nohup command is built into the C shell.

nomagic

A toggle in the ex and vi editors that turns off the magic variable.

nonomatch

A C shell environment variable that treats metacharacters as literal characters without any special meaning.

notify

A command that tells you when any new mail arrives.

Syntax

The syntax for this command is:

    notify [options]

Options and Arguments

If you use notify without options, the command displays the current state (on or off) of automatic mail notification. The options you can use with this command are listed in Table N.6.

TABLE N.6: Options for Use with notify

Option	Description
-m filename	Saves mail in the specified filename rather than the default file.
-n	Turns off automatic mail notification; this option must be used by itself.
-y	Turns on automatic mail notification.

Notes

notify is also a built-in C shell command that immediately informs users about completed jobs instead of waiting for the next prompt.

The syntax is:

    notify jobID

If you don't specify a jobID, the current background job is assumed.

See also biff, xbiff

novice

An environment variable in the vi editor that displays the name of the current editor mode at the bottom of the screen.

nroff

A text-processing program that creates a file suitable for output to a line printer; an acronym for New Runoff, nroff is pronounced "en-roff."

Unix often includes two programs for text processing, nroff and troff. The nroff program is used when you want to output formatted text to a line printer or to a line-oriented display, and troff is used when you want to send text to a laser printer, bitmapped display, or to a typesetter.

An input file for nroff contains lines of text interspersed with lines that begin with a period and contain one- or two-letter commands. nroff also allows you to define a macro as a series of input lines, and three major macro packages are available that automate complex formatting functions.

The main benefit to using nroff and troff rather than a commercial word processor is that their input files are simple text files. This allows you to use many other Unix utilities (grep, diff, and so on) with your files, which is something you can't do with the proprietary formats used by word processors.

See also eqn, **LATEX,** groff, me **macros,** mm **macros,** ms **macros,** pic, soelim, tbl, **TEX, TEXinfo,** troff

nslookup

A TCP/IP command that provides the IP address of any domain, as well as other information of interest to network administrators.

Used with no arguments, nslookup enters interactive mode, in which you can query name servers for information on hosts or print a list of the hosts in a domain. When you specify the name of a host as the first argument on the command line, nslookup prints the name and the requested information about a host or a domain.

null

Something that is empty, has zero length, and contains no characters.

See also null string

null argument

A command-line argument that has no value but is needed so that arguments are interpreted in their correct position. When you use explicit options, null arguments are not necessary.

null character

A special value used to indicate the end of a character string, the end of a file, or an empty pointer. By convention, the character is represented by all zeros.

null device

The Unix null device, also known as the *bit bucket*, is /dev/null. When you send output to the null device, it is discarded.

null string

A string that contains no characters; a string of zero length.

numbered buffer

In the vi editor, one of nine storage areas used to store text that has been deleted from a file; when the tenth deletion is made, the first buffer is overwritten.

O

od

A command used to make an octal, decimal, hexadecimal, or ASCII dump of a file.

Syntax

Here's the syntax to use with od:

```
od [options][filename]offset
```

Options and Arguments

The od command makes a dump of the specified *filename* in octal unless one of the options is used. The file is dumped starting at the beginning unless you specify an *offset*, which is normally in octal bytes; use a if you want to specify the *offset* in decimal, or b to specify that the *offset* represents blocks of 512 bytes. Table O.1 lists the options you can use with od.

See also bc, dd, hexdump, more

TABLE O.1: Options to use with od

Option	Description
-a	ASCII, text
-b	Octal, byte
-B	Short, octal
-c	ASCII, byte
-C	Extended ASCII
-d	Unsigned short, decimal
-D	Unsigned long, decimal
-e	Double-precision floating point
-f	Single-precision floating point
-F	Double-precision floating point; same as -e
-h	Short, hexadecimal
-H	Long, hexadecimal
-i	Short, signed decimal
-I	Long, signed decimal
-p	Even parity
-P	Odd parity
-s	Accepts a string
-v	Displays all data

olwm

The name of the Open Look window manager, developed by Sun Microsystems.

See also mwm, **Open Look**

onintr

A C shell keyword used to manage interrupts in a shell script. You can use onintr in three different ways: the command onintr *label* works like a goto and branches to the line beginning with *label*; the command onintr - allows the script to ignore interrupts; and the command onintr without arguments turns interrupt processing back on again.

Open Desktop

A graphical user interface (GUI) from SCO that provides access to system utility functions, SCO, and DOS on the desktop. Files, directories, and programs are represented by icons and displayed in windows.

See also OpenServer

open file

Any file currently in use is said to be open or open for use.

OpenGL

Acronym for Open Graphics Library; a set of graphics libraries originally developed by Silicon Graphics and now supported by IBM, Intel, Microsoft, and many other companies.

OpenGL lets developers create 3D graphical applications for work-stations running the Programmer's Hierarchical Interactive Graphics System (PHiGS) extensions to the X Window system.

See also X Window

Open Look

An X Window-based graphical user interface (GUI) developed by AT&T and Sun Microsystems. Open Look is used as the standard window man-ager on Sun's workstations, but it has not been adopted as widely as OSF's Motif.

See also olwm

OpenServer

A scalable set of Unix-based products from SCO, including the Desktop System, Host System, and Enterprise System, based on SVR3.2 but con-taining many significant SVR4 enhancements. The Desktop System is a single-user multitasking system that includes DOS emulation, Microsoft Windows 3.1 support, TCP/IP connectivity, a built-in World Wide Web browser, a graphical newsreader, and e-mail support.

The Enterprise and Host systems provide high-performance scalable servers for Intel-based platforms, supporting over 8,000 applications, with extensive networking support, UPS, and advanced power management support.

See also sysadmsh

open system

A term used to describe hardware and software that is not dependent on any specific vendor's proprietary systems but which follows well-known public standards.

openwin

A command used to start the X Window system and the OpenWindows window manager on a system running Solaris.

Syntax
The syntax for this command is:

```
openwin [options]
```

Options and Arguments
Table O.2 lists the options you can use with the openwin command.

See also xrdb

TABLE O.2: Options Used with openwin

Option	Description
-banner	Displays the OpenWindows startup banner.
-noauth	Lowers the security level.
-includedemo	Adds the demo directory to your path.
-nobanner	Disables the OpenWindows startup banner making startup slightly faster.

OpenWindows

A graphical user interface available with Solaris, based on Open Look. OpenWindows includes a set of applications, called DeskSet, used to perform common day-to-day tasks.

See also olwm

/opt

A root directory often used to contain additional application programs.

See also /bin

OPTARG

An environment variable that contains the last option argument processed by the getopts command.

See also OPTIND

OPTIND

An environment variable that contains the index of the last option argument processed by the getopts command.

See also OPTARG

ordinary file

A file that contains text or other user data accessible by a person or an application program. An ordinary file is what most users think of as a file and has no specific structure required by the system.

See also binary file, block special file, character special file, FIFO file

orphaned file

A file whose name has been lost but whose contents remain, usually as a result of damage to the file system. Such files are usually placed in the /lost+found directory by the fsck utility. Sometimes called an *unreferenced file*.

orphan process

A process whose parent has died.

See also child process, parent process, zombie

OSF/1

An operating system from the Open Software Foundation, released in 1990 and based on the Mach kernel developed by Carnegie Mellon University.

See also POSIX

OSIRM

See ISO/OSI model

OSx

A version of Unix from Pyramid Technology that includes elements of both AT&T and BSD systems.

P

pack

An SVR4 command used to compress files so that they occupy less hard disk space. The syntax is:

```
pack [options]filename...
```

The pack command compacts files and replaces them with compressed files with .z appended to the original filename. To restore the files to their original states, use the unpack command. The *filename* argument can be a single filename or a space-separated list of filenames for compression. File permissions and the modification date of the original file remain unchanged.

When you specify the – option, pack displays statistical information about the packing of files, and the -f option forces the file to be packed even though no space is saved. This option is useful when preparing a project archive and you have to pack all the project files.

See also cat, compress, gzip, uncompact, uncompress, unpack, zcat

page

A system level alias for the more command.

pagesize

A BSD command that displays the page size of system memory in bytes. This command has no options.

parameter

In programming, a variable that is passed to a program or function from the host environment and holds a constant value. A parameter can be a number, a date, a filename, or simple text—anything that customizes program operation.

See also argument, option, variable

parameter substitution

The mechanism used by the shell to replace a reference to a parameter by its value; sometimes called *variable substitution*.

parent directory

The directory immediately above the current directory in the filesystem; only the root directory has no parent. Two periods .. (dot dot) are short-hand for the name of the parent directory, and you can use:

```
cd ..
```

to change to the parent directory without having to type (or even remember) its name.

parent PID

See PPID

parent process

A process that forks other processes. Every process can identify its parent because the PPID number is stored in the process' user table.

See also **child process, exec, fork**

passwd

A command used to maintain users' login passwords.

Syntax
The syntax to use with passwd is simple:

```
passwd
```

The passwd command prompts you for your old password, then for the new password you want to use instead, and then asks you to confirm the new password a second time. Only your system administrator can change your password without knowing your current password.

This command has several options, which are not shown here because they can be used only by the superuser. Many modern Unix systems provide a system administrator's shell for password management; if yours does, you should use it because it is indeed the most convenient way to manage passwords and changes to passwords.

Notes
Many systems use NIS to share information. The original name for NIS was the Sun Yellow Pages, and so the yppasswd command is used to maintain the network-wide password database.

Some BSD systems use the Kerberos security system, which stores passwords in an authentication database; on these systems, use the kpasswd command to change passwords.

See also **password, password file**

password

A secret sequence of characters that you type to verify your identity when you log in to the system.

In general, passwords should be a mixture of uppercase and lowercase letters and numbers and should be longer than six characters. Here are some general guidelines:

- ▶ Passwords should be kept secret and changed frequently. The worst passwords are the obvious ones: people's names or initials, place names, names of pets, TV characters, or anyone associated with "Star Trek," phone numbers, birth dates, groups of the same letter or simple patterns of keys such as "qwerty," or complete English words. There are a limited number of words in the English language, and it is easy for a computer to try them all relatively quickly.

- ▶ Change all passwords at least every 90 days, and change those associated with high-security privileges every month.

- ▶ Some systems provide default passwords, such as MANAGER, SERVICE, or GUEST, as part of the installation process. These default passwords should be changed immediately.

- ▶ Limit concurrent sessions to one per system.

- ▶ Do not allow more than two or three invalid password attempts before disconnecting.

- ▶ Do not allow generic accounts.

- ▶ Promptly remove the accounts of transferred or terminated employees, as well as all unused accounts.

- ▶ Review the security log files periodically.

password encryption

In Unix, passwords are not stored as ordinary text but are encrypted. When you type your password as you log in to the system, it is encrypted, and the result is compared against the encrypted password stored in /etc/passwd. If they match, the login continues, and you can use the system; if not, you return to the Password: prompt.

password file

A file containing passwords and other information about users on the system. In Unix, the file is called /etc/passwd and contains the information in the seven fields listed in Table P.1.

See also passwd

TABLE P.1: Contents of /etc/passwd

FILENAME	DESCRIPTION
userID	Your username as defined by the system administrator, usually all in lowercase letters.
password	Your encrypted password.
userID number	Numeric value for your user ID.
groupID number	Numeric value for your group ID, indicating the groups you belong to. The names of the groups are in /etc/group.
text field	Sometimes called the GECOS field, after an ancient General Electric operating system. Traditionally, this entry has four comma-separated fields for your full name, your office number, your office phone number, and your home phone number.
users home directory	The name of your home directory.
shell	The name of the shell that automatically starts when you log in to the system.

paste

A command used to create columnar output from one or more files, each file contributing one column. Output is to the standard output.

Syntax
The syntax for paste is as follows:

    paste [*options*]*files*

The paste command merges corresponding lines in several files; each file is considered to represent one column, and the columns are joined horizontally. The newline character at the end of the first line is replaced by a tab, then the second file is pasted to the first, and so on.

Options and Arguments
In the syntax shown above, *files* specifies the list of files you want to paste together; if this argument is missing, you can use - to indicate that the standard input be used instead. The options available with paste are listed in Table P.2.

See also cat, cut, join, newform, pr

TABLE P.2: Options to Use with paste

Option	Description
-d *delim*	Specifies the character to use when delimiting columns; tab is the default.
-s	Merges lines serially from one file, combining them into one long line; if you use this option with more than one input file, you will get confused and meaningless results.

patch

A BSD command used along with the diff command to update a text file to a later version.

Syntax

The syntax to use with patch is as follows:

    patch [*options*] *filename*

The guardian of a file first uses diff to create a set of differences between two files; these differences are the patches. Another person who has a copy of the same original file can use the patch command to apply the differences and produce a patched copy that reflects the new version of the file.

By default, the patched file takes the place of the unpatched original, and the original is renamed *filename*.orig.

Options and Arguments

In the above syntax, *filename* represents the file you want to patch. The patches are read from the standard input unless a different file *pfile* is specified with the -i option; see Table P.3 for a complete listing of options available with patch.

See also diff, diff3

TABLE P.3: Options for patch

Option	Description
-b *extension*	Saves the original file in *filename*.*extension* rather than in *filename*.orig.
-c	Assumes that the patches were generated by diff -c.
-d *directory*	Changes to the specified *directory* before starting work.
-D	Makes patch use the C language #ifdef...#endif construct to mark changes.
-e	Assumes that the patches were generated by diff -e.

TABLE P.3 continued: Options for patch

OPTION	DESCRIPTION
-f	Turns off prompts for user input.
-F *n*	Sets the fuzz factor to *n*.
-i *pfile*	Reads patches from the specified *pfile*.
-l	Treats groups of spaces as equivalent.
-n	Assumes that the patches were generated by diff with no options.
-N	Ignores patches already applied.
-o *filename*	Writes the patched output to *filename*.
-p *n*	Deletes *n* pathname elements from the name of the file to be patched. This is useful if you keep your files in different directories than the person who sent you the patch.
-r *rfile*	Sends rejected patches to *rfile*.
-R	Reverses the patch.
-s	Sets silent working mode.

path

In the C shell, a variable that contains a list of directories separated by spaces and updated by the set command, as follows:

```
set path = ( /usr/bin /usr/bin/myprograms . )
```

The spacing also applies to the name of the current directory, represented here by the . (dot).

See also PATH

PATH

In the Bourne shell and Korn Shell, an environment variable that defines the system path for the shell, used to locate executable files or commands. Each time you ask the shell to execute a command, it searches each directory in this variable to find the command. Directory names in the PATH statement are separated by colons.

The best place to customize your path is in $HOME/.profile.

See also path, **pathname**

pathname

A list of directory names separated by slashes (/) that ends with the name of a file. The pathname is used to follow through a directory structure to locate a specific file. Sometimes written as pathname, and sometimes called *search path*.

See also **absolute pathname,** basename, **relative pathname**

pathname expansion

A term used in the Bash shell as a synonym for *filename expansion*.

See also **asterisk, filename substitution**

pattern matching

The process of searching for a character or string of characters.

See also grep, **regular expressions**

PB

See **petabyte**

pcat

A command used to display the contents of one or more packed files. The pcat command has no options.

See also compress, pack, unpack, zcat

percent sign

The % character, which is the default command prompt for the C shell. Also the modulo operator, used to determine the remainder after an integer division.

period

The . character, pronounced "dot."

- ▶ A symbol used to indicate the current directory in a pathname.
- ▶ A built-in Bourne shell and Korn shell command that reads a file and executes its contents as though you had typed them at the command prompt.
- ▶ A metacharacter used to match any single character in a regular expression.

See also **dot file**

perl

perl, an acronym formed from Practical Extraction and Report Language (also known as Pathologically Eclectic Rubbish Lister), is an interpreted language developed by Larry Wall, used to manipulate text, files, and processes and to print reports based on extracted information. It works something like a combination of awk, sed, the C language, and the C shell.

perl is rapidly becoming the system administrator's answer to all those problems that a C program does not seem to fit, and perl is well suited to perform other kinds of tasks. It does not have those arbitrary limitations that plague other commands—lines can be of any length, arrays can be of any size, variable names can be as long as you care to make them, and binary data does not cause problems.

You can get perl by anonymous ftp from prep.ai.mit.edu in the /pub/gnu directory. The file is called perlver.tar.gz, where *ver* represents the current version number. You can also get it from the comp .sources.unix archive. perl is public domain software, and several excellent books are available as both introductions to perl and advanced perl programming tutorials. You might also check the USENET newsgroup comp.lang.perl.

See also awk, sed

permission bits

A special binary number associated with a file that specifies who can access the file and in what way.

There are three independent permissions—read, write, and execute:

▶ Read permission lets you read the file.

▶ Write permission lets you write to the file and change it if you wish.

▶ Execute permission means that you can execute the file.

You can set and change the file permissions for your own files; the main reasons for doing this are to prevent others from accessing your files and to protect yourself against accidental changes or deletions to important files.

The permissions are divided into three sets of three: one set (rwx) for the user or owner of a file, one set (rwx) for the group owner, and another set (rwx) for everyone else.

See also chmod, ls, umask

permissions

See file permissions

permuted index

A special kind of index used in several of the Unix system manuals. Many of the Unix manuals treat each command on a separate page, and the pages are not numbered continuously, they are only numbered within each command. This makes it easy to add or remove pages as the system changes but can make it difficult to find specific information. The permuted index is a solution to this problem.

The permuted index has three columns; the middle column is in alphabetical order and that is where you start your search. The column to the right lists the command that performs the function and the section number of the manual (or the man pages) where you can find a detailed description, and the column to the left contains additional keywords to help confirm you have found the correct entry.

See also man, man **pages**, ptx

peta-

Abbreviated P. A prefix for one quadrillion, or 10^{15}. In computing, based on the binary system, peta has the value of 1,125,899,906,842,624 or the power of 2 (2^{50}) closest to one quadrillion.

petabyte

Abbreviated PB. Usually 1,125,899,906,842,624 bytes (2^{50}) but may also refer to one quadrillion bytes (10^{15}).

pfbtops

A BSD command that translates a PostScript font file in .pfb format into ASCII, which can then be used with groff.

pg

A Unix filter that displays the contents of a text file on the screen, one screenful at a time.

Syntax
Here's the syntax to use with pg:

```
pg [options] filenames
```

The command displays the contents of *filenames* and waits for you to press the Return key to view the next screenful.

When the pg command pauses, it interprets several keystrokes as commands; you can press h for help information, q to quit, even / followed by a regular expression to search. Table P.4 lists the most common commands.

TABLE P.4: pg Commands

COMMAND	DESCRIPTION
! *command*	Executes *command*.
/*pattern*/	Searches forward for the next occurrence of *pattern*.
?*pattern*? or ^*pattern*^	Searches backward for the next occurrence of *pattern*.
. or Ctrl-1	Redisplays the current page.
d	Displays the next half page.
f	Skips to the next page forward.
h	Displays help information.
1	Displays the next line.
n	Displays the next file.
p	Displays the previous file.
q or Q	Quits the more command.
nw	Sets the window size to *n* lines and displays the next page.
$	Displays the last page.

Options and Arguments

You can use the options listed in Table P.5 with the pg command.

TABLE P.5: Options to Use with pg

OPTION	DESCRIPTION
-c	Clears the screen before displaying the file's contents.
-e	Does not pause between files.
-f	Does not split lines longer than the screen width.
-n	Issues a pg command without waiting for you to press Return.
-p *string*	Uses *string* as the command prompt; the default prompt is a colon (:).
-s	Displays messages in inverse video.
-n	Sets the display window to *n* lines; the default is to use the whole screen.
+*number*	Starts the display at line *number*.
+/*pattern*/	Starts the display at the line containing *pattern*.

Examples
To look at the contents of your .profile file, use:

pg .profile

You can also use pg with a pipe on the command line; this is a good way to slow down the display of a long listing so that you can read it before it flashes past:

ls -R | pg

This command displays all files in all directories, and so can be a very long listing. Using pg lets you read each screenful; press the Return key to see the next screenful, and press q when you are ready to quit.

See also cat, less, more, MORE, pr

pic

A preprocessor for the troff text-processing system capable of translating a graphics language into simple pictures.

Syntax
The syntax for pic is:

pic [*options*][*filename*]

pic reads a troff file that contains pairs of special codes; .PS starts special typesetting, and .PE ends special typesetting. The graphic for typesetting is located between these two directives. Because pic requires full typesetting capabilities, you cannot use pic with nroff.

pic provides facilities for:

▶ Drawing boxes, circles, arcs, arrows, and lines

▶ Placing text inside graphical elements

▶ Joining objects with various kinds of line types

▶ Exact placing of graphical objects in relation to other objects

Options and Arguments
The options you can use with pic are listed in Table P.6.

TABLE P.6: Options Available with pic

OPTION	DESCRIPTION
-c	Enables tpic compatability.
-C	Recognizes .PS and .PE, even when they are followed by a character other than a space or a new line.
-D	Draws lines using \D escape sequence.

TABLE P.6 continued: Options Available with pic

OPTION	DESCRIPTION
-n	Turns off the GNU groff extensions to the troff drawing commands.
-t	Enables TEX mode.
-T *dev*	Specifies the output device.
-v	Displays version number.
-z	Draws dots as zero-length lines in TEX mode.

Notes

The pic command is often used in a pipeline containing several commands to format a file:

```
myfile.doc |pic|troff|lpr
```

In this example, myfile.doc is piped into pic, and output from that command is passed to troff for final output to the default printer.

See also eqn, groff, nroff, tbl, troff

pico

A popular text editor often used in conjunction with the Pine mailer.

See also emacs, ex, jove, vi

PID

An acronym that is formed from process ID and is normally followed by a unique number. This number is assigned to the process by Unix when the process first starts running and lets you refer to that process at a later time. PID numbers are usually within the range of 0 to 30,000; all systems have a limit to the number of processes that can be active on the system at any given time, as well as a limit to how many processes any specific user can have. These limits vary from system to system and are set in the Unix kernel.

See also kill, **managing processes,** ps

ping

Acronym formed from packet internet groper. A command used to test for network connectivity by transmitting a special diagnostic packet to a specific node on the network, forcing the node to acknowledge that the packet reached the correct destination. If the system responds, the link is operational; if not, something is wrong. The word ping is often used as a verb, as in "ping that workstation to see if it is awake."

ping is designed for network testing, trouble-shooting, and measurement, and because of the large load it can impose on a busy, working network, it should not be used during normal operations, unless the system administrator is tracing a specific problem on the network.

The syntax for this command is usually:

ping *hostname*

Here's an example of the command and a typical response:

ping elvis
elvis is alive

Most Unix systems (as well as other operating systems, such as Novell NetWare or Microsoft Windows NT) implement their own options for this command, so see the man pages on your system if you want to learn more about ping.

pipe

A mechanism used by one command to pass information to a second command for processing; a pipe connects the standard output of one command to the standard input of the next, without creating an intermediate file.

A pipe is symbolized by the vertical bar (|) character, and if you want to pause output from a long directory listing, you could type the following at the command prompt:

ls -l | **more**

This sequence creates the long directory listing and then pipes the output from ls to the more command, which displays the results on the standard output, usually the screen, one page at a time.

A pipe is a one-way conduit for information, but a special form of pipe, known as a *named pipe*, allows two processes to exchange information; this concept has been extended in several network operating systems as a method of interprocess communications, allowing data to be exchanged between applications running on networked computers.

See also FIFO file

pipeline

A group of commands connected by a pipe. Commands in a pipeline are executed simultaneously, with the output of one command serving as the input for the next.

pipelining

▶ In microprocessor architecture, a method of fetching and decoding instructions that ensures that the processor never needs to wait; as soon as an instruction is executed, another is waiting.

▶ In parallel processing, the method used to pass instructions from one processing unit to another.

.plan

A file in your home directory, originally intended to contain information about your location and immediate plans, but is normally used for humorous purposes. The `finger` command displays the contents of your `.plan` file to the person using `finger`.

See also `finger`, `.profile`

plot

A BSD command used to plot data contained in a file, or input from the standard input, onto a terminal screen.

plus symbol

The + character. A metacharacter used by `awk` and `grep` to locate one or more characters placed before the symbol when searching a regular expression. The plus symbol matches one or more occurrences of the previous character, whereas the question mark matches zero or one occurrence.

See also asterisk

popd

A built-in C shell command that removes the current entry from the directory stack. The C shell stores a list of directories you are using, and you manipulate the stack using `popd` and `pushd`; the `dirs` command lists the contents of the directory stack.

See also `dirs`, `pushd`

POSIX

Acronym for portable operating system interface. An Institute of Electrical and Electronics Engineers (IEEE) standard that defines a set of portable operating system services similar to those found in Unix. The seven adopted POSIX standards are listed in Table P.7; at least 20 more standards are still in the draft stage.

Each of the standards defines a specific aspect of an operating system, and the additional standards still under development will cover areas such as system administration, system security, networking, the user interface, and other topics.

When a program meets or exceeds the appropriate POSIX standard, it is said to be "POSIX-compliant."

TABLE P.7: Adopted POSIX Standards

STANDARD	DESCRIPTION
POSIX.1	The original POSIX standard describes the basic system-level interfaces for C programs. Adopted in 1988 and revised in 1990, it was adopted as an international standard by the ISO and the International Electrotechnical Commission (IEC) and is available as ISO/IEC IS 9945-1:1990.
POSIX.2	The shell and utilities standard, based on the Korn shell, describes the way that the shell and utilities work with different character sets and with location-specific information, such as time and date formats. Adopted in 1992.
POSIX.3	The test suite standard, adopted in 1991, defines the tests used to determine POSIX compliance. For POSIX.1, the test suite POSIX.3.1 specifies over 2400 individual test elements, and the draft test suite for POSIX.2 details over 10,000 individual items for testing.
POSIX.4	The standard that defines C language interfaces for real-time applications, in which real-time is defined as "the ability of the operating system to provide a required level of service in a bounded response time." Adopted in 1993.
POSIX.5	The version of POSIX.1 for the Ada programming language, adopted in 1992.
POSIX.9	The version of POSIX.1 for the Fortran 77 programming language, adopted in 1992.

pound sign

The # character, sometimes called a *hash symbol*. Some British keyboards also have a pound sterling currency symbol (£).

The pound sign (#) is used as the shell prompt for the superuser as a reminder of the superuser's special powers.

You can also start a comment line in a shell script or awk script with a pound sign, and the shell ignores everything that follows on that same line.

In the .cshrc file, a pound sign indicates that the rest of that line is a comment and should be ignored.

See also **Bourne shell**

PPID

An environment variable that contains the process ID number of the parent shell.

See also kill, ps, who

PPP

Abbreviation for Point-to-Point Protocol. A TCP/IP protocol used to transmit IP packets over serial lines and modem/telephone connections.

PPP establishes a temporary but direct connection to an Internet host, eliminating the need for connecting to an interim system. PPP also provides a method of automatically assigning an IP address, so that remote or mobile systems can connect to the network at any point.

pr

A command used to format text files according to certain specified options.

Syntax
The syntax to use is:

```
pr [options]filename...
```

If you don't specify any options for pr, each printed page consists of a five-line header, a 66-line page, and a five-line footer. The header contains the page number, filename, and the file's date and time. Output is to the standard output and is usually redirected by pipe to a printer.

Options and Arguments
The pr command formats *filename*, which can be a single file or a list of filenames. If you omit *filename*, or use -, the pr command reads from the standard input. Table P.8 lists the options you can use with pr.

TABLE P.8: Options to Use with pr

OPTION	DESCRIPTION
+*page*	Starts formatted output at *page*; the default is page 1.
-*n*	Formats output with *n* columns; the default is 1 column.
-a	Displays the file in multicolumn format; long lines that don't fit are truncated.
-d	Double-spaces the output.
-e*cn*	Expands spaces into tabs every *n*th position, with *c* as the tab character.
-f	Separates pages using a formfeed rather than a series of blank lines.
-F	Folds input lines to avoid truncation by -a or -m.

TABLE P.8 continued: Options to Use with pr

OPTION	DESCRIPTION
-h *string*	Uses *string* as the page header text; ignored when -t is used or when the -1 option sets the page length to ten or fewer lines.
-i*cn*	Converts spaces to the *c* character at every *n*th position; the default is a tab set at every eighth position.
-1*n*	Sets the page length to *n* lines; the default is 66 lines.
-m	Merges up to eight files, displaying them all, one in each column. Long lines are truncated; this option cannot be used with -n or -a.
-n*cn*	Provides *n* digit line numbers followed by the field separator specified by *c*.
-o*n*	Offsets each line by *n* spaces; the default is 0 spaces.
-p	Pauses before displaying each page on a terminal.
-r	Suppresses error messages.
-s*c*	Uses *c* as a column separator.
-t	Omits header and footer lines at the top and bottom of each page.
-w*n*	Sets the line length to *n* characters; the default is 72 characters.

Examples

To print two files side-by-side on the default printer, use:

```
pr -m results.jan results.feb | lp
```

To print a file containing C language source code with line numbers, use:

```
pr -n program.c | lp
```

See also cat, grep, lp, paste, more, nl, pg

precedence

The order in which a program performs arithmetic operations; usually multiplication, division, addition, and subtraction. By placing parentheses around an expression, you can control the order in which expressions are calculated.

Programming languages also follow a strict precedence in their execution of mathematical operations.

print

A built-in Korn shell command used to display text. The syntax to use with print is:

```
print [options][string]
```

The `print` command displays *string* on the standard output, and you can use the options shown in Table P.9 with this command.

See also echo

TABLE P.9: Options for use with print

OPTION	DESCRIPTION
-or —	Ignores all following options.
-n	Suppresses the final newline character.
-p	Sends *string* to the process created by |& rather than to the standard output.
-r	Ignores any echo escape sequences.
-R	Ignores any echo escape sequences, and ignores subsequent options except -n.
-s	Sends *string* to the history file.
-u*n*	Sends *string* to file descriptor *n*; the default is file descriptor 1.

printenv

A command that prints the names and values of the variables in the environment. If you specify a *name*, only that value is printed.

See also env

printf

A command used to print formatted output. `printf` is based on the C library function of the same name and works in the same sort of way. The syntax looks like this:

```
printf format [string...]
```

and *string* is printed on the standard output according to *format*, which can be text characters, C language escape characters, or a set of conversion arguments. See the man pages on your system for more details.

See also echo, print

privileged account

Another name for the superuser or root account on a Unix system.

/proc

An SVR4 directory that contains a list of all the processes running on the system.

See also ps

process ID

See PID

process status

The status of a process. Unix has eight different process states: running in user mode, running in kernel mode, waiting, sleeping, idle, swapping, stopped, and dead or zombie.

prof

A command that displays an object file's profile data.

See also gprof, ldd, lorder, lprof

.profile

A startup file located in your home directory, which is executed by the Bourne and Korn shells when you first log in to the system. You can use the .profile file to set variables, define functions, and run commands.

See also .cshrc, .login

prompt

A C shell environment variable that contains the prompt string. You can use set prompt ="*string*" in your .cshrc file to customize your prompt.

See also PS1, PS2, PS3, PS4

ps

A command that displays information about active processes.

Syntax

The syntax to use with ps is as follows:

```
ps [options]
```

The ps command provides a snapshot of system activity; if you re-execute the command later, you may see completely different information.

If you use ps without options, you will see the status of all the processes controlled by your terminal arranged in the four columns described in Table P.10.

If you use the -l option to produce a long listing, you will see information arranged in the columns described in Table P.11.

TABLE P.10: ps Output Without Options

Column	Description
PID	The process ID number of the process.
TTY	The number of the terminal that controls this process.
TIME	The length of CPU time, in minutes and seconds, that this process has been running.
COMD	The command name with which this process was called; if you use the -f option, you will see the whole command line.

TABLE P.11: Long Listing of ps Output

Column	Description
F	Lists the status flags.
S	Shows the state of the process as a single character; B and W indicate the process is waiting, I indicates idle, O indicates it is running, R means that it is loaded into a queue as a runnable process, S shows the process is sleeping, T means it is being traced, X indicates it is waiting for more memory, and Z indicates that the process is a zombie, meaning it has terminated.
UID	User ID of the owner of the process.
PID	The process ID number of the process.
PPID	The process ID of the parent process.
C	Processor utilization; this number is used for scheduling.
STIME	The starting time of the process (Solaris only).
PRI	The priority of the process; the higher the number, the lower the priority.
NI	The nice value for priority.
ADDR	The memory or disk address of the process.
SZ	The size, in blocks, of the core image of the process.
WCHAN	If the process is waiting or sleeping, this indicates the event it is waiting for.
TTY	The number of the terminal that controls this process.
TIME	The length of CPU time, in minutes and seconds, that this process has been running.
COMD	The command name with which this process was called; if you also use the -f option, you will see the whole command line.

Options and Arguments

For the SVR4 version of ps, the options you can use are listed in Table P.12. Any arguments contained in *list* should be either enclosed in double quotes or separated by commas.

In the BSD version, options work differently, as shown in Table P.13.

TABLE P.12: SVR4 ps Options

Option	Description
-a	Displays information about all processes except group leaders and those processes that are not associated with a terminal.
-c	Displays scheduler data set by prioctrl.
-d	Displays information about all processes except group leaders.
-e	Displays information about all processes.
-f	Creates a full listing.
-g *list*	Displays output for the specified process groups.
-j	Displays the process group ID and session ID.
-n *list*	Displays information for processes running on *list*.
-p *list*	Displays information for the specified process IDs.
-s *list*	Displays information for the specified session leader IDs.
-t *list*	Displays information for the specified terminals.
-u *list*	Displays information for the specified users.

TABLE P.13: BSD ps Options

Option	Description
-a	Displays information about all processes.
-C	Uses an alternative CPU time calculation.
-e	Displays the environment as well as the command.
-h	Repeats the display header to give one header per page.
-j	Creates a full report.
-l	Creates a long report.
-L	Lists all the keywords.
-m	Sorts by memory usage rather than by process ID.
-M *name*	List information for *name*.
-N *name*	Extracts the name list from *name*.
-o *keywords*	Displays information in space- or comma-separated lists of *keywords*.
-O *keywords*	Adds the information specified by space- or comma-separated lists of *keywords* to the default display.
-p *list*	Displays information on the specified process ID.
-r	Sorts by CPU usage rather than by process ID.
-S	Uses an alternative process time calculation.
-t *list*	Displays information for the specified terminals.
-T	Displays information for the process associated with the standard input.
-u	Specifies a different set of information for the full display.

TABLE P.13 continued: BSD ps Options

OPTION	DESCRIPTION
-v	Specifies a different set of information for the long display.
-w	Uses 132-column display.
-W *filename*	Specifies *filename* as the source of swap information rather than /dev/swap.
-x	Displays information for processes not associated with terminals.

Examples

To display information about active processes, use:

```
ps
  PID      TTY      TIMECOMD
  24559    tty12    0:07sh
  25668    tty12    0:12ps
```

The first process is the shell, and the second is the process executing the ps command. If you run the long version of ps, use the more filter to stop the extensive output from scrolling off the screen:

```
ps -el | more
```

See also kill, nice, **process status**, pstat, whodo

PS1

A Bourne shell and Korn shell variable that contains the primary prompt string that, by default, is a dollar sign ($). You can customize your prompt if you wish.

See also PS2, PS3, PS4

PS2

A Bourne shell and Korn shell variable that contains the secondary prompt string that, by default, is a greater than sign (>). This secondary prompt is used to indicate that the shell is expecting more input and is not often customized by the user.

See also PS1, PS3, PS4

PS3

A Korn shell variable that contains the prompt string used inside a shell select loop to read replies from the standard input.

See also PS1, PS2, PS4

PS4

A Korn shell variable that contains the prompt string used when in debug mode, a plus sign (+). Use the -x option to the shell, which you can use with set, to turn on this debug mode.

See also PS1, PS2, PS3

pstat

An SCO command that displays system information for the process table, i-node table, and open file table.

Syntax
The syntax for pstat is as follows:

```
pstat [options][filename]
```

pstat displays information from *filename*, if specified; otherwise, it displays information from /dev/mem and /dev/kmem.

Information in the open file table display is arranged in the columns described in Table P.14.

Information in the i-node table display is arranged in the columns described in Table P.15.

Information in the process table display is arranged in the same columns as shown for the long (-1) form of the SVR4 ps command provided earlier in this chapter.

TABLE P.14: Open File Information in pstat

COLUMN	DESCRIPTION
LOC	Location of this table entry
FLAGS	Assorted stream state variables
CNT	Number of processes related to this open file
INO	Location of the i-node table entry for this file
OFFS	File offset

TABLE P.15: I-Node Table Information in pstat

COLUMN	DESCRIPTION
LOC	Location of this table entry
FLAGS	Assorted state variables
CNT	Number of open file table entries for this i-node

TABLE P.15 continued: I-Node Table Information in pstat

Column	Description
DEVICE	Major and minor device numbers for the filesystem
INO	I-number
FS	Filesystem type
MODE	Mode bits
NLK	Number of links to this i-node
UID	User ID of the owner
SIZE/DEV	Number of bytes in an ordinary file, or the major and minor device numbers of a special file

Options and Arguments

The options you can use with pstat are shown in Table P.16.

See also kill, nice, **process status**, ps

TABLE P.16: Options Available with pstat

Option	Description
-a	Displays information for all processes.
-f	Displays the open file table.
-I	Displays the i-node table.
-n *list*	Displays information for the system specified in *list*.
-p	Displays the process table.
-s *filename*	Displays swap information from *filename* rather than from /dev/swap.
-u	Displays information for a specific process.

ptx

A BSD command used to create a permuted index.

Syntax

The syntax for this command is:

```
ptx [options][infile[outfile]]
```

If you don't specify an *infile* or an *outfile*, standard input and standard output are used instead.

Options and Arguments

The options listed in Table P.17 are available with ptx.

TABLE P.17: Options to Use with ptx

OPTION	DESCRIPTION
-b *filename*	Use the characters specified in *filename* as word separators.
-f	Ignores case when sorting keywords.
-g *n*	Specifies *n* characters as the gap between columns.
-i *filename*	Ignores the keywords listed in *filename*; opposite of -o.
-o *filename*	Uses only the keywords specified in *filename*; opposite of -i.
-r	Uses the first field in *infile* as a page or chapter reference identifier separate from the rest of the line text.
-t	Prepares the output for phototypesetting; maximum line length is 100 characters.
-w *n*	Sets the line length; the default is 72 characters.

pushd

A built-in C shell command that swaps the top two directories in your directory stack. The C shell stores a list of directories you are using, and you manipulate the stack using popd and pushd; the dirs command lists the contents of the directory stack. If you use a numeric argument to pushd, that directory is placed at the top of the stack; directories are listed in numerical order starting with 0 at the top of the stack.

See also dirs, popd

pwd

A command that displays the full pathname of the current working directory. The Bourne shell and Korn shell both have built-in commands of the same name, and the C shell has the dirs command. These shell commands are often faster than the Unix utility.

See also cd

Q

question mark

The ? character, used as a metacharacter representing a single character in a filename or in a regular expression.

See also asterisk

quota

A BSD command used to display a user's disk usage and limits.

Syntax

The syntax for quota is as follows:

```
quota [options] username
```

Options and Arguments

With no options, quota displays information on all the filesystems detailed in /etc/fstab. Only the superuser can use the -u option with a *username* to inspect information for other users. The other options are listed in Table Q.1.

TABLE Q.1: Options for Use with quota

OPTION	DESCRIPTION
-g	Displays group quotas.
-q	Displays information only on filesystems that are over quota.
-v	Displays quotas for filesystems on which no storage is allocated.

quote

To remove any special meaning a character might have for the shell by preceding the character with a backslash (\). You can also quote several characters by placing single quotes around them.

See also C shell, escaped character

quoting

▶ To place a backslash (\) before a single metacharacter or to surround a group of characters with single quotes so that any special meaning the metacharacter had is removed.

▶ To include a relevant portion of someone else's article when posting a followup to a USENET newsgroup. It is considered to be poor "netiquette" to quote more of the original post than is absolutely necessary to make your point.

See also escaped character

R

r

A built-in Korn shell command that re-executes the last command. The r command is an alias of fc -e - and is predefined by the shell. To run the last command in the background, use r &, and to repeat the second last command, use r -2. You can also repeat a command if you can remember how the command line started; for example, to repeat the last command that used grep, type r grep.

See also fc, history

RAID

Acronym for redundant array of inexpensive disks. In networking and mission critical applications, a method of using several hard disk drives—often SCSI or Integrated Drive Electronics (IDE) drives—in an array to provide fault tolerance in the event that one or more drives fail.

Each of the different levels of RAID is designed for a specific use:

RAID 0   Data is striped over one or more drives, but there is no redundant drive. RAID 0 provides no fault tolerance because the loss of a hard disk means a complete loss of data. Some classification schemes omit RAID 0 for this reason.

RAID 1   Two hard disks of equal capacity duplicate or mirror each other's contents. One disk continuously and automatically backs up the other disk. This method is also known as *disk mirroring* or *disk duplexing*, depending on whether one or two independent hard disk controllers are used.

RAID 2   Bit-interleaved data is written across several drives, and then parity and error-correction information is written to additional separate drives. The specific number of error-correction drives depends on the allocation algorithm in use.

RAID 3   Bit-interleaved data is written across several drives, but only one parity drive is used. If an error is detected, the data is reread to resolve the problem. The fact that data is reread in the event of an error may add a small performance penalty.

RAID 4   Data is written across drives by sectors rather than at the bit level, and a separate drive is used as a parity drive for error detection. Reads and writes occur independently.

RAID 5   Data is written across drives in sectors, and parity information is added as another sector, just as if it were ordinary data.

The appropriate level of RAID for any particular installation depends on network usage. RAID levels 1, 3, and 5 are available commercially, and levels 3 and 5 are proving popular for networks.

See also **disk striping, disk striping with parity, SLED**

random

An SCO command that generates a random number between 0 and *scale* on the standard output and returns this value as the exit value. The syntax is:

```
random [option][scale]
```

If you don't specify *scale*, the number will be either 0 or 1. The single option available with this command, -s, just prevents the number from being printed on the standard output.

RANDOM

A Korn shell environment variable that stores a random number between 0 and 32,767. A new random number is generated each time this variable is referenced.

ranlib

A BSD command that makes a table of contents for archive libraries used by the loader ld.

See also ar, ld, lorder, nm

raw

Jargon for anything that has not completed processing to produce a final product. Unprocessed data is often called *raw data*.

raw device

Any device that is written to or read from directly, without any intermediate buffering; sometimes called an *unbuffered device*.

raw mode

A mode that bypasses the usual Unix input/output system and writes characters directly to the device, usually a terminal. Raw mode is fast but is device-dependent, and so removes some of the portability benefits that Unix provides.

See also cbreak **mode, cooked mode**

rbash

The command used to start the restricted Bourne Again shell (bash) from the FSF. rbash limits users to read-only access to files and directories and does not let them change to another shell or use a different pathname.

See also Bash, Unix shell

rc

A small elegant shell that replaces the Bourne shell, developed by Tom Duff and extended by Byron Rakitzis. rc eliminates many of the technical shortcomings of the Bourne shell but does not have some of the advanced features that you find in some of the other shells, including job control or command-line editing. Its programming language is based on the C language.

See also Unix shell

.rc file

A file containing commands that establish custom values for environment variables for individual users.

See also dot file, .exrc, .kshrc, .mailrc, .netrc

rcp

A TCP/IP command used to copy files between two different computer systems that can communicate over a network.

Syntax
The syntax for rcp is as follows:

```
rcp [options] source-file destination-file
```
or
```
rcp [options] source-file-list  destination-directory
```
Like the cp utility, rcp has two modes; the first mode copies one file to another, while the second mode copies one or more files to a directory.

Options and Arguments
source-file is the pathname of the file to copy. If you want to copy a file from a remote computer to your own, you must precede the pathname with the name of the remote computer followed by a colon (:). The *destination-file* is the pathname that rcp assigns to the resulting copy of the file, and to copy a file to a remote computer, add the name of the system followed by a colon.

The *source-file-list* contains a list of the files you want to copy, and if you use the -r option, this can include directories, too. The *destination-directory* is the name of the directory where rcp places the copied files; again, add the name of the remote computer to the beginning of this path, separated by a colon.

The options you can use with rcp are listed in Table R.1.

TABLE R.1: Options to Use with rcp

OPTION	DESCRIPTION
-p	Preserves the modification times and file-access permissions from the original files.
-r	Used when working with directories; causes rcp to copy the contents of a directory and all subdirectories within that directory.

Examples

To copy a file called memo from the /home/jenny directory on the fullerton computer into your home directory, use:

```
rcp fullerton:/home/jenny/memo .
```

To copy two files, memo and file.log, to the /pub directory on the system called fullerton, use:

```
rcp memo file.log fullerton:/pub
```

Notes

The 4.4BSD version of rcp has several options that deal with Kerberos authentication; see your system documentation for more details.

You must have a login account on the remote system before you can use rcp to copy files.

See also cp, ftp, rlogin, rsh, telnet

RCS

Abbreviation for Revision Control System; a set of programs designed to keep track of multiple revisions to files, usually in a software development environment, and to minimize the amount of hard disk space needed to store the revisions. The RCS system is not usually a standard part of SVR4; you can get RCS from the Free Software Foundation.

Using RCS, you can automatically store and then retrieve revisions, compare and merge revisions, keep a complete change log, and specifically identify particular revisions. Table R.2 lists the major programs in the RCS suite and describes their use.

On many systems, you find a `man` page called `rcsintro` included with the RCS programs. To look at the page that includes basic RCS information as well as examples of how to use the programs, enter the following:

    man rcsintro

See also SCCS, version number

TABLE R.2: RCS Programs

PROGRAM	DESCRIPTION
ci	Stores the contents of the working files into their corresponding RCS files, and deletes the original.
co	Retrieves a previously checked-in revision.
ident	Extracts keyword or value symbols.
merge	Performs a three-way merge of files using the `diff` utility.
rcs	Lets you set up the RCS system and specify certain default attributes of RCS files.
rcsclean	Tidies up the RCS files by comparing checked-out files against the appropriate revision and, if there is no difference, by deleting the working file.
rcsdiff	Compares revisions using `diff`.
rcsfreeze	A shell script that assigns a name to a set of RCS files to mark them as a single unit.
rcsmerge	Performs a three-way merge of revisions, merging two different versions and incorporating the differences into a third working file.
rlog	Displays log messages associated with each revision, the number of lines added or removed, date of last check in, and so on.

rcsclean

See RCS

rcsdiff

See RCS

rcsfreeze

See RCS

rcsmerge

See RCS

rdist

A utility that makes sure that files are consistent on different computer systems.

Syntax

The syntax for this command is:

```
rdist [options][name...]
```

The rdist command runs commands contained in a file called distfile, located in the current directory and specified using the -f or -c options; if you use -, the standard input is used instead. On most systems, cron runs rdist automatically.

Options and Arguments

The options for use with rdist are detailed in Table R.3.

TABLE R.3: Options to Use with rdist

OPTION	DESCRIPTION
-b	Performs a binary comparison and updates files if they are different.
-c name[login@] host[:dest]	Makes rdist interpret name[login@]host[:dest] as a distfile.
-d variable=value	Sets variable equal to value; this option overrides definitions contained in the distfile.
-f distfile	Uses the specified distfile.
-h	Follows symbolic links.
-I	Ignores unresolved links.
-m host	Specifies a host computer to receive the update.
-n	Prints the commands without executing them; used for debugging a distfile.
-q	Turns off the printing of modified filenames on the standard output.
-R	Deletes any extra files found on the remote system that do not exist in the original master directory.
-v	Verifies that all files on the remote systems are up-to-date. The names of out-of-date files are displayed, but no changes are made.
-w	Preserves the directory structure of the files being copied.
-y	Does not update files that are younger than the master copies; prevents newer files from being overwritten.

Notes

On some systems, you find that the system administrator does not allow use of rdist; this is usually for security reasons.

See also rcp

read

A built-in Bourne shell and Korn shell command that reads the standard input and assigns each word read to the corresponding variable. All left-over words are assigned to the final variable; if you only specify one variable, all input is assigned to that variable. For example:

```
read first last address
Peter Dyson 2021 7th Avenue

Peter Dyson
2021 7th Avenue
```

In the Korn shell, you can use the options detailed in Table R.4, as well as use a ? syntax for prompting. When you follow a variable name with ?*string*, *string* is displayed as a prompt for the user and the input stored in the variable.

TABLE R.4: Korn Shell read Options

Option	Description
-p	Reads from the output of a |& coprocess.
-r	Ignores \ as the line-continuation character.
-s	Saves the input into the history file.
-u[*n*]	Reads input from the file descriptor specified by *n*.

readnews

An older and mostly obsolete newsreader used to access posts to USENET newsgroups.

See also nn, rn, tin, trn

readonly

A built-in Bourne shell and Korn shell command that prevents you from changing a variable value; variables can be read but not overwritten.

read-only filesystem

A filesystem set up by the system administrator as read-only so that no one can make changes to the files it contains. Most filesystems are mounted to allow write access for those users with the appropriate permissions.

rebuilding the kernel

The Unix kernel usually looks after itself and does not normally need much in the way of attention or maintenance; however, from time to time, the system administrator may have to rebuild the kernel for one or more of the following reasons:

▶ You receive a new version of the kernel.

▶ You want to reduce the size of the kernel by removing unused device drivers.

▶ You are experiencing problems automatically sensing certain hardware.

▶ You are upgrading certain hardware elements on your system.

The amount of effort needed to rebuild the kernel varies tremendously from system to system; some require long manual procedures while others automate as much of the process as they can. On other systems, you may need to recompile all or part of the kernel. A partial recompilation is needed if your kernel is in two parts: a set of configuration files you can change and a group of object files that you cannot change. A full recompilation occurs when you recompile the whole kernel.

As an example, here are the steps you follow on a Linux system to rebuild the kernel. All these steps are carried out from /usr/src:

1. Run make config, which asks you questions about which device drivers you want to include in the new kernel.

2. Run make depend to collect the appropriate dependencies for each source file and add them to the makefiles.

3. If you have built a kernel from this source tree in the past, run make clean to throw away all the old object files and make sure that the kernel is rebuilt from scratch.

4. Run make (with no arguments) to rebuild the kernel.

5. When the recompilation is complete, you will find a file called zImage in /usr/src/linux, an executable image of the kernel compressed by gzip; when the kernel boots, it will uncompress itself into memory.

6. Place the kernel image file on a boot floppy, or configure LILO to boot the new kernel from the hard disk.

red

A command used to access a restricted version of the ed text editor. Using red, you can only change text files located in the current directory, and you cannot use ! shell commands.

RedHat Linux

See Linux

redirection

A mechanism in the shell that causes the standard input for a program to come from a file rather than from the terminal. It also causes the standard output and standard error to go to a file rather than to the terminal. Table R.5 shows the most common redirection operations in the C shell, Bourne shell, and Korn shell.

Because Unix is a file-based operating system, and terminals and other devices are treated as files, a program doesn't care or even know if its output is going to your terminal or to a file.

See also **pipe,** tee

TABLE R.5: Common Redirection Operations

FUNCTION	C SHELL	BOURNE & KORN SHELLS
Sends standard output to *file*.	*command* > *file*	*command* > *file*
Sends standard error to *file*.		*command* 2> *file*
Sends standard output and standard error to *file*.	*command* >& *file*	*command* > *file* 2>&1
Reads standard input from *file*.	*command* < *file*	*command* < *file*
Appends standard output to end of *file*.	*command* >> *file*	*command* >> *file*
Appends standard error to end of *file*.		*command* 2>> *file*
Appends standard output and standard error to end of *file*.	*command* >>& *file*	*command* >> *file* 2>&1

refer

A GNU groff command that reads in a bibliography file and creates troff formatted output. groff is the Free Software Foundation's implementation of the Unix text processing commands nroff and troff. groff is distributed with many systems, including BSD and Linux.

See also indxbib, lkbib, lookbib

regcmp

An SVR4 command that compiles the regular expressions in one or more files into C language source code. The default source code file is called *filename*.i; but if you use the – option, the file is called *filename*.c instead.

register

A BSD command used to register a new user with the Kerberos authentication system. You are prompted to enter your current password and then to enter a new password for use only with Kerberos. You can register with Kerberos only once.

See also kdestroy, kinit, klist

regular character

A character that always represents itself in an ambiguous file reference or regular expression and has no special meaning.

See also metacharacter

regular expressions

A sequence of characters that can match a set of fixed-text strings used in searching for and replacing text. Many Unix programs, including ed, vi, emacs, grep, awk, and sed use regular expressions.

A regular expression is just a series of characters, most of which represent themselves; for example, the regular expression moth matches any string containing these letters in this sequence, including moth, mothball, mother, and behemoth. Several special characters have a much more general meaning, as Table R.6 shows.

You can use these symbols together. For example, the regular expression moth matches the string moth, ^moth matches moth at the beginning of a line, moth$ matches moth at the end of a line, and ^moth$ matches moth when it is the only word on a line. Obviously, these symbols can be combined to create some very complex and powerful regular expressions. Regular expressions form the basis of text processing in Unix, and you should take the time to learn how to use them properly.

TABLE R.6: Symbols Used in Regular Expressions

Symbol	Description
.	Matches any single non-null character except a newline.
*	Matches zero or more of the preceding character.
^	Matches the following regular expression at the beginning of a line.
$	Matches the following regular expression at the end of a line.
\<	Matches characters at the beginning of a word.
\>	Matches characters at the end of a word.
[ ]	Matches any one of the enclosed characters. A hyphen indicates a range of consecutive characters.
[^]	Matches any character that is not enclosed.
\	Takes the following symbol or character literally and turns off any special meaning.
\(\)	Saves the pattern enclosed between \(and \). Up to 9 patterns can be saved on a single line, and they can be repeated in substitutions by the escape sequences \1 to \9.
+	Matches one or more instances of the preceding regular expression.
?	Matches zero or one instances of the preceding regular expression.
|	Matches the regular expression specified before or after; the | acts as an OR.
( )	Applies a match to the enclosed group of regular expressions.

rehash

A built-in C shell command that rebuilds the hash table used in the path variable. You may have to use `rehash` as you add new commands from time to time to make sure that your path is up-to-date.

See also unhash

relational operators

An operator that allows for the comparison of two or more expressions.

The six relational operators are: equal to (==), not equal to (!=), less than (<), less than or equal to (<=), greater than (>), and greater than or equal to (>=).

See also Boolean, conditional statement

relative pathname

A pathname that begins in your current directory. A relative pathname does not begin with /.

See also absolute pathname, parent directory

relogin

An SVR4 command that changes the login entry to reflect the current window running under `layers` to ensure that commands such as who or `write` use the latest login information. One option is available, `-s` to suppress error messages.

remote

An SCO command that runs commands on a remote system.

Syntax

The syntax for this command is:

    remote [options]hostname command [options]

Options and Arguments

In the syntax above, *hostname* is the name of the remote computer, and *command* [*options*] represents the command and the command options that you want to run on that remote computer; if you use – instead of *command* [*options*], then input comes from the standard input on the local computer, not from the remote host. The options available with `remote` are listed in Table R.7.

TABLE R.7: Options to Use with remote

Option	Description
-f *filename*	Uses the specified local *filename* as the standard input for the *command* on the local computer.
-m	Mails the user to report the completion of *command*; normally, only errors are mailed.
-u *user*	Sends any mail to *user*.

Examples

To run the `ls` command on the /pub directory on a remote computer called sybex, use:

    remote sybex ls /pub

Remote File System

See RFS

remote filesystem

Any filesystem on a remote computer that has been set up so that you can access the files and directories it contains as though they were stored on your own computer's hard disk. This is usually done over a network with NFS.

See also **mounting a filesystem, RFS**

remote login

The action of logging in to a remote computer to access files and directories just as a local user would.

See also `rcp`, `remote`, `rlogin`, `rsh`, `rusers`, `rwho`, `telnet`

remote mapping

A security mechanism under RFS for controlling access by remote users to shared files and directories. Remote mapping can create groups and group permissions.

Remote Procedure Call

See RPC

repeat

A built-in C shell command that repeats a command a specified number of times. The syntax for `repeat` is:

```
repeat n command
```

where *n* specifies the number of times you want to repeat *command*.

reset

An SVR4 command used to reset a hung or confused terminal. `reset` uses the value of the TERM environment variable to reset the terminal.

See also `tset`

reset string

A string that your system administrator can send to your terminal to reset it when your terminal is hung or in an indeterminate state.

See also `reset`

resolver

A library of programs used by host systems with DNS to resolve host names into IP addresses.

resource

Any separately identifiable hardware element found on a network, including memory, hard disks, printers, tape drives, and CD-ROMs.

resource sharing

The ability of an operating system to share separate resources between different processes at the same time, without causing any interference.

return

A built-in Bourne shell and Korn shell command that is used inside a function definition.

See also exit

return code

See exit status

return value

See exit status

rev

A BSD command that reverses lines in a file. The syntax is:

```
rev filename...
```

rev copies the specified *filename* to the standard output, reversing the order of the characters in each line; if you don't specify a *filename*, then rev reads from the standard input.

Revision Control System

See RCS

RFC

Abbreviation for Request for Comments. A document or set of documents in which proposed Internet standards are described or defined. Well over a thousand RFCs are in existence, and they represent a major method of online publication for Internet technical standards.

See also IAB, RFD

RFD

Abbreviation for Request for Discussion. In USENET, a post sent to news.announce.newsgroups proposing the formation of a new newsgroup. Followup postings to this newsgroup will contain for and against opinions, and if most opinions are positive, the original proposer will issue a Call for Votes.

RFS

Abbreviation for Remote File System. A distributed file system network protocol that allows programs running on a computer to use network resources as though they were local. Originally developed by AT&T, RFS has been incorporated as a part of Unix System V Interface Definition.

See also NFS

.rhosts

A file in your home directory on a remote system that contains a list of the computers that you are allowed to log on to without using a password.

See also rlogin

rksh

A restricted version of the Korn shell used on certain systems. This version prevents you from leaving your home directory, changing the PATH variable, and re-directing output. On some systems this program is called krsh.

See also rsh

rlog

See RCS

rlogin

A command used to log in to a remote computer.

Syntax
The syntax to use with rlogin is:

    rlogin [options]hostname

You will be prompted to enter a password unless the .rhosts file in your home directory on the remote machine contains the host name and your username. *hostname* is a computer system you can access over a network.

Options and Arguments

The options you can use with `rlogin` are listed in Table R.8.

See also `ftp`, `rcp`, `.rhosts`, `telnet`

TABLE R.8: Options to Use with rlogin

OPTION	DESCRIPTION
-8	Allows 8-bit data (instead of 7-bit data) to pass across the network.
-e *c*	Sets the escape character to *c*; the default is a tilde (~). The escape character can be specified as a literal character or as an octal number in the form *nnn*.
-1 *username*	Logs in to the remote computer with *username* rather than the current user's name.

rm

A command used to remove files.

Syntax

The syntax for the `rm` command is as follows:

```
rm [options] filename
```

You must have write permission for the directory that holds the file or files you want to remove, but you do not have to have write permission for the file; the permissions are displayed and you are prompted to confirm that you want to delete the file.

Options and Arguments

The options available with `rm` are detailed in Table R.9.

TABLE R.9: Options to Use with rm

OPTION	DESCRIPTION
-f	Forces the removal, even if the permissions do not allow it.
-i	When used with the -r option, asks whether to delete each file or to examine each directory.
-P	A BSD option that overwrites each file three times before it is deleted.
-r	Recursively deletes the files and subdirectories associated with a directory as well as the directory itself; be careful—this can be a dangerous option if used without care.

Examples

To remove one of your own files even though the file is write-protected, use:

```
rm -f myfile.doc
```

and to ask for confirmation before deleting every file in the current directory, use:

```
rm -i *
```

Notes
New users should use the -i option until they are comfortable with this command, because rm normally runs without displaying any output at all, and this can result in files being deleted by accident.

See also rmdir

rmail

The mail facility built into some versions of emacs.

rmb

A SCO filter command that removes blank lines from a text file; any series of more than two blank lines is reduced to two lines.

rmdel

See SCCS

rmdir

A command used to remove empty directories.

Syntax
Here's the syntax for rmdir:

```
rmdir [options] directories
```

The directory must be empty before you can use rmdir.

Options and Arguments
This command deletes the named *directories* but not their contents; use rm -r for this task if a directory is not empty. Some versions of rmdir (4.4BSD and Solaris, for example) do not have any options; other versions have the options listed in Table R.10.

TABLE R.10: Options to Use with rmdir

Option	Description
-p	Removes the specified *directories* as well as any subdirectories that become empty as a result.
-s	Turns off any error messages generated by the -p option.

Examples

To remove the empty `elvis` directory, use:

```
rm elvis
```

To remove the directory `documents` using an absolute pathname:

```
rm /home/brenda/documents
```

See also `mkdir`, `rm`

rn

A widely available and popular newsreader, used to subscribe to USENET newsgroups, written by Larry Wall and Stan Barber. `rn` is not a threaded newsreader and so cannot organize posts into threads, but it does have very powerful pattern-matching features used when searching through the text of posts.

Table R.11 lists the `rn` commands you can use while selecting a newsgroup or executing a shell command. Table R.12 lists the commands used when selecting an article within a newsgroup.

See also `tin`, `trn`

TABLE R.11: rn Commands Used When Selecting a Newsgroup

COMMAND	DESCRIPTION
BASIC COMMANDS	
h	Displays help information.
q	Quits rn.
v	Displays the rn version number.
x	Quits rn and abandons all updates to your .newsrc file.
READING ARTICLES	
space	Performs the default operation.
y	Starts displaying the current newsgroup for reading.
WORKING WITH NEWSGROUPS	
^	Goes to the first newsgroup that contains unread articles.
$	Goes to the end of the list of newsgroups.
c	Marks all the articles in the newsgroup as having been read; catch up mode.
g *newsgroup*	Goes to the specified *newsgroup*.
l *pattern*	Lists the unsubscribed newsgroup names that contain *pattern*.

TABLE R.11 continued: rn Commands Used When Selecting a Newsgroup

COMMAND	DESCRIPTION
WORKING WITH NEWSGROUPS	
L	Lists the current state of newsgroups in .newsrc.
n	Goes to the next newsgroup that contains unread articles.
p	Goes to the previous newsgroup that contains unread articles.
/*pattern*	Searches forward for a newsgroup name containing *pattern*.
?*pattern*	Searches backward for a newsgroup name containing *pattern*.
/	Searches forward for previous *pattern*.
?	Searches backward for previous *pattern*.
EXECUTING UNIX COMMANDS	
! *command*	Executes the specified *command*.
!	Pauses rn and starts a shell.

TABLE R.12: rn Commands Used When Selecting an Article

COMMAND	DESCRIPTION
BASIC COMMANDS	
c	Marks all articles in the newsgroup as read.
h	Displays help information.
k	Marks as read all articles with the same subject; effectively kills unread articles.
n	Goes to the next unread article.
q	Quits this newsgroup.
u	Unsubscribes from the current newsgroup.
Ctrl-N	Goes to the next unread article on the same subject.
REDISPLAYING THE CURRENT ARTICLE	
b	Goes back one page.
v	Redisplays the current article with its header.
X	Decodes the current page using rot13.
Ctrl-L	Redisplays the current page.
Ctrl-R	Redisplays the current article.
Ctrl-X	Decodes the current article using rot13.

TABLE R.12 continued: rn Commands Used When Selecting an Article

COMMAND	DESCRIPTION
SELECTING ANOTHER ARTICLE	
-	Redisplays the last article displayed.
N	Goes forward to the next article.
$	Goes forward to the end of the last article.
p	Goes backward to the previous article.
Ctrl-P	Goes backward to the previous article with the same subject.
P	Goes backward to the next article, read or unread.
^	Goes backward to the next unread article.
USING ARTICLE NUMBERS	
=	Displays a list of all the unread articles.
number	Goes to the article with the specified *number*.
#	Displays the number of the last article.
SEARCHING FOR AN ARTICLE	
/pattern	Searches forward for a subject containing *pattern*.
?pattern	Searches backward for a subject containing *pattern*.
/	Searches forward for previous *pattern*.
?	Searches backward for previous *pattern*.
RESPONDING TO AN ARTICLE	
f	Starts the Pnews program to create a followup post.
F	Starts the Pnews program to create a followup post and includes a copy of the original message.
r	Sends a mail message to the author of the article.
R	Sends a mail message to the author of the article and includes a copy of the original message.
SAVING AN ARTICLE	
s *filename*	Saves the article in the specified *filename*.
w *filename*	Saves the article without the header in the specified *filename*.
EXECUTING UNIX COMMANDS	
! *command*	Executes the specified *command*.
!	Pauses rn and starts a shell.

roffs

Jargon for the Unix text-processing commands `nroff`, `roff`, and `troff`.

root

- ▶ The name of the directory at the top of the directory tree from which all other directories are descended.
- ▶ The name of the superuser, user number 0.

rootdev

A kernel variable used to set the major and minor device numbers for the root filesystem.

root directory

The common ancestor for all directories in the Unix filesystem and the start of all absolute pathnames. The name of the root directory is /.

root filesystem

The filesystem available when Unix is brought up in single-user mode. The root filesystem is called / and cannot be mounted or unmounted. Only the programs and files in the root directory are available until the user mounts other filesystems.

root login

The login name of the superuser.

rot13

Pronounced "rote-13." A simple encryption scheme often used to scramble posts to USENET newsgroups. rot13 works by swapping each alphabetic character with one of 13 characters from its location in the alphabet, so that a becomes n; numbers and punctuation symbols are unaffected.

rot13 makes the article unreadable until the text is decoded and is often used when the subject matter might be considered offensive. Many newsreaders have a built-in command to unscramble rot13 text, and if you use it, don't be surprised by what you read; if you think you might be offended, don't decrypt the post.

You will also find other, unoffensive material encoded by rot13, including spoilers that give away the ending of a book or film and answers to puzzles or riddles.

See also tr

RPC

Abbreviation for Remote Procedure Call, a set of procedures used to implement client/server architecture in distributed programming. RPC describes how an application initiates a process on another network node and how it retrieves the appropriate result.

rpcgen

A BSD software development tool that generates C language source code to implement a Remote Procedure Call (RPC) protocol.

See also cc, cpp

rsh

A command used to start a shell on a remote system and execute a single command. When the command terminates, rsh also terminates.

Syntax

The syntax for this command is:

```
rsh [options] hostname [command]
```

The commands that you can use on the remote system are determined by the system administrator for that system.

Options and Arguments

The rsh command attempts to connect to the remote computer *hostname* and execute the specified *command*. If you don't specify *command*, you can use rlogin to log in to the system. The options you can use with this command are shown in Table R.13.

TABLE R.13: Options to Use with rsh

OPTION	DESCRIPTION
-l *user*	Logs in as *user* rather than under your own login name.
-n	Allows you to run rsh in the background without expecting any input.
-x	Turns on DES encryption for all data exchange; using this option causes a significant delay in response times (BSD only).

Examples

To list the contents of your home directory on the remote computer system called `bigone`, use:

```
rsh bigone ls
```

This command:

```
rsh bigone ls > dirfile
```

makes a directory listing on the remote system called `bigone`, and redirects the output from the `ls` command to a file called `dirfile` on your local system. To create `dirfile` on the remote system instead, you must quote the redirection symbol like this:

```
rsh bigone ls ">" dirfile
```

You can also use the append symbol (>>) in the same way.

Notes

On some systems the `rsh` command is known as `remsh`.

Remember that shell metacharacters are interpreted on the local computer but not on the remote computer, unless you quote them.

See also `rcp`, `rlogin`, `telnet`

rsh

A command used to start the restricted version of the Bourne shell. This version of the shell won't let you change directories, change PATH or SHELL variables, or specify a command or path that contains a /. Also, you may not use redirection.

See also `rksh`, `Rsh`

Rsh

Another name for the restricted Bourne shell, which is usually called `rsh`. The advantage of using `Rsh` is that there is no confusion with the `rsh` remote shell command.

See also `sh`

rstat

A BSD command that displays a summary of the system status of a specified host computer. The syntax is:

```
rstat host
```

Output from this command details how long the computer system has been running, and the one-, five-, and 15-minute load averages.

See also ruptime, uptime

rup

A Solaris command that shows host status of local systems.

Syntax
Here's the syntax for rup:

```
run [options] hostname
```

Options and Arguments
The options you can use with rup are listed in Table R.14.

See also ping, ruptime, who

TABLE R.14: Options to Use with rup

OPTION	DESCRIPTION
-h	Sorts the listing alphabetically by host name.
-l	Sorts the listing by load average.
-t	Sorts the listing by up time.

ruptime

An SVR4 command that displays the status of all systems on the local area network.

Syntax
The syntax to use with ruptime is:

```
ruptime [options]
```

This command displays each system name, how long each host has been running, the number of users on each host, and the load average of each host.

Options and Arguments
When used without options, this command displays the status information sorted by host name. Available options are listed in Table R.15.

See also finger, rup, rusers, rwho, uptime

TABLE R.15: Options to Use with ruptime

Option	Description
-a	Includes information on users who have been inactive for longer than one hour; these users are normally not counted.
-l	Sorts the list of systems by load average.
-r	Reverses the sort order.
-t	Sorts the list of systems by the amount of time each system has been up and running.
-u	Sorts the list of systems by the number of users on each system.

rusers

A command that displays information about who is logged on to the local area network.

Syntax
Here's the syntax:

```
rusers [options] hostname...
```

Options and Arguments
When used with a *hostname* argument, *rusers* queries only the specified remote computer, and to respond, the remote computer must be running the rusers daemon. Options for rusers are given in Table R.16.

See also finger, rup, ruptime, rwho, uptime, who

TABLE R.16: Options to Use with rusers

Option	Description
-a	Displays a report even if no users are currently logged on.
-h	Sorts alphabetically by host name.
-I	Sorts by idle time.
-l	Creates a long listing, similar to that provided by who.
-u	Sorts by the number of users.

rwall

A command that broadcasts a message to all users on the network.

Syntax
The syntax to use with rwall is as follows:

```
rwall [options] hostname
```

Options and Arguments

The `rwall` command reads a message from the standard input and, when it sees an end-of-file character, it then broadcasts the message to all the users who are logged in to *hostname*. The text, `Broadcast Message`, appears before the text of the message. Options are listed in Table R.17.

See also `talk`, `wall`, `write`

TABLE R.17: Options to Use with rwall

OPTION	DESCRIPTION
-n *netgroup*	Sends the message to those users defined by *netgroup*, rather than to all users logged in to *hostname*.
-h *hostname*	Sends the message to the specified *hostname*. This option is used when both a *netgroup* and a *hostname* are specified.

rwho

A TCP/IP command that displays who is logged on for all machines on the local area network. You can use the -a option with `rwho` to list all users, even if they have been inactive for more than an hour.

See also `finger`, `rup`, `ruptime`, `rusers`, `users`, `who`

RZSZ

A package of tools used to implement the Zmodem file-transfer protocol. You will find these utilities in the package:

rz Receives files using the Zmodem protocol; if the sending program does not initiate a transfer within 50 seconds, rz changes to rb mode.

rb Receives files using the Ymodem protocol.

rx Receives files using the Xmodem protocol.

sz Sends files using the Zmodem protocol.

sb Sends files using the Ymodem protocol.

sx Sends files using the Xmodem protocol.

Table R.18 lists the most useful `rz` options, while Table R.19 lists the most useful `sz` options.

You can get RZSZ from `ftp.cs.pdx.edu` in the directory `/pub/zmodem`, as well as from other sites that archive the standard Unix source files, including `ftp.cs.unm.edu` and `plaza.aarnet.edu.au`.

Because most of the popular PC terminal emulation and communications programs support Zmodem, this package makes it easy to swap files between Unix systems, PCs, and Macintosh computers.

***See also* Kermit**

TABLE R.18: Useful Options to Use with rz

Option	Description
-+	Appends rather than overwrites existing files.
-a	Receives ASCII text files.
-b	Receives binary files.
-D	Sends output to /dev/null; a useful test mode.
-e	Makes the sending program escape control characters.
-p	Skips a transfer if a file of the same name already exists; this can prevent the completion of an interrupted file transfer.
-q	Turns off messages.
-t *n*	Sets the timeout to *n* in tenths of a second.
-v	Adds a list of transferred filenames to a log file /tmp/rzlog.

TABLE R.19: Useful Options to Use with sz

Option	Description
-+	Makes the receiving program append transmitted data to an existing file.
-a	Sends ASCII text.
-b	Sends binary files.
-d	Tries to reconcile filename differences between systems.
-e	Escapes control characters.
-f	Forces the full pathname to be sent in the transmitted filename.
-l *n*	Sets the packet length to *n* bytes.
-L *n*	Sets the Zmodem subpacket length to *n* bytes.
-n	Overwrites a file if the source file is newer than the destination file.
-N	Overwrites a file if the source filename is longer than the destination filename.
-p	Doesn't transfer the file if the destination file exists.
-q	Turns off messages.
-r	Resumes an interrupted transfer.
-t *n*	Sets the timeout to *n* tenths of a second.

TABLE R.19 continued: Useful Options to Use with sz

Option	Description
-v	Adds the names of transferred files to the log file /tmp/szlog.
-y	Overwrites existing files with the same name.
-Y	Overwrites existing files with the same name, but does not send files with the same pathname on the destination system.

S

SA

See system administrator

sact

See SCCS

sash

Acronym for standalone shell, a program started during the boot process as the system initializes and begins running.

save

To write a new file or to overwrite an existing file after you have made modifications to it.

savehist

A C shell environment variable that displays the number of commands saved in the /home/.history history file at the end of a session.

/sbin

An SVR4 directory that contains programs for starting the system and for system recovery.

SCCS

Abbreviation for Source Code Control System; a set of programs designed to keep track of multiple revisions to files, usually in a software development environment, and to minimize the amount of hard disk space needed to store the revisions.

Using SCCS, you can automatically store and retrieve revisions, compare and merge revisions, keep a complete change log, and identify particular revisions. Table S.1 lists the major programs in the sccs suite and describes their use.

In SCCS, each set of changes is known as a "delta" and is assigned a SCCS ID (sometimes abbreviated sid) consisting of either two components (a release and a level number in the form of $a.b$) or four components (release, level, branch, and sequence numbers in the form of $a.b.c.d$).

Each time a delta is entered into SCCS, the system notes which lines have been changed or deleted since the most recent version, and from this information, SCCS can re-create the file on demand. This means that each change depends on all previous changes.

See also RCS, version number

TABLE S.1: SCCS Programs

Program	Description
admin	Creates and configures a new SCCS file.
cdc	Changes the comments associated with a particular delta.
comb	Combines consecutive deltas into a single delta.
delta	Creates a new delta.
get	Retrieves a text file from the SCCS archive.
help	Opens the SCCS help system; at the prompt you can enter a command name or an error code and read a brief explanation.
prs	Prints a portion of the specified SCCS file.
rmdel	Removes an accidental delta from the SCCS file.
sact	Reports which files are being edited but that have yet to be updated using delta.
sccsdiff	Reports the differences between two SCCS files.
unget	Cancels a get operation without creating a new delta.
val	Validates an SCCS file.
what	Searches SCCS files for a specified pattern and then prints out the following text.

sccsdiff

See SCCS

SCO

Abbreviation for Santa Cruz Operation, the developers of several important strains of Unix, including XENIX, SCO UNIX, and the SCO OpenServer series of Unix products.

SCOadmin

A set of graphical system administrator tools provided with SCO Open-Server. SCOadmin lets you add or remove users, manage printers and filesystems, and check your network configuration quickly and easily. You can also run SCOadmin in text mode if you wish.

See also sysadmsh

SCO OpenServer

A set of Unix products from SCO; OpenServer Desktop, OpenServer Host, and OpenServer Enterprise.

OpenServer includes a journaling filesystem, integrated symmetrical multiprocessing, and a set of graphical system administration tools, as well as Merge, which allows you to run your DOS applications, and WABI, which lets you run selected Microsoft Windows 3.1 applications in an X Window.

See also SCO UNIX, XENIX

SCO UNIX

A popular version of Unix from SCO, based on System V Release 3.2 with many SVR4 enhancements. SCO UNIX includes the Korn shell, X Window, Level C2 security, multiprocessor support, and full network support, as well as the ability to run DOS programs and read and write DOS files on a floppy disk.

See also XENIX

script

A list of commands in a text file to be executed by an interpreter. The terms "script" and "shell program" are often used interchangeably, with the vague suggestion that a script is usually simpler; for example, a login script may execute the same specific set of instructions every time a user logs in to the system.

See also shell script

script

A command that saves a copy of everything you type during your current session into a file that is called `typescript`. The syntax to use is:

```
script [option][filename]
```

You can also specify the *filename* you want to use, and the single option, -a, lets you append the current session to the end of *filename* rather than overwrite its contents. This command is useful for occasional users who might want to document their sessions or for when the system administrator performs some particularly grueling task and wants to collect all the output from a time-consuming command for later reuse or as a record.

When you press Ctrl-D or type **exit**, you see the message:

```
Script is done, file is typescript
```

(unless you specified a different name), before you are returned to the system prompt.

`script` places everything that appears on your screen during your session into the file, including commands such as backspace and form feed. So be careful when you print out the file; you may get more than you bargained for.

sdb

A symbolic debugger for C, for assembly language, and for Fortran. `sdb` is used to check programs and to examine core files from aborted programs.

See also adb, dbx, gdb

sdiff

A command that creates a side-by-side comparison of two files.

Syntax
Here's the syntax:

```
sdiff [options] filename1 filename2
```

This command is very useful for comparing two versions of a file because the output is much easier to read than that created by the regular version of `diff`.

Options and Arguments
You can use the options listed in Table S.2 with `sdiff`.

TABLE S.2: Options to Use with sdiff

Option	Description
-l	Lists only the lines from *filename1* that are identical.
-o *outfile*	Sends identical lines from *filename1* and *filename2* to *outfile*. You can then enter one of the following commands to edit *outfile*:
	l Adds left column to output file.
	r Adds right column to output file.
	s Suppresses printing of matching lines.
	v Turns off the s option.
	e l Invokes ed to work on the left column.
	e r Invokes ed to work on the right column.
	e b Invokes ed to work on both columns.
	e Invokes ed.
	q Quits ed and sdiff.
-s	Does not print matching lines.
-w *n*	Sets the line length to *n*; the default is 130.

Examples

The output from sdiff has two columns. The text on the left is from *filename1*, the text on the right is from *filename2*, and you may also see the following:

text text	Indicates that the two lines are identical.
text <	Indicates that text only occurs in filename1.
> text	Indicates that text only occurs in filename2.
text | text	Indicates that the two lines are different.

To list the lines from sales.95 on the left side of the screen that match lines in sales.96, use:

```
sdiff -l sales.95 sales.96
```

See also bdiff, diff, diff3, ed

search path

That list of directories that the shell searches to locate the program file you want to execute. Your search path usually includes your home directory, the /bin directory, and the /usr/bin directory, although it may include others too. You can add directories to your search path by changing the path or PATH environment variables.

See also path, PATH, **pathname**

SECONDS

A Korn shell environment variable that contains the number of seconds since the shell was started.

sed

The Unix stream or batch editor. sed is more like a filter command than the traditional Unix text editors vi or emacs. It takes data from the standard input or from a file, applies a transformation to the data, and sends the changed data to the standard output. If you want to capture this output to a file, you must redirect standard output to the file.

Syntax
The syntax for sed is:

```
sed [options][files]
```

Here's how sed operates:

- ▶ Each line of input is copied into a buffer called the *pattern space*.

- ▶ All the editing commands in the sed script are applied to the data in the order in which they are specified. This can sometimes have unexpected results because sed applies every editing command to the first input line before reading the second input line, rather than, as some people imagine, applying the first editing command to all lines in the file before applying the second editing command.

- ▶ Editing commands are applied to all lines globally, unless they are restricted by line addressing.

- ▶ If a command changes the input, all subsequent commands will act on the current, changed line, rather than the original text. A pattern that once matched the original text may no longer match if that text has been changed.

- ▶ Output is written to the standard output, but you can redirect it to a file.

Options and Arguments
The options listed in Table S.3 are available with sed.

TABLE S.3: Options to Use with sed

Option	Description
-e *command*	Applies the editing *command* to the file.
-f *script*	Applies the editing instructions contained in *script*.
-n	Turns off echoing of lines to the standard output once all commands have been applied.

sed Scripts

The general form of a sed script is:

    [address[,address]]function[arguments]

where the addresses are optional. If you leave them out, sed applies the *function* to all input lines; otherwise, they are restricted to the specified address or range of addresses. The *function* is a sed editing command, and the *arguments* depend on which *function* you use. An *address* can be zero, one, or two line numbers; an *address* can also be a regular expression. Table S.4 lists the main sed editing commands.

You can also use ! as a NOT, and you can enclose a group of commands in braces so that they all act upon a single address.

See also awk, ed, grep

TABLE S.4: Major sed Editing Commands

Command	Description
d	Deletes a line.
n	Processes the next line of input with the next function, rather than resuming at the beginning of the sed script.
a	Appends one or more lines to the currently selected line.
i	Inserts one or more lines before the currently selected line.
c	Changes the selected line.
s	Substitutes a replacement pattern with a new pattern for each addressed line.
p	Writes selected lines to the standard output.
w *filename*	Writes selected lines to the specified *filename*.
r *filename*	Reads the contents of the specified *filename* and appends it to the selected line.
q	Stops sed processing.

select

A Korn shell programming construct that displays a numbered list of items and lets a user select one of them. A `select` statement might look like this:

```
select element [in list]
do
        commands
done
```

If no `list` is specified, items are read from the standard input. After the items in `list` are displayed, `select` displays the PS3 prompt string to receive the user's selection; if the user makes a valid selection, *commands* are executed.

semicolon

▶ The ; character. Used as a command separator in C programming and shell scripts.

▶ A special character used to separate multiple commands on the command line.

In speech, the semicolon is often referred to as simply "semi," as in "semi-semi-star" meaning ; ; *.

sendbug

A BSD command that sends a bug report, written in a standard format, to 4bsd-bugs@Berkeley.edu.

sendmail

A Unix program that acts as a mail transport agent in an e-mail system, receiving messages from a user's e-mail program such as Pine or `elm`, and then routing the mail to the correct destination. Normal Unix users rarely come into direct contact with `sendmail`.

See also `elm`, `smail`, **SMTP**

sentence

In the `vi` text editor, any string of characters ending in a period, comma, question mark, or exclamation mark, which is followed by at least two spaces or a newline character.

set

A built-in shell command used to set variable values. When used without arguments, set lists the values of all variables known to the current shell.

See also **Bourne shell, C shell, Korn shell,** setenv

set uid bit

A file permission that gives the file the permissions of its owner rather than the permissions of the user who called it. This is often done so that a person running a program can access files that he or she would normally not be allowed to access. For example, a multiuser database system might use a process validation program with superuser privileges to allow it to gain access to system process information every time a user (who does not have superuser privileges) logs on to the system.

setenv

A built-in C shell command that assigns a value to a named environment variable; by convention, the name must be in uppercase. The syntax is:

```
setenv [name[value]]
```

value can be either a single word or a quoted string; if no *value* is specified, the null value is used. If you don't specify any arguments, setenv lists the names and values of all environment variables.

See also set

sh

Command used to invoke the Bourne shell, the original Unix command processor.

Syntax

Here's the syntax:

```
sh [options][arguments]
```

Options and Arguments

Table S.5 lists the command-line options you can use with sh.

You may find that different implementations of sh vary somewhat; it is available in some form on almost all Unix systems because it is the preferred shell for running shell scripts.

TABLE S.5: Options to Use with sh

Option	Description
-a	Automatically exports variables after they have been defined or changed.
-c *string*	Reads commands from the specified *string*.
-e	Exits if a command returns a non-zero exit status.
-f	Ignores the filename metacharacters * ? [ ].
-h	Locates commands as they are defined.
-i	Starts an interactive shell.
-k	Assignment of a value to a variable can take place anywhere on the command line.
-m	Enables job control.
-n	Reads commands but does not execute them.
-p	Starts up without processing commands contained in .profile.
-r	Starts a restricted shell; same as rsh.
-s	Reads commands from the standard input, sends output from built-in commands to file descriptor 1, and all other shell output goes to file descriptor 2.
-t	Executes one command and then exits.
-u	Treats unset variables as errors rather than null.
-v	Displays the shell command line.
-x	Turns on shell-script debugging.

Examples

To run sh in a mode to debug shell scripts, use:

    sh -vx

The -x option echoes each command you enter, and -v echoes any data replacement in the shell script.

See also Bash, csh, ksh, rksh, rsh, Tcsh, Zsh

shar

A widely used archiver, written by Bill Davidsen, that allows you to create an archive in text form that you can then include in an e-mail message.

Syntax

The syntax for this command is:

    shar [options]file...

Options and Arguments

Table S.6 lists the command-line options available with shar; use redirection to send output from this command to a file.

TABLE S.6: Options to Use with shar

Option	Description
-b	Assumes all files are binary and converts them to text using uuencode.
-c	Adds a "cut here" line at the beginning of each output file.
-d*delim*	Uses *delim* as the delimiter character between files in the archive.
-D	Includes the date, user, and name of the current directory when the archive was created.
-f	Uses just the filename part of each pathname for the output file in the archive; this lets you unpack each file from the archive into the current directory.
-l*size*	Limits the archive to *size* kilobytes.
-M	Assumes files are both text and binary; binary files are converted to text using uuencode.
-o*filename*	Sends output to the specified *filename*.
-s	Checks files for damage using the sum command.
-v	Displays all messages; verbose mode.
-x	Prevents overwriting of existing files when unpacking an archive.

Examples

To place a group of files in a shar archive and put this archive into a file called document.shar, use:

```
shar memo.one memo.two memo.three > document.shar
```

To unpack and extract these files, use the sh command. This runs the file as a shell script to unpack the archive automatically:

```
sh document.shar
```

E Notes

A file created by this utility will have the filename extension .shar.

See also compress, mail, tar, uuencode

shell

The Unix system command processor. The shell accepts commands from the user, interprets them, and passes them on to the operating system for processing. Most shells also include a programming language interpreter so that users can write small programs without having to invoke a complete language compiler.

The three major shells are the Bourne shell (the original Unix shell from AT&T), the C shell (developed as part of the BSD Unix efforts), and the Korn shell (also developed by AT&T). In recent years several public-domain shells have become very popular, including Bash (the Bourne-again shell) often used on Linux, Tcsh, and Zsh.

SHELL

An environment variable that contains the name of the user's preferred shell.

shell escape

The ! character, when used from within a program to indicate that the next command should be passed to the shell for processing, rather than acted upon locally inside the program. Once the command executes, you exit from the shell and automatically return to your previous state within the program.

See also shell out

shell file

See shell script

shell function

A series of commands stored by the shell for execution at some later time. Shell functions are similar to shell scripts but they run faster because they are stored in memory rather than in files on disk. Also, a shell function is run in the same environment as the shell that calls it, whereas a shell script is usually run in a subshell.

shell option

In the Korn shell, a variable that acts like a toggle or an on/off switch. In the C shell, such a variable is known as a *shell variable*.

shell out

Jargon for creating a new shell while you are still in an existing program such as an editor or mailer.

See also shell escape

shell program

Any program written in the shell programming language and interpreted by a shell process; also known as a *shell script*. The shell programming languages are all very similar, with the most important differences appearing in the flow-control structures, including if...then and while loops.

Shell programs are usually written to automate complex or infrequently used tasks. When the shell program gets too large and cumbersome, you are often better off translating the program into C, particularly if speed of execution is important.

See also Bash, Bourne shell, C shell, shell programming language

shell programming language

A programming language provided by the Unix shell. A shell program is often developed quickly to speed up a mundane task or automate a little-used procedure.

The shell programming languages are interpreted and provide flow control, the ability to execute Unix utilities, input/output redirection, and simple variable manipulation. The shell programming languages are best suited to those tasks that can take advantage of existing Unix utilities and are not good at tasks that perform extensive arithmetic or require high performance.

See also Bash, Bourne shell, C shell, perl, shell script

shell prompt

An indication from the shell that it is ready to receive the next command from the command line. By default, the percent sign (%) is the C shell prompt, and the dollar sign ($) is the Bourne shell prompt.

See also PS1, PS2, PS3, PS4

shell script

Any program written in the shell programming language and interpreted by a shell process; also known as a *shell program*.

See also shell program

shell variable

In the C shell, a variable that represents a value. Some shell variables act as on/off switches, while others contain a string of characters.

In the Korn shell, a shell variable is the same as a global variable.

See also environment variables, shell option

shift

> ▶ A C shell programming keyword used to shift the words in a specified wordlist variable. The syntax is:
>
> shift [*variable*]

If no *variable* is specified, this command shifts the command-line arguments; $2 becomes $1, $3 becomes $2, and so on. shift is typically used in a while loop.

> ▶ A Bourne shell and Korn shell programming keyword used to shift the command-line arguments; $2 becomes $1, $3 becomes $2, and so on. If you specify an integer value, the command-line arguments are shifted the specified number of places to the left. In the Korn shell, this value can be an integer expression.

shl

An SVR4 command used to run more than one shell from a single terminal.

See also layers

shutdown

> ▶ A shell script used by the system administrator to shut down the system in a logical and orderly manner.
>
> ▶ Turning off the power to the system.

See also shutdown, **shutting down the system**

shutdown

An SVR4 command used by the system administrator or superuser to perform an orderly system shutdown.

Syntax

The syntax to use with shutdown is:

shutdown [*options*]

On SVR4 systems you find shutdown in /usr/sbin, on BSD systems in /usr/etc, and on SCO systems in /etc.

Options and Arguments

The options you can use with shutdown do vary somewhat between different Unix systems; Table S.7 lists the options available on SVR4.

The shutdown command goes through an orderly sequence of events to ensure a safe and complete system halt. First, it terminates all user processes and goes from a multiuser state to a single-user state. `shut-down` then posts a warning message, waits for 60 seconds, posts a final message, and then prompts for confirmation that you still want to take the system down.

See also `init`, `state`

TABLE S.7: Options to Use with shutdown

Option	Description
-gn	Uses a grace period of *n* seconds rather than the default 60 seconds.
-ik	Tells the `init` command to place the system in the state specified by *k*.
-y	Suppresses the default confirmation prompt.

shutting down the system

A procedure performed by the system administrator to stop the operating system in an orderly way so that users do not lose work. The system may be shut down for a variety of reasons, including preventative maintenance, troubleshooting hardware problems, or the installation or upgrade of hardware.

The system administrator usually runs a shell script named `/usr/sbin/shutdown` on SVR4, `/usr/etc` on Solaris, or `/etc` on SCO; refer to your system manual for more details. This script brings the system down gracefully by killing existing processes and synchronizing disks by writing the contents of the cache out to disk.

See also `init`

signal

A short message that the Unix kernel or the user can send to a process, usually indicating some sort of abnormal condition.

When a process receives a signal, one of three things may happen: the process may follow the default action of the signal if there is such a default; the process may be forced to terminate; or the process may execute special code to handle the signal.

See also kill

single quote symbol

The ' character. You can use single quotes around a part of the command line where you want the shell to override the meaning of any metacharacters in your commands. For example, the asterisk (*) is often used as a wild card, but becomes merely an asterisk when enclosed in single quotes.

See also **backquote, double quote, quoting**

single-user state

A Unix state in which only the system administrator has access to the system, and only the root filesystem is mounted. No multiuser processes can run, and the system can be accessed only through the console. Single-user state is most often used when the system administrator is troubleshooting the system or making repairs to the filesystem. Single-user state is also used just after the system boots and just before it shuts down.

See also `init`

size

A software development command used to display the data and text segment sizes of an object or binary file.

See also `gprof`, `lprof`, `nm`, `prof`

Slackware Linux

See **Linux**

slash

The / character. The slash is used to separate elements (file and directory names) in a pathname and is also the name of the root filesystem.

See also **absolute pathname, relative pathname, root**

sleep

To suspend execution of a process. Processes in Unix sleep when waiting for input/output to complete, when waiting for the death of a child process, or when suspended by a user. When a process wakes up again, it continues execution from the point at which it was suspended.

See also `sleep`, **wakeup**

sleep

A command that suspends animation for a specified time.

The syntax is:

```
sleep seconds
```

where *seconds* represents the length of time that you want to delay the process. This command is often used in shell scripts.

See also at

smail

A Unix program that acts as a mail transport agent in an e-mail system, receiving messages from a user's e-mail program, such as Pine or elm, and then routing the mail to the correct destination. Most users of Unix will never come into contact with smail.

See also elm, sendmail

smit

The system administration program on IBM's AIX. smit has both X Window and ASCII terminal user interfaces, as well as extensive online help. You can use smit to configure networking options and devices, install and upgrade software, manage and tune the system operating parameters, and look at and change print job priorities. There are also troubleshooting and diagnostic routines available.

See also sysadmsh

SMP

See symmetrical multiprocessing

SMTP

Abbreviation for simple mail transport protocol. The TCP/IP protocol for exchanging e-mail. Many third-party vendors sell host software for Unix capable of exchanging SMTP e-mail with proprietary e-mail systems such as IBM's PROFS.

SMTP provides a direct end-to-end mail delivery, which is rather unusual; most mail systems use store-and-forward protocols.

See also MIME

socket

An interprocess communications mechanism used in networking. Sockets allow processes that are not running at the same time or on the same system and that are not children of the same parent to exchange information; pairs of cooperating sockets manage communications between the processes on your computer and those on the remote system in a networked environment.

You can read data from, or write data to, a socket just as you can to a file. Socket pairs are bidirectional; either process can send data to the other. Sockets allow the utilities `telnet`, `rlogin` (remote login), and `rcp` (remote copy) to work.

Sockets were first implemented in the BSD-based versions of Unix and are identified by the letter `s` in the file type character of a long format `ls` file listing.

See also FIFO file, pipe

soelim

A Unix text processing command that reads an `nroff/troff` input file and strips out all of the `.so` commands, replacing them with the contents of the specified file. The `.so` (switch out) command reads the contents of another file into the current input file.

soft link

To reference one file to another by using a pathname rather than by a specific i-node address. By using an absolute pathname, soft links can cross filesystems.

See also hard link, link

Solaris

A version of Unix from SunSoft that runs on Intel-based PCs and Sun workstations; SunSoft is a subsidiary of Sun Microsystems.

Solaris is based on Unix System V Release 4, and includes networking support, the OpenWindows graphical user interface, and DeskSet, an integrated desktop that includes almost 20 productivity tools.

See also SunOS

sort

To arrange a set of individual elements into some kind of logical sequence, usually into alphabetical, numerical, or ASCII order, although files can be sorted by some other criteria such as time and or date. Additionally, a sort may be ascending or descending.

sort

A command that sorts the contents of text files.

Syntax
Here's the syntax to use:

```
sort [options][files]
```

The sort command sorts lines within a text file and then writes the output to the standard output or to a specified file. Output lines are sorted character by character, left to right; if you specify more than one file as input, the files are sorted and collated.

Options and Arguments
If you don't specify an option, sort orders the file in the machine collating sequence, which is usually ASCII. The options for use with sort are detailed in Table S.8.

sort is often used in conjunction with uniq to remove duplicate or partially duplicate lines from a text file.

TABLE S.8: Options to Use with sort

Option	Description
-b	Ignores leading blanks (tabs or spaces), making sort treat blanks as field delimiters with no value.
-c	Checks to see if the file is already sorted and, if it is, performs no action.
-d	Sorts in dictionary order, ignoring all punctuation and control characters.
-f	Considers all lowercase letters to be in uppercase; used when sorting files that contain both uppercase and lowercase text.
-i	Ignores nonprinting characters (those outside the range of decimal 32 to 126) when performing a non-numeric sort.
-m	Assumes multiple input files are already in sorted order and merges them without checking.
-M	Selects the first three nonblank characters, shifts them to uppercase, and sorts them into month order from JAN to DEC; invalid entries are placed at the beginning of the list.
-n	Performs a numeric sort, observing minus signs and decimal points; blanks are ignored.

TABLE S.8 continued: Options to Use with sort

OPTION	DESCRIPTION
-ofilename	Stores the output from sort in the specified file rather than sending it to the standard output.
-r	Reverses the direction of the sort.
-tc	Specifies c as the separator character in the input file.
-u	Identical lines from the input file are output only once.
-ymemory	Reduces the amount of memory available to sort; without this option, sort uses all available space. Specify memory in kilobytes; use 0 to make sort run in the smallest possible space.
-zrec	Specifies rec as the maximum line length when merging files and prevents sort from abnormally terminating if it reads an extremely long line; do not use this option if you are sorting files.

Examples

To sort the file names and write the output to the sorted file names .sort, use:

```
sort -o names.sort names
```

You can sort the contents of several files, combining the output into a single file:

```
sort section[a-d] -o section.sorted
```

This command sorts four files, sectiona through sectiond and stores the output in the file called section.sorted.

See also comm, join, uniq

source

A built-in C shell command used to read and execute commands from a C shell script file. If you use:

```
source ~/.cshrc
```

you can re-execute the contents of the .cshrc startup file without logging out and immediately logging back in again.

In the Bourne shell and Korn shell, the dot, or period, command (.) performs the same function.

spell

A command that compares the contents of a file to the system dictionary and reports all the misspelled words.

Syntax

Here's the syntax to use with `spell`:

```
spell [options][files]
```

The output from `spell` is a list of words that cannot be found in the dictionary. The list is arranged in alphabetical order and is sent to the standard output. If you specify more than one file, `spell` generates one list of words for all the files.

Options and Arguments

Table S.9 details the options you can use with `spell`.

The `spell` command is by no means a foolproof way of finding errors; in English, so much depends on context. `spell` does not identify correctly spelled but misused words.

TABLE S.9: Options to Use with spell

Option	Description
-b	Accepts British spelling of words such as *colour*, *honour*, *centre*, and *travelled*.
-l	Follows all `nroff` and `troff` include files (all files referenced in `.so` and `.nx` requests).
-v	Displays all words not literally in the system dictionary; words that can be derived from the dictionary are displayed, showing a possible derivation.
-x	Displays every possible stem for each word on the standard error.
+*wordlist*	Specifies *wordlist* as an additional dictionary file; *wordlist* should be a sorted file containing one word per line. This option is very useful for adding proper names and technical terms.

Examples

To check the file `chapter.one` for errors and write any words not in the system dictionary to a file called `corrections`, use:

```
spell chapter.one > corrections
```

See also `sort`, `uniq`

splat

Jargon for the asterisk character (*) that you can yell across a crowded, noisy room without fear of being misunderstood.

See also **bang**

spline

A BSD and SCO command that interpolates a smooth curve between data points.

Syntax

The syntax for the spline command is:

```
spline [options]
```

The spline command takes pairs of numbers from the standard input as abscissa and ordinates of a function and plots them on the standard output; there is a limit of 1,000 input points.

Options and Arguments

The options available for use with this command are listed in Table S.10.

See also graph, plot

TABLE S.10: Options Available with spline

Option	Description
-an	Automatically provides the abscissa with spacing of n or 1 if n is not a number.
-kn	Specifies the constant n used in the boundary value calculation.
-nn	Specifies the spacing n between x-axis values; the default is 100.
-p	Makes the output periodic.
-x$l u$	Sets the l lower and u upper x-axis limits.

split

A command that divides a text file into a number of smaller pieces. The syntax is:

```
split [option][infile][outfile]
```

infile is the name of the input file, and this file remains untouched during the processing. It is divided into files called *outfile*aa, *outfile*ab, and so on. If you don't specify an *infile*, the standard input is used instead.

The single option, -n, lets you specify the number of lines each *outfile* should contain; the default is 1000 lines.

See also cat, csplit, cut, sed

spool

Acronym formed from simultaneous peripheral operation online. Software designed to manage one or more peripheral devices, particularly printers, by temporarily storing the output on disk until the printer is available.

See also queue, /spool

/spool

A directory that contains any print jobs waiting to be printed by the spooler.

spooler

The software that manages print jobs sent to a shared or network printer when that printer is busy. Each print job is stored on disk in a separate file and is printed in turn when the printer becomes available. Sometimes called a *print spooler.*

See also queue, spool, /spool

SPX

Abbreviation for Sequenced Packet Exchange. A set of Novell NetWare protocols implemented on top of IPX to form a transport layer.

SPX provides additional capabilities over IPX. For example, it guarantees packet delivery by having the destination device verify that the data was received correctly; if no response is received within a specific time, SPX retransmits the packet. If several retransmissions fail to return an acknowledgment, SPX assumes that the connection has failed and informs the operator. All packets in the transmission are sent in sequence, and they all take the same path to their destination.

See also IPX

square brackets

The characters [ ]. Special characters that enclose character sets in regular expressions. In the C shell, square brackets enclose array indices.

See also braces

srchtxt

A command used to search message files for a regular expression.

See also exstr, gettxt, mkmsgs

stack

A reserved area of memory used to keep track of a program's internal operations, including functions' return addresses, passed parameters, and so on. A stack is usually maintained as a "last in, first out" (LIFO) data structure, so that the last item added to the structure is the first item used.

standard directories

The basic layout of the Unix filesystem is fairly constant with some variations occurring between systems from different vendors. Table S.11 lists the main directories you will encounter in SVR4; your own system will undoubtedly add many more directories.

TABLE S.11: Unix Standard Directories

DIRECTORY	DESCRIPTION
/	The root directory, which is always present, and the ancestor of all files in the filesystem.
/dev	Contains device files, including terminals, printers, and hard disks.
/etc	Contains system administration and configuration files, the most important of which is /etc/passwd.
/home	The directory containing the home directories of all users on the system.
/opt	The root directory for filesystems used by add-on applications.
/sbin	Contains programs used when booting the system and in system recovery.
/spool	Contains the directories for spooling files.
/spool/lp	Contains spooling files for the printer.
/spool/uucp	Contains files queued for UUCP.
/spool/uucppublic	Contains files placed here by UUCP.
/stand	Contains the standard programs and configuration files used when booting the system.
/tmp	Contains temporary files created by Unix.
/usr	Contains user-accessible programs.
/usr/bin	Contains executable programs and utilities.
/usr/ucb	Contains the BSD compatability package.
/usr/sbin	Contains executable programs for system administration.
/usr/games	Contains Unix games.
/usr/lib	Contains libraries for programs and for programming languages.
/var	Contains files whose contents vary as the system runs.
/var/admin	Contains system logging and accounting files.
/var/mail	Contains user mail files.
/var/news	Contains messages for users.
/var/opt	The root of a subtree of files for add-on applications.
/var/tmp	Contains temporary files.
/var/uucp	Contains UUCP files.

standard error

A file to which a program can send output, usually of error messages. Standard error is associated with file descriptor 2. Unless you use redirection, standard error output goes to the terminal. Also called *stderr*.

See also Bourne shell, C shell, Korn shell

standard input

A file from which a program can receive input. Standard input is associated with file descriptor 0. Unless you use redirection, standard input comes from the keyboard.

Also called *standard in* or *stdin*.

See also Bourne shell, C shell, Korn shell

standard output

A file to which a program can send output. Standard output is associated with file descriptor 1. Unless you use redirection, standard output goes to the terminal. Also called *standard out* or *stdout*.

See also Bourne shell, C shell, Korn shell

start bit

In asynchronous communications, a start bit is transmitted to indicate the beginning of a new data word.

See also data bits, parity, stop bit

startup file

A file that the login shell executes when you first log in to the system. Both the Bourne shell and Korn shell run a file called .profile; the C shell runs a file called .login; and bash runs .bash_profile. The C shell also runs a file called .cshrc when you invoke a new C shell; the Korn shell runs a file called .kshrc; and bash runs a file called .bashrc.

Startup files are used to customize shell functions and to store aliases.

See also dot file

state

The level of access granted to a user. The two fundamental Unix states are the single-user state, which limits access to the system administrator, and the more usual multiuser state, which gives access to many users.

Both of these states can be divided into further states by the system administrator; the most important states are shown in Table S.12.

TABLE S.12: Unix System States

SYSTEM STATE	DESCRIPTION
state 0	Shutdown state
state 1	Administrative state
state 2	Multiuser state
state 3	Remote file sharing state
state 4	User-defined state
state 5	Firmware state
state 6	Stop and reboot state

status

In the C shell, an environment variable used to indicate the status of the last command you executed; 0 represents a successful completion, while 1 represents failure.

stderr

See standard error

stdin

See standard input

stdout

See standard output

stop

A built-in Bourne shell command used to suspend a background job specified by its job identifier. The syntax is:

```
stop jobID
```

stop bit

In asynchronous communications, stop bits are transmitted to indicate the end of the current data word. Depending on the convention in use, either one or two stop bits are used.

See also parity, start bit

strings

A command that extracts printable ASCII strings from a binary file.

Syntax

The syntax to use is:

```
strings [options] files
```

Options and Arguments

The `strings` command defines a printable string as being four or more characters in length, terminated by a newline or a null. The options you can use with `strings` are detailed in Table S.13.

See also hexdump, od

TABLE S.13: Options for Use with strings

Option	Description
-a	Searches the whole file; you can also specify this option as -.
-n*n*	Specifies the minimum length of a string as *n* characters; the default is 4.
-o	Displays the string's offset position before the string.

strip

A command that removes unnecessary information from executable files, reducing their size to save disk space. `strip` deletes information used by debuggers, assemblers, and some loaders. This is a one-way process, so make sure that you no longer need the information before you run `strip`.

See also ld

struct

A BSD software development command used to translate a specified Fortran program into Ratfor.

stty

A command used by the superuser to display or set terminal parameters.

Syntax

Here's the syntax:

```
stty [options][modes]
```

Options and Arguments

Using `stty` you can control many terminal settings, including baud rate and parity, character size, and the type of handshaking. The *modes* are chosen from an extremely long list of terminal attributes; see your system documentation for more details. The options you can use with `stty` are listed in Table S.14.

TABLE S.14: Options to Use with stty

Option	Description
-a	Lists all settings.
-g	Lists the current settings in a way that can be used as input to `stty`.

Notes

Both the physical settings on the terminal and the system setup must match; otherwise, communications will stop.

The `stty` command changes the way in which the system's `tty` driver works.

See also `tput`, `tset`

style

A BSD command that reports on the writing style used in a document.

Syntax

The syntax for `style` is as follows:

```
style [options] filename...
```

Options and Arguments

The options you can use with `style` are listed in Table S.15. `style` displays a readability index and reports on sentence length and construction, word length, word usage, verb type, and expletives.

See also `diction`

TABLE S.15: Options to Use with style

Option	Description
-a	Calculates sentence length and readability index.
-e	Displays all sentences starting with an expletive.
-l*n*	Displays all sentences longer than *n* words.

TABLE S.15 continued: Options to Use with style

OPTION	DESCRIPTION
-ml	Skips lists contained in the document.
-mm	Skips macros contained in the document.
-p	Displays all sentences containing a passive verb.
-P	Labels text in the document according to word type.
-rn	Displays all sentences with a readability index of more than n.

su

A command that temporarily substitutes another user ID for your own.

Syntax
The syntax to use with su is as follows:

```
su username arguments
```

The su command is often used by the system administrator when changing to the superuser account.

E Options and Arguments
The su command temporarily switches your user ID to that specified by *username*. *su* prompts you to enter a password, just as if you were logging in, and the contents of your shell configuration file are executed. Any *arguments* specified on the command line are passed to the shell.

On many systems, specifying a dash tells su to execute a full login to the user's environment. The command:

```
su -name
```

runs the .login file in the C shell or the .profile file in the Bourne and Korn shells for the specified *name*. If you don't use the - option, your current environment is transferred to the new login.

See also env, **login**, passwd

subdirectory

A directory that is located within another directory. In Unix, all directories except the root directory are subdirectories. In day-to-day conversation subdirectory is often abbreviated to directory.

subshell

A shell, forked as a duplicate of the parent shell, that executes a specified command or list of commands within that shell. Also, when you surround commands with parentheses, they are run in a subshell.

sum

A command that calculates and prints a checksum for a file and displays the number of 512-byte blocks the file occupies. The syntax is:

```
sum [option]filename
```

The single option, -r, calculates an alternative checksum used by BSD systems.

See also wc

supercomputer

The most powerful class of computer. The term was first applied to the Cray-1 series. Supercomputers can cost over $50 million each. The Cray T3E has a top speed of more than two trillion operations per second, or two teraflops. They are used by large government agencies and major companies for tasks such as weather forecasting and complex three-dimensional modeling.

See also parallel processing

superuser

A specially privileged user who has access to anything that a normal user has access to and more. The system administrator must become the superuser to create new accounts, change passwords, and perform other administrative tasks that ordinary users are not allowed to carry out for security reasons. The superuser's login name is usually root with a user ID of 0.

swconfig

An SCO command used to display software configuration information.

Syntax
The syntax for this command is:

```
swconfig [options]
```

Options and Arguments

swconfig lists information located in /usr/lib/custom/history.
You can use the options listed in Table S.16 with this command.

See also hwconfig

TABLE S.16: Options to Use with swconfig

OPTION	DESCRIPTION
-a	Lists all information sorted in reverse chronological order.
-p	Lists software package information.

switch

A C shell programming construct used to execute commands based on
the value of a variable. switch is often used when a shell script must
manage more than the three choices handled by an if-then-else
statement. If the value of the variable matches the first pattern, the first
set of commands are executed; if it matches the second pattern, then the
second set of commands are executed, and so on. If the variable does not
match any of the patterns, then the commands under the default case
are executed. A breaksw statement exits from the switch after the
commands are executed.

See also breaksw, case, endsw, esac

sync

A command that is either run automatically or is initiated by the system
administrator when preparing to shutdown the system. The sync command ends all input/output operations, updates changes made in memory,
and writes all these changes out to disk, flushing the disk cache buffers so
that the information on the hard disk is absolutely up-to-date.

syntax

The formal rules of grammar as they apply to a specific programming language or operating system command; in particular, the exact sequence
and spelling of command elements required for the command to be correctly interpreted.

syntax error

An error in the use of a programming language or operating system command syntax—for example, misspelling a keyword or omitting a required space.

/sys

A BSD root directory that is reserved for utilities used for working with the kernel.

sysadmsh

A menu-driven system administration package from SCO, which can be started from the command line or from the Open Desktop. Using sysadmsh you can add and remove users; perform backups; manage the print system, files, and directories; prepare disks and tapes; configure system resources; and prepare reports on system status.

system administrator

The person charged with the responsibility of managing the system; often abbreviated to SA. On a very large installation, the system administrator may in fact be several people or even a small department; if you are running Linux on your PC at home, then you have to be your own system administrator.

See also SAGE, superuser

T

tabs

A command used to set tab stops on your terminal. The default Unix tabs are set eight spaces apart across the screen, but you can use tabs to set them wherever you like. Input is a comma-separated list of numbers or a filename containing this information. Your terminal must support host-set tab stops for this command to work correctly.

See also newform

tail

A command that displays the last ten lines of a text file.

Syntax

The syntax to use with `tail` is as follows:

```
tail [options][filename]
```

Options and Arguments

The `tail` command used without options displays the last ten lines of *filename*; if no *filename* is specified, `tail` reads from the standard input.

If a plus sign precedes an option, `tail` displays characters, lines, or blocks counting from the beginning of the file; if a hyphen precedes the option, `tail` counts from the end of the file. The options you can use with `tail` are detailed in Table T.1.

TABLE T.1:   Options to Use with tail

Option	Description
+*n*	Displays the number of characters, lines, or blocks specified by *n*, counting from the beginning of the input.
-*n*	Displays the number of characters, lines, or blocks specified by *n*, counting from the end of the input.
-b	Specifies blocks when used after +*n* or -*n*.
-c	Specifies characters when used after +*n* or -*n*.
-f	Enters an endless loop after displaying the last part of the file and waits for additional input. This can be useful for monitoring a background process which is sending its output to the file; use the `kill` command to terminate `tail`.
-l	Specifies lines when used after +*n* or -*n*.
-r	Reverses the specified order.

Examples

To display the last three lines of the file `phonelist`, use:

```
tail -3l phonelist
```

See also head, `less`, `more`, pg

talk

A command that opens a two-way, terminal-to-terminal communications path. Here is the syntax you need to use with `talk`:

```
talk [username][tty]
```

where *username* is the name of the other person you want to talk to. If the person uses the same computer that you do, you can use their login name; otherwise, you have to add the name of their system in the form *user@hostname*. Once the connection is established, you send messages back and forth just by typing them in. If the user you want to contact is logged in more than once, use the `tty` argument to specify which terminal you want to talk to. Type Ctrl-L to redraw your screen, and type Ctrl-D when you are ready to exit. The `talk` command has no options.

See also mail, mailx, mesg, who, write

tar

A command that can create, list, add to, and retrieve files from an archive file, which is usually stored on tape.

Syntax
The syntax for `tar` is:

```
tar option[modifiers][file-list]
```

The *options* and *modifiers* for `tar` vary considerably from Unix system to system, even among SVR4- or BSD-style systems. In the discussion that follows, only the most common arguments are covered; see the `tar` man pages for specific information on your own system.

Options and Arguments
You tell `tar` what you want it to do by specifying one *option* from Table T.2 and then adding one or more *modifiers* from Table T.3 to fine-tune the *option*. The modifiers do not require a leading hyphen.

Following these arguments is the *file-list* that lists the filenames of the files you want to read in or write out. If you use a directory name in *file-list*, `tar` references all files and subdirectories within that directory.

TABLE T.2: Options to Use with tar

OPTION	DESCRIPTION
c	Creates a new archive file, overwriting any previous archive on the tape or disk.
r	Appends the *file-list* to an existing archive; existing files are unchanged.
t	Lists the contents of the archive.
u	Performs an update, appending files to the archive if they are not already present or if they have been modified since they were originally written to the archive. This option can run very slowly due to all the checking it must do, so use it with care.
x	Extracts *file-list* from an archive; if *file-list* is not specified, this option extracts all the files from the archive.

TABLE T.3: Modifiers to Use with tar

MODIFIER	DESCRIPTION
b*n*	Specifies a blocking factor of *n*; the default is 1, and the maximum is 20.
f *device*	Uses the specified archive *device*. If *device* is specified as -, tar uses the standard input, and this lets you use tar in a pipeline.
L	Displays error messages if links to archived files cannot be resolved.
M	Updates file modification times to the time of extraction from the archive.
o	Disregards ownership information when extracting a file from an archive.
v	Displays the name of each file as it is archived or extracted.
w	Waits for user confirmation before taking any action.
z	Compresses and expands the archive using gzip and gunzip.
Z	Compresses and expands the archive using compress and uncompress.

Examples

To store all the files in your home directory and all files and subdirectories in that directory in an archive on the default tape drive, use:

```
tar -cv /home/pd
a /home/pd/ch.one 51 blocks
a /home/pd/ch.two 41 blocks
a /home/pd/ch.three 47 blocks
a /home/pd/ch.four 67 blocks
```

The v modifier makes tar list all the files as it writes them to tape, erasing anything that was previously on the tape.

Notes

You can use ambiguous file references or wildcards when you write files but not when you read them; this is because tar does not perform filename expansion. Filename expansion is done by the shell, and the results are passed to tar. This can be a problem when you have deleted a file by accident and want to extract the file from an archive. Because the file doesn't exist as part of the filesystem, the shell cannot complete the filename expansion to match these nonexistent files.

Files are extracted from an archive in the same way that they were originally created. If you write a file using a relative pathname, it will appear with that same relative pathname, starting from the current directory, when you read it back. If you use an absolute pathname, tar uses the same absolute pathname when it reads the file back.

See also cpio, ls

Tar archive

A tape or file in `tar` format. A `tar` archive has the filename extension `.tar`.

See also `tar`

tbl

A preprocessor for the `nroff/troff` text-processing system capable of formatting tables.

Syntax

The syntax to use with `tbl` is:

```
tbl [options][filename]
```

`tbl` reads a `troff` file that contains pairs of special codes. The beginning of a table is always marked by the `.TS` macro, and the end of a table by the `.TE` macro, while the internal structure of the table is defined by other macro commands that can:

- ▶ Left or right justify or center data in a column
- ▶ Align numbers on their decimal points
- ▶ Add horizontal or vertical lines to a table
- ▶ Allow entries to span several rows
- ▶ Transform a block of text into table entries

The output from `tbl` is a `troff` input file that includes `troff` instructions for creating the table on the printed page.

Options and Arguments

The options available with `tbl` are listed in Table T.4.

TABLE T.4: Options to Use with tbl

OPTION	DESCRIPTION
-me	Prepends the me macro package to the beginning of the specified *filename*.
-mm	Prepends the mm macro package to the beginning of the specified *filename*.
-ms	Prepends the ms macro package to the beginning of the specified *filename*.
-TX	Creates output using only full linefeeds and not partial linefeeds.

Examples

When you use the Unix text-processing commands in a pipeline, make sure you specify that `tbl` precedes `eqn`; this makes processing more efficient:

```
tbl textfile | troff | lp
```

This sequence formats textfile first with tbl and then with troff, sending the formatted output to the printer.

See also eqn, groff, **LATEX,** me **macros,** mm **macros,** ms **macros,** nroff, pic, **TEX**

/tcb

A directory found on certain SCO systems that contains program files for the Trusted Computing Base (TCB), which give the system a C-2 level security.

tcopy

A BSD command used to copy or verify magnetic tapes.

Syntax

The syntax for this command is:

```
tcopy [options][source[destination]]
```

Options and Arguments

If you specify only a *source*, tcopy displays record and file information for the contents of that tape. If you also specify *destination*, tcopy makes an exact copy of the *source*. The options you can use with tcopy are listed in Table T.5.

TABLE T.5: Options to Use with tcopy

OPTION	DESCRIPTION
-c	Copies *source* to *destination*, and then verifies that the two tapes are identical.
-s*n*	Sets the maximum block size to *n*.
-v	Verifies that the two tapes are identical.
-x	Sends all messages to the standard error.

Examples

To copy the tape on /dev/rmt0 to the tape on /dev/rmt1, use:

tcopy /dev/rmt0 /dev/rmt1

Notes

The tcopy command assumes that there are always two end-of-tape markers at the end of the tape.

See also cp, cpio, tar

TCP

Abbreviation for Transmission Control Protocol. The connection-oriented, transport-level protocol used in the TCP/IP suite of protocols.

See also IP, UDP

TCP/IP

Abbreviation for Transmission Control Protocol/Internet Protocol. A set of communications protocols first developed by the Defense Advanced Research Projects Agency (DARPA) in the late 1970s. The set of TCP/IP protocols encompasses media access, packet transport, session communications, file transfer, e-mail, and terminal emulation:

- ▶ Address Resolution Protocol (ARP), which translates between Internet and Ethernet addresses
- ▶ Internet Control Message Protocol (ICMP), an error-message and control protocol
- ▶ Point-to-Point Protocol (PPP), which provides synchronous and asynchronous network connections
- ▶ Reverse Address Resolution Protocol (RARP), which translates between Ethernet and Internet addresses
- ▶ Serial Line Internet Protocol (SLIP), which implements IP over serial lines
- ▶ Simple Mail Transport Protocol (SMTP), used for mail over TCP/IP
- ▶ Simple Network Management Protocol (SNMP), which performs distributed network management functions
- ▶ User Datagram Protocol (UDP), which provides data transfer but without the reliability of TCP

TCP/IP is supported by a large number of hardware and software vendors and is available on many different computers, from PCs to mainframes. Many corporations, universities, and government agencies use TCP/IP, and it is also the basis of the Internet. To find out more, consult one of the excellent books that have been written on TCP/IP for readers of all technical levels.

See also ftp, IP, TCP, telnet, tn3270

TCP/IP architecture

The TCP/IP set of protocols exist as four layers of software built on top of the fifth layer—the network hardware itself. The four layers are:

▶ Application layer, consisting of applications that use the network

▶ Host-to-host Transport layer, providing end-to-end data delivery services

▶ Internet layer, defining the datagram and managing the routing

▶ Network Access layer, consisting of routines to access the network hardware

Below these theoretical layers, you find the network hardware. When data is received from the network, it travels up through these layers, and when it is sent to the network, it travels down.

See also ISO/OSI model

Tcsh

An upward-compatible replacement for the C shell; pronounced "tee-see-shell."

Development of Tcsh was started in the late 1970s by Ken Greer at Carnegie Mellon University and was continued in the 1980s by Paul Placeway at Ohio State University. Since then, many people have contributed to Tcsh, and it is now maintained by a group at Cornell University. Tcsh is GPLsoftware.

Tcsh adds the following to the C shell:

▶ Easy retrieval of previously executed commands, which can then be edited and re-executed

▶ Interactive editing of the command line

▶ Interactive filename and command name completion

▶ Immediate documentation access as you type a command

▶ Addition of timestamps to the history list

▶ Ability to schedule a command for periodic execution

tee

A program, used within a pipe, that saves data in a specified file and at the same time sends the data to another program. Typically used when you want to review a program's standard output on the screen, while storing it in a file at the same time.

tee

A command that reproduces the standard input to its standard output and to one or more specified files.

Syntax

The syntax for this command is:

```
tee [options]filename ...
```

tee lets you capture in a file the information going to the standard output, while still allowing that information to flow through standard output.

Options and Arguments

The options available with tee are listed in Table T.6.

TABLE T.6: Options to Use with tee

Option	Description
-a	Appends the output to the specified *filename* instead of overwriting the existing contents.
-i	Ignores interrupts.

Examples

To print a report file called draft.final and also save a formatted copy of this report in a file called printed.report, use:

```
pr draft.final | tee printed.report | lp
```

See also cat, echo, script

telnet

A command that lets you communicate with a remote computer using the Telnet protocol. The resulting session behaves as if you had a standard terminal connected directly to the remote host.

Syntax

The usual telnet syntax is:

```
telnet [hostname[port]]
```

Where *hostname* is a domain address or IP address, and *port* specifies the port number on that system you want to log into. Once the connection is established, anything you type on your keyboard is passed to the remote computer, and anything displayed by the remote computer appears on your screen.

Using Command Mode

You can also start the program in command mode if you do not specify a *hostname* on the command line. When you type:

```
telnet
```

command mode starts, and you see the prompt:

```
telnet>
```

on your terminal, which indicates that the program is ready to accept one of the common `telnet` commands listed in Table T.7. If you started `telnet` with a *hostname*, you can also enter command mode by typing Ctrl-].

TABLE T.7: Common telnet Commands

COMMAND	DESCRIPTION
?	Displays a list of `telnet` commands.
close	Closes the connection to the remote system but continues to run `telnet`.
display	Lists the current `telnet` operating parameters.
open *hostname*	Opens a connection to *hostname*.
quit	Closes the connection to the remote system and exits from `telnet`.
set *value*	Sets the `telnet` operating parameters.
status	Displays the current status of `telnet`, including the name of the remote system you are connected to.
unset	Unsets the `telnet` operating parameters.
z	Suspends the session with the remote computer and returns to the login shell on your local system; to resume your `telnet` session, use `fg` at a shell prompt.

Examples

To connect to Internic to find various information on the ownership of domains and their availability, you could use:

```
telnet internic.net
```

Notes

`telnet` does not have a built-in file-transfer mode. To copy a file from the remote system, you must use `ftp`.

Many non-Unix systems also support the Telnet protocol, allowing you to use `telnet` to connect to many different types of systems. Once you use `telnet` to log in, you can often access other services, such as specific applications or special databases.

See also cu, ftp, rlogin, rsh, tn3270

term

> ▸ A C shell variable that holds the name of the terminal type you are using.

> ▸ A client/server application that lets you open several login sessions over the same modem and dial-up connection. This utility is often included with Linux, and other freely available Unix systems.

See also **PPP, SLIP**

termcap

Acronym formed from terminal capability. On BSD systems, the `termcap` file contains a list of terminals and their visual attributes. In SVR4, this function is found in `terminfo` instead.

See also `terminfo`

terminfo

Acronym formed from terminal information. On SVR4 systems, the `terminfo` directory contains many subdirectories, each containing many files. Each of these files is named for, and contains information on, a specific terminal. In BSD systems, this function is found in `termcap` instead.

See also `termcap`

test

A built-in Bourne shell and Korn shell command used to evaluate a condition, and, if the condition is true, return a zero exit status. Otherwise, it returns a non-zero exit status. You can use `test` from the command line, but it is most often used within a shell script.

Syntax

You can use the `test` command in three different ways:

    test condition

or you can use square brackets rather than the word `test`:

    [condition]

and in some versions of the Korn shell, you can use an additional form with two sets of square brackets:

    [[condition]]

In these examples, you must type the square brackets.

Options and Arguments

The *condition* contains one or more criteria for test to evaluate; see Table T.8 for a list.

Because each element within *condition* is a separate argument, you must separate one from another with a space. You can use -a as a logical AND between two criteria—both must be true for test to return a zero exit status—and -o as a logical OR. You can negate any criterion by placing an exclamation mark (!) before it, and you can group criteria using parentheses.

TABLE T.8: test Expressions

EXPRESSION	DESCRIPTION
FILE TESTS	
-b*filename*	True if *filename* exists and is a block special file.
-c*filename*	True if *filename* exists and is a character special file.
-d*filename*	True if *filename* exists and is a directory.
-f*filename*	True if *filename* exists and is an ordinary file.
-g*filename*	True if *filename* exists and its set group ID bit is set.
-G*filename*	True if *filename* exists and its group is the effective group ID.
-k*filename*	True if *filename* exists and its sticky bit is set.
-L*filename*	True if *filename* exists and is a symbolic link.
-O*filename*	True if *filename* exists and its owner is the effective owner.
-p*filename*	True if *filename* exists and is a FIFO special file or named pipe.
-r*filename*	True if *filename* exists and you have read access permission to it.
-s*filename*	True if *filename* exists and its size is greater than zero bytes.
-S*filename*	True if *filename* exists and is a socket special file.
-t*n*	True if the file associated with file descriptor *n* is a terminal.
-u*filename*	True if *filename* exists and its set user ID bit is set.
-w*filename*	True if *filename* exists and you have write access permission to it.
-x*filename*	True if *filename* exists and you have execute access permission to it.
filename1 -ef *filename2*	True if *filename1* is another name for *filename2*; the files are linked or point to the same i-node.
filename1 -nt *filename2*	True if *filename1* is newer than *filename2*.
filename1 -ot *filename2*	True if *filename1* is older than *filename2*.
INTEGER COMPARISONS	
n1 -eq *n2*	True if *n1* equals *n2*.
n1 -ge *n2*	True if *n1* is greater than or equal to *n2*.

TABLE T.8 continued: test Expressions

EXPRESSION	DESCRIPTION
INTEGER COMPARISONS	
n1 -gt *n2*	True if *n1* is greater than *n2*.
n1 -le *n2*	True if *n1* is less than or equal to *n2*.
n1 -lt *n2*	True if *n1* is less than *n2*.
n1 -ne *n2*	True if *n1* is not equal to *n2*.
STRING COMPARISONS	
string	True if string is not null.
string1=*string2*	True if *string1* is identical to *string2*.
string1!=*string2*	True if *string1* is not identical to *string2*.
-n*string*	True if *string* is not empty.
-z*string*	True if *string* has zero length.
COMBINED COMPARISONS	
!*condition*	True if *condition* is false.
(*condition*)	True if *condition* is true.
condition1 -a *condition2*	True if *condition1* and *condition2* are both true.
condition1 -o *condition2*	True if either *condition1* or *condition2* is true.
OPTION TEST	
-o*option*	True if *option* is turned on.

Examples

To test whether a file exists, use:

```
test -r /home/pmd/chapter.one
```

Notes

You must quote any special characters you use within the *condition* so that the shell does not interpret them but passes them on to test.

See also if

TEX

A typesetting language developed by Donald E. Knuth of Stanford University, capable of professional quality typeset text, particularly of mathematical equations and scientific, Japanese, Chinese, Cyrillic, and Arabic text.

The input file to TEX is an ordinary text file that contains control sequences to add the special formatting instructions. Each control sequence starts with a backslash and may appear anywhere, not just at the beginning of the line. Output from TEX does not go to the standard output but goes instead to a file. TEX is not easy for the casual user to master, and there are several TEX macro packages available containing macros designed to solve specific typesetting problems.

TEX is available for DOS, OS/2, Microsoft Windows NT, and the Macintosh, as well as for Unix systems. You can access a very large collection of public-domain tools and documents with anonymous `ftp` at `ftp.shsu.edu`, at `ftp.tex.ac.uk`, or at `ftp.dante.de`. Several commercially supported TEX packages are also available.

See also eqn, **LATEX**, nroff, pic, tbl, troff

Texinfo

A text processing system used by the GNU Project to create both online documentation and printed manuals using TEX. If the GNU Info pages are installed on your system, you will find that they contain complete `Texinfo` documentation.

tfmtodit

A command that creates font files for use with `groff`. This topic is beyond the scope of this book; see the man pages on your system for more details.

tftp

An interactive command, often called *trivial ftp*, used to transfer files between remote systems. Because it has no security associated with it, many system administrators do not support its use and recommend the `ftp` utility instead.

then

A shell programming construct that is normally part of an `if` statement; `then` begins the execution of subsequent commands. A typical statement might look like this:

```
if condition1 then
    statement1
else
    statement2
fi
```

See also elif, else, fi, if

Thread

▶ A concurrent process that is part of a larger process or program. In a multitasking operating system, a single program may contain several threads, all running at the same time. For example, one part of a program can be making a calculation while another part is drawing a graph or chart.

▶ A connected set of postings to a USENET newsgroup. Many newsreaders present postings as threads rather than in strict chronological sequence.

See also multiprocessing, session

tilde escape commands

A command used within the Unix mail program that is always preceded by a tilde (~). Tilde escape commands can be issued while you are entering a message; the tilde must always be the first character on a line, and each tilde escape command must be on a line by itself. Table T.9 summarizes the tilde escape commands.

TABLE T.9: Summary of Tilde Escape Commands

COMMAND	DESCRIPTION
~?	Help. Displays a list of tilde escape commands.
~b *address*	Add the specified *address* to the Blind Copy line.
~c *address*	Add the specified *address* to the Copy line.
~d	Reads in the contents of the dead.letter file.
~e	Starts the preselected text editor.
~f *messages*	Reads in the text of the specified old messages.
~h	Opens a prompt for the header information, including the Copy and Blind Copy information.
~m *messages*	Reads in the text of the specified old messages and shifts right one tab.
~p	Prints the current message with no header.
~q	Quits the mail program and cancels the current message.
~r *filename*	Reads in the contents of the specified *filename*.
~s *subject*	Changes the Subject line to that specified by *subject*.
~t *address*	Adds the specified *address* to the Address line.
~v	Starts the preselected text editor; same as ~e.
~w *filename*	Writes the current message to the specified *filename*.
~! *Command*	Executes the specified shell *command*, then returns to the message.
~| *filter*	Pipes the current message through the specified *filter*.
~~	Ignores the tilde escape and places a tilde in the text of the message.

tilde symbol

The ~ symbol. Used to represent the name of the user's home directory in the Korn shell, the C shell, `bash`, `tcsh`, and Zsh, but not in the Bourne shell. In the Korn shell, you can also use ~+ as a shortcut for the name of the current directory and ~- as the name of the previous directory. In the C shell, you can use ~*name* to represent the home directory of the user specified by *name*.

Also used to separate a command from normal text entry in the `mail` and `mailx` programs.

In the `vi` editor, a tilde in the first character position on a line shows that the line is empty.

See also tilde escape commands

time

A command that displays (in seconds) the total elapsed time, execution time, and system time taken by a specified command. The syntax looks like this:

```
time command
```

You can also specify any appropriate arguments for *command*.

The Bourne shell also has a similar `time` command, with which you can use the built-in command to time other built-in commands as well as all the commands in a pipeline.

This command has no options.

See also `nice`, `ps`, `times`

TIMEOUT

A Bourne shell variable containing the time limit on entering commands at the prompt; if this interval elapses before you enter a command, the shell automatically logs you out.

See also TMOUT

times

A built-in Bourne shell command that displays the accumulated times for user and system. The user time is the amount of time that a command takes to execute, and the system time reflects the time used by Unix to execute the `times` command.

See also `nice`, `ps`, `time`

tin

A threaded newsreader for reading posts and subscribing to USENET newsgroups, originally developed by Ian Lea. Start the newsreader by typing:

`tin`

at the command prompt; you can also include the name of a newsgroup you want to access. `tin` reads the contents of your `.newsrc` file and compares it to the master list of newsgroups. If there are new newsgroups, `tin` asks if you want to subscribe. `tin` then presents you with a newsgroup selection list, and when you make a choice, `tin` shows you a list of all the threads currently active in the newsgroup. You can choose a thread to read, and as you read you can save an article to a file on your computer, mail a copy of an article to someone else, kill all the posts with the same subject, decode an article using rot13, or respond to an article by posting a followup post or mailing directly to the original author.

Table T.10 lists the main `tin` commands, Table T.11 details the command you use when selecting a newsgroup, Table T.12 lists the commands you use when selecting a thread, and Table T.13 shows the commands used when reading articles.

For all single-letter commands, you do not have to press the Return or Enter key; just press the command letter and `tin` will immediately do as you ask.

Sometimes `tin` will display a list of possible choices and suggest one of the options as the most likely choice; just press the Return key to accept this default.

See also `.newsrc, nn, rn, trn`

TABLE T.10: Main tin Commands

COMMAND	DESCRIPTION
QUITTING	
q	Returns to the previous level.
Q	Exits `tin`.
GETTING HELP	
h	Displays a list of commands.
H	Toggles the help line at the bottom of the screen on and off.
M	Displays a menu of configurable options.

TABLE T.10 continued: Main tin Commands

COMMAND	DESCRIPTION
DISPLAYING INFORMATION	
PgDn or space	Displays the next page.
Ctrl-D or Ctrl-F	Displays the next page.
PgUp or b	Displays the previous page.
Ctrl-U or Ctrl-B	Displays the previous page.
POSTING AN ARTICLE	
w	Posts an article to the current newsgroup.
W	Displays a list of all the articles you have posted.
ENTERING UNIX COMMANDS	
!	Pauses tin and starts a new shell.
!command	Executes the specified Unix command.

TABLE T.11: Commands for Selecting a Newsgroup in tin

COMMAND	DESCRIPTION
DISPLAYING THE SELECTION LIST	
↓ or j	Moves down one line.
↑ or k	Moves up one line.
n Return	Goes to the newsgroup number n.
$	Goes to the last newsgroup in the list.
N	Goes to the next newsgroup containing articles you have not yet read.
g name	Goes directly to the specified newsgroup.
/name	Searches forward for the specified newsgroup.
?name	Searches backward for the specified newsgroup.
CONTROLLING THE DISPLAY	
d	Toggles between showing the newsgroup name and showing the newsgroup name and description.
r	Toggles between showing all newsgroups and showing the newsgroups with unread articles.

TABLE T.11 continued: Commands for Selecting a Newsgroup in tin

COMMAND	DESCRIPTION
	CONTROLLING NEWSGROUPS
m	Moves the newsgroup.
s	Subscribes to the current newsgroup.
S	Subscribes to all newsgroups that match a specified pattern.
u	Unsubscribes from the current newsgroup.
U	Unsubscribes from all newsgroups that match a specified pattern.
	READING NEWSGROUPS
→ or Return	Starts displaying the articles in the current newsgroup.
Tab or n	Goes to the next newsgroup containing articles you have not yet read.

TABLE T.12: Commands for Selecting a Thread in tin

COMMAND	DESCRIPTION
	SELECTING A THREAD
n Return	Goes to thread number *n*.
$	Goes to the last thread.
/	Searches forward for a subject containing a specified pattern.
?	Searches backward for a subject containing a specified pattern.
K	Marks a thread as read and then opens the next unread thread.
N	Goes to the next unread thread.
P	Goes to the previous unread thread.
	READING AN ARTICLE
→	Opens the current thread for reading.
Tab	Opens the next unread thread for reading.
-	Returns to the last thread you were reading.
	CONTROLLING THE DISPLAY
d	Toggles between showing the subject and showing the subject and author.
r	Toggles between showing all threads and showing unread threads only.

TABLE T.12 continued: Commands for Selecting a Thread in tin

COMMAND	DESCRIPTION
	CHANGING NEWSGROUPS
n	Goes to the next newsgroup.
p	Goes to the previous newsgroup.
	WORKING WITH THREADS
m	Mails the thread.
o	Prints the thread.
s	Saves the thread in a file.

TABLE T.13: Commands for Reading an Article in tin

COMMAND	DESCRIPTION
	DISPLAYING AN ARTICLE
↓	Displays the next page.
↑	Displays the previous page.
d	Decodes the current article using rot13.
g or Ctrl-R	Goes to the first page of the article.
G or $	Goes to the last page of the article.
Ctrl-H	Redisplays the article showing the header.
	SELECTING ANOTHER ARTICLE
→ or Tab or N	Goes to the next unread article.
Return	Goes to the next thread.
K	Marks the thread as read, goes to the next unread article.
K	Marks the entire thread as read, and goes to the next unread article.
N	Goes to the next article.
P	Goes to the previous article.
P	Goes to the previous unread article.
–	Returns to the last article you read.
	RESPONDING TO AN ARTICLE
F	Posts a followup including the original post.
F	Posts a followup without including the original post.

TABLE T.13 continued: Commands for Reading an Article in tin

COMMAND	DESCRIPTION
RESPONDING TO AN ARTICLE	
R	Replies to the original author by mail, and includes the original post.
R	Replies to the original author by mail without including the original post.

tip

A Solaris and BSD command used to log in to a remote computer using a dial-up connection and a modem.

Syntax

The syntax for tip is as follows:

    tip [phonenumber]

Once the connection is established, a remote session behaves just like any other interactive session on your terminal, and you can copy files between the two systems. tip does not support Xmodem protocols and cannot transfer binary files. The appropriate hardware to support the connection must be installed on both local and remote computers, and you must have an account on the remote system.

Commands

Once you have connected to the remote computer, you must use tilde commands to perform tasks on your local system; Table T.14 lists some of the most common tilde commands.

TABLE T.14: tip Tilde Commands

COMMAND	DESCRIPTION
~?	Displays a summary of all the tilde commands.
~!	Escapes to a new shell so you can access your local system and remain connected to the remote system. When you exit from this shell, you return to tip.
~.	Disconnects from the remote system; you may still be logged on to the remote system.
~cdirectory	Changes the directory on your local system.
~p	Puts a file on (or sends a file to) the remote system.
~t	Takes (or receives) a file from the remote system.

Examples

To connect to a system at the telephone number 444-1212, use:

```
tip 4441212
```

`tip` displays the message `dialing...` then places the call using your system's modem. When the remote system answers, you see `connected`, and you can log on to the system.

See also cu, rlogin, rsh

TMOUT

A Korn shell variable containing the time limit on entering commands at the prompt; if this interval elapses before you enter a command, the shell automatically logs you out.

See also TIMEOUT

/tmp

A directory used to hold temporary files or data.

See also /lost+found

tn3270

A variation of the `telnet` program designed to give access to an IBM 3270 series computer with 3278 page-mode terminals. Most of the computers on the Internet use Unix, but if you ever encounter an IBM mainframe, you will definitely need `tn3270`.

So how do you know when to use `tn3270` rather than `telnet`? If you try to connect to an Internet host using `telnet` and one of the following happens, it's time to load up `tn3270`:

▶ The on-screen messages are all in uppercase letters rather than the usual Unix mix of uppercase and lowercase letters.

▶ You see "VM" or "VMS" anywhere in the login message. These are both names of IBM operating systems.

▶ Your session is aborted before it really gets started.

For information on starting and using `tn3270`, see the `telnet` entry; in command mode, `tn3270` accepts and executes all the `telnet` commands.

touch

A command used to change the file access and modification times.

Syntax

The syntax for touch is as follows:

```
touch [options][time]file-list
```

The touch command sets the modification and access time to the current time or to a time that you specify. If the file doesn't exist, it is created with default permissions and the specified or current times. You cannot change the file creation time.

Options and Arguments

The *file-list* contains the pathname of the files that you want to update. The *time* argument specifies the new date and time, using this format:

```
MMddhhmm[yy]
```

where *MM* is the month number (01-12), *dd* is the day of the month (01-31), *hh* is the hour (00-23), *mm* is the minutes (00-59), and *yy* is an optional two-digit year number. On some systems, you can use this form for the time:

```
[[CC]yy]MMddhhmm[.ss]
```

where *CC* and *yy* specify the century and the year, and *ss* the number of seconds (0 to 61). If you don't specify a year, touch uses the current year, and if you don't specify a *time*, touch uses the current system time.

Table T.15 lists the options available with touch.

If you don't use the -a or the -m options, touch updates both the access and modification times.

TABLE T.15: Options to Use with touch

OPTION	DESCRIPTION
-a	Changes the file's access time, leaving the modification time unchanged.
-c	Does not create a file if the specified file does not exist.
-f	Attempts to force the update even if the file permissions do not allow it.
-m	Changes the file's modification time, leaving the access time unchanged.
-r*filename*	Changes the access and modification times to those of the specified *filename* rather than the current time.
-t*time*	Changes the access and modification times to the specified *time*.

Examples

Certain commands such as make and find use a file's access and modification time, and so touch can be very useful in forcing these commands to treat files in a specified way.

To set the access and modification times of all files in the current directory to the current time, use:

```
touch *
```

See also date, time

tput

A command that displays information from the term-info database or sends setup instructions to your terminal. The tput syntax is:

```
tput [option]attribute
```

The -Tterminal option specifies your terminal type, and the attribute can be one of the ones listed in Table T.16.

See also stty, termcap, terminfo, tset

TABLE T.16: Attributes to Use with the -Tterminal Option to tput

ATTRIBUTE	DESCRIPTION
clear	Sends the string that clears *parameter* the screen.
init	Sends the terminal initialization *parameter* string.
Longname	Displays the complete name of the terminal.
reset	Sends the terminal reset string.*parameter*.

tr

A command that translates characters in a file from one form to another. A common use of tr is to convert the text in a file from lowercase to uppercase or to change all the tabs into spaces.

Syntax

Here's the syntax:

```
tr [options][string1][string2]
```

tr copies the standard input to the standard output, translating occurrences from *string1* into corresponding characters in *string2*.

Options and Arguments

By using one argument, *string1*, and an option from Table T.17, you can use tr to delete the characters specified in *string1*. Used with no arguments, tr just copies its standard input to its standard output. Table T.17 lists the options you can use with tr.

You can also specify a range of characters by hyphenating them and enclosing them in square brackets.

TABLE T.17: Options to Use with tr

Option	Description
-c	Complements the set of characters in *string1*; the complement consists of all non-null characters that are not in *string1*, taken in their machine collating order.
-d	Deletes characters that match those specified in *string1*.
-s	Reduces any sequence of several identical characters in *string2* to a single occurrence.

Examples

To translate all the uppercase and lowercase letters in the file chapter
.one into lowercase and store the result into a file called chapter
.lower, use:

```
cat chapter.one | tr "[A-Z]" "[a-z]" > chapter.lower
```

See also comm, cut, dd, expand, fold, paste, translate, unexpand,
uniq

translate

An SCO command that translates files from one format to another.

Syntax

The syntax to use with translate is:

```
translate [options][input-file][output-file]
```

Options and Arguments

translate used without arguments reads from the standard input and
writes to the standard output. The options you can use are listed in
Table T.18.

See also comm, cut, dd, expand, fold, paste, tr, unexpand, uniq

TABLE T.18: Options to Use with translate

Option	Description
-ae	Translates from ASCII to EBCDIC.
-af*format*	Translates from ASCII to a user-defined *format*.
-bm	Translates from binary to uuencode ASCII.
-ea	Translates from EBCDIC to ASCII.
-ef*format*	Translates from EBCDIC to a user-defined *format*.
-fa*format*	Translates from a user-defined *format* to ASCII.
-fe*format*	Translates from a user-defined *format* to EBCDIC.
-mb	Translates from uuencode ASCII to binary.

trap

A built-in Bourne shell and Korn shell command that executes a specified command if one or more signals are received. `trap` can be used from the command line but is most often used in shell scripts.

The syntax looks like this:

```
trap [[commands]signals]
```

`trap` executes the *commands* when any of the *signals* is received; multiple commands should be quoted as a group and separated by semicolons.

If you use a null string as *commands*, then `trap` ignores the specified *signals*; for example:

```
trap "" 1 2 3 15
```

ignores the hangup, interrupt, quit, and software termination signals.

If both *commands* and *signals* are omitted, `trap` lists the current `trap` assignments.

See also exec, kill, **signal,** trap

trn

A public-domain threaded newsreader for reading posts and subscribing to USENET newsgroups, originally developed by Wayne Davison and based on the rn newsreader. Most, if not all, the standard rn commands are available in trn, and the online help in trn assumes a working knowledge of rn and focuses almost entirely on the trn-specific features of the program.

Table T.19 lists the trn commands you can use while selecting a newsgroup or executing a shell command. Table T.20 lists the commands used when selecting an article within a newsgroup.

See also .newsrc, nn, rn, tin

TABLE T.19: Commands for Selecting a Newsgroup in trn

COMMAND	DESCRIPTION
BASIC COMMANDS	
H	Displays help information.
Q	Quits trn.
V	Displays the trn version number.
X	Quits rn and abandons all updates to your .newsrc file.

TABLE T.19 continued: Commands for Selecting a Newsgroup in trn

COMMAND	DESCRIPTION
READING ARTICLES	
Space	Performs the default operation.
+	Invokes the thread selector to read the current newsgroup.
=	Displays a list of subjects in the current newsgroup.
Y	Starts displaying the current newsgroup for reading.
WORKING WITH NEWSGROUPS	
^	Goes to the first newsgroup that contains unread articles.
$	Goes to the end of the list of newsgroups.
A	Abandons all read and unread changes to this newsgroup.
C	Catchup mode: marks all the articles in the newsgroup as having been read.
g *newsgroup*	Goes to the specified *newsgroup*.
l *pattern*	Lists the unsubscribed newsgroup names that contain *pattern*.
L	Lists the current state of newsgroups in .newsrc.
N	Goes to the next newsgroup that contains unread articles.
P	Goes to the previous newsgroup that contains unread articles.
U	Unsubscribes from the current newsgroup.
/pattern	Searches forward for a newsgroup name containing *pattern*.
?pattern	Searches backward for a newsgroup name containing *pattern*.
/	Searches forward for previous *pattern*.
?	Searches backward for previous *pattern*.
EXECUTING UNIX COMMANDS	
! *command*	Executes the specified *command*.
!	Pauses trn and starts a shell.

TABLE T.20: Commands for Selecting an Article in trn

COMMAND	DESCRIPTION
BASIC COMMANDS	
+	Invokes thread selection mode.
C	Marks all articles in the newsgroup as read.
H	Displays help information.

TABLE T.20 continued: Commands for Selecting an Article in trn

COMMAND	DESCRIPTION
	BASIC COMMANDS
K	Marks all articles with the same subject as read; effectively kills unread articles.
N	Goes to the next unread article.
Q	Quits this newsgroup.
Ctrl-N	Goes to the next unread article on the same subject.
	REDISPLAYING THE CURRENT ARTICLE
B	Goes back one page.
V	Redisplays the current article with its header.
X	Decodes the current page using rot13.
Ctrl-L	Redisplays the current page.
Crtl-R	Redisplays the current article.
Ctrl-X	Decodes the current article using rot13.
	SELECTING ANOTHER ARTICLE
-	Redisplays the last article displayed.
N	Moves forward to the next article.
$	Moves forward to the end of the last article.
P	Moves backward to the previous article.
Ctrl-P	Moves backward to the previous article with the same subject.
P	Moves backward to the next article, read or unread.
^	Moves backward to the next unread article.
	USING ARTICLE NUMBERS
=	Displays a list of all the unread articles.
Number	Goes to the article with the specified *number*.
#	Displays the number of the last article.
	SEARCHING FOR AN ARTICLE
/pattern	Searches forward for a subject containing *pattern*.
?pattern	Searches backward for a subject containing *pattern*.
/	Searches forward for previous *pattern*.
?	Searches backward for previous *pattern*.

TABLE T.20 continued: Commands for Selecting an Article in trn

COMMAND	DESCRIPTION
	RESPONDING TO AN ARTICLE
F	Starts the Pnews program to create a followup post.
F	Starts the Pnews program to create a followup post, and includes a copy of the original message.
R	Sends a mail message to the author of the article.
R	Sends a mail message to the author of the article, and includes a copy of the original message.
	SAVING AN ARTICLE
s *filename*	Saves the article in the specified *filename*.
w *filename*	Saves the article without the header in the specified *filename*.
	EXECUTING UNIX COMMANDS
! *command*	Executes the specified *command*.
!	Pauses trn and starts a shell.

troff

A text-processing command used to format a text file for output to a type-setter; pronounced "tee-rof" for "typesetter runoff."

Unix often includes two programs for text processing, nroff and troff. The nroff program is used when you want to output formatted text to a line printer or to a line-oriented display, and troff is used when you want to send text to a laser printer, bitmapped display, or to a typesetter. troff supports proportionally spaced fonts, while nroff supports only mono-spaced fonts.

An input file for troff contains lines of text interspersed with lines that begin with a period and contain one- or two-letter commands. troff also allows you to define a macro as a series of input lines, and three major macro packages are available that automate complex formatting functions.

The main benefit to using nroff and troff rather than a commercial word processor is that their input files are simple text files. This allows you to use many other Unix utilities (grep, diff, and so on) with your files, which is something you can't do with the proprietary formats used by word processors. These files also tend to be smaller than equivalent files from commercial packages, and they can be quickly and easily copied from machine to machine.

See also eqn, **LATEX**, groff, me **macros**, mm **macros**, ms **macros**, nroff, pic, soelim, tbl, **TEX**, Texinfo

troff macros

A macro designed to manage a standard formatting function and create a standard document such as a letter, report, memo, manual, or book. Several important macro packages are available, including:

- ▶ me macros. A set of over 80 nroff and troff macros distributed with BSD systems, originally created by Eric Allman while at Berkeley. The me macro package is equivalent to the ms and mm macro packages on SVR4 systems and supports all common preprocessors such as eqn, tbl, and refer.

- ▶ mm macros. A set of almost 100 nroff and troff macros distributed with SVR4 systems. The mm macro package is equivalent to the me macro package on BSD systems.

- ▶ ms macros. The original set of approximately 50 nroff and troff macros. The ms macro package is no longer supported but is often found on many systems.

- ▶ man macros. A macro package used to format Unix man pages

- ▶ mview macros. A package of macros used to create overhead transparencies.

true

A shell command used in shell scripts to test whether a task has been completed. true is often used in a while loop; as long as a successful response (a value of zero) is received, the loop continues to run. If any other value is returned, the loop terminates.

See also false, if, test, while

truss

A troubleshooting command used to trace system calls and signals and to display information on the standard output. Only used by the system administrator.

tset

A command for setting the system interface to terminals and dial-up modems, designed for use with `termcap`.

Syntax
The syntax to use is:

```
tset [options][type]
```

`tset` is most often used in shell scripts; it is not often used from the command line.

Options and Arguments
In the syntax above, *type* is your terminal type; the options are listed in Table T.21.

Used without options, `tset` displays the settings for the erase, kill, and interrupt keys:

```
tset
Erase set to Delete
Kill set to Ctrl-U
Interrupt set to Ctrl-C
```

See also stty, termcap, terminfo, tput, tty

TABLE T.21: Options to Use with tset

OPTION	DESCRIPTION
-	Displays the terminal name without initializing the terminal.
-e*c*	Sets the erase character to *c*; the default is Ctrl-H, backspace.
-i*c*	Sets the interrupt character to *c*; the default is Ctrl-C.
-I	Suppresses the terminal initialization setting.
-k*c*	Sets the kill-line character to *c*; the default is Ctrl-U.
-m[*port*[*baud*]:*tty*]	Maps the specified parameters from a port type to a terminal. *port* is the port type (often dialup), *baud* is the baud rate of the port, *tty* is the terminal type.
-Q	Suppresses the display of the erase, interrupt, and kill-line information.
-r	Displays the terminal type on the standard error.
-s	Displays the commands used to set TERM.
-S	Displays the terminal type and termcap entry.

tty

A command that displays the pathname of your terminal's device file.

Syntax

The syntax for this command is:

```
tty [options]
```

Options and Arguments

You can use the options listed in Table T.22 with `tty`; the command takes no arguments.

See also stty, tput, tset, tty

TABLE T.22: Options to Use with tty

OPTION	DESCRIPTION
-1	Prints the synchronous line number.
-s	Causes tty not to print any output but still to set the exit status to 0 if the standard input file is a terminal, and to 1 if it is not.

Twm

The name of the Tab Window Manager included with the X Window system. `twm` has served as the model for many window managers, including the Motif and the Open Look window managers.

See also mwm, olwm

type

A command used to show whether a name is a Unix command, a built-in shell command, or a defined shell function.

In the Korn shell, this is an alias for whence -v.

See also whence

typeset

A built-in Korn shell command used for several different purposes in shell scripts.

Syntax

The syntax to use is:

```
typeset [options][variable[=value...]]
```

Options and Arguments

The `typeset` command assigns a type to each *variable*, as well as an optional initial *value*. When you specify a *variable*, *+option* enables it, while *-option* disables it. With no *variable*, *+option* prints the names, and *-option* prints the names and the values of all the set variables. You can use the options listed in Table T.23.

TABLE T.23: Options to Use with typeset

OPTION	DESCRIPTION
-f	Defines the current *variable* as a function; if no *variable* is given, lists the current function names.
-H	Maps Unix filenames to host filenames on non-Unix systems.
-i*n*	Defines *variable* as an integer of base *n*.
-L*n*	Defines *variable* as a flush-left string *n* characters in length.
-l	Converts uppercase to lowercase.
-r	Marks *variable* as read-only.
-R*n*	Defines *variable* as a flush-right string *n* characters in length.
-t	Marks *variable* with a user-defined tag.
-u	Converts lowercase to uppercase.
-x	Marks *variable* for automatic export.
-Z*n*	When used with –L, strips leading zeros.

Examples

To list the names, values, and types of all set shell variables, use:

```
typeset
```

To list the names, values, and types of all exported shell variables, use:

```
typeset -x
```

See also autoload, integer

U

u1

A BSD command that translates underlining in a text file into characters that your current terminal can display.

Syntax

The syntax for ul is as follows:

```
ul [options]filename...
```

Options and Arguments

The ul command reads from the specified *filename* or the standard input if no filename is given and translates any underlining into characters understood by your terminal. If the terminal cannot display any form of underlining, underlining is ignored. The options you can use with ul are listed in Table U.1.

TABLE U.1: Options to Use with ul

Options	Description
-i	Indicates that underlining is contained in a separate line containing dashes.
-t *terminal*	Overrides your current terminal type with *terminal*.

Examples

To display the contents of the file chapter.txt with underlining support for a VT100 ASCII terminal, use:

```
ul -t vt100 chapter.txt
```

See also colcrt, man, nroff, pg, term

Ulimit

A built-in Korn shell command used to limit system resources.

Syntax

Here's the ulimit syntax:

```
ulimit [options][number]
```

ulimit displays the value of one or more resource limits or, if *number* is specified, sets the resource limit to that value.

Options and Arguments

Resource limits can be either hard or soft limits; only the superuser can increase a hard limit, although anyone can lower one. Soft limits must be lower than the hard limit. Using ulimit, you can set either type of limit and display the value of the soft limits. Table U.2 lists the options available with ulimit.

See also env, printenv, set

TABLE U.2: Options to Use with ulimit

Option	Description
-H	Sets a hard limit.
-S	Sets a soft limit.
-a	Displays all limits.
-c	Sets the maximum block size of core files.
-d	Sets the maximum size of the data segment or heap in kilobytes.
-f	Sets the maximum block size of files; this is the default option.
-n	Sets the maximum file descriptor plus 1.
-s	Sets the maximum stack segment in kilobytes.
-t	Sets the maximum number of CPU seconds.
-v	Sets the maximum amount of virtual memory in kilobytes.

Umask

A built-in Unix command and shell command that lets you display or change the current file creation mask that determines the default permissions when you create a new file. Typically this value is set in the login script for each shell: the most common value is 022.

Syntax
Here's the umask syntax:

    umask [*number*]

Options and Arguments
Using umask without arguments displays the current file creation mask, and if you specify an octal *number*, you can set the file creation mask. This mask is a three-digit octal number, where each digit corresponds to permissions for the owner of the file and members of the group that the file is associated with, as well as everyone else. When you create a new file, Unix subtracts these numbers from the numbers corresponding to the access permissions and so arrives at an appropriate set of permissions. Table U.3 illustrates how these octal numbers work. The umask command has no options.

By default, new files are given the permission mode 666 (rw-rw-rw-), which gives everyone read and write access, while directories are given the permission mode 777 (rwxrwxrwx), which gives everyone read, write, and search permission.

The umask command is available in almost all the popular shells, including the C shell, Bourne shell, and Korn shell, and is often used in one of the shell startup files such as .profile or .login.

TABLE U.3: umask Permissions

Number	File Permission	Directory Permission	Description
0	rw–	Rwx	Grants read and write permission for files, and read, write, and search permission for directories.
1	rw–	Rw–	Grants read and write permission for files and directories.
2	r–	r–x	Grants read permission for files, and read and search permission for directories.
3	r–	r–	Grants only read permission for files and directories.
4	–w–	–wx	Grants write permission for files, and write and search permission for directories.
5	–w–	–w–	Grants only write permission for files and directories.
6	––	–x	Grants no permissions for files and only search permission for directories.
7	––	––	Denies all permissions for files and directories.

Examples

To set the file creation mask so that the owner and group have all permissions but the rest of the world only has read permission (equivalent to –r–), use:

umask 002

You can omit the leading zeros if you wish.

See also chmod, chown, ls

umask value

An octal number that specifies the file permissions to be masked out when a file is created.

See also chown, chmod, ls, umask

umount

A command that unmounts a removable device such as a floppy diskette or CD-ROM.

See also mount

unalias

A built-in command found in the Korn shell and the C shell that removes an alias created by the alias command.

Syntax
The syntax for unalias is:

```
unalias name
```

where *name* is the name of a previously created alias. For once, the C shell and Korn shell versions of this command are identical. unalias has no options.

See also alias

uname

A command that reports system information to the standard output.

Syntax
The syntax for uname is as follows:

```
uname [options]
```

Options and Arguments
The options you can use with this command are detailed in Table U.4.

See also hostid, hostname

TABLE U.4: Options to Use with uname

Option	Description
-a	Displays a complete report as though all the remaining options were specified.
-m	Displays the name of the system hardware.
-n	Displays the name of the network node.
-r	Displays the operating system's current release level.
-s	Displays the name of the operating system.
-v	Displays the operating system version level.

uncompact

A BSD command that restores an original file from a file compressed by compact.

Syntax

The uncompact syntax is:

    uncompact [*option*]*filename*

The single option, -v, displays the names of the files as they are processed. If no *filename* is specified, the standard input is uncompressed to the standard output.

See also ccat, compact

uncompress

A command that uncompresses compressed files.

Syntax

The uncompress syntax is:

    uncompress [*option*]*file-list*

where *file-list* contains the names of the files you want to expand; the filename extension .Z is assumed, so you don't have to specify it on the command line.

Options and Arguments

uncompress has one option, -c, which writes the compressed file to the standard output but does not change any files. This is the same as using the zcat command.

See also compact, compress, gzip, pack, uncompact, zcat

unexpand

A Solaris command that copies a file (or the standard input) to the standard output, replacing leading whitespace by a sequence of tabs and spaces. This command reverses the effects of the expand command.

Syntax

The syntax is:

    unexpand [*option*]*filename*

Options and Arguments

The single option, -a, inserts tab characters when replacing a run of two or more space characters and creates a smaller output file.

See also expand

unhash

A built-in C shell command that removes the internal hash table. After you invoke unhash, the C shell stops using hashed values to locate a command and spends more time searching directory pathnames.

See also hash, rehash

uniq

A command used to remove or report adjacent duplicate lines in a sorted text file.

Syntax

Here's the syntax to use:

```
uniq [options][inputfile[outputfile]]
```

Repeated lines in the input to uniq are not detected unless they are adjacent, so it may be wise to sort the file before using uniq.

Options and Arguments

uniq removes the adjacent duplicate lines from the sorted *inputfile* sending one copy of each line to the standard output or to outputfile. Table U.5 lists the options you can use with uniq.

TABLE U.5: Options to Use with uniq

Option	Description
-c	Precedes each line by a count of the number of times it occurred in the input.
-d	Displays all duplicate lines once, but does not display unique lines.
-f *n*	Ignores the first *n* fields in a file and any spaces preceding them; not available in all versions of uniq.
-s *n*	Ignores the first *n* characters and any spaces preceding them; not available in all versions of uniq.
-u	Displays only unique lines; does not display repeated lines.
-*n*	Ignores the first *n* fields in a file; this option is obsolete in some versions of uniq.
+*n*	Ignores the first *n* characters in a field; this option is obsolete in some versions of uniq.

Examples

The uniq command is often used as a filter and is good at combining two files to produce one output file with all duplicates removed. To combine two lists of names into one that contains no duplicates, use:

```
cat mylist yourlist | sort | uniq > ourlist
```

which combines mylist and yourlist using the cat command, sorts the result, removes any duplicates, and stores the result into the file ourlist.

See also comm, sort

units

An interactive program used to convert between different units of measure. The units program can only do multiplicative conversions, so while it can convert temperatures from Kelvin to Rankine, it cannot convert from Fahrenheit to centigrade. In addition, many of the currency conversion rates fluctuate and may not be up-to-date. Here's a short example of how it works:

```
units
You have: inch
You want: cm
        *2.54000e+00
        / 3.93701e-01
```

British units that differ from their U.S. counterparts are prefixed with br as in:

```
brgallon
```

and currency as:

```
germanmark
```

or

```
britainpound
```

Most familiar units are recognized, including metric prefixes and abbreviations. For a complete list of the 500 or so units recognized, look in /usr/share/units on BSD and SunOS systems, /usr/lib/units on SVR4, /usr/lib/unittab on SCO, and /usr/share/lib/unittab on Solaris and AIX.

See also bc, dc

Unix

Pronounced "yoo-nixs." An operating system designed and developed in 1969 at AT&T's Bell Labs by Ken Thompson and Dennis Ritchie. Since the initial development, the Unix environment has been enriched with a large number of utilities and other programs. The real turning point was the period between 1972 and 1974 when Unix was rewritten in the C language with portability as a major design goal. Unix has gone on to become the most widely used general-purpose operating system in the world. Table U.6 lists the names and developers of Unix and Unix-like operating systems.

See also **K&R**

TABLE U.6: Unix Systems and Their Developers

UNIX SYSTEM	DEVELOPER
386BSD	Free from the Internet and other sources
AIX	IBM
A/UX	Apple
BSD	University of California, Berkeley
BSD-Lite	University of California, Berkeley
BSD/386	Berkeley Software Design
Coherent	Mark Williams Company
DC/OS	Pyramid Technology
Dynix	Sequent Computer Systems
FreeBSD	Free from the Internet and other sources
HP-UX	Hewlett-Packard
Hurd (GNU)	Free Software Foundation
Interactive Unix	Sun Microsystems
Irix	Silicon Graphics
Linux	Linus Torvalds, et. al.; free from the Internet and other sources
Mach	Carnegie Mellon University
Minix	Andrew Tannenbaum
MKS Toolkit	Mortice Kern Systems
NetBSD	Free from the Internet and other sources
NeXTStep	NeXT
OSF/1	Digital Equipment Corporation (DEC)
SCO OpenServer	Santa Cruz Operation
SCO UNIX	Santa Cruz Operation
Solaris	Sun Microsystems
SunOS	Sun Microsystems
Ultrix	Digital Equipment Corporation (DEC)

TABLE U.6 continued: Unix Systems and Their Developers

Unix System	Developer
Unicos	Cray Research
UnixWare	Novell/Santa Cruz Operation

unlimit

A command that removes a resource limit. It is used to undo any `limit` commands, and the syntax is:

    unlimit [resources]

where *resources* is one of the elements listed in Table U.7.

If you don't specify *resources*, all limits are removed.

See also limit

TABLE U.7: Resource Names Used with unlimit

Resource	Description
Cputime	Maximum number of processor seconds
Filesize	Maximum size of any file
Datasize	Maximum size of data, including the stack
Stacksize	Maximum size of the stack
Coredumpsize	Maximum size of a core dump file

unpack

A command that expands a file compressed with `pack`. The syntax is:

    unpack file-list

where *file-list* contains the names of the packed files you want to uncompress. All such files have the filename extension `.z`; this is assumed so you don't have to type it on the command line.

See also compact, compress, gzip, pack, pcat, uncompact, uncompress, zcat

unset

A built-in command that removes one or more variables. The Bourne shell syntax is:

    unset names

where *names* specifies the variable or variables you want to remove.

In the Korn shell, functions must be explicitly stated using the `-f` option, as in:

```
unset -f names
```

if you want to turn off a shell option.

And in the C shell, you can specify variable names using filename metacharacters. You can also unset C shell variables by setting them to their opposite value.

See also `set`, `setenv`, `unsetenv`

unsetenv

A built-in C shell command that removes an environment variable. The syntax is:

```
unsetenv name
```

where *name* represents the variable you want to remove. You cannot specify environment variable names using filename metacharacters.

See also `set`, `setenv`, `unset`

until

A Bourne shell and Korn shell programming construct often used with `test` to set up a loop. The loop continues to run as long as the results are false (returns a non-zero value). When a true value is returned, the loop terminates. An example might look like this:

```
until condition
do
        commands
done
```

See also `do`, `done`, `fi`, `for`, `if`, `then`, `until`, `while`

unvis

A BSD command that reverses the effect of the `vis` command, and converts nonprinting characters back into their original forms.

See also `vis`

uptime

A command that shows how long the system has been up by displaying the current time, how long the system has been running, the number of users currently logged in, and the system load averages for the last one, five, and fifteen minutes.

See also `ruptime`, `w`, `who`

URL

Acronym for Uniform Resource Locator, pronounced "earl." A method of accessing Internet resources.

URLs contain information about both the access method to use and also about the resource itself. They are used by Web browsers to connect you directly to a specific document or page on the World Wide Web, without your having to know where that resource is located physically. A sample URL might look like this:

```
http://www.austin.ibm.com
```

The first part of the URL, before the colon, specifies the access method. On the Web, this is usually `http` (for Hypertext Transfer Protocol), but you might also see file, `ftp`, or gopher instead. The second part of the URL, after the colon, specifies the resource. The text after the two slashes usually indicates a server name, and the text after the single slash defines the directory or individual file you will connect to. If you are linking to a document, it will usually have the filename extension `.html`, the abbreviation for Hypertext Markup Language.

URLs are always case-sensitive, so pay particular attention to uppercase and lowercase letters and to symbols as well.

users

A command that displays the currently logged-in users as a space-separated sorted list. `users` has no options.

See also `finger`, `last`, `rusers`, `rwho`, `w`, `who`

/usr

A general-purpose directory that contains the subdirectories and files that make up most of the Unix system software and documentation. In SVR4, `/usr` has a number of important subdirectories, as shown in Table U.8.

If you are working on a proprietary Unix or an earlier release of System V, you may find the contents of `/usr` are slightly different.

See also `/bin`, `/etc`, `/home`, `/lost+found`, **root directory**, `/tmp`, `/var`

TABLE U.8: /usr Subdirectories

Directory	Description
/usr/bin	Contains executable versions of Unix commands and utilities.
/usr/include	Contains header files for C programs.
/usr/games	Contains Unix games.
/usr/lib	Contains compiled C program library files, daemons, and the like.
/usr/local	Contains programs specific to your installation.
/usr/sbin	Contains executable programs used when the system first starts running (on older systems these programs may be in /bin or /etc) and system administration programs.
/usr/share	Contains platform-independent documentation, including man pages and source files, if they are available.
/usr/src	Contains Unix source files if they are available.
/usr/ucb	Contains BSD-specific versions of certain programs, and you may also find the BSD compatability package in this directory.

---

uucp

A command used to copy files from one Unix system to another using a dial-up line and a modem.

Syntax

The syntax to use for uucp is:

```
uucp [options][source!]file[destination!]file
```

Options and Arguments

The uucp command copies one or more files from the *source* to the *destination*, where *destination* is usually a remote Unix system; sometimes *destination* specifies a directory. *source* and *destination* can also be preceded by an optional host name followed by a bang or exclamation point in the form:

```
hostname!filename
```

and any wildcards used are expanded on the appropriate machine. See Table U.9 for a description of the options you can use with uucp.

TABLE U.9: Options to Use with uucp

Option	Description
-c	Uses the original source file, rather than copying the file to the spool directory first; this is the default mode on most systems.
-C	Copies the original file to the spool directory and transmits this copy.

TABLE U.9 continued: Options to Use with uucp

OPTION	DESCRIPTION
-d	Creates all the necessary directories if they do not already exist.
-f	Does not create intermediate directories if they do not already exist.
-g*n*	Sets a priority of *n*; use uuglist to display the values available for *n*.
-j	Displays the uucp job number; you can then use uustat to check the status of the job.
-m	Sends an e-mail message to the person requesting the transfer when the job is complete.
-n *user*	Notifies *user* on the remote system by e-mail that the transfer is complete.
-r	Queues the job without starting the transfer.
-s *filename*	Sends a status report to *filename*.
-x *n*	Sets the debug level to *n*, where *n* is between 0 and 9 with the higher numbers giving more detailed output.

Examples

To copy all the `prog` files from /home/jenny on the remote manor system to /home/pmd, use:

```
uucp manor\!/home/jenny/prog.\* /home/pmd/
```

In this example, note that the exclamation point (!) and the wildcard (*) must be escaped with a backslash (\); these metacharacters must be protected from expansion on the local computer.

Notes

If the file being transferred is an executable file, the file permissions are preserved after the transfer.

uucp cannot connect to just any Unix system; certain files on the remote machine must be configured properly first; see your system administrator for more details.

uucp is a spooled process; it takes your requests and executes them for you so you do not have to interact with or watch the program work.

See also uudecode, uuencode, uuglist, uulog, uuname, uupick, uuq, uusend, uustat, uuto, uux

UUCP configuration

UUCP is a Unix-to-Unix communications package, developed at Bell Laboratories by Mike Lesk in the mid-1970s for serial communications between in-house Unix systems. It was revised in 1978, and in the early 1980s, a package known as BNU (basic networking utilities) was developed by P. Honeyman, D.A. Nowitz, and B.E. Redman. This version became known as HoneyDanBer UUCP. An even newer version, known as Taylor UUCP, is also available on some systems, particularly Linux.

UUCP provides:

- ▶ File transfer between two hosts
- ▶ A communications protocol for e-mail and USENET newsgroups
- ▶ Control of communications devices
- ▶ A set of utilities for managing the UUCP package

UUCP is usually set up by a system administrator, and configuration consists of:

- ▶ Telling your system what kind of modems you have on your computer and where they are located
- ▶ Describing how to talk to these modems
- ▶ Listing all the other systems that you would like to connect with, along with their phone numbers and passwords

The directory structure on System V Release 4 HoneyDanBer uses four major directories and subdirectories within these directories: `/etc/uucp` contains control files, `/usr/lib/uucp` contains `uucp` utilities, `/var/uucp` contains temporary files, and `/var/spool/uucp` contains public files. Other systems may be different: SCO stores control files in `/etc`, utilities and data files in `/usr/lib/uucp`, and temporary files and log files in `/usr/spool/uucp`.

UUCP is a set of utilities just like other Unix utilities. Table U.10 summarizes the various utilities in the UUCP system.

Because UUCP was designed for in-house use, it has some features that are less than secure in these days of crackers, viruses, and worms; talk to your system administrator about security. UUCP networks are found throughout the world and continue to perform important functions, such as connecting users who cannot directly access the Internet. Because UUCP is available on all sorts of systems, many other applications have been made compatible with it. UUCP is a big subject, and several very good books are available, covering system administration issues, security, and using `uucp` with USENET.

See also uucp, uudecode, uuencode, uuglist, uulog, uuname, uupick, uuq, uusend, uustat, uuto, uux

TABLE U.10: UUCP Utilities

UTILITY	DESCRIPTION
Uucico	Manages file transport for the UUCP system.
Uucp	Sends files between Unix systems, and lets you request files from other systems.
Uuglist	Lists options available for uux and uucp.
Uuname	Lists names of UUCP hosts.
Uupick	Obtains files from a remote system.
Uuq	Manages the UUCP queue (BSD systems only).
Uusend	Sends a file to a remote host (BSD systems only).
Uustat	Displays the status of the UUCP queue for both local and remote systems.
Uuto	Sends a file from one Unix system to another.
Uux	Executes commands on the remote system.

uucp network address

See bang path

uudecode

A command that reads a file encoded by uuencode and recreates the original file. The syntax is:

    uudecode *filename*

See also uucp, uuencode, uuglist, uulog, uuname, uupick, uuq, uusend, uustat, uuto, uux

uuencode

A command that reads a binary file and converts it into an ASCII text file that can be sent over communications links that do not support binary transfers. This technique is often used to send binary files to a USENET newsgroup as e-mail. The recipient of the encoded file must use uudecode to restore the file back to binary form before the file can be used.

The syntax for uuencode is as follows:

    uuencode *filename pathname*

where *filename* is the name of the binary file and *pathname* specifies where the decoded file should be stored.

When you encode a binary file with uuencode, the file grows by approximately 35 percent, so you often find that a particularly large file is divided into several smaller sections. For example, if the file is divided into four parts it might be labelled 1/4, 2/4, 3/4, and 4/4. You must find all the parts before you can decode and use the file. A large file may also be compressed before being encoded.

Due to the current popularity of the Internet and USENET, uuencode and uudecode programs are available on many operating systems, including DOS, OS/2, and Microsoft Windows.

See also uucp, uudecode, uuglist, uulog, uuname, uupick, uuq, uusend, uustat, uuto, uux

uuglist

A command that lists the priority levels available for use with the -g option of uucp or uux. A single option, -u lists the priorities available to the current user.

See also uucp, uudecode, uuencode, uulog, uuname, uupick, uuq, uusend, uustat, uuto, uux

uulog

A command that displays the contents of the uucp and uux log files using the tail command.

See also tail, uucp, uudecode, uuencode, uuglist, uuname, uupick, uuq, uusend, uustat, uuto, uux

uuname

A command that lists the names of known remote UUCP hosts. The syntax is:

    uuname [*options*]

Two options are available; -c lists the names of the systems known to the cu command, and -l displays the name of your own system.

See also uucp, uudecode, uuencode, uuglist, uulog, uupick, uuq, uusend, uustat, uuto, uux

uupick

An SVR4 command used to retrieve files sent to you by a user on a remote system using the uucp command. When files arrive from a remote system, they are stored in a special directory, usually /usr/spool/uucppublic/ receive/*user*/*system*, where *user* is your username and *system* is the name of the computer from which the files were transferred. You can use uupick to move the files to a more appropriate location. uupick has one option, -s *system,* which limits it to locating files transferred from that remote *system.*

The program is interactive and presents you with the names of the files sent to you one-by-one. You can use the interactive options listed in Table U.11 to tell uupick what to do with them.

See also uucp, uudecode, uuencode, uuglist, uulog, uuname, uuq, uusend, uustat, uuto, uux

TABLE U.11: Options to Use with uupick

OPTION	DESCRIPTION
? or *	Displays a summary of commands.
Enter or Return	Goes to the next item.
a *directory*	Moves all the files to the specified *directory;* if *directory* is not specified, the current directory is assumed.
D	Deletes the current entry.
m *directory*	Moves the current entry to the specified *directory;* if the current item is a directory, all its subdirectories are also moved.
P	Sends the current file to the standard output; does not apply to directories.
Q	Quits uupick.
! *command*	Executes *command* in a subshell.

uuq

A BSD command that displays the entries in the uucp queue.

Syntax

The syntax for this command is as follows:

    uuq [options]

Options and Arguments

The options available for use with uuq are listed in Table U.12; the default display only shows each job's number.

See also uucp, uudecode, uuencode, uuglist, uulog, uuname, uupick, uusend, uustat, uuto, uux

TABLE U.12: Options to Use with uuq

OPTIONS	DESCRIPTION
-b*baud*	Uses the specified *baud* when calculating transfer times; the default is 1200.
-d*jobnumber*	Deletes the specified *jobnumber.*

TABLE U.12 continued: Options to Use with uuq

Options	Description
-h	Displays summary information for each file, including system name, number of jobs, and total number of bytes to send.
-l	Displays complete information for each file, including job number and username, number of files waiting for transmission, number of bytes to send, and the type of command (S for sending files, R for receiving files, and X for remote uucp).
-r*sdir*	Uses the specified *sdir* directory as the spool directory, rather than the default directory.
-s*system*	Displays information for the specified *system*.
-u*user*	Displays information for the specified *user*.

uusend

A BSD command used to send a file to a remote host. This remote host does not have to be directly connected to your system, but a chain of uucp links must exist between the two systems so that the file can be transmitted.

The syntax is:

```
uusend [option]source hostname!...!destination
```

where *source* is the name of the file you wish to transmit, *hostname* is a uucp network address or bang path to the remote computer, and *destination* is the name for the file once it reaches the remote system.

A single option, -m *number*, sets the file mode to the specified octal number. If you don't use this option, the original mode of the source file is used.

See also uucp, uudecode, uuencode, uuglist, uulog, uuname, uupick, uuq, uustat, uuto, uux

uustat

An SVR4 command that shows you the status of jobs waiting transmission by uucp and the status of uucp communications with remote systems. You can also use uustat to cancel uucp requests.

Syntax
Here's the syntax:

```
uustat [options]
```

Options and Arguments
You will find that the uustat options vary from system to system; check the man pages on your system before using this command. Table U.13

lists the most common command-line options; others are available but only to the superuser.

The -s and -u options can be used together; all other options must be used by themselves.

See also uucp, uudecode, uuencode, uuglist, uulog, uuname, uupick, uuq, uusend, uuto, uux

TABLE U.13: Common Options to Use with uustat

Option	Description
-a	Displays the names of all jobs waiting to be transmitted.
-k *id*	Kills the job with the identifier of *id*; you must be the owner to execute this option.
-s *system*	Reports the status of jobs destined for *system*.
-u *user*	Reports the status of jobs originated by *user*.

uuto

An SVR4 command that sends a set of files or directories to a remote system, where a user can retrieve the file using uupick. The syntax is:

    uuto [options] files destination

where *files* represents the files or directories you want to transmit, and *destination* is in the form of:

    system!user

Two command-line options are available, as shown in Table U.14.

See also bang path, uucp, uudecode, uuencode, uuglist, uulog, uuname, uupick, uuq, uusend, uustat, uux

TABLE U.14: Options to Use with uuto

Option	Description
-p	Copies each file to be transmitted into a spool directory; any subsequent changes to the original are not reflected in the transmitted file.
-m	Sends an e-mail message to the sender when the transmission is complete.

uux

A command that lets you transfer files to a remote system and then execute a command on the specified system.

Syntax

The syntax to use with uux is as follows:

```
uux [options][[system]!command]
```

Options and Arguments

The options you can use with uux are listed in Table U.15.

TABLE U.15: Options to Use with uux

OPTION	DESCRIPTION
-	Makes the standard input to uux the standard input to *command*; same as -p.
-a*name*	Uses *name* instead of original username.
-c	Uses the original source file, rather than copying the file to the spool directory first; this is the default mode on most systems.
-C	Copies the original file to the spool directory and transmits this copy.
-g*n*	Sets a priority of *n*; use uuglist to display the values available for *n*.
-j	Displays the uux job number.
-n	Does not send e-mail if the job fails.
-p	Makes the standard input to uux the standard input to *command*; same as -.
-r	Queues the job without starting the transfer.
-s *filename*	Sends a status report to *filename*.
-x *n*	Sets the debug level to *n*, where *n* is between 0 and 9 with the higher numbers giving more detailed output.
-z	Notifies user on successful completion.

Notes

Some system administrators will not let you use this command on their systems for security reasons.

See also **bang path**, uucp, uudecode, uuencode, uuglist, uulog, uuname, uupick, uuq, uusend, uustat, uuto, uux

V

vacation

A command that tells anyone who sends you e-mail that you are on vacation.

Syntax

The syntax for this command is:

```
vacation [options]
```

Options and Arguments

You can use the options listed in Table V.1 with the vacation command.

TABLE V.1: Options to Use with vacation

OPTION	DESCRIPTION
-aalias	Handles messages for alias in the same way as those received for your normal login name.
-i	A BSD option that initializes the vacation database file.
-Iusername	A Solaris option that forwards your mail to username, and sends back a message that you are on vacation.
-rdays	A BSD option that sets the reply interval to days; the default is seven days.
-tn	A Solaris option used to set the time interval between repeat replies to the same sender to the value n; the default is one week.

Examples

Once you return from vacation, you can disable this command by entering:

```
mail -F " "
```

See also mail, mailx

val

See SCCS–

/var

An SVR4 directory that contains system files that often change, such as files waiting to be printed, log files, and mail files. On older Unix systems, these files are scattered through several subdirectories of /usr.

Subdirectories include /var/admin, which contains accounting information and other files used by the system administrator, and /var/spool, which holds spool files, temporary files waiting for processing. You can also find the subdirectories /var/adm, /var/cron, /var/lp, /var/mail, /var/news, and /var/uucp on most systems.

See also /dev, /etc, /sbin, /home, /lost+found, /tmp, /usr

vedit

A command that is an alias for the vi editor specially configured for beginning users. Using vedit is just like using vi, except that certain internal vi variables are set so that the user easily avoids problem areas.

See also vi, view

vgrind

A BSD command used to format program listings using `troff`. Any comments in the source code are printed in italic, keywords are printed in bold, and the name of the current function is listed in the margin.

vi

A popular Unix screen editor based on `ex`, originally written by Bill Joy as part of the BSD Unix systems. Pronounced "vee-eye," it is an acronym for visual editor.

Syntax

The syntax used to start `vi` is as follows:

    vi [options][filenames]

Here are some of the most common ways you can start `vi`:

    vi filename

opens the editor on the specified file starting at line one. If you don't include a *filename*, `vi` opens an empty buffer.

To open the specified file starting at line *n*:

    vi +n filename

To open the file at the last line:

    vi + filename

To open the specified file at the first line containing *pattern*:

    vi +/pattern filename

If you are using `vi` to recover files after a system failure, the following command displays the names of files that you can recover:

    vi -r

To start `vi` and recover the specified file:

    vi -r filename

Options and Arguments

The command-line options you can use with `vi` are similar to those used with `ex` and are listed in Table V.2.

TABLE V.2: Options to Use with vi

OPTION	DESCRIPTION
-c*command*	Starts an editing session by executing the specified vi command.
-C	Same as -x but assumes that *filename* is in encrypted form.
-l	Runs in LISP mode.

TABLE V.2 continued: Options to Use with vi

Option	Description
-L	Lists filenames saved due to an editor or system crash.
-r*filename*	Recovers and opens the specified *filename*.
-R	Opens vi in read-only mode; files cannot be changed.
-t *tag*	Edits the file containing *tag*.
-w*n*	Sets the window size to *n*.
-x	Requires a key to encrypt or decrypt *filename*.
+	Starts vi on the last line of the file.
+*n*	Starts vi on the line of the file specified by *n*.
+/*pattern*	Starts vi on the line of the file that contains *pattern*.

Command Mode and Input Mode

Unlike some of the other editors you encounter in the Unix world, vi operates in two quite different modes: input mode and command mode. When vi is in input mode, everything you type is inserted as text into the current editing buffer. When vi is in command mode, all the characters you type are interpreted as commands.

vi starts an editing session in command mode, and you can:

- ► Use the vi editing commands.
- ► Move the cursor to a new location in the editing buffer.
- ► Invoke a Unix shell, and use Unix utilities or commands.
- ► Change to insert mode.
- ► Save the current version of the editing buffer into a file.

Several commands put vi into input mode, including Append, Change, Insert, Open, and Replace. Table V.3 briefly describes these commands.

When you are in input mode, everything you type is treated as text and is added to the edit buffer; you can press the Escape key to return to command mode. To enter a control character, use Ctrl-V followed by the control character you want to use.

TABLE V.3: Commands That Invoke Input Mode in vi

Command	Description
a	Initiates input mode, and appends new text after the current cursor position.
A	Initiates input mode, and appends new text at the end of the current line.

TABLE V.3 continued: Commands That Invoke Input Mode in vi

COMMAND	DESCRIPTION
c	Initiates input mode, and starts a change operation.
C	Initiates input mode, and starts a change to the end of the line.
i	Initiates input mode, and lets you insert new text before the cursor position.
I	Initiates input mode, and allows you to insert new text at the beginning of the current line.
o	Initiates input mode, and opens a new line before the current line; the cursor moves to the start of this new blank line.
O	Initiates input mode, and opens a new line after the current line; the cursor moves to the start of this new blank line.
R	Initiates input mode, and begins overwriting text with as many new characters as you specify until you press the Escape key. vi then returns to command mode.

Moving Around in vi

There are many vi commands for moving the cursor to a new location, and for moving through the edit buffer. These commands are listed in Table V.4.

TABLE V.4: vi Cursor Movement Commands

COMMAND	DESCRIPTION
	MOVING THE CURSOR
h or ← or backspace	Moves the cursor one position to the left, without moving past the beginning of the current line. If you precede this command with a count *n*, the cursor moves *n* characters.
j or ↓	Moves the cursor one position down.
k or ↑	Moves the cursor one position up.
l or → or space	Moves the cursor one position to the right, without moving past the end of the current line. If you precede this command with a count *n*, the cursor moves *n* characters.
-	Moves the cursor to the beginning of the previous line.
+ or Return.	Moves the cursor to the beginning of the next line.
0	Moves the cursor to the beginning of the current line.
$	Moves the cursor to the end of the current line.
^	Moves the cursor to the first nonspace or tab in the current line.
b	Moves the cursor backward to the first character of the previous word. If you precede this command with a count *n*, the cursor moves back *n* words.
e	Moves the cursor forward to the last character of the next word.

TABLE V.4 continued: vi Cursor Movement Commands

COMMAND	DESCRIPTION
MOVING THE CURSOR	
w	Moves the cursor forward to the first character of the next word. If you precede this command with a count *n*, the cursor moves forward *n* words.
B	Same as b ignoring punctuation. If you precede this command with a count *n*, the cursor moves back *n* words.
E	Same as e, ignoring punctuation.
W	Same as w, ignoring punctuation. If you precede this command with a count *n*, the cursor moves forward *n* words.
)	Moves the cursor forward to the beginning of the next sentence.
(	Moves the cursor backward to the beginning of the previous sentence.
}	Moves the cursor forward to the beginning of the next paragraph.
{	Moves the cursor backward to the beginning of the previous paragraph.
]]	Moves the cursor forward to the next section boundary.
[[	Moves the cursor backward to the previous section boundary.
H	Moves the cursor to the first line of the editing buffer.
L	Moves the cursor to the last line of the editing buffer.
M	Moves the cursor to the middle line of the editing buffer.
MOVING THROUGH THE EDITING BUFFER	
Ctrl-B	Moves up one screenful.
Ctrl-D	Moves down half a screenful.
Ctrl-F	Moves down one screenful.
Ctrl-U	Moves up half a screenful.
GOING TO A LINE NUMBER	
*n*G	Goes to line number *n*.
1G	Goes to the first line in the buffer.
G	Goes to the last line in the buffer.

Editing Commands

In vi, editing commands look like this:

```
[n] operator [m] item
```

where the *operator* might be c to begin a change, d to begin a deletion, or y to begin a yank (copy) operation, and *n* and *m* are multipliers indicating how many times the operation is to be performed. The *item* can be a word, sentence, paragraph, or whole section of text. vi uses a large number of editing commands, and some of the most useful are listed in Table V.5.

The editing commands in Table V.5 that start with a colon (:) are actually ex commands invoked from inside vi.

TABLE V.5: vi Editing Commands

COMMAND	DESCRIPTION
	MAKING CHANGES
~	Changes the case of a letter.
c*move*	Replaces from the cursor location to *move* by inserting new text.
cc	Replaces the entire contents of the line by inserting new text.
C	Replaces from the position of the cursor to the end of the line by insertion.
ddp	Transposes two lines.
deep	Transposes two words.
r	Replaces one character but does not enter input mode.
R	Replaces by overstrike.
S	Replaces the current line by insertion.
Xp	Transposes two characters.
	UNDOING AND REPEATING CHANGES
.	Repeats the last command to modify the editing buffer.
u	Undoes the last command that modified the editing buffer. To undo the undo, use uu, which leaves the line in its original state.
U	Restores the current line.
Ctrl-1	Refreshes the screen.
	DELETING TEXT
d*move*	Deletes from the cursor to *move*.
dd	Deletes the current line.
dG	Deletes from the current line to the end of the buffer.
:*line*	Goes to the start of the specified *line*.
:*line*d	Deletes the specified line.
:*line*,*line*d	Deletes the specified range of lines.
D	Deletes from the cursor to the end of the line.
x	Deletes the character at the position of the cursor.
X	Deletes the character to the left of the cursor.

TABLE V.5 continued: vi Editing Commands

COMMAND	DESCRIPTION
INSERTING TEXT	
:*liner filename*	Inserts contents of *filename* after the specified *line*.
:r *filename*	Inserts contents of *filename* after the current line.
:*liner !command*	Inserts the output of *command* after the specified *line*.
:r *!command*	Inserts the output of *command* after the current *line*.
:r *!lookpattern*	Inserts words that begin with the specified *pattern*.
COPYING AND MOVING LINES	
:*linecotarget*	Copies the specified line, and inserts it after *target*.
:*line,linecotarget*	Copies the specified range, and inserts it after *target*.
:*linemtarget*	Moves the specified line, and inserts it after *target*.
:*line,linemtarget*	Moves the specified range, and inserts it after *target*.
EXECUTING SHELL COMMANDS	
:!*command*	Pauses vi, and executes the specified shell *command*.
:!!	Pauses vi, and executes the previous shell *command*.
:sh	Pauses vi, and starts a shell.
:!csh	Pauses vi, and starts the C shell.
SAVING YOUR WORK	
:w	Writes data out to the original file without quitting vi.
:w *filename*	Writes data out to the specified *filename*.
:w> *filename*	Appends data to the end of the specified filename.
QUITTING vi	
:q!	Quits vi without saving data.
ZZ	Saves data, and quits vi.

Searching for Patterns

Searching for a specific pattern of characters is an excellent way to navigate through the edit buffer. If you type /, vi displays a / on the command line at the bottom of the screen. Enter a pattern, press Return, and vi searches for the next occurrence of that pattern. Press / followed by

Return to repeat the same search. Table V.6 lists the commands you can use when searching for and replacing a pattern, as well as the characters you can use in regular expressions.

TABLE V.6: Search and Replace Commands in vi

COMMAND	DESCRIPTION
SEARCHING FOR A PATTERN	
/*expression*	Searches forward for the next occurrence of the specified regular expression.
/	Repeats the forward search for the same regular expression.
?*expression*	Searches backward for the previous occurrence of the specified regular expression.
?	Repeats the backward search for the same regular expression.
n	Repeats the last / or ? command in the same direction.
n	Repeats the last / or ? command in the opposite direction.
REPLACING A PATTERN	
:s/*pattern*/*replace*/	Substitutes *replace* for *pattern* in the current line.
:*lines*/*pattern*/*replace*/	Substitutes *replace* for *pattern* in the specified *lines*.
:*line*,*lines*/*pattern*/ *replace*/	Substitutes *replace* for *pattern* in the specified range of lines.
:%s/*pattern*/*replace*/	Substitutes *replace* for *pattern* in all lines.
SPECIAL CHARACTERS USED IN REGULAR EXPRESSIONS	
.	Matches any single character except newline.
*	Matches zero or more of the preceding characters.
^	Matches the beginning of a line.
$	Matches the end of a line.
\<	Matches the beginning of a word.
\>	Matches the end of a word.
[ ]	Matches any of the enclosed characters.
[^]	Matches any of the characters not enclosed.
\	Interprets the following character literally, removing any special meaning the character may have had.

Notes

When vi first starts up, it looks for a file called .exrc in your home directory and executes any ex commands that it contains.

See also emacs, ex, vedit, view, vi **local variables**

vi LOCAL VARIABLES

The vi editor has approximately 40 local variables you can set to customize your vi editing sessions. You can look at or change their values using the vi :set command. Some of these variables are either enabled or disabled, while others have a number or a string as their value. You can include commands for setting these variables in the .exrc file in your home directory.

See also vedit, vi

view

A command that starts the vi text editor in read-only mode, which is the same as using vi -R.

See also vedit, vi

view mode

In emacs, a read-only mode where you can look at but not change the contents of a file.

virtual console

A feature found in Linux, UnixWare, and certain other systems that allows you to log on as though you were different users. To open a new virtual console, press and hold the Alt key as you press one of the function keys F1 through F8. As you press each function key, you see a new screen complete with its own login prompt. Each virtual console displays its own output on its own virtual screen.

See also virtual terminal

virtual memory

A memory management technique that allows information in physical memory to be swapped out to a hard disk. This technique provides application programs with more memory space than is actually available in the computer.

True virtual memory management requires specialized hardware in the processor for the operating system to use; it is not just a question of writing information out to a swap area on the hard disk at the application level.

In a virtual memory system, programs and their data are divided into smaller pieces called *pages*. At the point at which more memory is needed, the operating system decides which pages are least likely to be needed soon (using an algorithm based on frequency of use, most recent use, and program priority), and it writes these pages out to disk. The memory space that they used is then available to the rest of the system for other application programs. When these pages are needed again, they are loaded back into real memory, displacing other pages.

virtual terminal

A simulated terminal that behaves as though it is an independent connection to the computer but actually shares the same keyboard and screen. Linux, UnixWare, and several other systems that run on Intel-based hardware support virtual terminals.

See also **virtual console**

vis

A BSD filter command that displays non-printing characters.

See also unvis

VISUAL

A Korn shell environment variable that invokes the visual command-line editing option in emacs, gmacs, or vi.

See also emacs, vi

vmstat

A command that reports statistics on virtual memory and how it is being used. It shows the number of processes, the amount of RAM and swap area available, paging information, and disk statistics.

w

A command that reports on system usage, logged-on users and what they are doing, and the load average. The load average is the average number of processes in the last 1, 5, and 15 minutes.

Syntax
Here's the syntax to use:

    w [options]username

Options and Arguments
Normally, w reports on all users, but if you specify *username* as a comma-separated list of names, the report is restricted to information on just these names. The options available with this command are listed in Table W.1.

See also finger, ps, uptime, who, whodo

TABLE W.1: Options to Use with w

Option	Description
-h	Turns off the report header line.
-l	Creates a long listing, including the following columns:
	User The name of the logged on user
	Tty The number of the terminal
	Login@ Time the user logged in
	Idle Number of minutes since the user typed anything at the terminal
	JCPU CPU minutes accumulated by all jobs run during this login session
	PCPU Minutes accumulated by the current process
	What Name of the current process and its arguments
-q	Creates a quick listing that consists of User, Tty, Idle, and What.
-t	Displays only the heading line; equivalent to the output from uptime.

wait

A command used in shell scripts that waits for all background processes to complete. If you specify a process ID, this command waits for that process to complete.

wall

A command that broadcasts a message to all logged on users.

Syntax

The syntax is:

```
wall message
```

where *message* is read from the standard input and is terminated with Ctrl-D. When you receive such a *message*, you see:

```
Broadcast Message:
```

on your terminal, followed by the text of the message.

This command is often used by the system administrator to tell everyone that the system will shut down shortly. There are no options for this command.

See also mesg, write

WC

A command that counts all the characters, words, and lines in a file.

Syntax

The syntax for wc is as follows:

```
wc [options][filename]
```

Options and Arguments

If you don't specify *filename*, wc reads from the standard input instead. If you specify more than one file, wc displays totals for each file and a grand total from all the files in the group. The options for wc are listed in Table W.2. The default report is equivalent to specifying all the options at once.

TABLE W.2: Options to Use with wc

OPTION	DESCRIPTION
-c	Counts the bytes in the specified *filename*.
-C	Counts the characters in the specified *filename*.
-l	Counts the lines in the specified *filename*.
-w	Counts the words in the specified *filename*.

Examples

The wc command is very useful in pipelines, as in the following sequence, which combines the ls command with wc to count the number of lines in the ls output—that is, the number of files in a directory:

```
ls | wc -l
```

Notes

The wc command defines a word as any sequence of characters bounded by space, tab, or newline, or any combination of these elements.

what

See SCCS

whatis

A command that gives a quick, one-line description of a Unix keyword summarizing the header line of the appropriate man page entry.

Syntax

The syntax is:

```
whatis command
```

where *command* represents the keyword you are interested in. The result is the same as using man -f.

whence

A built-in Korn shell command that shows whether a command is a Unix command, a built-in shell command, a defined shell function name, or an alias. The syntax is:

```
whence [options] command
```

where *command* represents the keyword you are interested in. whence has two options, as shown in Table W.3.

See also type, which

TABLE W.3: Options to Use with whence

Option	Description
-p	Searches for the pathname of *command*.
-v	Displays a long report; same as type -v.

whereis

A BSD command used to locate a program; when a copy of the program is found, whereis displays the complete pathname. Here's the syntax:

```
whereis program...
```

On some systems, the -m option displays the locations of the manual page files corresponding to the specified program name.

See also find, whence, which

which

A command that locates a Unix command and displays its pathname; which cannot locate built-in shell commands. The syntax to use is:

```
which command
```

which returns the name of the file that would be executed if you ran *command* by searching your shell configuration file .cshrc for aliases and searching the path variable. This command has no options.

See also type

while

A C shell programming construct used to set up a loop. The loop continues to run as long as the results are true (returns a zero value). When a false value is returned, the loop terminates. An example might look like this:

```
while condition
       commands
end
```

You can use break to terminate the loop and continue to continue the loop.

See also do, done, fi, for, if, shift, then, until

who

A command used to list the names of all users currently logged in to the system.

Syntax
The syntax for this command is:

```
who [option] filename
```

Options and Arguments
With no options, who lists the names of the users currently logged on to the system. Some versions of who, including those from Solaris and the BSD, have no options, while versions from other sources have the options listed in Table W.4.

You can use an optional argument *filename* to supply additional information; the default is /var/adm/utmp.

TABLE W.4: Options to Use with who

OPTION	DESCRIPTION
-a	Turns on all options except –T.
-b	Indicates when the system was last booted.
-d	Lists dead processes that have not been respawned by init.
-H	Adds the heading line to the report.
-l	Lists the terminals on which no one is logged in.
-p	Lists the active processes started by init.
-r	Displays the current run level of init.
-q	Displays only a space-separated list of usernames and a count of users.
-s	Displays only the name, terminal, and login time for each user.
-t	Indicates when the system clock was last changed.
-T	Displays the terminal state as writable (+), not writable (–), or unknown (?).
-u	Lists only the current users.
am I	Displays the username of the person invoking who.

Examples

The who report on most systems includes the following fields:

- ▶ NAME: login name of the user
- ▶ STATE: state of the terminal (see –T in Table W.4)
- ▶ LINE: the device number
- ▶ TIME: date and time the user logged in
- ▶ IDLE: length of time since the terminal was last used. A period indicates it was used within the last minute, and the word old indicates it has not been used for at least 24 hours.
- ▶ PID: process ID
- ▶ COMMENTS: any optional comments

See also finger, ps, rwho, users, w, whoami, whodo

whoami

A command that displays your login name.

See also finger, ps, rwho, users, w, who

whodo

An SCO command that formats who and ps command output to show you who is doing what, where.

See also finger, ps, rwho, users, w, who, whoami

whois

A TCP/IP command that searches an Internic Registry for the person, login, or organization specified on the command-line. The syntax is:

    whois [*option*]*name*

The single option, -h *host name*, limits the search to the specified *host name*.

See also finger, who

widget

A high-level programming element that is in the X Window system and is used by programmers to create the windows, buttons, scrollbars, and pull-down menus that form the user interface.

widget library

A library of programming elements in the X Window environment, used by programmers to create larger pieces of the user interface, including windows, buttons, scrollbars, and pull-down menus.

wildcard

A character appearing in a filename that stands for a set of possible characters. Sometimes it is written as *wild card* and is also known as a *metacharacter*. In filenames, a question mark (?) stands for any single character, while an asterisk (*) stands for any sequence of zero or more characters. You can also use square brackets to match any characters listed in the brackets; for example, a[ab] matches aa or ab.

Wildcards do not match files whose names begin with a dot to prevent you from deleting these important files by accident.

See also **filename completion, filename substitution, globbing**

window

A BSD command that implements a windowed environment on an ASCII terminal. When window starts running, it executes the commands contained in the .windowrc file in your home directory. If this file doesn't exist, two equally sized windows are created by default. window supports up to nine different windows, but only one window at a time can receive input from the keyboard.

See also X Window

wksh

A special version of the Korn shell that includes X Window system extensions and is used to provide an X Window interface for applications developed for the Korn shell.

working directory

Jargon for the current working directory, also known as the *current directory*.

write

A command that opens an interactive communications session with another user. The syntax for the write command is as follows:

```
write user tty
```

where *user* is the login name of the person you want to talk to and *tty* is an optional argument to resolve any ambiguity if the person is logged in to more than one terminal.

When you use write, a message appears on the specified *user* terminal, telling the user that you are about to send a message. Type the text of your message, and then press Ctrl-D when you are finished to terminate the write command. You can use an exclamation mark (!) followed by a command in the middle of a write session to execute a shell command; the other user does not see the exclamation mark, the command, or the output from the command.

See also mail, mailx, mesg, talk, wall

write permission

Permission for your programs to write data to a certain file or to create files in a directory.

See also execute permission, file permissions

X

xargs

A command that lets you pass a long list of arguments to a command, often a list of filenames passed by a pipe.

Syntax

The syntax to use with xargs is as follows:

```
xargs [options] [command]
```

Options and Arguments

xargs repeatedly invokes *command* using arguments read from the standard input as command-line arguments until the standard input is exhausted. The *command* must not read from the standard input, and if no *command* is specified, it defaults to the echo command. The options you can use with xargs are listed in Table X.1.

TABLE X.1: Options to Use with xargs

Option	Description
-estring	Stops passing arguments when *string* is encountered; the default is the underscore character (_).
-I	Passes arguments to *command*, replacing any curly braces on the command line with the current line of input.
-ln	Executes *command* for *n* lines of input.
-nn	Calls *command* with up to *n* arguments.
-ssize	Calls *command*, limiting the length of the command line to *size* characters.
-t	Enables trace mode, and echoes each *command* before it is executed.
-x	Terminates if the argument list is longer than the -s option allows.

xbench

A public domain X Window benchmark program that runs approximately 40 individual tests consisting of different X operations. The results of these tests are combined into a single measurement of the performance of your system called an *Xstone*; the higher the number, the faster your system. As with many benchmark programs, the tests may not give an accurate representation of actual performance when running your mix of applications.

See also x11perf

xbiff

An X Window version of the biff program; xbiff lets you know when the mail has arrived. xbiff is a picture of a mailbox in a small window on your screen; when the flag on the mailbox is up, you have mail. When the flag is down, you are up-to-date on reading your mail.

See also biff, mail, mailx, **X client**

xcalc

An X Window version of a scientific calculator operated by using a mouse. xcalc can emulate a Texas Instruments TI-30 or a Hewlett-Packard 10C. To run the TI calculator in the background, enter:

```
xcalc &
```

To use the HP 10C, enter:

```
xcalc -rpn &
```

See also bc, dc, **X client**

X client

An X Window program, that uses an X server to act as its interface with a terminal.

X is not limited to one server and one client; many combinations are possible. Clients can interact with a single server when several applications display on the same terminal, or a single client can communicate with several servers and display the same information on many different terminals.

The command-line options for an X client can be long and complex. A - usually turns an option on, while a + turns an option off—just the opposite of what you might expect. You can also abbreviate an option to its shortest unambiguous form, so you can use -bg rather than -background or -fn rather than -font. Table X.2 lists the most commonly used X client command-line options; most of these options define characteristics of the window in which the application runs and can be used with most X programs. Other options may be available on your system; see your documentation for details.

Many common Unix programs are available in X versions; there are X-based troff and TEX viewers, X-based editors and debuggers, X-based Internet-access programs, including xgopher, xarchie, and xmosaic, and even X-based plotting and display programs. See the FAQ in the USENET newsgroup comp.windows.x for more details.

See also **X server**

TABLE X.2: Common X Client Command-Line Options

OPTION	DESCRIPTION
-bd *color*	Specifies *color* as the window border color.
-bg *color*	Specifies *color* as the window background color.
-bw *width*	Specifies a window border of *width* pixels.
-e *program*	Executes *program*, and uses *program* as the window title, unless you also use the -title option.
-fg *color*	Specifies *color* as the window foreground color.
-fn *font*	Specifies the name of the fixed-width font to use.
-help	Displays a list of command options.
-rv	Simulates reverse video by swapping the foreground and background colors. Use +rv to prevent this swapping when reverse video is set as the default.
-title *string*	Specifies *string* as the title of the window if the window manager requests a title.

xclock

An X program that displays a clock on your terminal. You can use the command-line options detailed in Table X.3 to configure the clock display to your liking.

A variation of xclock, called oclock, displays a round clock face instead of the rectangular face used by xclock.

See also X client

TABLE X.3: Options to Use with xclock

OPTION	DESCRIPTION
-analog	Displays an ordinary 12-hour clock face, the default.
-chime	Chimes once on the half hour and twice on the hour; a good way to annoy your coworkers.
-digital	Displays a 24-hour digital clock.
-hd *color*	Specifies *color* as the color of the hands.
-hl *color*	Specifies *color* as the color of the edges of the hands.
-padding *n*	Specifies *n* pixels of space around the clock; the defaults are 8 for an analog clock and 10 for a digital clock.
-update *n*	Specifies that the clock be updated every *n* seconds; the default is 60. Any value of less than 60 adds a second hand to the analog clock, and the clock is updated every second.

xcolors

An X program that displays a color chart so you can see what the different colors actually look like.

See also X client

.Xdefaults

An X Window configuration file in your home directory that sets window-related values for all X clients.

.Xdefaults is a text file, and the syntax used to set a resource requires the name of a general resource such as background or a program name and a resource such as xclock*background. To establish a blue background for all instances of xclock, include the following in your .Xdefaults file:

```
xclock*background: blue
```

You can enter statements in any order, but it makes good sense to group like statements together; use an exclamation point to begin a comment line, and X Window ignores anything else on that same line. Use the xrdb program to display or edit the values in .Xdefaults.

See also X client, xinit, .xinitrc, xrdb

xdm

The X Window display manager. A program that starts your X server and opens a window that you can use to log in to the system. xdm then starts xterm, a shell script, or an application that you specify. When you finish and log out, xdm resets the server and displays the login window once again, ready for the next user.

See also X client, xterm

xdpr

An X Window program that captures and prints a standard screen dump.

See also X client, xwd

x11perf

An MIT X Window benchmark program that tests over 150 different aspects of an X server operation. The results of these tests are not combined into a single measurement of system performance but are listed so you can make your own judgment for your own particular application mix. The x11perfcomp program takes output from x11perf and presents it in tabular form.

See also xbench

X11R5

Abbreviation for the 1991 X 11 Release 5 specification for the X Window system. This release of the specification added the ability to support scalable fonts, certain international symbols, as well as 2D and 3D graphics.

X11R6

Abbreviation for the 1994 X 11 Release 6 specification for the X Window system, which added an object-oriented interface, improved 3D graphics, servers capable of performing multiple tasks, screen savers, and improved performance over a dial-up modem.

XENIX

A version of Unix developed from Unix Version 7 as a joint venture between Microsoft and SCO and released in 1980. XENIX was intended to support commercial applications on the IBM PC (versions were also developed for the Motorola 68000 and Zilog Z8000), and for a while XENIX was the most successful Unix in terms of sheer numbers sold. Microsoft sold its interest in XENIX to SCO in 1987.

xfd

An X Window program that displays the characters in a specified font in their own window.

Syntax
The syntax is:

```
xfd -font font-name
```

where *font-name* indicates the name of the font you want to look at. The window contains the name of the font being displayed, a grid containing one character per cell, and three buttons: Prev Page, Next Page, and quit. The characters are displayed in increasing ASCII order from left to right and from top to bottom.

See also X client, xfontsel, xlsfonts

X.500

A recommended standard, first released in 1988 and revised in 1992, for a global directory system for locating e-mail users, to be used with the X.400 e-mail services. X.500 is similar to a worldwide telephone book. The Lightweight Directory Access Protocol (LDAP) is a component of X.500

xfontsel

An X Window program that lists and displays the fonts available to the X server.

See also X client, xfd, xlsfonts

X.400

A recommended standard, released in 1984 and revised in 1988, for public or private international e-mail distribution systems, defining how messages will be transferred across the network or between two or more connected heterogeneous networks. X.400 defines the components of an electronic address, as well as the details of the envelope surrounding the message and the rules to follow when converting between message types, such as text or fax.

See also X.500

XFree86

A version of the X11R6 X Window system freely available for Intel-based Unix systems such as Linux and FreeBSD. You can get XFree86 using anonymous ftp to sunsite.unc.edu in the /pub/Linux/X11 directory.

xinit

An X Window program used to manually start the X server and an initial X client program; if your system does not start X Window automatically, you can use xinit. xinit executes the configuration commands in the .xinitrc file; if this file does not exist, xinit opens an xterm window.

See also X client, .xinitrc, X server

.xinitrc

An X Window initialization file executed by xinit when starting X. On SCO's Open Desktop, this file is called .startxrc instead.

xkill

An X Window program that forces the X server to close its connection to an X client. You can use xkill to get rid of a hung window, but the clients that it kills may not always terminate cleanly.

See also kill, **X client, X server**

xlax

An X Window program used by system administrators to execute the same commands on many different host computers, where each host has its own xterm window.

See also **X client**, xterm

xlib

A library of over 300 C language routines that provide the basics of the X Window system. The library includes groups of functions for:

▶ Opening connections to servers

▶ Issuing X requests

▶ Receiving events and information from the server

▶ Performing X-related tasks

▶ Improving X performance

See also library

xlock

An X Window program that locks your terminal and displays a screen saver to prevent anyone from using your system if you leave your office for a few moments and would rather not log off the system. The screen saver also prevents anyone from looking at your work while you are out of the office.

To regain control of your system, press a key or click the mouse; you will be prompted to enter your login password.

See also **X client**, xset

xlsfonts

An X Window program that lists the available fonts. Specify the font you are interested in with:

```
xlsfonts font-name
```

where *font-name* is the name of the font you are interested in; if you omit *font-name*, information is displayed for all the fonts. You can also use the wildcard characters ? and * to match characters.

See also **X client**, xfd, xfontsel

xman

An X Window program that provides an X interface to the Unix man pages. When xman starts, the initial Manual Browser window displays three buttons: Help, Quit, and Manual Page. Click on the Manual Page or Help buttons to see a set of instructions on how to use xman. At the top of the window you see two menus: Options and Sections. Options determines what you do next, and Sections lets you choose between the major sections of the Unix online documentation. See the help screen for more details.

See also cat, man, man **pages**, **X client**

x protocol

A UUCP protocol, designed for use over X.25 connections. The x protocol is similar to the g protocol, except that there is no per-packet checksum and the packet size is larger at 512 rather than 64.

See also e **protocol**, f **protocol**

xrdb

An X Window program used to create and display the collection of global X resources available to all X clients using your X server.

Syntax
The syntax for xrdb is:

    xrdb [options]filename

where *filename* specifies a file containing a set of resources that you want to load and use rather than the existing resources. The normal filename is .Xdefaults. The most important options for xrdb are listed in Table X.4; you can also use those options listed with the X client entry earlier in this book.

See also .Xdefaults, xinit, .xinitrc, xset, xsetroot

TABLE X.4: Options to Use with xrdb

OPTION	DESCRIPTION
-load	Loads the global resource database from the standard input.
-merge	Merges the standard input into the global resource database.
-query	Displays the current contents of the global resource database on the standard output.
-remove	Empties the global resource database.

xrn

An X Window interface to the `rn` newsreader used to access USENET newsgroups.

See also rn, **X client**

xsend

A set of BSD utilities that implements an encrypted e-mail system on top of the normal `mail` program. There are three parts to the system:

- ▸ `enroll` asks you to specify a password. You must use this password to access the other two parts of the system.
- ▸ `xsend` works just like `mail`, except that it does not send copies of your message to cc recipients.
- ▸ `xget` is used to read encrypted e-mail.

X server

An X Window display server. X is not limited to one server and one client, and many combinations are possible. Several clients may interact with a single server when several different applications display on the same terminal, or a single client can communicate with several servers and display the same information on several different terminals.

See also **X client**

xset

An X Window program used to configure several user-selected items, including the pathname for font directories, keyboard adjustments, screen-saver parameters, and mouse speed settings. The command:

```
xset q
```

lists the current settings; note that the option is q and not -q as you might expect.

Any X settings that you change are lost or reset to their default values when you log off unless you add them to the .xinitrc file in your home directory.

See also set, X client, .xinitrc, xsetroot

xsetroot

An X Window program used to change the appearance of the root window, the background behind all the other windows. See your system manual for information on the options available with this command.

See also X client, xset

xstr

A BSD software development command that removes text strings from a program and replaces them with references to a strings database.

xterm

An X Window command that opens a text-based terminal emulation window on a graphics terminal. xterm emulates a VT100 and a Tektronics 4015 graphics terminal; you are unlikely to have either of these terminals, but the purpose of these emulations is to provide a consistent interface.

The name of the X terminal emulator may vary depending on the version of Unix you use. In the SCO Open Desktop, xterm is known as scoterm, and in Hewlett-Packard systems as hpterm; in Sun systems, you find cmdterm and shelltool in addition to xterm, and in UnixWare, you find a Terminal window.

Because xterm acts just like a real terminal running your shell, you can still run all the old familiar character-based commands and utilities, such as ls, pwd, even vi, all without leaving X. Running these character-based applications with xterm gives you other advantages, including:

▶ You can cut and paste between xterm and other X windows, giving a degree of communications between the older programs and your X clients.

▶ You can customize your keyboard and map function keys separately for each window.

▶ You can scroll text output or log your session to a file.

▶ You can connect each xterm window to a different host computer so you can perform work on several different computers, all from the same physical terminal.

▶ You can open multiple terminals in different windows and run several simultaneous copies of the same program.

▶ By using telnet from an xterm window, you can run applications on computers that do not have X Window support.

You can activate the xterm menus by holding down the Ctrl key and using the mouse as follows:

▶ Ctrl and clicking the left mouse button opens the xterm menu, which contains selections you can use to start logging and to send signals of various kinds to the current foreground process.

▶ Ctrl and clicking the middle mouse button opens a menu containing options to set the various terminal modes. On some systems with a two-button mouse, you have to press both buttons simultaneously to simulate this option.

▶ Ctrl and clicking the right mouse button may open a menu containing font selections; on some systems, this combination does nothing.

The main command-line options you can use with xterm are listed in Table X.5. You can also use those options listed in Table X.2.

See also **virtual terminal, X client,** xlax

TABLE X.5: Options to Use with xterm

OPTION	DESCRIPTION
-j or +j	Turns jump scrolling on or off, which makes xterm much faster when scanning long files; also called *speed scrolling*.
-l	Sends xterm input and output to the default log file XtermLog.*n*, where *n* is a five-digit number that represents the process ID number.
-sb or +sb	Turns the scroll bars on or off, and saves text that rolls off the top of the screen in a buffer so you can look at it later.
-sl *n*	Specifies the number of lines in the text buffer.

xtod

A command that converts Unix text files into DOS format.

Syntax
The syntax is:

```
xtod filename > outputfile
```

where *filename* is the name of the Unix file you want to convert, and *outputfile* is the name you want to give to the DOS file after the conversion.

Unix uses the newline character to indicate the end of a line, while DOS uses two characters: a carriage return and a linefeed. DOS also uses Ctrl-Z as an end-of-file marker. xtod adds an extra carriage return to the end of each line, and Ctrl-Z to the end of the file. You cannot use xtod on binary files.

See also dtox

xtract

An SCO command that extracts one file from a cpio archive.

Syntax
The syntax is:

```
xtract options filename archive
```

Options and Arguments
Where *options* are cpio options, and *filename* defines the name of the file that you want to extract from the *archive*. The extraction is actually done using cpio -iv.

See also cpio

xwd

An X Window program that writes a copy of the screen to a file and then uses the xwud program to display or print the image.

See also X client, xdpr

X Window

A windowing system originally developed at MIT and now jointly owned and distributed by the nonprofit X Consortium.

X is a windowing system that allows multiple resizable windows so that you can have many applications displayed on your screen at the same time. Unlike most windowing systems that have a specific built-in user interface, X is a foundation upon which you can construct almost any style of user interface. The unique feature of X is that it is based on a network protocol rather than the more usual programming procedure calls.

The X system consists of three main parts:

▶ The X server software, which controls your display, keyboard, and mouse. It accepts requests sent across the communications link from client application programs to open a window on the screen, change the size or position of a window, and display text and draw graphics in these windows. The server sends back events to the clients, telling them about keyboard or mouse input.

▶ The X client software or application programs, which are completely separate from the server. X is not limited to one server and one client; many combinations are possible.

▶ A communications link that connects the client and the server. This link can be implemented in one of two ways, either as an interprocess communications mechanism such as shared memory, when both client and server are running on the same computer, or over a network, when client and server are running on different computers.

This definition separates the X client software from the X server to the extent that they can run on hardware from different vendors

The protocol is the real definition of X Window, and it defines four types of messages that can be transferred over the communications link. Requests are sent from the client to the server, and replies, events, and error messages are sent from the server to the client. The X Window system is complex enough so that whole books are devoted to it; one publisher in particular, O'Reilly & Associates, has produced a library of about twenty technical books in its X Window System series. Check out http://www.ora.com with your World Wide Web browser for details.

X Window versions of many popular programs are available; what usually happens is that the programmer indicates the X Window version by prefacing the old program name with an x, so biff becomes xbiff, man becomes xman, gopher becomes xgopher, and so on.

See also **Motif, Open Look, widget,** window, .Xdefaults, **X client, X server,** xterm

Y

yacc

A program used to create a parser (a program that converts text files into something else) from a simple set of rules contained in a file. yacc reads in the set of rules or the language syntax from the file and outputs a C or Ratfor (a version of Fortran originally called rational Fortran) program to recognize that language. The name yacc is an acronym formed from yet another compiler compiler.

See also lex

yes

A BSD and SCO command that prints either the y character or a specified string, continuously.

Syntax
The syntax is:

    yes [string]

This command is used in pipes to commands that prompt for input and require a y response. The yes command terminates when the command it pipes to terminates.

yppasswd

An NIS command used to change your NIS password. When you type this command, you are prompted first for your current NIS password, then for your new NIS password.

See also passwd

yyfix

A BSD command used to extract tables from yacc-generated files.

See also yacc

Z

zcat

A command that uncompresses one or more compressed files to the standard output leaving the compressed files unchanged.

Syntax
The syntax is:

    zcat filename...

The zcat command has no options.

See also compact, compress, pack, pcat, uncompact, uncompress, unpack

zcmp

A BSD command that invokes the cmp command on a compressed file.

Syntax
The syntax is:

    zcmp [cmp-options]filename1 [filename2]

where *cmp-options* are passed directly to the cmp command. See the cmp entry earlier in this book for details.

See also cmp, diff, gzip, zmore, znew

zdiff

A BSD command that invokes the diff command on a compressed file.

Syntax
The syntax is:

    zdiff [diff-options]filename1 [filename2]

where *diff-options* are passed directly to the diff command. See the diff entry earlier in this book for details.

See also cmp, diff, gzip, zmore, znew

zforce

A BSD command that forces a .gz filename extension on all gzip files so that gzip will not compress them twice. On systems with a 14-character limitation on filenames, you may find that a long filename is truncated to make room for the `.gz` suffix.

See also `gzip`, `zcmp`, `zdiff`, `zgrep`, `zmore`, `znew`

zgrep

A BSD version of `grep` for use on compressed files. Any command-line options you specify are passed directly to `grep`, and files you specify are automatically uncompressed and then passed to `grep`.

See also `gzip`, `zcmp`, `zdiff`, `zmore`, `znew`

zmore

A BSD filter command used to view compressed files. `zmore` works on files compressed by `gzip`, `pack`, or `compress`, as well as files that have not been compressed.

`zmore` works just like `more`, and displays:

```
– More –
```

at the bottom of the screen; press Return to display the next line, or press Space to display the next screenful.

See also `gzip`, `more`

znew

A BSD command that recompresses files from `compress` format (with a `.Z` filename extension) to files in `gzip` format (with a `.gz` filename extension).

Syntax
Here's the syntax:

```
znew [options]filename.Z...
```

Options and Arguments
The options you can use with `znew` are listed in Table Z.1.

See also `compress`, `gzip`, `zforce`

TABLE Z.1: Options to Use with znew

OPTIONS	DESCRIPTION
-9	Uses the slowest compression method for the greatest degree of compression.
-f	Forces a recompression from `.Z` format to `.gz` format even if a file in `.gz` format already exists.
-K	Keeps the `.Z` format file when it is smaller than the `.gz` format file.

TABLE Z.1 continued: Options to Use with znew

OPTIONS	DESCRIPTION
-P	Uses pipes during the conversion to conserve disk space.
-t	Tests the new files before deleting the originals.
-v	Displays the filename and percentage compression as each file is processed.

Zsh

A replacement for the Bourne shell and C shell developed by Paul Falstad; pronounced "zee-shell." Zsh is a relatively new shell, first released in 1990, and offers command-line editing among other advanced features. Zsh has developed something of a cult following among C programmers and advanced Unix users.

See also Bourne shell family

INDEX

Note to the Reader: Throughout this index *italics* page numbers refer to figures; **boldfaced** page numbers refer to primary discussions of the topic.

SYMBOLS AND NUMBERS

& (ampersand)
  for background process-
    ing, **125–127**, 236,
    486
  to terminate command,
    136
! (bang), **487**, **624**
  to escape to shell for
    command execution,
    857
  for file name generation,
    230
  in ftp, 656
  to reverse matching in
    sed, **299**
  in UUCP addresses, 369
! (bang) command, 129
! (bang) command (ftp), 391
! (NOT) operator (awk), 309,
  310
&& (AND) operator, 309
&& operator for branching, **351**
\ (backslash), **226–227**
- command (mailx), 755
- (dash), for grep range, 281
- (dash), in command syntax,
  18
" (double quotes), **228–229**,
  596

\# command (mailx), 755
\# (pound sign), **807**
  in awk, 302
  for C shell script, 203
  as comment character,
    227–228, 558
  for root prompt, 58
/ (slash), 26–27, **861**
  for root symbol, 31–32
$ (dollar sign), 213, **591**
  and double quotes, 225
  in grep command, 279
  in v command, 285
  variable name with,
    95–96
$ prompt
  for Bourne shell, 10
  for Korn shell, 709
$ shell variable, 556
$? shell variable, 334–335
$! shell variable (Bourne), 504
$# shell variable (Bourne), 504
$$ shell variable (Bourne), 504
$* shell variable (Bourne), 504
$- shell variable (Bourne), 504
$? shell variable (Bourne), 504
$! shell variable (Korn), 714
$# shell variable (Korn), 714
$$ shell variable (Korn), 714
$* shell variable (Korn), 714
$? shell variable (Korn), 714

$_ shell variable (Korn), 714
$@, to scan argument list,
  358–359
$0 shell variable (Bourne), 504
$0 variable (awk), 484
% prompt (C shell), 10, **799**
' (single quote), **861**. *See also*
  quoting
  in grep commands, 209
* (asterisk), 866
  for file name generation,
    230
  in grep command, 281
  in v command, 285–286
  as wildcard, 41, **475–476**
+ (plus) symbol, **806**
++ (postincrement) operator,
  313
. (dot) command, **210**
. (period), **799**
  and file searches, 42–43
  in filenames, 26
  in grep command, 280
  in v command, 285
  as vi repeat command,
    179
.. (two periods), for home directory, 35, 103
: (colon)
  to indicated Bourne shell
    script, 203
  in vi command mode, 187

: command, 505, **535**
    for command argument,
      345
: command (C shell), 558
: command (Korn shell), 716
; (semicolon), **853**
    in case statement, 349
    in multicommand line,
      135
    to terminate command,
      136
;login, **737**
< command (vi), 184
<< command (vi), 184
< (less than) symbol, **728**
= assignment operator, 95
== (relational operator),
    307–308
> command (vi), 184
>> command (vi), 184
> (greater-than) symbol, 39,
    665
>> redirection operator, 54
? command (ftp), 391
? command (Mail), 752
? command (mailx), 755
? command (telnet), 394, 886
? (question mark), 41, **817**
    for file name generation,
      230
    in ftp, 656
    for mail command mode
      prompt, 65
@ command (C shell), 558
@(#) (what string), 203
[] (square brackets), **868**
    for file name generation,
      230
    in grep command, 281
    for optional arguments,
      18
    regular expressions with,
      286–287

^ (caret), **512**
    in grep command, 279,
      281
    with square brackets ([ ]),
      286–287
    in v command, 285
` (backquote), **486–487**
    in shell script, **224–226**
\ (backslash), 487
|| operator, for branching, **351**
|| (OR) operator, 309
| (vertical bar), for piping, 20
~ (tilde), **892**
    in C shell, 380
    for empty lines in vi, 169
    for home directory, 679
~ (tilde) escape sequences, **891**
4.4BSD Lite, **651**

A

.a filename extension, 638
a keyword (bc), 492
abbr command (vi), **189–195**
ABI (Application Binary
    Interface), **463**
aborting command (vi), 161
absolute mode for chmod com-
    mand, 112, 527, 528
absolute path names, **32**, **463**
    displaying, 33
accent grave, 486
access modes, 104
account, **464**
account command (ftp), 656
acct command, **464**
ACK (acknowledgment), **464**
Acsii command (ftp), 392
active processes, information
    about, **811–814**
active window, **464**, **648**
adb (debugger), **464**

Address Resolution Protocol
    (ARP), 385, 883
admin program (SCCS), 847
Advanced interactive Executive
    (AIX), **466**
AFS (Andrews File System),
    465
Aho, Alfred, 776
AIX (Advanced interactive
    Executive), **466**
alarm system, sleep command
    to create, 137
ali command (MH), 764
alias command (C shell),
    151–153, **466–467**, 558
alias command (Korn),
    466–467, 716
alias command (Mail), 752
alias command (mailx), 755
aliases
    listing setup, 152
    removing, 153, **913**
allexport option (Korn shell),
    713
alloc command (C shell), **467**,
    558
almanac, 733
Alt key, 5
    as Meta key, 608
alternate command (Mail), 752
alternate command (mailx),
    755
ambiguous file reference, **467**
American National Standards
    Institute (ANSI), **468–469**
ampersand (&)
    for background process-
      ing, **125–127**, 236,
      486
    to terminate command,
      136

AND (&&) operator, 309

AND operator (-a), in test command, 339

Andrews File System (AFS), **465**

anno command (MH), 764

anonymous ftp, 391, **467–468**

anonymous server, **468**

ANSI (American National Standards Institute), **468–469**

ANSI C, **469**

ansitape command, **469–470**

a.out file, **470**

API (application programming interface), **470**

append command (ed), 623

append command (ftp), 656

append mode, in vi editor, 170, 181

appending, **470**

    output to files, **54–55**

    text in sed stream editor, **300**

    vi buffer to file, 172

    yank, 185

Application Binary Interface (ABI), **463**

application interface in X, 425, 426

application layer (ISO/OSI), 696

Application layer (TCP/IP), 884

application programming interface (API), **470**

apropos command, **471**

ar command, **471–473**

archive, **473**

    copying files and directories to, 545–547

    creating in text form, 855–856

    work with, –880

archive libraries, 471–472

    table of contents for, **820**

arctangent, from bc, 492

ARGC variable (awk), 312

ARGC variable (nawk), 484

argument list, **474**

arguments, **17–21**, **474**, **538**

    empty vs. no, 337

    passing long list to command, **947**

    testing for, **355–356**

argv shell variable, **474**, 556

ARGV variable (awk), 312, 474

ARGV variable (nawk), 484

arithmetical values

    awk and, **313–316**

    sorting by, **245**

ARP (Address Resolution Protocol), 385, 883

array, **474**

    splitting string into, 316

as command, **474–475**

ascii command (ftp), 393, 657

ASCII control codes, backslash (\) to generate, 226–227

ASCII files, 16

    converting between EDCDIC and, 574

    dd command to convert, 266

    executable, 236

ASCII set, 5

ASCII strings, extracting from binary file, **872**

ASCII windowing system, starting, **724**

assembler, command to run, **474–475**

assignment statement, 214

asterisk (*), 866

    for file name generation, 230

    in grep command, 281

in v command, 285–286

    as wildcard, 41, **475–476**

at command, 138, **476–478**

    redirecting in, 140

at job queue

    listing contents, **478**

    removing jobs from, **478–479**

AT&T, 429

atan2 command (awk), 314, 482

atan2 command (nawk), 777

atq command, **478**

atrm command, **478–479**

.au filename extension, 638

auto keyword (bc), 492

AUTOEXEC.BAT file (DOS), 91

autoindent feature (vi), 160

autoindent (set argument), 192

autoload (Korn), **479**, 716

automatic check, overriding, 624

automounter, **479**

autoprint (set argument), 192

autowrite (set argument), 192

awk, 273, **301–319**, **479–485**

    ARGV variable, 474

    BEGIN and END, **311–313**

    commands in, 481, 482–484

    data types in, 312

    error in, 319

    -F option, **306–308**

    fields, **303–304**

    flow control, **316–319**

    general syntax, 302

    logical operators, **309–310**

    and math, **313–316**

    new awk, **776–779**

    operators in, 481–482

    predefined variables, 312

printf command, **306**
records, **304-306**
relational operators,
  308-309

B

backbones, 367
background, **485**
background processing, 124,
  486
  & (ampersand) for,
    125-127, 236, 486
  bringing to foreground,
    126-127
  waiting for, 940
backquote (`), 95, 98,
  486-487
  in shell script, **224-226**
backslash (\), **226-227**, 487
backspace, 223, 265, 564
  in vi editor, 161
Backspace key, 8, **487**
  in vi text-entry mode, 181
backup, **410-417**
  cpio command, **414**
  find command for selec-
    tive, 260-261
  frequency, 411
  incremental, **685**
  process, **413-417**
  responsibility for, 412-413
  strategies, 411
  tar command for,
    879-880
backward searches, 283
  in vi editor, 186
bang (!), **487, 624**
  to escape to shell for
    command execution,
    857
  for file name generation,
    230
  in ftp, 656

to reverse matching in
  sed, **299**
  in UUCP addresses, 369
bang (!) command, 129
bang (!) command (ftp), 391
bang path, **487**
banner command, **487-488**
banner page, 145, **488**
  default for printing, 148
Barber, Stan, 836
basename, **488**
basename utility, **488-489**
bash (Bourne Again shell), 91,
  489-490
.bash_logout file, 595
.bash_profile file, 595
.bashrc file, 595
Basic Networking Utilities
  (BNU), 679, 923
basic regular expressions. *See*
  regular expressions
basis, 130
batch command, 140
batch queue, **490-491**
batch utility, **490**
bbc command (MH), 764
bc, **491-494**
BCD (binary coded decimal),
  494
bdes utility, **494-495**
bdiff utility, **495-496**
beautify (set argument), 192
BEGIN (awk), **311-313**
bell, 265
bell command (ftp), 657
Besel function (bc), 492
bg command, 127, 486, **496**
bg command (C shell), 558
Bg command (Korn), 716
bgnice option (Korn shell), 713
bib, **496-498**
bibliographic databases
  creating inverted index

file for, **685-686**
  searching, **734-735**
  searching for specified
    keyword, **739**
bibliography file
  creating troff formatted
    output from, **827-828**
  preprocessor to format,
    496-498
biff utility, **498**
bin login name, 90
/bin/passwd file, 84
/bin subdirectory, 89, **498**
  in path, 90
binary command (ftp), 392,
  393, 657
binary files, 16, 89, 236, **499**
  displaying data and text
    segment sizes, 861
  extracting ASCII strings
    from, **872**
  mailing, **370-371**
binary numbers, **499**
bind, **499**
BISON, **499**
bit, **499**
bitmap program (X), 435
bitwise operator, **499**
blank, 144, 170, **499**
blind courtesy copy, 75, **500**
block device, **500**
block special file, 578, 636
blocks, **500**
  command to report size,
    531
BNU (Basic Networking
  Utilities), 679, 923
body, for mail message, 65
bookmarks, in vi editor, 187
Boolean expression, 317
  test command with,
    339-341
/boot directory, **500**

booting up, **405–406**
Borden, Bruce, 77
Bourne Again shell (bash),
 489–490
 starting, **821**
Bourne shell, 90, 200,
 500–507, 856
 $ prompt for, 10
 : command to indicate
  script for, 323
 commands, 501, 505–506
 curly braces ({ }) in, 507
 dot (.) command, **210**
 and Korn shell, 709
 login profile, **92**
 logout, 13
 metacharacters in,
  501–502
 predefined variables in,
  504–505
 quoting in, 503
 redirecting in, 502–503
 restricted version, 841
 scripts for, 201
 set command options,
  506–507
 special commands, 208
 starting, **854–855**
 startup files, 501
 Zsh as replacement, **963**
braces ({ }), 507
brackets ([]). *See* square brackets ([ ])
branching, logical operations
 for, **351**
break command, 326, 345, **507**
 for for loop, 357
break command (awk), 482
break command (Bourne), 505
break command (C shell), 558
Break command (Korn), 716
break command (nawk), 777
break (Ctrl-C), **563**

breaksw command (C shell),
 507, 558
broadcasting message, to all
 network users, 843–844
BSD terminal handler, cbreak
 mode, **514–515**
buffers, 8
 for file changes, 406–407
 numbered, **788**
 in vi editor, 185
bunzip function, 508
Burrows-Wheeler-Fenwick
 block-sorting text compression, 508
burst command (MH), 765
bye command (ftp), 656
bzip program, **508**

C

c command (vi), 183
.c filename extension, 638
c keyword (bc), 492
C language, 301
 bitwise operators, 499
 creating error message file
  from source code, 769
 curly braces ({ }) in, 507
 gcc C compiler, **659–660**
 lint to check source code,
  731
 source code formatting,
  514
 standard, 468, **469**
 X Window library of rou-
  tines, 953
C++ language, 301
 standard, 468
The C Programming Language,
 702
C shell, 91, 200, **552–561**, 856.
 See also csh command
 % prompt for, 10, **799**

alias command, **151–153**
 syntax, 467
 commands, 558–560
 curly braces ({ }) in, 507
 environment variables in,
  557–558
 login profile, **92–93**
 logout, 13
 metacharacters, 554
 quoting in, 555
 redirecting in, 554–555
 repeating commands, 624
 scripts for, 201
 startup files, 553
 Tcsh as replacement, 884
 Zsh as replacement, **963**
CAE (Common Application
 Environment), **508**
cal command, 19, **509**
 month argument, 20
 year argument, 20–21
calculator
 bc, **491–494**
 dc command for, **572**
calendar utility, **509–510**
calendars, **19**
 printing, **509**
call, **510**
call by reference, **510**
call by value, **511**
calling environment, **511**
cancel command, **156**,
 511–512
canceling, scheduled jobs, 138
Caps Lock key, and login error, 9
Car Ret key, 6
carbon copy, 74
caret (^), **512**
 in grep command, 279,
  281
 with square brackets ([ ]),
  286–287
 in v command, 285

carriage return, 223, **512**

case, **512**

case command

    in C shell, 558

    esac to end, **619**

    in Korn shell, 716

case-insensitive, **513**

case-sensitive, **513**

case sensitivity, 27

    of command options, 44

    in grep searches, **276–278**

    for password, 9

    and sort command, 243

    for user variables, 213

case statement, **349–351**

cat command, **45–46, 513–514**, 640

    to examine /etc/passwd file, 85–86

    for file creation, **47–48**

catenate, **514**

cb utility, **514**

cbreak mode, **514–515**

cc (C language compiler), **515–521**

cc command (vi), 184

ccat shell script, **521–522**

cd command, 34, 102, **522**

cd command (Bourne), 505

cd command (C shell), 559

cd command (ftp), 392, 656

Cd command (Korn), 716

cd command (mailx), 755

cd command (Samba), **449**

CD-ROM, command to eject from drive, 604

cdc program (SCCS), 847

CDE (Common Desktop Environment), **522**, 543

CDPATH shell variable (Bourne), 94, 504, **523**

cdpath shell variable (C shell), **522**, 556

CDPATH shell variable (Korn), **523**, 715

cdup command (ftp), 392, 656

central printers, **144–145**

change command, in ed editor, 623

character-based programs, running in X, 432

character class, **523**

character set, converting file between, 683

character special file, **523**, 578

characters, 636

    counting for file, 49–50

    erasing, 8

    invisible, **692**

    quoting, **818**

    regular, **828**

    tr command to translate, **264–265**

    translating between forms, **900–901**

chdir command (C shell), **523**, 559

chdir command (Mail), 752

chdir command (mailx), 755

checkmail command, **523–524**

checknr command, **524–525**

checksum, calculating and printing, **875**

chflags command, **525**

chgrp command, 111–112, **526**

child process, 123

    waiting for, 126

chkey command, **526**

chmod command, 112, 150–151, 323, **527–529**

chown (change owner id) command, 111, **529**

chpass command, **530**

ci program (RCS), 823

cksum command, **531**

cleanup daemon, 383

clear command, **531**

click command, **531**

client software in X, 424, **424**, **948–949**, 959

    configuration file for window-related values, 950

    killing, 436

    xkill to close connection, 953

close call, 578

close command (awk), 482

close command (ftp), 392, 656

close command (nawk), 777

close command (telnet), 394, 886

cmchk command, **531**

cmdedit, **531**

cmdterm, 431, 956

cmp command, **531–532**

    for compressed files, 961

co program (RCS), 823

cof2elf command, **532–533**

COFF (common object file format) files, **533**

    converting to ELF format, 532–533

col command, **533–534**

colcrt command, **534–535**

colon (:)

    to indicated Bourne shell script, 203

    in vi command mode, 187

colon (:) command, 505, **535**

colon commands in vi, 172

color chart, displaying, 950

colrm command, **535**, 640

column command, **535–536**

columns

    creating output from multiple files, 796–797

    cut command to extract, **567–568**

    input formatted in, **535–536**

listing in, 49

printing in, 156

removing from text file, **535**

COLUMNS shell variable (Korn), 715

comb program (SCCS), 847

comm command, **536**

command directories, **537**

command file, **537**

command history list, displaying or editing, **630–631**

command-line, **537–538**

    command to parse options, **662**

    parsing, 218

command-line argument, **538**. *See also* arguments

command-line editing, **531**

command mode, 73, 160, 538

    confirming, 172

    macros for, 189

    in vi editor, 167, 932–933

    vi keystroke for, 161

command substitution, 224, 228, 487, **538–539**

command text, 236

commands, **11–12**

    arguments, **17–21**

    in awk, 481, 482–484

    backslash (\) for long, 227

    in Bourne shell, 501

    checking status in UUCP, 382

    combining, **267–270**

    displaying information on executed, **723**

    displaying type, 908

    embedded, **614**

    executing remote, **373**, **625**, 928–929

    multiple on one line, 12

online reference manual, 17

pipe to pass information between, **805**

re-executing the previous, **818–819**

script to force failure, 219

shell script as, **208–209**

storage in history file, 677

terminators, 136

comments, 324, **539**

Common Application Environment (CAE), **508**

Common Desktop Environment (CDE), **522**, 543

common object file format (COFF) files, **533**

Common Open Software Environment (COSE), **543**

communications

    interprocess, **690**

        printing information, **693–694**

    two-way, terminal-to-terminal, **878–879**

communications link, accuracy check on data transmission, 548

comp command (MH), 765

compact command, 522, **539**

comparing

    directories, **585–586**

    expressions, 829

    file revisions, **584–585**

    file versions, **583–584**

    files, **531–532**

    floppy disks, **589**

comparing files, **531–532**

compile, **539**

compiler, **540**

    cc (C language), **515–521**

    f77 (Fortran compiler), **654**

    gcc (C language), **659–660**

compiler compiler, **540**

    eyacc (extended yacc), **628**

    yacc, 540, **960**

compose mode, 73

    for e-mail messages, 72

compress command, **540–541**

compression

    bzip program for, **508**

    compact command for, **539**

    executable file, 671

    lossless, **740**

    lossy, 700, **740**

    pack command for, **793**

    uncompressing after, **914**

    unpack to expand, **918**

    zcat to uncompress, **961**

    zmore to view files, 962

concatenating, 46, **541**

    cat command for, **513–514**

condition code, 219

/config directory, **541**

configuration, listing information, 681–682

confirmation, before file deletion, 53

connect time, quotas for, 13

connected terminals, 62

connections, 4

console, 5

    virtual, **938**

constants, in shell scripts, 663

contents of file, displaying, 45–46

context of suspended program, 120

continue command, 326, **542**

continue command (awk), 482

continue command (Bourne), 505

continue command (C shell), 559

Continue command (Korn), 716
continue command (nawk), 777
control characters, 5, **542**
    inserting in vi editor, 162
    octal values, 265
control codes, inserting in macro, 190
converting, COFF to ELF format, 532–533
copies, printing multiple, 149
coprocesses (Korn shell), 719
copy command, 71, **542–543**
copy command (ed), 623
copy command (Mail), 752
copy command (mailx), 755
copying
    directories in UUCP, 375
    files over network connection, **821–822**
    floppy disks, **589–590**
    mcopy command, **456–457**
    uucp command for, 366–367, **379–382**, **921–922**
copyleft command, **543**
core image, command to obtain, 660
corrupted files, check for, 405
cos command (awk), 314, 482
cos command (nawk), 777
COSE (Common Open Software Environment), **543**
cosine, from bc, 492
counting, words, **49–50**
cp (copy) command, 103, **544–545**
cpio archive, extracting one file from, **958**
cpio command, **414**, **545–547**
cpp command, **547–548**
CR, 6, 265
crackers, 87

CRC (Cyclic Redundancy Check), **548**
creation mask, **548**, 911–912
cron command, 132, 139, **548**
crontab command, 140, **549–550**
cross-reference table, 569
crypt command, **87–88**, **550–551**, 640
cscope utility, **551**
csh command, **551–552**
.csh filename extension, 638
.cshrc file, 465, 553, **561**, 595
    alias commands in, 152
csplit utility, **561–562**
ct utility, **562–563**
ctags command, **563**
ctrace command, **563**
Ctrl-C (break), **563**
Ctrl-D (^D), **564**
    for EOF (end-of-file) character, 47
    to terminate program, 62
Ctrl-H (backspace), 564
Ctrl key, 5, 542, **564**
    in emacs editor, 608
Ctrl-L (redraw), 564
Ctrl-Q (restart), 564
Ctrl-\ (quit), **563**
Ctrl-R, 564
Ctrl-S (pause), 564
Ctrl-U, 564
Ctrl-W, 565
Ctrl-X, 565
Ctrl-Z, 565
cu command, 373, **565–567**
curly braces ({ }), 507
current directory, 90, **594**, 946
    changing, **522**, **523**
    command to list, **587**
    listing contents, 43
curses, **567**

cursor movement, in vi editor, **173–175**, 178–179, 933–934
cursors, 7
    controlling location, 567
    in emacs editor, 609
    in xterm window, 433
cut-and-paste, **568–569**
    in vi editor, **184–186**
cut command, **253–254**, **567–568**, 640
cut, selected text, **568**
cwd shell variable, 556
cxref command, **569**
Cyclic Redundancy Check (CRC), **548**
cylinders on floppy disks, 454

D

daemons, 124, 132, 382, **569–570**
DARPA (Defense Advanced Research Projects Agency), 570
dash (-)
    in command syntax, 18, 44
    for grep range, 281
Data Encryption Standard (DES), 494–495, **576**
data-link layer (ISO/OSI), 696
data segment, 121
data types, in awk, 312
database applications, 387
date
    formatting in awk, 315–316
    Julian, **701**
    scheduling jobs to run on specific, 477
date command, 11, **570–572**
Davidsen, Bill, 855
dbx (debugger), **572**
.dbxinit file, 572

dc command, **572**

dd command, **266**, **573–574**

DDI (Device Driver Interface), **574**

DDRM (Device Driver Interface/Driver Kernel Interface Reference Manual), **575**

dead.letter file, 73

debugger

    adb, **464**

    dbx, **572**

    gdb (debugger), **660–661**

    sdb, **849**

debugging

    ctrace command for, **563**

    shell script, **207–208**, 362

decimal numbers, sorting, 245

decryption, 614

default: command (C shell), 559

default shell, 89

defaults, **10**, **575**

    for nice number, 133

    permissions, **110–111**

    printers, 154

    for printing, 147

    system administrator and, 65

    text editor, 631

Defense Advanced Research Projects Agency (DARPA), 570

define keyword (bc), 492

del command (Samba), **449**

delete command

    in ed editor, 623

    for e-mail messages, 71

    repeating in vi, 179

delete command (awk), 482

delete command (ftp), 656

delete command (Mail), 752

delete command (mailx), 755

delete command (nawk), 777

deleting

    characters, 8

    directories, **35**

    e-mail messages, **70–72**

    e-mail messages when quitting, 66–67

    empty directory, **835–836**

    file from archive file, 473

    files, **52–54**, **834–835**

    line of input, 564, 565

    old jobs in UUCP, 383

    in sed stream editor, **299–300**

    text in vi editor, **181–183**

    words, 565

delimiter, 223, **575**

delta, 847

delta program (SCCS), 847

deroff command, **575–576**

des command, **576**

DES (Data Encryption Standard), 494–495, **576**

descriptor table, **576**

DeskSet, 437

Desktop System (OpenServer), 790

destination file, for cp (copy) command, 103

destructive yank, 185

detached processing, 486

/dev directory, 409, **576–577**, 869

/dev/lp0, 145

/dev/null file, 346

/dev/ttyn, 145

devconfig file, 577

"device busy" message, 410

device-dependent, **577**

device driver calls, **578**

Device Driver Interface (DDI), **574**

Device Driver Interface/Driver Kernel Interface Reference Manual (DDRM), **575**

device drivers, 146, **577**

    directory for, **576–577**

device file, **578**

device filename, 578

device-independent, 578

device-independent troff, **590**

device interrupt, 120

device number, 578

    major, **757**

    minor, **766**

    variable to set, 839

df command, **579–580**

DFS (Distributed File System), **580**

dfspace script, **580**

/dgn directory, **580**

dial-up connection

    system interface setup to, 907

    tip command to login, **897–898**

diction command, **580–581**

dictionary

    comparing file contents to, **865–866**

    finding words in system, **738–739**

    running against password file, 87

dictionary sort, 244

diff command, 296, **581–583**, 797

    for compressed files, 961

diff3 command, **583–584**

diffmk command, **584–585**

dig command, 390, **585**

dir command (ftp), 392, 656

dir command (Samba), **449**

dircmp command, **585–586**

directories, 16, **24–31**, **586**
  changing in Samba, **449**
  changing working, **522**,
    523
  for commands, **537**
  comparing contents,
    585–586
  copying in UUCP, 375
  copying to archive files,
    545–547
  creating, **767**
  deleting, **35**
  deleting empty, **835–836**
  empty, 29
  file organization sugges-
    tion, 102
  home, 33–34
  listing contents, **40–45**,
    746–747
  moving to parent, 35
  mtools to manipulate,
    456–458
  NFS exporting for shar-
    ing, 386
  ownership of, **104**
  parent, **794**
  paths, **28–29**
  permissions, **105–106**,
    107, 635
  report on disk space use
    by, 599
  root, **31–35**, **839**, 869
  and script troubleshoot-
    ing, 207
  shell variable for, 225
  standard, **869**
  swapping in stack, **817**
  trees and hierarchies,
    27–31
  working, 33–34
"directory: does not exist" message, 35
directory (set argument), 193
dirname command, **586–587**

dirs command (C shell), 559,
  587
dis command, **587**
disable command, **588**
disassembler, 587, **589**
discard command (mailx), 755
disconnect command (ftp), 656
disk block number, from grep
  command, 278
disk drives, device number, 757
disk I/O, and program swapping, 119
disk image copy, of floppy disk,
  456
disk space
  report on free, **579–580**
  use report for directory,
    599
diskcmp command, **589**
diskcp command, **589–590**
display command (telnet), 886
dist command (MH), 765
distributed file-sharing system,
  782
ditroff command, **590**
dividing files into smaller segments, 561–562
DNS (Domain Name System),
  389
  query of name servers,
    585
do command, **590**
Do command (awk), 482
Do command (Korn), 716
Do command (nawk), 777
document instance, **590**
document type definition
  (DTD), **597**
documents, report on writing
  style, **873–874**
dollar sign ($), 213, **591**. See
  also $ (dollar sign)
domain, **591**

domain address, **591**
  vs. UUCP address,
    389–390
domain information groper, 585
domain member list, **591**
domain name, **592**
domain name server, **592**
Domain Name System (DNS),
  389
domainname command, **592**
done command, 325, **592**
DOS (disk operating system),
  592–593
  access to files on Unix
    server. See Samba
  AUTOEXEC.BAT file, 91
  converting text file to
    Unix, **597**
  converting Unix text files
    to, **958**
  hierarchical file structure,
    28
  Unix system file manipu-
    lation in, **452–453**
doscat command, 593
doscp command, 593
dosdir command, 593
dosemu program, 593, **594**
dosformat command, 593
dosls command, 593
dosmkdir command, 593
dosrm command, 593
dosrmdir command, 593
dot (.), **594**, **799**
dot (.) command, **210**, **594**
dot dot, **594**
dot file, **594–595**
dot requests, **595**
double-line spacing
  from pr command, 51, 157
  in sed stream editor, 299
double quotes ("), **228–229**,
  596. See also quotation
  marks

dp command (Mail), 752

dp command (mailx), 755

dpost command, **596–597**

dt command (Mail), 752

dt command (mailx), 755

DTD (document type definition), **597**

dtox command, **597**

dtype command, **597–599**

du command, **599**

Duff, Tom, 821

dumb terminals, 5

dump command, 413–414

dump of file, **788–789**

duplex, **600**

duplicates, suppressing in sorted lists, 246–247

E

e command, **600**

e keyword (bc), 492

e protocol, **617**

eb (error bells), **600**

EBCDIC (Extended Binary Coded Decimal Inter-change Code), **600**

dd command to convert, 266

echo, 5, 8, **600**

echo area, **602**

echo command, 96, 221, **222–223**, **600–601**

echo command (Bourne), 505

echo command (C shell), 559

Echo command (Korn), 716

echo command (mailx), 755

echo shell variable, 556

echoing, **602**

ed editor, **602**

starting within mail, 74

EDCDIC file format, converting between ASCII and, 574

edit, **603**

edit command (Mail), 752

edit command (mailx), 755

editing buffer, saving in vi, 171

EDITOR shell variable (Korn), 715

Effective User Identifier (euid), **621**

egrep command, **289–292**, **603**

regular expressions, 294

regular expressions in descending precedence, 292

summary, 293

eject command, **603–604**

electronic mail. *See* e-mail messages

electronic mail service, 11

ELF (Executable and Link Format) files, **533**, **604**

converting COFF to, 532–533

manipulating comments sections, 761–762

elif command, **348–349**, **604**

.elm file, 595

elm (mail program), 77, **604**, 749

else command, **605**

in awk, 317

emacs editor, 77, **605–613**, 749

cursor, 609

editing commands, 610–612

help for, 609

key combinations, 608–609

killed text, 610

major and minor modes, 606–608

mark, 610

point, 609

region, 610

.emacs file, 595

emacs option (Korn shell), 713

e-mail, **613**. *See also* e-mail messages

e-mail address, **613**

displaying, 753

e-mail messages, 57, **940–941**

appending to database, **662**

broadcasting to all network users, 843–844

command to manage, **662–663**

controlling receipt during vi session, 166

deleting when quitting, 66–67

display options, 69

displaying current, 66

encryption, **955**

headers, **67–68**

to indicate completed printing, 149

indicator for current, 68

MIME for binary elements, **766**

more filter to control display, 66

notification of arrival, 498, **786**, **948**

for notification of file arrival, 381

open to receiving, 59

printing, **67**

reading from another source, **72**

report on status, **523–524**

responding to, 73–74

retaining when exiting, 66

saving and deleting, **70–72**

searches for regular expressions in, **868**

selecting, **68–70**

sending, **72–75**

sending to multiple users, 73

sendmail as transport agent, **853**

smail as transport agent, **862**

standard for distribution systems, **952**

summary of messages waiting delivery, 753

vacation command to respond, **929–930**

e-mail programs. *See also* mail

elm, **604**

MH message handling system, **764–765**

embedded command, **614**

empty directory, 29

removing, **835–836**

empty string, 333

emulation software, 5

enable command, **614**

.enc filename extension, 638

encryption, **614**

bdes utility for, 494–495

crypt command for, **550–551**

makekey utility for, **758**

of password, **795**

rot13, **839–840**

encryption key, 88

chkey command to change, **526**

end command (C shell), 559, **614**

END, in awk, **311–313**

end-of-file (EOF) character, 564, **615**

for /dev/null file, 346

environment variables to ignore, **684**

and read cancel exit status, 343

end-of-file (EOF) message, 30

end-of-text (ETX) character, **615**

end-of-transmission (EOT), **615**

endif command (C shell), 559, **615**

endless loops, **326–328**

endsw command, **615**

Enter key, 6, **9**, **615**

env command, 211, **615–616**

ENV environment variable, **616**

ENV shell variable (Korn), 715

ENVIRON variable (gawk), 485

environment, 511, **616**

environment file, **616**

environment variables, 65, 210–211, **616–617**. *See also* shell variables

assigning value, **854**

in boot up, 235

in C shell, 557–558

displaying, 211

displaying or changing, **615–616**

null value vs. unset, 214

removing, **919**

EOF (end-of-file) character, **615**

Ctrl-D (^D) for, 47

EOF (end-of-file) message, 30

EOT (end-of-transmission), **615**

epoch, **617**

eqn preprocessor, **617–618**

removing formatting from file, 575–576

equations, formatting text containing, 779

erasing. *See* deleting

errexit option (Korn shell), 713

$ERRNO shell variable (Korn), 714

error handling, **346–349**, **618–619**

error message file, creating from C source code, 769

error messages. *See* messages

sending to standard error, 347

errorbells (set argument), 193

errors, standard, 55

esac command, 349, **619**

Esac command (Korn), 716

Esc key, in macro, 191

escape, **619**

escape character, **619**

escape commands, **619**

Escape key, 265

as Meta key, 609

escape sequences, **620**

for echo, 222–223

removing from file, 575–576

escaped character, **619**

/etc/cshrc file, 92

/etc/default/lpd file, 148

/etc directory, 84, 402, 869

files and directories in, **620–621**

/etc/dump command, 413–414

/etc/haltsys command, 407

/etc/initab file, 234

/etc/passwd file, **84–88**, 234–235, 307

cat command to examine, 85–86

password encryption in, 86–87

/etc/profile file, 92

/etc/restor command, 413–414

/etc/shutdown command, 407–408

/etc/termcap file, 162–163

ETX (end-of-text) character, **615**

euid (Effective User Identifier), **621**

eval command, **621**

eval command (Bourne), 505

eval command (C shell), 559

Eval command (Korn), 716

ex command (mail), 66
ex command (Mail), 752
ex command (mailx), 755
ex command mode, **187–188**
ex editor, 160, **621–623**
  commands, 623
  line addressing in, 622
ex Escape mode, in vi editor, 167–168
ex mode commands (vi), **188–196**
  abbr command, **189–195**
ex mode, for vi editor, 166
exa-, **623**
exabyte, **624**
exclamation point (!), **624**. *See also* ! (bang)
exec command, **624**
exec command (Bourne), 505, 624
exec command (C shell), 559, 624
Exec command (Korn), 716
exec system call, 123
Executable and Link Format (ELF) files, **533**
executable file, 236
  compressing and uncompressing, **670**
  default name, 470
"execute permission denied" message, 205
execute permissions, 104, 108, 527, **624–625**, 635, 800
  for directories, 105
  owner, group and public, 107
  for script file, 323
  testing for, 338
executing remote commands, **625**
EXINIT environment variable, 191, 557

exit command, 219, 327, 346, **625**
exit command (awk), 482
exit command (Bourne), 505
exit command (C shell), 559
Exit command (Korn), 716
exit command (mail), 66
exit command (Mail), 752
exit command (mailx), 755
exit command (nawk), 777
exit command (Samba), **449**
exit statement, 319
exit status, 219, 325, **625**
  of last executed command, 335
  of read command, 343
  test command to return, 329
exit to shell, signal generated on, 327
exit value, return by command, 215
exiting, vi editor, 173
exp command (awk), 482
exp command (nawk), 777
exp operation (awk), 314
expand command, **625–626**
explain program, **626**
export command, 99, **626**
export command (Bourne), 505
export command (Korn), 716
/export directory, **626**
exportfs command, **626**
exporting, shell variables, **216–218**
expr command, 362–363, **626–628**
expressions. *See* regular expressions
.exrc file, 166, **195**, 595, **628**
  abbreviations in, 189
  macros in, 191
exstr command, **628**

ext2fs (Second Extended Filesystem), **628**
Extended Binary Coded Decimal Inter-change Code (EBCDIC), **600**
extracting
  files from archives, 880
  from tar backup, 416
eyacc (extended yacc), **628**

F

.f filename extension, 638
.F filename extension, 638
f (finger) command, 629
f protocol, **651**
f77 (Fortran compiler), **654**
face command, **629**
FACE (Framed Access Command Environment), **629**
factor command, **630**
false, **630**
FAQ (frequently asked questions), **630**
fault tolerance, RAID (redundant array of inexpensive disks) for, **819–820**
fc command, **630–631**
FCEDIT environment variable, **631**
FCEDIT shell variable (Korn), 715
fd (file descriptor), for open files, 347
FDDI (Fiber Distributed Data Interface), standard, 469
fdformat command, **631–632**
fg command, 126–127, 486, **632**
fg command (C shell), 559
Fg command (Korn), 716

fgrep command, **288–289, 632**
    regular expressions, 294
    summary, 293
fi command, **632**
Fi command (Korn), 716
Fiber Distributed Data Interface
    (FDDI), standard, 469
field separators, **684**
    in awk, 306, 311
fields
    in awk, **303–304**
    removing from file,
        253–254
    for uniq command,
        249–250
    for who command
        response, 60
FIFO file, **633**, 636
    creating, 767
fignore variable, 556, **633**
file allocation tables, and
    mtools, 452
file attributes, **634**
    mattrib to change, 456
file command, **84–87**,
    633–634
file command (Mail), 752
file command (mailx), 755
file commands, **634**
file creation mask, **548**,
    911–912
file descriptor (fd), for open
    files, 347
file extension in DOS, 26
file flags, command to change,
    525
file formats
    converting, **573–574**
    ELF (Executable and Link
        Format) files, **604**
file locking, **635**
"file not found" message, 17,
    28, 206
file server, **636**

file size, 30
file transfer. *See also* ftp com-
    mand
    to remote system,
        928–929
file types, **636**
    command to determine,
        84–85
    on Internet, **689–690**
filec environment variable, **636**
Filec shell variable, 556
filename completion, **638**
filename expansion, **638**
filename extension, **638–639**
    disabling, 785
    types on Internet,
        689–690
filename generation, 230–231,
    475, **639**
"filename: not found" message,
    28
filename substitution, 475,
    639, 663
FILENAME variable (awk),
    312, 484
filenames, 16, **26–27, 637**
    changing, 774–775
    characters to avoid, 637
    DOS vs. Unix, 593
    duplicates, 29–30
    extracting from path
        statement, 488–489
    as ls argument, 40–41
    for output redirection, 39
files, **16–17**
    adding to archive file, 473
    ambiguous reference, **467**
    appending output to,
        54–55
    bdiff utility to compare,
        495–496
    buffers for changes,
        406–407

cat command to create,
    47–48
changing modification
    and access time for,
    898–900
combining content of
    multiple in columns,
    255–257
comparing, **531–532,
    849–850**
comparing 3 versions,
    583–584
comparing revisions,
    584–585
compressing, **540–541**
copying, 544–545
copying and converting,
    573–574
copying to archive files,
    545–547
deleting in Samba, **449**
displaying, **674**
displaying contents,
    45–46
displaying contents of
    packed, **799**
displaying is specified
    format, 675–676
distribution over net-
    works, **386–387**
dump of, **788–789**
encrypting, 87–88
find to search for,
    257–263
finding by searching
    database, 736
forcing overwrite in vi, 171
grep to search contents,
    274
hierarchical structure, 27,
    676–677
invisible, **692**
linking, 31
listing, 40

mtools to manipulate, 456–458
open, **789**
ordinary, **792**
orphaned, **792**
overwriting, 30, 54
ownership of, **104**
permissions, **104–105, 635**
printing multiple, 147–148
removing, **834–835**
renaming and moving, **774–775**
restoring, 914
rm to erase, **52–54**
and sed output, 296
separating into smaller pieces, 561–562
shell manipulation within vi, 188
sort command for multiple, **246**
splitting, **252–253**
suggestions for directory organization, 102
testing, **338–339**
tracking multiple revisions of, **846–847**
filesystem, **409–410, 639**
remote, **830–831**
root, **839**
filesystem check command, **653**
filesystem data block, fragment of, **651**
filter command, **640**
filters, 20, 50
for pipelines, 52
for printers, 147
scripts for, 201
find command, **257–263, 640–643**
-cpio option, 261

-exec option, 260
logical operations, 259
-perm option, 261–262
primary expressions, 262–263
-type option, 261
finger command, **643–645**
and .plan file, 806
finger entry, **645**
firewall, **645**
fixed strings, fgrep to search for, **288–289**
flat files, 30–31
flex, **645**
floppy disks
for backup medium, 412
backup to, 415
command to eject from drive, 603–604
comparing, **589**
copying, **589–590**
determining type, 597–599
formatting, **631–632, 650**
splitting files when backing up, 414
floppy drives
configuration file properties for, 454–455
drive parameters for mtools, **453–458**
floppyd command (mtools), **455–456**
flow control, 202. *See also* if command
awk, **316–319**
branching with && and ||, **351**
case statement, **349–351**
elif command, **348–349**
if command, **683–684**
for loop, **356–360**

of script
exit status for, 219
switch command, 560, 610, **876**
until loop, **328–329**
while loop, **324–329**
/flush command (IRC), 694
flushing pending file I/O, 407
fmli command, **646**
FMLI (Forms and Menu Language Interpreter), **646**
fmt command, 640, **646–647**
fmtmsg command, **647–648**
FNR variable (awk), 312, 484
focus, **648**
fold command, **648**
folder command (Mail), 752
folder command (mailx), 755
folder command (MH), 765
folder environment variable, 71
folders. *See* directories
folders command (Mail), 752
folders command (mailx), 755
folders command (MH), 765
followup command (mailx), 755
Followup command (mailx), 755
fonts
creating files, 890
listing available, 953
xfd to display, **951**
for command (awk), 482
For command (Korn), 716
for command (nawk), 777
for keyword, **649**
for keyword (bc), 491
for loop, **356–360**
foreach command (C shell), 559, **649**
end to terminate, 614
foreground, 125, **649**
bringing background job to, 486, 632

foreground processing, **649**
fork system call, 123–124, **650**
format command, **650**
formatting
  floppy disks, **631–632, 650**
  with pr command, **156–157**
  text files, 50, **780–781**
formfeed, 223, 265, **650**
Forms and Menu Language Interpreter (FMLI), **646**
Fortran language
  filter for translating file, 651
  splitting source code into routines, **654**
  standard, 468
forw command (MH), 765
forward quotes, 95
forward searches, 283
  in vi editor, 186
forwarding mail, in UUCP, 371–372
for.while, in awk, 318–319
4.4BSD Lite, **651**
Fox, Brian, 489
FPATH environment variable, **651**
FPATH shell variable (Korn), 715
fpr filter, **651**
fragment, **651**
fragmentation, **651–652**
Framed Access Command Environment (FACE), **629**
free blocks, **652**
free disk space, report on, **579–580**
Free Software Foundation (FSF), 605, 612, **654**
  BISON, 499
  file compression utilities, **670–672**

General Public License, 543
GNU Project, 489
Hurd project, **681**
FreeBSD, **652**
freeware, **652**
frequently asked questions (FAQ), **630**
from command, **653**
from command (Mail), 752
from command (mailx), 756
frontware, 434
FS variable (awk), 311, 312, 484
fsck command, 405, 410, **653**, 740
fsplit command, **654**
fstat command, **654**
ftp
  anonymous, 391, **467–468**
  file transfer with, **390–393**
ftp command, **654–657**
FTP (File Transfer Protocol), **658**
  configuration information file for, 780
ftpd daemon, 569
full duplex, 600
full-screen editor, 658
function, call to, 510
function command (awk), 482
Function command (Korn), 716
Function command (nawk), 778
fvwm, **658**

G

g (global) command, 283
G (global) command, 284
G protocol, **664**
g++ shell script, **658**

gadgets, **658**
Gaines, Stockton, 77
gateway, 367
gawk command, 479, **659**
gcc C compiler, **659–660**
gcore command, **660**
gdb (debugger), **660–661**
GDS (Global Directory Service), **661**
gencat command, **662**
General Sherman, 185
geographical domains, 389
get command (ftp), 392, 393, 656
get command (Samba), **450**
get program (SCCS), 847
getline command (awk), 483
getline command (nawk), 778
getoptcvt command, **662**
getopts command, **662**
getopts command (Bourne), 505
getopts command (Korn), 716
gettxt command, **662–663**
getty command, in boot up, 234
Ghostview, **663**
Gid, chpass to change, 530
.gif filename extension, 638, 690
.gl filename extension, 638
glob command (C shell), 559, **663**
global command, in ed editor, 623
global commands, **283–284**
  inverse, **284–287**
Global Directory Service (GDS), **661**
global login profile, 91
  in Bourne shell, 92
global variables, 217, **663**
globbing, **663**
gmacs option (Korn shell), 713

GNU, **663–664**

GNU C compiler preprocessor, 547

goodpw command (SCO UNIX), 84

.gopherrc file, 595

goto command (C shell), 559, **664**

gprof tool, **664**

grace period, for shutdown, 408

graph command, **664–665**

graphical desktop, 437

Graphical User Interface (GUI), 6, 200–201, 422. *See also* X WIndows systems
  Open Desktop, **789**

grave accent. *See* backquote

greater-than (<) symbol, 39, **665**

Greer, Ken, 884

grep command, 209, 273, **274–278**, 640, **665–667**
  -b option, **278**
  -c option to count matching lines, **277**
  case-sensitive searches, **276–278**
  for compressed files, 962
  -e option, **278**
  egrep command, **289–292**
  family summary, **292–294**
  fgrep command, **288–289**
  -h option for multiple files, **277**
  -l option, **278**
  -n option, **276–277**
  quoting search pattern, **275**
  regular expressions, **278–288**, 294

regular expressions in descending precedence, 292
  -s option, **278**
  -v option, **277–278**
  -w (word) option, **275**

grodvi command, 668

groff command, **667–668**
  refer command for, **827–828**

grog command, 668

grops command, 668

grotty command, 668

group, **669**

group command (mailx), 756

group ID, **669**, 761

group permissions, 107
  viewing, 108–109

groups
  changing, **111–112**
  changing file association, **526**
  find command to select files belonging to, 261
  membership, 104–105

groups command, **669**

groupware, **669**

gsub command (awk), 483

gsub command (nawk), 778

GUI (Graphical User Interface), 6, 200–201, 422. *See also* X Window systems
  Open Desktop, **789**

gunzip command, 670, 671

gwm (window manager), **670**

.gz filename extension, 638, 690
  recompressing .Z files to, 962

gzexe command, **670**

gzip, **670–672**

gzip files, 961–962

H

.h filename extension, 638

hacking, 200

half-duplex, 600

haltsys command, 407

hanpug signal, 327

hard copy, 143

hard drives
  fragmentation, **651–652**
  fsck command to check and repair problems, **653**
  incremental backup, **685**

hard link, **672**, 735, 736

hard-wired, **673**

Hardpaths shell variable, 556

hardware interrupt, **672**

hardwired connection, 4

hash command (Bourne), 506, **673**

hash command (ftp), 392, 657

Hash command (Korn), 716

hash symbol (#). *See* # (pound sign)

hash table, **673**
  rebuilding, **829**
  removing internal, 915

hashing, **673**

hashstat command (C shell), 559, **673**

hd command, **674**

head command, **250–251**, 269, 640, **675**

header file, 684

headers
  for e-mail messages, 65, **67–68**
    skipping, 70
  as pr default, 50

headers command (Mail), 752

headers command (mailx), 756

heads on floppy disks, 454

hello command, **675**

help command (ftp), 391, 656

/help command (IRC), 694

help command (Mail), 752

help command (mailx), 756

help command (Samba), **450**

help, for mail program, 65–66

help program (SCCS), 847

Hewlett-Packard 2640 terminal series, 680

hexdump command, **675–676**

hidden characters, **676**

hidden files, 594

hierarchical file structure, 27, **676–677**

    leaf in, **725**

high-level backups, 411

histchars environment variable, **677**

Histchars shell variable, 556

HISTFILE shell variable (Korn), 715

history, **677**

history command (C shell), 559, **677–678**

History command (Korn), 716

.history file, 595, **678**

history shell variable, 556

HISTORY shell variable (Korn), 715

HISTSIZE environment variable, **678**, 718

hold command (Mail), 752

hold command (mailx), 756

home, **678**

home directory, 33–34, 38, 101, 465, **678**, **678–679**, 869

    changing, 616

    chpass to change, 530

    .login, 92

    moving to, 102

    .profile file, 92

    returning to, 34

HOME environment variable, 557

home page, **679**

HOME shell variable, 94, 211, 556, **678**

HOME shell variable (Bourne), 504

HOME shell variable (Korn), 715

HoneyDanBer UUCP, **679**, 923

Honeyman, Peter, 679, 923

Horton, Mark, 567

host, **679**

host command, 390

host computer, summary of system status, **841–842**

Host-to-host Transport layer (TCP/IP), 884

hostid, **679**

hostname, **679**

hp commmand, **680**

HP-UX, **680**

hpterm, 431, 956

HQX filename extension, 690

HTML (Hypertext Markup Language), **680**

HTTP (Hypertext Transfer Protocol), **680–681**

Huffman coding, 539

Hurd project, **681**

hwconfig command, **681–682**

hypermedia, **682**

hypertext, 395, **682**

Hypertext Markup Language (HTML), **680**

Hypertext Transfer Protocol (HTTP), **680–681**

hyphen (-)

    in command syntax, 18, 44

    for grep range, 281

HZ environment variable, 212

I

i-node table, **688**

i-nodes, **30**, **687–688**

i-number, **691**

I/O devices, file-like interface for, 145–146

ibase keyword (bc), 492

ICMP (Internet Control Message Protocol), 385, 883

icon in X, 428

iconv command, **683**

id command, **683**

ident program (RCS), 823

if command, 344–346, **683–684**

    alternative to, **351**

    fi to terminate, **632**

    then keyword, **890**

if command (awk), 317, 483

if command (C shell), 559

if command (Korn), 716

if command (nawk), 778

if keyword (bc), 491

IFS shell variable, 94, 211, 214, **684**

IFS shell variable (Bourne), 504

IFS shell variable (Korn), 715

ignore command, 70

ignore command (Mail), 752

ignore command (mailx), 756

ignorecase (set argument), 193

IGNORECASE variable (gawk), 485

ignoreeof environment variable, **684**

ignoreeof option (Korn shell), 713

Ignoreeof shell variable, 556

image copy, **684**

image in Unix, 121, *122*

images, JPEG file compression, **700–701**

imake, 684

in-line input, 55

in statement, in for loop, 357

inactive window, **684**

inc command (MH), 765

include file, **684**

inclusive OR, 309–310

incremental backup, 411, **685**

incremental search, **685**

indent command, **685**

indenting, 299

    when printing, 157

index command (awk), 483

index command (nawk), 778

index, permuted, **801**

    creating, **816–817**

indxxbib command, **685–686**

inetd daemon, 569

info command, **686**

InfoExplorer, 686

information node, 687

inheritance, **686**

init level, for shutdown, 408

init process, 124, **686–687**

    in boot up, 234

initialization file, **687**

    for X, 430

initialization string, **687**

input, 5

    buffer for, 8

    erasing line, 564, 565

    redirecting, 40, **50–51**

    typing errors, **8**

input mode, in vi editor,
932–933

input/output streams, 295

input stream, 295

insert command

    in ed editor, 623

    repeating in vi, 179

Insert key, 5

insert mode, in vi editor, 167,
170, 181

inserting, text in sed stream
editor, **300**

installing, UUCP network software, 367–368

Institute of Electrical and
Electronics Engineers, 806

int command (awk), 483

int command (nawk), 778

int operation (awk), 314

integer command, **688**

Integer command (Korn), 716

integers

    comparing, **337–338**

    remainder after division,
769

Intel-based PCs

    Linux for, 731

    NetBSD for, **779**

    Solaris for, **863**

intelligent terminals, 5

interactive, **688**

interactive global command,
284

Interactive UNIX, **688**

interface definition, for character device, 523

internal command, 508

International Organization for
Standardization (ISO), 468,
695

International Organization for
Standardization/Open
System Interconnection
model, **696**

Internet, **388–396**, **688**

    anonymous ftp access,
467–468

    file transfer with ftp,
390–393

    file types, **689–690**

    Internet Relay Chat (IRC),
395–396

    telnet to connect to
remote computer,

    394–395

    URL (Uniform Resource
Locator), **920**

    USENET, **396**

    what it is, **388**

    World Wide Web, **395**

    for X System files, 437

internet, **688**

Internet address, **689**

Internet Control Message
Protocol (ICMP), 385, 883

Internet layer (TCP/IP), 884

Internet Packet Exchange
(IPX), **694**

Internet Protocol (IP), **692**

Internet Relay Chat (IRC),
395–396, **694–695**

internetwork, 688

interpreter, 690

interprocess communications,
690

    printing information,
693–694

interrupt handler, 691

interrupting program, 563

interrupting program, in endless loop, 326–327

interrupts, **672**, **691**

    for peripherals, 120–121

inverse global commands,
284–287

invert command, **691–692**

invisible character, **692**

invisible file, **692**

ioctl call, 578

IP address, command to provide, **787**

IP (Internet Protocol), **692**

    address, 389

ipcrm command, **692**

ipcs command, **693–694**

IPX (Internet Packet
Exchange), **694**

IRC (Internet Relay Chat),
  395-396, 694-695
ismpx command, **695**
ISO (International Organization
  for Standardization), 468,
  695
ISO/OSI model, **696**
isochronous, **696**

J

J (join) command, in vi editor,
  181
j keyword (bc), 492
Java, **697**
job control, **697-698**
job number, **698**
jobs, **697**
  at job queue, **478-479**
  scheduling, 549-550
jobs command, **698**
  to list running jobs, 486
jobs command (C shell), 559
Jobs command (Korn), 716
Jobs, Steve, 422
joe (editor), **698**
join command, **699**
/join command (IRC), 695
jot command, **699-700**
jove editor, **700**
Joy, Bill, 552, 621
JPEG filename extension, 690,
  700-701
.jpg filename extension, 638,
  690
jsh, **701**
jterm command, **701**
jukebox, **701**
Julian date, **701**
jwin command, **701**

K

K&R, **702**
kdestroy command, **702**
kdump command, **702-703**
Kerberos, **703**
  ksrvtgt utility, **720**
  login after ticket expira-
    tion, **707-708**
  register command for,
    828
Kerberos tickets, 703
  destroying, 702
  listing current, **708**
kernel, 119, **704**
  boot program to load, 405
  rebuilding, **826**
kernel address space, **704**
kernel description file, **704**
kernel process tracing, 720-721
kernel trace information, displaying, **702-703**
Kernighan, Brian, 702, 776
key binding, **704**
keyboard, **5-6**
  click control, 531
  Ctrl key, **564**
  Enter key, **9**
  file creation from input,
    47
  mapping for vi editor,
    161-162
  stdin to reference, 38
keylogin, **704**
keylogout, **704**
keys, for sort command, 240
keyword, **704-705**
keyword lookup, in online manual pages, 471
keyword option (Korn shell),
  713

kill character, **706**
kill command, **127-129,
  705-706**
kill command (C shell), 559
Kill command (Korn), 717
kill file, **707**
kill ring, in emacs editor, 610
kill signal, **707**
killall command, 129
killer signal, 327
kinit command, **707-708**
klist command, **708**
Knuth, Donald, 889
Korn, David, 708
Korn shell, 89, 91, **708-719,**
  856
  alias command syntax,
    466-467
  arrays and arithmetic
    expressions, 719
  Bourne shell scripts in,
    201
  command history,
    718-719
  commands, 709-710,
    716-718
  coprocesses, 719
  filename metacharacters,
    710
  options, 712-713
  quoting in, 712
  redirecting in, 710-712
  rksh, **833**
  shell variables, 713-715
  startup files, 709
kpasswd command, 795
ksh command, **719-720.** *See
  also* Korn shell
.kshrc file, 465, 709, **720**
ksrvtgt utility, **720**
ktrace command, **720-721**

L

l, 721
l filename extension, 690
l keyword (bc), 492
lam cmmand, **721–722**
Lamport, Leslie, 723
LAN (local area network), **722.**
    See also local area network
    (LAN)
LANG shell variable (Korn),
    715
laser printer, formatting text
    file for, 905
last command, **722–723**
"last in last out" data manage-
    ment, 729
lastcomm command, 723
LATEX, **723–724**
layers command, **724**
LBX (low-bandwidth X), **724**
lc command, **48–49**
lcd command (ftp), 392, 656
lcd command (Samba), **450**
ld (link editor), **725**
    library file maintenance
        for, 472
LDAP (Lightweight Directory
    Access Protocol), 952
ldd utility, **725**
Lea, Ian, 893
leader, of spawned processes,
    129
leaf, **725**
learn command, **725**
leave command, **725–726**
/leave command (IRC), 695
Lempel-Ziv (LZ) algorithm, 672,
    740, **748**
length command (awk), 483
length command (nawk), 778
length function (awk), 309
length keyword (bc), 492

less command, 640, **726–727**
less than (>) symbol, **728**
Let command (Korn), 717, **728**
lex command, **728**
lexical analysis, **728**
/lib directory, **728**
library, **728**
library function, **729**
Lightweight Directory Access
    Protocol (LDAP), 952
LILO, **729**
limit command (C shell), 559,
    729
Lincoln, 185
line command, **730**
line editor, **730**
line erase character, 706
line numbers
    adding to text file,
        783–785
    from pr command, 157
line of text
    counting for file, 49–50
    deleting, 8
line printers, 144, **730**
    creating file for output to,
        787
linefeed, **730**
LINENO shell variable, **730**
$LINENO shell variable (Korn),
    714
lines
    counting, 941–942
    extracting common from
        sorted files, 699
    reversing in file, 832
LINES shell variable (Korn),
    715
link, **730–731**
link editor, 725, **731**
lint, **731**

Linux, **731–733**
    minimum RAM, 119
    steps to rebuild kernel,
        826
Linux Journal, 733
Linux loader, 729
/list command (IRC), 695
list command (mailx), 756
list (set argument), 193
listserver, **733–734**
listusers command, **734**
lkbib command, **734–735**
ln (link) command, 31,
    735–736
local area network (LAN), **722**
    displaying status of sys-
        tems on, **842–843**
    displaying users logged
        on, 844
    users logged on, **843**
local printers, **144–145**, 156
    printing to, **744**
local systems, host status of,
    842
local variables, 216, 217, **736**
locate command, **736**
lock command, **736**
lockd daemon, 569
locking files, **635**
log command (nawk), 778
log operation (awk), 314
logger command, **736**
logging in, 6, **7–8**, 737
    changing entry, **830**
    checkiing for mail when,
        64
    errors, **9**
    greetings, **10–11**
    report on last, **722–723**
    as root, 58
    X Window systems, **430**
logging off, **12–13**, 737

logical operators, in awk, **309–310**

login, **737**

remote, **831**

root, **839**

login command (C shell), 559

login command, in boot up, 234

.login file, 202, 465, 553, 595, **737**

login group, assigning user to, 418

"Login incorrect" message, 9

login name, **737**

displaying, 683, 944

process owner from ps command, 131

login profile, **91–93**

Bourne shell, **92**

in C shell, **92–93**

chpass to change, 530

personal, **93–99**

login: prompt, 7, 8

login shell, **737**

logname command, **738**

LOGNAME environment variable, 557

logon, 8. *See also* user name

command to list, 18

grep command to check for, 286

logout command, **738**

.logout file, 553, 595, **738**

logs, for security, 403

long filename, **738**

look command, 640, **738–739**

lookbib command, **739**

loops

debugging, 362

endless, **326–328**

lorderr utility, **739**

lossless compression, **740**

lossy compression, 700, **740**

/lost+found directory, **740**

low-bandwidth X (LBX), **724**

low-level backups, 411

lowercase

for logon, 8

translating to uppercase, 900

LP daemon, 145

lp (line print) command, 144, **147–153**, **740–741**

-i (inquire) option, **155**

immediate copies of files in, 153

lpd daemon, 569

lpq command, **741–742**

lpr command, 67, **742–743**

lprint command, **156**, **744**

lprm command, **744**

lprof command, **744**

lpstat command, **154–155**, **745–746**

for print request id, 155

lptest command, **746**

ls command, **40–45**, **746–747**

online manual pages for, 43

and permissions, 105

wildcards for, **41–43**

ls command (ftp), 656

ls command (Samba), **450**

ls-lR.Z filename extension, 689

ls-ltR.Z filename extension, 689

Lynx, **748**

Lyrix, and /etc/termcap, 163

LZ (Lempel-Ziv) algorithm, **748**

M

m (mark) command (vi), 187

m4 (macro language preprocessor), **764**

Mach operating system, **748**

machid command, **748**

Macintosh interface, 425

macros, 151, 189

assignments to avoid, 189–190

mm, **769**

ms, **773**

removing during session, 191

removing from file, 575–576

troff, **906**

magic (set argument), 193

magnetic tapes

command to read and write to, 469–470

copying and verifying, **882**

manipulating, 773–774

mail, **748–750**

mail alias file, recreating database for, 780

Mail command, 73, 749, **751–753**

mail command, 58, 64, **750**

? for command mode prompt, 65

escape character for command entry, 74

help for, 65–66

leaving, **66–67**

mail, 73

summary, 75–77

mail command (Mail), 752

mail command (mailx), 756

Mail command (mailx), 756

MAIL environment variable, 557

mail headers, printing, 653

MAIL shell variable, 94

mail shell variable, 556

MAIL shell variable (Bourne), 504

MAIL shell variable (Korn), 715

mail transport agents, 77

mail user agents, 77

mailalias command, **753**

MAILCHECK shell variable, 94, 214

MAILCHECK shell variable (Bourne), 504

MAILCHECK shell variable (Korn), 715

mailing list, 733–734

MAILPATH shell variable (Korn), 715

mailq command, **753**

mail.rc file, **753**

.mailrc file, **372–373**, 595, **754**

mailserv, 733

mailx command, 77, 749, **754–756**

    escape commands, **619**

mailx.rc file, **757**

maintenance mode, 405

major device number, **757**, 839

major mode, **757**

majordomo, 733

make utility, **757**

makefile file, **757–758**

makekey utility, **758**

man command, **43–45**, **758–759**

    options for customizing and printing, 45

    syntax in, 44–45

man- command, 17

man macros, 906

man pages, **759–760**

    X interface to, **954**

managing processes, **760–761**

manuscript macros, **769**

map, **761**

map command, **189–192**

map! command, **189–192**

mapping

    files to i-nodes, 30

    remote, **831**

mark command (MH), 765

mark, in emacs editor, 610

markdirs option (Korn shell), 713

marking text, in vi editor, 187

mask, **761**

mass-storage device, unmounting removable, 410

master map, **761**

match command (awk), 483

match command (nawk), 778

math, awk and, **313–316**

mathematical symbols, formatting text containing, 779

mattribcommand (mtools), **456**

mbox command (Mail), 752

mbox command (mailx), 756

mbox file, 67, **761**

mcatcommand (mtools), **456**

mcdcommand (mtools), **456**

mcopycommand (mtools), **456**

mcs command, **761–762**

md command (Samba), **451**

mdelcommand (mtools), **457**

mdeltreecommand (mtools), **457**

mdircommand (mtools), **457–458**

mducommand (mtools), **458**

me macros, **762**, 906

measurement units, converting, **916**

memory

    stack, **868**

    status of blocks, 467

    in terminal, 5

    virtual, **938–939**

menu, **762**

    code for, 352–353

    quit variable in, 341–342

    read command, **342–343**

    shell script to create, **322–363**

user response to prompt, 344–346

    in xterm window, 434

Merge, **459**, 593

merge, **762**

merge command, **763**

merge program (RCS), 823

mesg command, 59, **763**

mesg (set argument), 193

message of the day (motd), 11, 93

messages

    "device busy", 410

    "directory: does not exist", 35

    EOF (end-of-file), 30

    "execute permission denied", 205

    "filename: not found", 17, 28, 206

    "Login incorrect", 9

    "Mismatch - password unchanged", 83

    "not found", 12

    permission denied, 60–61

    "remote access to path/file denied", 375

    shutdown warning for users, 408

    suppressing from grep command, **278**

    "Using open mode", 163

    You have mail, 64

Meta key, **764**

    in emacs editor, 608–609

metacharacters, 95, 218, **226–233**, **763**

    # (pound sign) for comments, **227–228**

    backslash (\), **226–227**

    in Bourne shell, 501–502

    in C shell, 554

    " (double quotes), **228–229**

in grep command, 279
in Korn shell, 710
quoting, 333, **818**
sequences, **229–232**
summary, 232–233
metafile, **764**
mformatcommand (mtools), **458**
mget command (ftp), 392, 657
MH message handling system, 77, 749, **764–765**
mhl command (MH), 765
mhmail command (MH), 765
mhn command (MH), 765
mhook command (MH), 765
mhparam command (MH), 765
mhpath command (MH), 765
MIME (Multipurpose Internet Mail Extensions), **766**
minibuffer, **766**
minor device number, **766**, 839
minor mode, **766**
"Mismatch - password unchanged" message, 83
mkdep command, **766**
mkdir command, 34, 103, **767**
mkdir command (ftp), 656
mkfifo command, **767**
mkfs command, 409
mklocale command, **768**
mkmsgs command, **768**
mknod command, **768**
mksrt command, **769**
.mm filename extension, 638
mm macros, **769**, 906
mmdcommand (mtools), **458**
mmovecommand (mtools), **458**
/mnt directory, **769**
mode, **769**
mode argument for chmod command, 112
/mode command (IRC), 695
mode line, **769**

modem connection, 4
hanging up, 13
utility for, 562–563
modules, 363
modulo, **769**
monitor. *See also* screen display
monitor option (Korn shell), 713
Montoulli, Lou, 748
MORE environment variable, **771**
more filter, 19–20, 640, **769–770**
for mail message display, 66
Mosaic browser, 395
motd (message of the day), 11, 93
Motif window manager (mwm), 428–429, 436, **771**, **776**
mount, **771**
mount command, **771–772**
mount point, **772**
mounting filesystem, 409, **772**
manual, 410
mouse cursor, in xterm window, 433
move command, in ed editor, 623
moving, files, 774–775
MPEG filename extension, 690
.mpg filename extension, 638, 690
mput command (ftp), 392, 657
mrencommand (mtools), **458**
.ms filename extension, 639
ms macros, **773**, 906
mscreen command, **772**
mset command, **772**
/msg command (IRC), 695
msgchk command (MH), 765
msgs command, **773**
msh command (MH), 765

mt utility, **773–774**
mtools, 442, **452–453**
drive parameters for, **453–458**
floppyd command, **455–456**
mattrib, **456**
mcat, **456**
mcd, **456**
mcopy, **456**
mdel, **457**
mdeltree, **457**
mdir, **457–458**
mdu, **458**
mformat, **458**
mmd, **458**
mmove, **458**
mren, **458**
mtype, **458**
running, **455–458**
mtypecommand (mtools), **458**
multicommand line, **134–136**
Multiplan, and /etc/termcap, 163
multiprocessor system, 118
multiprogramming operating systems, **118–120**
multitasking, **120–121**
multiuser environment, 118
security for, 7
multiuser mode, 405, **406**
mush (mail user's shell), 749, **774**
mv command, 377, **774–775**
mview macros, 906
mwm (Motif window manager), **776**
mymenu file, 322

N

NAK (negative acknowledgment), **776**

name generation, 226
named daemon, 569
named pipe, **776**, 805
names
    for printers, 146
    of shell, **90–91**
nawk, 479, **776–779**
negative numbers, sorting, 245
neqn, **779**
Net News software, 396
NetBIOS connectivity, 444
NetBSD, **779**
.netrc file, 595, **780**
Network Access layer (TCP/IP),
    884
network connections
    copying files over,
        821–822
    sockets for, **863**
    testing, 804–805
network filesystem (NFS), **386**
Network Information Service
    (NIS) domain, **783**
        setting or displaying
        name, 592
network layer (ISO/OSI), 696
networking reference model,
    696
networks, **384–388**
    client-server computing,
        387–388
    file distribution over,
        386–387
    NIS (Network Information
        Service), **387**
    TCP/IP and Ethernet,
        385–386
new accounts, **417–418**
newalias command, **780**
newform command, **780–781**
newgrp command, **781**
newgrp command (Bourne),
    506
Newgrp command (Korn), 717

newline, 47, 223, 265, **781**
    from echo command, 222
    in quoted string, 97
    to terminate command,
        136
    in vi editor, 161
news command, **781–782**
newsgroups, for Linux,
    732–733
.newsrc file, 595, 893
newsreader, **396**
    kill file, **707**
    readnews, **825**
    rn, **836–838**
    tin, **893–897**
    trn, **902–905**
    xrn to interface, 955
next command (awk), 483
next command (Mail), 752
next command (mailx), 756
next command (MH), 765
next command (nawk), 778
NeXT operating system, 748
NF variable (awk), 312, 484
NFS (network filesystem), **386**,
    782–783
nfsd daemon, 570
nice command, **133–134**, **783**
nice command (C shell), 559
/nick command (IRC), 695
NIS (Network Information
    Service), **387**, **783**
        password changes, **960**
nl command, 640, **783–785**
nm command, **785**
nmbd (Samba), **444–445**
nn (newsreader), 396
Nobeep shell variable, 556
noclobber environment vari-
    able, **785**
noclobber option (Korn shell),
    713
Noclobber shell variable, 556

node, **785**
node name (UUCP), 368
noexec option (Korn shell), 713
noglob environment variable,
    785
noglob option (Korn shell), 713
Noglob shell variable, 556
Nohup command (Korn), 717
nohup (no hangup), 128, 560,
    785–786
    killing, 129
nolog option (Korn shell), 713
nomagic, **786**
nonomatch environment vari-
    able, **786**
Nonomatch shell variable, 556
nonprintable characters
    displaying, 939
    and sort command, **244**
    unvis to convert, **919**
"not found" message, 12
NOT (!) operator
    in awk, 309, 310
    in test command, 339,
        342
NOT option, in find command,
    259
notify command, **786**
notify command (C shell), 560
Notify shell variable, 557
nounset option (Korn shell),
    713
novice environment variable,
    787
novice mode for vi editor, 165
    turning off and on, 166
Nowitz, David, 679, 923
NR variable (awk), 306, 312,
    484
nroff, **787**
    error check for input file,
        524–525
    macros, **762**, 773

output display on screen, 533–534

removing dot requests from file, 575–576

vs. troff, 905

nslookup command, 390, **787**

null, **787**

null argument, **788**

null character, **788**

null device, 577, **788**

null path, 211

null string, 333, **788**

null value, 214

number (set argument), 193

numbered buffer, **788**

.o filename extension, 639

O

o (over), 62

obase keyword (bc), 492

object file, profile data of, 811

object files, 540

displaying data and text segment sizes, 861

listing dependencies for group, **739**

object-oriented programming, inheritance, **686**

oclock program, 949

octal notation, 223

for chmod command argument, 112–113

for control characters, 265

od command, **788–789**

offline, 4

offsets, when printing, 157

OFMT variable (awk), 312, 484

OFS character, 305

OFS variable (awk), 312, 484

Oikarinen, Jarkko, 694

$OLDPWD shell variable (Korn), 714

olwm (Open Look window manager), 427–429, 789

onintr keyword, **789**

online, 4

online manual pages. *See* man command

displaying, **758–759**

keyword lookup in, 471

open call, 578

open command (ftp), 392, 656

open command (telnet), 394, 886

Open Desktop, **789**

open files, **789**

identifying and reporting on, 654

Open Look window manager (olwm), 428–429, 436, 789, **790**

open new line, in vi editor, 181

open system, **791**

OpenGL (Open Graphics Library), **789**

opening file, 38

OpenServer, **790**

openwin command, **791**

OpenWindows window manager, **791**

operating system, shutting down, **860**

Operating System System Administrator's Guide, 400

operators

in awk, 481–482

in bc, 493

/opt directory, **791**, 869

OPTARG environment variable, **792**

$OPTARG shell variable (Korn), 714

OPTIND environment variable, **792**

$OPTIND shell variable (Korn), 714

options for commands, 17

OR (||) operator, 309

OR operator (-o), in test command, 339

OR option, in find command, 259

Orange Book guidelines, 403

ordinary files, 636, **792**

orphan process, **792**

orphaned file, **792**

ORS variable (awk), 312, 484

OSF/1, 748, **792**

OSx, **792**

output, 5

appending to files, **54–55**

redirecting, **39–40**, **46–47**

output stream, 295

overwriting files, 30, 54

owner permissions, 107

viewing, 108–109

ownership of file, 16, **104**

changing, **111–112**, **529**

in home directory, 465

P

pack command, **793**

packed files, displaying contents, **799**

packet internet groper (ping), **804–805**

packf command (MH), 765

page, **793**

page length, setting for printing, 149

pager utility, less command as, **726–727**

pages in virtual memory, 939

pagesize command, **793**

parallel port, 145

parallel processing, pipelining in, 806

parameter, **793**. *See also* variables

parameter substitution, 228, **793**

parent directory, **794**
  listing contents, 43
  moving to, 35

parent directory (..), 103

parent process, 123, 124, **794**

parent shell, 236

parentheses to control precedence, 290–291

parsing command line, 218

passive system, UUCP link as, 368

passwd command, 82, **794–795**

password, 8, **795**
  case sensitivity for, 9
  changing, **82–84**
  changing NIS, **960**
  choosing, **13**
  chpass to change, 530
  for crypt command, 550
  encryption, **795**
  encryption in /etc/passwd file, 86–87
  good and bad, **83–84**
  minimum length, 84
  for new accounts, 417
  for root, 402

password file, **796**

paste command, **255–257**, 640, **796–797**

patch command, **797–798**

path database, to route mail, 372

path environment variable, 851

PATH environment variable, 207, 211, 214, 558, **798**, 851
  working directory in, 323

path names
  absolute, **463**
  including in alias, 466

PATH shell variable, 94

path shell variable, 557, **798**

PATH! shell variable, 93

PATH shell variable (Bourne), 504

PATH shell variable (Korn), 715

pathname, **798–799**
  relative, **829**

pathname extension, 475, **799**

paths, **28–29**, **89–90**
  absolute names, **32**
  to environment file when starting shell, 616
  extracting directory name from, **586–587**
  extracting filename from, 488–489
  for find command, 258
  specifying for function definitions, 651

pattern, in awk, 481

pattern matching, **799**

pattern space for sed, 851

pause, 343, 564
  code in menu for, 353
  in scrolling display, 19

PC (personal computer), 5
  X server to run, 426

pcat command, **799**

percent sign (%) prompt, 10, **799**

period (.), **799**
  and file searches, 42–43
  in filenames, 26
  in grep command, 280
  in v command, 285
  as vi repeat command, 179

peripherals, interrupts for, 120–121

perl (Practical Extraction and Report Language), **800**

permission bits, **800**

permission denied message, 60–61

permissions, 16, **103–111**, 338, **635**
  access modes, **107–110**
  changing, **112–114**, **527–529**
  creation mask for, 548
  defaults, **110–111**
  directories, **105–106**
  and executable scripts, 205–206
  files, **104–105**
  finding files with specific, 261–262
  script files, 111
  in UUCP, 374
  viewing, 108–110

permuted index, **801**
  creating, **816–817**

personal login profile, 92, **93–99**

personal mail resource file, 372

personal shell variables, 94

personalizing Unix
  login profile, **91–93**
  password, **82–88**
  personal login profile, **93–99**
  shell, **88–91**

peta-, **801**

petabyte, **801**

pfbttops command, **801**

pg command, 640, **801–803**

phone number, utility to dial, 562–563

physical layer (ISO/OSI), 696

physical links, 735

physical option (Korn shell), 713

pic, **803–804**

pick command (MH), 765

pico, **804**

PID (process ID), **804**

pid (process identifier), 122
    of parent process, 131
    ps (process status) com-
        mand to find, 131

Pine (mail program), 749

.pinerc file, 595

ping (packet internet groper),
    804–805

pipe, 123, 269, **805**
    command output into
        grep, 274
    and split command, 253

pipe command (mailx), 756

pipelines, **20**, **805**
    redirecting vs., **51–52**

pipelining, **806**

Placeway, Paul, 884

.plan file, 595, **806**

pling (!), **487**. *See also* ! (bang)

plot command, **806**

plus (+) symbol, **806**

point, in emacs editor, 609

Point-to-Point protocol (PPP),
    808, 883

popd command (C shell), 560,
    806

port, for printer, 145

positional parameters, 150,
    270, **354–362**
    set to assign values,
        360–362
    in shell script, **220–221**

POSIX (portable operating sys-
    tem interface), **806**

postincrement (++) operator,
    313

PostScript files
    translating font file into
        ASCII, 801
    viewing in X Window
        system, **663**

PostScript printing, translating
    troff-formatted files for, 596

pound sign (#), **807**

PPID environment variable,
    808

$PPID shell variable (Korn),
    714

PPP (Point-to-Point protocol),
    808, 883

pppd daemon, 570

pr command, 50–51, **156–157**,
    640, **808–809**

Practical Extraction and Report
    Language (perl), **800**

precedence, **809**
    in awk, 310
    in egrep command,
        290–292
    for test operations,
        340–341

predefined variables. *See also*
    shell variables

prepending, 67

presentation layer (ISO/OSI),
    696

preserve command (Mail), 752

preserve command (mailx), 756

prev command (MH), 765

print command, **809–810**
    in ed editor, 623

print command (awk), 483

Print command (Korn), 717

print command (Mail), 752

Print command (Mail), 752

print command (mailx), 756

Print command (mailx), 756

print command (nawk), 778

print command (Samba), **451**

print request id, 147

print spooler, 125
    removing jobs from, **744**

printenv command, 617, **810**

printer ports, 144

printers
    advancing paper, 650
    central and local,
        144–145
    device number, 757
    displaying queue status,
        741–742
    enabling, 614
    port for, 145
    testing, 146
    turning off temporarily,
        588

printf command, **810**

printf command (awk), **306**,
    483

printf command (nawk), 778

printing, 143
    in awk, 304–305
    -c copy option, **153**
    canceling, **156**
    canceling request,
        511–512
    changing requests, **155**
    e-mail messages, **67**
    to local printers, **744**
    man command options
        for, 45
    messages from shell
        scripts, **647–648**
    multiple files, 147–148
    sending text files to print
        queue for, 742
    sequential or random
        data, 699–700
    smbd for Windows users,
        442–443
    specific e-mail message,
        68–69
    symbol table, **785**

"printing on the screen", 50

printout, banner page in, **488**

priorities
    nice command to lower, 133–134, **783**
    for print request, 150
private (symmetrical) key schemes, 614
privileged account, **810**
privileged option (Korn shell), 713
/proc directory, 810
procedure, in awk, 481
process IDs (PID), 760, **804**
    of shell, 215
    terminating, **705–706**
process in Unix, 121
    biography, **122–123**
    information about active, **811–814**
    parent, 123, 124, **794**
    priority of, **783**
    spawning by, 123–124
    suspending, **861**
process paths, 234
process status, **811**
processes
    managing, **760–761**
    scheduling, **138–140**, **476–478**
prof command, **811**
profile data
    of object file, 811
    of program, **744**
.profile file, 92, 191, 202, 210, 465, 595, **811**
    viewing, **98–99**
program
    interrupting, 563
    quit signal for, 563
program code, 16. *See also* binary files
programming languages. *See also* awk; C language
    Java, **697**

perl, **800**
shell, **858**
standards, 468
programs, 121
    multiple in memory, 119
    profile data of, **744**
.project file, 595
prompt, 7, **811**
    ? for mail command mode, 65
    for information, 10–11
    in Samba, 448
    shell, 10, **858**
prompt command (ftp), 392, 657
prompter command (MH), 765
protected option (Korn shell), 713
protocol stack, 696
protocols
    AFS (Andrews File System), **465**
    e, **617**
    f protocol, **651**
    FTP (File Transfer Protocol), **658**
    G protocol, **664**
    HTTP (Hypertext Transfer Protocol), **680–681**
    IP (Internet Protocol), **692**
    LBX (low-bandwidth X), **724**
    LDAP (Lightweight Directory Access Protocol), 952
    Point-to-Point protocol (PPP), **808**
    RFS (Remote File System), **833**
    SMTP (Simple Mail Transfer Protocol), **862**
    SPX (Sequenced Packet Exchange), **868**

TCP/IP (Transmission Control Protocol/Internet Protocol), **385–386**, **883**
    TCP (Transmission Control Protocol), **883**
    x protocol, **954**
    Zmodem file transfer protocol, **844–846**
prs program (SCCS), 847
.ps filename extension, 393, 639, 690
ps (process status) command, 128, **130–133**, **811–814**
PS1 shell variable, 94, 95, 214, **814**
PS1 shell variable (Bourne), 504
PS1 shell variable (Korn), 715
PS2 shell variable, 94, 97, 214, **814**
PS2 shell variable (Bourne), 504
PS2 shell variable (Korn), 715
PS3 shell variable (Korn), 715, **814**
PS4 shell variable (Korn), 715, **814**
pseudocode, 326
pstat command, **815–816**
ptx command, **816–817**
PUBDIR directory, 374
    moving files from, 377
    uuto command to send files to, 376
public (asymmetrical) key schemes, 614
public permissions, 105, 107
    viewing, **108–109**
pushd command (C shell), 560, **817**
put command (ftp), 392, 393, 657

put command (Samba), **451**
Pwd command (Bourne), 506
pwd command (ftp), 392, 656
Pwd command (Korn), 717
PWD environment variable, 558
pwd (print working directory)
  command, **33–34**, 38, **817**
$PWD shell variable (Korn),
  714

Q

/query command (IRC), 695
question mark (?), 41, **817**
  for file name generation,
    230
  in ftp, 656
  for mail command mode
    prompt, 65
queue. *See also* at job queue
  batch, **490–491**
queue command (Samba), **451**
quit command (ed), 623
quit command (ftp), 391, 656
quit command (mail), 66–67
quit command (Mail), 752
quit command (mailx), 756
quit command (Samba), **449**
quit command (telnet), 394,
  886
quit (Ctrl-\), **563**
quota command, **817–818**
quotation marks, 222,
  223–226
  for date in awk, 315
  double quote, **596**
  double quote and back-
    quotes, 225
  forward vs. backward, 95
  for sed edit command,
    296
quote, **818**
quoting, **818**
  in Bourne shell, 503

in C shell, 555
  for echo, 331
  for find command file
    arguments, 258
  grep search pattern, **275**
  in Korn shell, 712
  and metacharacters, 333
  parentheses for text, 341
  single quote ('), **861**

R

r command, **818–819**
R command (Korn), 717
r command (vi), 183
R command (vi), 183
-r (recursive) option, for rm
  command, 53
RAID (redundant array of inexpensive disks), **819–820**
Rakitzis, Byron, 821
RAM (Random Access
  Memory), 119
Ramey, Chet, 489
rand command (awk), 314, 483
rand command (nawk), 778
Rand operation (awk), 314
random access, 16
Random Access Memory
  (RAM), 119
random command, **820**
RANDOM environment vari-
  able, **820**
$RANDOM shell variable
  (Korn), 714
ranlib command, **820**
RARP (Reverse Address
  Resolution Protocol), 385, 883
raw, **820**
raw device, **820**
raw mode, **820**
rbash command, **821**
.rc file, **821**
rc shell, **821**

rcp command, **821–822**
.rcrc file, 595
rcs program (RCS), 823
RCS (Revision Control System),
  822–823
rcsclean program (RCS), 823
rcsdiff program (RCS), 823
rcsfreeze program (RCS), 823
rcsmerge program (RCS), 823
rcvstore command (MH), 765
rd command (Samba), **451**
rdist utility, **823–824**
read call, 578
read command, **342–343**, **825**
  in ed editor, 623
read command (Bourne), 506
read command (Korn), 717
read-only filesystem, **825**
"read-only" version of vi editor,
  164
read permission, 104, 108, 527,
  635, 800
  for directories, 105
  owner, group and public,
    107
  testing for, 338
read protected file, 106
reading e-mail messages, from
  another source, **72**
readnews, **825**
readonly command, **825**
Readonly command (Bourne),
  506
Readonly command (Korn), 717
rebuilding kernel, **826**
receive directory, 374
record locking, 635
records, in awk, 302, **304–306**
recurring jobs, scheduling, 140
red command, **827**
redirecting, **827**
  in Bourne shell, 502–503
  in C shell, 554–555
  in at command, 140

input, 40, **50–51**

input to shell scripts, **204–205**

in Korn shell, 710–712

output, **39–40**

for pasting, 257

vs. pipelines, **51–52**

to save sort command results, 241–242

to send mail, 74

Redman, Brian D., 679, 923

redundant array of inexpensive disks (RAID), **819–820**

refer command, **827–828**

refile command (MH), 765

regcmp command, **828**

region, in emacs editor, 610

register command, **828**

regular character, **828**

regular expressions, 160, **278–288, 828–829**

with [ ], 286–287

in awk, 302, 305

for egrep command, 289

for grep and egrep in descending precedence, 292

in sed stream editor, 298

tagged, **287–288**

regular files, 636

rehash command (C shell), 560, **829**

relational operators, **829**

in awk, **308–309**

relative mode, for chmod command, 113

relative pathname, **829**

relogin, **830**

remapping keyboard, 5

"remote access to path/file denied" message, 375

remote command, **830**

remote commands, executing, **625**

remote connections, 4, **565–567**

ftp for file transfer, **654–657**

logging in, 833–834

running commands on, 830

sending file, 927

shell to execute single command on, **840–841**

telnet command for, **394–395**

tip command to login, **897–898**

Remote File System (RFS), **833**

remote filesystem, **830–831**

remote login, **831**

remote mapping, **831**

Remote Procedure Call (RPC) protocol, 387, **840**

remote system, executing commands on, **373**

removable mass-storage device, unmounting, 410, **913**

removing. See deleting

remsh command, 841

repeat command, **831**

period (.) as in vi, 179

repeat command (C shell), 560

repeating search in vi editor, 186

repl command (MH), 765

reply command (Mail), 752

Reply command (Mail), 752

reply command (mailx), 756

Reply command (mailx), 756

$REPLY shell variable (Korn), 714

report (set argument), 193

report threshold, 165

Request for Comments (RFC), **832**

Request for Discussion (RFD), **833**

reset command, **831**

reset string, **831**

resolver, **831**

resource, **832**

resource allocation, in multiprogramming operating systems, 118

resource sharing, **832**

uux command for, 373

resources, automounting, 479

respond command (Mail), 753

respond command (mailx), 756

responding to e-mail message, 73–74

restor command, 413–414

restoring files, from tar backup, 416

Retain command (Mail), 753

return code, 219

return command, **832**

return command (awk), 483

return command (Bourne), 506

Return command (Korn), 717

return command (nawk), 778

Return key, 6, 615

Ctrl-M for, 190

return keyword (bc), 492

return value, 325, 625

rev command, 640, **832**

Reverse Address Resolution Protocol (RARP), 385, 883

reverse polish notation, 572

reverse slash. See backslash (\)

Revision Control System (RCS), **822–823**

RFC (Request for Comments), **832**

RFD (Request for Discussion), **833**

RFS (Remote File System), **833**

.rhosts file, **833**

ripple test, to standard output, **746**

Ritchie, Dennis, 702, 917

rksh (Korn shell), **833**

RLENGTH variable (awk), 484

rlog program (RCS), 823

rlogin command, **833–834**

rm command, **52–54**, **834–835**

rmail, **835**

rmb command, **835**

rmdel program (SCCS), 847

rmdir command (ftp), 656

rmdir (remove directory) command, **35**, **835–836**

rmf command (MH), 765

rmm command (MH), 765

rn (newsreader), 396, **836–838**

robust program, 337

roffs, **839**

Romine, John, 77

root, **839**. *See also* superuser

root account, 810

root directory, **31–35**, **839**, 869

root filesystem, 409, **839**

root login, **839**

root login name, 402
    capabilities, 402–403
    logging in, 58, 404

rootdev variable, **839**

Rose, Marshall, 77

rot13, **839–840**

RPC (Remote Procedure Call) protocol, 387, **840**

rpcgen, **840**

RS (record separator) variable, 304

RS variable (awk), 312, 484

rsh command, **840–841**

Rsh command, **841**

RSTART variable (awk), 484

rstat command, **841–842**

run levels, 234, 405
    for shutdown, 408

rup command, **842**

ruptime command, **842–843**

rusers command, **843**

rwall command, **843–844**

rwho command, **844**

RZSZ tools, **844–846**

S

s command (vi), 184

S command (vi), 184

.s filename extension, 639

s keyword (bc), 492

s (substitute) command, **282–283**

sact program (SCCS), 847

Samba, **442–451**
    cd command, **449**
    del command, **449**
    dir command, **449**
    exit command, **449**
    get command, **450**
    help command, **450**
    lcd command, **450**
    ls command, **450**
    md command, **451**
    nmbd, **444–445**
    print command, **451**
    put command, **451**
    queue command, **451**
    quit command, **449**
    rd command, **451**
    running, **448–451**
    setmode command, **451**
    smbclient, **445–448**
    smb.conf file, **443**
    smbd, **442–443**
    swat program, **443**

Santa Cruz Operation (SCO), **848**

sash (standalone shell), **846**

save, **846**

save command (Mail), 753

save command (mailx), 756

savehist environment variable, **846**

savehist shell variable, 557

Saveignore command (Mail), 753

Saveretain command (Mail), 753

saving, e-mail messages, **70–72**

/sbin directory, **846**, 869

scale keyword (bc), 492

scan command (MH), 765

SCCS (Source Code Control System), **846–847**

sccsdiff program (SCCS), 847

sched process, 124

scheduled jobs, 549–550
    at command for, **138–140**, **476–478**

scientific calculator. *See also* bc

SCO (Santa Cruz Operation), **848**

SCO OpenServer, **848**

SCO UNIX, **848**
    C compiler options, 517–521
    goodpw command, 84
    Merge, **459**
    minimum RAM, 119
    sysadmsh (system administration shell), 85
    text-only screen, 6
    VisionFS, **459**

SCOadmin tools, **848**

scoterm, 431, 956

screen display, **6**
    command to clear, 531
    pause in scrolling, 19
    pausing output, 564
    redrawing, 564
    restarting output, 564

stdout to reference, 38
troubleshooting garbled, 163
screen redraw, 170
screen refresh, 170
script command, **849**
script files, **848**. *See also* shell script
permissions, 111
scroll bars, for xterm window, 433
scroll (set argument), 193
scrolling display
pause in, 19
in vi editor, 161
SCSI (Small Computer System Interface), standard, 468
sdb (symbolic debugger), **849**
sdiff command, **849–850**
search path, **850–851**
search permissions, for directories, 105
searches. *See also* find command; grep command
incremental, **685**
for patterns in files, **665–667**
searching text, in vi editor, **186–187**
Second Extended Filesystem (ext2fs), **628**
secondary prompt, 97
SECONDS environment variable, **851**
$SECONDS shell variable (Korn), 714
section coding scheme, 44
sectors on floppy disks, 454–455
security, 7, 307. *See also* password
firewall, **645**
Kerberos, **703**
logs for, 403

Orange Book guidelines, 403
remote mapping, **831**
UUCP network software, **374–384**
sed stream editor, 273, **295**, **851–852**
! (bang) to reverse matching, **299**
appending and inserting text, **300**
d (delete) function, **299–300**
edit_command, **297–301**
-f (file)option, 296–297
g (global) option, 297
p function, **301**
q (quit) option, 297
regular expressions in, 298
s (substitute) function, **298–299**
syntax, **295–301**
y function, **300**
Select command (Korn), 717
select statement (Korn), **853**
selecting e-mail messages, **68–70**
semicolon (;), **853**
in case statement, 349
in multicommand line, 135
to terminate command, 136
send command (MH), 765
sendbug command, **853**
sending, e-mail messages, **72–75**
sendmail environment variable, 371
sendmail program, **853**
sentence, **853**
definition in vi, 171

Sequenced Packet Exchange (SPX), **868**
Serial Line Internet Protocol (SLIP), 883
serial port, 145
server, anonymous, **468**
Server Message Block (SMP) protocol, 442
server software in X, **423**, *424*, **955**, 959
benchmark program to test, **950–951**
session layer (ISO/OSI), 696
set command, 191, **192–194**, 207–208, **360–362**, 854
to display shell variables, 217
set command (Bourne), 506
options, 506–507
set command (C shell), 560
Set command (Korn), 717
set command (Mail), 753
set command (mailx), 756
set command (telnet), 395, 886
set ignorecase ex command, in vi editor, 186
/set novice off command (IRC), 695
set uid bit, **854**
setenv command, 560, 617, **854**
setmode command (Samba), **451**
SGML (Standard Generalized Markup Language), document instance, 590
sh command, **854–855**
.sh filename extension, 90, 639
SHACCT shell variable, 94, 505
shadow password file, 87
Shapiro, Norman, 77
shar (archiver), **855–856**
.shar filename extension, 639, 690

shared objects, utility to list, 725

shar.Z filename extension, 690

shell, **856–857**
    choosing, **88–91**
    chpass to change, 530
    launching new temporarily, 552
    names of, **90–91**
    as process, **124–125**
    temporary escape to, 129
    terminating, 236
    using within vi, **188**

shell command (Mail), 753

shell command (mailx), 756

shell command, ˜! to execute, 75

SHELL environment variable, 212, 558, **857**

shell escape, **857**

shell function, **857**

shell option, **857**

shell out, **857**

shell program, **857–858**

shell programming language, **858**

shell prompt, 10, **858**

shell script, 95, **201–210**, 537, 857, **858**. *See also* .login file; .profile file
    arithmetical tools, **362–363**
    backquote (`) in, **224–226**
    basic steps, 207
    as command, **208–209**
    creation basics, **202–204**
    debugging, **207–208**, 362
    execute permissions for, 323
    executing directly, **205–206**
    to force command failure, 219

how they work, **218–223**
menu creation, **322–363**
for multiple commands, 270
naming, **204**
positional parameters, **220–221**
for printing, **150–151**
printing messages from, **647–648**
redirecting input to, **204–205**
scheduling from, 140
while command in, **329–342**
white space in, 323
for X resources, 430

shell (set argument), 193

shell shell variable, 557

SHELL shell variable (Bourne), 505

SHELL shell variable (Korn), 715

shell variables, **93–97**, **210–218**, 617, **858**. *See also* environment variables
    in Bourne shell, **504–505**
    in C shell, 556–557
    echo to display contents, 96
    evaluating, **621**
    exporting, **216–218**, **626**
    in Korn shell, 713–715
    personal, 94
    set command to display, 217
    setting and unsetting, **214–215**
    setting automatically by shell, 214–215

shells, 200

shelltool, 956

shift command, 220–221

shift command (Bourne), 506

shift command (C shell), 560

shift command (Korn), 717

Shift key, 5

shift keyword, **859**

shiftwidth (set argument), 193

shl command, **859**

show command (MH), 765

showmatch (set argument), 193

showmode, in vedit, 165, 166

showmode (set argument), 193

shutdown, **406–408**, **859**
    sync command to prepare for, **876**

shutdown command, 407–408, **859–860**

shutting down system, **860**

signal, **860**
    between processes, 327

.signature file, 595

Simple Mail Transfer Protocol (SMTP), 57, 385, **862**, 883

Simple Network Management Protocol (SNMP), 385, 883

simultaneous peripheral operation online (spool), 144, **867**

sin command (awk), 483

sin command (nawk), 778

sin operation (awk), 314

sine, from bc, 492

single quote ('), **861**
    in grep commands, 209

single-user mode, 405, **406**

single-user state, **861**

SIT filename extension, 690

size command, **861**

Size command (Mail), 753

size command (mailx), 756

slash (/), 26–27, **861**
    for root symbol, 31–32

sleep, **861**

sleep command, **137**, **862**

sleeping state, 123

SLIP (Serial Line Internet Protocol), 883

slocal command (MH), 765

smail program, **862**

SMB (Server Message Block) protocol, 442

smbclient (Samba), **445–448**

smb.conf file (Samba), **443**

smbd (Samba), **442–443**

smit program, **862**

SMP (symmetrical multiprocessing), 118

SMTP (Simple Mail Transfer Protocol), 57, 385, **862**, 883

SNMP (Simple Network Management Protocol), 385, 883

sockets, 636, **863**

soelim command, **863**

soft links, 735, **863**

software, displaying configuration information, **875–876**

Solaris, **863**

Solaris source code debugger (dbx), **572**

sort, **864**

sort command, **240–250**, 268, 640, **864–865**

   -d option, **244**

   -f option, **243–244**

   foreign language variations, **242–243**

   -i option, **244**

   for multiple files, **246**

   -n option, **245**

   -o (output) option, 241–242

   redirecting to save results, 241–242

   -u option, **246–247**

sorted files, finding common lines in, 536

sortm command (MH), 765

Source Code Control System (SCCS), **846–847**

source code, maintaining file dependencies, **757**

source command, **865**

   in ed editor, 623

source command (C shell), 560

source command (mailx), 756

source file, for cp (copy) command, 103

spaces. *See also* white space

   as argument separator, 223

   converting tab character to, **625–626**

spawned processes, leader of, 129

special characters. *See also* metacharacters

   restricting in vedit, 165

special file, 578

special users, 403–404

spell command, 640, **865–866**

splat, **866**

spline command, **866–867**

split command, **252–253**, **867**

split command (awk), 316, 483

split command (nawk), 779

/spool directory, **868**, 869

spool (simultaneous peripheral operation online), 144, **867**

spooler, 125, 144–145, **868**

   displaying status information for lp, **745–746**

   removing print jobs from, **744**

sprintf command (awk), 483

Sprintf command (nawk), 779

SPX (Sequenced Packet Exchange), **868**

SQL (Structured Query Language), 387–388

sqrt command (nawk), 779

sqrt keyword (bc), 492

sqrt operation (awk), 314

square brackets ([]), **868**

   for file name generation, 230

   in grep command, 281

   for optional arguments, 18

   regular expressions with, 286–287

srand command (awk), 484

srand command (nawk), 779

srand operation (awk), 314

srchtxt command, **868**

stack, 121, **868**

Stallman, Richard, 605, 654

/stand directory, 869

standard directories, **869**

standard error, 55, **870**

   redirecting, 827

   sending error messages to, 347

standard files, 347

standard input, 38–39, **870**

   assigning to variables, 825

   reading line from, 730

   redirecting, 827

   sorting, 240

standard output, **38–39**, **870**

   echo to write to, **600–601**

   redirecting, 827

   reporting system information to, **913**

   ripple test to, **746**

   testing for running under layers software, 695

standards, 468

start bit, **870**

start-up shell, 235–236

startup files, **870**

   for Bourne shell, 501

   for C shell, 553

   for Korn shell, 709

.startxr file, 430

state, **870–871**

status command (ftp), 392, 657

status command (telnet), 395, 886

status command (vi), 170

status environment variable, **871**

status message, displaying in vi, 170

status shell variable, 557

stderr, 55. *See also* standard error

   and streams, 295

stdin, **38–39**. *See also* standard input

   and streams, 295

stdout, **38–39**. *See also* standard ouput

   redirecting output from, 46

   and streams, 295

stop bit, **871**

stop command (C shell), 560, **871**

storage allocation blocks, **500**

stream, sed to edit, **851–852**

string options, 192

strings, **872**

   empty, 333

   extracting from C language source code, **628**

   splitting into array, 316

strip command, **872**

struct command, **872**

Structured Query Language (SQL), 387–388

stty command, 97, **97–98**, **872–873**

   to change interrupt key, 326

style command, **873–874**

su command, 404, **874**

sub command (awk), 484

sub command (nawk), 779

subdirectories, 28, **874**. *See also* directories

   listing, 40

subject, for e-mail messages, 72

subprocesses, 234

subroutine, call to, 510

SUBSEP variable (awk), 485

subshell, 205, 206, **875**

   exporting variables for, 216

substitute command, in ed editor, 623

substr command (awk), 484

substr command (nawk), 779

sum command, **875**

summary, of printer service, 155

Sun Microsystem, 429

Sun workstation, Meta key, 608

Sun Yellow Pages, 387

super-block, 408

supercomputer, **875**

superuser, 58, 810, **875**

   for backup operation, 412–413

   becoming, **404**

   messages from, 59

   process priority increase by, 134

   for system administration, **402–405**

suspend command (C shell), 560

suspended programs, 565

   context of, 120

   swapping, 119

swap spaces, 409

swapper, 124

swapping suspended programs, 119

swat program (Samba), **443**

swconfig command, **875–876**

switch command, 560, **876**

   end to terminate, 614

switch options, 192

switches for commands, 17

symbol cross-reference, **551**

symbol table, printing, **785**

symbolic links, 636, 735

symbolic mode, for chmod command, 113, 527, 528–529

symmetrical multiprocessing (SMP), 118

sync command, **876**

synonyms, explain to look up, **626**

syntax, 17, **876**

syntax error, **877**

/sys directory, **877**

sysadmsh (system administration shell), 85, 400, 418, **877**

syslog system log module, shell command interface to, 736

system administration, **400–401**

   backup, **410–417**. *See also* backup

   booting up, **405–406**

   filesystems, **409–410**

   new accounts, **417–418**

   required tasks, 401–402

   shutdown, **406–408**

   smit program for, **862**

   superuser access for, **402–405**

system administrator, 7, 400, **877**

   overriding mesg n user setting, 63

   and security, 8

System Administrator's Reference Guide, 400

system calls, 121

   truss command to trace, **906**

system command (awk), 484

system command (nawk), 779

system console, 5

system diagnostics, 580

system mailbox, 64

system messages, reading, 773

system resources

    displaying or setting limits, **729**

    limiting, 910–911

system time, 892

T

tab character, 223, 265

    as argument separator, 223

    converting to spaces, **625–626**

table of contents, for archive libraries, **820**

tables, formatting, **881–882**

tabs command, **877**

tagged regular expressions, **287–288**

tail command, **251–252**, 640, **877–878**

talk command, **878–879**

tape drives

    for backup medium, 412

    device number, 757

Tar archive, **881**

tar command, **414–417**, **879–880**

    display options, 416

.tar filename extension, 393, 639, 689

.tar.gz filename extension, 393

.tar.Z filename extension, 393, 689

tasks, 120

Tauber, Dan, *The Complete Linux Kit*, 732

Taylor, Dave, 77, 604

tbl, **881–882**

    output display on screen, 533–534

    removing formatting from file, 575–576

/tcb directory, **882**

tcopy command, **882**

TCP/IP (Transmission Control Protocol/Internet Protocol), **385–386**, **883**

    architecture, **884**

TCP (Transmission Control Protocol), **883**

Tcsh, **884**

.tcshrc file, 595

tee command, 135–136, *136*, **885**

tee program, **884**

telecommunications, 366

teletypewriter (TTY), 144

telnet command, **394–395**, 425, **885–886**

    tn3270, **898**

temporary files, directory for, **898**

term, **887**

TERM environment variable, 558

term-info database, displaying information from, **900**

term (set argument), 193

TERM shell variable, 94, 163, 164

term shell variable, 557

TERM shell variable (Bourne), 505

TERM shell variable (Korn), 715

termcap, **887**

TERMCAP environment variable, 558

terminal emulator, 427

Terminal window, opening, 6

terminals, **4–5**

    command to list name, 18

    connected, 62

    device number, 757

    enabling, 614

    files for managing, 577

    Hewlett-Packard 2640 series, 680

    locking, **736**, **953**

    multiple login screens, 772

    output to, 143

    pathname of device file, 908

    prompt for type, 10–11

    sending message to, 675

    stty to set options, **97–98**

    system interface setup to, 907

    turning off temporarily, 588

    vi editor and type, 163

    virtual, **939**

    in X Windows, **426–427**

    xterm to emulate, **956–957**

terminating, shell, 236

terminfo directory, 887

terminfo file, 146, 169

terse (set argument), 194

test command, **329–342**, **887–889**

    with Boolean expressions, **339–341**

    to compare two strings, 332

Test command (Bourne), 506

test command (Korn), 717

testing

    for arguments, **355–356**

    empty variables, **333–337**

    files, **338–339**

    numbers, **337–338**

.tex filename extension, 639

TEX (typesetting language), **889–890**

text-based approach, 6

text cursor, in xterm window, 433

text editor

to compose letter, 74

default, 631

ed editor, **602**

edit, **603**

emacs editor, **605–613**

ex editor, **621–623**

joe (editor), **698**

jove, **700**

pico, **804**

vedit, **930**

vi editor, **931–938**

text-entry macros, 189

text-entry mode, 160

in vi editor, 167, **180–181**

text files, 16

adding line numbers to, **783–785**

breaking long lines in, **648**

converting DOS to Unix, **597**

converting Unix to DOS, **958**

displaying differences, **581–583**

displaying last lines of, **877–878**

displaying screen at a time, **801–803**

dividing, **867**

fmt command for formatting, **646–647**

formatting, **780–781**, **808–809**

printing beginning, **675**

removing blank lines from, **835**

removing duplicate lines

from sorted, **915–916**

sending to print queue, 742

sorting, **864–865**

troff to format, **905–906**

updating to later version, **797–798**

text, print command to display, **809–810**

text segment, 121–122

text streams, 295

text window, accessing, 6

tfmtodit command, **890**

tftp command, **890**

then keyword, **890**

Thompson, Ken, 199, 917

thrashing, 119

threads, 120, **891**

TIF filename extension, 690

tilde (~), 192

in Cshell, 380

for empty lines in vi, 169

for home directory, 679

tilde (~) escape sequences, **891**

in mt command, 77

time command, **892**

time command (C shell), 560

time command (Korn), 717

time-of-last-access, for file list order, 49

time-of-last-modification, for file list order, 49

time, scheduling jobs to run at specific, 4–477

time shell variable, 557

time slice, 118

TIMEOUT shell variable, **892**

times command, 892

Times command (Bourne),

times command (Korn), 71

tin (newsreader), 396, **893–897**

tip command, 373, **897–**

TMOUT shell variable, 715, **898**

/tmp directory, 869, **898**

tn3270, **898**

to-do list, calendar utility for, **509–510**

tolower command (awk), 484

tolower command (nawk), 779

toolkit, 431

top command, for e-mail messages, 69

Top command (Mail), **753**

top command (mailx), **756**

top-level domains, 389

Torvalds, Linus, 731

touch command, **898–900**

touch command (mailx), **756**

toupper command (awk), 484

toupper command (nawk), 779

tput command, **900**

tr (translate) command, **264–265**, 267–268, 640, **900–901**

trace mode, 362

trackall option (Korn shell), 713

tracks on floppy disks, 454

trailer, as pr default, 50

translate command, **901**

Transmission Control Protocol (TCP), **883**

transmission speeds, 366

transparent file sharing, 386

transport layer (ISO/OSI), 696

trn command, **326–328**, **902**

trap command (Bourne), 506

Trap command (Korn), 717

trapdoor syndrome, 403

"trash can" system file, 346

trivial ftp, 890

trn (newsreader), 396, **902–905**

troff
> device-independent, **590**
> eqn preprocessor,
> **617–618**
> macros, **762**, 773, **906**
> pic preprocessor for,
> **803–804**
> translating files for
> PostScript printing,
> 596

troff command, **905–906**

troff dot requests, removing
from file, 575–576

troff input file, error check for,
524–525

Trojan Horses, **374**

troubleshooting
> garbled screens, 163
> gcore to obtain core
> image, 660
> hard drive problems, **653**
> truss command to trace
> system calls, **906**

true command, **906**

truss command, **906**

truth table, 340–341

tset command, 98, **907**

tty command, **908**

TTY (teletypewriter), 144

Twm (Tab Window manager),
908

.txt filename extension, 639,
690

type command, **908**

~~type~~ command (Bourne), 506

~~type c~~ommand (Korn), 717

~~type~~ command (Mail), 753

~~type~~ command (Mail), 753

~~type~~ command (mailx), 756

~~type~~ command (mailx), 756

~~type~~ command (Korn), 717,

typesetting
> formatting text file for,
> **905–906**
> TEX for, **889–890**

TZ environment variable, 212

U

u (undo) command (vi), 179
> after deleting, 182

UDP (User Datagram Protocol),
385, 883

uid, chpass to change, 530

ul command, **909–910**

ulimit command (Bourne), 506

ulimit command (Korn), 717,
910–911

umask command, 93, 99, 11,
911–912

umask command (Bourne), 506

umask command (C shell), 560

umask command (Korn), 717

umask value, 912

umount command 0, **913**

unab command,

unalias command 3, **913**

unalias command (C shell), 560

unalias command (Korn), 717

unalias command (Mail), 753

uname command 3

unbuffered dev 20

uncompact command, **914**

uncompress command, **914**

delete command (Mail), 753

delete command (mailx), 756

deleting e-m messages,
72

uuencoding, translating for display, 909–91

uucp command, **914–915**

uu program (SCCS), 847

uu command, 560, **915**

Uniform Resource Locator

(URL), **920**

uniq command, **247–250**,
268–269, 640, **915–916**
> fields for, 249–250
> options, 248

units command, **916**

Unix, **917–918**. *See also* personalizing Unix; system
administration
> booting up, **405–406**
> bootup steps, 234
> check for mail at login, 64
> date used for beginning of
> time in, 617
> developers, 917–918
> displaying length of time
> running, **919–920**
> file types in, **636**
> kernel, **704**
> origins, 199
> security features, 7
> system manual divisions,
> 759–760
> system usage statistics,
> **940**
> XENIX, **951**

Unix prerequisites, **4–6**
> keyboard, **5–6**
> screen display, 6
> terminals, **4–5**

unlimit command, 560, **918**

unmap command, 191

unnamed buffer, in vi editor,
185

unpack command, **918**

unread command (Mail), 753

unreferenced file, 792

unset command, 214, 334,
918–919

unset command (Bourne), 506

unset command (C shell), 560

unset command (Korn), 717

Unset command (Mail), 753

unset command (mailx), 756
unset command (telnet), 886
unsetenv command, 560, 617, **919**
until command (Korn), 717
until loop, **328–329**, **919**
unvis command, **919**
update process, 132
uppercase, translating to lowercase, 900
uptime command, **919–920**
urgent messages, from root, 63
URL (Uniform Resource Locator), **920**
USENET, **396**. *See also* newsreader
USENIX Association, 737
user command (ftp), 392, 656
User Datagram Protocol (UDP), 385, 883
user-defined variables, 311
   placing standard input in, 342
USER environment variable, 558
user filesystem, 409
user ID, 761
user id
   access using another, 404, **874**
   euid (Effective User Identifier), **621**
   login name and, 86
user name, 8
   command to list, 18
user shell variable, 557
user time, 892
user variables, 212–213
users
   adding new, **465**
   authenticating for server drive access, **455–456**
   changing database information, **530**

checking for online, 59–60
displaying disk usage and limits, 817–818
displaying login name and ID, 683
find command to select files belonging to, 261
information about, 796
information about logged on, **643–645**
limiting use of crontab, 550
listing group memberships, 669
listing in /etc/passwd, 85
message warning about shutdown for, 408
users command, **920**
"Using open mode" message, 163
/usr directory, 869, **920–921**
.uu filename extension, 639
uucico utility, 924
uucp command, 366–367, **379–382, 921–922**, 924
   syntax, 381
UUCP job id, 383
UUCP network software, **366–373**
   address syntax, 369
   address vs. Internet domain address, **389–390**
   configuration, **922–924**
   forwarding mail, 371–372
   HoneyDanBer UUCP, **679**
   installing, 367–368
   job tracking, **383–384**
   mailing binary files, **370–371**
   .mailrc file, **372–373**
   making contact, **367–368**
   security, **374–384**

uucp command, **379–382**
uulog command, **382**
uuname command, **369–370**
uustat command, **382**
uuto command, 370
uucp user name, 374
uucpd daemon, 570
uudecode command, 370–371, **924**
uue filename extension, 690
uuencode command, 370–371, **924–925**
uue.z filename extension, 690
uuglist command, 924, **925**
uulog command, **382**, 384, **925**
uumail program, 372
uuname command, **369–370**, 924, **925**
uupick command, **375–379**, 377, 924, **925–926**
uuq command, 924, **926–927**
uusend command, 924, **927**
uustat command, **382**, 383, 924, **927–928**
uuto command, 370, **375–379**, 924, **928**
   vs. uucp command, 379
uux command, 373, 924, **928–929**

V

v command, 284–285
V command, 284–285
vacation command, **929–930**
val program (SCCS), 847
/var directory, 869, **930**
variable identifier, 93
variable substitution, 793

variables. *See also* environment variables; shell variables
  assigning standard input words to, 825
  assigning value to, 330
  defining within shell, 334
  displaying value, 331
  global, 217, **663**
  local, 216, 217, **736**
  removing, 918–919
  setting, **854**
  to store test results, 356
  testing empty, **333–337**
  unset command for, 334
  user, 212–213
  user-defined, 311
vedit, 164. *See also* vi editor
vedit command, **930**
verbose mode, 207–208
verbose option (Korn shell), 713
verbose shell variable, 557
version command (mailx), 756
vertical bar (|), for piping, 20
vertical tab, 223
vgrind command, **931**
vi editor, 159–160, **931–938**
  autoindent feature, 160
  changing text, **183–184**
  command mode and input mode, 932–933
  cursor movement, **173–175**, 178–179
  editing commands, 934–936
  entering and leaving, **195–196**
  ing, 173
  file overwrite in,
  apping for,
  77, 178

local variables, **938**
mode-switching maneuvers, **168–169**
moving around in, 933–934
operational mode, **166–168**
pattern searching, 936–937
preliminaries, **160–164**
saving editing buffer, 171
screen-control commands, **179–180**
searching text, **186–187**
starting within mail, 74
text creation with, **169–175**
text deletion, **181–183**
text entry, **170–173**
text-entry mode, **180–181**
unassigned printing keys, 189–190
using shell within, **188**
vedit, 164
view editor, 164
yanking and putting text, **184–186**
vi option (Korn shell), 713
view command, **938**
view editor, 164. *See also* vi editor
view mode, **938**
viraw option (Korn shell), 713
virtual console, **938**
virtual memory, **938–939**
  statistics on, 939
virtual terminal, 431, **939**
viruses, 374
vis command, 939
VisionFS, **459**
visual command (Mail), 753
visual command (mailx), 756

VISUAL shell variable (Korn), 715, **939**
Visual Systems Management (VSM), 466
vmh command (MH), 765
vmstat command, **939**
vnews (news reader), 396
VSM (Visual Systems Management), 466

W

w command, **940**
wait command, **126–127**, **940**
wait command (Bourne), 506
Wait command (C shell), 560
wait command (Korn), 717
wait for child process, 124
Wall, Larry, 800, 836
wall (write all) command, 63, **940–941**
warn (set argument), 194
wc filter, command output combined by, 135
wc (word count) command, 49–50, 122, 640, **941–942**
Weinberger, Peter, 776
what command, 203
what program (SCCS), 847
what string (@(#)), 203
whatis command, **942**
whatnow command (MH), 765
whence command (Korn), 718, **942**
whereis command, **942–943**
which command, **943**
while command, 326, **943**
  in scripts, **324–342**
  test for, 329–330
while command (awk), 318, 482, 484
while command (C shell), 560
while command (Korn), 718

while command (nawk), 779

"while forever' loop, null command for, 345

while keyword (bc), 491

The White Book, 702

white space, 499

    replacing with tabs and spaces, 914–915

    in scripts, 323

    and variable assignment, 330

    when testing strings, 332

who command, 12, **17–19**, 59–60, **943–944**

    grep command for output of, 286

/who command (IRC), 695

whoami command, 944

whodo command, **945**

whois command, 390, **945**

/whois command (IRC), 695

whom command (MH), 765

widget, 431, **945**

widget library, **945**

wildcards, **945**. *See also* metacharacters

    for ls command, **41–43**

window

    active, **464**

    with focus, **648**

    inactive, **684**

window command, **945–946**

window manager in X, *426*, *426*, 427–429

window (set argument), 194

windowed applications, 646

Windows (Microsoft), 425, 459

    access to files on Unix server. *See* Samba

wksh, **946**. *See also* Korn shell

words

    counting, **49–50**, **941–942**

counting in expression, 361

deleting, 565

finding in system dictionary, **738–739**

for for loop, 358

in vi editor, 174

wordy text, evaluating, **580–581**

working directory, 33–34, 946. *See also* current directory

World Wide Web

    home page, **679**

    Lynx browser, **748**

worms, 374

wrapmargin (set argument), 194

wrapscan (set argument), 194

write call, 578

write command, 58, **946**

    appropriate use, 63

    in ed editor, 623

write command (Mail), 753

write command (mailx), 756

write login command, **59–64**

write permissions, 104, 108, 527, 635, 800, **946**

    for directories, 105

    owner, group and public, 107

    for restoring backups, 416

    and rm command, 53

    testing for, 338

write protected file, 106, 108

writeany (set argument), 194

X

x command in mail command, 66

x command (Mail), 752

x command (mailx), 755

X Consortium, 423

X Protocol, **425**

x protocol, **954**

X server, **955**. *See also* server software in X

X Window systems, 6, **958–959**

    benchmark program, **947**

    benchmark program to test server, **950–951**

    benefits, **427**

    client software, 424, *424*, **434–436**

    communications link, **424–425**

    components, **425–426**, *426*

    future of, **436–437**

    introduction, **422–427**

    logging in, **430**

    Motif, **771**

    Motif window manager (mwm), 428–429

    obtaining files on Internet, 437

    Open Look window manager (olwm), 428–429

    vs. other windowing systems, **425**

    requirements, **429–436**

    resources, **430–431**

    server software, *424*

    standard, 469

    standard development, 436

    starting, **791**

    terminals, **426–427**

    Twm (Tab Window manager), **908**

    user configuration settings, **955–956**

    version number, 437

X11R5 (X Window specification), **951**

X11R6 (X Window specification), **951**

X.400 standard, **952**

X.500 standard, **952**

xargs command, **947**

xbench program, **947**

xbiff program (X), 435, 436, **948**

xcalc program (X), 435, **948**

xcalendar program (X), 435

xclock program (X), 435–436, **949**

xcolors program (X), 435, **950**

.Xdefaults configuration file, **950**

xdm (X Display Manager), 430, **950**

xdos program, 593

xdpr program (X), 435, 950

XENIX, **951**

Xerox Corporation, Palo Alto Research Center, 422

xfd program (X), 435, **951**

xfontsel program (X), 435

XFree86, **952**

xinit program, 430, **952**

.xinitrc file, 430, 595, **952**, 956

xit command (Mail), 752

xit command (mailx), 755

xkill program (X), 435, 436, **953**

xlax program, **953**

xlib library, **953**

xllperf program (X), **950–951**

·load program (X), 435

·ck program (X), **953**

·ts program (X), 435, ·954

·ram (X), 435, **954**

·n (X), **954–955**

·m (X), 435

·ewsreader

xsend utilities, **955**

.xsession file, 430, 595

xset program (X), 435, **955–956**

xsetroot program (X), 435, **956**

Xstone, 947

xstr command, **956**

xterm command, **431–434**, **956–957**

command line options, 432–433

xtod command, **958**

xtrace option (Korn shell), 713

xtract command, **958**

xwd program (X), 435, **958**

xwud program (X), 435

.xx filename extension, 639

Y

Y2K problem, 701

yacc compiler compiler, 540, **960**

yanking and putting text, vi editor, **184–186**

Yellow Pages, 783

yes command, **960**

You have mail message, 64

yppasswd command, **960**

yyfix command, **960**

Z

z command (mailx), 756

z command (telnet), 886

.Z filename extension, 393, 639, 689

recompressing to gzip format, 962

.z filename extension, 639, 689, 793

zcat command, 670, **961**

zcmp command, **961**

zdiff command, **961**

zforce command, **961–962**

zgrep command, **962**

.zip filename extension, 393, 689

.zlogin file, 595

.zlogout file, 595

Zmodem file transfer protocol, tools to implement, **844–846**

zmore command, **962**

znew command, **962–963**

.zprofile file, 595

Zsh, **963**

.zshenv file, 595

.zshrc file, 595

ABOUT THE CONTRIBUTORS

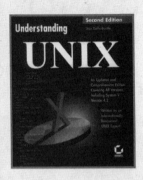

Stan Kelly-Bootle contributed chapters from Understanding Unix.

Stan has been computing since the 1950s when he graduated from Cambridge University in Pure Mathematics and helped pioneer the EDSAC I. He is a contributing editor to *Component Strategies Magazine*, a Jolt Judge for *Software Development Magazine*, and has written a regular column for Unix Review since 1984. His other books include *The Devil's Dictionary*, *The Computer Contradictionary*, *Lern Yorself Scouse*, and SYBEX's *Mastering Turbo C*. Stan welcomes e-mail at skb@crl.com and his Web site http://www.crl.com/~skb/.

Peter Dyson contributed chapters from *The Unix Desk Reference*.

Peter is a consultant with more than twenty years of experience in engineering, software development, and technical support. He first encountered Unix as a programmer in 1984, and has used several different versions as a system designer. Dyson is the author of more than two dozen books on operating systems and software, including *The Dictionary of Networking* and *Mastering Microsoft Internet Information Server*, both from Sybex.

John Heilborn revised and updated the material in this book, and also wrote Chapter 19 "Out of the Vacuum: The Door to Mainstream Applications".

John is an internationally syndicated computer columnist, author of more than fifty-five computer books, and a computer consultant. His syndicated columns, Ask Dr. John, ComputerTalk and High Tech Toys reach an audience of more than fifty million readers worldwide.

He has been involved in the computer industry for more than 35 years with more than fifteen years as an R&D engineer, developing technology that is still used in computers today. He also teaches computer classes covering everything from building PCs to programming, system repair, and maintenance.

Master Your
WINDOWS® 98
Destiny WITH THESE BESTSELLING SYBEX TITLES

Protect and Upgrade Your PC

Expert Advice for Everyone

STEP-BY-STEP, JARGON-FREE INSTRUCTIONS FOR PROTECTING AND UPGRADING YOUR PC

Of the more than 200 million computers in use today, nearly 75 percent are obsolete according to today's fast Pentium standards. If your machine is more than a year old, you need this book. Its clear, step-by-step explanations allow even complete computer novices to make all of the important software and hardware upgrades necessary to keep their computers running trouble-free. Tutorials, photos, and illustrations show you how to install memory, hard drives, CD players, and scores of other peripherals. A glossary of terminology rounds out this essential book for beginning and intermediate computer users.

ISBN: 0-7821-2137-3
544 pp.; 7½" × 9"; $24.99

"the best book on the subject today"

—Douglas M. Bonham, Manager Heathkit Educational Systems

This revised and updated eighth edition is the industry's ultimate hardware reference, written by Mark Minasi, the world's #1 hardware/networking authority. Inside is valuable information about every technology—from chips to hard drives to multimedia. The book also includes a buyer's guide, a 220-page manufacturer resource guide, a complete hardware dictionary, and a special chapter on how to upgrade from the Internet. The book's two CDs include professional upgrading video clips from Minasi's own $800 seminars, PC Tuning (a commercial, multimedia upgrading program), and scores of diagnostic and utility software.

ISBN: 0-7821-2151-9
1,520 pp.; 7½" × 9"; $59.99

SUMMARY OF COMMON UNIX COMMANDS (Continued)

COMMAND	ACTION
news	Display news item
nice	Run a command at (usually) lower priority
nohup	Run a command after logout (inhibit hangups)
nroff	Format files for printing
nslookup	Display IP information about a domain
od	Display file in octal
psswd	Create or change login password
paste	Merge lines of files
pr	Format and print file
ps	Report status of active processes
pstat	Report system status
pwcheck	Check /etc/passwd (default) file
pwd	Display current working directory
rm	Remove (erase) files or directories
rmdir	Remove (erase) empty directories
rsh	Invoke restricted Bourne shell
sed	The stream editor
set	Assign value to variable
setenv	Assign value to environmental variable (C Shell)
sh	Invoke Bourne shell
sleep	Suspend execution for given period
sort	Sort and merge files
spell	Find spelling errors
split	Split a file into smaller files
stty	Set options for a terminal
su	Make a user a superuser (or a different user) without logging out first
sum	Compute checksums and number of blocks for files
tabs	Set tabs on a terminal
ail	Display last few lines of a file
	Copy (archive) and restore files to diskette or tape
	Create a tee in a pipe
	Access remote systems